The De Soto Chronicles

VOLUME I

The De

THE EXPEDITION OF HERNANDO

VOLUME I

Soto Chronicles

DE SOTO TO NORTH AMERICA IN 1539–1543

EDITED BY

LAWRENCE A. CLAYTON
VERNON JAMES KNIGHT, JR.
EDWARD C. MOORE

THE UNIVERSITY OF ALABAMA PRESS ❧ TUSCALOOSA

The University of Alabama Press
Tuscaloosa, Alabama 35487-0380
uapress.ua.edu

First Paperback Edition 1995

Illustrations on cover and title page from *The Conquistadores* by Terence Wise, © 1980, reprinted 1990; courtesy of Osprey Publishing, London
Cover and interior design: Paula C. Dennis

ISBN: 978-0-8173-6177-8 (paper)
ISBN: 978-0-8173-9562-9 (electronic)

Cataloging-in-Publication data is available from the Library of Congress.
ISBN: 978-0-8173-0593-2 (cloth)

To

DOUGLAS E. JONES

Chairman of the Alabama De Soto Commission
and of
The De Soto Trail Commission

with many thanks.

Publication of this work has been supported in part by grants and donations from the following agencies, institutions, and individuals:

Alabama De Soto Commission

Anonymous Donor

Historic Chattahoochee Commission

J. Conrad Dunagan

National Endowment for the Humanities

Panamerican Consultants, Inc.

The Program for Cultural Cooperation
Between Spain's Ministry of Culture
and United States' Universities

Southeastern Archaeological Conference

The De Soto Trail Commission

Hernando de Soto, ca. 1495–1542
(From the Library of Congress copy of
Retratos de los Españoles ilustres
con un epítome de sus vidas [Madrid, 1791])

Contents

Illustrations

Board of Advisers

Contributors

DAVID BOST
Department of Classical and Modern Languages
Furman University
Greenville, South Carolina.

JEFFREY P. BRAIN
Peabody Museum of Salem
Salem, Massachusetts.

LAWRENCE A. CLAYTON
Department of History
The University of Alabama
Tuscaloosa, Alabama.

FRANCES G. CROWLEY
Department of Foreign Languages
Southeast Missouri State University
Cape Girardeau, Missouri.

CHARLES R. EWEN
Arkansas Archeological Survey
Fayetteville, Arkansas.

JOHN H. HANN
San Luis Archaeological and Historical Site
Tallahassee, Florida.

PAUL E. HOFFMAN
Department of History
Louisiana State University
Baton Rouge, Louisiana.

CHARLES HUDSON
Department of Anthropology
University of Georgia
Athens, Georgia.

VERNON JAMES KNIGHT, JR.
Department of Anthropology
The University of Alabama
Tuscaloosa, Alabama.

EUGENE LYON
Center for Historical Research
St. Augustine Restoration Foundation
St. Augustine, Florida.

EDWARD C. MOORE
Alabama Museum of Natural History
The University of Alabama
Tuscaloosa, Alabama.

ROCÍO SÁNCHEZ RUBIO
University of Extremadura
Cáceres, Spain.

JOHN E. WORTH
Department of Anthropology
University of Florida
Gainesville, Florida.

Foreword

by Lawrence A. Clayton

The De Soto expedition forms an integral part of the great age of discovery and conquest in the Americas triggered by the Columbian voyages. In the wake of Columbus there came other explorers and conquistadors who pushed through the islands of the Caribbean and into the American mainlands during the first half of the sixteenth century. They came as explorers and discoverers, as conquerors and settlers, spreading the best and the worst of European civilization through the Americas.

A great part of the Western world's interest in commemorating the Columbian voyages has been in how to assess the long-range impact of Europe on America. In this clash, new peoples and new cultures were born, and ancient peoples and indigenous cultures were destroyed. The De Soto expedition was the first major encounter of Europeans with North American Indians in the eastern half of the United States and, as such, is of monumental importance in the study and analysis of the origins of North American history after the arrival of the Europeans.

In the years 1989–93, the United States commemorated the 450th anniversary of the expedition of Hernando de Soto to the southeastern United States. De Soto and his expedition of over six hundred men, including two hundred cavalry, spent four years (1539–43) traveling through what is now Florida, Georgia, Alabama, North and South Carolina, Tennessee, Mississippi, Louisiana, Arkansas, and Texas. De Soto discovered the Mississippi River, died of a fever, and was buried in the river.

As leader of the first European penetration into the interior of the area, then called La Florida, De Soto saw American Indians in their native towns and with their native customs, untouched, as yet, by foreign people. Accordingly, scholars have found the accounts of the De Soto expedition to be of major importance in understanding the Native Americans and their way of life. De Soto's army spent six months in Alabama. They traveled over five hundred miles of Indian trails in the process and had their greatest battle in

Alabama. For these reasons especially, Alabama has always had a great interest in De Soto.

For anthropologists and archaeologists, the surviving De Soto chronicles are uniquely valued for the ethnological information they contain. These documents are the only detailed eyewitness record of the most advanced native cultural achievement in North America—the Mississippian culture—a culture that vanished in the wake of European contact. Scholars are now engaged in the exciting prospect of uniting the ethnological record displayed in the De Soto chronicles with modern archaeological, historical, and linguistic findings in order to yield the first comprehensive picture of southeastern Mississippian Indian chiefdoms at the time of European contact.

For the historical record, the De Soto *entrada* initiated a long period of intermittent contact between Europeans and Native Americans during the sixteenth and seventeenth centuries. De Soto's failures did not deter the Spanish from planting frontier outposts to protect their growing empire in Mexico and the Caribbean. St. Augustine, 1565, was perhaps the most famous, but it was followed by small missions and presidios that dotted the Southeast in the seventeenth century.

The Spanish, and their European rivals for colonial empire, vied for the control and loyalty of Native Americans in the seventeenth and eighteenth centuries, as Spaniards, Frenchmen, and Englishmen jockeyed for empire.

The Amerindian peoples, caught in this tangle of European rivalry, were but a ghostly specter of the densely populated, well-organized Indian chiefdoms encountered by De Soto and his men in 1539–43. With De Soto marched the sickle of diseases that cut down Amerindians with no immunities. Part of the Columbian legacy was not only the conquest and assimilation of native peoples, not only the creation of new races through miscegenation, not only the bringing of Christianity, but a terrible destruction brought on by disease and by the demoralizing defeats at the hands of the Europeans.

De Soto's expedition was one of those primary events in the transformation of North American life initiated by the Columbian voyages, and it is within this context that we view the accounts included in these volumes as being of extraordinary importance.

Preface

We have gathered in these two volumes English translations of the basic documents relating to the expedition of Hernando de Soto to the present-day United States in the years 1539–43.

In contrast to previous editions, where the items were published separately, at various times, and by various publishers, the four primary accounts of the expedition and some relevant supplementary documents have been included here. They appear in a single compact form, newly annotated, and with literary and historical introductions. As such, they should be readily available to scholars and to the general public alike.

Of the four primary accounts, one was originally written in Portuguese and three in Spanish. The one in Portuguese by the "Gentleman from Elvas" had a fine translation in 1933 and we use that translation. The remaining three appear in new translations. Two of them, the accounts by Luis Hernández de Biedma and Rodrigo Rangel, are most commonly referred to in translations published in 1866 and 1904, respectively. The third—the Garcilaso de la Vega account—was most recently done in 1951. Nevertheless, a new translation of the Garcilaso account by a leading scholar in the field was discovered recently, and we publish that translation for the first time. In sum, all three of the Spanish chronicles appear in new translations, newly annotated.

The classic literary account of the expedition, *La Florida*, was written by the Peruvian mestizo Garcilaso de la Vega, the Inca. This long, colorful narrative possesses an unchallenged literary quality lacking in the other three accounts. It has survived the ages and has been translated and republished many times in French, German, and English since first appearing in Spanish in 1605 in Lisbon, Portugal. Like other works by Garcilaso, it is considered by many to be a literary masterpiece. Its historical accuracy has not been so widely praised, however.

When we came upon a new translation several years ago in English, and realized the translation had never been published, we decided to include it in this volume. The translation, done by a supremely well qualified Hispanicist, Dr. Charmion Shelby, more than half a century ago, essentially takes up volume two of *The De Soto Chronicles.*

We realize that a great deal of controversy, both contemporary and modern, surrounds Garcilaso de la Vega's works: controversy over sources he used, over the literary merit versus the historical accuracy of his works, over his life and its significance as a mestizo son of a Spanish conquistador and an Inca noblewoman. He was, in essence, the first of a new race of people born of unions between the Spanish conquerors and the Native American peoples they conquered, and his perspective colored the way he wrote about Hernando de Soto. Accordingly, we asked a modern Garcilaso de la Vega scholar, Dr. Frances Crowley, to write an extended introduction to Garcilaso, and a Spanish specialist, Dr. David Bost, to review and edit the Shelby translation by comparing her work against the original. The results are volume two. We trust the reader will find Garcilaso as much of a "page turner" as have previous generations, providing us with insights into the age of the conquerors.

The other three chronicles form the bulk of volume one of *The De Soto Chronicles.* The longest of these three was written by an unknown gentleman from the Portuguese city of Elvas who marched with De Soto in the expedition. The other two are shorter accounts, one produced by Hernández de Biedma, the king's factor on the expedition, and the second by Rodrigo Rangel, De Soto's private secretary.

As with the Garcilaso de la Vega account, we have new translations of the Biedma and Rangel accounts. Both were translated for this work by a young scholar, John Worth, whose anthropological training has been supplemented by indispensable experience in the General Archive of the Indies in Spain with original Spanish documents. John combines the best training of two disciplines—anthropology and history—and his annotations, reviewed by one of his professors, Dr. Charles Hudson of the University of Georgia, reflect a sensitivity to both areas.

Acknowledgments

Thanks are due to the Alabama Museum of Natural History at The University of Alabama in Tuscaloosa—a town named after the great war chief Tascaluça, who figures so prominently in the accounts of the De Soto expedition. The editors wish to express their appreciation for the extensive assistance provided by the museum and its director, Dr. Douglas E. Jones, who, as chairman of the Alabama De Soto Commission, originally suggested this project, and to the assistant director for administration, Dr. Edward C. Moore.

Thanks are also due to The University of Alabama's Latin American Studies Program and to the History Department, which made the time of historian Dr. Lawrence A. Clayton available to serve as an editor; to the Department of Anthropology, which supported the services of a member of its faculty, Dr. Vernon James Knight, Jr., to serve as an editor; to Dr. Edward H. Moseley, director of the Capstone International Program Center, for his continuing support; to Dr. Spurgeon Baldwin, chairman of the Department of Romance Languages and Classics, for assistance with Spanish materials; and to Dr. Joseph Sánchez, director of the Spanish Colonial Research Center at the University of New Mexico, who provided us with insights into several of the De Soto documents.

Our contributing editors and the members of our board of advisers are listed on other pages of this volume, but we would be remiss if we did not acknowledge their support and assistance during every phase of the project. All busy scholars, with many demands on their time, they were always present when we needed them, and their enthusiasm for the project sustained its driving force during some difficult days. We are grateful and we thank them.

Other persons to whom we are indebted include Kathleen T. Baxter, reference archivist in the National Anthropological Archives of the National Museum of Natural History at the Smithsonian Institution, for assistance in locating the Charmion Shelby translation of *La Florida* in the papers of Dr.

John Swanton; Jane Garner, archivist at the General Libraries of the University of Texas at Austin, for providing help in reviewing the Charmion Shelby papers in the Nettie Lee Benson Latin American Collection there and for providing us with a microfilm copy of the 1605 edition of *La Florida;* John H. Hébert, director of the Quincentenary Program of the Library of Congress, for biographical information concerning Dr. Shelby; Dean Joyce Lamont and Andrea Watson, special collections archivists at The University of Alabama Library, for assistance in many ways; Dr. Jeffrey P. Brain of Harvard University and Dr. John C. Hall of the Alabama Museum of Natural History at The University of Alabama for assistance with illustrations; Charles M. Hudson of the University of Georgia; Richard Hite, Superintendent of the De Soto National Memorial, Bradenton, Florida, for advice and counseling; Eduardo Kortright for assistance in translating material from the Spanish; Anne R. Gibbons for preparing the indexes for both volumes; and two students who have helped on this project, Lisa Zimmerman at Furman University who assisted Dr. Bost in checking the Shelby translation and Anna Bryan who worked on a preliminary index for *La Florida*.

No project as complex as this one could ever be brought to print without extensive assistance from the publisher. We are very grateful to the staff of The University of Alabama Press, and to its director, Malcolm M. MacDonald, who gave the project unswerving support.

We also wish to acknowledge support from the following:

the Alabama De Soto Commission for a substantial grant in support of the project;

the National Endowment for the Humanities for their generous grant;

the Center for Early Contact Period Studies at the University of Florida at Gainesville and its director, Dr. Michael V. Gannon, for supporting the work of Dr. John H. Hann in updating the notes to the Elvas account;

the Program for Cultural Cooperation Between Spain's Ministry of Culture and United States' Universities for a grant in support of publication;

the Spain '92 Foundation;

the Consul General of Spain, New Orleans, Louisiana;

the Smithsonian Institution, Washington, D.C., for permission to use the Charmion Shelby translation of *La Florida del Inca* by Garcilaso de la Vega (BAE manuscript #4465, John R. Swanton), in their National Anthropological Archives;

the Smithsonian Institution Press for permission to use material from the *Final Report of the United States De Soto Expedition Commission*, by John

R. Swanton, published by Smithsonian Press, copyright 1985, Smithsonian Institution;

the University of Texas Press for permission to reproduce material from the *Royal Commentaries of the Incas and General History of Peru* by Garcilaso de la Vega, El Inca, translated and with an introduction by Harold V. Livermore, copyright 1966;

Osprey Publishing, Ltd., 59 Grosvenor Street, London W1X9DA, for permission to reproduce two illustrations from *The Conquistadores* in the Osprey Men-at-Arms Series, copyright 1980;

the De Soto National Memorial, Bradenton, Florida, for permission to use the illustration of the Hernando de Soto entrada by Dan Feaser, National Park Service, Harpers Ferry Interpretive Design Center;

the National Museum of the American Indian, Smithsonian Institution, for permission to reproduce the photograph of the monolithic ax and the photograph of the pottery jar in the form of a human head;

the Florida Division of Historical Resources for permission to reproduce the photograph of the four-maravedi coin;

the W. S. Hoole Special Collections Library, The University of Alabama;

Jan Pruitt, the Office of Publications, The University of Alabama;

Florida Museum of Natural History for permission to use the illustration of a carved wooden bird;

Etowah Mounds State Historic Site, operated by Georgia State Parks and Historic Sites Division, for permission to use an illustration of the Etowah figurines;

National Geographic Society for permission to use two illustrations, "A Southeast Village in 1491," by H. Tom Hall, and "Spanish Captain Juan Pardo Meets with the Ancestors of the Creek and Cherokee," by John Berkey;

and Cornell University Library for permission to print Delisle's map of Louisiana.

Notes on Translations and Names

Four full narratives that were produced in the years following the De Soto expedition have survived. One of these is known simply as the Elvas account because its author only identified himself as a Portuguese gentleman from Elvas. A second is that of Rodrigo Rangel, private secretary to De Soto. The third, "presented in the year 1544 to the King of Spain in Council," was written by Luis Hernández de Biedma, factor for the king. The fourth account, *La Florida,* was completed by the Inca, Garcilaso de la Vega, in 1591, although it was not published until 1605. It is generally thought to have been based on interviews with Gonzalo Sylvestre, an officer under De Soto and a survivor of the expedition. These four accounts are customarily referred to as Elvas, Rangel, Biedma, and Garcilaso (or the Inca).

The four accounts have had an erratic publishing history and an even less orderly translation history. The classic translation of Elvas, by Dr. James Alexander Robertson, was published in 1933 by the Yale University Press for the Florida State Historical Society. It was a limited edition of only 360 copies. It is still the most recent translation.

Garcilaso's *La Florida* is currently available in a translation by John and Jeannette Varner, published by the University of Texas Press in 1951.

Recently, there have been expressions of concern by scholars that most of the available translations were not literal enough to be really satisfactory, particularly for the needs of archaeologists and anthropologists. We have tried to meet this concern by being more literal in these translations.

Accordingly, we use the Robertson version of Elvas. This account, written originally in Portuguese, is currently out of print. It was completed by Robertson, then secretary of the Florida State Historical Society, in 1933 for that society and was published by the Yale University Press. It had excellent reviews at the time of its publication, and we see little likelihood of improving on it. At the time it appeared, Lesley Byrd Simpson wrote (*Hispanic American Historical Review* 14, no. 3 (August 1934): 346–48), "Dr. Robertson's method is to preserve the style of the original by reproducing in English as closely as possible, word for word, the Portuguese text. . . . This book is a monument of patient and thorough scholarship." To bring Robertson's material up to the current state of De Soto scholarship, Robertson's notes have been updated for this volume by Dr. John H. Hann.

For our version of the Garcilaso chronicle, we have identified in the National Anthropological Archives at the Smithsonian Institution a previously unpublished translation. Garcilaso's *La Florida* is the longest of the four accounts and occupies most of our second volume. This new translation was done by Dr. Clair Charmion Shelby for the 1935 U.S. De Soto Expedition Commission. In the final report of that commission, Dr. John Swanton, chairman of the commission, wrote, "The Commission employed Dr. Charmion Shelby, of Austin, Tex., an experienced translator of documents in sixteenth century Spanish, to provide an accurate translation of *La Florida of the Inca.* This translation covers 910 typewritten pages, double-spaced" (Swanton, John R., *Final Report of the United States De Soto Expedition Commission,* Washington: United States Government Printing Office, 1939; reprint the Smithsonian Institution Press, 1985, p. viii).

Dr. Shelby was indeed an experienced translator. She had earned a doctorate in Spanish history under Professor Charles Wilson Hackett at the University of Texas. She was cotranslator with him of *Pichardo's Treatise on the Limits of Louisiana and Texas,* a two-volume work, and was translator of the original documents for Professor Hackett's monumental *Revolt of the Pueblo Indians of New Mexico*. Dr. Shelby worked for thirteen years, until her death in 1955, as a reference librarian for the Hispanic Division of the Library of Congress.

Shelby's translation of *La Florida* was not published because Congress did not fund many of the projects of the 1935 Commission. At a later date (1950), the Hakluyt Society of England proposed to publish her translation and had it scheduled for publication when the Varner edition was published by the University of Texas Press. In the light of that, the Hakluyt Society dropped its plans for publication.

We believe interested parties should have both translations available. The Varners performed a great service to scholars in publishing the first complete English translation of *La Florida,* but Dr. Shelby was an expert in sixteenth-century Spanish, and her translation will give us the first translation of the longest chronicle done by a scholar whose expertise was in Spanish of the sixteenth century. It was edited for this book by Dr. David Bost of Furman University with notes by Dr. Vernon James Knight, Jr., of The University of Alabama. The editors have made a few small corrections in places where Garcilaso's table of contents does not exactly match his chapter headings and enumeration.

We are greatly indebted to Dr. Bost, who not only checked the Shelby translation of Garcilaso word-for-word against the 1605 edition but also found time in his schedule to translate for us the several documents from the General Archive of the Indies in Seville, which appear in volume one of these *De Soto Chronicles*.

The account by Garcilaso de la Vega was first published in Lisbon in 1605. A second edition was published in 1723. Dr. Shelby used the 1605 edition, with reference where necessary to the 1723 edition. Because Garcilaso was not a member of the expedition, and his version is thought to be based on what he was told many years later by Gonzalo Sylvestre, it is considered to be the least accurate of the four. In addition to what he was told by Sylvestre, Garcilaso says he had access to accounts by two other members of the expedition, Alonso de Carmona and Juan Coles. Their accounts have not survived except in quotations by Garcilaso.

We also owe thanks to Dr. Frances Crowley of Southeast Missouri State University for the version of Garcilaso's *Genealogy of Garci Perez de Vargas*, which appears as an appendix to volume two. This document appears here in English for the first time. Dr. Crowley identified the *Genealogy* in the Biblioteca Nacional in Madrid and translated it for our use.

The two shorter accounts, by Rangel and by Biedma, are translated anew for this edition by John Worth at the University of Florida at Gainesville with annotation support from Dr. Charles Hudson of the University of Georgia.

The account by Rodrigo Rangel, De Soto's secretary, is a detailed itinerary covering the first three years of the expedition. This account was not published until 1851, when it appeared in Gonzalo Fernández de Oviedo's *Historia general y natural de las Indias*. Our translation was made from Oviedo's *Historia*.

The account by Biedma, the king's representative on the expedition, is the only one for which the original manuscript has survived. We have based our translation on a photostatic copy of that manuscript. Although the manuscript was written in 1544, it was only published in 1857 by Buckingham Smith.

We owe special thanks to Dr. Paul E. Hoffman of Louisiana State University, whose extensive knowledge of the history of the period and of the Spanish language was frequently drawn upon.

In preparing his translation of Elvas, Dr. Robertson added an extensive collection of notes. We have reproduced these in full, at the end of the Elvas account, because they are a valuable part of Robertson's work. In addition, we have had them updated for this present work by Dr. John H. Hann, who has also provided some of his own original notes, which appear as footnotes in our volume. Dr. Hann's original notes cover points distinct from those made by Robertson and originated from his comparative reading of Robertson's translation with the original Portuguese text. Some minor additional updating of Robertson's notes has also been done by Dr. Vernon James Knight, Jr. Dr. Knight's notes are identified with VJK in brackets. The editors have taken the liberty to standardize the name Hernando de Soto from the normal usage of "Fernando" in the original text.

Some minor alterations in quotations from the Portuguese have been made to accommodate the style of modern fonts and spellings. Where Elvas used the tilde ˜ in certain cases (*q* with a tilde, *hu* or *hua* with a tilde over the *u*, *e* with a tilde to indicate the dropping of a following *n*, and *d* with a tilde to indicate the dropping of a following *e*), modern usage has been adopted.

Another thorny problem is that of names—both Indian names and Spanish names. The Indians had no written alphabet at this time in their history. Accordingly, when one of the chroniclers heard the name of a town or a person, he translated it into his own alphabet as well as he could. Partly for this reason, the same Indian person or town will be called by different names in different chronicles. We adopted John Swanton's solution in his report for the 1935 U.S. De Soto Expedition Commission; he included a table showing the various Indian proper names used in the four chronicles. We have reproduced his table of names within volume one. Nevertheless, variant spellings of the same name often appear in the same source document—and even on the same page. Where this occurs, we have not selected among the alternatives but have reproduced the variants as found in our original authors.

A somewhat different problem presents itself with Spanish surnames when they are preceded by the word *de*. The general rule is to use lowercase for the *de* except at the beginning of a sentence. We have followed this rule for all names except that of *De Soto* when it stands alone without the first name. The usage *De Soto* has become such a common term in English that we consider it preferable to *de Soto* when standing by itself.

We have also made some slight changes in punctuation and capitalization to follow modern practices. For example, a comma may have been added before "and" in a series of three or more items, and a word in a chapter title may have been capitalized.

Introduction: The De Soto Expedition, a Cultural Crossroads

by Paul E. Hoffman

Spanish Context and the Significance of De Soto's Expedition

We will probably never know when European seamen first laid eyes on peninsular Florida and lived to tell about it. The standard narrative accounts of early voyages, such as those of Peter Martyr, Gonzalo Fernández Oviedo y Valdés, and Bartholomé de Las Casas, and the manuscript correspondence, lawsuits, *residencias,* notarial records, and treasury records have failed, so far, to yield any clear evidence prior to the 1510s. Tantalizing clues exist: the Cantino Map, said to date to 1503; the discovery of Bermuda in 1505; the circumnavigation of Cuba in 1508; and in Juan Ponce de León's apparent knowledge of land west of the Bahamas when he asked for permission to seek "Bimini" in 1512. From the teens come more specific but still vague references to slaving voyages and the indirect evidence provided by the hostile reception that Ponce received.[1]

After Ponce de León's voyage of 1513, there was no doubt that land existed north of Cuba and west of the Bahamas. The extent of that land in either direction was, however, less clear and remained vague until the 1520s, because Spanish exploration was still driven, even in the 1510s, by various forms of the Columbian-Vespuccian effort to fit the "new world" (Vespucci) or "another world" (Columbus) into Ptolemaic concepts of world geography. In those concepts, the new discoveries were either islands off of Asia or

[1]The slaving voyages of Pedro de Salazar and Diego de Miruelo are discussed in Paul E. Hoffman, "A New Voyage of North American Discovery: The Voyage of Pedro de Salazar to the Island of Giants," *Florida Historical Quarterly* 58 (1980): 415–26.

various peninsulas jutting out from it.[2] The job of explorers, according to this conceptualization of the world, was to go around these islands and peninsulas to the southeast and south, or, if starting from the southern side of the Isthmus of Panama, to sail west across the "great gulf" thought to separate the "new world" peninsula (or island) from Asia proper. Ferdinand Magellan's voyage (1519–23), the explorations of Vasco Núñez de Balboa (1517–19) westward in the Gulf of Panama, and Gil Gonzalez Dávila's exploration up the west coast of Central America (1520–23) fit this pattern, as do the "minor voyages" along the northeastern coast of South America in the years 1499–1519.[3]

A better understanding of the extent of North America developed rapidly after 1517. In that year, Francisco Hernández de Córdoba was sent to Yucatan, first explored by Vicente Yáñez Pinzón and Juan Díaz de Solís (1508–9). Hernández de Córdoba's findings, soon amplified by Juan de Grijalva's voyage as far as Cabo Rojo (1518), set in motion not only Hernán Cortés's expedition of 1519, which resulted in the conquest of central Mexico two years later, but also the voyage of Alonso Alvarez de Pineda, sent in 1519 by Francisco de Garay, governor of Jamaica. Alvarez de Pineda was to seek the strait that one variant on the Ptolemaic theory suggested might lie north of the "new world," now conceived as a very large island off the coast of Asia. Alvarez de Pineda did not find any opening along the northern and eastern shores of the Gulf of Mexico, nor did he divine that the "River of Flowers" that he had passed drained the interior of a continent.[4] He did, however, visit Cortés's outpost at Vera Cruz and left a small Spanish force on the Pánuco River.

If, after Alvarez de Pineda's exploration, it was clear that a land mass enclosed the Gulf of Mexico, the questions then became how far to the north that land ran and if there was open water between it and the land areas associated with the cod fisheries in the far north. Answers to these questions

---

[2]John H. Parry, *The Discovery of South America* (New York: Taplinger Publishing, 1979), 78–79.

[3]In addition to Parry, see Louis-André Vigneras, *The Discovery of South America and the Andalucian Voyages* (Chicago: University of Chicago Press, 1976).

[4]Alvarez de Pineda's map has been published in William P. Cumming, R. A. Skelton, and David B. Quinn, *The Discovery of North America* (New York: American Heritage Press, 1972), 68–69; his record of his voyage is incorporated into Alonso de Chaves, *Alonso de Chaves y el libro de su "Espejo de Navegantes,"* ed. by Pablo Castañeda, M. Cuesta, and P. Hernández (Madrid: privately printed, 1977), 120–22. The identification of the Río de Flores as the Mississippi is mine.

were obtained in 1521–25. In 1521, slavers sailing on behalf of two companies, each involving judges of the Audiencia of Santo Domingo, made landfall at the South Santee River, in modern South Carolina. Subsequently, the Licenciado Lucas Vázquez de Ayllón, one of the judges, obtained a royal contract for the exploration and then settlement of this new discovery, which he claimed was at 35°, 36°, and 37°N latitude (it was actually at 33°20′), the same "parallel" as Andalucia in Spain. His pilot, Pedro de Quejo, explored the coast from near Delaware Bay to Saint Simon's Sound (1525) but found no evidence of a strait.[5] Meanwhile, from the north and in 1523, Esteban Gómez had sailed south to about the area of New York harbor, again finding no strait.[6] Thus, by the end of 1525, the Spaniards knew that North America stood between Europe and Asia. In addition, thanks to the Magellan-El Cano voyage (1519–22), they knew that the Pacific Ocean was very wide. The Americas, or, as the Spaniards called them, the Indies, truly were a "new world."

Spanish attempts to conquer and colonize the newly revealed North American land mass began in 1521, when Francisco de Garay received a royal contract to conquer "Amichel," and Ponce de León made a final, fatal attempt to gain control over the Indians of south Florida. Garay's Amichel was a province whose southern border was at or near the Pánuco River in Mexico. To the east and north, "Amichel" ended wherever Juan Ponce de León's "Florida" began, an undetermined point on the northern Gulf Coast. There is evidence that Garay intended all along to force his way into Mexico and that he had Alvarez de Pineda leave men on the Pánuco River in 1519 in preparation for that attempt. In the end, he failed because Cortés had control of the rich central provinces of New Spain, as the Spanish called Mexico, and so was able to suborn most of Garay's men into joining him. Garay died at Mexico City in 1524, vainly trying to obtain recognition of his claim over the Pánuco drainage.[7] Ponce de León died at San Juan, Puerto Rico, in 1522 from wounds received when he and his men had tried to land among the Caloosahatchee Indians in April 1521.[8]

---

[5]Paul E. Hoffman, *A New Andalucia and a Way to the Orient: The American Southeast in the Sixteenth Century* (Baton Rouge: Louisiana State University Press, 1990), 20–21, 35–36, 51–58.

[6]Samuel E. Morison, *The European Discovery of America*, 2 vols. (New York: Oxford University Press, 1971), 1:326–31.

[7]Robert S. Weddle, *Spanish Sea: The Gulf of Mexico in North American Discovery, 1500–1685* (College Station: Texas A&M Press, 1985), 95–108, 130–46.

[8]Morison, *European Discovery*, 2:506–12 (1513 voyage), 2:515–16 (1521 voyage).

Along the Atlantic Coast, the Spanish attempt at conquest and settlement began in 1526, when Ayllón landed a colony of six hundred persons at the Santee River-Winyah Bay area. His plan, apparently, was to have his native interpreters (captured in 1521) guide him to the Indian chiefdom of Duhae (also, Du-a-e), in the interior. However, the interpreters fled. Moreover, the coastal zone was found to be largely empty of inhabitants and lacking in foods familiar to the Spaniards. Scouting parties Ayllón sent to explore the coast to the south reported the existence of an area with an Indian population that grew maize. So Ayllón moved his colony to the area of the Guale Indians who lived around Sapelo and St. Catherine's sounds in modern Georgia. Established on or about September 29, 1526, as San Miguel de Gualdape, this new colony was abandoned in late October or early November, following Ayllón's death on October 18.[9]

The next Spanish intrusion into the Southeast was the result of accident rather than design. Pánfilo de Narváez obtained a grant in 1526 that made him heir to Ponce de León and Garay, thus allowing him to colonize anywhere from Amichel on the west to the Cape of Florida on the east. His intention was to move into Amichel, the gateway to Mexico. But bad luck, in the form of a storm as his fleet neared Havana, forced him to seek shelter on the middle west coast of Florida during Holy Week, 1528. He had evidently provisioned his ships only for the leg of the trip from Trinidad to Havana and so now found himself in a strange land on short rations.

Although not indisputable, the available evidence shows that he landed at Johns Pass, just north of the entrance to Tampa Bay. Alvar Núñez Cabeza de Vaca, whose account is almost all that we know of this expedition's history, indicates that the pilots and officials of the expedition were uncertain of their geography or location. In the end, over Cabeza de Vaca's objection, they decided to send the ships northward and then south to Havana for supplies and to march the army north, in the belief that they would soon find a "deep bay" reaching ten leagues into the land. There they would wait for the ships, meanwhile living off the stored food of the inhabitants.

Following this design, Narváez marched northward within a few leagues of the coast until he crossed the Withlacoochee River. In all of that area, his men found little to eat and no Indians. Once across the Withlacoochee, he turned inland and used Indian guides to move northward to Apalachee. According to Cabeza de Vaca, the army met few Indians but did encounter their maize fields at intervals of seven or eight leagues (seventeen to twenty-

[9] Hoffman, *New Andalucia*, 66–80.

five miles, depending on which league he was using). Apalachee was also a disappointment, apparently because they were fooled into thinking that an outlying, rather small village was the entire province. Having rested there, the Spaniards decided to go west to Aute, said to have abundant food, and then to the sea, with the intention of making boats, or making contact with their own ships, so that they might escape to Amichel or Mexico. And that, in summary, is what they did, except that the boats they built were wrecked on the Texas coast. Only Cabeza de Vaca and two other men survived to reach Mexico in 1536.[10]

When Hernando de Soto returned from Peru to Spain to seek his own area of government in Ecuador or Guatemala, or permission to conquer some new area, the fate of the Narváez expedition was still not known, although its disappearance was. That fact fit with the gradually building reputation of the Gulf and Atlantic coasts of North America. Alvarez de Pineda had summed up his findings along the upper Gulf Coast by saying that "all the land is low and sterile."[11] Ponce de León had found the Cape of Florida area inhabited by brave, skilled warriors who beat the Spaniards in pitched battles, an almost unheard-of event. The majority of Ayllón's surviving colonists spread the word that the Atlantic Coast, too, was not suitable for colonization, even where there were Indians. Although fish and fowl were abundant, few sources of carbohydrates that were familiar or acceptable to the Spaniards seemed available.[12] Ayllón's propaganda about it being a "new Andalucia" was false. Only the rumored pearls and "terrestrial gems" of an inland province called "Xapira" might still be true. But no one really knew, because Ayllón's people had not reached into the interior, having lost their guides to that area at the Santee-Winyah Bay landing site (which was the one known to give access to Xapira, according to a report by a native captured in 1521). Cabeza de Vaca's return to the Spanish world allowed De Soto to fill in this picture with knowledge of the experiences of Narváez on the west coast of peninsular Florida.

Hernando de Soto was the inheritor not only of all the previous grants,

[10]Paul E. Hoffman, "Narváez and Cabeza de Vaca in Florida," in Charles Hudson and Carmen McClendon, eds., *The Forgotten Centuries: Indians and Europeans in the American South, 1513–1704* (Athens: University of Georgia Press, 1993).

[11]Included in the text of Francisco de Garay's contract for the conquest of Amichel, June 4, 1521, in Martín Fernández de Navarrete, ed., *Colección de los viages y descubrimientos que hicieron por mar los Españoles desde fines del siglo XV,* 5 vols. (Madrid, 1825–1837), 3:160.

[12]Gonzalo Fernández de Oviedo, *Historia general y natural de las Indias,* 4 vols. (Madrid: Real Academia de la Historia, 1851–55), 3:631–33.

now consolidated into a single province of "La Florida," but also of his predecessors' painfully gained knowledge about the coast and interior.[13] Judging by his actions, he made as much use of this information as he could, beginning with the selection of a landing point and in deciding where to move next. The accuracy of this information was probably not very good, however, a fact that the modern reader should bear in mind.

Probably the first fruit that De Soto gathered from the work of his predecessors was that neither the Atlantic Coast nor the Gulf Coast was preferable. Neither offered deep, protected ports that also gave immediate access to large native populations. Ayllón's San Miguel, a possible exception to this rule, was of unknown location; not even the pilot major of the House of Trade in Seville recorded it in his collection of sailing directions and coastal descriptions.[14] Because neither coast offered any particular advantage, De Soto seems to have opted for the Gulf Coast of peninsular Florida because it was close to Cuba and easy to reach on both legs of a trip back and forth. An Atlantic Coast port, while easy to reach from the Antilles, would have required a return via a long detour east of the Bahamas, through the Mona Passage, or even farther east into the Atlantic Ocean. Then there was the long and sometimes difficult journey around western Cuba and back into the Gulf to Havana. A voyage using the counter-current along the coast of Florida and then across the Gulf Stream to Havana was less difficult and lengthy, but it was more dangerous because it required sailing close to the shore in relatively shallow water.

Having decided his general line of approach to La Florida, De Soto next made use of Cabeza de Vaca's information about the bay that Narváez had glimpsed and that his ships had found on their voyage south. According to Cabeza de Vaca, this bay, modern Tampa Bay, was "so uninhabited and so poor [a land] as had ever been found in those parts."[15] Accordingly, De Soto sent Juan de Añasco to seek a better harbor, which he found seventy-five to eighty leagues north of Havana, rather short of the hundred leagues that was the standard estimate of the distance to Bahía Honda, that is, Tampa Bay.[16]

---

[13]De Soto's contract is published herein, vol. 1.

[14]Chaves, *Alonso de Chaves,* 124–25.

[15]Alvar Núñez Cabeza de Vaca, *La relación de los naufragios de Alvar Núñez Cabeza de Vaca,* ed. Martín A. Favata and José B. Fernández (Potomac, Md.: Scripta Humanistica, 1986), 18, my translation.

[16]Chaves, *Alonso de Chaves,* 121, No. 9. De Soto and the treasury officials described this port as "inhabited and very secure," thus implicitly contrasting it to Narváez's Bahía Honda. Quoted in John R. Swanton, *Final Report of the United States De Soto Expedition Commission,*

Whether that newly discovered port is where De Soto actually landed is another, much-debated question. The point is that De Soto sought to avoid the sterile bay that Narváez had found.

In the same way, De Soto's path north in the interior (rather than close to the coast) of peninsular Florida seems to have been based on the experience of Narváez. De Soto had better scouting and an efficient policy of moving from the central town of each chiefdom to that of the next, a technique probably learned in Central America. This took him to Apalachee, where he found the central town. Then he subjected the entire province to foraging activities, unlike Narváez, who had been kept at a minor village with little food.

De Soto's pace may also have been determined, at least initially, by the experience of Narváez. Elvas says that De Soto marched five or six leagues a day in populated areas, and as rapidly as his men and swine would allow in unpopulated ones to avoid hunger from lack of maize.[17] Swanton presents evidence that De Soto moved at about twelve miles per day during the march to the Withlacoochee River.[18] These figures are estimated averages. They are very close to the minimum distance (seven leagues) that Cabeza de Vaca mentions as that between Indian maize fields. The figures suggest that De Soto intended to avoid Narváez's experience of hunger. Narváez attributed the difficulty in getting food to the fact that his men did not make a day's march between sources of maize. Jeffrey Mitchem has suggested that De Soto's inclusion of pigs in his expedition was another effort to avoid Narváez's hunger.[19]

Apalachee's nature and general location relative to the coast were the last useful information De Soto could have derived from Narváez's experience. Of the knowledge that his predecessors had gathered about La Florida, only Ayllón's province of pearls and "terrestrial gems" remained as a guide to

---

1938, reprint with introduction by Jeffrey Brain (Washington, D.C.: Smithsonian Institution Press, 1985), 101.

[17]"The Account by a Gentleman from Elvas," *True Relation of the Hardships Suffered by Governor Hernando de Soto & Certain Portuquese Gentlemen During the Discovery of the Province of Florida, Now newly set forth by a Gentlemen of Elvas,* trans. and ed. James Alexander Robertson, herein, vol. 1. Cited hereafter as Elvas, *Relation.*

[18]Swanton, *Final Report,* 302. See also his p. 105.

[19]Jeffrey M. Mitchem, "Initial Spanish-Indian Contact in West Peninsular Florida: The Archaeological Evidence," in *Columbian Consequences,* vol. 2: *Archaeological and Historical Perspectives on the Spanish Borderlands East,* ed. David Hurst Thomas (Washington, D.C.: Smithsonian Institution Press, 1990), 51.

future action. De Soto followed up on it because an Indian boy, Pedro, provided him with a description of Cofitachequi that matched part of the Ayllón material.

Once at Cofitachequi, De Soto's men found knives and beads that they recognized could have come from Ayllón's colony. Mistakenly believing that he had landed at only one place, they assumed that the river of Cofitachequi (probably the Wateree, which feeds into the Santee) was the river where Ayllón had died.[20] They called this river the Santa Elena and assumed that it came out at the point of the same name, a landmark that could be found because it was at 32°N according to Alonso de Chaves. They thus established, in their own minds, a way to approach the rich agricultural possibilities of Cofitachequi by using the sea and this river. A subsequent search in the mountains farther north and west failed to turn up any sign of the "terrestrial gems" (actually quartz and other types of crystal) or any minerals aside from some copper that the Native Americans had obtained by trade from mines located farther north than De Soto penetrated. In short, Ayllón's report of pearls in the interior was accurate, but the rest of his tale of "Xapira" seemed not to be.

De Soto was not interested in freshwater pearls and agricultural lands. Dreaming of new gold mines such as he and others had found in the mountains of Central America, he turned his army westward and continued the search. His next major stopping place was Coosa. It, like Cofitachequi, came to be remembered as a place of abundant food and good prospects for European agriculture. In fact, after the events of the next two years, Coosa took on the qualities of a Garden of Eden in the telling and retelling of the adventures of the army.

In sum, De Soto's expedition not only consolidated all prior grants into one, but it also used and checked the geographic knowledge deriving from those expeditions. It brought a closure to the early Spanish explorations and attempts at settlement in La Florida. At the same time, its experiences at Cofitachequi, and even more at Coosa, served to create a new piece of knowledge, perhaps better understood as a folkloric legend, about the Southeast: that these interior places would be good for Spanish settlement and might, because of dense Indian populations, allow the establishment of *encomiendas*, whose members would cultivate the soil for their new lords.

---

[20]Luys Hernández de Biedma, "Relations of the Island of Florida," herein, vol. 1; Rodrigo Rangel, "Account of the Northern Conquest and Discovery of Hernando de Soto," herein, vol. 1; Elvas *Relation*, herein, vol. 1.

This new belief in the idyllic Coosa is well reflected in the words that Francisco Cervantes de Salazar put into the mouth of Zuazo in the following dialogue from his *Life in the Imperial and Loyal City of Mexico in New Spain* (1554): "ZUAZO: . . . Florida, lying distant only an easy and very short voyage by sea, and by land neither a long nor a difficult journey, should be conquered. . . . ALFARO: What advantage and profit would your province derive from this action? ZUAZO: Very much indeed, for whatever is produced by the other Spain in the Old World, from which merchandise is imported into ours with so much delay and difficulty, all this would be supplied by Florida, which produces much more abundantly and is contiguous to us."[21]

Although later in date and of uncertain origins, Garcilaso de la Vega's report of Viceroy Mendoza's reaction to the De Soto story is along the same lines. Garcilaso says that although Mendoza was saddened by the loss of so many men and the hardships of the others, he was "very happy to hear of the spaciousness of that kingdom, the opportunity that it holds for raising all kinds of livestock, and the fertility of the land in corn, grains, fruits, and vegetables."[22]

This vision of Coosa's abundance and potential were among the main motives for the colonizing expedition of Tristán de Luna y Arellano. Luna went from Mexico to Florida in 1559 to build a series of Spanish settlements that would link Achuse (Pensacola Bay) on the Gulf of Mexico, with the Point of Santa Elena (Tybee Island at the mouth of the Savannah River) on the Atlantic Ocean. Each was to be built in the center of an Indian chiefdom, whose residents would in time be brought to obey the Spaniards and be placed in encomiendas awarded to the more meritorious colonists.[23] The expedition failed to achieve any of these goals. Its last soldiers withdrew from the shore of Pensacola Bay in 1561.

If the Luna expedition was the most direct consequence of De Soto's *entrada* so far as the Spaniards were concerned, there were others of less consequence. Knowledge of the agricultural possibilities of the interior, of the relatively dense Native American populations there, and that there was a way to reach and cross the mountains and continue westward toward Mexico all seem to have played some role in Pedro Menéndez de Avilés's decision

[21]Francisco Cervantes de Salazar, *Life in the Imperial and Loyal City of Mexico in New Spain* (1554), trans. Mimia Lee Barrett Shepard (Austin: University of Texas Press, 1953), 79.

[22]Garcilaso de la Vega, *La Florida,* herein, vol. 2.

[23]Hoffman, *New Andalucia,* 144, 151.

to send Captain Juan Pardo into the interior in 1566 and 1567. Pardo left from the new Spanish post at Santa Elena town, established in the spring of 1566 on Parris Island, S.C.[24]

Another consequence was the confusion of Alvarez de Pineda's Bay of the Holy Spirit and De Soto-Moscoso's River of the Holy Spirit. The latter is the Mississippi, but the former appears to have been one of the bays on the Louisiana coast west of the "father of waters." The similarity of the names led to their conflation on later maps, with the river shown as emptying into the bay, which is placed farther west than the actual location of the Mississippi's delta. This mistaken placement had little effect on the Spaniards, who apparently never tried to find the River of the Holy Spirit until the 1680s. Later, it may have helped to convince the Sieur de la Salle and his French patrons that his incorrect latitude for the river's delta was somehow right, since it placed the outlet on the western side of the Gulf of Mexico, in the general vicinity of the Bay and River of the Holy Spirit.[25]

The Native American Context and Significance

The De Soto expedition has long been recognized as vital to understanding the history of Native American cultures in the areas he visited. The accounts of the expedition provide a sort of snapshot of populations, political systems, and, seemingly, cultural ways that correspond to late phases of the Mississippian cultural horizon in the Southeast. As Ann Ramenofsky has recently noted, this information in the chronicles was a critical link in Cyrus Thomas's resolution of the so-called Mound Builder debate, and in most of the "direct historical" study of southeastern Indians since.[26] Much recent archaeological scholarship has tested data found in these accounts, while at the same time providing information and details that the Spaniards overlooked or thought unworthy of mention in their accounts. Ongoing controversies about "the route" have led to efforts to better understand selected

[24]Charles Hudson, *The Juan Pardo Expeditions: Exploration of the Carolinas and Tennessee, 1566–1568* (Washington, D.C.: Smithsonian Institution Press, 1990), provides details and transcriptions and translations of documents relating to these expeditions.

[25]Peter H. Wood, "La Salle: Discovery of a Lost Explorer," *American Historical Review* 89 (1984): 294–323. La Salle did not, however, mistake the River and Bay of the Holy Spirit as the outlets of the Mississippi, which he had named the Colbert.

[26]Ann F. Ramenofsky, "Loss of Innocence: Explanations of Differential Persistence in the Sixteenth-Century Southeast," in *Columbian Consequences,* vol. 2, 33–35.

sites and to synthesize archaeological findings into larger pictures of polities and their cultures. Jeffrey Brain summarized this research (to 1984) in his introduction to the reprint of the 1939 United States De Soto Expedition Commission report.[27] Brain and Charles Ewen herein provide a bibliography that brings Brain's earlier bibliography up to date. In general, it appears that we now have a better understanding of the geographic extent of, social stratification of, and general subsistence and cultural ways of the peoples De Soto encountered in his peregrination through their maize fields. Much remains to be learned, especially about the supposed effects of De Soto's passing on Native American cultures.

The De Soto expedition's effects on the native peoples of the American Southeast have been much debated, especially because those effects may be an explanation for the apparent demographic, cultural, and political collapse of the Mississippian cultures, and the subsequent cultural and political reorganization that occurred between De Soto's time and the European penetration of the region that began in the late seventeenth century. In the most common explanation of the changes, De Soto's men are said to have spread disease that destroyed the demographic basis of the societies he visited, causing the disintegration of the culture.[28]

The demographic consequences of European, and not just De Soto's, contact with the southeastern Indians are the subject of recent works by G. R. Milner, Henry F. Dobyns, Marvin Smith, and Ann Ramenofsky.[29]

---

[27]Swanton, *Final Report.*

[28]Rochelle A. Marrinan, John F. Scarry, and Rhonda L. Majors, "Prelude to De Soto: The Expedition of Pánfilo de Narváez," in *Columbian Consequences,* vol. 2, 78, suggest that the Spaniards confronted the Indians with a reality that could not be contained in their worldview and that somehow caused cultural collapse. The basis for this suggestion is the work of Mary W. Helms, *Ulysses' Sail: An Ethnographic Odyssey of Power, Knowledge, and Geographical Distance* (Princeton: Princeton University Press, 1988). For a different view, see Janet E. Levy, J. Alan May, and David G. Moore, "From Ysa to Joara: Cultural Diversity in the Catawba Valley from the Fourteenth to the Sixteenth Century," in *Columbian Consequences,* vol. 2, 164. The similar case of the collapse of the Classic Maya culture in southern Yucatan has been ignored by students of the southeastern Indians. Single-cause explanations such as disease, failure of priests to predict some celestial event, or the invasion of corn fields (*milpas*) by grasses have been suggested at one time or another for the Maya case. Recent work suggests the compounding effects of an invasion from Central Mexico.

[29]G. R. Milner, "Epidemic Disease in the Post-Contact Southeast: A Reappraisal," *Midcontinental Journal of Archaeology* 5 (1980): 3–17; Henry F. Dobyns, *Their Number Became Thinned: Native American Population Dynamics in Eastern North America* (Knoxville: University of Tennessee Press, 1983); Marvin T. Smith, *Archaeology of Aboriginal Culture Change in the Interior Southeast: Depopulation during the Early Historic Period* (Gainesville: University

Smith, especially, has better archaeological evidence (especially of mass burials) than was available to Dobyns. But all of these works rely heavily on analogy from modern epidemiological studies. They also sometimes accept unstated assumptions about the role of demographic change as a factor in cultural change. They extrapolate data from the rather vague numerical reports in the accounts of the De Soto and some other early expeditions and on the report of a disease that had caused the depopulation of a town near Cofitachequi the year before De Soto arrived.[30] They rely on the scanty evidence of what Coosa was like at the time of the De Soto and Luna expeditions and on the dating of artifacts.[31]

A nonspecialist in these matters often gets the impression that Old World diseases, arising *solely* from the De Soto expedition's passage, are a sort of "deus ex machina" that substitutes for what must in reality have been complex cause-and-effect relationships in a sequence of events. A step in the direction of a complex explanation of the changes and of demography's role in them is Ramenofsky's recent proposal for a Darwinian (environmental) model for responses to disease.[32] Clearly, some Old World diseases did reach epidemic levels among the southeastern Indians during the sixteenth century, but whether that was before or after or because of De Soto remains to be tested, as do their full effects on the political and social structures that De Soto's men recorded.

The very substantial problems presented by limited documentary data can be illustrated by the evidence from Coosa. De Soto's men described Coosa as flourishing; Luna's men found small villages and relatively little food eighteen years later. However, archaeologists and historians generally have not subjected these statements to skeptical examination as a possible example of "explorer's rhetoric" (De Soto's men) versus "settler's rhetoric"

---

of Florida Press, 1987); Ann F. Ramenofsky, *Vectors of Death: The Archaeology of European Contact* (Albuquerque: University of New Mexico Press, 1987); Ramenofsky, "Loss of Innocence," 31–48.

[30]Elvas, *Relation,* Biedma, "Relation," and Rangel, "Account of the Northern Conquest," herein, vol. 1; Garcilaso, *La Florida,* herein, vol. 2.

[31]Many strides have recently been made in isotope and trace-element analysis and in dating bead types, with the result that we have better dates, but still ones that are plus or minus a number, often a large number of years. Spanish artifacts, aside from beads, are nearly impossible to date to anything less than a century; the most datable beads, Nueva Cadiz, can be dated only as pre-1550 in manufacture. Native American ceramics are typically dated by the half-century or longer interval, and sometimes even by reference to their association with European objects!

[32]Ramenofsky, "Loss of Innocence," 37–44.

(Luna's men).[33] Nor have the folkloric qualities of the De Soto Coosa story been fully evaluated. Nor has much work been done on the narrative strategies of the De Soto chroniclers that might have led them to embellish Coosa's reality. Yet without such care to discover the biases behind the data, the data can give false impressions, leading to false conclusions. Put another way, historical "facts," like archaeological artifacts, have "proveniences" that give them meaning. They cannot be, as artifacts cannot be, simply "dug up."

In short, the proposition that De Soto's expedition, and its presumed diseases, largely if not completely accounts for the transformation of southeastern Indian societies remains a thesis or theory, whose verification awaits the development of archaeological and possibly ethnographic evidence that is better than any currently available for the 1540–1700 period.

The consequences for Native American societies of De Soto's activities that can be documented are limited to the diffusion of European manufactures, such as cloth, clothing, iron objects, and glass beads (all available from other contacts with Europeans), the deaths of large numbers (but probably not the thousands claimed) of Indians in battles with De Soto, and limited population movements caused by his forcing Indian burden bearers to leave their chiefdoms and enter neighboring, usually hostile, ones before he released them. An example of the latter is the Indian who explained to Alonso Velas, one of Pardo's soldiers, that he did not wish to accompany him any farther than Satapo because he had five brothers who had been captured by the Coosa while in the company of De Soto.[34] These were not insignificant consequences, but they may have been less important in the long run than other factors particular to the native cultures in question.

Recent Critiques of the Chronicles

Literary studies of those De Soto chronicles published in these volumes have been limited in number, but they do provide important perspectives on the interrelatedness of the texts and on the factual veracity of the chronicles,

---

[33]See Wayne Franklyn, *Discoverers, Explorers, and Settlers: The Diligent Writers of Early America* (Chicago: University of Chicago Press, 1979), 70–71, 122–24. The folkloric quality of the Coosa story was suggested by the comments of George E. Lankford in "Legends of the Adelantado," a paper he presented to the 2nd Arkansas De Soto Conference, Fayetteville, March 28, 1990. Copy in collection of the author.

[34]Testimony in the "Long Bandera Relation," trans. Paul E. Hoffman, in Hudson, *Pardo Expeditions*, 272.

and thus on their utility for the details of Native American culture. Patricia Galloway, picking up threads from the work of the late Daymond Turner, has probed the possible links between the Rangel/Oviedo text and that of the Gentleman of Elvas, going so far as to suggest that Oviedo's printer probably had the manuscript additions to Oviedo's *Historia general*, in which the Rangel material was found, at the time that the printer moved to Portugal, which was not long before the Elvas account appeared in print.[35] That is to say, Elvas's account may be based upon the Rangel/Oviedo original, with additions by a Portuguese survivor of the expedition or someone else who was familiar with its legends.[36] Galloway also suspects that Elvas was the basic source for Garcilaso de la Vega's account.[37]

Garcilaso de la Vega's *The Florida of the Inca* has long been recognized as the most literary, and possibly the least reliable, of the four main accounts of the expedition.[38] Recently, David Henige has suggested that Garcilaso's literary purposes and the literary conventions of his time need to be taken into account, especially when using his descriptions of Indian society.[39] Both Henige and Galloway have called for modern critical, original-language editions of the sources, especially Oviedo.

Luís Hernández de Biedma's account (herein newly retranslated by John Worth), the only one to come down to us in a contemporary manuscript, has not been subjected to the same scrutiny as the Rangel/Oviedo, Elvas, and

---

[35]Patricia Galloway, "Sources for the Hernando de Soto Expedition: Intertextuality and the Elusiveness of Truth," 12–13, 16. Paper presented to the Society of Spanish and Portuguese Historical Studies, New Orleans, April 1990. Collection of the author. This "intertextuality" of Rangel/Oviedo and Elvas was noticed as early as 1901 by Woodbury Lowery, *The Spanish Settlements Within the Present Limits of the United States* (New York: G. P. Putnam's Sons, 1901), 1:459, where, in commenting on the Rangel text he says "the account up to the burning of Chicaça appears to be independent of, while it substantially agrees with, those of the other writers. Beyond that, it follows very closely the Elvas narrative. . . . Many of the names correspond with those of the Elvas narrative."

[36]Lankford, "Legends of the Adelantado," chart 2, p. 7, shows that of the twenty-one legends found in the part of the expedition's story that the Elvas and Rangel/Oviedo texts have in common, eleven are about the same incidents. The other ten would have been contributed by some other source.

[37]Personal communication.

[38]Dennis Fernandez, "La Florida del Inca Garcilaso de la Vega." Ph.D. Dissertation. Florida State University. 1970.

[39]David Henige, "The Content, Context, and Credibility of *La Florida del Ynca*," *The Americas* 43 (1986): 1–23.

Garcilaso accounts. Swanton noted its brevity (and thus lack of utility for "route" studies) and that "it supported the Portuguese chronicler [Elvas] rather than the Inca," but the implications of this observation have not been explored.[40]

The Cañete Fragment, here published for the first time together with Eugene Lyon's commentary, also awaits comparative study with the other texts. Its concern with flora and fauna suggests that the complete account, if it can ever be found, will provide new information about De Soto and his men's interest in the resources of the Southeast, unless, that is, it is shown that Cañete compiled his materials from Martyr and Oviedo.

Less controversial than the Henige-Galloway critiques of the nature and uses of the four sources is George Lankford's recent examination of the accounts from the perspective of a folklorist. Lankford has suggested that the members of the De Soto expedition "emerged from their cocoon in La Florida with a common set of [folkloric] legends about most of the important events they had lived through. . . ."[41] He finds eighty-two legends in Garcilaso, many of which also appear in the other written accounts. Stripped of these legends, Garcilaso's account is a "bare-bones story not significantly different from Elvas and Rangel in tone, although the details may vary."[42] He concludes that Garcilaso probably used Elvas, the written sources he claimed to have used, and oral testimony in the form of folkloric legends gathered from Gonzalo Silvestre. All were woven into a text fitting certain literary cannons of his time. The result has been an enjoyable tale read ever since and used by most popular writers as the basis for their retellings of the De Soto story.

The thrust of this recent critical scholarship of the accounts as interrelated rather than independent accounts and as literary documents is to confirm that a sequential itinerary can be constructed from the Biedma and Rangel accounts, supplemented by the derivative Elvas and Garcilaso accounts. Swanton's "Parallel Itinerary of the Expedition," reprinted here, is such a construction.

A measured itinerary, on the other hand, can be only partially reconstructed because Elvas provides most of the league distances, estimated in

---

[40]Swanton, *Final Report*, 9. Ida Altman is preparing a deconstructionist analysis of Biedma's text [personal communication, Patricia Galloway to author, October 3, 1990].

[41]Lankford, "Legends of the Adelantado," 2.

[42]Ibid., 14

units of ten, and because the length of his league and those used by the other sources are uncertain.[43] Arguments about how far the army marched in a day, the other line of approach to a measured itinerary, seem problematical because they rest heavily on Garcilaso (for the day count) and on assumptions and partial data about actual distances made good.[44] This approach is useful to the extent that it points to particular archaeological sites that fit the accounts and date to the correct period, but those who use it are in constant danger of employing a circular argument from the sites to the estimated day's travel.

In sum, recent literary studies of the De Soto chronicles have raised new doubts about their use in reconstructions of "the route" while helping to sort out fact and possible fiction in studies of the Native American cultures that De Soto met.

The De Soto Chronicles Project

Most present-day students of the expedition would not agree with Lowery that "it is a matter of comparatively small importance to trace the path of these Spanish adventurers with the precision of a modern railway. . . ."[45] It thus seems especially important that an edition of the best-available translations of all four accounts, and selected ancillary materials, be published. With all four narratives together, the curious student can better compare them to reach his/her own conclusions about their interrelatedness, literary and folkloric qualities, and veracity. Such an edition provides a basis from which to make a fresh start and to eliminate some of the old, erroneous answers still bandied about.

In addition to the four main chronicles, these volumes include selected materials from the United States De Soto Expedition Commission's *Final Report* of 1939 and the documents that Buckingham Smith published in 1866. To round out the presentation, Rocío Sánchez Rubio's recent biographical sketch of De Soto has been translated from the Spanish to provide

---

[43]For the best modern scholarship on this controversy see Roland Chardon, "The Elusive Spanish League: A Problem of Measurement in Sixteenth-Century New Spain," *Hispanic American Historical Review* 60 (1980): 294–302, and Charles Hudson and Marvin Smith, "Reply to Eubanks," *The Florida Anthropologist* 43 (1990): 36–42.

[44]Keith J. Little and Caleb Curren are the leading critics of the estimated day's travel approach. See "Conquest Archaeology of Alabama," *Columbian Consequences*, vol. 2, 170–71.

[45]Lowery, *Spanish Settlements*, 1:464.

some insight into how De Soto is viewed by a modern Spanish historian. This author's somewhat longer biography of De Soto to 1539 provides a different perspective on his life and character.

Finally, an observation about the arguments that have grown up, again, around "the route." An excitable and injudicious man himself, Hernando de Soto might be amused to see how much heat and controversy his legacy has produced.

The Account by a Gentleman from Elvas

Translated and Edited by James Alexander Robertson
With Footnotes and Updates to Robertson's Notes by John H. Hann

The True Relation of the Hardships Suffered by Governor Hernando de Soto, by a Gentleman of Elvas, was translated from the Portuguese by James Alexander Robertson for the Florida State Historical Society and was published in two volumes for them by the Yale University Press as the society's publication number eleven. The first volume, published in 1932, was a photographic facsimile of the original Portuguese edition of Elvas in 1557. The second volume, published in 1933, was an English translation of volume one by Dr. Robertson, who was at that time the executive secretary of the Florida State Historical Society.

The Robertson translation has stood the test of over fifty years and is still considered to be an excellent translation. Relevant portions of the front material from volume one have been included here to clarify the context of Robertson's work. This is followed by the complete translation from volume two of the Robertson edition, which is reproduced below, followed by Dr. Robertson's notes.

In Robertson's notes, native towns and physical features are located according to a route reconstruction on modern maps by Theodore H. Lewis, published in the volume *Spanish Explorers in the Southern United States, 1528–1543* (1907). The decision to rely on Lewis was a rather eclectic one, because Lewis's reconstructions, though interesting, deviated widely from those of nearly all of his predecessors and contemporaries, leading John R. Swanton to call him the "great iconoclast" of De Soto route studies. No effort has been made in the present volume to update these locations, although the reader should be aware that in many, if not most, cases a better estimate might be had. Modern versions of De Soto's route, although they differ from each other, generally make use of ethnographic, linguistic, and archaeological data that were not available to Lewis. References to these more recent attempts may be found in our bibliography.

The notes in turn have been updated for this edition by Dr. John Hann, historic sites specialist for the state of Florida, the Bureau of Archaeological Research, under a grant from the Institute for Early Contact Period Studies at the University of Florida in Gainesville.

Foreword

[To Robertson volume one]

This facsimile reproduction of the narrative of the expedition by Hernando de Soto into Florida and regions to the north and west thereof was made from the copy of the original "Relaçam" of 1557 owned by the New York Public Library. This work is so rare that but two other copies [those of the Bibliotheca de Ajuda, in Portugal, and of the British Museum] are known to be in existence. The publication, therefore, of a source so important for the history of the United States can be regarded only as an epochal event. A new translation into English of the original, with copious annotations, has been made by James Alexander Robertson, executive secretary of the Society. . . . The Committee thanks the New York Public Library for its courtesy in allowing its priceless volume to be photographed for reproduction; and the Yale University Press for the care with which it has executed the work.

John B. Stetson, Jr.,
Chairman,
F. Franklin Jameson,
Charles B. Reynolds,
George Parker Winship.
Committee on Publications.

Preface

[To Robertson volume one]

The excuse for a new edition of the "Relaçam Verdadeira" of the "Fidalgo" of Elvas is many fold: the rarity of the original; its intrinsic merit; its importance for the early history of lands now a part of the United States; the greater exactness of the translation. This narrative forms, indeed, one of the most valuable of the existing sources whereby the veil was lifted, at least momentarily, from the darkness enshrouding the life of a great part of the lands bordering upon the northern shore of the Gulf of Mexico and the lands reaching north and northeast of that mighty inland water. The Florida of that early day, and for long after, covered an indefinite extent of territory. The name conveyed only a vague impression of vast space delimited perhaps at the west by the Las Palmas River, but extending northward no person knew whither. On that account, not only is this narrative of interest to the present State of Florida, but as well to Georgia, Alabama, Mississippi, North Carolina, [South Carolina], and Tennessee, and beyond the Father of Waters to Louisiana, Arkansas, Texas, and even other regions. One narrative only of the interior of the present United States is older than it—the account of that traveler of travelers, Alvar Núñez Cabeza de Vaca, whose adventures, unique among such annals, as truly as those of Hernando de Soto, form an epic of the New World.

The brief glimpse afforded by the narrative of the expedition of Hernando de Soto of an aboriginal population struggling painfully along the pathway toward civilization, exhibiting many of the characteristics of older known peoples, together with many of the virtues and the frailties of the barbarian—unaware of the civilization of the Old World and of the white man—was not to be renewed, except momentarily, until almost a score of years later when Tristán de Luna y Arellano thrust himself up through Florida and Alabama on his abortive expedition. So vivid was the tale of the unknown Portuguese and so avid his audience "new things for to hear" that his book must have been literally read to pieces, for but three known copies of it are known to have survived to the present day. Even so early after its publication as 1609, when that puissant man of letters, Richard Hakluyt, the father of English colonization, made the first translation of it into English, he seems to have been hard put to it to find a copy. The successive reissues of Hakluyt's translation; the new translation of the original into French and the translation of the latter into English near the end of the seventeenth century; the new translation from the Portuguese into English by Buckingham Smith and the latter reissues of this by Edward Gaylord Bourne and Theodore H. Lewis; and the reprint of the original Portuguese, albeit modernized in 1844; all these attest the abiding interest in, and the value of, the narrative.

As one of the basic documents of the early history of Florida, it appeared peculiarly fitting that the "Relaçam Verdadeira" should form one of the publications of the Florida State Historical Society. It was therefore planned, shortly after the foundation of the society, to publish it, not only in an English dress, but in its original form as well. This has now been done. The work is issued in two volumes, the first being the reproduction of the original and the second the translation. At first it was intended to reissue the translation by Buckingham Smith, but closer examination of this with the original proved the desirability of making a new and more exact translation. In performing this task, the work of the present writer was made much easier by virtue of the two preceding translations into English from the original Portuguese and the translation into French noted above. To these, especially to the translations by Richard Hakluyt and Buckingham Smith, of which the translator made continual use, his indebtedness is acknowledged.

In annotating the translation, constant reference was made to the translations of the narratives by Luis Fernández de Biedma and Rodrigo Rangel which appear in the second volume of Edward Gaylord Bourne's "Narratives of the Career of Hernando de Soto." The first was reprinted by Professor Bourne from the volume of Buckingham Smith; the second he translated himself from the narrative as incorporated in the great work of Gonzalo Fernández de Oviedo Valdez. Numerous citations have been made of each account, in each instance the fitting acknowledgment being rendered. It was thus possible to make some comparison of the incidents as related by the three chroniclers. A much less extensive use was made of the narrative by the Inca Garcilaso de la Vega, both for lack of space and because his account is the least dependable of the four narratives. Considerable use was made also of the footnotes of Theodore A. Lewis published in his edition of Buckingham Smith's translation of the "Relaçam Verdadeira," due acknowledgment being made for each citation. . . .

J. A. R. November, 1932

True Relation of the Hardships Suffered by Governor Hernando De Soto & Certain Portuguese Gentlemen During the Discovery of the Province of Florida. Now newly set forth by a Gentleman of Elvas.

¶Translated and Edited by James Alexander Robertson.

¶Volume Two. Translation and Annotations.

¶DeLand, The Florida State Historical Society, 1933.

[Title page to Robertson volume two]

Preface

[to Robertson volume two]

. . . Hernando de Soto seems to have been especially fortunate in most of the men who joined his expedition. They were recruited under his vigilant eye; and the enthusiasm with which they flocked to his standard is evidenced by the fact that many were left behind for lack of room in the vessels sailing to Cuba from San Lúcar; or because they were rejected as unfit. From all who offered themselves, he chose those whom he considered best fitted for the arduous undertaking that lay before them.

Some had campaigned with him in Peru. They were an asset, for they had been tried and had stood the test. They knew the hardships and uncertainties of a campaign in the wilderness. A considerable number were from De Soto's own town or province, and either they, or their families, were probably known by him. That Portuguese should join the expedition is not at all strange. Badajoz, a chief city of the then province of Extremadura, lay near the Portuguese town of Elvas. To this very day, each place is an active smuggling center. Each is a place of entry or departure into or from the other country. There is, and probably always has been, a constant passing from one place to the other. Still, the precaution seems to have been taken of enrolling the men who came from Elvas as being of the town of Badajoz—this undoubtedly to satisfy any official inquiry that might be made.

Some members of the expedition were of comparatively high rank—perhaps higher even than that of the commander. As such, they had behind them the power and prestige of family, and some, of wealth; and all had apparently been bred to the profession of arms. It is not strange to find some of them among the officers of the expedition. Lay priests and friars were also enrolled, one of whom had the name Soto, evidently a kinsman of the leader. Their primary function seems to have been the spiritual care of the men of the expedition, but their number would indicate that they were intended as well for the evangelization of the Indians whenever occasion might offer. Though the chroniclers do not so state specifically, the raising of a huge cross on a high hill overlooking an Indian village, as related by the "Fidalgo" of Elvas, was probably suggested by the ecclesiastics. For the rest, they probably fought side by side with and suffered equally with the other members of the expedition. After the reverses at Mavilla and Chicaça, they were reduced to saying "dry masses" because of the loss of the wheaten hosts by fire, together with all the sacred ornaments; and it was not considered proper to use hosts made from maize flour.

There were apparently no convicts among the men. So ready were men to enlist in an expedition led by one who had played so prominent a part in the brilliant Peruvian campaign—De Soto was next to Francisco and Hernando Pizarro, and in moral worth far above them—that it was not necessary to open the doors of the jails in order to get enough men. Some of the men were of coarser mold than others and many were reckless and ruthless enough. There was exploitation of the Indians, and cruelty and lust were not absent. This, indeed, has been the story of the contact between white and red man from the beginning to the present day, and no colonizing nation and no country in the Americas can boast of a clean escutcheon. De Soto's expedition, however, in comparison with some that preceded it and many that followed it, was of a superior tone. Much of the credit for this belongs to the leader himself. It can at least be said of him that he was not heedlessly cruel. He was impelled by the necessity for self-preservation. One may readily grant that to our present twentieth-century eyes the basic idea of the expedition was ethically wrong, but this conception was not that of the age of conquest in the Americas.

One and all, from the greatest to the least, were able to endure hardship and suffering. Even in times of plenty, they were dogged by the grim specter of hunger. A proof of De Soto's ability as a leader is the absence of any attempt to mutiny; though there were signs of unrest among the men at the time of his death. Luis de Moscoso was not at all to be classed as a leader with De Soto; and it is evident that the idea of self-preservation held the expedition together under him. It is quite probable that a mutiny, if led by such men as Baltasar de Gallegos or Juan de Añasco, would have succeeded. It is to the credit of them all that the expedition ended as a unit.

De Soto was fortunate also in his officers, who were, in most instances, of more than ordinary ability. The devotion he inspired among his men is evidenced by the determination of Nuño de Tobar, who had been "maese de campo" and whom De Soto had deposed, to follow him to Florida as a private in the ranks. He ever gave unwavering loyalty to his leader. One altercation De Soto seems to have had with Tobar's successor, Vasco Porcallo de Figueroa, who returned to Cuba shortly after the expedition had reached Florida; but Porcallo seems to have borne him no enmity and aided the expedition from Cuba on more than one occasion.

As compared with the expedition of Pánfilo de Narvaez and that of Tristán de Luna y Arellano, and even that of Francisco Vasquez de Coronado, the personnel of the De Soto expedition was unquestionably of a higher type and was better kept in hand. There is one instance only when the men of the Narvaez expedition approached those of De Soto—that is, when they built their crazy boats near the present St. Marks, and perished almost to a man on their attempt to reach Mexico. The exploits of Alvar Núñez Cabeza de Vaca form an epic of their own quite apart from [those of] Narvaez.

The records of the expedition show the conquering Spaniards at their best. It was no slight undertaking to plunge into a new land, of which all were ignorant. Not knowing what was to be encountered from red man, wild beasts, the terrain itself, and the forces of nature, the expedition was as venturesome an undertaking as was that of Admiral Byrd and his men to Antarctica—perhaps more so, for notwithstanding De Soto's careful planning (much more careful than was usual at that epoch), he had little aid from science and all his apparatus was crude and clumsy as compared to that of the present day. But, as in all great undertakings, the men, we are told, longed for the hour of departure and thought they would never get to the fabulously rich land of Florida. Lured on by their love of adventure and the hope of achieving great wealth, they expected to find another Mexico or another Peru and their imaginations ran riot with the glories they were to achieve.

Never were men more grievously fooled. There was no wealth as they understood the term. They could not see the Florida of today. They could not visualize wealth as the result of the patient exploitation of nature. They had chosen for themselves four years of grueling hardship and suffering which, while they might "yield a pleasant tale to tell," were hard enough to bear. The survivors returned "sans everything."

On the other hand, many days of the expedition must have been extremely pleasant. There were many fine marches along the Indian trails which led beside pleasing streams or the shores of lovely lakes and through more or less open forests. Sometimes they hunted and fished and played with friendly Indians and had plentiful living. They frequently suffered unnecessarily because they were untrained to woodcraft. The problem of a sufficient food supply was among their greatest and most continual worries. They were not of the kind to establish a base where they might grow their own food. They counted on getting most of this from the Indians, unmindful of the depredations they caused and the hostility they created for themselves. To build an enduring settlement was not to their taste. They were adventurers, and little else beside. If they could find another Peru, where settlements already existed, then they might settle down to a steady existence. They did not see even with the eyes of poor Tristán de Luna y Arellano, and they would have laughed to scorn the plans of that great colonial pioneer, Pedro Menéndez de Avilés.

They found no submission in the Indians as had been found in Peru or Mexico, where the Indians had long been disciplined into a partially sedentary life. Instead, they found that the plenty of today might turn to leanness tomorrow. The Indians were not to be coerced into obedience. Imprisoned or chained or mutilated they might be, but these things did not tame them nor calm the fury roused in them by the white strangers. Sometimes they killed their captors. Mavilla and Chicaça became grim reminders of what might be the common fate.

Gradually his men diminished in number—victims of disease, casualties, or sudden death from the Indians. Of the six hundred with which De Soto set out, three hundred and eleven only won through to Pánuco. The dwindling of his men and the loss of almost all his resources at last tempered the obstinacy of Hernando de Soto, and when sickness and death overtook him, near the shores of the "Great River" which he first of all white men is known to have crossed, he was intent on returning to Cuba, there to refit his expedition and set out once more on his quest of glory.

The death of the commander brought a new problem—how to get out of Florida and return to as much civilization as Cuba or Mexico had to offer. Moscoso, the leader appointed by De Soto while on his deathbed, was not the man De Soto had been. It would appear that Baltasar de Gallegos was more fitted for the leadership than was Moscoso, who, said the "Fidalgo" of Elvas, was fond of a gay life and of taking his ease. Still, however chaotic grew conditions, the expedition did not lose its heroic quality. The aimless marching and countermarching, without knowing directions, often through pathless forests and wildernesses, without reliable guide or interpreter, harassed by hostile Indians only too anxious to be rid of them, was no small thing. Quite lost at last, it is no wonder that the majority of them counseled a return to the "Great River" where they might build boats and pass out into whatever body of water it flowed into and so reach a land inhabited by Christians. The return was no easy thing in itself, for they passed through a land that had once learned to hate them. Not a little heroic was the building of the vessels near the banks of the Mississippi and their sailing down the mighty stream to the gulf, harassed on their way by the Indians who came at them from all directions like angry hornets. Not the least wonder was their safe arrival at Pánuco after suffering various storms in the Gulf of Mexico.

Even in that frontier town, the survivors must have presented a curious and semi-ludicrous spectacle, clad as they were in skins and bark garments with which they had replaced the clothing lost at Mavilla and Chicaça. No shipwrecked mariners were probably more thankful at rescue than were they. Their reception at Pánuco was characteristic of the frontier. They were welcomed wholeheartedly and given freely of the best that could be had. Some of them found acquaintances or people from the same towns in Spain as themselves. The same hospitality was shown them all the way to Mexico City.

So ended the expedition. Some, we are told, looked back with regret at the land of Florida and in later years more than one tried to get permission to return thither. The results of the expedition are more interesting to the present age than to its own. It established for one thing the immensity of the northern American continent; as well as the difficulty of passing through its forests and over its rivers and lakes, and its impassable swamps and the cold regions in the northern interior. It also established, jointly with the Coronado expedition of 1540–1542, the absence of great centers of barbaric or semi-civilized splendor such as had been found in Mexico and Peru. The northern continent, therefore, lost much of its interest, until the rivalry of other European nations once more focused Spain's attention on these inhospitable regions and caused the sending out of other expeditions for settlement and colonization lest its rich colonies to the southward be lost by attack from the north.

J. A. R.
[January, 1933]

Contents

TRUE RELATION OF THE HARDSHIPS SUFFERED BY GOVERNOR DON HERNANDO DE SOTO AND CERTAIN PORTUGUESE GENTLEMEN DURING THE DISCOVERY OF FLORIDA.

[Translation]

True Relation of the Hardships Suffered by Governor Don Hernando de Soto and certain Portuguese Gentlemen in the Discovery of the Province of Florida. Now newly set forth by a Gentleman of Elvas.

Examined by the Inquisitor

Fernando da Silveira,[1]
Senhor das Serzedas, great poet
and very illustrious, respecting
the material of this Book,
in praise of its
Author.

EPIGRAM

He who would see the New World,
The Golden Pole, according to
Other seas, other lands,
Achievements great, & wars;
And attempt such things
As amaze and give pleasure,
Strike terror and give delight:
Read by this author
This pleasing narrative;
And he will see not a fabulous [history]
[But one] worthy of being esteemed,
Made use of, read, and discussed.

Finis.

André de Burgos to the prudent reader.

Aristotle says that all or the most of men are always prone and inclined to see and hear new things, especially when those things pertain to very distant and remote countries. Those things, he says, furnish diversion to delicate and subtile minds, and re-animate dull minds; and this gives them a natural desire to see and to hear, and, if possible, to take part in them.* This desire is for two reasons greater among the Lusitanians than among other nations: the first, because they are a warlike people and of very subtile minds; the second, because they are by nature great navigators, and have discovered more land, with wider sailing, than all the other nations of the world. And as it appeared to me that I do some little service to those who might read this book, I resolved to publish it, taking courage inasmuch as it was written by a Portuguese and in his own language; and likewise because Portuguese citizens of the city of Elvas aided in the discovery, as the narrative itself makes mention.† I believe beyond doubt that he has written truthfully, and that he has not recounted fables or fictitious things; for one must believe that the author, not having any interest in so doing, would not swerve from the truth. Besides this, he asserts that all that is here written passed before him. Should the language, by chance, not appear to you very polished, lay not the fault on me, for I did not write it but only published it. May God have you in His keeping.

In these footnotes and in my updates of Robertson's notes (found at the end of the Elvas account), where sixteenth-century Portuguese spelling differed from modern spelling, I have used the modern spelling so that an interested reader may find the words in a modern Portuguese dictionary.—JH

*In the Portuguese text, the words for "if possible" (*se possível fôsse*) are placed within parentheses and include a verb, which Robertson deleted along with the parentheses. A strictly literal rendering of the Portuguese would be "if it should be possible."

†In the Portuguese text, the words for "as the narrative itself makes mention" were enclosed in parentheses.

Relation of what the adelantado of Florida, Don Hernando de Soto, suffered in conquering it: in which is set forth who he was, and some of those who went with him; some of the peculiarities and diversities of the country, and all they saw therein; and of what befell them.

[The Discovery of Florida]

FIRST.

WHICH DECLARES WHO DON HERNANDO DE SOTO WAS, AND HOW HE OBTAINED THE GOVERNMENT OF FLORIDA.[2]

Captain Soto was the son of an esquire of Jeréz de Badajóz. He went to the Indies of Castile when Pedrárias Dávila[3] was governor of the Indies of the Ocean Sea. There he found himself with nothing else his own except his sword and shield. Because of his good qualities and courage, Pedrárias made him captain of a troop of horse, and by his order he went with Hernando Pizarro[4] to conquer Peru. There, according to the report of many creditable persons who were there, he distinguished himself over the other captains and principal persons, both at the seizure of Atabalipa,[5] lord of Peru, and in making the entrance into the city of Cuzco, and in all other places where they encountered resistance, and where he happened to be. For that reason, aside from his part in the treasure of Atabalipa, he got good repartimiento, from which in time he collected one hundred and eighty thousand cruzados,[6] which he took to Spain, with what fell to him as his share. Of this, the emperor took [by loan] a certain part which was repaid to him [Soto] by six hundred thousand reales[7] with interest in the silks of Granada, while all the rest was delivered to him at the casa de contratación[8] in Seville. He employed servants, including a majordomo, grand master of ceremonies, pages, equerry, chamberlain, footmen, and all the other servants requisite for an establishment of a gentleman. From Seville, he went to court, and at court was accompanied by Juan de Añasco,[9] of Seville, Luis Moscoso de Alvarado,[10] Nuño de Tobar, and Juan Rodriguez Lobillo. With the exception of Juan de Añasco, all the others had come with him from Peru; and each brought fourteen or fifteen thousand cruzados. They all went well and expensively dressed; and Soto, although because of his cupidity he was not liberal, yet since that was the first time he had to appear at court, spent very liberally, and went about closely attended by those I have named and by his servants and many others who came to him at court. He married Doña Isabel[11] de Bobadilla, daughter of Pedrárias Dávila, conde de Puñonrostro. The emperor rewarded him by making him governor of the island of Cuba and adelantado of Florida, with the title of marquis to a certain part of the lands he might conquer.[12]

SECOND.

HOW CABEZA DE VACA CAME TO COURT AND GAVE ACCOUNT OF THE LAND OF FLORIDA; AND OF THE MEN WHO WERE GATHERED TOGETHER AT SEVILLE TO GO WITH DON HERNANDO DE SOTO.

After Don Hernando had obtained the government, a gentleman arrived at court from the Indies, Cabeza de Vaca by name, who had gone with Governor Narváez,[13] who had perished in Florida. He told how Narváez had perished at sea with all his men; and how he and four others had escaped and reached New Spain. He brought also a written relation of what he had seen in Florida. This stated in certain places, "In such a place I saw this. Most of what I saw there I leave for discussion between myself and his Majesty." He described in general the wretchedness of the land and the hardships he had suffered. To some of his kinsfolk, who were minded to go to the Indies and strongly urged him to tell them whether he had seen any rich land in Florida, he said that he could not tell this, because he and another (by name, Dorantes,[14] who had remained in New Spain with the intention of returning to Florida—for which purpose he [Cabeza de Vaca] came to Spain to beg the government from the emperor) had sworn not to divulge certain things which they had seen, lest some person might beg for it before hand. He gave them to understand that it was the richest land in the world. Don Hernando de Soto wished to take him [i.e., Cabeza de Vaca] with him and made him an advantageous proposal; but after they had come to an agreement, they fell out because Soto would not give him the money which he [Cabeza de Vaca] asked of him to buy a ship. Baltasar de Gallegos and Cristóbal de Espindola, his kinsmen, told him [Cabeza de Vaca] that since they had resolved to go to Florida with Soto because of what he had told them, he should advise them as to what they should do. Cabeza de Vaca told them that if he had given up going with Soto, it was because he expected to ask for another government and did not wish to go under the banner of another. Since Don Hernando de Soto already had the conquest of Florida, which he [Cabeza de Vaca] came to beg, he could not tell them, on account of his oath, what they wished to know. Nevertheless, he advised them to sell their estates and go with him [i.e., Soto], for in so doing they would act wisely. As soon as he had an opportunity, he spoke with the emperor and related to him all he had suffered and seen and the other things he had succeeded in learning. Of this relation, made orally to the emperor by Cabeza de Vaca, the marqués de Astorga was informed. He determined at once to send his brother, Don Antonio Osorio, with Don Hernando de Soto, and two of his kinsmen made ready to go with him, namely, Francisco Osorio and Garcia Osorio. Don Antonio disposed of an income of six hundred thousand reales[15] which he received from the Church, and Francisco Osorio of a village of vassals he owned in the district of Campos. They joined the adelantado at Seville, as did also Nuño de Tobar, Luis de Moscoso, and Juan Rodriguez Lobillo, with the wealth, amounting to fourteen or fifteen thousand cruzados, which each one had brought from Peru. Luis de Moscoso took two brothers with him. Don Carlos, who had married the governor's niece,[16] went also and took his wife. From Badajóz went Pedro Calderón and three kinsmen of the adelantado, namely, Arias Tinoco, Alonso Romo, and Diego Tinoco. As Luis de Moscoso passed through Elvas, André de Vasconcelos spoke with him, and requested him to speak to Don Hernando de Soto in his behalf, and gave him patents issued by the marqués de Vilareal, conferring on him the captaincy of Ceuta, so that he might exhibit them. The adelantado saw these and found out who he [Vasconcelos] was and wrote him promising that he would favor him in every way and would give him men to command in Florida. From Elvas went André de Vasconcelos, Fernan Pegado, Antonio Martinez Segurado, Mem Royz Pereyra, Joan Cordeiro, Estevan Pegado, Bento Fernandez, and Alvaro Fernandez;[17] and from Salamanaca, Jaen, Valencia, Albuquerque, and other parts of Spain many persons of noble family gathered in Seville; so much so that many men of good condition, who had sold their estates, remained behind in San Lúcar because there was no ship for them; although for other known and rich countries it was usual to lack men. The cause of this was what Cabeza de Vaca had told the emperor and given persons who conversed with him to understand respecting that land. Soto made him [i.e., Cabeza de Vaca] fine proposals but Cabeza de Vaca, having agreed to go with him as mentioned above,* because Soto would not give him money to pay for a ship which he had bought, they disagreed, and Cabeza de Vaca went as governor to Rio de la Plata. His kinsmen, Cristóbal de Espindola and Baltasar de Gallegos went with Soto. Baltasar de Gallegos sold houses, vineyards, a rent of wheat, and ninety geiras[18] of olive orchard in the district of Seville. He obtained the post of chief constable and took his

*In the Portuguese text, the words for "as mentioned above," *como se já disse,* were enclosed in parentheses.

wife with him. Many other persons of rank also went with the adelantado, and obtained the following posts aided by powerful influence, for they were posts which were desired by many, namely: Antonio de Biedma[19] obtained the post of factor; Juan de Añasco[20] that of contador; and Juan Gaytán,[21] a nephew of Cardinal de Ciquenza, obtained the post of treasurer.

III.

HOW THE PORTUGUESE WENT TO SEVILLE AND THENCE TO SAN LÚCAR; AND HOW THE CAPTAINS WERE APPOINTED OVER THE SHIPS, AND THE MEN WHO WERE TO GO IN THEM DISTRIBUTED.

The Portuguese left Elvas on the 15th of January. They reached Seville on St. Sebastian's eve and went to the governor's lodging. They entered the patio upon which looked some balconies where he was. He looked down and went to meet them at the stairs where they went up to the balconies. When they were up, he ordered chairs to be given them so that they might be seated. André de Vasconcelos told him who he and the other Portuguese were and how they had all come to accompany him and to serve him on his voyage. He [i.e., Soto] thanked him and appeared well pleased with their coming and proffer. The table being already laid, he invited them to eat; and while they were eating, he directed his majordomo to find lodgings for them near his inn. From Seville, the adelantado went to San Lúcar with all the men that were to go with him. He ordered a muster to be held, to which the Portuguese went armed with very splendid arms, and the Castilians very elegantly, in silk over silk, and many plaits and slashes. As such finery was not pleasing to the governor on such an occasion, he ordered a muster to be held on the next day and for every man to appear with his armor. To this the Portuguese came as at first, armed with very excellent armor, and the governor set them in order near the standard borne by his alferez. Most of the Castilians wore poor and rusty coats of mail, and all [wore] helmets and carried worthless and poor lances. Some of them managed to get a place among the Portuguese. Thus they passed in review, and those who were to the liking of Soto and whom he wished were counted and enrolled and went with him to Florida. Those who went numbered in all six hundred men.[22] He had already bought seven ships and had placed in them the provisions necessary, appointed captains, and assigned his ship to each captain, giving each one a list of the men he was to take.

IIII.

HOW THE ADELANTADO AND HIS MEN LEFT SPAIN AND ARRIVED AT THE CANARY ISLANDS, AND AFTERWARD AT THE ANTILLES.

In the month of April, of the year 1538, the adelantado delivered the ships over to the captains who were to go in them. He took a new and good sailing ship for himself and gave one to André de Vasconcelos, in which the Portuguese went. He left the bar of San Lúcar on Sunday morning, on the day of St. Lazarus in that month, and as was later written, amid great festivity, ordering the trumpets to be sounded and many rounds of artillery fired. For four days he sailed amid favoring weather and then the wind lulled. The calms with a rolling sea lasted for a week, during which no headway was made. On the fifteenth day after his departure from San Lúcar, he reached Gomera, one of the Canary Islands, on the morning of Easter Sunday. The count of that island was clad entirely in white—cloak, jerkin, hose, shoes, and cap—and resembled a Gypsy count. He received the governor very cordially. The latter was well provided with lodgings, and all the men were lodged there without expense. For his money, he [Soto] was provided with many provisions, bread, wine, and meat; and they took what was needful for the ships. On the following Sunday, a week after their arrival, they left the island of Gomera. The count gave Doña Isabel, the wife of the adelantado, a bastard daughter[23] of his, as her maid. They reached the Antilles at the island of Cuba, at the port of the city of Santiago on Whitsuntide.[24] As soon as they arrived there, a gentleman of the city sent a very beautiful and well caparisoned roan horse to the shore for the governor and a mule for Doña Isabel; and all the men of foot and horse who were in the town came to the shore to welcome them. The governor was lodged, visited, and served by all the citizens of that city, and all the men were lodged free of expense. Those who wished to go into the country were quartered among the dwelling and farm houses by fours and sixes, in accordance with the possibility of the owners of the dwellings, and were furnished by the latter with the provisions of which they had need.[25]

V.

OF THE CITIZENS OF THE CITY OF SANTIAGO AND THE OTHER TOWNS OF THE ISLAND; AND OF THE QUALITY OF THE LAND AND THE FRUITS THEREOF.

The city of Santiago has about eighty large and well-apportioned houses.[26] Most of them have wooden walls and roofs of hay. A few are of stone and lime and are roofed with tiles. They have large farms on which are many trees differing from those of Spain—fig trees which produce figs as big as the fist, yellow inside and of little savor; and other trees which produce a fruit called "anona," of the shape and size of a small pineapple.* It is a tasty fruit, and when the rind is removed, the pulp resembles a piece of curd. On the farms in the country are other large pineapples which grow on low trees that resemble the aloe. They are of excellent odor and of fine taste. Other trees yield a good fruit called "mamei,"[27] of the size of a peach, which the islanders consider the best of all the fruits of the land. There is another fruit called guava, resembling the hazel nut in form, the size of a fig. There are other trees as tall as a good lance, with a single stalk having no branches, with leaves broad and as long as a javelin, the fruit of the size and form of a cucumber (on one bunch twenty or thirty); and also as the fruit goes on ripening, the tree goes on bending lower with it. They are called plantains in that land and are of agreeable taste. They ripen after being gathered, although those that ripen on the tree itself are better. The tree produces fruit but once. When the tree is cut down, others grow at the root which yield fruit the next year. There is another fruit on which many people live, especially the slaves, which they call "batata."† These now grow in the island of

*The Portuguese that Robertson rendered as "They have large farms" is *têm qrandes quintaes. Quintaes* here is the modern *quintal,* which is "back yard," rather than the modern *quinta,* which means "country seat" or "rural residence." This interpretation is suggested also by Elvas's separate reference to "the farms in the country" as something distinct from the *quintaes* above. Consequently, the preferable translation is "They have large back yards." In the same context, Elvas used *estância* for farm.

†*Batata,* which Robertson left in Portuguese, is the same word as the one he rendered as "potatoes" in describing *manioc* as resembling potatoes. The *batata* to which Elvas referred is probably the plant known in Cuba and the Dominican Republic as *aje.* See Bernardo Vega, ed., *El aje, un enigma decifrado* (Santo Domingo: Ediciones Museo del Hombre Dominicano, 1978).

Terceira belonging to this kingdom of Portugal. They grow under ground and resemble the yam. They have almost the taste of chestnuts. The bread of that land is also made from roots which resemble potatoes.[28] The bread made from those roots resembles the pith of the alder. The earth is heaped up and in each heap four or five stalks are planted; and after they have been planted for a year and a half, the roots are gathered. Should any person, thinking it to be a potato, eat any of it, he runs great risk of death, as was found by experience in the case of a soldier who, as soon as he ate a very little of a root, died immediately. They pare those roots and grate them and crush them in a press. The juice that comes out has a bad smell. The bread has but little taste and less nourishment. Of the fruits of Spain, it [Cuba] has figs and oranges. They produce fruit all year long because the land is very hot and vigorous. In that land are many horses and cattle; and all through the year [there is] green grass. There are many wild cattle and hogs whereby the people of the island are well supplied with meat.[29] In the country outside the town are many fruits; and it sometimes happens that some Christian gets lost and wanders about lost for fifteen or twenty days because of the many paths made by the cattle crisscrossing from one part to another through the dense forests. Thus wandering about lost, he keeps alive on fruits and palmetto cabbage, for there are many large palm trees throughout the island which yield no other fruit of any value. The island of Cuba[30] is three hundred leagues in extent from east to southeast, and in some places thirty, and in others forty, leagues from north to south. There are six towns of Christians, namely, Santiago, Baracoa, the Bayamo, Puerto Principe, Sancti Spiritus, and the Havana. Each one has between thirty and forty citizens, except Santiago and the Havana, each of which has seventy or eighty houses.[31] They all have churches and a chaplain who confesses the people and celebrates mass for them. In Santiago there is a Franciscan monastery. It has few friars, but is well provided with alms, because of the richness of the land. The church of Santiago has a suitable income, a parish priest, benefices, and many secular priests, it being the church of that city which is the capital of all the island.[32] There is much gold in this land, but few slaves to get it out, for many hanged themselves because of the harsh treatment received in the mines from the Christians. An overseer of Vasco Porcallo, a resident of that island, having learned that his Indians were about to hang themselves, with a rope in his hands,[33] went to await them in the place where they were to meet and told them that they could do nothing nor think of anything which he did not know beforehand; that he was going to hang himself with them, for if he had given them a hard life in this world, he would give them a worse in the other. This caused them to change their minds and return to do what he ordered them.

V. [I.E., VI].

HOW THE GOVERNOR SENT DOÑA ISABEL WITH THE SHIPS TO THE HAVANA, AND HE WITH SOME OF HIS MEN WENT OVERLAND.

From Santiago, the governor sent Don Carlos, his brother-in-law [*sic*],[34] in the ships, together with Doña Isabel with orders to await him at the Havana, which is a port at the eastern[35] end of the island, one hundred and eighty leagues from the city of Santiago. The governor and those who remained with him bought horses and set out on their journey. The first town at which they arrived was the Bayamo,[36] and they were lodged by fours and sixes just as they went in company. And there where they were lodged they were given their food without expense. Nothing else cost them money except maize for their horses, because from town to town, the governor went to visit each one and assessed it a tax on the tribute and service of the Indians.[37] The Bayamo is twenty-five leagues from the city of Santiago. Near it runs a large river, larger than the Guadiana, called Tanto. In it are huge lizards[38] which sometimes do harm to the Indians or animals crossing the river. In all the land there are no wolves, foxes, bears, lions, or tigers. There are wild dogs which have left the houses for the woods and live on the hogs. There are some snakes as thick as a man's thigh and more.[39] They are very sluggish and do no harm. From Bayamo to Puerto Principe it is fifty leagues. Throughout the island, roads are made from town to town by means of the machete [*rocadoira*]; and any year they neglect to do this, the thickets grow to such an extent that the road does not show. So many are the paths made by the cattle that no one can travel without an Indian of the country for a guide, for most of it is covered with a very lofty and dense forest. From Puerto Principe, the governor went by sea in a canoe to the dwelling of Vasco Porcallo,[40] which is near the sea, in order to get news of Doña Isabel, who at that time (as was afterward learned) was in great distress—so much so that the ships were lost one from the other (two of them going within sight of the coast of Florida), and all suffered great need of water and food. After the storm ceased, and the ships were come together again, without knowing whither they had been driven, they came upon the cape of San Antón, an uninhabited district of the island of Cuba. There they got water, and forty days after they had left the city of Santiago they reached the Havana. The governor learned of this immediately and went to Doña Isabel. Those who came overland—in number one hundred and fifty of horse—divided into two divisions in order not to burden the islanders, made their way to Sáncti Spiritus,[41] sixty leagues from Puerto Principe. The food they took consisted of cassava bread, which is that I have mentioned above. It is of such quality that if water touches it, it immediately crumbles. On that account, it happened that some ate meat for many days without bread. They took dogs and a native of the country who hunted as they marched, or killed what hogs they needed at the place where they had to stop to sleep. They were well supplied with beef and pork on that journey. They suffered much annoyance from mosquitoes, especially in a swamp called the marsh of the watering trough [*pia*], which gave them considerable trouble in crossing from midday to night. There was more than a half league of water and for the distance of a good crossbow shot they had to swim it; and the rest of it reached to the waist. They were mired up to the knees; and on the bottom were clam shells which cut their feet badly, so that not a single sole of boot or shoe lasted whole for half the way. Their clothes and saddles were taken over on bits of bark from the palm trees. While crossing that swamp without their clothes, many mosquitoes attacked them, which when they stung raised a lump and smarted badly. They would strike at them with the hand, and from the slaps given they killed so many that the blood ran over the arms and bodies of the men. That night they got very little rest because of them, and the same thing was experienced on other nights at like places and seasons. They reached Sancti Spiritus, a town of thirty houses, near which flows a small river.[42] It is very pleasant and luxuriant, with many fine orange and citron trees and fruits native to the land. Half the men were lodged there, while the others went on twenty-five leagues farther to another town called Trinidad,[43] consisting of fifteen or twenty citizens. There is a hospital for the poor there, but no other in the whole island. They say that that town was once the largest of any in the island; and that before the Christians made an entrance into that land, while a ship was coasting along that shore, there came in it a very sick man who requested the captain to have him taken ashore. The captain did so and the ship proceeded on its way. The sick man remained on the shore in that land which so far had never been oppressed by Christians, where the Indians found him and took him and cared for him until he was well. The lord of that town gave him his daughter in marriage. He [the chief] was at war with all his neighbors, and by means of the skill and courage of the Christian, he subdued and brought under his command all the people of that island. A long time afterward, Governor Diego Velázquez went to conquer it and discovered New Spain from that place. That Christian who was with the Indians pacified them and brought them under the subjection and into the obedience of the governor. From that town of Trinidad to Havana, there is a stretch of eighty leagues without a town, which they traveled. They reached Havana at the end of March where they found the governor and all the rest of the men who had accompanied him from Spain. From Havana, the governor sent Juan de Añasco with a caravel and two brigantines with fifty men to explore the port of Florida. He brought two Indians from there whom he seized on the coast. Thereat (both because they would be needed as guides and interpreters, and because they said by signs that much gold existed in Florida), the governor and all the men were greatly pleased, and thought they would never see the hour of departure, for it seemed to them that was the richest land which had yet been discovered.

VII.

HOW WE LEFT THE HAVANA AND REACHED FLORIDA; AND OF WHAT HAPPENED.

Before our departure, the governor deprived Nuño de Tobar of the post of captain general and gave it to Porcallo de Figueroa,[44] a citizen of Cuba, who was to see that the ships should sail well-provisioned, and who gave a number of large loads of cassava bread and many hogs. The governor took the post from Nuño de Tobar because he had made love to the daughter of the conde of Gomera, the waiting maid of Doña Isabel. He, notwithstanding that the post was taken from him, took her to wife and went to Florida with Soto, in order to be restored to favor and because she was already pregnant by him.* The governor left Doña Isabel in the Havana[45] and with her the wives of Don Carlos, Baltasar de Gallegos, and Nuño de Tobar. As his lieutenant for the government of the island, he left a gentleman of the Havana, Juan de Rojas[46] by name. On Sunday, May 18, of the year 1539, the

*The words "in order to be restored to favor and because she was already pregnant by him" are enclosed in parentheses in the Portuguese text.

adelantado left the Havana with his fleet consisting of nine ships—five vessels with topsails, two caravels, and two brigantines. For seven days, they sailed attended by good weather. On Whitsunday, May 25, they sighted the land of Florida,[47] and for fear of shoals anchored a league from shore. On Friday, May 30, they disembarked on the land of Florida, two leagues from a town of an Indian chief called Ucita.[48] They disembarked the two hundred and thirteen horses which they carried, in order to lighten the ships so that they would need less water. All the men landed and only the seamen stayed aboard, who in a week, by going up with the tide for a short distance daily, brought the vessels near to the town. As soon as the men landed the camp was established on the shore near the bay which went up to the town. The captain general, Vasco Porcallo, taking with him seven horse, immediately overran the land for a half league round about and found six[49] Indians who tried to oppose him with their arrows—the weapons with which they are accustomed to fight. The horsemen killed two of them and the four [others] escaped, for the land being obstructed by woods and swamps, the horses, because of weakness from voyaging on the sea, became mired there and fell with their masters. That night following, the governor with one hundred men in the brigantines came upon a town which he found without people, because the Christians were perceived as soon as they came within sight of land; and they saw many smokes along the whole coast, which the Indians made in order to give information to one another. On the following day, Luis de Moscoso,[50] maese de campo, set the men in order, those on horse in three squadrons—the vanguard, the battle line, and the rear guard—and in that way they marched that day and the next, going around great mud flats which come from the bay. They arrived at the town of Ucita, where the governor was, on Sunday, June first, the day of the Trinity. The town consisted of seven or eight houses. The chief's house stood near the beach on a very high hill which had been artificially built as a fortress.[51] At the other side of the town was the temple and on top of it a wooden bird with its eyes gilded. Some pearls, spoiled by fire and of little value, were found there. The Indians bore them through in order to string them for beads, which are worn around the neck or arm, and they esteem them greatly.* The houses were of wood and were covered with palm leaves. The governor was lodged in the houses of the chief and with him Vasco Porcallo and Luis de Moscoso; and in the other houses which were located in the middle of the town, the

*The Portuguese that Robertson translated simply as "arm" is *no colo de braço,* which means literally, "on the neck (or lap) of the arm" or, more comprehensibly, "the upper arm."

chief constable, Baltasar de Gallegos. And apart in the same houses were placed the provisions carried on the ships. The other houses and the temple were destroyed, and a mess of every three or four built a small house in which they were lodged.* The land round about was greatly encumbered and choked with a vast and lofty forest. The governor ordered it to be cut down for the space of a crossbow shot about the town, in order that the horses might run and the Christians have the advantage of the Indians if the latter should by chance try to attack them by night. They posted foot soldiers as sentinels, in couples at each position along the roads and at proper places, who stood watch for four hours [*por quartes*]. The horsemen visited them and were ready to aid them if there should be an alarm. The governor appointed four captains over the horsemen and two over the foot soldiers. Those over the horse were: one, André de Vasconcelos,[52] and second, Pedro Calderón, of Badajóz, and the other two his kinsmen, the Cardeñosa (Arias Tinoco and Alfonso Romo), also natives of Badajóz. One of the captains over the foot soldiers was Francisco Maldonado of Salamanaca, and the other Juan Rodriguez Lobillo.[53] While they were in that town of Ucita, the Indians[54] whom Juan de Añasco had captured along that coast and whom the governor brought along as guides and interpreters escaped one night through the carelessness of two men who were guarding them. The governor and all were very sorry for this, for some forays had already been made, but no Indians could be captured, as the land was swampy and in many parts covered with very lofty and thick woods.

VIII.

HOW SOME FORAYS WERE MADE AND A CHRISTIAN WAS FOUND WHO HAD BEEN IN THE POWER OF AN INDIAN CHIEF FOR A LONG TIME.

The Governor sent the chief constable, Baltasar de Gallegos, from the town of Ucita with forty horse and eight foot into the interior to see whether any Indian could be captured; and in another direction, Captain Juan

*The Portuguese word *desbaratar,* which Robertson translated as "destroyed," can be rendered also as "dismantled." In this context "dismantled" seems to make more sense inasmuch as De Soto's men were building small huts for themselves to replace the ones that they allegedly "destroyed." "Destroy" suggests fire and destruction by fire would possibly have endangered the house in which the provisions were stored or the one chosen by Gallegos.

Rodriguez Lobillo, with fifty foot, most of them armed with swords and shields. Others were arquebusiers and crossbowmen. They went over a swampy land where the horsemen could not go. A half league from camp they came upon some Indian huts near the river; [but] the people who were inside them plunged into the river. They captured four Indian women, and twenty Indians came at us and attacked us so stoutly that we had to retreat to the camp, because of their being (as they are) so skillful with their weapons. Those people are so warlike and so quick that they make no account of foot soldiers; for if these go for them, they flee, and when their adversaries turn their backs they are immediately on them. The farthest they flee is the distance of an arrow shot. They are never quiet but always running and crossing from one side to another so that the crossbows or the arquebuses can not be aimed at them; and before a crossbowman can fire a shot, an Indian can shoot three or four arrows, and very seldom does he miss what he shoots at. If the arrow does not find armor, it penetrates as deeply as a crossbow. The bows are very long and the arrows are made of certain reeds like canes, very heavy and so tough that a sharpened cane passes through a shield.* Some are pointed with a fish bone, as sharp as an awl, and others with a certain stone like a diamond point. Generally when these strike against armor, they break off at the place where they are fastened on. Those of cane split and enter through the links of mail and are more hurtful. Juan Rodriguez Lobillo reached the camp with six men wounded, one of whom died. He brought the four Indian women whom he had captured in the quarters or huts.[55] Ablate de Gallegos, on going into the level terrain two leagues from town, saw ten or eleven Indians, among whom was a Christian, naked and on that account burned by the sun. He had his arms tattooed after the manner of the Indians and in no wise did he differ from them. As soon as the horsemen saw them they ran at them. The Indians took to flight and hid from them in a forest. They overtook two or three of them who had been wounded. The Christian, as one of the horsemen was about to charge him with his lance, began to cry out, "Sirs, I am a Christian; do not kill me. Do not kill these Indians, for they have given me my life."[56] Thereupon, he called the latter and reassured them; whereupon, they came out of the woods. The horsemen took both the Christian and the Indians before them and entered the camp at nightfall very joyful. When this was learned by the governor, and those who had remained in camp, they were received with the same rejoicing.

*The Portuguese word *rijas,* which Robertson translated as "tough," might be rendered also as "rigid" or "stiff" to reflect the nuance better.

IX.

HOW THAT CHRISTIAN WENT TO THE LAND OF FLORIDA, WHO HE WAS, AND WHAT TOOK PLACE WITH THE GOVERNOR.

That Christian was called Juan Ortiz and was a native of Seville, of a noble family. For twelve years he had been in the hands of the Indians. He had gone to that land with Governor Narvaez and had returned in the ships to the island of Cuba, where the wife of Governor Pánfilo de Narvaez had remained. At her order, with twenty or thirty others he returned to Florida in a brigantine. Arriving at the port, within sight of the town, they saw on land a cane sticking in the ground with its top split and holding a letter. They believed that the governor had left it in order to give news of himself when he resolved to go inland. They asked four or five Indians who were walking on the beach for it, but the latter told them by signs to come ashore for it, which Juan Ortiz and another did contrary to the wish of the others. As soon as they reached land, many Indians came out of the houses of the town and surrounded them and seized them so that they could not escape. The other man who tried to defend himself they killed immediately in that place, and Juan Ortiz they seized by the hands and led to their chief, Ucita. The men in the brigantine refused to land and made for the open sea and returned to the island of Cuba. Ucita ordered Juan Ortiz to be bound hand and foot on a grill laid on top of four stakes [*barra*]. He ordered a fire to be kindled under him in order to burn him there. The chief's daughter asked him not to kill him [Ortiz], saying that a single Christian could not do him any ill or good, and that it would be more to his [the cacique's] honor to hold him captive. Ucita granted this and ordered him taken care of; and as soon as he was well, gave him charge of the guarding of the temple, for at night wolves would carry off the corpses from inside it. He commended himself to God and watched over their temple. One night the wolves carried off from him the corpse of a child, the son of one of the principal Indians. Going after it, he threw a club, which struck the wolf carrying the body, which, finding itself wounded, abandoned it and went off to die nearby.* He [Ortiz], not knowing what he had done as it was night, returned to the temple. At day-

*The word *vara*, which Robertson rendered as "club," is more likely to have been a "spear."

break, when he found the body of the child gone, he became very sad. As soon as Ucita learned of it, he determined to have him killed. He sent [men] along the trail where he [Ortiz] said the wolves had gone, and they found the boy's corpse and farther on the dead wolf. Whereupon, Ucita was greatly pleased with the Christian and at the watch he had kept in the temple, and thenceforward showed him great honor. After being in captivity to him for three years, another chief named Mocoço, who lived two days' journey from the port, came and burned the town. Ucita went in flight to another town he had in another seaport. Juan Ortiz lost his post and the favor he enjoyed from him. And since they [the Indians] are servants of the devil, they are accustomed to offer him souls and blood of their Indians or of any other people they can get. They say that when he [the devil] desires that sacrifice be made to him, he talks with them and tells them he is thirsty and that they should offer a sacrifice to him. Juan Ortiz learned from the girl who had saved him from the fire that her father had determined to sacrifice him the next day; and she told him that he should go to Mocoço, that she knew he would show him honor for she had heard him say that he would ask for him; and she said he would be glad to see him. At night, since he did not know the way, the Indian woman went a half league from the town and put him on it, and in order that this might not be perceived, returned [to the town].[57] Juan Ortiz traveled that night and in the morning came to a river which was already within the boundary of Mocoço and there he saw two Indians fishing. And since they were hostile to those of Ucita and their languages were different, and he did not know that of Mocoço, he feared lest, inasmuch as he did not know how to say who he was and how he came nor how to give an explanation concerning himself, they would kill him thinking him to be an Indian of Ucita. Before they saw him, he came to where they had their weapons, and as soon as they saw him, they ran along the road to the town. And although he told them to wait, that he would do them no harm, they did not understand him and ran away as fast as they could. And when they reached the town, shouting, many Indians came out toward him and began to surround him in order to shoot him with arrows. Juan Ortiz, seeing himself in so great an emergency, hid behind some trees and began to call out very loudly and to cry out and to say that he was a Christian who was fleeing from Ucita and came to see and serve Mocoço, their chief. It was God's will that an Indian who knew the language came up at that time and understood him and made the other Indians keep still, telling them what he [Ortiz] said to him. Three or four Indians were dispatched from there who went to report to their chief, who came out to welcome him a quarter league from the town and was very glad to see him. He immediately made him swear according to his custom as a Christian that he would not run off to any other chief, and promised him that he would show him much honor and that, if at any time, Christians should come to that land, he would release him freely and give him permission to go to them. And so he swore according to his custom as an Indian. Three years after that, some Indians who were fishing in the sea two leagues from the town came to inform Mocoço that they had seen some ships. He called Juan Ortiz and gave him permission to go, who having bade him farewell reached the sea as soon as he could. But not finding the ships, he thought he had been deceived and that the cacique had done that to ascertain his desire. So he remained with Mocoço for nine years, now with little expectation of seeing Christians. As soon as the governor reached Florida, it was known by Mocoço. He immediately told Juan Ortiz that Christians were lodging in the town of Ucita. It seemed to the latter that he [Mocoço] was jesting with him as on the other occasion and told him that the Christians did not come to his mind nor anything else than to serve him. He [Mocoço] assured him of it and gave him permission to go to them, telling him that if he refused to do it, and the Christians returned, he must not hold him guilty, for he was accomplishing what he had promised him. So great was Juan Ortiz's joy that he could not believe it to be true. However, he thanked [Mocoço] and took his leave of him. Mocoço gave him ten or twelve[58] of the principal Indians to go in his company. On his way to the port where the governor was, he met Baltasar de Gallegos, as I have said above. As soon as he reached the camp, the governor ordered some clothes to be given him and some good arms and a beautiful horse. He asked him if he had heard of any land where there was gold or silver. He said no, he had never gone more than ten leagues round about from where he was, and that thirty leagues from there resided an Indian chief called Paracoxi,[59] to whom Mocoço and Ucita and all those of that coast paid tribute; that perhaps he might have some information of any good land; and that his land was indeed better than that of the coast and more fertile and abounding in maize. At this the governor was greatly pleased and said that he wished only to find provisions in order that he might go inland; that the land of Florida was so vast that there could not but be rich land at one end or the other. The cacique of Mocoço came to the port to visit the governor and made him the following talk:

"Very lofty and very mighty lord: In my own estimation, to obey you, least of all those whom you hold under your command but greatest in my desire to perform greater services for you, I appear before your Lordship with as much confidence of receiving favor as if, in fact, this my good will were manifest to you by deeds (not for the small service which I did you of the Christian whom I hold in my possession, by giving him his liberty freely, for I was obliged to do that in order to keep my honor and what I had promised him), but because it belongs to the great to exercise their office with great magnificence; and I hold that you precede all those of the land both in bodily perfections and in ruling good men, as well as in the perfections of the mind with which you can boast of the liberality of nature. The favor which I await from your Lordship is that you consider me as your own, and feel free to command me in whatever I may serve you."[60]

The governor answered him saying that, although in freeing and sending him the Christian, he had kept his honor and his promise, he thanked him and appreciated him so much that there was no comparison and that he would always consider him as a brother and that he would protect him in every way. He ordered a shirt and other clothing to be given him, with which the cacique very happy bade him farewell and went to his town.

X.

HOW THE GOVERNOR SENT THE SHIPS TO CUBA AND LEFT ONE HUNDRED MEN IN THE PORT WHILE HE AND THE REST OF THE MEN MARCHED INLAND.

From the port of Espiritu Santo,[61] where the governor was, he sent the chief constable, Baltasar de Gallegos, with fifty horse and thirty or forty foot to the province of Paracoxi, in order to note the disposition of the land and gather information of the land that lay beyond and to send him word of what he found. He sent the ships to the island of Cuba with orders to return with provisions at a certain time.[62] Since the principal intent of Vasco Porcallo de Figueroa, who came with the governor as captain general, was to send slaves from Florida to the island of Cuba where he had his lands and his mines, and since he had made some forays and found that he could not capture any Indians because of the dense thickets and vast swamps in that land, upon seeing the character of the land, he determined to return to

Cuba. And although there was some difference between him and the governor so that they did not willingly hold any communication or conversation with each other, he asked him [De Soto] courteously to leave and took his departure from him.[63] Baltasar de Gallegos reached Paracoxi and thirty Indians came to him on the part of the cacique who was absent from his town, one of whom spoke as follows:

"King Paracoxi, lord of this province, whose vassals we are, sent us to your grace to learn what you seek in this his land and in what he can serve you."

Baltasar de Gallegos answered them saying that he thanked him [the cacique] heartily for his offer and that they should tell their lord that he should come to his town and that there they could converse and make peace and friendship which he very greatly desired. The Indians went and returned next day saying that their lord was ill and on that account could not come; and that they came before him [Gallegos] to see what he ordered. He asked them if they knew or had information of any rich land where there was gold or silver. They said yes, that there was a province toward the west called Cale,[64] and that the people of that land were hostile to others living in other lands where it was summer most of the year. That land had gold in abundance and when those people came to make war on the people of Cale, they wore hats of gold resembling helmets. When Baltasar de Gallegos perceived that the cacique did not come, as it seemed to him that all these messages were pretense, in order that he [the cacique] might meanwhile get away safely, and fearing lest if he allowed the thirty Indians to go, they would never return, he ordered them put in chains and had the governor informed by eight horse of what was happening. At this the governor and all those in the port with him received great joy, for they believed that what the Indians said might be true. The governor left Captain Calderón in the port with thirty horse and seventy foot with food for two years.[65] He and all the rest of the men marched inland and reached Paracoxi where Baltasar de Gallegos was, and from there, with all the men of the latter, he took the road toward Cale. He passed through a small town, Acela[66] by name, and reached another town called Tocaste.[67] Thence, with thirty horse and fifty foot, he went on toward Cale. As they passed through a town which had been depopulated, they saw some Indians of that town in a shallow lake, to whom the interpreter spoke. They came and gave an Indian to act as guide. He [the governor] came to a river with a swift current and on a tree in the middle of it, a foot bridge was made on which the men crossed. The horses crossed by swimming by means of a tackle which was drawn by those on the other side, for the first horse they drove in without it was drowned. From there, the governor sent two horsemen to the men who had stayed behind, ordering them to hurry for the road was long and provisions were lacking.[68] He reached Cale and found the town without people. He seized three Indians who were spies. There he awaited the men who were coming behind, who were experiencing great hardship from hunger and bad roads, as the land was very poor in maize, low, and very wet, swampy, and covered with dense forests, and the provisions brought from the port were finished. Wherever any village was found, there were some blites [*bredos*],[69] and he who came first gathered them and, having stewed them with water and salt, ate them without anything else. Those who could not get any of them, gathered the stalks from the maize fields which being still young had no maize, and ate them. Having reached the river which the governor had crossed, they found palm cabbages in low palm trees like those of Andalusia. There came two horsemen whom the governor had sent, who told them that there was maize in abundance in Cale; at which all were rejoiced. As soon as they reached Cale, the governor ordered all the maize which was ripe in the fields to be taken, which was enough for three months.* When they were gathering this, the Indians killed three Christians, and one of two Indians who were captured told the governor that seven days' journey farther on was a very large province with maize in abundance, called Apalache.[70] He immediately set out from Cale with fifty horse and sixty foot, leaving the maestre de campo, Luis de Moscoso, with all the rest of the men and ordering him not to move thence until getting word from him. Inasmuch as there was no one to serve them, the bread each one had to eat, he ground in a mortar cannon or mortar made of a log, with a pestle like a window bar. Some sifted the meal through their coats of mail. The bread was baked in some flat pieces of earthen vessels which they set on the fire, in the same way as I have already said was done in Cuba.† It is so difficult to grind that many, who would not formerly eat it unless it was ground, ate the maize parched and sodden.

*The Portuguese term *sêco,* which Robertson rendered as "ripe," rendered literally is "dry."

†The Portuguese that Robertson translated as "in some flat pieces of earthen vessels" is *em uns têstos.* A *têsto* is a lid or cover of an iron or clay vessel.

XI.

HOW THE GOVERNOR REACHED CALIQUEN, AND THENCE, TAKING THE CACIQUE WITH HIM, WENT TO NAPETACA, WHERE THE INDIANS ATTEMPTED TO REMOVE HIM [THE CACIQUE] FROM HIS POWER, AND IN TURN MANY WERE KILLED AND CAPTURED.

On the eleventh day of August, in the year 1540,[71] the governor left Cale and went to sleep at a small town called Ytara,[72] the next day at another called Potano, and the third at Utinama.[73] He arrived at another town to which they gave the name of Mala Paz [i.e., Bad Peace][74] because an Indian came in peace saying that he was the cacique, that he wished to serve the governor with his people, [and asking] that he [the governor] should order twenty-eight Indian men and women, who had been seized from him the night before, to be set free; that he would order provisions taken to him and would give him a guide for the onward journey. The governor ordered the Indians freed and a guard put over him [the supposed cacique]. On the morning of the next day many Indians came and took position about the town near the forest. The Indian asked to be taken near them as he wished to speak to them and assure them, and that they would do whatever he ordered them. As soon as he found himself near them, he attacked the Christians stoutly and escaped and no one was able to overtake him; and all the Indians went fleeing through the woods. The governor ordered loosed a hound which he brought along, previously glutted on them, which passing by many other Indians went to seize the pretended cacique who had fled from the Christians and held him until the latter came to seize him. From there, the governor went to sleep at a town called Cholupaha; and as it had maize in abundance, they gave it the name Villafarta [Well-fed Town]. In front was a river over which a bridge of wood was built,[75] and he went for two days through an abandoned region. On August 17, he arrived at Caliquen[76] and got information of the province of Apalache. They told him that Narvaez had arrived there and that he had taken to boats there because he found no road on beyond; that there was no other village, but that it was all water in every direction. All were saddened at this news and advised the governor to return to the port and leave the land of Florida; so that he might not get lost as had Narvaez; that, if he went on, when he might wish to return he could not; that the Indians would end by seizing the little maize that was to be found. To this the governor answered that he would not turn back until seeing with his own eyes what they said, which he could not believe, and that we should be ready saddled.[77] He ordered Luis de Moscoso to set out immediately from Cale and [said] that he was awaiting him there [in Caliquen]. It appeared to Luis de Moscoso and to many others that they must turn back from Apalache and they buried iron and other things in Cale.* They reached Caliquen after great hardship for the land over which the governor had passed was destroyed and bare of maize. After all the men had gathered there, he ordered a bridge built over a river which flowed near the town. He left Caliquen on September ten,[78] taking the cacique with him. After a march of three days, Indians came in peace saying that they came to see their lord; and every day they came to the road playing on flutes, which is their sign by which they make known that they come in peace. They said that farther on a cacique called Uzachil,[79] a relative of the cacique of Caliquen, their lord, was waiting with great gifts. They asked the governor to free the cacique, but he refused to free him, for he feared lest they revolt and refuse to give him guides and from day to day he dismissed them with good words. He marched for five days, passing through several small towns, and reached a town, Napetuca[80] by name, on September 15. There fourteen or fifteen Indians came and asked the governor to set the cacique of Caliquen, their lord, free. He answered them saying that he did not hold him captive, but that he wished to keep him with him as far as Uzachil. The governor learned from Juan Ortiz that an Indian had revealed to him that they [the Indians] had decided to assemble and to come against him in order to give him battle and to take from him the cacique whom he was holding. On the day agreed upon, the governor ordered his men to be ready, and the horsemen armed and mounted, each one to be within his lodging, so that the Indians might not see them and would accordingly come to the town without fear. Four hundred Indians came within sight of the camp with their bows and arrows[81] and posted themselves in a wood. Then they sent two Indians to tell the governor to give up the cacique to them. The governor with six men of foot, taking the cacique by the hand and talking with him, in order to assure the

*The Portuguese, *ferragem,* which Robertson rendered as "iron," could better be rendered as "hardware" or "iron fittings" and especially as "horseshoes," as the meaning of *ferragem* is "things made of iron" rather than "iron" per se, which is *ferro.*

Indians, went toward the place where they were and seeing the time ready ordered a blast of the trumpet to be given. Immediately those who were in the houses in the town, both foot and horse, attacked the Indians, who were so surprised that their greatest thought was where they could escape. They killed two horses, one of which was that of the governor, who was immediately provided with another. Thirty or forty Indians were lanced. The rest fled toward two very large shallow lakes which were separated one from the other.* There they went swimming about, while the Christians round about—arquebusiers and crossbowmen—shot at them from the outside. But as they were far away and they [the Spaniards] shot at them from a long distance they did no hurt to them. That night the governor ordered one of the two lakes to be surrounded; for, because of their large size, his men were insufficient to surround both of them. Being surrounded, the Indians, upon the approach of night, having made up their minds to take to flight, would come swimming very softly to the edge, and so that they might not be seen, would place water-lily leaves on their heads. When the horsemen saw the leaves moving they would dash in until the water was up to the breasts of the horses and the Indians would return in flight within the lake. In that way they passed that night without the Indians or the Christians having any rest. Juan Ortiz told them that since they could not escape, they would better surrender to the governor, which, forced by necessity and the coldness of the water, they did; and one by one as soon as the suffering from the cold conquered them, they would cry out to Juan Ortiz saying that they should not be killed for now they were going to put themselves in the hands of the governor. At day dawn they had all surrendered except twelve of the principal men who, being more honored and valiant, resolved to perish rather than come into his power. The Indians of Paracoxi who were now going about unchained, went in swimming after them and pulled them out by their hair. They were all put in chains and on the day following were allotted among the Christians for their service. While captive there they resolved to revolt and charged an Indian interpreter whom they held as a valiant man that as

*In the Portuguese here, *duas alagoas muito grandes* there is no explicit mention of the lakes as being shallow. Although *alagoa* or *lagoa* normally means a small lake or pond or swamp even, which one usually would presume to be shallow, Elvas's use of the terms "very large" to describe the lakes suggest a distinct possibility at least that they were deep also.

The Portuguese for Robertson's "were separated one from the other" is *que desuiadas uma da outra estavam. Desuiadas* has the sense of "distant" or "remote" from one another as well as "separated." Elvas's use of *desuiadas* might indicate that the two lakes were on opposite sides of the settlement.

soon as the governor came to talk with him, he should seize him about the neck with his hands and choke him. As soon as he saw an opportunity he seized hold of the governor, and before he got his hands about his neck, struck him so hard on the nose that it was all covered with blood. Immediately they all rose in revolt. He who could get weapons in his hand or the pestle for crushing maize tried with all his might to kill his master or the first man he met. He who could get a lance or sword in his hand so handled himself with it as if he had used it all his life. An Indian with a sword surrounded by fifteen or twenty men on foot in the public place, uttered [a] challenge like a bull, until some halberdiers of the governor came up, who killed him. Another one with a lance climbed up on a cane floor* which they made to hold their maize (which they call barbacoa†) and there he made a noise as if ten men were inside; and while defending the door he was struck down by a javelin [*passador*]. In all, there were about two hundred Indians, all of whom were subdued. The governor gave some of the youngest boys to those who had good chains and cautioned them not to let them escape from them. All the rest he ordered to be punished by being fastened to a stake in the middle of the plaza and the Indians of Paracoxi shot them with arrows.

XII.

HOW THE GOVERNOR ARRIVED AT PALACHE AND WAS INFORMED THAT GOLD EXISTED IN ABUNDANCE IN THE INTERIOR OF THE LAND.

On September the 23rd, the governor left Napetaca [*sic*] and went to sleep at a river[82] where two Indians brought him a stag on the part of the cacique

*The Portuguese for Robertson's "Another one . . . climbed up on a cane floor" is *Outro se sobio . . . a um sobrado de canas. Sobrado de canas* has the sense of "upper story" as well as "cane floor." This structure is clearly the elevated granary supported by twelve beams described by Bishop Gabriel Días Vara Calderón (see Lucy L. Wenhold, ed. and trans., "A 17th Century Letter of Gabriel Días Vara Calderón, Bishop of Cuba, Describing the Indians and Indian Missions of Florida," Washington, D.C.: Smithsonian Miscellaneous Collections, vol. 95, no. 16, (1936), 13).

†The word *barbacoa,* which is of Arawakian derivation, was also used in Florida for a raised framework for smoking meat or fish (or the grill on which Ortiz was to be roasted by Ucita when he was first captured). *Barbacoa* was also the name for the chief's raised bench in the council house as well as for the benches that lined the council house wall.

of Uzachil. Next day he passed through a large town called Hapaluya[83] and went to sleep at Uzachil. He found no people there, for because of the news which the Indians had of the massacre of Napetaca they dared not remain. In the town he found an abundance of maize, beans, and pumpkins, of which their food consists, and on which the Christians lived there. Maize is like coarse millet and the pumpkins are better and more savory than those of Spain.* From there the governor sent two captains, each one in a different direction, in search of the Indians. They captured a hundred head, among Indian men and women. Of the latter, there, as well as in any other part where forays were made, the captain selected one or two for the governor and the others were divided among themselves and those who went with them. These Indians they took along in chains with collars about their necks and they were used for carrying the baggage and grinding the maize and for other services which so fastened in this manner they could perform. Sometimes it happened that when they went with them for firewood or maize they would kill the Christian who was leading them and would escape with the chain. Others at night would file the chain off with a bit of stone which they have in place of iron tools, and with which they cut it. Those who were caught at it paid for themselves and for those others, so that on another day they might not dare do likewise. As soon as the women and young children were a hundred leagues from their land, having become unmindful, they were taken along unbound, and served in that way, and in a very short time learned the language of the Christians. The governor left Uzachil for Apalache and, in a march of two days, reached a town called Axille.[84] And because the Indians had not heard of the Christians, they were careless, [but] most of them escaped because the town was surrounded by a forest.[85] On the morning of the next day, October first, the governor left there and ordered a bridge to be built over a river where he had to cross. It was necessary to swim for a stone's throw where the bridge was built, and beyond that a crossbow-shot's distance the water came up to the waist. And there was a very high, thick wood through which the Indians would come to see if they could prevent the passage and those who were building the bridge. The crossbowmen came to their aid and made the Indians take to flight. Some timbers were put in over which some men passed which assured the cross-

*The Portuguese that Robertson rendered as "coarse millet" is *Milho Zaburo.* Both Taylor's *A Portuguese-English Dictionary* and Hildebrando Lima and Gustavo Barroso's *Pequeno dicionario brasileiro da lingua portuguesa*, 2nd ed. (Rio de Janeiro: Civilização Brasileira S/A, Editôra, 1939), define *milho zaburro* as "sorghum." Millet is *painco, milho miudo,* or *milho da itália. Milho* by itself is the modern Portuguese word for "maize."

A Coin from De Soto's First Winter Camp. This four maravedi copper coin was excavated by archaeologists at the Governor Martin site in Tallahassee, Florida. These coins were minted in Spain between 1505 and 1517. The Martin site is the only one in the southeastern United States where there is compelling, direct evidence of the presence of De Soto's army. (Courtesy of the Florida Division of Historical Resources)

ing. The governor crossed over on Wednesday, the day of St. Francis. He went to sleep at a town called Vitachuco[86] which was subject to Palache. He found it burning, for the Indians had set fire to it. Beyond that place, the land was very populous and maize abounded. He passed through many open districts like villages. On Sunday, October 25, he arrived at a town called Uzela,[87] and on Monday, at Anhaica Apalache[88] where the lord of all that land and province lived. In that town, the maestre de campo, whose office it is to allot and provide lodgings, lodged them all. Within a league and a half league about that town were other towns where there was abundance of maize, pumpkins, beans, and dried plums[89] native to the land, which are better than those of Spain and grow wild in the fields without being planted. Food which seemed sufficient to last over the winter was gathered together from those towns on into Anhaica Apalache. The governor was informed that the sea was ten leagues from there. He immediately sent a captain and some horse and foot, and after going six leagues the captain found a town called Ochete.* He reached the sea and found a large tree which had been cut down and made into troughs [*couchos*] fixed with some posts which were used as mangers and saw skulls of horses.[90] With this message he came and what they said of Narvaez was considered true, namely, that he had there built the boats with which he left that land and in which he was lost at sea. The governor immediately sent Juan de Añasco with thirty horse to the port of Espiritu Santo, where Calderón was, ordering them to abandon that port and all to go to Apalache. He [Añasco] set out on Friday, November 17.[91] In Uzachil and at other towns on the way, he [Añasco] found many people already careless. He would not capture Indians in order not to be detained, for it did not suit him to give the Indians time to assemble. He passed through the towns at night and rested for three or four hours at a distance from habitation. In ten days he reached the port, brought twenty Indian women whom he captured in Utara and Potano near Cale, sent them to Doña Isabel in two caravels which he sent from the port to Cuba, and brought all the men of foot in the brigantines, coasting along toward Palache. Calderón with the men of horse and some foot crossbowmen went by land. In some places, the Indians attacked him and wounded some of his men. As soon as they reached Apalache, the governor immediately ordered planks hewn and spikes taken to the sea, with which was built a piragua large enough to hold thirty well-armed men who went by way of the bay to the sea and coasted about waiting for the brigantines. Several times they fought

*Whereas Elvas's account and Robertson's translation placed the sea ten leagues from Anhaica and Ochete six leagues distant from Anhaica, Buckingham Smith's translation rendered both distances as eight leagues. And in addition, Smith described Ochete as "eight leagues on the way to the sea." Despite the contradiction implicit in Smith's two distances of eight leagues, which should have made editors or publishers investigate, editions of the Smith translation as recent as that by Palmetto Books in 1968 have presented Smith's mistranslation of this passage without comment.

with Indians who were going along the keys in canoes.* On Saturday, November 29,[92] an Indian came through the sentinels without being seen and set fire to the town; and because of the high wind blowing, two-thirds of it were quickly burned. On Sunday, the 28th of December, Juan de Añasco arrived with the brigantines.[93] The governor sent Francisco Maldonado, captain of the foot soldiers, with fifty men to coast along toward the west and look for a port, for he had decided to go by land in order to explore in that direction. On that day, eight horse, by order of the governor, went out into the open country for two leagues about the town to look for Indians; for now the latter had become so daring that they would come within two crossbow-shots of the camp to kill the men. They found two Indians and one Indian woman gathering beans. Although the men could have escaped, in order not to abandon the Indian woman who was the wife of one of them, they resolved to die fighting. Before being killed they wounded three horses, one of which died a few days afterward. Calderón with his men marched along the seacoast. From a wood close to the sea some Indians came out to attack him and forced him to leave the road, and many of those with him to abandon some necessary food they were carrying. Three or four days after the time limit set by the governor to Maldonado for going and coming (although he had planned and determined not to await him longer if he did not come within a week from that time), he [Maldonado] came and brought an Indian from a province called Ochus,[94] sixty leagues from Apalache, where he had found a port of good depth and sheltered. And because he hoped to find farther on a good land, the governor was very happy and sent Maldonado[95] to Havana for provisions with orders to wait at the port of Ochus which he [Maldonado] had discovered; and that he [the governor] would go overland in search of it; and that if he [the governor] were delayed and should not go [to that port] that summer he [Maldonado] should return to

---

*The word that Robertson rendered as "keys" is *caez*. The Spanish *cayo* for "key" or "islet" does not seem to have passed into Portuguese. Elvas, of course, would have been familiar with the Spanish form, but his *caez* is more suggestive of the modern Portuguese *cais*, which is "wharf" or "pier." Buckingham Smith (1968:48) rendered *caez* as "estuary."

Almadias, the word Elvas used for "canoes" here, signifies a very long and narrow African or Asiatic vessel. Apropos of a possible sixteenth-century distinction made between *almadias* and *canoas*, Suzanne Lussagnet in her *Les Français en Amérique pendant la Deuxième Moitié du XVI*[e] *Siecle: Les Français en Floride* (Paris: Presses Universitaires de France, 1958) noted that René Laudonnière used *almadias* when speaking of small dugouts and *canoas* when speaking of larger ones.

the Havana, and the next summer return to wait at the port, for he [the governor] would do nothing else than go in search of Ochus. Francisco Maldonado went and Juan de Guzmán remained in his stead as captain of the foot soldiers of his company. From among the Indians captured at Napetuca, the treasurer, Juan Gaytán, brought along a youth who said that he was not of that land, but that he was from another very distant one lying in the direction of the sunrise, and that some time ago he had come in order to visit [other] lands; that his land was called Yupaha[96] and a woman ruled it; that the town where she lived was of wonderful size; and that the chieftainess collected tribute from many of her neighboring chiefs, some of whom gave her clothing and others gold in abundance. He told how it was taken from the mines, melted, and refined, just as if he had seen it done, or else the devil taught him; so that all who knew anything of this said it was impossible to give so good an account of it unless one had seen it; and all when they saw the signs he made believed whatever he said to be true.

XIII.

HOW THE GOVERNOR SET OUT FROM APALACHE TO LOOK FOR YUPAHA AND OF WHAT HAPPENED TO HIM.

On Wednesday, the 3rd of March, 1540,[97] the governor left Anhaica Apalache in search of Yupaha. He ordered all his men to provide themselves with maize for a journey of sixty leagues through uninhabited land. Those of horse carried the maize on their horses, and those of foot on their backs; for most of the Indians whom they had to serve them, being naked and in chains, died because of the hard life they suffered during that winter. After a march of four days, they came to a deep river,[98] where a piragua was made and, because of the strong current, a chain cable was made and fastened on each side of the river. The piragua crossed over alongside it and the horses crossed swimming by means of ropes and tackle which were pulled along by them. After crossing the river, in a day and a half they reached a town called Capachiqui.[99] On Friday,[100] March 11, they saw the Indians had risen [and gone into the woods]. Next day, five[101] Christians went to look for mortars which the Indians use for crushing their maize. They went to certain houses contiguous to the camp surrounded by a wood. Within the wood many

Indians were walking about who came to spy on us. Five of them separated from the others and attacked our men. One of the Christians came running to the camp, shouting "To arms." Those who were most ready attended to the alarm. They found one Christian dead and three badly wounded. The Indians fled through a swamp with a very dense wood where the horses could not enter. The governor left Capachiqui and crossed over an abandoned region. On Wednesday, the 21st of the month, he came to a town called Toalli. Beyond that place, a difference was seen in the houses, for those behind were covered with hay and those of Toalli[102] were covered with canes in the manner of tile.[103] Those houses are very clean and some have their walls plastered and appear to be made of mud.* Throughout the cold lands each of the Indians has his house for the winter plastered inside and out.† They shut the very small door at night and build a fire inside the house so that it gets as hot as an oven, and stays so all night long so that there is no need of clothing. Besides those houses they have others for summer with kitchens nearby where they build their fires and bake their bread. They have barbacoas in which they keep their maize. This is a house raised up on four posts, timbered like a loft and the floor of cane. The difference which the houses of the lords or principal men have from those of the others is that besides being larger they have large balconies in front and below seats resembling benches made of canes;‡ and round about many large barbacoas in which they gather together the tribute paid them by their Indians, which consists of maize and deerskins and native blankets resembling shawls, some being made of the inner bark of trees and some from a plant like daffodils [*abroteas*] which when pounded remains like flax.[104] The Indian women cover themselves with these blankets, draping one around themselves from the waist down and another over the shoulder with the right arm uncovered

*The Portuguese that Robertson rendered as "walls plastered and appear to be made of mud" is *paredes envaradas q pareciam de taipa. Envaradas* is from the modern *envarar,* meaning "to place wattles or laths horizontally." *Taipa* could be either "mud" or "tabby." A more literal rendering of this passage would be "wattled walls that appear to be of mud."

†The word that Robertson translated as "plastered" is again *envaradas* or "wattled."

For a description of a larger communal version of this structure in the Guale village of Asao at the mouth of the Altamaha River, see Gary N. Shapiro and John H. Hann, "The Documentary Image of the Council Houses of Spanish Florida Tested by Excavations at the Mission of San Luis De Talimali," in Thomas, ed., *Columbian Consequences,* vol. 2, p. 513.

‡The Portuguese that Robertson rendered as "resembling benches made of canes" is *assentos de caniços a maneira descanhos.* It might be rendered more literally as "cane seats resembling chairs." *Escano* in Spanish is a bench with a back.

in the manner and custom of Gypsies. The Indian men wear only one over the shoulders in the same way and have their privies covered with a truss of deerskin resembling the breech clouts formerly worn in Spain. The skins are well tanned and are given the color that is desired; and so perfectly that if the color is vermillion, it seems to be very fine grained cloth, and that colored black is splendid.* And of this same they make shoes. They give the same colors to the blankets. The governor left Toalli on March 24. At supper time on Thursday he came to a little stream where a footbridge was made on which the men crossed. Benito Fernandez, a Portuguese, fell off it and was drowned.[105] As soon as the governor had crossed the stream, he found a village called Achese[106] a short distance on. Although the Indians had never heard of Christians they plunged into a river. A few Indians, men and women, were seized, among whom was found one who understood the youth who was guiding the governor to Yupaha. On that account, the governor was more certain of what the latter said, for they had passed through lands having different languages, some of which he did not understand. The governor sent one of the Indians captured there to call the cacique who was on the other side of the river. He came and spoke as follows: "Very exalted and very mighty and very excellent Lord: Things which seldom happen cause wonder. Therefore, what must the sight of your Lordship and your men, whom we have never seen, be to me and mine; and the entrance into my land with so great haste and fury, and on animals so fierce as are your horses, without me having known of your coming. It was a thing so new and caused such terror and fear in our minds that it was not in our power to await and welcome your Lordship with the ceremony due so exalted and distinguished a prince as is your Lordship. Confiding in your greatness and singular virtues, not only do I hope to be held free of guilt but to receive rewards. The first thing I beg of your Lordship is that with my person and land and vassals, you do as with a thing [of] your own; and secondly, that you tell me who you are, whence you come, whither you go, and what you seek, so that I may better serve you." The governor answered him saying that he thanked him heartily for his offer and for his good will, as if he had welcomed him

*The Portuguese that Robertson rendered as "if the color is vermillion, it seems to be a very fine grained cloth" is *que se he vermelho parece muito fino pano de grã*. It might be rendered more literally as, "if it be red, it looks like a very fine grenadine cloth." *Graã* or *grã* in modern Portuguese is a red dye extracted from a type of oak-tree gall or from the cochineal insect or from other sources that produce a scarlet dye. As Elvas may not have been familiar with cochineal at this early date, grenadine seems a likely candidate for the tone of red he described.

and offered him a great treasure; that he [the governor] was a son of the sun and came from where it dwelt and that he was going through that land and seeking the greatest lord and the richest province in it. The cacique said that a great lord lived on ahead; that his domain was called Ocute.[107] He gave him a guide and interpreter for that province. The governor ordered his [the cacique's] Indians to be set free and departed from his town on the first day of April, marching through his land up along a river with many villages. He left a wooden cross raised very high in the middle of the public place. And as time did not allow more, he only declared that that cross was a memorial of that on which Christ suffered, who was God and man and created the heavens and the earth and suffered to save us and, therefore, they should reverence it. They signified that they would do so. On April 4, the governor passed through a town, by name, Altamaca;[108] and on the tenth day of the month reached Ocute. The cacique sent him two thousand Indians bearing gifts, namely, many rabbits, partridges, maize bread, two hens,[109] and many dogs, which are esteemed among the Christians as if they were fat sheep because there was a great lack of meat and salt. Of this there was so much need and lack in many places and on many occasions that if a man fell sick, there was nothing with which to make him well; and he would waste away of an illness which could have been easily cured in any other place, until nothing but his bones were left and he would die from pure weakness, some saying: "If I had a bit of meat or some lumps of salt, I should not die." The Indians do not lack meat; for they kill many deer, hens, rabbits, and other game with their arrows. In this they have great skill, which the Christians do not have; and even if they had it, they had no time for it, for most of the time they were on the march, and they did not dare to turn aside from the paths. And because they lacked meat so badly, when the six hundred men with De Soto arrived at any town and found twenty or thirty dogs, he who could get one and who killed it thought he was not a little agile. And if he who killed one did not send his captain a quarter, the latter, if he learned of it, upbraided him and gave him to understand it in the watches or in any other matter of worth that arose with which he could annoy him. On Monday, April 12, the governor left Ocute, the cacique having given him four hundred tamemes,[110] that is, Indians for carrying. He passed through a town, whose lord was called Cofaqui; and reached a province of an Indian lord called Patofa,[111] who, since he was at peace with the lord of Ocute and the other lords round about, had heard of the governor some days before and desired to see him. He came to visit him and spoke as follows:

"Powerful Lord: Now with reason I will beg fortune to pay me some slight adversity for so great happiness; and I call myself happy for I have obtained what I desired in this life—that of seeing your Lordship and being able to render you some service. Although speech is the image of what is in the heart and what my heart feels with this happiness it cannot conceal, yet my tongue is not sufficient to enable me to express that happiness entirely. From whence did this your land, which I am governing, merit the visit of so sovereign and so excellent a prince to whom all people in the world owe service and obedience? And from whence has come so great a good fortune to those who inhabit this land, they being so insignificant, unless to recall to their memory some great misfortune which might happen in accordance with the arrangement of fortune? Therefore, now and forever, if we are worthy of your Lordship holding us as yours, we can not cease to be favored and maintained in true justice and reason and called men; for those who lack reason and justice can be compared to brute beasts. In my heart with the respect due to such a prince as your Lordship, I offer myself, and beg you that in payment of this true good will, you may wish to be served by my person, land, and vassals."

The governor answered him saying that his offers and good will exhibited by deeds would greatly please him; that he would always remember to honor and protect him as a brother.

This land, from that of the first peaceful cacique to the province of Patofa—a distance of fifty leagues—is a rich land, beautiful, fertile, well watered, and with fine fields along the rivers. From thence to the port of Espiritu Santo, where we first reached the land of Florida—a distance of about three hundred and fifty leagues or so—it is a lean land, and most of it covered with rough pine groves, low and very swampy, and in places having lofty dense forests, where the hostile Indians wandered so that no one could find them nor could the horses enter there—which was annoying to the Christians because of the provisions which had been carried off and the trouble experienced by them in looking for the Indians to guide them.

Spaniards Meet with a Mississippian Chief. Chiefs in Mississippian societies were at the top of a highly structured and ranked social system. In some cases they were treated by their subjects almost as if they were gods. They were accustomed to courtesy and respect from visitors. De Soto, in seeking peaceful passage, burden bearers, women, and food supplies, would routinely arrest the local chief and take him along as a hostage to the border of the next chiefdom. (Painting by John Berkey © National Geographic Society)

XIIII.

HOW THE GOVERNOR LEFT THE PROVINCE OF PATOFA AND CAME UPON AN UNINHABITED REGION, WHERE HE AND ALL HIS MEN EXPERIENCED GREAT VICISSITUDES AND EXTREME NEED.

In the town of Patofa, the youth[112] whom the governor brought as interpreter and guide began to foam at the mouth and to throw himself to the ground as if possessed by the devil. They prayed the evangel over him and that fit left him. He said that four days' journey thence toward the rising sun was the province of which he spoke. The Indians of Patofa said that they knew of no settlement in that direction, but that toward the northwest they knew a province called Coça,[113] a well provisioned land and of very large villages. The cacique told the governor that if he wished to go thither, he would furnish him service of a guide and Indians to carry; and if in the direction indicated by the youth he would also give him all those he needed; and with mutual words of affection and promises they said farewell to each other. He [the chief] gave him [De Soto] seven hundred tamemes. He took maize for four days and marched for six days along a path which gradually grew narrower until it was all lost. He marched in the direction where the youth guided him and crossed two rivers[114] by fording, each of which was two crossbow-shots wide. The water came to their stirrups and had a swift current, so that it was necessary for the men on horseback to form a line one in front of the other in order that those on foot might cross above them by virtue of their support. He came to another river[115] with a more powerful current and wider which was crossed with greater difficulty, for the horses swam as they got out for the length of a lance. That river being crossed, the governor came out to a pine grove and threatened the youth and made as if he would throw him to the dogs because he had deceived him, saying that it was a march of four days, and for nine days he had marched making seven or eight leagues on each day; and now the men and horses were become weak because of the great economy which had been practiced with regard to the maize. The youth said that he did not know where he was. That there was no other whom Juan Ortiz understood availed in preventing him from being thrown to the dogs. The governor with them [the youth and Ortiz] and with some horse and foot, leaving the camp established in a pine grove, marched five or six leagues that day looking for a road, and at night returned greatly disheartened without having found any signs of habitation. Next day different opinions were expressed as to whether he should turn back or what he should do. Inasmuch as the land behind through which they had come was left very desolate and lacking in maize, and the maize they brought was finished, and the men very weak, as well as the horses, they were in great doubt as to whether they could reach a place where they might be aided. Moreover, they considered that if they went on like defeated men, if any Indians dared to attack them, they could not escape either because of hunger or war. The governor determined to send horsemen thence in all directions to look for habitation. On the next day he sent four captains in different directions, each one with eight horsemen. They returned at night some leading their horses by the bridle and others driving them before them with a stick, for they could not carry them they were so tired out, and without finding any road or sign of habitation. Next day, the governor sent four others [i.e., captains] each with eight horse, men who could swim, in order to cross the mud and streams which they might come to, and chosen horses, the best in the camp. The captains were Baltasar de Gallegos, who went upstream; Juan de Añasco, who went down; Alonso Romo and Juan Rodriguez Lobillo, who went inland.[116]

The governor had taken thirteen sows to Florida and was now driving three hundred pigs. He ordered half a pound of flesh to be given to each man daily, it having been three or four days since maize was lacking. With that small amount of meat and with some herbs boiled with considerable trouble, the men were sustained.

The governor sent the Indians of Patofa back since he had nothing to give them to eat. They, upon ceasing to accompany and serve the Christians in their need, and manifesting great sorrow to him at returning without leaving them in a village, returned to their own land.

Juan de Añasco came on Sunday afternoon and gave news of finding a small town twelve or thirteen leagues away. He brought an Indian woman and a boy whom he captured. With his coming and with the news, the governor and all were so glad that it seemed to them that they had then come back from greedy death. On Monday, the 26th of April, the governor set out for the town which was called Aymay,[117] to which the Christians gave the name of the town of Socorro [i.e., Relief]. At the place where the camp was established he left a letter buried at the foot of a pine tree and on the pine some words cut on the bark with a machete [*măchil*], as follows: "Dig at the foot of this pine tree and you will find a letter," doing this so that when the captains came, who had gone to look for a village, they might see the letter and might learn what the governor had done and where he had gone. There was no other way to the town than marks left cut on the trees by Juan de Añasco. The governor, with some of those who had the best horses, reached the town on Monday; and all striving to reach it as soon as possible slept, some at a distance of two, and others at three or four, leagues from the town, each one according as he could march and his strength aided him. In the town was found a barbacoa full of parched maize meal and some maize which was given out by rationing. There four Indians were captured, and no one of them would say anything else than that they did not know of any other village. The governor ordered one of them to be burned. Thereupon, another said that two days' journey thence was a province called Cutifachiqui.[118] On Wednesday arrived the captains, Baltasar de Gallegos, Alonso Romo, and Juan Rodriquez Lobillo, who had found the letter and followed to the town whither the governor had gone. Two men belonging to the company of Juan Rodriquez were lost because of their tired horses. The governor chid him severely for having left them and sent him to look for them, and as soon as they came set out for Cutifachiqui. On the way three Indians were captured who declared that the chieftainess of that land had already heard of the Christians and was awaiting them in one of her towns. The governor sent to her by one of them an offer of his friendship and the information that he was coming thither.

The governor arrived and immediately four canoes came to him in one of which was a sister[119] of the cacica. Coming to the governor, she said these words: "Excellent Lord: My sister orders me to kiss your Lordship's hands and say to you that the reason why she has not come in person is that she thought she could better serve you by remaining as she is doing to give orders that all her canoes should be made ready quickly so that your Lordship might cross and so that you might rest, for you will be served immediately." The governor thanked her and she returned to the other side of the river. Shortly thereafter, the cacica came from the town in a carrying chair in which certain principal Indians carried her to the river.* She entered a canoe with an awning at the stern and on the bottom of which was already spread a mat for her and above it two cushions one on top of the other, on which she seated herself. With her principal men and other canoes filled with Indians who accompanied her, she went to the place where the governor was; and on

*The Portuguese *andor*, which Robertson rendered as "carrying chair," has the primary meaning today of the litter or platform with poles used for carrying religious images in a procession.

her arrival spoke as follows: "O, Excellent Lord: May your Lordship's coming to these your lands be of very good augury, although my possibility does not equal my wishes and my services are not equal to what I desire and to the merits of so powerful a prince as your Lordship; for good will is more worthy of acceptance than all the treasures of the world which may be offered without it. With very sincere and open good will I offer you my person, my lands, my vassals, and this poor service." And she presented him a quantity of clothing of the country which she brought in the other canoes, namely, blankets and skins. And from her neck she drew a long string of pearl beads and threw it about the neck of the governor, exchanging with him many gracious words of affection and courtesy. She ordered canoes to go thither in which the governor and his men crossed. As soon as he was lodged in the town, another gift of many hens[120] was made him. That land was very pleasing and fertile, and had excellent fields along the rivers, the forest being clear and having many walnuts and mulberries. They said that the sea was two days' journey away. About the town within the compass of a league and a half league were large uninhabited towns, choked with vegetation, which looked as though no people had inhabited them for some time. The Indians said that two years ago there had been a plague in that land and they had moved to other towns. In the barbacoas of the towns there was considerable amount of clothing—blankets made of thread from the bark of trees and feather mantles (white, gray,* vermillion, and yellow), made according to their custom, elegant and suitable for winter. There were also many deerskins, well tanned and colored, with designs drawn on them and made into pantaloons, hose, and shoes.† The cacica, observing that the Christians esteemed pearls, told the governor that he might order certain graves in that town to be examined, for he would find many, and that if he wished to send to the uninhabited towns, they could load all their horses. The graves of that town were examined and fourteen arrobas[121] of pearls were found, babies and birds being made of them.

The people were dark, well set up and proportioned, and more civilized than any who had been seen in all the land of Florida;‡ and all were shod and clothed. The youth told the governor that he was now beginning to enter

*Robertson has mistranslated the Portuguese *verdes* as "gray." *Verdes* is "green."

†The Portuguese *calças, y meas calças,* which Robertson rendered as "pantaloons, hose," might be rendered also as "trousers, leggings."

‡The Portuguese *polida* that Robertson rendered as "civilized" might be rendered also as "polite" or "well mannered."

that land of which he had spoken to him. And since it was such a land and he understood the language of the Indians, some credence was given him. He requested that he be baptized, for he wished to become a Christian. He was made a Christian and was called Pedro. The governor ordered him to be loosed from the chain in which he had gone until then. That land, according to the statement of the Indian, had been very populous and was reputed to be a good land.* According to appearances, the youth whom the governor had taken as guide had heard of it, and what he learned from hearsay he asserted to have seen, and enlarged at will what he saw. In that town were found a dagger and some beads of Christians, whom the Indians said had been in the port two days' journey thence;† and that it was now many years since Governor Licentiate Ayllón[122] had arrived there in order to make a conquest of that land; that on arriving at the port, he died; and there ensued a division, quarrels, and deaths among several of the principal persons who had accompanied him as to who should have the command; and without learning anything of the land they returned to Spain from that port.

All the men were of the opinion that they should settle in that land as it was an excellent region; that if it were settled, all the ships from New Spain, and those from Peru, Santa Marta, and Tierra Firme,[123] on their way to Spain, would come to take advantage of the stop there, for their route passes by there; and as it is a good land and suitable for making profits.

Since the governor's purpose was to seek another treasure like that of Atabalipa, the lord of Peru, he had no wish to content himself with good land or with pearls, even though many of them were worth their weight in gold and, if the land were to be allotted in repartimiento, those pearls which the Indians would get afterward would be worth more; for those they have, inasmuch as they are bored by fire, lose their color thereby. The governor replied to those who urged him to settle that there was not food in that whole land for the support of his men for a single month; that it was neces-

---

*The Portuguese *os índios,* which Robertson rendered as "the Indian," is plural rather than singular. In translating *os índios* as singular, Robertson has changed the meaning of the Portuguese to make Perico the speaker. The Portuguese *esta terra segundo os índios diziam havia sido muito povoada* should be rendered thus, "that land, according to what the Indians were saying, had been very populated." In the context, the Indians speaking seem to be the Indians of Cutifachiqui in general.

†Robertson's "in the port two days' journey thence" is an obvious reference to goods left behind by the Vázquez de Ayllón settlers. Together with Charles Hudson's placement of Cutifachiqui near Camden, South Carolina, this raises questions for those who locate the Ayllón settlement on the Savannah River or even farther south in Guale territory.

sary to hasten to the port of Ochus where Maldonado was to wait; that if another richer land were not found they could always return to that one whenever they wished; that meanwhile the Indians would plant their fields and it would be better provided with maize. He asked the Indians whether they had heard of any great lord farther on. They said that twelve days' journey thence was a province called Chiaha which was subject to the lord of Coça. Thereupon, the governor determined to go in search of that land; and as he was a man, hard and dry of word, and although he was glad to listen to and learn the opinion of all, after he had voiced his own opinion he did not like to be contradicted and always did what seemed best to him. Accordingly, all conformed to his will, and although it seemed a mistake to leave that land, for another land might have been found round about where the men might maintain themselves until the planting might be done there and the maize harvested, no one had anything to say to him after his determination was learned.

FIFTEEN.

HOW THE GOVERNOR LEFT CUTIFACHIQUI TO GO IN SEARCH OF COÇA; AND OF THE THINGS THAT HAPPENED TO HIM ON THE WAY.

On May 3,[124] the governor set out from Cutifachiqui, and because the Indians had already risen, and it was learned that the cacica was minded to go away if she could without giving guides or tamemes for carrying because of offenses committed against the Indians by the Christians—for among many men there is never lacking some person of little quality who for very little advantage to himself places the others in danger of losing their lives—the governor ordered a guard to be placed over her and took her along with him; not giving her such good treatment as she deserved for the good will she had shown him and the welcome she had given him. He made true the old proverb which says "For well doing," etc. And so he took her along on foot with her slave women, so that they [the Indians] might show respect because of her. In all the towns through which the governor passed, the cacica ordered the Indians to come and carry the loads from one town to the other. We traversed her lands for a hundred leagues, in which, as we saw, she was very well obeyed, for all the Indians did with great efficiency and diligence what she ordered of them. Perico, the youth who was guiding us, said that she was not the ruler but that she was the ruler's niece* and that she had come to that town to execute justice on certain of the principal men under command of the ruler who had rebelled against her and kept the tribute. No credit was given to him because of the lies in which he had been found; but everything was endured in him because of the need of him to tell what the Indians said. In seven days, the governor reached a province, by name Chalaque,[125] the poorest land in maize seen in Florida. The Indians live on roots of herbs which they seek in the open field and on game killed with their arrows. The people are very domestic, go quite naked, and are very weak.† There was a lord who brought the governor two deerskins as a great act of service. In that land are many wild hens.[126] In one town they performed a service for him, presenting him seven hundred of them, and likewise in others they brought those they had and could get.

It took five days to go from this province to another one called Xualla.[127] They found little maize, and for that reason, although the men were tired and their horses very weak, the governor did not stop over two days. From Ocute to Cufitachiqui it was about one hundred and thirty leagues, eighty of which were without inhabitants. From Cutifa[chiqui] to Xualla it was two hundred and fifty leagues, over mountainous country.[128] The governor set out from Xualla for Guaxule, crossing over very rough and lofty mountains. Along that way, the cacica of Cutifachiqui, whom the governor brought as above said for the purpose of taking her to Guaxule[129]—for her lands reached that far—going one day with her slave women who were carrying

*Robertson's phrase "but that she was the ruler's niece" needs some comment. The word "ruler" does not appear explicitly in the Portuguese text, and the Portuguese could conceivably be rendered to make the ruler her niece. The Portuguese that Robertson rendered as "Perico . . . said that she was not the ruler, but that she was the ruler's niece" is *dizia Perico . . . que não era aquela a senhora mas que era uma sua sobrinha.* Rendered with extreme literalness, the sentence reads as follows: "Perico . . . said that the lady in charge was not that one, but that it (or she) was a (or one) her niece." Rendered more loosely the last phrase would be "but that she was a niece of hers." Consequently, one could read the Portuguese text either as saying that the Lady of Cutifachiqui was the ruler's niece or that the ruler was the niece of the Lady of Cutifachiqui. The use of the indefinite article *uma* with the possessive *sua* in this fashion is an odd construction. When *uma* is so used, it can have the meaning of "certain" in the sense, in this context, of "it was a certain niece of hers." Of the two possible renditions, the one that makes the ruler the niece of the Lady of Cutifachiqui seems preferable.

†The Portuguese *muy debilitados,* which Robertson rendered as "very weak," might be rendered more properly as "very debilitated," to reproduce the nuance suggested by Elvas's choice of that word rather than *fraco,* the one usually used for "weak."

her, stepped aside from the road and went into a wood saying that she had to attend to her necessities. Thus she deceived them and hid herself in the woods; and although they sought her she could not be found. She took with her a box of canes made like a coffer which they call "petaca,"[130] filled with unbored pearls. Some who had most knowledge of them said they were very valuable. An Indian woman was carrying them for her whom she took with her. The governor, in order not to cause her unhappiness in everything, left them, intending to ask them from her at Guaxule, when he should give her leave to return. She took it and went to stop at Xualla with three slaves who had escaped from the camp and with a horseman who remained behind, for being sick with fever he wandered from the road and was lost. This man, named Alimamos tried to have the slaves abandon their evil intention and go with him to the Christians—which two of them did. Alimamos and they overtook the governor fifty leagues from there in a province called Chiaha. They related how the cacica had remained in Xualla with a slave of André de Vasconcellos who refused to come with them; and it was very certain that they held communication as husband and wife, and that both had made up their minds to go to Cutifachiqui.[131]

In five days, the governor arrived at Guaxulle. The Indians there made him service of three hundred dogs, for they observed that the Christians liked them and sought them to eat; but they are not eaten among them [the Indians]. In Guaxulle and along that road there was very little maize. The governor sent an Indian thence with a message to the cacique of Chiaha,[132] asking him to order some maize brought them, so that they might rest several days in Chiaha. The governor left Guaxulle and after a march of two days reached a town called Canasagua.[133] Twenty Indians came out to meet him each carrying his basket of mulberries which grow in abundance and good from Cutifachiqui thither and also on into other provinces, as well as walnuts and plums. The trees grow wild in the fields without being planted or manured and are as large and as vigorous as if they were cultivated and irrigated in gardens. After the governor left Canasagua, he marched five days through an uninhabited region. Two leagues before reaching Chiaha, fifteen Indians, bearing maize, whom the cacique sent, met him and told him in behalf of the cacique that the latter was awaiting him with twenty barbacoas full, and [that] he with all the rest, including his person, land, and vassals, were all at his service.

On July 5,[134] the governor entered Chiaha. The cacique moved out of his houses in which he was lodging and welcomed him very hospitably, with the following words: "Powerful and excellent lord: I consider myself so fortunate in that your Lordship is pleased to use my services that no greater happiness could come to me nor any that I could esteem as much. Your Lordship ordered me from Guaxulle to have maize for you in this town for two months. I have here for you twenty barbacoas full of choice maize, and the best that can be found in all the land. If your Lordship was not received by me in accordance with what is due to so great a prince, have consideration for my few years which acquit me of guilt, and receive the good will which, with great, true, and sincere loyalty, I shall always have for what concerns your service."

The governor answered him saying that his service and offer pleased him greatly and that he would always consider him as a brother. In that town, there was an abundance of butter in gourds, in melted form like olive oil. They said it was bear's grease. There was also found considerable walnut oil which like the butter* was clean and of a good taste, and a pot of bee's honey; which before or after was not seen in all the land—neither honey nor bees.

The town was isolated between two arms of a river and was settled near one of them.[135] At a distance of two crossbow-shots above the town, the river divided into those two arms which were reunited a league below. The field between the one arm and the other was in places about the width of one crossbow-shot, and in places of two. They were of great width and both were fordable. Very excellent fields lay along them and many maize fields. Inasmuch as the Indians were in their town, only the governor was lodged in the houses of the cacique, and his men in the open field. Wherever there were any trees each one took his own. In this way the camp was established with some widely separated from the others and without any order. The governor overlooked this since the Indians were peaceable and the weather was quiet[136] and the men would have suffered great discomfort if they had not done this.

The horses reached there so weak that they were unable to carry their owners through weakness, because of having come from Cutifachiqui all the way with but little maize. They [the horses] had suffered hunger and fatigue all the way from the unpopulated region of Ocute. Since most of the men were not fit to fight on them even if it should be necessary, they put the horses out to pasture at night a quarter of a league from the camp.

The Christians were in great danger, for if at that time, the Indians had

*The Portuguese *mãteiga*, which Robertson translated as "butter" should probably be translated as "lard," which is the primary meaning of *manteca*, its Spanish equivalent.

attacked them, they were in a poor position for defending themselves. There the governor rested for thirty days, during which time the horses grew fat because of the luxuriance of the land. At the time of his departure, because of the importunity of some who wished more than was proper, he asked the cacique for thirty Indian women as slaves.[137] The cacique answered that he would talk with his principal men; but one night, before returning an answer, all the Indians left the town[138] with their wives and children and went away. Next day, when the governor had made up his mind to go to look for them, the cacique came, and on arriving spoke as follows to the governor: "Powerful Lord: I am ashamed and fearful of your Lordship, because my Indians, against my will, decided to go away. I fled without your permission; and having perceived the mistake I committed, I have come as a loyal vassal to deliver myself into your Lordship's power so that you may do what you please with my person, for my people do not obey me nor do anything except what an uncle of mine orders, who is governing these lands for me until I am of proper age. If your Lordship wishes to follow them and execute on them what they deserve for their disobedience, I will be your guide, for my fortune refuses at present to let me do more."

The governor immediately went in search of the Indians with thirty horse and a like number of foot. Passing through some towns of the principal Indians who had gone off, he cut down and destroyed their large maize fields; and went to hold the river above where the Indians were on an islet, whither the men of horse could not go. He sent word to them there by an Indian that they should return to their town and should have no fear and that they should furnish him tamemes for carrying as had been done by all the Indians before; that he did not wish any Indian women since it cost them so dearly to give them to him.

The Indians considered it well and came to the governor and made their excuses to him; and so they all returned to the town. A cacique from a province called Acoste[139] came there to visit the governor. After offering himself to him and exchanging words of politeness and courtesy with him, the governor asked him whether he knew of any rich land. He said he did; that there was a province to the north called Chisca,[140] and that there was a foundry for copper and other metal of that color, except that it was finer and of much more perfect color and much better in appearance; and that they did not make so much use of it as it was softer. The same thing had been told the governor in Cutifachiqui where we saw some copper hatchets which they said had a mixture of gold. However, the land was thinly populated as far as that region and they said that there were mountain ridges which the horses could not cross. On that account, the governor did not wish to go thither by direct road from Cutifachiqui, and thought that if he went through a populated region while the men and horses were in better condition and he more certain of the truth of what there was, he could turn hither through ridges and better populated land where he could travel better. He sent two Christians from Chiaha with Indians who knew the land of Chisca and its language, in order that they might examine it, with orders that they should go to report what they found at the place where he said he would await them.

XVI.

HOW THE GOVERNOR SET OUT FROM CHIAHA AND WAS IN DANGER OF BEING KILLED IN ACOSTE AT THE HANDS OF THE INDIANS, AND HOW HE ESCAPED THROUGH WARNING; AND OF WHAT HAPPENED TO HIM ON THIS JOURNEY, AND HOW HE ARRIVED AT COÇA.

When the governor made up his mind to go from Chiaha[141] to Acoste, he ordered the cacique to come[142] to him, and took leave of him with courteous words, and gave him some pieces of cloth with which he was very happy.* He reached Acoste in seven days. On the second of July, he ordered the camp made in the open field two crossbow flights from the town and with eight men of his guard he went toward the town where he found the cacique, who apparently received him with great friendliness. While he was talking with him, some of the foot soldiers went to the town from the camp to look for maize, and not being satisfied with it, went rummaging around and searching the houses and seized what they found. Annoyed at this the Indians began to get excited and to seize their arms. Some of them with clubs in their hands went to five or six Christians who angered them and with blows served them to their liking.

The governor seeing them all excited and himself among them with so few Christians, in order to escape out of their hands, practiced a stratagem quite

*The Portuguese that Robertson rendered as "some pieces of cloth" is simply *peças*. "Pieces of cloth" is among the meanings of *peças*, but *peças* could be pieces of various things. However, pieces of cloth is probably what De Soto gave him.

contrary to his usual disposition,† which was very direct and open; and although it grieved him greatly that any Indian should dare, either with or without reason, to show contempt for the Christians, he seized a club and went to their aid against his own men, which was done for the purpose of assuring them [the Indians]. Straightway he secretly sent a message to camp through a man for armed men to come to him. He took the cacique by the hand while conversing with him very courteously and with some of the principal Indians who were with him drew him from the town to a level road, and within sight of the camp whence the Christians began gradually to come, under an innocent guise, and to take position round about. Thus the governor led the cacique and his principal men until he got into the camp with them. When near his tent, he ordered them to be placed under guard and told them that they could not go until giving him a guide and Indians for carrying and until some sick Christians should come from Chiaha whom he had ordered to come down the river in canoes, and those also whom he had sent to the province of Chisca, who had not yet come. He feared lest the Indians had killed both parties.

Three days afterward they came. Those from Chisca said that the Indians had taken them through a land so poor in maize and so rough and with such lofty mountains that it was impossible for the camp to march through it; and seeing that the road was getting long and they were greatly delayed, they considered it advisable to return from a small, poor village where they saw nothing that might be of use. They brought a cowskin which the Indians gave them, as soft as the skin of a kid,[143] with hair like that of the soft wool of a sheep between that of the common and that of the merino. The cacique furnished a guide and tamemes, and with the governor's permission went away.

The governor set forth from Coste on July 9[144] and went to sleep at a town called Tali. The cacique came out to meet him on the road[145] and spoke as follows: "Excellent lord Prince, worthy of being served and obeyed by all the princes of the world. Just as one can judge in greater part of the inner virtue by the face, and since who you are and your power have been known to me before now, I do not wish to bear the consequence of how small I am in your presence by expecting that my poor service will be pleasing and

†The Portuguese *de mau jeito,* which Robertson rendered as "excited," would be better rendered as "in a bad disposition" in that context. The Portuguese that Robertson rendered as "usual disposition" is the same word, *geito,* preceded by *seu* ("his"). In this context and combined with *seu,* it would be better rendered as "his manner."

acceptable, for where the strength fails, it is not unbecoming for the good will to be praised and received. On this account I dare to beg your Lordship only to consider and observe, in this your land in which you command, how I may serve you."

The governor answered him saying that he thanked him as much for his good will and tenders as if he had offered him all the riches of the world, and that he would always be protected and esteemed by him as a true brother. The cacique ordered brought thither the provisions needed for the two days the governor should be there; and at the time of his leaving he made him service of four Indian women and two Indian men who were needed as carriers.

The governor marched for six days, passing through many towns subject to the cacique of Coça, and as he entered his lands, many Indians daily came to him on the way on the part of the cacique with messages, some going, others coming.

He reached Coça on Friday, July 16.[146] The cacique came out to welcome him two crossbow flights from the town in a carrying chair borne on the shoulders of his principal men, seated on a cushion, and covered with a robe of marten skins of the form and size of a woman's shawl.* He wore a crown of feathers on his head; and around about him were many Indians playing and singing.

As soon as he came to the governor, he saluted him and addressed the following words to him: "Excellent and powerful Lord, superior to all those of the earth: Although now I come to welcome you, long ago I have welcomed you in my heart, namely, from the day on which I heard of your Lordship. With so great a desire, joy, and happiness to serve you, what I show is nothing compared to what I feel, nor could it have any comparison. You may consider it as true that to receive dominion over the world would not gladden me so much as does the sight of you; nor should I consider it as great happiness. Do not expect me to offer you what is yours, namely, my person, lands, and vassals. I wish only to occupy myself in commanding my people to welcome you with all diligence and due reverence from this place to the town with music and singing, where your Lordship will be lodged and

---

*The Portuguese *tiros de besta,* which Robertson translated as "crossbow flights," might be better rendered as "crossbow shots," as "shot" is the primary meaning of *tiro.*

The Portuguese *andor,* which Robertson translated as "carrying chair," is more properly a platform on poles used by Latin peoples for carrying religious statues in street processions.

served by me and by them; and you will do with all I possess as though it were your own for, if your Lordship so do, I shall be favored."

The governor thanked him, and both talking together very joyfully, they went on to the town. He ordered his Indians to move out of their dwellings, in which the governor and his men were lodged. In the barbacoas and fields there was a great quantity of maize and beans. The land was very populous and had many large towns and planted fields which reached from one town to the other. It was a charming and fertile land, with good cultivated fields stretching along the rivers. In the open fields were many plums, both those of Spain and those of the land, and grapes along the rivers on vines climbing up into the trees. Beyond the streams were the low stocks of large, sweet grapes, but because they were not cultivated or well taken care of they had large seeds.[147]

The governor was accustomed to place a guard over the caciques so that they might not go away, and took them along with him until leaving their land; for by taking them, the people would await in their towns and they would give a guide and Indians as carriers. Before departing from their lands, he would give them leave to return to their homes—as well as the tamemes—as soon as he reached another dominion where others were given to him.

Those of Coça, seeing their lord detained, thought ill of it and revolted and went away to hide themselves in the woods—both those of their lord's town and those of other chief towns, who were his vassals. The governor sent four captains, each in a different direction, to look for them. They seized many Indians, men and women, who were put in chains. Upon seeing the harm they received and how little they gained in absenting themselves, they came, saying that they wished to serve in whatever might be commanded them. Some of the principal men among those imprisoned were set free on petition of the cacique. Of the rest, each man took away as slaves those he had in chains, without allowing them to go to their lands. Nor did many of them return except some whose good fortune and assiduous industry aided them, who managed to file off their chains at night; or some, who were able, while on the march, to wander away from the road upon observing any lack of care in their guard, who went off with their chains and with their loads and the clothes they were carrying.[148]

XVII.

HOW THE GOVERNOR WENT FROM COÇA TO TASTALUCA.

The governor rested in Coça for twenty-five days. He set out on Friday, August 20, to look for a province, by name, Tascaluca,[149] taking the cacique of Coça with him. That day he passed through a large town called Tallimuchase,[150] which was without people. He went to sleep a half league beyond near a stream. Next day he reached a town called Ytaua,[151] subject to Coça. He stayed there for six days because of a river which ran hard by the town, and was swollen at that time. As soon as the river allowed crossing, he set out, and went to sleep at a town called Ullibahali.[152] Ten or twelve of the principal Indians, all with feather plumes, and with bows and arrows, came to him on the road bearing a message on the part of the cacique of that province, to offer themselves to him. The governor, on reaching the town with twelve horse and some foot belonging to his guard, for he had left his men a crossbow flight from town, entered therein and found all the Indians under arms; and judging from their manner, he thought them evilly disposed. It was learned later that they had concerted to take the cacique of Coça out of the governor's possession, if he [the cacique] should request this of them. The governor ordered all his men to enter the town which was enclosed and near which flowed a small river. The enclosure, like that in other towns seen there afterward, was of thick logs, set solidly close together in the ground, and many long poles as thick as an arm placed crosswise. The height of the enclosure was that of a good lance, and it was plastered within and without and had loopholes. On the other side of the river was a town where the cacique was at the time. The governor ordered him to be summoned and he came immediately. After exchanging some verbal promises with the governor, he gave him the necessary tamemes and thirty Indian women as slaves. A Christian of noble parentage, named Manzano, a native of Salamanca, who wandered away to look for grapes which are abundant and excellent there, was lost in that place.[153] On the day the governor set out thence, he went to sleep at a town subject to the lord of Ullibahali, and next day reached another called Toasi.[154] The Indians gave the governor thirty Indian women and the necessary tamemes. He marched ordinarily five or six leagues daily when going through a peopled region, and as much as he could through a depopulated region, in order to avoid the necessity of a lack of maize. From Toasi, passing through some towns subject to a cacique, the lord of a province called Talise,[155] he marched for five days. He reached Tallise on September 18. The town was large and was located near a deep river. On the other side of the river were other towns and many fields of maize. On both sides, it was a land very well supplied with maize in abundance. They [the inhabitants] had abandoned the town. The governor ordered the cacique summoned. He came and an exchange of words of courtesy and of promises took place between them. He gave him [the governor] the service of forty Indians.[156] At that town one of the principal Indians came to the governor in the name of the cacique of Tascaluca and spoke to him as follows: "Very powerful, virtuous, and esteemed Lord: The great cacique of Tascaluca, my lord, orders me to kiss your Lordship's hands and to report to you that he is aware that you deservedly excel all those of the land, because of your perfections and power; that all, wherever your Lordship goes, serve and obey you, which he knows is your due. He desires as he does life to see and serve your Lordship. Therefore, he sends to offer with his person his land and his vassals, in order that whenever your Lordship should please to go through his lands, you may be received in all peace and love, and be served and obeyed; and that as payment of this desire which he has to serve you, you grant him the favor of informing him when you will come, for the earlier you come the greater favor and happiness will he receive." The governor received and dismissed him graciously, giving him some beads (which were not much regarded among them) and other pieces of cloth to take to his lord; and gave the cacique of Coça permission to return to his lands. The cacique of Tallise gave him the tamemes necessary; and after resting there for twenty days he set out for Tascaluca. The day he left Tallise, he went to sleep at a large town called Casiste,[157] and next day he passed through another town and reached a small town of Tascaluca. The next day he slept in a wood two leagues from the town where the cacique lived and was at that time.[158] He sent the maestre de campo, Luis de Moscoso, with fifteen horse to inform him that he was coming. The cacique was in his dwelling under a balcony.* Outside, in front of his dwelling, on an elevated place, was spread a mat

*The Portuguese *apousentos,* which Robertson translated as "dwelling," is plural and consequently should be rendered as "dwellings" or "lodgings." It was customary for Creek leaders to have compounds containing a winter house and a summer house. The protruding balcony, indicating a two-story structure, suggests that this structure was the cacique's summer house. Robertson's "dwelling" in the next sentence, which is *pousadas* in the Portuguese, is also plural.

for him and on it two cushions, one above the other, where he came to seat himself. His Indians gathered about him, separated somewhat, so that they formed a courtyard and open space where he was—his most principal Indians being nearest him, and one holding a sort of fan of deerskin which kept the sun from him, round and the size of a shield, quartered with black and white, with a cross made in the middle.† From a distance it looked like taffeta, for the colors were very perfect. It was set on a small and very long staff. This was the device he bore in his wars. He was a man, very tall of body, large limbed, lean, and well built.[159] He was greatly feared by his neighbors and vassals. He was lord of many lands and many people. In his aspect he was very dignified. After the maestre de campo talked with him, he [the maestre de campo] and his men came, galloped their horses in front of him, turning them from one side to the other, and at times toward the cacique. He with great gravity and unconcern from time to time raised his eyes and looked as if in disdain. The governor arrived but he made no movement to arise. The governor took him by the hand and both went to seat themselves on a seat below the balcony. The cacique spoke to him as follows: "Powerful Lord: May the coming of your Lordship be very propitious. At sight of you, I receive as great pleasure and happiness as if you were one of my brothers whom I hold in great affection. Regarding this, it is unnecessary to discuss further, for it is not wise to utter in many words what can be said in few; for as it is one's desire that determines deeds, and deeds give testimony of truth, therefore you will perceive how determined and clear is my will to serve you, and how pure my motive.[160] The favor which you showed me by reason of the pieces of cloth which you sent me, I esteem as much as it is proper to esteem them, and chiefly because they were yours. Now, see in what you may command me to serve you." The governor made him happy with pleasing and very brief words. When he set out thence, he determined, for several reasons, to take him [the cacique] with him. After a march of two days he reached a town called Piache.[161] Near it flowed a large

---

†The Portuguese that Robertson translated as "courtyard and open space" is *terreiro i cãpo despejado. Terreiro* can be rendered also as "public square" or "plaza" and *cãpo despejado* as "cleared field." This possibility suggests the Creek "square ground," in an informal sense at least, but with a low mound for the chief to sit on.

The Portuguese that Robertson translated as "cross" is *aspa.* An *aspa* is an instrument of torture made in the form of an X or, in this case, the somewhat more horizontal St. Andrew's Cross, rather than the standard cross suggested by Robertson's unannotated translation of the word as simple "cross." The cross on the deerskin fan described was thus probably a St. Andrew's Cross.

The Hernando de Soto Expedition Encounters Chief Tascaluça. "The cacique was on a balcony which was made on a mound to one side of the plaza, about his head a certain headdress, like an almaizar, worn like a Moor, which gave him an appearance of authority, and a pelote or blanket of feathers down to his feet, very authoritative, seated upon some high cushions, and many principals of his Indians with him" (Rangel, Ch. 7). In this Dutch engraving the cacique is seated to the left, while one of De Soto's men attempts to intimidate him with a show of horsemanship. The architecture in the background is entirely fanciful and inaccurate. (From De Gedenkwaardige Voyagie van don Ferdinand de Soto, *Leyden: P. Van der Aa, 1706, courtesy of the W. S. Hoole Special Collections Library, The University of Alabama)*

river. The governor asked the Indians for canoes. They said that they did not have any, but that they would make rafts of canes and dry wood on which he could cross. Diligently and quickly they made them and steered them; and since the water was quiet, the governor and his men crossed in great safety. From the port of Espiritu Santo to Palache—a distance of about one hundred leagues—the governor marched from east to west; from Apalache to Cutifachiqui—a distance of about four hundred and thirty leagues—from southwest to northeast; from Cutifachiqui to Xualla—a distance of about two hundred and fifty leagues—from south to north; and from Xualla to Tascaluca—a distance of about two hundred and fifty leagues also—he marched one hundred and ninety from east to west, namely, to the province of Coça, and sixty from Coça to Tascaluca from north to south.[162] After crossing the river of Piache, a Christian left the ranks there and went to look for an Indian woman who had escaped from him, and the Indians captured or killed him. The governor urged the cacique to inform him of the man and threatened him that if he did not appear, he would never let him [the cacique] go. The cacique sent an Indian from that place to Mavilla,[163] whither they were marching—a town of one of the principal Indians, his vassal—saying that he was sending him [the messenger] to advise him [his vassal] to have provisions prepared and Indians for carrying; but as it afterward appeared he ordered him to assemble there all the warriors whom he had in his land. The governor marched for three days, the third day through a continuously peopled region. He reached Mavilla on Monday, the eighteenth of October,[164] he going in the vanguard with fifteen horse and thirty foot.[165] A Christian, whom he had sent with a message to the chief three or four days before, in order that the latter might not go away, and also in order to see the disposition of the Indians, came out of the town. He told him [the governor] that it appeared to him [the messenger] that they [the Indians] were evilly disposed, because when he was there many men and many arms had entered the town and they had made great haste to strengthen the stockade. Luis de Moscoso told the governor that it would be well to camp in the open field since the Indians were so disposed. The governor answered that he would lodge in the town, and that he was tired out with sleeping in the open field. On his arrival near the town, the cacique came out to welcome him with many Indians playing music and singing, and after tendering his services to him, gave him three blankets of marten skin. The governor, with the caciques and with seven or eight men from his guard, and three or four horse, who dismounted in order to accompany him, entered the town and seated himself under a balcony. The cacique of Tascaluca asked him to let him stay in that town and not to give him more trouble of marching; and seeing by his talk that he did not grant him permission, changed his purpose and, dissembling, pretended that he wished to talk with some of the principal Indians. He rose from the place where he was with the governor, and entered a house where were many Indians with their bows and arrows. When the governor saw that he did not come, he called him, but he said that he would not come out of there and that he would not leave that town and that if he [the governor] wished to go in peace he should go immediately and should not insist on trying to take him out of his lands and dominion by force.

XVIII.

HOW THE INDIANS ROSE AGAINST THE GOVERNOR AND OF WHAT HAPPENED.

The governor, on seeing the determination and furious reply of the cacique, endeavored to soothe him with pleasant words. To them he made no reply but, on the contrary, he withdrew very haughtily and disdainfully to a place where the governor could not see or talk with him. As one of the principal Indians was passing that place, the governor called him in order to send him to tell him [the cacique] that he could stay and welcome in his land, but that he should consider it well to have a guide and Indians for carrying sent him, in order to see whether he could pacify him [the cacique] with soft words. The Indian with great haughtiness said that he would not do it. Baltasar de Gallegos, who was there, seized him roughly by a cloak of marten skin which he wore as a covering, but he slipped it off over his head and left it in his [Gallegos's] hands. And because all the Indians straightway rose in revolt, Baltasar de Gallegos gave him a slash which opened up his back. Immediately, all the Indians came out from the houses shouting loudly and discharging their arrows. The governor, seeing that he could not escape if he stayed there, and that if he should order his men who were outside the town to enter, the Indians could kill the horses for him from inside the houses and do much damage, went out running; but before getting out of the town, he fell two or three times, and those who were with him helped him to rise. He and those with him were severely wounded. In the town five Christians were immediately slain. The governor went out from the town shouting for all his men to go outside, for they were doing him much damage from the stockade. The Indians, seeing that the Christians were withdrawing but some or most of them nevertheless at a walk, with great boldness continued to shoot at them and to bring down those they could overtake. The Indians, whom the Christians were bringing in chains, had set down their loads near the stockade, and as soon as the governor and his men became separated, those of Mavilla put the loads on their backs and took them [the Indians] within the town and immediately freed them from their chains and gave them bows and arrows with which to fight. In this way they got possession of all the clothing and pearls, and everything the Christians had and which their Indians were carrying for them. And inasmuch as the Indians had been peaceful thitherto, some [of the Christians] were bringing their weapons in the packs and were left without arms. From others of those who had entered with the governor, they [the Indians] took away their swords and halberds and fought therewith. When the governor found himself in the open field, he asked for a horse, and with some men who accompanied him, turned about and struck two or three Indians through with a lance. Most of the Indians withdrew into the town and continued to shoot their arrows from the stockade. Those who dared would insolently go out to fight for the distance of a stone's throw; and from there would again retire from time to time when the Christians turned on them. At the time when the return [of the Christians] began, there were a friar and a secular priest in the town, as well as a servant of the governor with a slave woman, and they did not have time to go outside but shut themselves in their house. Thus they remained inside the town after the Indians got control of it. They closed the door with a grating;* and they had one sword among them, which the governor's servant owned. He stationed himself behind the door with it, thrusting at the Indians who tried to effect an entrance; with the friar and the secular priest, on the other side, each with a club in his hands,† to strike down whomever might first enter. The Indians, seeing that they could not enter through the door, began to uncover the house at the top. At this time, all the horse and foot who came marching behind, happened to reach Mavilla. They were of different opinions there as to whether they should attack the Indians in order to enter into the town or whether this should be avoided as the entrance was doubtful, but at last, it was decided to attack them.

*The Portuguese *cancela,* which Robertson rendered as "a grating," is a "lattice-work door" or "gate."

†The Portuguese *tranca,* which Robertson translated as "club," is a "door-bar" rather than a club per se.

XIX.

HOW THE GOVERNOR DREW HIS MEN UP IN ORDER AND ENTERED THE TOWN OF MAVILLA.

As soon as the battle line and rear guard reached Mavilla, the governor ordered all those who were best armed to dismount and made four companies of foot. The Indians, on seeing how the governor was drawing up his men, urged the cacique to leave, telling him, as was later learned from some Indian women who were captured there, that he was only one man and could fight for one only; that there were many principal men of the Indians there, very daring and skillful in matters of war, any of whom could direct all the other men; that since matters of war and victory were a hazard of fortune and there was no certainty as to which of the sides would be victorious, he should endeavor to place his person in safety, so that if they should end their lives there, as they had resolved to do rather than allow themselves to be vanquished, he would be left to govern the land. However, he refused to go, but so much did they urge him that he went out of the town with twenty or thirty of his Indians. From the clothing of the Christians he took a scarlet cloak and some other pieces—all that he could carry and which pleased him most. The governor was advised that the Indians were going out of the town, and he ordered those who were mounted to surround it. In each foot company, he ordered a soldier with a firebrand to set fire to the houses so that the Indians would have no shelter. Having arranged all his men in order, he ordered an arquebus fired. At the signal, all four companies, each in its own position, attacked with great fury and doing great damage entered the town from one side and the other. The friar and the secular priest and those who were with them in the house were rescued, which cost the life of two men of ability and courage who went thither to help them.

The Indians fought with so great spirit that they drove us outside again and again. It took them so long to get back that many of the Christians, tired out and suffering great thirst, went to get a drink at a pond located near the stockade, but it was tinged with the blood of the dead and they returned to the fight. The governor, seeing this, with those who accompanied him entered the town on horseback together with the returning foot. This gave an opportunity for the Christians to succeed in setting fire to the houses and overthrow and defeat the Indians. As the latter fled outside the town from those on foot, those on horse again drove them within the gates, where,

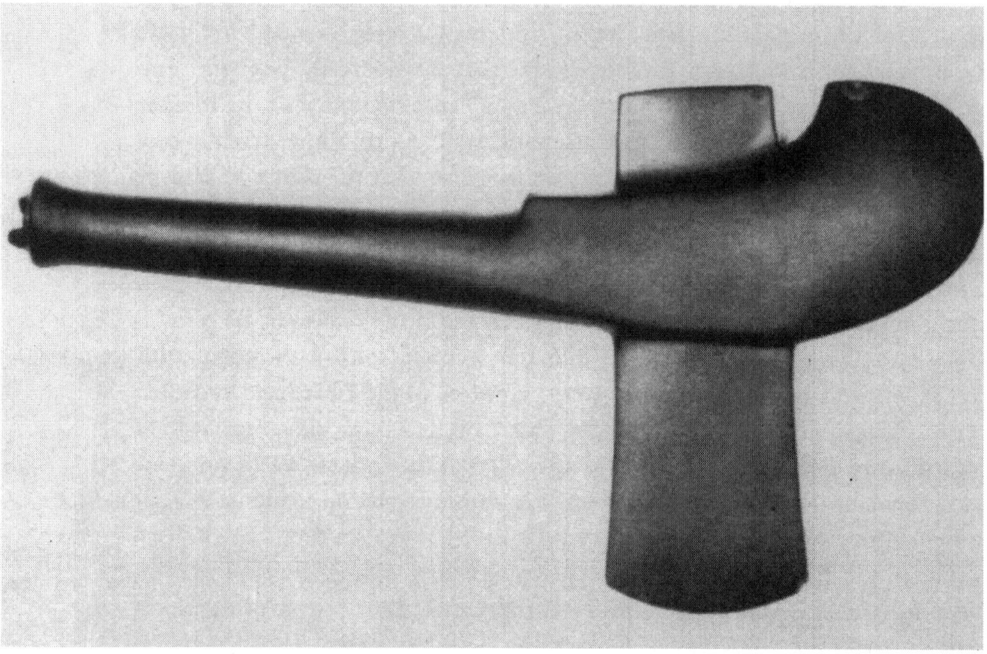

Monolithic Ax. This Mississippian artifact is meticulously made from a single piece of stone. Such a piece would undoubtedly have had more symbolic than practical value. A more typical example would have a stone blade set in a wooden handle of the same form. Mississippian warfare was conducted using battle axes and clubs, in addition to the bow and arrow. Moundville site, Hale County, Alabama. (Courtesy of the National Museum of the American Indian/Smithsonian Institution)

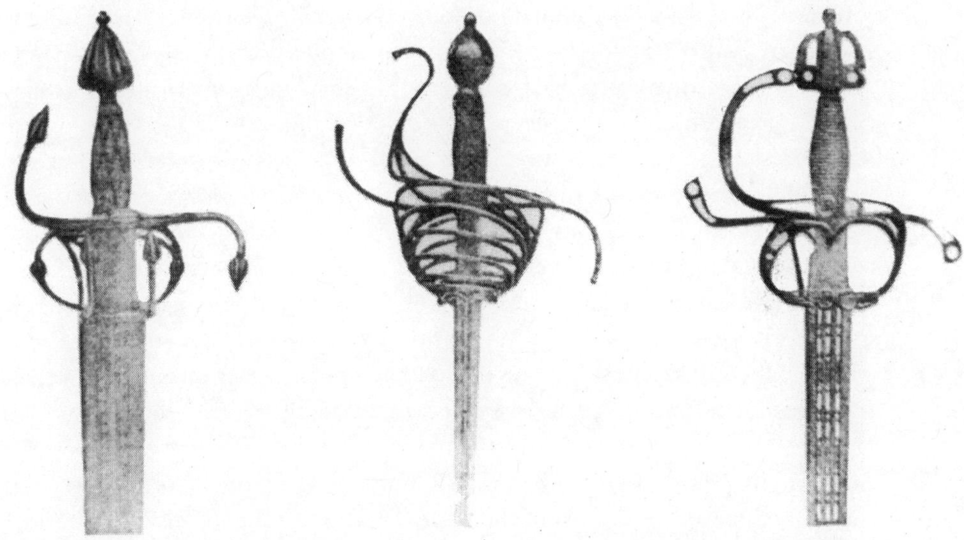

Spanish Swords. Swords of the period were individually crafted and came in a wide variety of styles. Most were long with straight, double-edged blades. The swords shown here are among the more elaborate ones. A similar example has been found at a native village site in northwest Georgia. (From Albert F. Calvert, Spanish Arms and Armour, *London: John Lane, 1907)*

having lost hopes of escape, they fought courageously; and after the Christians had come among them cutting with the sword, seeing that they were assailed beyond repair, many fled into the burning houses, where, piled up one on top of the other, they were suffocated and burned to death. In all, those who were killed there numbered two thousand five hundred or thereabout. Of the Christians eighteen[166] were killed there, one of whom was Don Carlos, the governor's brother-in-law, another, his nephew, another, Juan Gamez, [and others including] Mem Rodriquez, a Portuguese, and Juan Vázquez of Villanova de Barcarota—all men of honor and pride. The others [killed] were foot soldiers. Besides those killed, one hundred and fifty Christians were wounded, receiving seven hundred arrow wounds. It was God's will that they were healed shortly of very dangerous wounds. Twelve horses were also killed and seventy wounded. All the clothing carried by the Christians, the ornaments for saying mass, and the pearls were all burned there. The Christians set fire to them; for they considered as more annoying the hurt which the Indians could do them from within the houses where everything was gathered together.[167] The governor learned there that Francisco Maldonado was awaiting him in the port of Ochuse and that it [Ochuse] was six days' journey from there. He arranged with Juan Ortiz that he should keep still about it, so that the men might not oppose his determination, and because the pearls which he desired to send to Cuba as samples had been burned; for if the news [of the ship] were noised about the men might desire to go to that land [Cuba]. And fearing that if news were heard of him, unless they saw gold or silver, or anything of value, it [Florida] would acquire such a reputation that no man would desire to go thither when people might be needed; consequently, he determined not to give news of himself so long as he did not find a rich land.

XX.

HOW THE GOVERNOR SET OUT FROM MAVILLA FOR CHICAÇA, AND OF WHAT HAPPENED TO HIM.

From the time the governor entered Florida until leaving Mavilla, one hundred and two Christians had died, some of their illnesses and others being killed by the Indians. He remained in Mavilla for twenty-eight days because of the wounded, during which he was always in the open field. It was a very populous and fertile land. There were some large enclosed towns and a considerable population scattered about over the field, the houses being separated from one another one or two crossbow flights.* On Sunday, November 18,[168] now that it was learned that our wounded men were getting well, the governor set out from Mavilla, all the men having provided themselves with maize for two days. They marched for five days through an unpeopled region, and arrived at a province called Pafallaya and a town called Taliepataua. Thence, they went to another town by name Cabusto,[169] near which flowed a large river. The Indians on the other side of it gave loud cries, telling the Christians that if they crossed over the river to them they would have to kill them. The governor ordered a piragua built inside the town, so that the Indians might not perceive it. It was made in four days. When it was finished, he ordered it to be transported one night a half league up stream.† In the morning, thirty well-armed men entered it. The Indians perceived what was being planned and those who were nearest ran up to forbid the crossing. They resisted it as well as they could until the Christians were near them; and seeing that the piragua was about to land fled through some canebrakes. The Christians mounted their horses and went upstream to assure a crossing where the governor, with all those who remained with him, crossed over. Along the river were some towns well provided with maize and beans. From that place to Chicaça,[170] the governor marched for five days through an unpopulated region. He reached a river where some Indians on the other side tried to forbid him crossing. In two days another piragua was made. When it was finished, the governor ordered an Indian to announce to the cacique that he should desire his friendship and should await him peacefully. But the Indians on the other side of the river killed him in his [the governor's] sight, and immediately went away uttering loud cries. Having crossed the river next day, December 17, the governor reached Chicaça, a small town of twenty houses. After they were in Chicaça they suffered great hardships and cold, for it was already winter, and most of the men were lodged in the open field in the snow before having any place where they could build houses. This land was very well peopled, the population being spread out as was that of Mavilla. It was fertile and abounding in maize, most of this being still in the fields. The amount necessary for passing

*The Portuguese *tiros de besta,* which Robertson translated as "crossbow flights," would be better rendered as "crossbow shots."

†In his translation of the passage, "he ordered it to be transported one night a half league upstream," Robertson deleted a detail found in the Portuguese stating that the pirogue was transported *em carretões* or "in carts."

the winter was gathered. Certain Indians were captured, among whom was one who was greatly esteemed by the cacique. By means of an Indian the governor sent word to the cacique that he desired to see him and wished his friendship. The cacique came to offer himself to him, together with his person, land, and vassals. He said that he would cause two caciques to come in peace. A few days afterward they came with him accompanied by their Indians, one being named Alimamu and the other Nicalasa. They presented the governor with one hundred and fifty rabbits and some clothing of their land, namely blankets and skins. The cacique of Chicaça came to visit him frequently and sometimes the governor ordered him summoned and sent him a horse to go and come. He [the cacique] made complaint to him [the governor], that one of his vassals had risen against him, withholding his tribute, and asked that he protect him against him, saying that he was about to go to seek him in his land and punish him as he deserved—all pretense, for it was planned that while the governor went with him and the camp was divided into two parts, some would attack the governor and others those who remained in Chicaça. He [the cacique] went to the town where he lived and came with two hundred Indians with their bows and arrows. The governor took thirty horse and eighty foot and went to Saquechuma,[171] as the province of the principal man was called, who he [the cacique] told him [the governor] had rebelled against him. They found an enclosed town which had been abandoned by the Indians, and those who were with the cacique set fire to the houses in order to conceal their treachery. But since the men taken by the governor were very watchful and prudent, as well as those who remained in Chicaça, on that occasion they did not dare attack us. The governor invited the cacique and certain of the principal Indians [to visit him] and gave them some pork to eat. And although they were not accustomed to it, they lusted after it so much that Indians would come nightly to certain houses a crossbow shot away from the camp where the hogs were sleeping and kill and carry off as many as they could. Three Indians were seized in the act, two of whom the governor ordered to be shot with arrows and the hands of the other cut off. In that condition he sent him to the cacique, who expressed regret that they had troubled the governor and was glad that justice had been executed on them. He [the cacique] was in an open plain a half league from where the Christians were.* Four of the horsemen went thither without orders, namely, Francisco Osorio, a servant of the Marquis de As-

*The Portuguese *campina,* which Robertson rendered as "open plain," has the sense of "extensive meadow without trees," or "rangeland," or "natural pasture."

torga, named Reynoso, and two servants of the governor, one his page, named Ribera, and the other his chamberlain, named Fuentes.[172] They seized some skins and blankets from the Indians, at which the latter were greatly offended and abandoned their houses. The governor learned of it and ordered them [the four horsemen] seized. Francisco Osorio and the chamberlain he sentenced to death, as being the principals, and all to the loss of their possessions. The friars and secular priests and other principal persons importuned him to leave Francisco Osorio alive, and to moderate the sentence, which he refused to do for anyone. And while he was already giving the order to take them to the public place to behead them, certain Indians came who had been sent by the cacique to make complaint against them. Juan Ortiz, at the request of Baltasar de Gallegos and other persons, changed their words, telling the governor that the cacique said that he had learned that his Lordship had seized those Christians on his account; that they were not guilty nor had they done any wrong to him; that if he [De Soto] would do him a favor, he should let them go free. To the Indians, he [Ortiz] was to say that the governor said that he had seized them and would give them such punishment that it would be an example to others. The governor ordered the prisoners released. As soon as March was come, he determined to leave Chicaça and asked the cacique for two hundred tamemes. The latter replied to him that he would talk it over with his principal men. On Tuesday, the eighth of March, the governor went to where the cacique was to ask him for the tamemes. He said he would send them next day. As soon as the governor came to Chicaça, he told Luis de Moscoso, the maestre de campo, that the Indians looked ill-disposed to him, and that night he should keep careful watch, which the latter heeded but slightly. The Indians came at the quarter of the modorra [second or sleepy watch]* in four companies, each company coming from a different direction. As soon as they were perceived, they beat a drum and with loud cries rushed forward, and so rapidly that they arrived at the same time as the spies who had carelessly gone out a distance from the camp; and when they were perceived by those who were within the town, half the houses were burning from the fire which they kindled. That night, three horsemen were by chance at watch, two of whom were of low degree, the most worthless of the camp, and the other was the governor's nephew, who until then had been considered a good man.[173] There he proved himself as cowardly as each one of them [i.e., the other two], for they all fled, and the Indians not finding any resistance came and

*The word *modórra* means sleepiness, or drowsiness, or sluggishness.

set fire to the town and awaited the Christians outside behind the doors, who came out of the houses without having time to arm themselves; and as they rose, maddened by the noise and blinded by the smoke and flame of the fire, they did not know where they were going nor did they succeed in getting their arms or in putting saddle on horse; neither did they see the Indians who were shooting at them. Many of the horses were burned in their stables, and those which could break their halters freed themselves. The confusion and rout were of such a nature that each one fled wherever it seemed safest, without any one resisting the Indians. But God who punishes His own as is His pleasure, and in the greatest needs and dangers holds them in His hand, blinded the Indians so that they might not see what they had done, and they thought that the horses which were running about loose were the horsemen gathering together to assault them. The governor alone, and with a soldier called Tapia, got mounted and attacked the Indians, and giving the first one he met a thrust with his lance, went down and his saddle with him; for in the haste he had badly fastened the girth and fell from his horse. All the men who were afoot and were in flight through a wood outside the town, sought protection there. And as it was night and the Indians thought the horses, as above said, were mounted men who were attacking them, they fled away and only one remained there dead, namely, the one the governor had struck with his lance. The town was consumed by fire. A woman was burned there who had gone there with her husband. Both of them going outside the house, she returned for some pearls which they had forgotten; and when she tried to get out, already the fire was at the door and she could not, and her husband could not help her.[174] Three other Christians got away from their houses so badly hurt by the fire that one of them died three days later, and each of the other two was carried for many days in his bed upon some poles which the Indians carried on their shoulders, for they could not have journeyed in any other way. In that turn of fortune eleven Christians and fifty horses died. Of the swine, one hundred were left, and four hundred were burned. If, perchance, any one still had had any clothing left from the fire at Mavilla, it was now all burned up in that place [Chicaça]; and many were naked as they had no time to snatch their jerkins.[175] There they endured great suffering from the cold, for which they got relief in large fires. The whole night was passed turning from one side to the other without sleeping, for if they were warmed on one side they froze on the other. They managed to make some mats out of dry grass woven together, and placed one mat below and the other above. Many laughed at this contrivance, but afterward necessity forced them to do likewise. The

Christians were become so demoralized, together with the lack of saddles and weapons, which had been burned, that if the Indians had returned the second night, they would have routed them with little trouble. They moved thence to the village where the cacique usually lived as it was a site in the open field.[176] A week later they had made many saddles and lances. There were some ash trees there from which they were made as good as those of Vizcaya.

XXI.

HOW THE INDIANS AGAIN ATTACKED THE CHRISTIANS; AND HOW THE GOVERNOR WENT TO ALIMAMU, WHERE THEY AWAITED HIM ON THE WAY TO THE FIGHT.

On Wednesday, the 15th of March, 1541,[177] after the governor had been for a week in a level field, a half league from the place where he had lodged during the winter, having already set up a forge and having tempered the swords which had been burned in Chicaça and having made many shields, saddles, and lances, on Tuesday night, at the hour of dawn, many Indians came to attack the camp, formed into three companies, each company coming from a different direction. Those who were on watch sounded the alarm. The governor, with great quickness, drew up his men in order in three other companies, with some men staying behind to guard the camp, and hastened to the attack. The Indians were thrown into confusion and took to flight. The land was flat and suitable for the Christians to profit thereby. Already the dawn had come bright and clear, but there was some confusion, which was the reason why they did not kill thirty or forty more Indians, namely, a friar in the camp raised a loud cry "To the camp! To the camp!" without any reason for so crying out. On that account, the governor and all the men ran to the rescue, and the Indians had time to get away safely. Some Indians were captured, from whom the governor got information relative to the land beyond. On April 25,[178] he left Chicaça and went to sleep at a small village called Alimamu.[179] It had very little maize and it was necessary after leaving there to commit themselves to an unpopulated region for seven days' journey. Next day, the governor sent three captains with horse and foot—each one taking a different direction—to search out provisions in order to cross the unpopulated region. Juan de Añasco, the accountant, went with fifteen horse and forty foot along the road where the governor was to go, and found a strong stockade where the Indians were waiting.[180] On top of it were many armed men daubed over with red ochre and with their bodies, legs, and arms painted black, white, yellow, and red, in the manner of stripes which made them look as though they were in breeches and doublet. Some had feather plumes on their heads and others horns, with their faces black and the eyes ringed round in red in order to look more ferocious. As soon as they saw the Christians approach, with loud cries and beating two drums, they came out in great fury to meet them. It seemed best to Juan de Añasco and those with him to keep away from them and to inform the governor. They withdrew over a level ground for the distance of a crossbow flight from the stockade and in sight of it. The men of foot, the crossbowmen, and those having shields placed themselves before the horsemen so that the horses might not be wounded. The Indians came out by sevens and eights to shoot their arrows and then to retire. In sight of the Christians, they made a fire and seized an Indian—one by the feet and others by the head—and pretended they were going to throw him into the fire, first giving him many blows on the head, signifying that so they would do to the Christians. Juan de Añasco sent three horse to inform the governor. The latter came immediately, and since he thought he should drive them thence, saying that if he did not do so, they would become emboldened to attack him at a time when they could do him more hurt, he ordered the horsemen to dismount and having divided them into four companies gave the signal and they attacked the Indians. The latter resisted until the Christians reached the stockade; and as soon as they saw that they could not defend themselves they fled along a way where a stream flowed near the stockade, and from the other shore shot some arrows. And inasmuch as no crossing was found for the horses for the time being, they [the Indians] had time to get away. Three Indians were killed there, and many Christians were wounded, fifteen of whom died on the march a few days later. It seemed to all that the governor was much to blame in not having had an examination made of the disposition of the land which lay on the other side of the stream and of ascertaining the crossing before attacking them; for with their hope of escaping by flight in that direction whenever they might not be seen by his men, they fought until they were routed; and they were thus enabled to defend themselves until then and to offend the Christians with safety.

XXII.

HOW THE GOVERNOR WENT FROM ALIMAMU TO QUIZQUIZ AND THENCE TO A LARGE RIVER.

Three days having passed since they had looked for some maize (and it was little that was found in proportion to what was needed), and for this reason, even though rest was needed because of the wounded, on account of the great need of finding a place where there was maize, the governor was obliged to set out immediately for Quizquiz.[181] He marched seven days through an unpopulated region of many swamps and thick woods, but all passable on horseback except several marshes or swamps which were crossed by swimming. He reached the town of Quizquiz without being perceived. He seized all the people of the town before they got out of their houses. The cacique's mother was captured there, and then he [the governor] sent to him [the cacique] one of the Indians who had been seized there, bidding him come to see him and [saying] that he would give him his mother and all the other people who had been taken there. For reply, he [the cacique] said that his Lordship should order them released and sent [to him] and that he would come to visit and serve him. Inasmuch as his men were ill and weary for lack of maize and the horses were also weak, he [De Soto] determined to pleasure him, in order to see whether he could have peace with him. So he ordered the mother and all the others released and dispatched them and sent them [to the cacique] with words of kindness. Next day when the governor was awaiting the cacique, many Indians came with their bows and arrows with the intention of attacking the Christians. The governor ordered all the horsemen to be armed and mounted and all in readiness. When the Indians saw that they were on guard, they stopped a crossbow flight from the spot where the governor was, near a stream, and after they had stayed there for a half hour, six of the principal Indians came to the camp and said that they were come to see what people they were and that they had learned from their ancestors that a white race would inevitably subdue them; and that they were about to return to the cacique to tell him to come immediately to render obedience and service to the governor. And after offering him six or seven skins and blankets which they brought they took leave of him and, together with the others who were waiting on the shore, returned. The cacique did not again come, nor did he send another message. Inasmuch as there was little maize in the town where the governor was, he moved to another town located a half league from the large river,[182] where maize was found in abundance. He went to see the river and found there was an abundance of timber near it from which piraguas could be constructed and an excellently situated land for establishing the camp. He immediately moved thither, houses were built, and the camp was established on a level place, a crossbow flight from the river. All the maize of all the towns behind was collected there, and the men set to work immediately to cut timber and square the planks for canoes. Immediately the Indians came down the river, landed, and told the governor that they were vassals of a great lord called Aquixo, who was lord of many towns and people on the other side of the river. On his behalf they informed him [the governor] that he [the cacique] would come the next day with all his men to see what his Lordship would command him. Then next day, the cacique came with two hundred canoes full of Indians with their bows and arrows, painted with red ocher and having great plumes of white and many colored feathers on either side [of the canoes] and holding shields in their hands with which they covered the paddlers, while the warriors were standing from prow to stern with their bows and arrows in their hands. The canoe in which the cacique came had an awning spread in the stern and he [the cacique] was seated under the canopy. Also other canoes came bearing other Indian notables. The chief [of each canoe] from his position under the canopy, controlled and gave orders to the other men. All the canoes were together and came to within a stone's throw from the bluff. From there, the cacique told the governor, who was walking along the river with others whom he had brought with him, that he had come to visit him and to serve and obey him, for he had heard that he was the greatest and most powerful lord of all the earth and that he should bethink him in what to command him. The governor thanked him and asked him to land so that they might better be able to talk, but without answering this, he [the cacique] ordered three canoes to come up in which he brought a quantity of fish and loaves made of the pulp of plums in the shape of bricks. All having been received, he [the governor] thanked him and again asked him to land. But since his intent was to see whether he might do some damage by means of that pretense, upon seeing that the governor and his men were on their guard, they began to withdraw from land. With loud cries, the crossbowmen who were ready, shot at them and struck five or six. They withdrew in splendid order; no one abandoned his paddle even though the one near him fell. Flaunting[183] themselves, they retired. Afterward they came frequently and landed, and when they [the Christians] went toward them, they would return to their canoes. Those canoes were very pleasing to see, for they were very large and well built; and together with the awnings, the plumes of feathers, the shields, and banners, and the many men in them, they had the appearance of a beautiful fleet of galleys. During the thirty days the governor was there, they made four piraguas, in three of which, one early morning three hours before it became light, he ordered a dozen horse to enter, four to each one—men whom he was confident would succeed in gaining the land in spite of the Indians and assure the crossing or die in doing it—and with them some of foot—crossbowmen and rowers—to place them on the other side. In the other piragua, he ordered Juan de Guzmán to cross with men of foot, he having become captain in place of Francisco Maldonado. And because the current was strong, they went up stream along the shore for a quarter of a league and in crossing they were carried down with the current of the river and went to land opposite the place where the camp was. At a distance of two stones' throw before reaching shore, the men of horse went from the piraguas on horseback to a sandy place of hard sand and clear ground where all the men landed without any accident. As soon as those who crossed first were on the other side, the piraguas returned immediately to where the governor was and, in two hours after the sun was up, all the men finished crossing. It [the crossing] was nearly a half league wide, and if a man stood still on the other side, one could not tell whether he were a man or something else. It [the river] was of great depth and of very strong current. Its water was always turgid and continually many trees and wood came down it borne along by the force of the water and current. It had abundance of fish of various kinds, and most of them different from those of the fresh waters of Spain as will be told hereafter.[184]

XXIII.

HOW THE GOVERNOR WENT FROM AQUIXO TO CASQUI AND THENCE TO PAC[A]HA; AND HOW THAT LAND DIFFERS FROM THAT BEHIND.

Having got across the great river, the governor marched a league and a half and reached a large town of Aquixo, which was abandoned before his arrival. Over a plain they saw thirty Indians coming whom the cacique had sent to learn what the Christians were intending to do, but as soon as the latter had sight of them they fled. Those of horse pursued them killing ten and capturing fifteen. And since the town whither the governor was marching, was near the river, he sent a captain with the men he deemed sufficient to take the piraguas up stream. And because by land they frequently turned away from the river in order to get around arms which thrust out of the river, the Indians had opportunity to attack those in the piraguas and put us in great danger. For because of the strong current of the river, they did not dare to go any distance from land and they [the Indians] shot arrows at them from the bluff. As soon as the governor reached the town, he immediately sent some crossbowmen down stream who were to come as his rear guard. When the piraguas reached the town he [the governor] ordered them taken apart and the nails kept for other piraguas when they might be needed. He slept there one night and next day marched in search of a province called Pac[a]ha, which he was informed lay near Chisca where the Indians said there was gold. He marched through large towns in Aquixo which had been abandoned for fear of the Christians. From some Indians who were captured, he learned that a great cacique lived three days' journey thence, called Casqui.[185] He reached a small river where a bridge was made on which he crossed.[186] On that day, they walked continually through water until sunset, which in places reached to the middle and in places to the knee. When they came to dry land, they were very glad, for it seemed to them that they would be walking about lost through the water all night. At noon they arrived at the first town of Casqui. They found the Indians off guard for they had not heard of them [the Christians]. Many Indians, both men and women, were seized, besides a quantity of clothing—blankets and skins—both in the first town and in another which was within sight of it [the first town] in an open field a half league from it, whither the horsemen had galloped. That land is more high, dry, and level than the land of the river behind which they had thus far seen. In the open field were many walnut trees with soft nuts shaped like acorns;[187] and in the houses were found many which the Indians had stored away. The walnut trees did not differ in any other way from those of Spain, or from those seen before except only in having a smaller leaf. There were many mulberry trees and plum trees having red plums like those of Spain, and others gray,[188] differing, but much better, and all the trees as verdant all year as if set out in gardens and in a clear grove. For two days the governor marched through the land of Casqui before arriving at the town[189] where the cacique was, and most of the way continually through land of open field, very well peopled with large towns, two or three of which were to be seen from one town. He sent word to the cacique through an Indian that he was coming to where he was for the purpose of procuring his friendship and of considering him as a brother. To which he [the cacique] answered that he [the governor] would be welcome, that he would receive him with special pleasure, and that he would do everything his Lordship ordered. He sent his offerings to him on the road, namely, skins and blankets and fish. After these gifts, the governor found all the towns through which he passed inhabited, in which the Indians were awaiting him peacefully and offered him blankets and skins and fish. The cacique, accompanied by many Indians, came out of the town where he was living for a half league on the road to welcome the governor, and meeting him spoke as follows: "Very lofty, powerful, and illustrious Lord: May the coming of Your Lordship be very propitious. As soon as I had notice of your Lordship, of your power and perfections, although you entered my land killing and making captive the inhabitants of it and my vassals, I resolved to conform my will to yours, and as yours to consider as good all that your Lordship might do; believing that it is proper that it might be so for some just consideration, in order to provide for some future event, revealed to your Lordship, but concealed from me; for, indeed, one evil may be permitted in order to avoid another greater evil, and therefrom good may result, which I believe will be so; for from so excellent a prince it is not right to presume that the nobility of your heart and the effect of your good will would allow you to permit an injustice. My capacity to serve you as your Lordship merits is so slight that if my good will should abundantly and humbly offer every kind of service, you would acquire no honor [thereby]. In your Lordship's presence, I merit very little. But if it is proper that that capacity may be esteemed, may you receive it, and me and my land and vassals as your own, and of me and them make use according to your pleasure; for if I were lord of all the world, your Lordship would be received, served, and obeyed with the same good will." The governor replied to him fittingly and in few words made him happy. For a while after that, they both went on exchanging words generous in offers and of great courtesy, and he [the cacique] begging that he [the governor] should lodge in his houses. The governor, in order to preserve peace better, excused himself, by saying that he preferred to lodge in the open field; and because the heat was very great, the camp was established a quarter league from the town among some trees. The cacique went to his town and returned with many Indians singing. As soon as they came to the governor, they all bowed themselves to the ground. Among them were two blind Indians. The cacique made a speech which, in order not to be prolix, I will relate in a few words only the substance of the matter. He said that since he [the governor] was the son of the sun and a great lord, he begged him to do him the favor of giving health to those blind Indians. The blind men immediately rose and with great earnestness begged this of the governor. He replied saying that in the lofty heaven was He who had power to give them health and everything they might ask of Him, whose servant he [the governor] was; and that that Lord made the heavens and the earth and man in His likeness; that he suffered[190] on the tree of the true cross to save the human race, and rose again on the third day; that inasmuch as He was man He died, and inasmuch as He was divinity, He is immortal; that He ascended to heaven where He was with open arms in order to receive all those who wished to be converted to Him. He [the governor] immediately ordered him [the chief] to make a very high wooden cross which was set up in the highest part of the town, [the governor] declaring to him that the Christians adored it in conformity to, and in memory of, that on which Christ suffered. The governor and his men knelt before it and the Indians did the same. The governor told him [the cacique] that thenceforth they should adore and beg the Lord, of whom he had told them and who was in heaven, for everything of which they had need. He asked him [the cacique] how far it was from there to Pacaha. He said it was a day's journey and that on the edge of his land was a marsh like an estuary which gave into the large river; that he would send men to build in advance a bridge by which he might cross. The day on which the governor left, he went to sleep at a town of Casqui; and the next day he passed in sight of the other towns and reached the swamp, which was half a crossbow flight in width and very deep and flowing.[191] When he reached it, the Indians had just finished building the bridge, which was constructed of wood in the manner of beams [*viroes*] extending from tree to tree, and at one of the sides a line of wood higher than the bridge in order to support those who should cross. The cacique of Casqui went to the governor and took his men with him. The governor sent word by an Indian to the cacique of Pacaha that although he [the cacique of Pacaha] was hostile to the cacique of Casqui and the latter should be there, he would make no quarrel with him or do him no harm if he waited peacefully and wished his friendship, but that he would treat him as a brother. The Indian whom the governor had sent came and said that the cacique gave no heed to what he had told him but that he had gone away in flight with all his people out of the other side of the town. The governor immediately entered and together with the men of horse charged ahead where the Indians were fleeing; and at another town situated a quarter of a league from that place captured many Indians. And as the horsemen captured them, they delivered them over to the Indians of Casqui, who, being their enemies, carefully and with great pleasure took them to the town where the Christians were; and the greatest sorrow they had was in not having permission to kill them. Many blankets, deer, lion, and bear skins, and many cat skins were found in town. Many [of the men] were still poorly clad and there clothed themselves. From the blankets were made loose coats and cassocks; and some made gowns and lined them with the catskins, as well as the cassocks. From the deerskins were also made some jerkins, shirts, stockings,* and shoes and from the bear skins very good cloaks, for water would not go through them.[192] They found there shields made of raw cowhide[193] with which the horses were provided with armor.

XXIIII.

HOW THE CACIQUE OF PACAHA CAME IN PEACE, AND HE OF CASQUI WENT AWAY AND RETURNED TO EXCUSE HIMSELF; AND HOW THE GOVERNOR MADE HIM AND THE CACIQUE OF PACAHA FRIENDS.

On Wednesday, June 19,[194] the governor entered Pacaha. He lodged in the town where the cacique lived, which was very large, enclosed, and furnished with towers; and in the towers and stockade many loopholes. In the town was abundance of old maize and new maize in the maize fields in great quantity. Located at a league and half a league were large towns, all enclosed. Where the governor was lodged, there was a large marsh which came near to the enclosure, and entered through a ditch round about the town so that but little of the town remained to enclose.† A channel had been made from the

*The Portuguese *calças,* which Robertson rendered as "stockings," could be rendered also as "trousers" or "leggings." "Trousers" is probably the preferable rendering here.

†The Portuguese that Robertson translated as "large marsh" is *grande alagoa. Alagoa* can be rendered also as "lake," but Robertson's rendition seems the preferable one here.

The clause, *que perto da cêrca chegaua,* which Robertson translated as "which came near to the enclosure," might be rendered more clearly as "which came close to the palisade."

The Portuguese *i por uma caua que aorredor do pouo hia entrava com que pouco delle quedaua por cercar,* which Robertson translated as "and entered through a ditch round about the town so that but little of the town remained to enclose," might be rendered a little more literally and clearly as "and it entered by way of a ditch, which ran around the settlement, so that it almost encircled it."

marsh to the large river through which the fish entered the former.* This the cacique had there for his recreation and pleasure.† As many fish as they wished were caught with nets which were found in the town; and however many of them were drawn out, there was never lack of them found. In many other swamps thereabout, there were also many fish, but they were soft and not so good as those which came from the river, and most of them were different from those of the fresh water of Spain. There was a fish called "bagre," a third of which was head; and it had large spines like a sharp shoemaker's awl at either side of its throat and along the sides. Those of them which were in the water were as large as a "pico." In the river there were some of one hundred and one hundred and fifty pounds. Many of them were caught with the hook. Another fish resembled the "barbel" [*barbo*]; and others were like the "choupa," with a head like that of the "*besugo*" and between russet and brown.‡ This was the one that was most relished. There was another fish called the "pexe palla." Its snout was a cubit in length and the tip of its upper lip was shaped like a shovel. There was another fish which resembled a shad [*savel*]. All had scales except the "bagres" and the "pexe palla." There was another fish which the Indians brought sometimes, of the size of a hog, called "pexe pereo." It had rows of teeth below and above.[195] The cacique of Casqui frequently sent gifts of fish in abundance, and blankets, and skins. He told the governor that he would give the cacique of Pacaha into his hands. He went to Casqui, ordered many canoes brought up the river, while he went overland with many of his people. The governor, with forty of horse and sixty of foot, took him [the cacique] with him up the river. His Indians who were in the canoes discovered where the cacique of Pacaha was on an islet between two arms of the river. Five Christians embarked in a canoe, among whom went Don Antonio Osorio, going ahead to see what people the cacique had with himself. There were five or six thousand souls on the islet. As soon as they saw them, thinking that the Indians in the canoes were Christians also, the cacique and those who belonged to three canoes they had there, fled in great haste to the other side of the river. The rest, in great fear and confusion, betook themselves hastily to the water

*The Portuguese *acéquia,* which Robertson rendered as "channel," might be rendered more literally and clearly as "irrigation ditch."

†The Portuguese *deporte,* which Robertson rendered as "pleasure," might be rendered more literally as "sport."

‡The Portuguese *ruiuo,* which Robertson rendered as "russet," is literally "reddish-yellow" or "red." *Ruiuo* is the word used to denote red-headed people.

swimming, where many people were drowned, principally women and children. Then the governor, who was on land, not knowing what was happening to Don Antonio and those who went with him, ordered Christians and Indians to enter with great haste in the canoes of the Indians of Casqui; and they immediately went to Don Antonio on the islet where they captured many Indians—men and women—and a quantity of clothing, from the abundance of clothing which the Indians [of Pacaha] had in hurdles and on wooden rafts in order to take it across from the other side.* It went floating down stream; and the Indians of Casqui filled their canoes with it. And fearing lest the Christians would seize it, the cacique and his men went down stream with them to his land without taking leave of the governor. On that account the governor was indignant at him. Immediately returning to Pacaha, two leagues away, along the road from Casqui, he made a raid, on which he seized twenty or thirty of his [the cacique's] Indians. And because the horses were tired and there was no time to go farther that day, he returned to Pacaha, planning to attack Casqui from there three or four days later. He immediately released one of the Indians of Pacaha, and sent him to tell the cacique that if he wished for his friendship he should come to him and that they would go to make war on Casqui. Immediately many of the Indians of Pacaha came and brought an Indian under the name of cacique, which was revealed by a brother of the cacique who was a prisoner. The governor told the Indians that their lord should come, for he knew well that that one was not he, and that they could do nothing that he did not know before they thought of it. Next day came the cacique accompanied by many Indians bringing a gift of many fish, skins, and blankets. He made a talk which all were glad to hear and concluded by saying that even though his lordship had wrought damage to his land and vassals without him having deserved it, nevertheless he would not cease to be his, and would always be at his service. The governor ordered his brother and some others of the principal Indians whom he had captured to be released. That day came an Indian on the part of the cacique of Casqui and said that his lord would come immediately next day in order to beg pardon for the error he had committed in having gone away without the governor's permission. The governor told him [the Indian messenger] to tell him [the cacique of Casqui] that if he did not come in his own proper person he would go to get him and give him the

*The Portuguese *em caniçadas i balsas de madeira,* which Robertson rendered as "in hurdles and on wooden rafts," would be better rendered as "on fences (or trellises) and wooden rafts." *Caniçados* connotes a wickerwork type of fence made of reeds or canes.

punishment he deserved. Immediately next day came the cacique of Casqui, and made the governor a gift of many blankets, skins, and fish. He gave him one of his daughters, saying that his greatest desire was to unite his blood with that of so great a lord as he was. On that account he brought his daughter and begged him to take her as his wife. He made a long and discreet argument, praising him highly, and concluded by asking that he pardon him, by the love of that cross which he had left him, for having gone off without his permission; that he had gone away for shame of what his people had done without his consent. The governor answered him saying that he had taken a good protector and that if he had not come to beg pardon, he had planned to go to get him and burn his towns for him and kill him and his people and ravage his land for him. He replied to him saying "Lord, I and mine are your Lordship's, and my land is yours. Therefore, if you should go, you would destroy your own land and kill your own people. All that comes to me from your hand, I shall receive as from my lord, both punishment and favor. Know that what you did for me in leaving me that cross, I consider a very notable thing and greater than I have ever deserved. For you will know that the maize fields of my lands were lost because of the great drouth; but as soon as I and my people knelt down before the cross and begged it for waters, our need was alleviated." The governor made him and the cacique of Pacaha friends and placed them at table with him so that they might eat with him. In regard to the seats, the caciques had a quarrel as to who was to sit at his right hand. The governor made peace between them by saying that among Christians one side was accounted as the other, and that so they should consider it. Since they were his guests no one would pay any attention to them; and each should seat himself in the first seat he should find.[196] Hence he sent thirty men of horse and fifty of foot to the province of Caluça[197] to see whether they could bend back toward Chisca by that way where the Indians said there was a foundry for gold and copper. They went for seven days through an uninhabited region and returned after much hardship, eating green plums[198] and maize stalks which they found in a poor town of six or seven houses. From there on toward the north, the Indians said that the land was very poorly inhabited because it was very cold, and that there were so many cattle[199] that no field could be protected because of them, and that the Indians sustained themselves on their flesh. The governor, seeing that in that direction the land was so poor in maize that they could not sustain themselves, asked the Indians where the most populous district lay. They said that they had heard of a large province and of a very well provided land called Quiguate[200] and it was toward the south.

XXV.

HOW THE GOVERNOR WENT FROM PACAHA TO QUIGUATE AND TO COLIGOA AND ARRIVED AT CAYAS.

The governor rested in Pacaha for forty days. During all that time, the two caciques gave him service of abundance of fish, blankets, and skins, and they tried to see which of them could perform the greater services. At the time of his departure, the cacique of Pacaha, gave two of his sisters to him, saying that if he would remember him he should take them as wives as a testimonial of love. The name of the one was Macanoche, and of the other Mochila.[201] They were very well disposed, tall of body and plump in figure. Macanoche was of good appearance, and in her address and face appeared a lady; the other was robust. The cacique of Casqui ordered the bridge repaired, and the governor gave a turn through his land and lodged in the open field, near his town, whither he [the cacique] came with a quantity of fish and two Indian women whom he exchanged with two Christians for two shirts. He gave a guide and tamemes. The governor went to sleep at one of his towns and next day at another near a river, where he ordered canoes brought for him in which to cross and with his permission returned. The governor took his way toward Aquiguate.[202] On the fourth of August, he reached the town where the cacique was living. On the way, the latter sent him a service of many blankets and skins, but not daring to remain in the town went away. The town was the largest which had been seen in Florida. The governor and his men were lodged in half of it; and a few days afterward seeing that the Indians were going about deceitfully, he ordered the other half burned, so that it might not afford them protection, if they came to attack him at night, and be an obstacle to his men of horse in resisting them. An Indian well attended by many Indians came saying that he was the cacique. He [the governor] delivered him to his guard that they might look after him. Many Indians went off and came bringing blankets and skins. Seeing poor opportunity for carrying out his evil thought, the pretended cacique going out of the house one day with the governor, started to run away so swiftly that there was no Christian who could overtake him; and plunged into the river which was a crossbow shot's distance from the town. As soon as he had crossed to the other side, many Indians who were walking about there, uttering loud cries, began to shoot arrows. The governor crossed over to them immediately with men of horse and of foot, but they did not dare await him. On going in pursuit of them, he arrived at a town which had been abandoned, and on beyond it a swamp[203] where the horses could not cross. On the other side were many Indian women. Some men of foot crossed over and captured many of the women and a quantity of clothing. The governor returned to the camp; and soon after on that night a spy of the Indians was captured by those who were on watch. The governor asked him whether he would take them to the place where the cacique was. He said yes, and he [the governor] went immediately to look for him [the cacique] with twenty men of horse and fifty of foot. After a march of a day and a half he found him [the cacique] in a dense wood, and a soldier, not knowing him, gave him a cutlass stroke on the head. He [the cacique] cried out not to kill him saying that he was the cacique. He was taken captive and with him one hundred and forty of his people. The governor went to Quiguate and told him that he should make his Indians come to serve the Christians; and after waiting for some days hoping for them to come, but they not coming, he sent two captains, each one on his own side of the river, with horse and foot. They captured many Indians, both men and women. Upon seeing the hurt they received, because of their rebellion, they came to see what the governor might order them. Thus they came and went frequently and brought gifts of clothing and fish. The cacique and two of his wives were left unshackled in the governor's house, being guarded by the halberdiers of the governor's guard. The governor asked them in what direction the land was more densely populated. They said that on the lower part of the river toward the south were large settlements and caciques who were lords of wide lands and of many people, and that there was a province called Coligoa[204] toward the northwest, situated near some mountain ridges. It seemed advisable to the governor and to all the rest to go first to Coligoa, saying that perhaps the mountains would make a difference in the land and that gold or silver might exist on the other side of them. Both Aquiguate and Casqui and Pacaha were flat and fertile lands, with excellent meadow lands along the rivers where the Indians made large fields. From Tascaluca to the great river, the distance was about three hundred leagues, the land being very low and with many marshes.[205] From Pacaha to Quiguate, the distance is about one hundred and ten leagues.[206] The governor left the cacique of Quiguate in his town; and an Indian who guided him through large pathless forests conducted him for seven days through an uninhabited region where they lodged each night amid marshes and streamlets[207] of very shallow water. So plentiful were the fish that they killed them by striking them with clubs; and the Indians whom they took along in chains roiled the water with the mud of the waters, and the fish, as if stupefied would come to the surface, and they caught as many as they wished. The Indians of Coligoa had not heard of Christians, and when they [the Christians] came within sight of the town[208] so that they [the Indians] saw them, they took to flight up a river which flowed near the town. Some plunged into the river, but Christians who went along both banks captured them. Many Indians were captured there, both men and women, and among them, the cacique. At his command, many Indians came three days afterward bearing gifts of blankets and deerskins and two cowhides. They said that five or six leagues beyond toward the north were many cattle, but because the land was cold, it was poorly populated; that the best land they knew of, as being more plentifully supplied with food and better inhabited, was a province toward the south called Cayas. From Quiguate to Coligoa, the distance was about forty leagues. That town of Coligoa was situated at the foot of a mountain in a field of a river half the size of the Caya River which flows through Estremadura. It was a fertile land and so abundant in maize that the old was thrown out in order to store the new. There was also a great quantity of beans and pumpkins, the beans being larger and better than those of Spain; and the pumpkins likewise. When roasted the latter have almost the taste of chestnuts. The cacique of Coligoa gave a guide to Cayas and remained in his town. We traveled for five days and reached the province of Palisema.[209] The house of the cacique was found with coverlings of colored deerskins drawn over with designs, and the floor of the house was covered with the same material in the manner of carpets. The cacique left it so, in order that the governor might lodge in it as a sign that he was desirous of peace and his friendship, but he did not dare remain. The governor, upon seeing that he had gone away, sent a captain with horse and foot to look for him. He [the captain] found many people, but because of the roughness of the land they captured only some women and young persons. It was a small and scattered settlement and had very little maize. On that account, the governor left it immediately. He came upon another settlement called Tatalicoya,[210] taking with him the cacique who guided him to Cayas.[211] From Tatalicoya it is a distance of four days' journey to Cayas. When he reached Cayas and saw the scattered settlement, because of the information he had received, namely, that it was well populated land, he believed that the cacique was lying to him and that that was not the province of Cayas. He threatened the cacique, bidding him to tell him where he was; and both the latter and the other Indians who had been captured near that place asserted that that settlement was that of Cayas, and the best settlement of that province; and that although the houses were separated from one another, the populated land was considerable, and it had many people and many maize fields. The name of the settlement was Tanico.[212] The camp was made in the best part of it near a river. The day on which the governor reached there with some men of horse, he went a league farther on and, although he found no Indians, found on a road many skins which the cacique had left there for him to find as a sign of peace; for this is the custom of that land.

XXVI.

HOW THE GOVERNOR WENT TO SEE THE PROVINCE OF TULLA AND WHAT BEFELL HIM THERE.

The governor abode in the province of Cayas for a month. During that interval, the horses grew fat and throve more than after a longer time in any other region because of the abundance of maize and the leaf thereof, which is, I think, the best that has been seen. They drank from a very warm and brackish marsh of water,* and they drank so much that it was noticed in their bellies when they were brought back from the water. Thitherto the Christians had lacked salt, but there they made a good quantity of it in order to carry it along with them. The Indians carry it thence to other regions to exchange it for skins and blankets. They gather it along the river, which leaves it on top of the sand when the water falls. And since they cannot gather it without more sand being mixed with it, they put it into certain baskets which they have for this purpose, wide at the top and narrow at the bottom. They hang the baskets to a pole in the air and put water in them, and they place a basin underneath into which the water falls.† After being

---

*The words *muito quente,* which Robertson rendered as "very warm," might be rendered more properly as "very hot," as *quente* by itself means "hot" or "very warm," and here it is reinforced by *muito.* The word *alagoa,* which Robertson rendered as "marsh," could be rendered also as "pond."

†The Portuguese that Robertson rendered as "They hang the baskets to a pole in the air" is *poeno no ar sobre hua barra.* That passage might be rendered more accurately as "They place it in the air above (*sobre*) a frame (*barra*)." *Sobre* can only mean "on" or "above." *Barra* suggests something horizontal rather than a vertical "pole." This suggests that the baskets are not hung to the *barra,* but sitting on or over it. *Barra,* strictly speaking, means "bar" or "rod" rather than "pole." Among *barra's* other meanings is that of "crude bed frame." I think that it is something of that sort which is intended here, which provides support for the basket. The verb *poe* means simply "put" or "place" without any necessary connotation of "hang."

strained and set on the fire to boil, as the water becomes less, the salt is left on the bottom of the pot.[213] On both sides of the river, the land had cultivated fields and there was an abundance of maize. The Indians did not dare to cross [the river] to the place where we were. When some [Indians] appeared, some soldiers who saw them called to them. The Indians crossed the river and came with them [the soldiers] to the place where the governor was. He asked them for their cacique. They declared that he was friendly, but that he did not dare to appear. Thereupon, the governor ordered that he be told to come to see him and to bring a guide and interpreter for the region ahead, if he wished to be his friend; and that if he did not do this, he would go to fetch him and his hurt would be greater. He waited three days, and seeing that he [the cacique] did not come, went to look for him, and brought him back a prisoner with one hundred and fifty of his Indians. He [the governor] asked him whether he had knowledge of any great cacique and where the most populated land was. He [the cacique] said that the best populated land thereabout was a province situated to the south, a day and a half away, called Tulla, that he could give him a guide, but that he did not have an interpreter, for the speech of Tulla was different from his; and because he and his forebears had always been at war with the lords of that province, they had no converse, nor did they understand each other. Thereupon, the governor set out for Tulla with men of horse and fifty foot in order to see whether it was a land through which he might pass with all his men. As soon as he arrived and was perceived by the Indians, the land was summoned. When fifteen or twenty Indians had gathered together, they came to attack the Christians. On [the Indians'] seeing that they [the Christians] handled them roughly, and that when they took to flight the horses overtook them, they climbed on top of the houses, where they tried to defend themselves with their arrows; and when driven from some [of the housetops] would climb on top of others; and while they [the Christians] were pursuing some [of the Indians], others [of the Indians] would attack them [the Christians] from another direction. In this way, the running lasted so long that the horses became tired and could no longer run. The Indians killed one horse there and wounded[214] several. Fifteen Indians were killed there, and captives were made of forty women and young persons; for they [the Christians] did not leave any Indian alive who was shooting arrows if they could overtake him. The governor determined to return to Cayas before the Indians should have time to gather themselves together. Thereupon, that evening, after having marched part of the night, in order to get some distance from Tulla, he went to sleep on the road, and reached Cayas next day. Three days after that he set out with all his men for Tulla, taking the cacique with him. Among all the Indians of the latter, he did not find a single one who understood the speech of Tulla. He was three days on the way, and the day he reached the town, he found it abandoned, for the Indians did not dare await him. But as soon as they knew he was in Tulla, at the hour of dawn of the first night, they came in two bands from two different directions with their bows and arrows and long poles resembling pikes. As soon as they [the Indians] were perceived, both those of horse and those of foot sallied out against them and there many Indians were killed, and some Christians and horses wounded. Some Indians were captured, six of whom the governor sent to the cacique with their right hands and their noses cut off. He ordered them to tell him that if he did not come to make his excuses and obey him, he would go to get him; and that he would do to him and to as many of his men as he found what he had done to those whom he sent to him. He gave him the space of three days in which to come. This he gave them to understand the best he could by signs as he had no interpreter. After three days came an Indian whom the cacique sent laden with cowhides. He came weeping bitterly, and coming to the governor cast himself at his feet. He [the governor] raised him up, and he made him talk, but no one could understand him. The governor told him by signs that he should return and tell the cacique to send him an interpreter whom the people of Cayas could understand. Next day, three Indians came laden with cowhides and three days after that twenty Indians came. Among them was one who understood those of Cayas. After a long discourse of excuses from the cacique and praises of the governor, he concluded by saying that he and the others were come thither on behalf of the cacique to see what his lordship ordered; and that he was ready to serve him. The governor and all the men were very glad, for they could in no wise travel without an interpreter. The governor ordered him under guard and told him to tell the Indians who had come with him to return to the cacique and tell him that he pardoned him for the past and that he thanked him greatly for his gifts and for the interpreter whom he had sent him and that he would be glad to see him and for him to come next day to see him. The cacique came after three days and eighty Indians with him. Both he and his men entered the camp weeping in token of obedience and repentance for the past mistake, after the manner of that land. He brought many cowhides as a gift, which were useful because it was a cold land, and were serviceable for coverlets as they were very soft and the wool like that of sheep.[215] Nearby to the north were many cattle. The Christians did not see them nor enter their land, for the land was poorly settled where they [the cattle] were, and had little maize. The cacique of Tulla made his address to the governor in which he excused himself and offered him his land and vassals and person. No orator could more elegantly express the message or address both of that cacique and of all those who came to the governor in their behalf.

XXVII.

HOW THE GOVERNOR WENT FROM TULLA TO AUTIAMQUE, WHERE HE WINTERED.

The governor informed himself of the land in all directions and learned that there was a scattering of population toward the west and large towns toward the southeast, especially in a province called Autiamque, ten days' journey from Tulla—a distance of about eighty leagues—and that it was a land abounding in maize. Since winter had already come and on account of the cold, rains, and snows, they could not travel during two or three months of the year; fearing lest they could not feed themselves for so long a time because of its scattered population; also because the Indians said there was a large body of water near Autiamque—and according to what they said, the governor believed it to be an arm of the sea—and because he now wished to give information of himself in Cuba,* for it was three years and over since Doña Isabel, who was in the Havana, or any other person in a Christian land, had heard of him, and now two hundred and fifty men and one hundred and fifty horses were wanting: he determined to go to winter at Autiamque, and in the following summer to reach the sea and build two brigantines and send one of them to Cuba and the other to New Spain, so that the one which should go safely might give news of him; hoping from his property in Cuba to refit, take up his expedition again, and explore and conquer [the land] farther west than he had yet reached, whither Cabeza de Vaca had gone. He dismissed the two caciques of Tulla and Cayas, and set out toward Autiamque. For five days he proceeded through very rough ridges[216] and reached a village called Quipana,[217] where he was unable to capture any Indian because of the roughness of the land and because the town was located among ridges. At night he set an ambush in which two Indians were

*In his translation Robertson omitted the following Portuguese phrase, *pera que lhe fosse socorro de gente i caualos*. The phrase should be inserted after "Cuba" and rendered as "so that relief in the form of people and horses might come to him."

captured. They said that Autiamque was six days' journey away and that another province called Guahate lay a week's journey southward—a land plentifully abounding in maize and of much population.* But since Autiamque was nearer and more of the Indians mentioned it to him, the governor proceeded on his journey in search of it. He reached a town called Anoixi in three days and sent a captain with thirty horse and fifty foot on ahead. The latter surprised the Indians unawares and captured many Indian men and women. Two days later, the governor arrived at another town called Catamaya[218] and made camp in the open field of the town. Two Indians came with a false message from the cacique in order to ascertain what he was going to do. The governor told them to tell their lord that he should come to talk with him. The Indians went away but did not return, nor was there any other message from the cacique. Next day the Christians went to the town, which was without people, and took what maize they needed. They went to sleep on that day in a forest and next day reached Autiamque.[219] They found considerable maize hidden away, as well as beans, nuts, and dried plums, all in great quantity.† They seized some Indians who were collecting their clothing, and who had already placed their women in safety.[220] That land was cultivated and well peopled. The governor lodged in the best part of the village and immediately ordered a wooden stockade to be built about the place where the camp was established at some distance from the houses, so that the Indians without might not harm it with fire. Having measured off the land by paces, he allotted to each one the amount that was proper for him to build, in proportion to the number of Indians he had. Thereupon, the wood was brought in by them, and within three days the stockade was built of very high timbers set close together in the ground and with many boards placed crosswise.‡ Near this village flowed a river of Cayas and above and below it was densely populated.§ Indians came there on behalf of the

*The Portuguese *pera ho sul oito jornadas dalli,* which Robertson rendered as "week's journey southward," is literally "toward the south eight days' travel from there."

†The Portuguese *encerrado,* which Robertson rendered as "hidden away," rendered literally is simply "stored" without the nuance of being "hidden."

‡The Portuguese *latas,* which Robertson translated as "boards," may well have been boards, but *latas* does not have the specific meaning of "boards." The literal meaning of *latas* is merely "wide pieces."

§The Portuguese *por junto deste pouoaçã,* which Robertson rendered as "near this village," rendered literally is "next to this village." *Junto* usually has the sense of "next to" or "on," although it can be translated as "near." That its rendition as "near" is not proper in this instance is made clear later in this chapter: "He reached a town near the river which flowed through cacique with gifts of blankets and skins, and a lame cacique subject to the cacique of Autiamque,[221] lord of a town called Tietiquaquo,[222] came frequently to visit the governor and brought him gifts of what he had. The cacique of Autiamque sent to ask the governor how long he intended to remain in his land. Upon seeing that he was a guest for more than three days, he sent no more Indians to him, nor any further message; but, on the contrary, he conspired with the lame cacique to revolt. Forays were made in which many Indians, both men and women, were seized, and the lame cacique was captured. The governor, in consideration of the gifts he had received from him, rebuked and warned him, and gave him back his liberty, giving him two Indians to carry him on their shoulders. The cacique of Autiamque, desirous of driving the governor from his land, set spies on him. An Indian coming during the night to the gate of the stockade, a soldier who was on guard saw him and, taking position behind the gate, thrust at him as he entered it and knocked him down; and in that condition brought him to the governor. On asking him why he had come, he fell down dead without being able to answer. Next night, the governor ordered a soldier to sound to arms and to say that he had seen Indians, in order to ascertain how soon they would hasten to the alarm. And both there and in other places, he did the same at various times when he thought his men were growing careless. Those who were slow in standing by, he reproved. And both on this account and because of what was his duty toward him, each one strove to be the first to respond when the alarm was given. They stayed three months in Autiamque, and had great abundance of maize, beans, walnuts, dried plums, and rabbits, which until then they had no skill in killing. In Autiamque, the Indians showed them how they snared them, namely, by means of stout springs which lift the feet off the ground and a noose of strong cord fastened to which is a joint of cane which runs to the neck of the rabbit, so that it can not gnaw the cord. Many were taken in the maize fields, especially when it froze or snowed. The Christians were there a month amid snow during which they never left the town. When firewood was needed, the governor with those of horse going frequently to and from the woods, a distance of two crossbow flights from the town, made a road by which those of foot went in a line. During that time, some Indians, whom they were now taking

---

Cayas and Autiamque." There Elvas mentioned that the same River of Cayas flowed "through" Cayas and Autiamque, which would place the village literally on the river. By contrast, in chapter XXVIII (p. 130), in speaking of another village as being "near the river," Elvas used the word *perto*, meaning "near" rather than *junto*.

along unshackled, killed many rabbits with their snares and arrows. The rabbits were of two kinds—some like those of Spain and others of the same color, form and size as large hares, but larger and with larger loins.

XXVIII.

HOW THE GOVERNOR WENT FROM AUTIAMQUE TO NILCO AND THENCE TO GUACHOYA.

On Monday, March six of the year 1542, the governor set out from Autiamque to go in search of Nilco, which the Indians said was near the great river, with the intention of reaching the sea and obtaining aid of men and horses; for he now had only three hundred fighting men and forty horses, and some of them lame and useful only for making a body of horse. For a year, because of lack of iron they brought them along all unshod; but because they [the horses] were now accustomed to going in a flat country, this did not make their need felt much. In Autiamque died Juan Ortiz,[223] which the governor felt deeply, for without an interpreter, not knowing where he was going, he feared lest he enter a region where he might get lost. After that, a youth who had been seized in Cutifachiqui, and who now knew something of the language of the Christians, served as interpreter. So great a misfortune was the death of Juan Ortiz, with regard to the exploring or trying to leave the land, that to learn from the Indians what he stated in four words, with the youth the whole day was needed; and most of the time he understood just the opposite of what was asked, so that many times it came about that the road they took one day, and at times, two or three days, they would return on, and they would wander about lost from one side of those woods to the other. From Autiamque, it took the governor ten days to reach a province called Ayays.[224] He reached a town near the river which flowed through Cayas and Autiamque. There he ordered a piragua to be constructed, by which he crossed the river.[225] After crossing, such weather occurred that he could not march for four days because of the snow. As soon as it stopped snowing, he marched for three days through an unpopulated region and a land so low and with so many swamps[226] and such hard going that one day he marched all day through water that in some places reached to the knees and in others to the stirrups, and some passages were swum over. He came to a deserted village, without maize called Tutelpinco.[227] Near it was a lake which emptied into the river and had a strong current and force of water. As five Christians, accompanied by a captain whom the governor had sent, were crossing it in a canoe, the canoe overturned. Some caught hold of it [the canoe] and others of trees which were in the lake. One Francisco Bastian,[228] an honorable person, a native of Villanueva de Barcarota, was drowned there. The governor went for a day along the lake looking for a crossing place, but he did not find it all that day nor any road leading from any other direction. Returning at night to the town, he found two peaceful Indians who showed him the crossing and the road he must take. Reed frames and rafts were made there from reeds and wood from the houses, on which they crossed the lake. They marched for three days and reached a town of the district of Nilco, called Tianto. Thirty Indians were captured there, among them being two of the principal men of that town. The governor sent a captain on ahead to Nilco with horse and foot, so that the Indians might not have any opportunity to carry off the food. They went through three or four large towns, and in the town where the cacique lived—located two leagues from where the governor remained—they found many Indians with their bows and arrows, and in appearance as if they wished to give battle, and who were surrounding the town. As soon as they saw that the Christians were coming toward them without any hesitation, they set fire to the cacique's house and escaped over a swamp[229] that lay near the town, where the horses could not cross. Next day, Wednesday, March 29, the governor reached Nilco.[230] He lodged with all his men in the cacique's town which was located on a level field, and which was all populated for a quarter of a league; while a league and a half-league distant were other very large towns where there was a quantity of maize, beans, walnuts, and dried plums. This was the most populous region which had been seen in Florida and more abounding in maize, with the exception of Coça and Apalache. An Indian came to the camp, accompanied by others, and in the cacique's name presented the governor with a blanket of marten skins and a string of pearl beads. The governor gave him some "margaridetas"[231]—a kind of bead much esteemed in Peru—and some other trifles with which he was much pleased. He promised to return two days later, but he never did return. On the other hand, Indians came in canoes at night and carried off all the maize they could and set up their huts on the other side of the river in the thickest part of the forest, so that if they [the Spaniards] should go in search of them, they might escape. The governor, on seeing that he [the Indian] did not come at the promised time, ordered an ambush to be made at some barbacoas near the swamp[232] where the Indians came for maize. Two Indians were captured there, who told the governor that the one who came to visit them was not the cacique, but one sent at the latter's command under pretense that it was he, in order to ascertain whether the Christians were off their guard, and whether they planned to settle in that region or go on farther. Thereupon, the governor sent a captain across the river with men of horse and foot, but on crossing they were perceived by the Indians, and for that reason, he [the captain] could not capture more than ten or twelve Indians, men and women, with whom he returned to the camp. That river which flowed through Anilco was the same that flowed through Cayas and Autiamque and emptied into the large river which flowed through Pacaha and Aquixo hard by the province of Guachoya.[233] The lord of the upper part came in canoes to make war on the lord of Nilco. Sent by him, an Indian came to the governor and told him that he was his servant and as such he should consider him and that two days later he would come to kiss the hands of his Lordship. He came at that time with some of his principal Indians who accompanied him. With words of great promise and courtesy, he presented many blankets and deerskins to the governor. The governor gave him some trifles and showed him great honor. He questioned him about the settlement down the river. He said that he knew of none other except his own; and that on the other side was a province of a cacique called Quigaltam.[234] He took his leave of the governor and returned to his town. A few days later, the governor made up his mind to go to Guachoya,[235] in order to ascertain there whether the sea were nearby, or whether there were any settlement nearby where he might subsist himself while brigantines were being built which he intended to send to the land of Christians. As he was crossing the river of Nilco, Indians came up it in canoes from Guachoya, and when they saw him, thinking that he was going after them to do them some hurt, they turned back down the river and went to warn the cacique. The latter, abandoning the town with all his people, with all they could carry off, on that night crossed over to the other side of the great river. The governor sent a captain and fifty men in six canoes down the river, while he, with the rest of his men, went overland. He reached Guachoya on Sunday, April 17,[236] and lodged himself in the cacique's town, which was surrounded by a stockade, a crossbow flight from the river. There, the river was called Tamaliseu, at Nilco, Tapatu, at Coça, Mico, and at the port, Ri [i.e., River].[237]

XXIX.

OF THE MESSAGE SENT BY THE GOVERNOR TO QUIGALTAM AND OF THE ANSWER GIVEN BY THE LATTER; AND OF WHAT HAPPENED DURING THIS TIME.

As soon as the governor reached Guachoya, he sent Juan de Añasco up the river with as many men as could get into the canoes; for when they were coming from Anilco, they saw newly made huts on the other side. Juan de Añasco went and brought back the canoes laden with maize, beans, dried plums, and many loaves made from the pulp of the plums. On that day, an Indian came to the governor in the name of the cacique of Guachoya and said that his lord would come next day. On the following day, they saw many canoes coming from downstream. They assembled together for the space of an hour on the other side of the great river, debating as to whether they should come or not. At last, they made up their minds and crossed the river. The cacique of Guachoya came in them, bringing with him many Indians bearing a considerable quantity of fish, dogs, skins, and blankets. As soon as they landed at the town, they went immediately to the town to the governor's lodging and presented the gifts to him; and the cacique spoke as follows: "Powerful and excellent lord; May your Lordship pardon me for the mistake I made in going away and not waiting in this town to receive you and serve you; for the obtaining of this opportune occasion was, and is, a great victory for me. But I feared what I should not have feared and on that account did what it was not proper to do. However, since hasty actions cause unfavorable results, and I had acted without deliberation, as soon as I reflected on this, I made up my mind not to follow the advice of the foolish, which is to persist in their error, but to imitate the wise and prudent ones in changing one's opinion; and I am come to see what your Lordship might command me in order to serve you in so far as my possibility suffices." The governor welcomed him with much hospitality and gave him thanks for his gifts and promises. He asked him [the cacique] whether he had any knowledge of the sea. He said he did not, nor of any settlement down the river from that place, except that there was a town of one of his principal Indians subject to him two leagues away, and on the other side three days' journey downstream the province of Quigaltam, who was the greatest lord of that region. It seemed to the governor that the cacique was lying to him in order to turn him aside from his towns, and he sent Juan de Añasco downstream with eight horse to see what population there was and to ascertain whether there were any knowledge of the sea. He was gone for a week and on his coming said that during that whole time he could not proceed more than fourteen or fifteen leagues because of the great arms leading out of the river, and the canebrakes and thick woods lying along it; and that he found no settlement. The governor's grief was intense on seeing the small prospect [*mao remedio*] he had for reaching the sea; and worse, according to the way in which his men and horses were[238] diminishing, they could not be maintained in the land without succor. With that thought, he fell sick, but before he took to his bed, he sent an Indian to tell the cacique of Quigaltam that he was the son of the sun and that wherever he went all obeyed him and did him service. He requested him to choose his friendship and come there where he was, for he would be very glad to see him; and in token of love and obedience that he should bring him something of what was most esteemed in that land. By the same Indian, he [the cacique] answered him saying that with respect to what he [the governor] said about being the son of the sun, let him dry up the great river and he would believe him. With respect to the rest [that the governor said], he was not accustomed to visit any one. On the contrary, all of whom he had knowledge visited and served him and obeyed him and paid him tribute, either by force or of their own volition. Consequently, if he [the governor] wished to see him, let him cross there. If he came in peace he would welcome him with special good will; if he came in war, he would await him in the town where he was, for not for him or any other would he move one foot backward.[239] When the Indian came with this reply, the governor was already in bed, badly racked by fever. He was very angry that he was not in condition to cross the river forthwith and go in quest of him [the cacique] to see whether he could not lessen that arrogant demeanor. However, the river was now very powerful there, being about half a league wide and sixteen brazas[240] deep, and very furious because of its strong current. On both sides of it were many Indians; and his strength was now no longer so great that he did not need to take advantage of cunning rather than force. The Indians of Guachoya came daily with fish, so many that the town was filled with them. The cacique said that the cacique of Quigaltam was going to come on a certain night to do battle with the governor. The governor, believing that he [the cacique of Guachoya] was planning thereby to drive him out of his land, ordered him placed under guard. That night and every other night a very strict watch was kept. Asking him why Quigaltam did not come, he [the cacique] said that he had come, but saw that he [the governor] was on the watch and he did not dare to attack him. He [the cacique] importuned him [the governor] frequently, to order his captains to cross to the other side of the river and [said] that he would give him many men to attack Quigaltam. The governor told him that as soon as he got well, he would go to look for him [Quigaltam]. Noting how many Indians came to the town daily, and how many people were in that land, and fearing lest some of them conspire with others and plan some treason against him, and because the town, having no gates by which advantage could be taken, had some openings which had not been completely closed: he left them in that condition without repairing the stockade in order that the Indians might not think he feared them. He ordered that men of horse be stationed at them and at the gates. All night long the horses were left bridled and from each company mounted men rode by couples and went to visit the sentinels who were stationed on the roads at their posts outside the town, and the crossbowmen who were guarding the canoes on the river. In order that the Indians might fear him, the governor determined to send a captain to Nilco, which those of Guachoya had told him was inhabited, in order that by treating them cruelly, neither the one town nor the other should dare attack him. He sent Nuño de Tobar with fifteen horse and Juan de Guzmán, captain of men of foot, with his men upstream in the canoes. The cacique of Guachoya sent for canoes and for many Indian warriors who went with the Christians. A captain of the Christians, Nuño de Tobar, by name, with the men of horse went overland. At a distance of two leagues before reaching Nilco, he awaited Juan de Guzmán and at night they crossed the river at that place. Those of horse arrived first. At daybreak next morning, in sight of the town they came upon a spy, who, on seeing the Christians, ran away uttering loud cries in order to give the alarm to those of the town. Nuño de Tobar and those who accompanied him set such a pace that before the Indians of the town had all come out, they were on them. The land was open, that part which was peopled being about a quarter of a league [in extent]. There were about five or six thousand souls in that settlement. And since many of the people came out of the houses and went fleeing from one house to the other, and many Indians were gathering together in all directions, there was not a single one of the horse who did not find himself alone among many. The captain had ordered that no male Indian's life should be spared. So great was their confusion that not an Indian shot at a Christian. The cries of the women and little children were so loud that they deafened the ears of those who pursued them. A hundred or so Indians were killed there and many were badly wounded with the lances, who were let go in order that they might strike terror into those who did not happen to be there. There were men there so cruel and such butchers that they killed old men and young men and all they came upon without any one offering them little or much resistance. Those who trusted in themselves, who went to prove themselves wherever there was any resistance, and who were considered as such men, broke through the Indians, overthrowing many with the stirrup and breasts of their horses; and some they lanced and let them go in that condition; but on seeing a child or a woman, they would capture and deliver such a person to those of foot. Those who were cruel, because they showed themselves inhuman, God permitted their sin to confront them, very great cowardice assailing them in the sight of all at a time when there was greater need of fighting, and when at last they came to die.[241] Of the Indians at Nilco, eighty women and children were seized, and much clothing. The Indians of Guachoya stopped before reaching the town and stayed outside, beholding how the Christians dealt [*se avinhã*] with the people of Nilco; and seeing them defeated and those of horse going about lancing them, they went to the houses to loot, and from the booty loaded their canoes with clothing and went to Guachoya before the Christians came. And full of wonder at what they had seen done to the Indians of Anilco, they told their cacique with great fear everything as it had happened.

XXX.

HOW THE ADELANTADO, DON HERNANDO DE SOTO, DIED AND HOW LUIS MOSCOSO DE ALVARADO WAS CHOSEN GOVERNOR.

The governor realized within himself that the hour had come in which he must leave this present life. He had the royal officials summoned, and the captains and principal persons. To them he gave a talk, saying that he was about to go to give an accounting before the throne of God of all his past life; and that since He [God] was pleased to take him at such a time, and to arrive at a time when he could perceive his death, he a very unworthy servant gave Him many thanks; and to all those present and absent, to whom he confessed his great obligation for their singular virtues, love, and loyalty toward himself, which he had well proven in the hardships they had suffered. This he had always had in mind and had hoped to recompense and to reward when God should be pleased to give leisure to his life with greater prosperity of his estate. He asked them to pray God for him and in His mercy to pardon him his sins, and place his soul in glory. He asked them to give him release and remission from the obligation in which he stood to them and of what he was owing to them all; and to pardon any feelings of offense they might have received from him. In order to avoid any disunion that might arise at his death with regard to the one who was to act as governor, he asked them to consider it fitting to elect one of the principal and capable persons to govern, in whom they all might be satisfied, and before whom having been elected they should take oath to obey him. For this, he would be very grateful, for it would soften somewhat his grief and the sorrow he felt at leaving them in so great confusion as he was doing in a land in which they did not know where they were. Baltasar de Gallegos answered him in the name of all, and first consoling him, spoke to him of how brief was the life of this world and of how many hardships and sufferings; that he who earliest left it, to him God showed signal mercy; saying to him [also] many other things proper at such a time; and lastly, that since God was pleased to take him to himself, although his death, with much reason they greatly grieved over, it was necessary and proper for him as it was for all to conform to the will of God. And as to the governor whom he ordered them to choose, let his Lordship appoint him whom he might delegate and they would obey him. Therefore, he [the governor] appointed Luis de Moscoso de Alvarado[242] as their captain general, and by all those who were present he was immediately sworn and elected as governor. Next day, May 21, died the magnanimous, virtuous, and courageous captain, Don Hernando de Soto, governor of Cuba and adelantado of Florida, whom fortune exalted as she is wont to do with others, so that he might fall from a greater height. He died in a land and at a time when his illness had very little solace. The danger of being lost in that land, which stared all of them in the face, was the reason why each one himself had need of consolation and why they did not visit him and wait upon him as was fitting.[243] Luis de Moscoso determined to conceal his death from the Indians, for Hernando de Soto had given them to understand that the Christians were immortal. Also because they knew him to be bold, wise, and courageous, if they should learn of his death, they would be emboldened to attack them [the Spaniards] even though they were at peace, because of their nature and their entire lack of constancy. They [the Indians] believe everything told them. The adelantado had made them believe that [he knew] certain things which had happened among them in secret, which he had succeeded in discovering without their knowing how or in what manner, and that the face which appeared within the mirror (which he showed them) told him whatever they were planning and thinking about. Consequently, they did not dare by word or deed to attempt anything which might be to his hurt. As soon as he died, Luis de Moscoso ordered him [i.e., his corpse] to be placed secretly in a house where he was kept for three days; and from thence he ordered him to be buried at night inside at a gate of the town. And since the Indians had seen that he was sick and found him missing, they suspected what might have happened; and passing by where he was buried and seeing the earth had been disturbed, looked and talked among themselves. Luis de Moscoso, having learned this, ordered him disinterred at night, and a considerable quantity of sand was placed with the blankets in which he was shrouded, and he was taken in a canoe and cast into the middle of the river.[244] The cacique of Guachoya asked for him, inquiring what had been done with his brother and lord, the governor. Luis de Moscoso told him that he had gone to the sky as he had often done before; and since he was to stay there for some days, he had left him in his stead.* The cacique believed that he [De Soto] was dead and ordered two young and well-built Indians to be taken there. He said it was the custom in that land when any lord died to kill Indians to accompany him and serve him on the way; and on this account, those [Indians] had come thither at his order; and he told Luis de Moscoso to have them beheaded so that they might accompany and serve his brother and lord. Luis de Moscoso told him that the governor was not dead but that he had gone to the sky and that he had taken from among his soldiers Christians who were sufficient for his service; and that he requested him to order those Indians freed and from thenceforth not to follow so evil a custom. Thereupon, he ordered them set free and commanded them to go to their homes. One of them refused to go saying that he did not wish to remain under the power of any one who had sentenced him to death undeservedly, and that he desired to serve, while life lasted, him who had freed him. Luis de Moscoso ordered the property of the governor to be sold at auction, namely, two men slaves, two women slaves, three horses, and seven hundred hogs.[245] For each horse or slave, two or three thousand cruzados were given, which were to be paid at the first melting of gold or silver, or from their repartimientos. They pledged themselves that, even though there might be nothing in the land, they would make payment within a year, and for that purpose, those who had no property in Spain gave bonds. For a hog,

*The Portuguese *ceo,* which Robertson translated as "sky," might be rendered also as "heaven."

two hundred cruzados, pledged in the same way [were given]. Those who had property in Spain bought more timidly and bought less. Thenceforward, most of the men had hogs and reared and ate them. They observed Fridays and Saturdays and the vespers of holidays, which they had not done before; for two or three months would pass without their eating meat, and they had eaten it on any day they could get it.

XXXI.

HOW GOVERNOR LUIS DE MOSCOSO DEPARTED FROM GUACHOYA AND WENT TO CHAGUATE AND THENCE TO AGUACAY.

There were some who rejoiced at the death of Don Hernando de Soto, considering it as certain that Luis de Moscoso (who was fond of leading a gay life) would rather prefer to be at ease in a land of Christians than to continue the hardships of the war of conquest and discovery, of which they had long ago become awearied because of the little profit obtained.[246] The governor ordered the captains and principal men to assemble in order to consult them and plan what should be done. Having obtained information of the population all thereabout, he learned that there was a more populous land toward the west and that the river below Quigaltam was uninhabited and had little food. He asked each to express his opinion in writing and to sign his opinion with his name, so that having the opinions of them all, he might make up his mind whether to descend the river or to penetrate inland. It seemed advisable to all to take the road overland toward the west, for New Spain lay in that direction; and they considered as more dangerous and of greater risk the voyage by sea; for no ship could be built strong enough to weather a storm, and they had no master or pilot, and no compass or sailing chart, and they did not know how far away the sea was, nor had they any information of it; nor whether the river made some great bend through the land or whether it fell over any rocks where they would perish. Some men who had seen the sailing chart found that the distance to New Spain along the coast in the region where they were was about five hundred leagues[247] or so. They declared that even although they might have to make some detours by land, because of looking for a settlement, they would not be prevented from going ahead that summer except by some great uninhabited district which they could not cross. If they found food to pass the winter in some settlement, the following summer they would reach the land of Christians. It might be also that by going by land, they would find some rich land from which they might get profit. Although the governor's desire was to leave the land of Florida in the shortest time possible, on seeing the difficulties which lay before him in making the voyage by sea he resolved to follow what seemed best to all. On Monday, June 5,[248] he left Guachoya. The cacique gave him a guide to Chaguate and remained in his village. They passed through a province called Catalte[249] and after passing through an uninhabited region for six days, they reached Chaguete[250] on the twentieth of the month. The cacique of that province had gone to visit the governor, Don Hernando de Soto, at Autiamque where he brought him gifts of skins, blankets, and salt. A day before Luis de Moscoso arrived at his village, a sick Christian got lost, and he suspected that the Indians had killed him. He [Moscoso] sent word to the cacique to have him looked for and sent to him, and said that he would consider him a friend as formerly; but that if he did not do so, there was no place of escape for him or his people, and that his land would be burned. The cacique came forthwith and brought a rich gift of blankets and skins and the Christian, and made the following speech: "Excellent Lord: For all the treasure in the world, I would not desire the opinion you have of me. Who forced me to go to visit the excellent lord governor, your father, at Autiamque (which you should have remembered) where I offered myself with all loyalty, fidelity, and love to serve and obey him as long as I lived? Therefore, what could be the reason, after I had received favors from him and without you or he having done me any injury that I could be induced to do what I ought not do? Believe me, neither injury nor human interest were enough to make me act so, nor would it have blinded me. But since it is a natural thing in this life for many griefs to happen after one pleasure, fortune has pleased by your indignation to moderate the gladness which my heart felt at your coming, and that I should err wherein I thought to succeed, in sheltering that Christian who had become lost and in treating him in such manner as he can tell; for it seemed to me that by so doing I was rendering a service and I planned to go to deliver him to you at Chaguete, and to serve you in everything for which my strength sufficed. If I merit punishment from your hand on this account, I shall receive it as from a lord, as if it were a reward;[251] for the love I bore to the excellent governor and that which I have for you has no limit. Therefore, whatever punishment you give me, you will do me a favor. And what I now ask of you is that you declare your will to me and those things in which I can best serve you." The governor answered him saying that because he did not find him in that town he was angry at him, as it appeared to him that he had gone away as others had done; but since he now understood his loyalty and love, he would always consider him as a brother, and would favor him in all his affairs. The cacique accompanied him to the town where he was living, which was a day's journey thence. They passed through a small town where there was a lake[252] where the Indians made salt. The Christians made some on a day they rested there from some briny water which rose near the town in pools like springs. The governor stayed six days in Chaguete. There he got information of the people to the west. They told him that three days' journey from there was a province called Aguacay. The day he left Chaguete, a Christian named Francisco de Guzmán,[253] bastard son of a gentleman of Seville, remained behind. He went away to the Indians in fear lest they [the Christians] seize from him as a gaming obligation an Indian woman whom he had as a mistress and whom he took away with him. The governor marched for two days before he found he was not with them. He sent word to the cacique to look for him and send him to Aguacay, whither he was going, which he [the cacique] never did. On behalf of the cacique of Aguacay, before reaching that province, fifteen Indians came to meet him on the way with a present of skins and fish and roasted venison. The governor reached his town on Wednesday, July 4.[254] He found the town abandoned and lodged therein. He stayed there for some time, during which he made several inroads, in which many Indians, both men and women, were captured.* There they heard of the south sea. There a considerable quantity of salt was made from the sand which they gathered in a vein of earth like slate and which was made as it was made in Cayas.†

---

*The Portuguese *entrada,* which Robertson rendered as "inroads," would be better rendered in this context as "raid" or "sortie." Elvas's *alguma entrada* also is singular rather than plural.

†The Portuguese *como piçarra,* which Robertson rendered as "slate," might be rendered more accurately in this context as "shale."

XXXII.

HOW THE GOVERNOR WENT FROM AGUACAY TO NAGUATEX AND WHAT HAPPENED TO HIM.

On the day the governor left Aguacay, he went to sleep near a small town subject to the lord of that province. The camp was pitched quite near to a salt marsh, and on that evening some salt was made there.[255] Next day he went to sleep between two ridges in a forest of open trees. Next day he reached a small town called Pato. The fourth day after he left Aguacay, he reached the first settlement of a province called Amaye. An Indian was captured there who said that it was a day and a half journey thence to Naguatex, all of which lay through an inhabited region. Having left the village of Amaye, on Saturday, July 20,[256] camp was made at midday beside a brook in a luxuriant grove between Amaye and Naguatex.[257] Indians were seen there who came to spy on them. Those of horse rushed at them, killing six and capturing two. On being asked by the governor why they had come, they said it was to ascertain what people he had and of what manner they were,[258] and that they had been sent by their lord, the cacique of Naguatex; that the latter, with other caciques, who were in his company and under his protection, had made up their minds to give him battle that day. While this questioning and answering was going on, many Indians came in two bands from two directions. As soon as they saw they had been perceived, uttering loud cries they rushed upon the Christians with great fury, each band in its own part. But on seeing the resistance they met with from the Christians, they turned and fled, and in their flight many of them lost their lives. While most of the horse were going in pursuit of them, quite forgetful of the camp, two other bands of Indians who had been concealed, attacked them. They were also resisted and had their pay as the first had. After the Indians had fled and the Christians had gathered together, they heard a loud cry at the distance of a crossbow flight from where they were. The governor sent twelve horse to see what it was. They found six Christians, two of horse and four of foot, among many Indians, those on horse with great difficulty defending those on foot. These had got lost from those who pursued the first two bands of Indians, and while returning to camp, met those with whom they were fighting. Both they and those who went to their aid killed many of the Indians. They brought one Indian to camp alive, whom the governor asked who those were who had come to do battle with him. He said that they were the cacique of Naguatex and he of Maye and another of a province called Hacanac, lord of vast lands and many vassals; and that he of Naguatex came as captain and head of all. The governor ordered his right arm and his nostrils cut off and sent him to the cacique of Naguatex, ordering him to say that on the morrow he would be in his land to destroy him and that if he wished to forbid him entrance, he should await him. That night he slept there and next day reached the village of Naguatex which was very extensive. He asked where the town of the cacique was and they told him it was on the other side of a river[259] which ran through that district. He marched toward it and on reaching it saw many Indians on the other side waiting for him, so posted as to forbid his passage. Since he did not know whether it [the river] was fordable, nor where it could be crossed, and since several Christians and horses were wounded, in order that they might have time to recover in the town where he was, he made up his mind to rest for a few days. Because of the great heat, he made camp near the village, a quarter of a league from the river, in an open forest of luxuriant and lofty trees near a brook. Several Indians were captured there. He asked them whether the river was fordable. They said it was at times in certain places. Ten days later he sent two captains, each with fifteen horse up and down the river with Indians to show them where they could cross, to see what population lay on the other side of the river. The Indians opposed the crossing of them both as strongly as possible, but they crossed in spite of them. On the other side they saw a large village and many provisions; and returned to camp with this news.

XXXIII.

HOW THE CACIQUE OF NAGUATEX CAME TO VISIT THE GOVERNOR; AND HOW THE GOVERNOR LEFT NAGUATEX AND WENT TO NONDACAO.

From the town of Naguatex, where the governor was, he sent word by an Indian to the cacique to come to serve and obey him and said that he would pardon him for the past; and that if he did not come he would go to look for him and give him the punishment he merited for what he had done against him. Two days later the Indian came and said that the cacique would come next day. The very day before he came he [the cacique] sent many Indians ahead, among whom were some of the principal men. He sent them to see in what mood they found the governor, in order to make up his mind with himself whether to go or not. The Indians reported he was coming and immediately returned. The cacique came two hours later well attended by his men. They all came after this manner, one ahead of the other in double file, leaving a lane in the middle through which the cacique came. They reached the place where the governor was, all weeping after the manner of Tula which lay to the east not very far from that place. The cacique paid his respects fittingly and spoke as follows: "Very exalted, very mighty Lord, to whom the whole world owes service and obedience: I venture to appear before your Lordship after having committed so enormous and vile an act, for which even because it passed through my mind I merit punishment, trusting in your greatness, that although I have not even deserved pardon, but because it is your custom, you will observe clemency toward me, considering how insignificant I am in comparison with your Lordship, so that you will not be mindful of my weaknesses, which, because of my evil, I have come to know for my greater good. I believe that you and your men must be immortal and that your Lordship is lord of the realm of nature, since everything submits to and obeys you, even the hearts of men. For, seeing the death and destruction of my men in the battle, which I fought with your Lordship through my ignorance and the counsel of a brother of mine, who was killed in the action, I immediately repented me in my heart of the mistake I had committed and desired to serve and obey you. I come, therefore so that your Lordship may punish me and order me as your own." The governor answered him saying that he pardoned him for the past, that thenceforth and in the future he should act as he ought and that he would consider him his friend and protect him in all his affairs. Four days later he departed thence, but on reaching the river[260] could not cross, as it had swollen greatly. This appeared a wonderful phenomenon to him because of the season then and because it had not rained for more than a month. The Indians declared that it swelled often in that way without it having rained anywhere in the land. It was conjectured that it might be the sea which came up through the river. It was learned that the increase always came from above, and that the Indians of all that land had no knowledge of the sea. The governor returned to the place where he had been during the preceding days. A week later, hearing that the river could be crossed, he passed to the other side and found a village without any people.[261] He lodged in the open field and sent word to the cacique to come where he was and give him a guide for the forward journey. A few days later, seeing that the cacique did not come or send, he sent two captains, each in a different direction, to burn the towns and capture any Indians they might find. They burned many provisions and captured many Indians. The cacique, on beholding the damage that his land was receiving, sent six[262] of his principal men and three Indians with them as guides who knew the language of the region ahead where the governor was about to go. He immediately left Naguatex and after marching three days reached a town of four or five houses, belonging to the cacique of that miserable province, called Nisohone.[263] It was a poorly populated region and had little maize. Two days later, the guides who were guiding the governor, if they had to go toward the west, guided them toward the east, and sometimes they went through dense forests, wandering off the road. The governor ordered them hanged from a tree, and an Indian woman, who had been captured at Nisohone, guided him, and he went back to look for the road. Two days later, he reached another wretched land called Lacane.[264] There he captured an Indian who said that the land of Nondacao[265] was a very populous region and the houses scattered about one from another as is customary in mountains, and that there was abundance of maize. The cacique and his Indians came weeping like those of Naguatex, that being their custom in token of obedience. He made him [the governor] a gift of a great quantity of fish and offered to do as he should order. He took his leave of him and gave him a guide to the province of Soacatino.[266]

XXXIIII.

HOW THE GOVERNOR WENT FROM NONDACAO TO SOACATINO AND GUASCO, AND CROSSED THROUGH AN UNPEOPLED REGION, WHENCE FOR LACK OF A GUIDE AND INTERPRETER, HE RETURNED TO NILCO.

The governor departed from Nondacao for Soacatino and after he had marched for five days arrived at the province called Aays.[267] The Indians who lived there had not heard of Christians, and as soon as they perceived that they had entered their lands, the country was aroused. As soon as fifty or a hundred had gathered together, they would go out on the road to fight.[268] While some were fighting, others came and attacked them [the Christians] on another side, and when some [of the Christians] pursued [them], the Indians pursued them. The affair lasted the greater part of the day before they [the Christians] reached the village. Some horses and Christians were wounded, but not so badly that it presented any obstacle to their march, for no one had a dangerous wound. Great damage was done the Indians. The day the governor departed thence, the Indian who was guiding him said that he had heard Nondacao[269] say that the Indians of Soacatino had seen other Christians.[270] At this all were very glad, as they thought it might be true and that they might have entered by way of New Spain, and that, if it were so, they would have it in their power to get out of Florida, since they had found nothing of profit, for they feared lest they get lost in some unpeopled region. That Indian led him [the governor] off the road for two days. The governor ordered him to be tortured. He said that the cacique of Nondacao, his lord, had ordered him to lead him in that way, because they were his enemies; and that he had to do so, since his lord so ordered. The governor ordered him thrown to the dogs, and another one guided him to Soacatino,[271] whither he arrived the next day. It was a very poor land and there was great lack of maize there. He asked the Indians whether they knew of other Christians. They said they had heard it said that they were traveling about near there to the southward.[272] He marched for twenty days through a very poorly populated region where they endured great need and suffering; for the little maize the Indians had they hid in the forests and buried it where, after being well tired out with marching, the Christians went about trailing it, at the end of the day's journey looking for what they must eat.* On reaching a province called Guasco,[273] they found maize with which they loaded the horses and the Indians whom they were taking. Thence they went to another village called Naquiscoça. The Indians said they had never heard of other Christians. The governor ordered them put to the torture, and they said that they [the Christians] had reached another domain ahead called Naçacahoz[274] and had returned thence toward the west whence they had come. The governor reached Naçacahoz[275] in two days and some Indian women were captured there. Among them was one who said that she had seen Christians and that she had been in their hands but had escaped. The governor sent a captain and fifteen horse to the place where the Indian woman said she had seen them, in order to ascertain whether there were any

*The Portuguese *rastrejãdo*, which Robertson rendered as "trailing it," might be better rendered in this context as "looking for signs of it."

trace of horses or any token of their having reached there. After having gone three or four leagues, the Indian woman who was guiding them said that all she had said was a lie; and so they considered what the other Indians had said about having seen Christians in the land of Florida. And inasmuch as the land thereabout was very poor in maize, and there was no tidings of any village westward, they returned to Guasco. There the Indians told them that ten days' journey thence toward the west was a river called Daycao[276] where they sometimes went to hunt in the mountains and to kill deer; and that on the other side of it they had seen people, but did not know what village it was. There the Christians took what maize they found and could carry and after marching for ten days through an unpeopled region reached the river of which the Indians had spoken. Ten of horse, whom the governor had sent on ahead, crossed over to the other side, and went along the road leading to the river. They came upon an encampment of Indians who were living in very small huts. As soon as they saw them [the Christians], they took to flight, abandoning their possessions, all of which were wretchedness and poverty. The land was so poor that, among them all, they [the Christians] did not find half an "alqueire"[277] of maize. Those of horse captured two Indians and returned with them to the river where the governor was awaiting them. They continued to question them in order to learn from them the population to the westward, but there was no Indian in the camp who understood their language. The governor ordered the captains and principal persons summoned, in order to plan what he should do after hearing their opinions. Most of them said that in their opinion they should return to the great river of Guachoya, for there was plenty of maize at Anilco and thereabout. They said that during the winter they would make brigantines and the following summer they would descend the river in them to look for the sea, and once having reached the sea, they would coast along it to New Spain which, although it seemed a difficult thing, because of what they had already said, yet it was their last resort because they could not travel by land for lack of an interpreter. They maintained that that land beyond the river of Daycao, where they were, was the land which Cabeza de Vaca said in his relation he had traversed, and was of Indians who wandered about like Arabs[278] without having a settled abode anywhere, subsisting on prickly pears, the roots of plants, and the game they killed. And if that were so, if they entered it and found no food in order to pass the winter, they could not help but perish, for it was already the beginning of October; and if they stayed longer, they could not turn back because of the waters and snows, nor could they feed themselves in such a poor land. The governor, who was desirous now of being in a place where he could sleep out his full sleep, rather than to govern and conquer a land where so many hardships presented themselves to him, at once turned back to the place whence they had come.[279]

XXXV.

HOW THEY RETURNED TO NILCO AND WENT TO MINOYA, WHERE THEY SET ABOUT MAKING SHIPS IN ORDER TO GET OUT OF THE LAND OF FLORIDA.

When the plan determined on was published in the camp, there were many who regretted it keenly, for they considered the journey by sea as doubtful on account of their lack of equipment, and as risky as the journey overland; and they hoped to find a rich land before reaching the land of Christians, because of what Cabeza de Vaca had told the emperor. This was that, while he had found cotton cloth, he had seen gold and silver and precious gems of much value. They had not yet reached the place where he had gone, for he had gone continually along the coast up to that point and they had gone inland. If they traveled toward the west, they would of necessity have to come out whither he had gone. For he said that he had traveled many days in a certain direction and had penetrated inland toward the north. Already at Guasco, they had found some turquoises and cotton blankets which the Indians gave them to understand by signs were brought from the west; and if they took that way, they would reach the land of Christians. But in addition to this they were greatly discontented, and it grieved many of them to turn back, for they would rather have risked death in the land of Florida than to leave it poor. They were unable to prevent what had been determined upon, because the principal men were of the governor's mind. But afterward there was one who said he would willingly put out one of his own eyes if he could put out one of Luis de Moscoso, for it grieved him greatly to see him prosperous; for which he [Moscoso] would have maltreated both him and others, his friends, but he did not dare do it, seeing that two days later he [Moscoso] was to leave the command. From Daycao, where they were, it was one hundred and fifty leagues to the great river—a distance they had marched continually to the westward. On the backward journey, they found maize to eat with great difficulty, for where they had already passed the land was left devastated, and any maize which the Indians had, they had hidden. The towns which they had burned in Naguatex, which was now regretted by them, had now been rebuilt and the houses were full of maize. This region is very well populated and well supplied with food. Pottery is made there of refined clay, which differs but little from that of Estremoz or Montemor.[280] At Chaguete, the Indians, by order of the cacique, came in peace and said that the Christian[281] who had remained there had refused to come. The governor wrote to him and sent him ink and paper so that he could reply. The substance of the words of the letter was to declare to him his determination, namely, to leave the land of Florida, and to remind him that he was a Christian and should not desire to stay in the power of infidels; that he pardoned him the error he had committed in going to the Indians, and that he should come; and if they [the Indians] tried to detain him, he should so inform him [Moscoso] in writing. The Indian went with the letter and came without other reply than on its back his name and rubric so that they might know he was alive. The governor sent twelve men of horse to look for him, but having his spies, he hid himself so that they could not find him. For lack of maize the governor could not stop longer to look for him. He left Chaguete and crossed the river before Aays,[282] and going down it came to a town called Chilano,[283] which they had not seen until then. Reaching Nilco, they found so little maize that it did not suffice for the building of ships. The cause of this was that when the Christians were at Guachoya at seed time, the Indians had not dared sow the lands of Anilco for fear of them; and they knew no other land thereabout where there was any maize. That was the most fertile land thereabout and where they had most hope of finding maize. They were all thrown into confusion; and most of them thought it had been a bad plan to have turned back from Daycao and not to have followed their fortune by going ahead by land in the way they had taken, for it seemed impossible that they could escape by sea unless a miracle were performed for them; for there was neither pilot nor chart, they did not know where the river entered the sea, they had no information concerning the latter; they had nothing with which to make sails nor enough "henequen" (a plant like tow which grew there)[284] and what they found they were keeping to calk the brigantines; nor was there anything with which to pitch them; nor could they build ships strong enough so that they would not be placed in great danger of any untoward happening. They feared greatly the fate that had befallen Narvaez who had perished on that coast; and especially the disadvantage in not finding maize, for without it they could not sustain themselves; nor could they do anything of the things they had to accomplish. All were thrown into great confusion. For their relief they commended themselves to God and besought Him to show them how to save themselves. By His goodness it was pleasing to Him that the Indians of Anilco should come in peace and say that at a distance of two days' journey thence, near the great river were two towns of which the Christians had never heard, called Aminoya,[285] and that the region was fertile. They did not know whether there was any maize there now or not, because there was war between them. But they would be very glad to go to destroy them with the help of the Christians. The governor sent a captain thither with men of horse and foot and the Indians of Anilco with him. He reached Aminoya and found two large towns which were in an open and level region, at a half league's distance apart; and in them he captured many Indians and found a great quantity of maize. He immediately took up his lodging in one of them and sent word to the governor of what he had found, whereat all were very joyful. They left Anilco at the beginning of December. On that journey, as on that before from Chilano, they suffered great hardship, for they had to cross many waters, and often it rained with a north wind and it became very cold; added to which they found themselves in the open fields with water below and above. While on the way, if they found any dry land to rest on at night, they gave many thanks to God. Almost all the Indians of service died from these sufferings, and after they had reached Aminoya, many Christians, and most of them were ill with severe and dangerous diseases which were akin to lethargy.[286] There died André de Vasconcelos and two Portuguese of Elvas, who were of kin to him, who were brothers and called by the nickname of the Sotis.[287] The Christians lodged in one of the towns, the one which appeared to them to be the better. It was surrounded with a stockade and was a quarter of a league from the great river. The maize of the other town was withdrawn thither—in all estimated at six thousand "fanegas."[288] For building ships there was there the best wood they had seen in all the land of Florida. Thereupon, all gave hearty thanks to God for so notable a mercy and took hope of their desire being realized, namely, that they would come into a Christian land.

XXXVI.

HOW SEVEN BRIGANTINES WERE CONSTRUCTED AND HOW THEY DEPARTED FROM AMINOYA.

As soon as they were come to Aminoya, the governor ordered the chains which each one had brought for his Indians to be taken and all the iron shot and all the iron in the camp to be collected together. He ordered a forge set up, nails made, and timber cut for the brigantines. A Portuguese of Ceuta who had been taught to saw with saws while a captive at Fez—and they brought him for that reason—taught others who were aiding him to saw timber; and a man from Genoa whom it was God's will to preserve (for without him they [the Christians] could not have left that land, as there was no other who knew how to build ships), together with four or five other Basque carpenters who hewed the planks and knees [*ceruatões*] for him, built the brigantines. Two calkers, one a Genoese, and the other from Sardinia, calked them with tow from a plant like daffodils[289] (of which I have previously spoken and which is there called "henequen"). But because there was not enough of it, they calked them with flax of the country and blankets which were unraveled for that purpose. A cooper among them fell sick and was at the point of death and there was no other man who could do that work. It pleased God to give him health; and though he was very weak and could not work, two weeks ere they departed, he made for each brigantine two hogsheads called quarter casks by sailors because four of them make a water cask. The Indians of a province located two days' journey up the river, by name Tagoanate,[290] as well as those of Anilco and Guachoya and others roundabout seeing that the brigantines were being built and thinking that since their harvests lay along the water,[291] it was for the purpose of going to look for them;[292] and because the governor asked them for blankets which were needed for use as sails, they came frequently and brought many and an abundance of fish. It surely seems that it was God's will to protect them in so great need, disposing the Indians to bring them; for there would have been no remedy except to go to take them; for, in the town where they were, as soon as winter set in, they became isolated and surrounded by water, so that it was impossible to go more than a league or a league and a half by land; and they could not take their horses to get away from there, and without them there was no place where they could attack them [the Indians] because there were many of them; and opposed on foot, one to the other, on water or land, they [the Indians] had the advantage, because they were more cunning and agile; and because of the lay of the land which suited their wishes in the manner of their warfare. They also brought some ropes and what was lacking for the cables were made from the bark of mulberry trees. They made stirrups out of wood and made anchors out of the [iron] stirrups. In the month of March, although it had not rained in that land for over a month, the river rose in such manner that it stretched clear to Nilco, nine leagues away; and the Indians said that it spread over another nine leagues of land on the other side. In the town where they [the Christians] were—which was higher land where one could go about better—the water rose to the stirrups. Wood was piled up in heaps, and many branches laid on top, and there they fastened the horses; and in the houses they did likewise. Finding that nothing was sufficient, they climbed up above.* And if they left the house they used canoes or went horseback in places where the land was higher. Thus they lived for two months, during which the river did not fall and during which no work was done. The Indians did not cease to come to the brigantines, for they came and went in canoes. The governor feared lest they attack him during that time, and ordered one of those who came to the town to be seized secretly and kept until the others should be gone. One was seized and the governor ordered him tortured in order to get him to tell whether the Indians were preparing any act of treachery. He stated that the caciques of Anilco, Guachoya, Taguanate, and others—in all about twenty caciques—had planned to attack him [the governor] with a great number of men, and that three days before doing so they were to send a gift of fish in order to conceal their great treason and ill will; and on the very day [of the attack] they were to send some Indians on ahead with another gift. These latter, with those who served [the Christians] and who had conspired with them, were to set fire to the houses, but were first to possess themselves of the lances which were leaning against the doors of the houses. The caciques, with all their men, were to be placed in ambush in the woods near the town, and when they saw the fire lit, they were to hasten and rout the horsemen. The governor ordered the Indians to be chained; and on the day of which he [the tortured Indian] spoke, thirty Indians came with fish. He [the governor] ordered their right hands cut off, and in that condition sent them to the cacique of Guachoya to whom they belonged. He ordered them to tell him

*The Portuguese *aos sorberados,* which Robertson rendered as "above," might be rendered more clearly as "to the upper story." A *soberado* or *sobrado* in modern Portuguese is a house of more than one story.

that he and the others could come whenever they wished, for he desired nothing better; but that he should know that they could think of nothing which he did not know before they thought of it. Thereupon, they were all greatly terrified. The caciques of Anilco and Taguanate came to excuse themselves; and a few days later the cacique of Guachoya came, accompanied by one of his principal Indians and vassals. He said that by trustworthy information which he had, the caciques of Anilco and Taguanete had made an agreement to come to make war on the Christians. As soon as Indians came from Anilco, the governor questioned them and they confessed that this was true. He immediately handed them over to the principal man of Guachoya who led them outside the town and killed them. On the morrow others came from Taguanete and they also confessed. The governor ordered their right hands and nostrils cut off and sent them to the cacique. Thereupon, those of Guachoya were very happy and came frequently bearing gifts of blankets, fish, and hogs which had been bred from some sows which had got lost there the year before. As soon as the waters fell, they agreed with the governor that he should send men to Taguanate. They came with canoes in which men of foot went down the river and a captain with men of horse and the Indians of Guachoya who guided him went overland until reaching Taguanete.[293] They assaulted the town, capturing Indian men and women and blankets, which with those they had, were sufficient for their needs. The building of the brigantines[294] having been completed in the month of June, although the Indians had declared that the river rose only once during the year, namely, when the snows melted—at the time I have already mentioned it as having risen—it now being summer and a long time having passed since it had rained, it was God's will that the water rising came up to the town until it reached the brigantines, whence they were taken by water to the river; for had they been taken over by land, there would have been danger of their breaking and their bottoms opening up and being altogether disjointed, because for lack of iron the spikes were short and the planks and timbers thin. During their stay there, the Indians of Aminoya, forced by necessity, came to serve them, so that they might give them some of the ears of maize they had taken from them. And since the land was fertile and they were accustomed to eat maize, and they [the Christians] had taken from them [the Indians] all they had, and the people were many in number, they could not sustain themselves. Those who came to the town were so weak and enfeebled that they had no flesh on their bones; and many near the town died of pure hunger and weakness. The governor ordered, under grievous penalties, that no maize should be given them. However, seeing that they had no lack of hogs and that they were submitting themselves to serve them; and seeing their wretchedness and pitiful condition; having shared with them their maize out of pity for them; when they came to the time of embarking, there was not as much as was necessary. What there was they loaded into the brigantines and into large canoes[295] fastened together in pairs. They put twenty-two[296] horses aboard—the best ones in camp—and the rest were made into salt meat; and they did the same with the hogs they had. They left Aminoya on the second day of July, 1543.

XXXVII.

HOW THE INDIANS OF QUIGALTAM ATTACKED THE CHRISTIANS ON THE RIVER WHILE GOING ON THEIR VOYAGE AND OF WHAT HAPPENED.

One day before they left Aminoya, they made up their minds to dismiss the Indians of service whom they had—both men and women—with the exception of some hundred or so whom the governor embarked or let those whom he wished embark. And because there were many persons of quality to whom he could not refuse what he granted to others, he made use of a trick, saying that while they were on the river they [the Indians] might serve them, but that as soon as they reached the sea, they would have to abandon them because of the need of water, there being but few casks. To his friends he said in secret that they should take them [their Indians], that they could take them to New Spain; and all those for whom he did not have good countenance—who were in the majority—ignorant of what was concealed from them (which time later made known), thought it inhuman for so short a time of service, in payment of the great service they had performed, to take them away in order to abandon them outside their lands to become captives of others. They abandoned five hundred head of Indians, male and female, among whom were many boys and girls who spoke and understood Spanish. Most of them were overcome with weeping, which was a great pity seeing that they had all readily become Christians and were now lost. Three hundred and twenty-two Spaniards left Aminoya in seven brigantines, of good construction except that the planks were thin because of the shortness of the spikes and they were not pitched. They had no decks by which to keep the water from coming in. In place of decks, they laid planks so that the sailors could go above to fasten the sails and the men might be sheltered below and above. The governor appointed captains of them and gave each one his brigantine, taking from each one his oath and word that he would be obedient to him until reaching the land of the Christians. The governor took one of the brigantines for himself—the one he considered best. The day they left Aminoya, they passed Guachoya where the Indians were awaiting them in canoes on the river. They [the Indians] had built a large arbor on land and besought them to disembark. But he [the governor] excused himself and passed by at a distance. The Indians accompanied him in their canoes. Coming to where an arm of the river led off to the right,[297] they said the province of Quigualtam lay nearby. They importuned the governor to go to make war on them, and said that they would aid him. But since they had said that it [Quigaltam][298] lay three days' journey below, it seemed to the governor that they had planned some treachery against him. There he took his leave of them and proceeded on his voyage where the force of the water was greater. The current was very powerful and, aided by their oars, they journeyed at a good rate. The first day they landed in a wood on the left side of the river and at night they collected in the brigantines. Next day they came to a town where they landed, but the people there did not dare await them. An Indian woman whom they captured there, on being questioned, said that that town belonged to a cacique called Huhasene, a vassal of Quigaltam, and that Quigaltam was awaiting them with many men. Men of horse went down the river and found some houses in which was considerable maize. They immediately went there and stopped for a day, during which they threshed out and gathered what maize they needed. While they were there many Indians came down the river in canoes and placed themselves somewhat carelessly in form of battle in front on the other side. The governor sent in two canoes what crossbowmen he had and what men could get into them. They [the Indians] took to flight, but seeing that the Spaniards could not overtake them, gaining courage they turned back and coming nearer and shouting menaced them. As soon as they left there, they [the Indians] followed after them, some in canoes and others on land along the river. Going ahead of them, when they reached a town near the bluff,[299] they all united, as if to show that they were a mind to wait there. Each brigantine had a canoe fastened astern for its use. Men immediately entered them all and put the Indians to flight. He [the governor] burned the town. Then on that day they landed at a large open field where the Indians did not dare await them. Next day, they [the Indians] got together one hundred canoes, some of which held sixty or seventy Indians, and those of the principal men with their awnings, and they [the principal Indians] with white and colored plumes of feathers as a device. They came within two crossbow flights of the brigantines, and sent three Indians in one small canoe with a false message so that they might see the nature of the brigantines and the weapons they had. On coming up to the governor's brigantine, one of the Indians went in and told the governor that the cacique of Quigaltam, his lord, sent him to implore his protection, and to inform him that whatever the Indians of Guachoya had told him was false, namely, that they had revolted because they were his enemies; that he was his servitor and considered himself as such. The governor answered him saying that he believed all he said to be true and that he appreciated his friendship highly. Thereupon, they went to the place where the others were awaiting them in their canoes; and from that place, they [the Indians] all came down and came upon the Spaniards yelling and threatening them. The governor sent Juan de Guzmán, who had been captain of foot in Florida, in the canoes with twenty-five[300] armed men to get them [the Indians] out of the way. As soon as the Indians saw them coming, they divided into two bands and remained still until the Spaniards reached them, when putting out from each side, they came together, taking between them Juan de Guzmán and those who came ahead with him, and closed with them with great fury. Since their canoes were larger and since many of them jumped into the water in order to keep them upright, and others to seize the canoes of the Spaniards and cause them to overturn, they immediately overturned them. The Christians fell into the water and because of the weight of their armor sank to the bottom. And if any, by swimming or laying hold of a canoe, were able to keep afloat, they [the Indians] struck them over the head with their paddles and the clubs they were carrying and made them sink. When the men in the brigantines beheld their defeat, although they desired to aid them, they were unable to turn back because of the current of the river. Four Spaniards escaped to that brigantine which was nearest the canoes; and these only of all who had gone to the Indians escaped. Eleven men were killed there, among them being Juan de Guzmán and a son of Don Carlos called Juan de Vargas. Most, also, were persons of honor and men of much bearing. Those who escaped by swimming said they saw the Indians enter one of their canoes by the stern with Juan de Guzmán, but whether they bore him away dead or alive, they could not determine.[301]

XXXVIII.

WHICH RELATES HOW THEY WERE PURSUED BY THE INDIANS.

The Indians, on seeing that they had gained the victory, were so greatly encouraged that they went out to engage the brigantines which they had not dared to do before. First they went to that in which Calderón was captain. It was going in the rear guard. At the first flight of arrows twenty-five men were wounded. In the brigantine were only four men with armor. These were stationed at the side in order to defend it. Those who had no armor, seeing that they were being wounded, abandoned the oars and hid away below the covering. The brigantine began to run crosswise and to go whither the current of the water might bear it. On seeing this one of the men in armor, without awaiting the captain's approval for his action, forced a foot soldier to take the oar and steer the brigantine, placing himself before him and covering him with his shield. The Indians did not come up nearer than an arrow's flight, where they took the offensive without being attacked and without receiving any injury, for there was not above one crossbow in each brigantine, and those that there were, were now in very bad condition; so that the Christians did nothing else except to stand as a mark waiting for their arrows. Having left that brigantine they [the Indians] went to another and fought against it for half an hour. And in this way they circulated from one to another of them all. The Christians had brought mats to put under themselves which were doubled and very close and strong so that the arrows did not pierce them. As soon as the Indians gave them time, the brigantines were hung with them. The Indians seeing that they could not shoot direct, shot their arrows haphazardly into the air which fell down into the brigantines and wounded some of the men. Not satisfied with this, they tried to get at those who were coming in the canoes with the horses. Those of the brigantines came about in order to protect them and convoyed them in their midst. And now, finding themselves so closely pursued by them and so tired out that they could not endure it, they resolved to travel all that night following, thinking that they would pass by the land of Quigualtam and that they [the Indians] would leave them. But when they were going along more freely,* thinking that they [the Indians] had already left them, they heard

*The Portuguese that Robertson rendered as "more freely" is *mais descuydados*. Rendered more literally it should be "more unpreoccupied" or "more unworried."

very loud cries hard by, which stunned them. In this manner, they followed us that night and the next day, until noon, when we had now reached the land of others whom they advised to treat us in the same way; and so they did. Those of Quigualtam returned to their own lands, and the others in fifty canoes continued to fight us for a whole day and night. They boarded one of the brigantines which was coming as a rear guard by means of the canoe which it bore astern, and they took away an Indian woman whom they found in it. And from there they wounded some of those in the brigantine. Those who came in the canoes with horses, wearied out with paddling night and day, sometimes allowed themselves to rest.[302] Then the Indians were on them at once, and the men in the brigantines would wait for them. The governor made up his mind to land and kill the horses, because of the slowness with which they sailed on account of them. As soon as they saw a place suitable for this, they went thither and killed the horses there, and loaded the meat into the brigantines after salting it. They left four or five of the horses alive on the shore and the Indians went up to them after the Spaniards had embarked. The horses were unused to them and began to neigh and to run about in various directions, whereat the Indians jumped into the water for fear of them. Entering their canoes behind the brigantines, they continued to shoot at them without any pity and followed us that afternoon and the night following until ten o'clock next morning, and then went back up stream. Soon seven canoes came out from a small town located near the river and followed them for a short distance down the river shooting at them. But seeing that because of their small number they were doing them [the Christians] little injury, they went back to their town. After that they had no trouble, until they came almost to the sea.[303] They went for seventeen[304] days along the river, a distance of about two hundred and fifty leagues or so.[305] Near the sea, it [the river] divided into two branches each of which was about a league and a half wide.

XXXIX.

HOW THEY REACHED THE SEA; AND WHAT HAPPENED TO THEM BEFORE AND AFTER THEY STARTED THEIR VOYAGE.

A half league before they came to the sea, they anchored there for a day to rest, for they were very tired from rowing and greatly disheartened because of the many days during which they had eaten nothing but parched and boiled maize, which was doled out in a ration of a leveled-off helmet to each mess of three. While they were there, seven canoes of Indians came to attack those in the canoes they [the Christians] brought. The governor ordered armed men to enter [the canoes] and go out against them [the Indians] and put them to flight. They [the Indians] also came to attack them by land through a thicket and a swamp. They had clubs set with very sharp fish bones, and with these they fought courageously with those of us who sallied out to oppose them. The others who came in their canoes were awaiting with their arrows those who went out to them; and as soon as we came up, both those on land and those in canoes wounded some of us. When they saw that they [the Christians] were approaching, they would turn about face, and like swift horses before foot soldiers, would make off, and after turning hither and thither, and again gathering together without ever getting farther away than an arrow's flight, for thus gathering they would come on shooting without receiving any injury from the Christians. For, although they [the Christians] had some bows, they did not know how to shoot with them and came on rowing, breaking their arms to come up [to the Indians]. The Indians kept circling tirelessly around them in their canoes, waiting and turning about as if in a skirmish. Those [Christians] who went after them [the Indians] seeing that they could do them no harm; and that the closer they [the Christians] obstinately tried to approach them [the Indians], the more injury they received; as soon as they managed to drive them off, they returned to the brigantines. They stayed there two days. From thence they went to the place where that branch of the river flowed into the sea.[306] They took soundings in the river near the sea and found a depth of forty fathoms. They stopped there and the governor ordered all and every one of them to state his opinion regarding their voyage—whether, committing themselves to the sea, they should cross direct to New Spain, or whether they should go coasting along. There were various opinions about this. In this matter, Juan de Añasco, who had great self-conceit and set high value on his understanding of navigation and sea matters, but who really had small experience in its practice, influenced the governor. His opinion accorded with that of some others who said that it was much better to take to the open sea and cross the gulf—a voyage one-fourth as long—for if they coasted along, they would make many windings, because of the bends in the land: Juan de Añasco saying that he had seen the sailing chart and that where they were, the coast ran east and west to the river Las Palmas,[307] and from the river Las Palmas to New Spain, it ran north and south, and for that reason, if they went continuously within sight of land, they would make a great circuit and their course would be very slow. They would also run great danger of winter overtaking them ere they could reach a Christian land. They could arrive within ten or twelve days by crossing if they had good weather. The majority opposed this opinion and said it would be safer to coast along even if it did take longer, for their ships had little strength, had no decks, and a slight storm would be enough to wreck them, and if calm or contrary weather should come upon them because of the small space they had for water, they would also run great risk. Even were the ships such that they could venture in them, since they had no pilot or sailing chart by which to steer, to cross over was not a good counsel. This opinion of the majority was confirmed, and they agreed to coast along. When they were about to depart, the cable by which the anchor of the governor's brigantine was cast, broke, and the anchor was lost in the river; and although they were near land, so great was the depth of water that however much swimmers looked for it, it could not be found. This was the cause of great distress to the governor and to all in his brigantine. With a stone for grinding maize which they had brought along, and the bridles still remaining to some of those hidalgos and gentlemen who had horses, they made a weight which passed by way of remedy for an anchor. On July 18, they put out to sea and undertook their voyage amid calm and fair weather. The governor, accompanied by Juan de Añasco, put out to sea in their brigantines, and all followed them.[308] On seeing that they had got two or three leagues offshore, the captains of the other brigantines overtook them and asked the governor why he was holding offshore, [and said] that if he intended to leave the coast, he ought to say so, but that he should not do so without getting the opinion of all, and that if he tried to act in any other manner, they would not follow him, but each one would do what seemed best to him. The governor answered saying that he would do nothing without their advice, but that he desired to leave the land in order to be able to sail better and safer by night, and that next day when it was time he would return within sight of land. They sailed that day with a fine wind, the night following and the next day until vespers always in fresh water, at which they were greatly surprised, for they were very far offshore. But so great is the force of the current of the river, and the coast there so shallow and gentle that fresh water runs out very far into the sea.[309] That night, they saw some keys[310] on the right, whither they went. They rested there that night. There Juan de Añasco, by means of his arguments, finished by getting all to consent and consider it proper to take to the open sea, saying, as he had said already, that it would be a great advantage and would shorten their voyage greatly. They sailed for two days and when they tried to return within sight of land, they could not, because the wind was blowing offshore. On the fourth day, seeing that the water was giving out, and fearing want and danger, they all cursed Juan de Añasco and the governor who had taken his advice. Each one of the captains declared that he would never again get away from the land, although the governor could go wherever he wished. It was God's will that the wind should shift, although only a bit, and four days after having taken to the open sea, and now in need of water, they came within sight of land by dint of rowing and, after great labor, reached it along an unsheltered beach. That afternoon, the wind veered to the south, which is a cross wind along that coast and drove the brigantines ashore, for it was a very stiff wind; and the anchors straightened out because they had little iron and went dragging. The governor ordered them all into the water, and by placing themselves on the land side and by forcing the brigantines seaward when the wave passed by, they kept them up until the wind softened.

XL.

HOW SOME [OF THE BRIGANTINES] GOT LOST FROM OTHERS BECAUSE OF THE STORM AND AFTERWARD CAME TOGETHER ON A KEY.[311]

After the storm had ceased, they landed on the beach where they were and by means of some hoes they had brought along they dug some holes which filled with fresh water with which they filled their water casks. Next day they left that place and sailed for two days; and entered a small creek like an estuary sheltered from a south wind which was then blowing and which was contrary to them. Four days passed before they could leave there; and as soon as the sea became quiet, they went out by rowing. They went along that day and about eventide the wind strengthened so that it drove them ashore and they regretted having left there, for as soon as night fell the storm began to rage on sea and the wind to strengthen more and more because of the storm. The brigantines got lost one from the other. The two farthest out to sea went two leagues beyond the place where the others were that night and entered an arm of the sea which ran up into the land. The five which were behind separated one from the other by a distance of a league or a half league found themselves without knowing anything of one another on a very unsheltered beach where the wind and wave drove them ashore, for the anchors straightened out and went dragging and the oars could not keep them [the brigantines] upright, although seven or eight men laid hold of one oar and rowed seaward. All the other men leaped into the water and as the wave which was driving the brigantine ashore passed by, they pushed it seaward with as much force as possible. Before another wave came, other men bailed out with bowls the water they had shipped. While suffering this hazard of fortune,[312] in great fear of being lost there, from midnight on they had to endure an insufferable torment from myriads of mosquitoes which came upon them and which caused an irritation whenever they stung as if they were poisonous. In the morning the sea calmed and the wind softened, but not the mosquitoes; and although the sails were white, in the morning, they appeared black with them. The men who were at the oars, could not row unless other men drove them [the mosquitoes] away. The terror and danger of the storm having subsided, upon beholding the disfigurement of their faces and slaps which they had given one another to drive them [the mosquitoes] away, they laughed. They [the brigantines] came together in the estuary where were the two brigantines which had gone on ahead. There a scum was found called "copee"[313] which the sea cast up and which resembles pitch (with which they pitch their ships in certain regions where pitch is lacking). There they pitched their brigantines. They stayed [there] two days and then resumed their voyage. They sailed another two days and anchored at a bay or arm of the sea where they stayed two days. The day they left, six men went up the bay in a canoe but did not come to its head. They left there with a south wind which was against them, but since it was light and their desire to shorten their voyage great, they went out by rowing into the sea, and journeyed for two days in that way and with great toil, a very little distance, and entered behind an islet[314] by means of a branch of the sea which surrounded it [the islet]. While they were there, such weather ensued that they gave fervent thanks to God that they had reached such a shelter. There was an abundance of fish there which they caught with nets and a hook. A man threw out a hook with a line, tying the end of it about his arm. A fish seized it and drew him into the water until he was up to his neck. It was God's will that he remembered his knife which he drew out and cut the line therewith. They stayed there fourteen days, at the end of which God was pleased to send them good weather. Because of that, they very devoutly arranged a procession and walked along the beach praying God to take them to a land where they might serve Him better.[315]

XL [I.E., XLI].

HOW THEY CAME TO THE RIVER OF PANICO.

All along the seacoast wherever they dug, they found water. There they filled their casks and after the procession was ended, they embarked, and always keeping within sight of land, sailed for six days. Juan de Añasco said that they would do well to put out to sea, for he had seen the sailing chart and remembered that the coast ran north and south from the river of Palmas[316] on, and that so far it had run east and west. According to his opinion, judging by his reckonings, the river of Palmas ought not to be far from where they were. That night they put out to sea and in the morning, over the rim of the water, beheld palm trees and the coast running north and south; and from noon on great mountains which they had not seen thitherto; for from that point to the port of Espiritu Santo where they had entered Florida, it was a very level and low land, and for that reason it could not be seen except when they were very close to it. From what they saw, they believed that that night they had passed the river of Palmas, which is sixty leagues from that of Panico,[317] which is in New Spain. All gathered together. Some said that they would do well not to sail by night in order not to pass the river of Panico; and others, that it was not advisable to lose time during favoring weather, and that it could not be so near that they would pass it that night. They agreed to set the sails half reefed and sail in that way. Two brigantines which sailed that night with all sails set passed the river of Panico at dawn without seeing it. The first to arrive of the five which were behind was that of which Calderón was captain. For a quarter of a league before they reached it, and before they saw it, they saw the water was muddy and perceived that it was fresh. Coming opposite the river, they saw that water was breaking over a shoal where it flowed into the sea. Because there was no one there who knew it, they were in doubt as to whether they should enter or pass by at a distance. They made up their minds to enter, and they put in to land before reaching the current, and entered the port. As soon as they were inside, they saw Indians, both men and women, on the shore, clad according to the Spanish custom, whom they asked in what land they were. They replied in the Spanish language that that was the river of Panico and that the town of the Christians was fifteen leagues inland. The joy received by all at this news could not be wholly told. For it seemed to them that then they had received birth. Many leaped ashore and kissed the ground and kneeling down with hands and eyes raised to heaven, one and all ceased not to give thanks to God. As soon as those who were coming behind saw Calderón with his brigantine anchored in the river, they immediately set out thither and entered the port. The two other brigantines which had passed beyond, put out to sea in order to turn back to look for the others, but they could not because the wind was against them and the sea was choppy. Fearing lest they be lost, they ran toward the land and anchored. While there, a storm came up, and seeing that they could not hold themselves there, nor less in the sea, they determined to run up on the land. And as the brigantines were small, they drew but little water, and as there was a sandy beach there, the force of their sails drove them to dry land without harm coming to the men in them. At that time, if those in the port were very joyful, these [on the beach] felt a double sadness in their hearts, for they knew nothing of the others, nor in what land they were, and feared lest it be one of hostile Indians. They came out two leagues below the port, and as soon as they found themselves free of the sea, each one took as much of his clothing as he could carry on his back. They went inland and found Indians who told them where they were, whereat their sorrow was turned into joy.* They gave many thanks to God for having delivered them from so many dangers.

XLII.

HOW THEY REACHED PANICO AND HOW THEY WERE RECEIVED BY THE INHABITANTS.

From the time they went out from the great river of Florida into the sea until they reached the river of Panico, they took fifty-two days. They entered Panico on the tenth of September of the year 1543. They went upstream with their brigantines for four days; and as the wind was light and frequently useless to them because of the many windings of the river; and in towing them up because of the powerful current in many places they could for this reason make but little headway, and with heavy toil;† and seeing that the

*In the Portuguese, the clause that Robertson translated as "where they were" is followed by the words *i os agasalharã,* which means "and welcomed them." Robertson has deleted this phrase in his translation.

†The Portuguese that Robertson translated as "and in towing them up" is *leuãdo os a strga.* There is no such word in Portuguese as "strga." It obviously has been misspelled or lost one or more of its vowels. It could be a misspelling for *atrasar* (to hold back or delay) or for *atrair* (to pull back or attract). There is no word meaning "towing" that remotely resembles "strga."

accomplishment of their desire—namely, to see themselves among Christians and to see the divine offices celebrated which they had not seen for so long—was delayed: they left the brigantines to the sailors and went overland to Panico. All were clad in deerskins, tanned and dyed black—namely cassocks, breeches, and shoes.‡ Upon entering Panico, they went immediately to the church to pray and give thanks to God for having so miraculously saved them. The inhabitants, whom the Indians had already advised and who knew of their coming, took them to their homes and entertained them—some among them whom they knew and with whom they had had contact, or because they had come from their districts. The alcalde mayor took the governor to his home, and all the others, as soon as they arrived, he sent to lodgings in groups of six and ten, according to the capacity of each of the inhabitants; and all were supplied by their hosts with many hens, maize bread, and fruits of the land, which are identical with those of Cuba, of which I have spoken above. The town of Panico[318] has about seventy householders. Most of them have houses of cut stone; some are of wood [*rama*], and all are thatched with hay.* The land is poor and there is no gold or silver in it. People there are very well supplied with food and service. The richest do not have an income of five hundred cruzados at the outside, which they get in cotton clothing, fowls, and maize, paid to them as tribute by the Indians, their vassals. Of those who left Florida, three hundred and eleven Christians entered that port. The alcalde mayor immediately sent one of the citizens by post to inform the viceroy, Don Antonio de Mendoza[319] (who was living in Mexico) that of the men who had gone with Hernando de Soto to conquer and explore Florida, there had ported there three hundred men,[320] for whom he had determined to provide since they came in the service of his Majesty. At this, the viceroy and all those of Mexico were surprised, for they considered them lost because they had plunged into the land of Florida, and they had had no news of them for a long time. It seemed to them a marvel that they could sustain themselves for so long a time among heathen being without a fortress where they might build strongholds and without any other relief. The viceroy immediately issued an order in which

‡The Portuguese *sayos,* which Robertson rendered as "cassocks," would be better rendered as "military greatcoat." *Saio,* the modern form of *sayo,* is not used for "cassock" except in the feminine form of *saia,* meaning "skirt." When it is so used, it is used in a derogatory sense intended as an insult to the cleric or clerics to whom it is addressed.

*Robertson's translation of the Portuguese *algumas de rama,* as "some are of wood" could be misleading. *Rama* is branches or foliage. The structures made of *rama* are something more primitive than a wooden house, more of an arbor-type structure or one with wattle walls.

he decreed that, wherever they should be ordered, the necessary food and Indian porters should be given them; and wherever any refused to make provision, they could take by force what they needed without incurring any penalty. That order was so well obeyed that on the way before they reached the towns the people went out to meet them with fowls and food.

XLIII.

OF THE FAVOR THEY FOUND WITH THE VICEROY AND INHABITANTS OF MEXICO.

From Panico to the great city of Mestitam[321] Mexico is a distance of sixty leagues. There are another sixty leagues, both from Panico and from Mexico to the port of Vera Cruz[322] where one embarks for Spain and where those on their way to New Spain land. Those three towns, which were settled by Spaniards, form a triangle, to wit, with Vera Cruz at the south, Panico at the east,[323] and Mexico at the west, with a distance of sixty leagues one from the other. The land is so thickly populated with Indians that from town to town those which are farthest apart are separated only by a league or half a league. Some of those who came from Florida remained in Panico for a month resting and others for a fortnight—each as long as he wished, for no one showed a long face toward his guests, but gave them everything they had, and showed they were sorry when they bade them goodbye. This can be believed, for the food which the Indians gave as tribute was more than enough for them, and there was nothing to buy or sell in that town. Few Spaniards were there and rejoiced to talk with them. The alcalde mayor divided among all who wished to go to get it all the clothing there belonging to the emperor (which is paid there [by the Indians] as taxes). Those who still had coats of mail rejoiced, for each one found a horse there [in exchange] for it. Some got mounts, and those who could not (the majority of them) set out on their journey afoot. On their way they were well received by the Indians who abode in their towns, and better served than they could have been in their own homes, even though they lived decently as to food.[324] For, if they asked an Indian for a hen, he would bring four; and if they asked for some fruit, they would go off running for it, even if it were a league away. And if any Christian were ill, they would carry him from one town to the next in a chair. To whatever town they came, the cacique, through the agency of an

Indian who carried a rod of justice in his hand (whom they call "tapile,"[325] signifying magistrate [*Merinho*]),* ordered them to be supplied with provisions and Indians as bearers of any clothing they had and for carrying those who were ill, as many as were needed. The viceroy sent a Portuguese to a distance of twenty leagues from Mexico with a quantity of sugar, raisins, pomegranates, and other things given to sick people, for those who might have need of them. He had determined to clothe them all at the emperor's cost. And the inhabitants of Mexico, having heard that they were coming, went out to meet them; and with great courtesy requesting it as a favor, each one took to his home those whom he could and gave them clothing—each the best he could—so that he who was least well clad had clothing worth thirty cruzados and upward. To all who cared to go to the lodging of the viceroy, the latter ordered clothing to be given, and those who were persons of quality ate at his table. For men of lesser sort, he had a table in his house for all who cared to eat at it. He was immediately informed who each one was, in order to show him the honor he merited. Some of the conquistadors placed them all, both gentlemen and peasants, at the same table with themselves and frequently made the servant sit shoulder to shoulder beside his master. This was mainly done by artisans and men of low sort. However, those of better breeding, asked who each one was and differentiated among persons. But all did what they could with great goodwill, each telling those he had in his house not to be vexed or hesitate to take what was given them, for they had formerly beheld themselves in like circumstances and others had helped them and that such was the custom in that land. May God reward them; and those whom He was pleased to let escape from Florida and come to the land of Christians, may it please Him that this be for His service; and to those who died there and all those who believe in Him and confess His holy faith, may He grant them through His mercy the glory of paradise. Amen.

*Robertson's "(whom they call 'tapile,' signifying magistrate)" is not enclosed in parentheses in the Portuguese text.

XLIIII.

WHICH DECLARES CERTAIN DIVERSITIES AND PECULIARITIES OF THE LAND OF FLORIDA; AND THE PRODUCTS AND BIRDS AND ANIMALS OF THAT LAND.

From the port of Espiritu Santo, where they landed when they entered Florida, to the province of Ocute, a distance of about four hundred leagues or so, the land is very level and has many lakes and thick woods. In places there are wild pine groves and the soil is lean, and without a mountain or hill in it.* The land of Ocute is the most fertile and vigorous and has the most open forest and very excellent fields along the rivers.† From Ocute to Cutifachiqui is a distance of about one hundred and thirty leagues, eighty of which are without inhabitants and covered with many wild pine groves. Large rivers flow through the uninhabited part. From Cutifachiqui to Xuala is a distance of about two hundred and fifty leagues, all the land being mountainous. Cutifachiqui and Xuala are located on level ground, high, and with excellent river meadows.[326] Thence, as far as Chiaha, Coça, and Talise, the land is level, dry and fertile, and greatly abounding in maize. From Xuala to Tascaluça is a distance of about two hundred and fifty leagues. From Tascaluça to the great river it is about three hundred leagues, the land being low and having many swamps.[327] From the great river onward, the land is higher and open and the most densely populated of all the land of Florida. And along this river, from Aquixo to Pacaha and Coligoa, a distance of one hundred and fifty leagues, the land is level and covered with open forest, and in places has very fertile and pleasant fields. From Coligoa to Autiamque is a distance of about two hundred and fifty leagues of mountainous country. From Autiamque to Guacay is a distance of about two hundred and thirty leagues of level land. From Aguacay to Daycao, a distance of one hundred and twenty leagues, is all a mountainous country. From the port of Espiritu Santo to Apalache, they marched from east to west and northeast;[328] from Cutifachiqui to Xuala, from south to north; from

*In talking about soil, the Portuguese *delgado,* which Robertson rendered as "lean," would be better rendered as "thin."

†The Portuguese *ten o arvoredo mais ralo,* which Robertson translated as "has the most open forest," would catch the nuance of the Portuguese better if rendered as "has the forest more open."

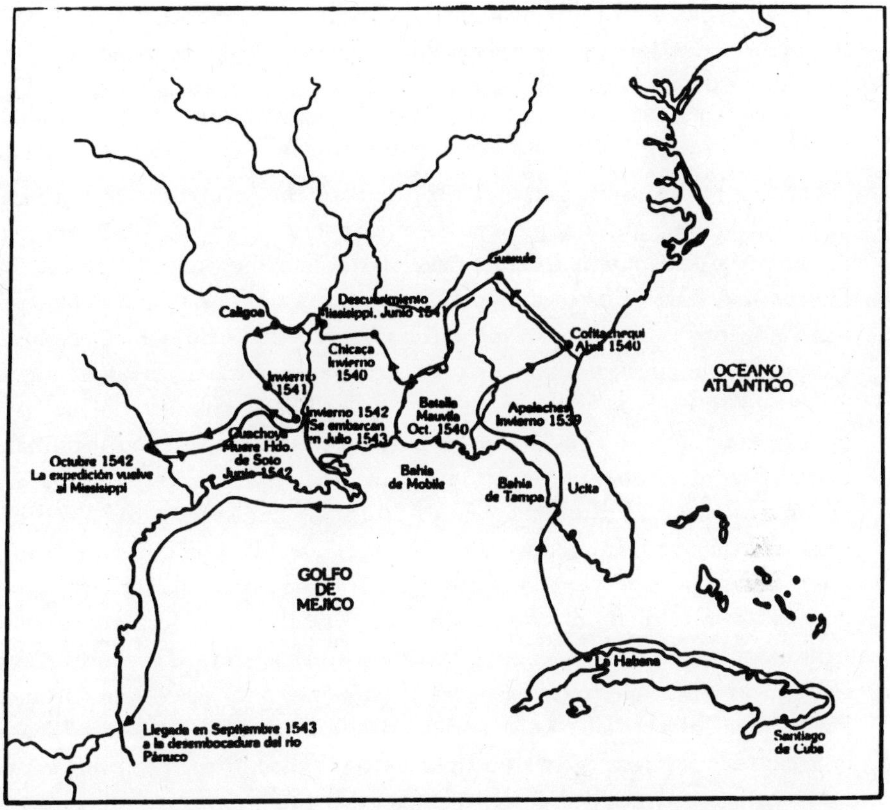

De Soto's Route in North America. This modern map, first published in Spain by Rocío Sánchez Rubio, follows the expedition from the landing of the fleet in Santiago Harbor in Cuba, to the arrival of the survivors four years later at the Panuco River in Mexico. The southeastern United States portion of this version of the route closely follows the findings of the 1935 United States De Soto Expedition Commission. (Courtesy of Rocío Sánchez Rubio)

Xuala to Coça, from east to west, from Coça to Tascaluça, and to the great river as far as the provinces of Quizquiz and Aquixo, from east to west; from Aquixo to Pacaha, northward; from Pacaha to Tula, from east to west; and from Tula to Autiamque, from north to south, as far as the province of Guachoya and Daycao.[329] The bread which is eaten in all the land of Florida is of maize which resembles coarse millet. This maize is found in all the islands and Indies of Castile from the Antilles on. In Florida, there are also many walnuts, plums, mulberries, and grapes. They sow and harvest the maize, each one cultivating his own. The fruits are common to all, for they grow very abundantly in the open fields, without it being necessary to plant or cultivate them. Wherever there are mountains, there are chestnuts. They are somewhat smaller than those of Spain. From the great river westward, the walnuts differ from the others,[330] for they are easier to crush and shaped like acorns.[331] From the great river to the port, they are, for the most part, hard and the trees and walnuts seem similar to those of Spain. In all parts of the country is a fruit which comes from a plant like "ligoacam,"[332] which the Indians sow. The fruit resembles the royal pear, and has an excellent smell and a delicious taste. Another plant grows in the open field, which produces a fruit near the ground like the strawberry, which is very tasty. The plums are of two kinds, red and gray, of the form and size of walnuts.[333] They have three or four stones. They are better than all those of Spain and they make much better dried ones of them. Only in the grapes can one perceive the lack of cultivation, which although they are large have large seeds.* All the other fruits are very perfect and less harmful than those of Spain. In Florida, are many bears and lions, wolves, deer, jackals, cats, and rabbits. There are many wild fowl there, as large as peafowls, small partridges like those of Africa, cranes, ducks, turtledoves, thrushes, and sparrows. There are certain black birds[334] which are larger than sparrows and smaller than starlings. There are goshawks, falcons, sparrowhawks, and all the birds of prey found in Spain. The Indians are well proportioned. Those of the flat lands are of taller stature and better built than those of the mountains. Those of the interior are better supplied with maize and clothing native to the country than those of the coast. The land along the coast[335] is lean and poor; and the more warlike people are along the coast. From the port of Espiritu Santo to Apalache, and from Apalache to the river of Palmas [the land runs] from east to west; from the river of Palmas to New Spain from north to south, with a gentle coast, but with many shoals and high sand hills.

DEO GRATIAS.

*Although lack of cultivation may well be what Elvas had in mind in his use of the expression *falta de adobio,* rendered literally the Portuguese means "lack of fertilizer (or manure)."

This relation of the discovery of
Florida was printed in the
house of André de Burgos,
printer and gentleman
of the house of the
Lord Cardinal
Infante.[336]
It was finished on the tenth day of
February of the year one thousand
five hundred and fifty-seven in
the noble and ever loyal
city of Evora.

Notes to the Elvas Narrative

by James A. Robertson

1. *Silveira.* Undoubtedly the Fernáo da Silveira who died at Evora in 1569, the son of Francisco da Silveira. He fought in Africa and India; and on his return to Portugal was held in high esteem by Joao III and Queen Catharina. He was called the "heroic poet." His family, which was localized about Evora, produced a number of poets. See Maximiliano Lemos, *Encyclopedia Portugueza Illustrada,* X, 162.

2. *Soto.* The best biography in English of Hernando de Soto is that by Theodore Maynard, *De Soto and the Conquistadores* (London, New York, and Toronto: Longmans, Green and Co., 1930). Soto's full name (see Antonio del Solar y Taboada and José de Rújula y de Ochotorena, *El Adelantado Hernando de Soto* [Badajoz, Spain: Ediciones Arqueros, 1929], pp. 29–34, 41–46, 53–60) was Hernán (Hernando, Fernando) Méndez de Soto y Gutiérrez Cardeñosa; and on both sides he was descended from illustrious forebears. His parents were Francisco Méndez de Soto and Leonor Arias Tinoco, the latter of whom came from the city of Badajoz and was of Portuguese ancestry. Considerable confusion exists with regard to various details of his life. He is said, for instance, to have been born in Villanueva de la Serena, Villanueva de Barcarrota (today simply Barcarrota), the city of Badajoz, and Jerez de los Caballeros. The last place is probably the correct one for that was the home of his parents (see Solar and Rújula, pp. 38–39). Again, his birth has been placed as early as 1496 and as late as 1501. If he was forty-two at the time of his death, he must have been born in 1500 or 1501. His first journey to the new world probably occurred in 1519 instead of in 1514 as some say. In the Indies, he served under the notorious Pedrárias Dávila, by whom he was sent on several raiding and punitive expeditions, and, in 1524, he took part in the expedition against Gil Gonzáles Dávila under the command of Francisco Fernández de Córdoba, during which he was captured and then released by the former. Later, he was made regidor of León, in Guatemala, and shortly after was invited to take part in the conquest of Peru. For this he furnished a contingent of men and a number of horses, and was considered next in importance after Francisco and Hernando Pizarro. He succeeded in capturing the last Inca ruler, Atahuallpa (the Atabalipa of the text), and shared heavily in the spoils of the conquest. In Peru, he contracted relations with Leonor Coya, daughter of the chief Guaynacapac, by whom he had a natural daughter, also called Leonor (see "Testamento de Doña Leonor Coya," Archivo de Indias, 109-1-15-20/4; published in Solar

and Rújula, *ut supra*, pp. 191–197). While still in Guatemala he had formed a partnership with Hernán Ponce de León and Francisco Campañón, each obligating himself to share equally in all his possessions with the other two. The latter died shortly after the triple compact was made. A later agreement made with Ponce de León, however, became the matter of a long lawsuit between Ponce de León and his heirs and Isabel de Bobadilla. A copy of this latter agreement, dated at Cuzco, June 27, 1535, as reaffirmed at Havana, May 13, 1539, five days before the expedition left for Florida, is in AI, 50-2-55/10, Papeles de Justica, no. 750 (a), pieza 1(2). fols. 56–62 (published in Solar and Rújula, *ut supra*, pp. 79–89; copy of the original contract of 1535 also among the Harkness Papers in the Library of Congress, *q.v.*, below). Shortly after his return to Spain in 1536, Soto married Isabel de Bobadilla (the daughter of Pedrárias), whose mother (also Isabel de Bobadilla) was a relative of that Beatrice de Bobadilla, the friend and confidante of Isabel the Catholic. It might be of interest to recall here that the sister of his wife had married Balboa, the discoverer of the Pacific, who was also from Jerez de los Caballeros. In Spain, prior to his departure on his Florida Expedition, he was admitted into the Order of Santiago (see Solar and Rújula, *ut supra*, pp. 123–155). By nature, Soto, although a product of his age, seems to have been far more humane than most of his contemporaries, but on occasion (and generally only when he deemed it necessary) he could be ruthless enough. He inspired almost unquestioning obedience in his followers, but by his rashness and lack of judgment at times, joined with a streak of obstinacy, notwithstanding many admirable traits, he seems to have lacked some of the qualities of a great leader. For accounts and estimates of Soto, see the following: Oviedo, in Bourne, *Narratives of the Career of Hernando de Soto*, II, 59; Prescott, *Conquest of Peru;* Buckingham Smith, *Narratives of the Career of Hernando de Soto* (New York, 1866), pp. ix–xxvi (reprinted in Bourne, *ut supra*, II, 169–192); Maynard, *ut supra;* and Francis Borgia Steck, *Neglected Aspects of the De Soto Expedition*, a reprint from *Mid-America*, July, 1932.

Among the papers of the Harkness Collection in the Library of Congress, three have reference to Soto: 1. A "Carta de compañia e hermandad," signed by Captains Hernán Ponce de León and Hernando de Soto: "a renewal and ratification of a fraternal partnership which had existed between them for eighteen or nineteen years, in which they agree to share whatever they may have or obtain by profit, mining, in war, or from any other source; also any royal commissions for offices or commands" (Cuzco, June 27, 1535; see above for mention of a third renewal of this contract). 2. A "Carta de poder" given by Ponce de León to Captain Hernando de Soto: "Full authority to recover gold, jewels, merchandise, horses, ships, negroes, Indians, and give receipts therefor; to conduct all phases of suits; to petition the Crown for offices and cedulas and *provisiones* of *haciendas* in reward for his services; to enter into contracts; to purchase and rent property; to appoint procuradores in his place and revoke such appointment" (Cuzco, July 12, 1535). 3. A "bill for merchandise" bought by Soto. The "items include velvet, silk, linen, satin, gloves, a velvet cap, a brush, some thread. Some of them were taken by Roman, some by Piçarro, the tailor, and one item by De Soto's Indian" (July 10–31, 1536). See *The Harkness Collection in the Library of Congress. Calendar of Spanish Manuscripts Concerning Peru,* 1531–1651 (Washington, 1932), compiled by Stella R. Clemence, Nos. 83, 86, and 97. Other papers are listed in the calendar of documents in Vol. II of *Catálogo de los Fondos Americanos del Archivo de Protocolos de Sevilla* (Madrid, 1930), published by the Instituto Hispano-Cubano de Historia de América. In the first (No. 222), dated February 27, 1538, "Don Fernando de Soto, adelantado of Florida and governor of the Island of Cuba, in the name of Nuño de Tovar, obligates himself to pay to Nicolas de Aramburu, acting for Pascual de Andagoya, regidor of Panama, two hundred ducats of gold, which the aforesaid Nuño de Tovar, in the name of the abovementioned Andagoya collected from Pedro and Melchor de Espinosa" (the entire document is reproduced in Appendix VI, [ibid.] pp. 469–471). In the second (No. 469), dated January 8, 1540, "Captain Fernán Ponce de León, acting for Doña Isabel de Bobadilla, wife of Don Fernando de Soto, governor and captain general of the conquests of Florida and the island of Fernandina, gives his power of attorney to Francisco Hurtado and to Diego del Castillo, to solicit the certification of the 792,000 maravedis which were taken from him for his Majesty's service" (p. 112). In the third (No. 497), dated March 13, 1540, "Cristobal Francesquin and Diego Martínez, public bankers, acting for Don Hernando de Soto, adelantado of Florida, give power of attorney to Gonzalo de Herrera to collect for the aforesaid adelantado, the 300,000 maravedis *de juro* corresponding to the two preceding years" (reproduced in Appendix X, [ibid.] pp. 478–479). Much material, still unpublished in full, exists in the Archives of the Indies (AI) in Seville.

3. *Pedrárias Dávila.* His correct name was Pedro Arias de Avila. He was probably born at Segovia about the year 1440 and died at León, Nicaragua, in July, 1530. For information concerning his career, see Clement R. Markham's translation of Pascual de Andagoya, *Narrative of the Proceedings of Pedrárias Dávila in the Provinces of Tierra Firme or Castilla del Oro, and of the Discovery of the South Sea and the Coasts of Peru and Nicaragua* (Hakluyt Society Publications, No. XXXIV, London, 1865)—taking note that Markham's translations are not always above reproach; Martín Fernández de Navarrete, *Colección de los Viages* (Madrid, 1825–1837); Helps, *Spanish Conquest in America* (London, 1861), I, 373–520, 76–86; Maynard, *ut supra.*

4. *Pizarro.* Probably Francisco Pizarro is meant here. Hernando (Fernando) Pizarro was the half brother of the great commander and of all the sons of their common father the only legitimate child. Francisco Pizarro, the conqueror of Peru, marqués de las Charcas y de los Atabillos, was born in Trujillo, Cáceres, in 1470, or somewhat later, and was assassinated in Lima, June 26, 1541. For information relative to his career, see Prescott, *Conquest of Peru;* Helps, *Spanish Conquest in America;* Rómulo Cúneo-Vidal, *Vida del Conquistador del Perú* (Barcelona, 1925); Maynard, *ut supra.* There are a number of Pizarro letters in the Henry E. Huntington Library and Art Gallery, at San Marino, California. See also the calendar of *The Harkness Collection*

in the Library of Congress, for various material connected with Pizarro and his expedition; also the early Peruvian manuscripts in the New York Public Library.

Hernando Pizarro was born in Trujillo some time before Francisco and is said to have died in the same city in 1578. Reared to the profession of arms, he fought with his father in the Italian and other campaigns. He only (after Francisco Pizarro) exceeded Soto in authority during the Peruvian conquest. Before his death he apparently became blind (see Clemence, *The Harkness Collection,* p. 252, "Carta de poder," of May 25, 1578, given by Pizarro and his wife to Martin de Anpuero). Three documents concerning him are recorded in the *Catálogo de los Fondos Americanos del Archivo de Protocolos de Sevilla,* II, namely, Nos. 196, 451, and 606. See also Prescott, *Conquest of Peru;* and *Enciclopedia Universal* (Espasa), XLV, 183–184; and Cúneo Vidal, *ut supra.*

5. *Atabalipa.* That is, Atahuallpa, the last Inca ruler.

6. *Cruzados.* The cruzado was a silver coin first minted in Castile during the reign of Enrique II. It took its name from the cross on the obverse. At first it was valued at one silver maravedí, but the value was later reduced to a third that amount. The cruzado of the text, however, was a later gold coin minted during the reign of Ferdinand and Isabella. At first this was equivalent to seven pesetas, but by the end of the seventeenth century, the value had risen to ten pesetas. A document of 1489 states that it was equal to a ducat. See *Enciclopedia Universal* (Espasa), XVI, 683; and Fray Liciniano Saez, *Demostración histórica del verdadero Valor de todas las Monedas que corrian en Castilla durante el Reynado del Señor Don Enrique IV* (Madrid, 1805), p. 283.

7. *Reales.* Hakluyt in his translation of the *Relaçam (Virginia richly valued,* London, 1609) says wrongly 60,000, as do the French translation of 1685 and the translation of the latter into English (1686). The real was a silver coin first minted in Castile. The earliest coin struck was probably equivalent to the sixty-sixth part of a marco (or 50 castellanos), but this was later changed by the Catholic Kings to the sixty-seventh part. The present real, which is no longer coined as such, is valued at twenty-five centimos. Values are still largely quoted in reals, especially by the common people. See *Enciclopedia Universal* (Espasa), XLIX, 1008–1009.

8. *Casa de Contratación.* The Casa de Contratación or India House of Trade intervened largely in the early Spanish expeditions to America. It was created by royal cédula of February 14, 1503, and was to consist of three officials, namely, a factor, a treasurer, and a notary (see Joseph de Veitia Linage, *Norte de la Contratacion de las Indias Occidentales,* Seville, 1672, pp. 2–3). See also Bernard Moses, "The Casa de Contratacion of Seville," in *Annual Report of the American Historical Association for 1894* (Washington, 1895), pp. 93–123.

9. *Juan de Añasco.* Juan de Añasco, who was evidently born in Seville, joined Soto there after the latter's return from Peru; and on the organization of the expedition was made its accountant, this being one of the royal official positions of the expedition. On November 14, 1536, he witnessed the "conveyance of dower by the widow

of Pedrárias Dávila to Hernando de Soto, in consideration of the espousal of her daughter" (see Buckingham Smith, *Narratives of the Career of Hernando de Soto*, p. 264, note). Smith also (p. 273) publishes a translation of a royal cédula of Valladolid, May 4, 1537, granting him authority to trade with the Indians of Florida "so long as there are no duties on imports in that province." On May 13, 1539, five days before the expedition left Havana for Florida, he witnessed two documents, namely the second renewal of the contract between Soto and Hernan Ponce de León, and the full authorization given by Soto to Ponce de León to redeem his right in the silks of Granada in which Soto had made an investment (see Solar and Rújula, *ut supra*, pp. 89, 206). On the day of departure from Havana, together with Juan Gaytán, the treasurer, and Luis Hernández de Biedma, the factor, he wrote to the king to the effect that Soto had been detained in Cuba longer than he had wished (see B. Smith, *ut supra*, p. 273). Soto, as is shown by the text, seems at all times to have reposed considerable reliance upon him.

10. *Luis Moscoso de Alvarado.* Luis Moscoso de Alvarado was born in Badajoz in 1505 and died in Peru about 1561. He was the son of Comendador Alonso Hernández de Diosdado and Isabel de Alvarado, inhabitants of Zafra (see Solar and Rújula, p. 329). He was a relative of Pedro de Alvarado and participated with the latter in some of his enterprises, thereby gaining considerable profit; and took part in the early Peruvian campaign. He later went to Spain, where he entered upon a life of dissipation and soon lost most of his possessions. He joined Soto's expedition and after the death of the latter led the remnant of the band to Mexico, reaching Pánuco on September 10, 1543. Two of his brothers, namely Juan de Alvarado and Cristóbal de Mosquera, accompanied him (see Solar and Rújula, p. 329). He witnessed the agreement made between Soto and Ponce de León at Cuzco, on June 27, 1535 (see *ante*, note 2); and on July 10, 1535, at Cuzco, he gave a "Carte de poder" to Antón Ruiz de Guevara "to claim and collect all gold, silver, jewels, Negro slaves, horses, and Indians belonging to him as assignee of Adelantado Pedro de Alvarado and to give letters of payment and quittance therefor, with full powers to act in any conflict arising therefrom" (see Clemence, *The Harkness Collection in the Library of Congress*, No. 90).

The only Tovar mentioned in the "Relacion de las Personas que pasaron a la Florida para la Empresa de Hernando de Soto" (see Solar and Rújula, pp. 275–334) is one Diego de Tovar, son of Rodrigo de Tovar and Beatrice de Segovia, inhabitants of Marchena (see p. 327). He is not mentioned in the list reproduced by Buckingham Smith of those who returned from Florida (Smith, pp. 292–299). Garcilaso de la Vega, *La Florida del Inca* (Lisbon, 1605), says (fol. 10) that Nuño Tovar was one of the sixty conquistadors of Peru and that he was a native of Xerez de Badajoz.

Juan Rodriquez Lobillo is called Johan Ruiz Lobillo by Rangel (see *post*, note 53). He is given in the list of those who returned from Florida, and the place of his residence as Ronda (see Buckingham Smith, *Narratives*, p. 296). A Juan Ruiz Lobillo gave a "Carta de poder" to one Beranga in Xauxa, Peru, on February 22, 1534 (see

Clemence, *The Harkness Collection,* No. 58). Documents Nos. 161 and 163 of *Catálogo de los Fondos Americanos del Archivo de Protocolos de Sevilla* also treat of Juan Ruiz Lobillo, former conquistador and settler of Peru. It is probable that this is the same man as the Juan Rodriquez Lobillo of our text.

11. *Isabel de Bobadilla.* See *ante,* note 2. She married Hernando de Soto in 1537. Upon his departure for Florida, Soto left her in virtual charge of the government of Cuba (but see *post,* note 46). She was an able and strong-willed woman. On the occasion of her marriage, her mother executed a document ("Escritura de dote y arras de Doña Isabel de Bobadilla") by which the dower given with her daughter amounted in value to six thousand ducats, and consisted of the cattle, mares, and their increase, as well as all the buildings of a ranch in Panama owned by Pedrárias Dávila (see Solar and Rújula, *ut supra,* pp. 157–166; original of this document in AI, 50-2-55/10, Papeles de Justicia, 750). Before he left Havana for Florida, Soto gave his wife (May 17, 1539) power of attorney, by which she was authorized to administer all his properties during his absence (see this in Solar and Rújula, pp. 167–177; original in AI, 50-2-55/10). On June 2, 1539, only about a fortnight after her husband's departure for Florida, Isabel, by virtue of the power of attorney given her, summoned Hernán Ponce de León by due course of law to state whether he were in accordance with the documents of partnership contract he had signed with Soto (see *ante,* note 2), for it had been reported that he had stated before royal notary that he had signed the contracts under compulsion (see Solar and Rújula, pp. 179–184; original in AI, 50-2-55/10). This was the beginning of the long lawsuit between these two and the heirs of Ponce de León. It is perhaps doubtful that Isabel died shortly after hearing of her husband's death.

12. *Conquer.* A long document of April 20, 1537 (conserved in AI, 32-4-29/35; another copy in 50-2-55/10), granted to Hernando de Soto the titles of governor, captain general, and adelantado of Florida. This specified fully the conditions under which the expedition was to be undertaken. Another royal decree of equal date conferred on him also the governorship of the island of Cuba (see *Colección de Documentos inéditos . . . de América y Oceanía,* XXII, 534–546; see English translation by Buckingham Smith in his *Narratives,* pp. 266–272). Another decree, dated Valladolid, May 4, 1537, also set forth that Soto was to be governor of Cuba during the period of the conquest, but that he was to appoint an alcalde mayor (who must also be a lawyer) to act as his agent during his absence (see *Col. de Doc. inéd. . . . de Ultramar,* IV, 431–437; original in AI, 79-4-1). A separate decree of the same date (AI, 50-2-55/10) also granted him the titles of adelantado and captain general of Florida (see this in Solar and Rújula, pp. 289–290). By a decree of August 18, 1537, Soto was granted permission to take what food was necessary from Cuba (AI, 32-4-29/35) and on August 20, he was granted additional privileges (AI, *ibid.*). On August 14, 1543, a decree dispatched from Valladolid granted the title of governor of the island of Fernandina (an early name of the island of Cuba) to Licentiate Juanes de Avila in place of Soto, from whom no news had been received (*Col. de Doc. inéd. . . .*

de Ultramar, VI, 190–195; original in AI, 46-4-1/33). Licentiate Bartolomé Ortiz had been alcalde mayor for Soto in Cuba (*Col. de Doc. inéd. . . . de Ultramar,* VI, 204–209; original in AI, 47-2-23/18).

13. *Narváez.* Alvar Núñez Cabeza de Vaca, treasurer of the expedition of Pánfilo de Narváez to Florida in 1527, was one of four survivors of that expedition to reach Mexico. His narrative of 1542 will be reproduced in facsimile, with a new translation into English in a future volume to be published by the Florida State Historical Society. [The plans of the Florida State Historical Society to sponsor a new translation of the Cabeza de Vaca manuscript and to publish it were not realized. That failure is regrettable, as the translation into English by Fanny Bandelier is an extremely free one, although, for the Apalachee portion at least, her editing of Cabeza de Vaca's account is not as extensive as her prefatory warning to her readers might lead them to suspect. In those remarks, she noted that it was "impossible to follow the original more than remotely, and paraphrasing had to be resorted to."—JH] For information relative to the Narváez expedition, see Buckingham Smith, *Relation of Alvar Nuñez Cabeça de Vaca* (New York, 1871); Lowery, *The Spanish Settlements* (New York, 1901), pp. 172–212; and Bolton, *Spanish Borderlands* (New Haven, 1921), pp. 26–45.

14. *Dorantes.* Andrés Dorantes, one of the four survivors of the Narváez expedition.

15. *Reales.* Buckingham Smith in his translation, following Hakluyt (1609), the French translation of 1685, and the English of 1686, says wrongly 60,000 reales.

16. *Niece.* In his will, which is dated San Cristobal de la Habana, May 10, 1539, Soto makes provision for this relative as follows: "Also, I order that, inasmuch as I gave Isabel de Soto, my niece, in marriage to Don Carlos Enriquez, and it was arranged that I should give her at her marriage whatever dowry I might wish to give, I order that three thousand ducats be given him from my property, which are included in the dowry of marriage of the said Doña Isabel de Soto, my niece" (Solar and Rújula, p. 214). Buckingham Smith (*Narratives,* p. 276) also translates this passage of the will, but mistranslates "sobrina" as "cousin."

17. *Fernandez.* It has been generally assumed that one of these Portuguese who accompanied Soto was the author of the present relation.

18. [The Portuguese for the words Robertson rendered as "a rent of wheat," *pão de renda,* translated literally would be "bread of rent" or "bread revenue."—JH]

Geiras. A land measure denoting the area a team of oxen can plough in a day. By some it is given as a rectangle 120 x 240 feet. Roughly it might be considered as the equivalent of the French arpent or the English acre.

19. *Biedma.* The correct name is Luis Fernández de Biedma, not "Antonio" as here. He was appointed factor of the expedition by royal decree of Madrid, December 10, 1537; and his duties were outlined in a later decree of Valladolid, January 14, 1538 (original in AI, 32-4-29–35). He wrote a relation of the expedition which was published in a rather free French translation by Henri Ternaux-Compans (*Voyages Relations et Mémoires orignaux pour servir á l'Histoire de l'Amérique,* Paris, 1841,

XX, 51–106). An English adaptation made from the French of Ternaux-Compans was published by B. F. French, *Historical Collection of Louisiana* (Philadelphia, 1850), and a translation from the same source appeared in William B. Rye, *Discovery and Conquest of Terra Florida* (London, 1851). It was published in Spanish for the first time by Buckingham Smith in *Colleción de varios Documentos para la Historia de la Florida* (Londres, 1857); and in his *Narratives of the Career of Hernando de Soto* (New York, 1866), Smith published a new English translation (pp. 229–261). It was also published in Spanish in *Colleccíon de Doc. inéd. . . . de América,* III, (1865), pp. 414–441. Fernández de Biedma also signed the letter from the royal officials to the Spanish monarch, written from Havana on May 18, 1539, announcing that the expedition was about to leave Cuba for Florida (see *Col. de Doc. inéd. . . . de Ultramar,* VI. 54–56; original manuscript in AI, 51-1-34, No.1, and translation into English by Buckingham Smith, *Narratives,* pp. 281–282). His account (probably official) of the expedition is short, but on the whole an excellent report.

20. *Añasco.* See *ante,* note 9.

21. *Juan Gaytán.* A document in AI, 32-4-29/35, contains a decree of May 4, 1537, outlining the duties of the treasurer of the expedition, Diego de Corral, but this man evidently did not go on the expedition after all. Another decree in the same legajo is addressed to one Jorge Gaytán. Gaytán signed the letter of May 18, 1539 (see *ante,* note 19). He was one of those who returned from Florida (see Buckingham Smith, *Narr.,* p. 295, where he is mentioned as a native of Talavera la Reina).

22. *Six hundred men.* Fernández de Biedma says there were 620 men and 223 horses (see B. Smith, *Narr.,* p. 221). Solar and Rújula (pp. 275–334) give a list of those who went on the expedition—almost 650 in number. However, the list (original in AI, 45-1-1/17) is not altogether accurate, for the names of some who actually went do not appear; and others whose names are in the list evidently did not go. In the list, it is interesting to note, is the name of Juan Coles, the witness cited by Garcilaso de la Vega in his *La Florida del Inca,* who he said furnished him valuable material for his book. The entry relative to Coles is as follows: "Juan Coles, son of Juan Coles and Luisa Rodriguez, inhabitants of Zafra" (p. 323). All but three of the Portuguese mentioned in the text can be identified in this list, but they are mentioned as being inhabitants of Badajoz (probably in order to avoid any charge of taking foreigners on the expedition). Those who have been identified are André de Vasconcelos, Men Rodriquez (probably the "Mem" of the text), Alvaro Hernandez (for Alvaro Fernandez), Benito Hernandez (for Bento Fernandez), Juan Cordero (for Ioam Cordeiro), and Esteban Pegado. See also *post,* note 24.

23. *Daughter.* The governor of the Canaries was a cousin of Isabel de Bobadilla, and his natural daughter was named Leonor. See Maynard, *De Soto and the Conquistadores,* p. 132.

24. *Whitsuntide.* The cabildo of the city of Santiago, in a letter of July 26, 1538 (abstract in *Col. de Doc. inéd. . . . de Ultramar,* VI, 36–37; and apparently given in full in B. Smith, *Narr.,* pp. 288–291, where he wrongly dates it 1539), mentions the

arrival in Cuba of Soto and his men on June 7 with five ships and 600 men and says that preparations were being made for the voyage to Florida. As his alcalde mayor he had appointed Licentiate Bartolomé Ortiz. The arrival in Cuba is noted also in a letter of July 20, 1538 (*Col. de Doc. inéd. . . . de Ultramar,* VI, 27–35), by Gonzalo de Guzmán, formerly lieutenant governor in Cuba, as follows: "On June 7, Adelantado Don Hernando de Soto reached this port with six vessels and a fine body of men, about five hundred in all, who say they comprise the whole body" (p. 33). The arrival is mentioned also in a letter of August 1, 1538, written by Bernardo de Quesada, procurator of Santiago (*ibid.,* pp. 39–42), who says: "On June 9 of this present year, there arrived in this island of Cuba and city of Santiago, Hernando de Soto, governor of this island and adelantado of Florida, with over five hundred men" (p. 39).

25. *Need.* In his letter of July 20, 1538 (see *ante,* note 24), Gonzalo de Guzmán says (pp. 33–34) in speaking of the arrival of Soto and his men in Cuba: "They disembarked at this port and were lodged in this city, and in the farms of the inhabitants thereof, from which all have received much inconvenience; for since many ships coming from the coast of Tierra Firme are always putting in at this port, the greatest and sole profit of the inhabitants of this city is that of selling them all the provisions which they obtain and possess. And on that account and because this year has been very unproductive, we have had so great a lack of food that there was not even enough for all the inhabitants. And it comes to pass that, although the people had need of it, he has so much need of it that it seems to me that, without abundance of food, neither war nor pacification can be made. And, together with this, [there is] less money with which to provide food, wherever it can be found. What I have regretted in him is that he is planning to stay in this island until this may be remedied in one way or another; and that, in fact, the inhabitants have suffered and are suffering much inconvenience because of the food which they are giving to all his men at their own expense. Outside of this, I see ability and so good a manner in his person that I believe he will achieve a better result than the previous ones. Please God that this may not be so prejudicial to the island, that we inhabitants thereof may have to abandon it; for, besides having supported and supporting him and his men, we learn that they are going to take some of our young men and inhabitants away with them; and without them we can give up everything and live with difficulty in the land. He has his eyes and his thought so fixed on Florida that he will give little heed to the loss of this land. We can not help complaining loudly for the present and because of what I have mentioned, for especially we are expecting the Indians in revolt to cause great harm daily, and since the aforementioned Soto came they have done us a great deal of hurt, so that, although the island has greater need of aid, a greater loss comes upon it. For we are sure that he can not leave here these eight months, and although there is not enough to feed the natives, the necessity of feeding five hundred men at the latters' expense, whatever remedy is sought it can not but come late."

Quesada (see *ante,* note 24) says also (pp. 39–40): "He was lodged in this city of Santiago and its environs and on the farms of the inhabitants of this city, and they have been fed until now without the inhabitants having any gain therefrom. The inhabitants of this city are in revolt, because for two years, one after the other, the weather has been very poor for the raising of provisions. On this account, the inhabitants are experiencing considerable trouble in supporting so many people at their own expense. Since this island has been a mother for the settling of New Spain and the supplying of Tierra Firme, and since after the discovery of Peru, many provisions and horses and Spanish Christians have left this island, it is considerably depopulated and bereft of any one to act for it, and if your Majesty does not remedy it, it is headed clear for destruction.

"Its destruction is that Governor Hernando de Soto is going away on his conquest of Florida and will try to take all the Spaniards who are most useful in keeping this island peaceful, and prevent the inhabitants of this island from selling horses or provisions to Tierra Firme or Peru; for hitherto, the inhabitants have been aided by selling horses and provisions to the ships coming to look for them for Tierra Firme and Peru. Since Governor Hernando de Soto is now preventing that, as I have said, the inhabitants of this island and your Majesty's subjects are receiving very great injury and the country is being depopulated. And although your Majesty has little income in this island at present, it has been because of supporting other places where your Majesty has many subjects and much income." See also, *post,* note 37.

26. *Houses.* For the early history of Santiago de Cuba, see Irene A. Wright, *The Early History of Cuba, 1492–1586* (New York, 1916).

27. *Mamei.* The mammee apple, sometimes called the St. Domingo apricot (*Mammea Americana*). Both tree and fruit were described by Gonzalo Fernández de Oviedo y Valdés in his *Historia general y natural de las Indias* (Madrid ed., 1851–1852), I, book VIII, chapter XX, "Del Arbol mamey ó de su fructa, llamada assi mismo mamey," pp. 305–307; and by Bernabé Cobo, *Historia del Mundo Nuevo* (Seville, 1890–1893), II, 20–21. The fruit, which is still much esteemed today, has also medicinal value.

28. *Potatoes.* The cassava root has played an important role in the history of the world. The land of its origin is still a moot question (see Wiener, *Africa and the Discovery of America,* Philadelphia, 1920–1922, I, 210–216). The name "cassava" properly designates the starchy content of the plant, but has been extended to the plant itself. The proper common name is "manioc" and the commercial product is called "tapioca." There are two varieties, the bitter and the sweet, so designated from the amount of prussic acid present. The sweet variety has been grown extensively in Florida for many years and to some extent in other southern states of the United States. See Harvey W. Wiley, *Sweet Cassava: Its Culture, Properties, and Uses,* Bull. No. 44, Division of Chemistry, United States Department of Agriculture (Washington, 1894); and Charles C. Moore, *Cassava: Its Content of Hydrocyanic Acid and Starch and other Properties,* Bull. No. 106, *ibid.* (Washington, 1907). Much has been written about this plant, both in old and modern works. Among early writers, consult Gonzalo Fernández de Oviedo y Valdés, *Historia general y natural de las Indias*

(Madrid, 1851), I, book VII, chap. II, "Del pan de las Indias que so llama caçabi"; José de Acosta, *Historia natural y moral de las Indias* (Seville, 1590), pp. 239–240 (Eng. transl.); *The naturall and morall Historie of the East and West Indies* (London, 1604), pp. 257–258; and Jean Baptiste du Tertre, *Histoire Generale des Antilles habitées par les François* (Paris, 1667–1671), II, Traite III, section XIV, pp. 112–118. [Elvas's allusion to potatoes here probably refers to the sweet potato or yam rather than to the so-called "Irish potato." As the conquest of Peru occurred only a little over twenty years before the publication of Elvas's account, it is doubtful whether knowledge of this new "potato" from the Peruvian and Bolivian highlands had yet spread very widely.—JH] [The work by the eccentric Weiner, here cited by Robertson, is now almost universally disregarded. Cassava is quite certainly a Native American domesticate.—VJK]

29. *Meat.* These wild cattle and hogs had escaped from the Spaniards who introduced them into the island of Española and others of the West Indies. The wild cattle, especially, were destined to play a large part in the conquering and peopling of America. To exploit them, men of various nationalities formed themselves into bands, especially in Española and later in Jamaica; and from the method employed in curing the carcasses of the cattle, were called buccaneers (from the Indian word *boucan*). See Exquemelin's interesting narrative, *Bucaniers of America,* which first appeared in Dutch, but was later translated into many languages. Many dogs also escaped from civilization.

30. *Cuba.* The island of Cuba, exclusive of the Isle of Pines and many of the nearby keys, has an area of about 43,000 sq. mi. It is 730 miles long by 20 to 90 miles wide.

31. *Houses.* For the early history of Havana, see Irene A. Wright, *Historia documentada de San Cristóbal de la Habana en el Siglo XVI* (Havana, 1927); and *The early History of Cuba.*

32. *Island.* Santiago was the metropolitan see for Florida during the Spanish occupation of the latter. See James Alexander Robertson, "Notes on Early Church Government in Spanish Florida," in *Catholic Historical Review,* XVII, July, 1931, pp. 151–174.

33. *Hands.* Buckingham Smith, evidently following Hakluyt, who makes the same error, mistranslates this passage, saying "with a cudgel in his hands."

34. *Brother-in-law.* The French translation of 1685 and its English translation of 1686 call Carlos a cousin of Soto. In reality he had married Soto's niece (see *ante,* note 16).

35. *Eastern.* So in our text, but certainly an error for "western." This was probably an error of the printer, who must have mistaken the word "loeste" meaning "west" for "leste" meaning "east." Hakluyt corrected the error without comment.

36. *Bayamo.* The Spanish town of Bayamo—called from its old Indian name—was founded by the conquistador Diego Velázquez (see Wright, *Early History of Cuba*). The town is located on the Bayamo River, a branch of the Cauto. In his letter of July 20, 1538, Gonzalo Guzmán notes (*Col. de Doc. inéd. . . . de Ultramar,* VI, 32–33)

that the inhabitants of Bayamo were considering changing its location, and asks that they be forbidden to do this.

37. *Indians.* The Bishop of Cuba, writing to Charles V on August 15, 1539 (*Col. de Doc. inéd. . . . de Ultramar,* VI, 58), said: "As soon as Soto arrived, he ordered that no person, under penalty of death, should sell horses or provisions outside the island. He has taken 250 horses, has supported 500 men for almost a year, and has taken provisions for another year—all this without paying scarcely any money. How much hurt he has caused the inhabitants who maintain themselves by their farms and their animals! Add to this that he has taken with him the men of the island who are of use in war. This will cause the Indians to revolt and it is to be feared that they will leave not a single Christian alive." See also, *ante,* note 25.

Gonzalo de Guzmán, in a letter to the monarch on August 28, 1539 (abstract by Muñoz in *Col. de Doc. inéd. . . . de Ultramar,* VI, 59–60), said: "Soto, in addition to having been a year with his men eating at the expense of the inhabitants, committed two very grievous wrongs: 1. By depriving the island of its greatest source of gain, for he ordered that neither provisions nor horses be exported, since which time no vessels have been coming here and the people are in a desperate condition. 2. By taking Porcallo, who was in the province of the city of Trinidad in the middle of the island, who by himself had more wealth than four ports together and was greatly feared. Soto is sending everything to Florida where he will have to stay and this island is done for." The account of Juan de Agramonte, written at Santiago, on September 3, 1539 (AI, 54-1-34, No. 2; also published in (*Col. de Doc. inéd. . . . de Ultramar,* VI, 61–68), says: "The other reason [for the desperate condition of the island] is that Governor Don Hernando de Soto ordered, under penalty of death, that no person withdraw from this island any horses or provisions. . . ."

The royal officials in their letter to the king on May 18, 1539 (see *ante,* note 19), stated that Soto was about to leave for Florida with nine ships, 237 horses, 330 foot, and altogether 513 men excluding the sailors. He also had 300 loaves of cassava bread, 2500 shoulders of bacon, and 2500 fanegas of maize; and in order to insure a continuous supply of provisions he had bought up many pasturages.

38. *Lizards.* Alligators.

39. *More.* The maja (*Epicrates angulifer*), which is still found. As the narrator says, it is harmless to people. It reaches a length of twelve feet and feeds on birds and small mammals. The name is also applied in Cuba to another snake (*Tropidophis malanurus*) which seldom reaches over a yard in length.

40. *Porcallo.* Vasco Porcallo de Figueroa was born in Cáceres, Spain, in the second half of the fifteenth century and died in Puerto Príncipe, Cuba (which he had founded), in 1550. His family was of noble extraction and related to the Dukes of Feria. Entering upon the profession of arms, he served with distinction in Spain and Italy; and when still a young man went to America and soon settled in Cuba, becoming the original settler in the province of Camaguey. There he founded the settlement of San Juan de los Remedios, which soon attained to considerable importance. He was Di-

ego Velázquez's first choice for the leader of the expedition on which Cortés entered. He became one of the wealthiest landowners in Cuba and one of the most ruthless. He was very active. He became procurator in Sancti Spiritus and aided Velázquez in the founding of Baracoa. The Bishop of Santiago in his letter of August 15, 1539 (see *ante*, note 37), reported that Soto had taken Porcallo, who was powerful, wealthy, and feared, to Florida, on which account the Indians had lost their fear of the Spaniards. However, the Florida campaign not being much to his liking because of the hardships and the small chance of getting Indian slaves, he returned to Cuba almost immediately, as related in the text. However, he left his natural son, Gómez de Figueroa, with Soto. See Garcilaso de la Vega, *La Florida del Inca*, book II, chap. XI, pp. 48–50, for an amusing account of Porcallo's discomfiture on the expedition to the district of Paracoxi; and Lowery, *Spanish Settlements . . . 1513–1561*, pp. 220–222. See also *Enciclopedia Universal* (Espasa), XLVI, 459–460; and Wright, *Early History of Cuba, passim.* Buckingham Smith, *Collección de varios Documentos* (Londrés, 1857) reproduces a "Declaración" made by him on February 28, 1522 (pp. 45–87).

41. *Sancti Spiritus.* In 1544, Sancti Spiritus (founded in 1514 by Diego de Velázquez) had a population of eighteen citizens, fifty-eight free Indians on encomiendas, fourteen Negro, and fifty Indian slaves. See *Enciclopedia Universal* (Espasa), XIII, 1189; and Wright, *Early Hist. of Cuba, passim.*

42. *River.* Probably the Yayabo.

43. *Trinidad.* Founded in 1514. Las Casas was one of its original settlers. See Wright, *Early Hist. of Cuba, passim.*

44. *Porcallo de Figueroa.* See *ante*, note 40.

45. *Havana.* By a royal cédula, issued in Valladolid, March 20, 1538, Soto was ordered to construct a fort at Havana (see Wright, *Historia documentada de . . . Habana en el Siglo XVI*, I, 184). Soto delegated the building of the fort to Francisco Aceituno, an aged inhabitant of Santiago de Cuba, to whom an annual salary of 100,000 maravedís was assigned. The fort was built in seven months and Aceituno was appointed its governor with an annual salary of 75,000 maravedís (*ibid.*, pp. 16–17).

46. *Juan de Rojas.* Juan de Rojas was for many years one of the most prominent citizens of Havana. See Wright, *Early Hist. of Cuba, passim;* and *Col. de Doc. inéd. . . . de Ultramar*, VI, *passim.*

47. *Florida.* Probably at a point on Tampa Bay and not on Charlotte Harbor as some have contended. Such is the opinion of Lowery, *Spanish Settlements . . . 1513–1561*, p. 219; as well as of Mr. John C. Cooper, Jr., of Jacksonville, Florida, who has made a careful study of this question from the evidence of narratives and maps; and of Mrs. Isabel Garrard Patterson, of Atlanta, Georgia, who is now endeavoring to establish Soto's route with more accuracy than has yet been done. Rangel (see Bourne, *Narratives*, II, 51–54) gives many details of the landing. [Robertson did this translation in 1933, before very much work on the De Soto trail was published. In 1939, John R. Swanton published the *Final Report of the United States De Soto Expedition Commission*, representing a major effort to establish De Soto's route.

More recently, many scholars have suggested various revisions of the route that Swanton suggested, affecting particularly the route followed by De Soto during his second year of exploration after breaking his winter camp in Apalachee.—JH]

48. *Ucita.* Called Oçita by Rangel, Soto's private secretary, in his account of the expedition (see Bourne, *ut supra,* II, 52). The place is called the port of Baya Honda by Luis Fernández de Biedma, the factor, in his relation (see *ibid.*, II, 3). Soto probably took possession for Spain of Florida (June 3, 1539) on the shore of the bay opposite this place (see Rangel, in Bourne, *ut supra,* II, 56).

49. *Six.* Rangel (Bourne, *ut supra,* II, 54–55) says: "they lighted upon ten Indians . . . and they [the Indians] shot two horses and the Spaniards slew two Indians and put the rest to flight."

50. *Luis de Moscoso.* See *ante,* note 10.

51. [*Junto à praya* are the Portuguese words that Robertson rendered as "near the beach." The Portuguese *junto* as used here has the same sense of "next to" or "on" rather than simply "near," which is *perto* or *cêrca.* The Portuguese word that Robertson translated as "artificially" (*à mão*) rendered literally would be "by hand."—JH] *Fortress.* The remains of this artificial mound are still to be seen a few miles from Gadsdens Point (Lowery, pp. 219–220). Garcilaso de la Vega gives the name of the town as Hirriga.

52. *Vasconcelos.* One of the Portuguese from Elvas. Pedro de Calderón was the son of Rodrigo Calderón and Beatriz de Hoces, of Badajoz. He took with him his two sons, Rodrigo Calderón and Gregorio de Hoces. All three returned from Florida. See Solar and Rújula, *Hernando de Soto,* pp. 276–277; and B. Smith, *Narratives,* p. 292. Solar and Rújula (p. 281) say that there were three of the Cardeñosa, namely, Arias Tinoco, Alonso Romo, and Diego Tinoco, sons of Gutierre Garcia Calderón and María Romo. All three returned from Florida (see B. Smith, *Narr.*, p. 293). The name Tinoco shows that they were related to Soto through his mother.

53. *Lobillo.* See *ante,* note 10. Captain Francisco Maldonado was the son of Rodrigo Maldonado and Beatriz Ordoñez, of Salamanca (Solar and Rújula, p. 333). He made repeated voyages in search of Soto, on one occasion going as far north as Newfoundland (see Lowery, pp. 250–251).

54. *Indians.* Hakluyt, who is followed by the French edition of 1685 and its English translation of 1686, says "two" Indians. Rangel (Bourne, *Narr.*, II, 55) says that Añasco had seized four Indians when he went in search of a harbor in Florida before the expedition actually left Cuba. One Indian, he says, was sent by Soto to persuade the cacique to make peace. Two of the others escaped.

55. *Huts.* Hakluyt (p. 20) mistranslates, saying that Baltasar de Gallegos had captured the four Indian women.

56. *Life.* Rangel (Bourne, *Narr.*, II, 56–57) says that Ortiz was in a band of twenty Indians, all painted red, adorned with feathers, and armed with bows and arrows. According to him, the salutation of Ortiz was "Sirs, for the love of God and of Holy Mary, slay not me; I am a Christian like yourselves and was born in Seville, and my

name is Johan Ortiz." Fernández de Biedma says (Bourne, II, 4) that for more than four days, Ortiz could not speak without uttering four or five Indian words to one of Spanish.

57. *Returned.* Various writers have attempted to weave a romance about this early "Pocahontas," but with no real authority for so doing. Garcilaso de la Vega recites the episode of Ortiz with great detail (*La Florida del Inca*, fols. 39–46). Rangel (Bourne, II, 57–58) says that Mucoço was peaceful and for that reason was threatened by the other chiefs of his vicinity.

58. *Twelve.* Hakluyt (p. 25) says "ten or eleven." Fernández de Biedma (Bourne, II, 3) says there were nine Indians, and Rangel (see note 56) twenty. Lewis, "The Narrative of the Expedition of Hernando de Soto," in *Spanish Explorers in the Southern United States, 1528–1543* (p. 150, note), conjectures that the town of Mucoço was located west of Miakka River (Macaco of the old maps), but this is doubtful, for Lewis locates the first landfall in Florida on Charlotte Harbor instead of Tampa Bay.

59. *Paracoxi.* Paracoxi (Hurripacuxi in Fernández de Biedma, Bourne, II, 5, and Orriparacogi in Rangel, *ibid.*, p. 60) was evidently not the name of the cacique, but the title of the superior chief of the region. The name apparently reappears in the relation of Jacques le Moyne de Morgues (Frankfort, 1591) and in Laudonniére's *Histoire Notable* (Paris, 1586), where it has the forms Paraousti and Paracousi and is said to be the equivalent of king. For variants of the name, see John R. Swanton, *Early History of the Creek Indians and their Neighbors*, Bulletin No. 73, Bureau of American Ethnology, Washington, 1922, p. 327. See also Lowery, *Span. Settlements*, p. 221.

60. *You.* This and all subsequent talks attributed to the Indian caciques are undoubtedly apocryphal and simply put into the mouths of the speakers. After leaving this cacique, Fernández de Biedma says (Bourne, II, 5) that they went for fifteen or twenty leagues to a town called Etocale (the Cale of our text) where they found food and stayed for about a week.

61. *Espiritu Santo.* "So called from the day when the governor and his fleet arrived" (Rangel, Bourne, II, 63).

62. *Time.* With the ships was dispatched the celebrated letter of Soto to the cabildo of Santiago de Cuba, dated July 9, 1539. An English translation will be found in B. Smith, *Letter of Hernando de Soto, and Memoir of Hernando de Escalante Fontaneda* (Washington, 1854), pp. 7–10, and *Narr.*, pp. 288–291; and in Bourne, II, 159–165. See also J. A. Robertson, *Documents in Span. Archives relating to the History of the U.S.*, p. 7, for location of copies of the original.

63. *Him.* See Rangel's account of Porcallo's departure in Bourne, II, 61–62. Among other things, Rangel says: "The departure of this cavalier was regretted by many since he was a friend of good men and did much for them." It was agreed that Porcallo should still look after the provisioning of the expedition from Cuba. He seems to have kept on good terms with Isabel de Bobadilla.

64. *Cale.* The word probably survives in the modern name "Ocala" (Rangel uses the form "Ocale"). Swanton (Bull. No. 73) says (p. 327) that it was a province north of the Withlacoochee, not far from the present Ocala. He gives the variants Ocale, Ocaly, Etocale, Ologale. See Rangel's statement (Bourne, II, 62–63) relative to Soto's instructions to Gallegos regarding the dual reports he was to make on his explorations. In his letter of July 9, 1539, Soto says of this town: " . . . Afterwards, farther on, at the distance of two days' journey, there is another town, called Ocale. It is so large, and they so extol it, that I dare not repeat all that is said. . . . On our coming together we will march to join Baltazar de Gallegos, that we may go thence to pass the winter at Ocale, where, if what is said be true, we shall have nothing to desire." See B. Smith, *Narratives,* pp. 285–286. [If Elvas's recollection is reliable here, Paracoxi's town must have been deep in the center of the peninsula for Cale to have been "toward the west" from it. The Portuguese, *para ponente* ("toward the setting sun") leaves no doubt that "toward the west" was intended by Elvas.—JH]

65. *Years.* Rangel (Bourne, II, 63) says that the men ordered to remain behind with Calderón "were heavy in spirit." He puts them at forty horse and sixty foot.

66. *Acela.* Called "Vicela" by Rangel (Bourne, II, 65). Swanton (Bull. No. 73, p. 330) says it was a small town somewhat south of the Withlacoochee.

67. *Tocaste.* The same form is used by Rangel. Swanton (Bull. No. 73, p. 329) says it was located on a large lake some distance south of the Withlacoochee. See Lewis's conjecture in *Spanish Explorers,* p. 155, note 1.

68. *Lacking.* Rangel appears to have been sent on this errand (see Bourne, II, 65–66).

69. *Blites.* Probably greens of some sort. [As Henry F. Dobyns noted on pages 221–22 of *Their Number Become Thinned* (Knoxville: University of Tennessee Press, 1983), the Portuguese term *bredos,* which Robertson translated as "blites" and speculated were "probably greens of some sort," is more specific. James L. Taylor, in his *Portuguese-English Dictionary* (Stanford, Calif.: Stanford University Press, 1958), gives the following range of possibilities for *bredo:* princess feather *(Amaranthus hypochondriacus),* the blite goosefoot (*Chenopodium capilatum*), spiny amaranth (*A. spinosus*), the tumbleweed amaranth (*A. graecizans*), amaranth or love-lies-bleeding (*A. caudatus sanguineus*), among others. An English equivalent more comprehensible than "blites" would be "pigweed" or "lamb's quarters."—JH]

70. *Apalache.* Rangel (Bourne, II, 69) says that Apalache "was reported to be populous." Fernández de Biedma (Bourne, II, 5) says that several forays were made in order to get Indians for guides. [The Portuguese that Robertson rendered as "one of two Indians who were captured told" is *e dos que se tomaram disse um.* Here *dos* is the Portuguese contraction of *de* and *os,* meaning "of those," rather than the Spanish *dos,* meaning "two," which is what Robertson has taken *dos* for. In order for this phrase to be rendered as Robertson has rendered it, it would have to be, *e de os dois índios que se tomaram disse um.* The usual Portuguese for

"two" is *dois*. The passage should be rendered as "one of those who were captured said."—JH]

71. *1540. Sic* in our text, but an error for 1539. This is corrected by Hakluyt and by B. Smith. The date of the departure is the same in Rangel.

72. *Ytara.* Itaraholata in Rangel (Bourne, II, 69). The word *holata* means "chief" (see Swanton, Bull. No. 73, p. 323).

73. *Utinama.* The name Potano is given also by Rangel (Bourne, II, 70); but Utinama becomes Utinamocharra in the latter.

74. *Mala Paz.* This story is also related by Rangel (Bourne, II, 70). [The five villages mentioned by Elvas may have been the total for the province. At the beginning of the seventeenth century, Potano was spoken of as having five settlements.—JH]

75. *Built.* The river over which the bridge was built is called the River of Discord by Rangel (Bourne, II, 71) because of certain quarrels which are not explained.

76. *Caliquen.* Aguacalecuen in the narrative by Fernández de Biedma (Bourne, II, 5), and Aguascaleyquen in Rangel (*ibid.*, p. 71). Swanton (Bull. No. 73, p. 323) says this town and province seem to have been located between the Suwanee and its branch, the Santa Fe.

77. *Saddled.* Hakluyt (p. 32) mistranslates this passage as follows: "and that we should be put out of doubt before it were long."

78. *Ten.* Rangel gives the date of departure as September 9 (Bourne, II, 72).

79. *Uzachil.* Called Veachile by Fernández de Biedma (Bourne, II, 6), Uchachile and Uçachile by Rangel (*ibid.*, p. 73), and Ossachile by Garcilaso de la Vega, *La Florida del Inca,* fols. 88–90; see also Barnard Shipp, *History of Hernando de Soto and Florida* (Philadelphia, 1881), pp. 299–301. This region may have been the seat of the Indians called Osochi, perhaps an offshoot of the Timucua (see Swanton, Bull. No. 73, pp. 165–167). [There seems to be no good reason for identifying Uzachil as other than a Yustagan settlement, as De Soto was clearly on the trail to Apalachee and from Uzachil passed on to Axille, which is the Asile of the mission era on the border of Apalachee.—JH]

80. *Napetuca.* Rangel mentions two towns on the way to Napetuca (Napituca, Napetaca), namely Uriutina (a village of pleasant aspect and abundant food) and one called Many Waters (so called because of the heavy rains). Napetuca is located by Swanton (Bull. No. 73, p. 327) as lying apparently in the province of Aguascalecuen, between the Suwanee and Sante Fe rivers. Rangel (Bourne, II, 73) describes Napetuca as "a very pleasant village, in a pretty spot, with plenty of food." Rangel and the text agree here as to date. [Inasmuch as Elvas referred to Uzachil as paramount for all the Timucua territory between Caliquen and Uzachil, it would seem more logical to refer to the region as the Province of Uzachil. In mission times, the territory from Caliquen to the river just beyond Napetuca (the Suwannee) was part of the Province of Utina, and the chief of the settlement that is believed to have been Caliquen was the paramount chief for all the Timucua-speaking territory west to Apalachee.—JH]

81. *Arrows.* See Rangel's account of these happenings, which differs considerably in detail from that of our text (Bourne, II, 73–77).

82. *River.* Called Deer River by the men because of the occurrence noted here (see also Rangel, in Bourne, II, 77).

83. *Hapaluya.* Apalu in Rangel (Bourne, II, 78). The form Apalou appears in Laudonnière (*Histoire Notable,* fol. 93), as applied to one of the caciques. Swanton (Bull. No. 73, p. 324) locates this district in the northwestern part of Timucua country near Uzachil (see *ante,* note 79) in the province of Hostaqua; and says that the word signifies "fort" in Timucua. [There apparently was more than one settlement bearing the name Apalo. The Le Moyne map shows an Appalou located a little to the northeast of Potano. In 1616, Fray Gerónimo de Oré described Apalo as a mission station two and one-half days' journey by foot from the Fresh Water Timucua mission of San Antonio on the route to San Francisco Potano. Maynard Geiger, the translator of Oré's work, placed Apalo south of Lake Orange.—JH]

84. *Axille.* Aguile in Fernández de Biedma (Bourne, II, 7) and Agile by Rangel (*ibid.,* p. 78). This was Asile (Swanton gives many other variants) which was an important town in the westernmost part of the Timucua country, and which later gave its name to the mission of San Miguel de Assile and to the Ocilla River (Swanton, Bull. No. 73, p. 324). [There is nothing in the De Soto accounts or in the mission-era documentation that indicates that Asile was an important town. In 1675, Asile was listed as having only forty people, while the other three Yustagan missions each had about three hundred people (see Juan Fernández de Florencia to Pablo de Hita Salazar, San Luis de Apalachee, July 15, 1675, AGI, Santo Domingo 839, Stetson Collection of the P. K. Yonge Library of Florida History of the University of Florida at Gainesville).—JH]

85. *Forest.* The last clause of this sentence is omitted by Hakluyt.

86. *Vitachuco.* Ivatachuco in Fernández de Biedma (Bourne, II, 17) and Rangel (*ibid.,* p. 79). See also Swanton, Bull. No. 73, p. 112, for other information regarding this Apalache town. Lewis (*Spanish Explorers,* p. 161, note 1) points out that the day of St. Francis falls on October 4, but that this day did not come on Wednesday in 1539. Rangel (Bourne, II, 79) says the crossing was made on Friday, October 3. [During the mission era, Vitachuco's chief was referred to repeatedly as the most prestigious or the most important of Apalachee's chiefs, rather that the chief of San Luis, who was heir to the chiefdom of Anhaica Apalachee (see John H. Hann, *Apalachee: The Land between the Rivers* (Gainesville: University Presses of Florida, 1988), 98–100.—JH]

87. *Uzela.* Rangel says (Bourne, II, 79) that on Sunday, October 5, the Spaniards reached the town of Calahuchi, an Apalache town. Lewis (*Span. Explorers,* p. 161, note 3) identifies this with Uzela, but it may have been one of the other small towns thereabout.

88. *Anhaica Apalache.* Iniahico in Fernández de Biedma (Bourne, II, 7) and Iviahica in Rangel (*ibid.,* p. 79). Swanton seems to accept the form Iniahica as the

correct one (see Bull. No. 73, p. 111). The town was evidently in the neighborhood of the present Tallahassee. The Apalache Indians were a Muskhogean group, whose name in Hitchiti apparently means "on the other side." Their habitat at the time of their first discovery by Europeans was that portion of the present western part of Florida lying between the Ocilla River on the east and the Ocklochnee and its branches on the west. The center of their territory seems to have been at about the location of the present Tallahassee, but they probably extended as far north as southern Georgia. In culture they were probably midway between the other Florida Indians and their own Muskhogean relatives toward the north. Many Spanish missions were established among them in the seventeenth century.

They were first mentioned by Cabeza de Vaca in his narrative (see Adolphe Bandelier, *Journey of Alvar Núñez Cabeza de Vaca*, New York, 1922, pp. 12–13, 24, 25–26, 27, 28–34). In addition to the short notice in our text, they are mentioned by Fernández de Biedma (Bourne, II, 6–7); Rangel (*ibid.*, pp. 78–80, 82); Hernando de Escalante Fontaneda, in his memoir written about 1575 (B. Smith's translation, *Letter of Hernando de Soto and Memoir of Hernando de Escalante Fontaneda*, Washington, 1854); Garcilaso de la Vega, *La Florida del Inca* (from Alonso de Carmona; see Bourne, II, 151–152). These references as well as later ones, are given in Swanton, Bull. No. 73 (*q.v.*, pp. 109–129). See also Hodge, *Handbook of the American Indian* (Washington, 1907), I, 67–68.

[Robertson's surmise about the location of Anhaica Apalachee has been borne out by discovery of the location of De Soto's winter camp at the Martin site in downtown Tallahassee. The site is on a hill adjacent to the one on which the state's Capitol complex stands. The alternate names of Anhaica and Iniahico used by the De Soto chroniclers reappeared in the 1657 visitation record for the San Luis mission, which was referred to variously as San Luis Xinayca and San Luis Nixaxipa (see Hann, "Translation of Governor Rebolledo's 1657 Visitation of Three Florida Provinces and Related Documents," *Florida Archaeology* 2 (1986): 93, 95). There appears to be little evidence for Robertson's statement that Apalachee territory "probably extended as far north as southern Georgia." B. Calvin Jones, in his surface-collecting expeditions, has found little evidence of an Apalachee presence much north of Lakes Jackson and Iamonia. Gary Shapiro speculated that southern Georgia's lack of such bodies of water was a reason the Apalachee did not move into that territory (personal communication).

Robertson's remark "In culture they were probably midway between the other Florida Indians and their own Muskhogean relatives toward the north" is not very clear. If Robertson meant to say that the Apalachee were only half as Mississippian or half as advanced as their neighbors to the north, his remark is open to serious question.

Robertson's statement "Many Spanish missions . . ." might be changed to "Eleven Spanish missions."—JH]

89. *Plums.* The dried plums were probably persimmons. Swanton (Bull. No. 73, p. 117, note) calls attention to a possible misprint in the original near this point. The

sentence beginning "In that town" translates as follows, if the punctuation of the original be kept, "In that town, the maestre de campo, . . . lodged them all within a league and a half league about that town." The reading as suggested by Swanton is more logical and has been adopted in the present translation.

90. *Horses.* Fernández de Biedma (Bourne, II, 7) says they found the place where "the forge had stood, and many bones of horses"; and adds: "The Indians told us, through the interpreters, what others like us there had done." Rangel (*ibid.*, p. 79–80) says that Añasco recognized the place "by the headpieces of the horses and the place where the forge was set up and the mangers and the mortars that they used to grind corn and by the crosses cut in the trees." Lewis (*Spanish Explorers*, p. 162, note 2) says that the Spaniards knew this place as Bahia de Caballos or Horse Bay, and identifies it as Bay Ocklockonee. [For the most recent scholarship on the location of Horse Bay, see Rochelle A. Marrinan, John F. Scarry, and Rhonda L. Majors, "Prelude to De Soto: The Expedition of Pánfilo De Narváez," in *Columbian Consequences*, vol. 2, *Archaeological and Historical Perspectives on the Spanish Borderlands East*, ed. David Hurst Thomas (Washington, D.C.: Smithsonian Institution Press, 1990), 76–77.—JH]

91. *November 17.* This sentence showing the date of Calderón's [Añasco's] departure was omitted by B. Smith. Hakluyt says that Añasco set out on Saturday. The seventeenth of November really fell on Monday.

92. *November 29.* November 29 fell on Saturday as here given.

93. *Brigantines.* Rangel (Bourne, II, 81), gives the date of Añasco's arrival at the port as November 19, but this is an evident error. December 28 fell on Sunday as given in our text (see Bourne, II, 81, note 13).

94. *Ochus.* This name appears later in the accounts of the expedition of Tristán de Luna y Arellano as Ochuse. Luna gave it the name Bahia de Santa Maria Filipina because he entered it on August 14 (the assumption of the Virgin) and in honor of Philip II. This was the harbor of Pensacola (see H. I. Priestley, *The Luna Papers*, index).

95. *Maldonado.* Maldonado never again saw the men of the expedition. Fernández de Biedma (Bourne, II, 9) says: "as we were about to set off in quest of the country which that Indian stated to be on another sea, he must return with the brigantines to Cuba, where Doña Ysabel de Bobadilla, his wife, remained, and if within six months' time he should hear nothing of us, to come with the brigantines, and run the shore as far as the River Espiritu Santo, to which we should have to resort." Rangel (*ibid.*, pp. 81–82) says that Maldonado left Apalache on February 26, 1540.

96. *Yupaha.* Probably a reference to Cufitachiqui.

97. *1540.* This date agrees with that given by Rangel (Bourne, II, 82).

98. *River.* Called Guacuca by Rangel (Bourne, II, 82).

99. *Capachiqui.* Acapachiqui in Fernández de Biedma (Bourne, II, 9) and Capachequi in Rangel (*ibid.*, p. 83). Swanton conjectures that this region belonged to the Indians now known as Hitchiti (see Bull. No. 73, p. 118).

100. *Friday.* Bourne (II, 52, note 1) points out that the 11th of the month in 1540 fell on Thursday.

101. *Five.* Rangel says "one hundred," which Bourne (II, 84, note) conjectures to be an error in transcription, "cient" being set down instead of "cinco."

102. *Toalli.* Otoa in Fernández de Biedma (Bourne, II, 10) and Toa in Rangel (*ibid.,* 84). Swanton (Bull. No. 73, p. 12) says these various forms are synonyms of "Tamali," the name of a tribe living in what is now southern Georgia, and probably speaking a Hitchiti dialect. Rangel says they reached this place on the 23rd of the month. Bourne (I, 52, note 2) notes that Wednesday fell on the 24th.

103. *Tile.* Fernández de Biedma (Bourne, II, 9–10) notices the difference of the habitations, saying: "There was a change in the habitations which were now in the earth, like caves; heretofore they were covered with palm leaves and with grass."

104. *Flax.* The bark cloth was probably made from the inner lining of the bark of the mulberry tree. Le Page du Pratz (*Histoire de la Louisiane,* Paris, 1758, II, 191–193) describes the method of manufacture of cloth from the mulberry bark much as does our text. The fiber mentioned by our author might have been the *Urena lobata* (popularly called Caesar's weed in Florida) or the so-called false sisal (*Agave decipiens*), both of which abound in Florida. See J. H. McCulloh, Jr., *Researches Philosophical and Antiquarian Concerning the Aboriginal History of America* (Baltimore, 1829), p. 153; Charles Richard Dodge, *A Report on the Uncultivated Bast Fibers of the United States* (Washington, 1894), p. 14, and *A Report on the Leaf Fibers of the United States* (Washington, 1893), pp. 28–33 (these being respectively "Fiber Investigations," Nos. 6 and 5 of the Department of Agriculture). On the clothing of the Indians in Florida, see also, Swanton, Bull. No. 73, pp. 112, 346, 387, 391.

105. *Drowned.* Rangel (Bourne, II, 85) says: "On Tuesday morning they arrived at Toa, a large village, and the Governor wanted to go on further, but they would not suffer him. On Wednesday, the Governor went at midnight in secret with about forty horse, knights and gentlemen and some others, who for various reasons had not wished to be under another captain." Fernández de Biedma (*ibid.,* p. 10) says that before reaching this village, they crossed two rivers, over which they passed on bridges made by tying the trees together.

106. *Achese.* Called Chisi by Fernández de Biedma (Bourne, II, 10) and Rangel (*ibid.,* p. 85). The latter says that this place was reached on the morning of Holy Thursday; and adds that "though it was Holy Thursday there was not so strict a Christian that he scrupled to eat flesh." Swanton (Bull. No. 73, p. 226) conjectures that the Chisi, Ichisi, or Achese (the people inhabiting this village) belonged to the Coweta, the principal body of the Lower Creeks. He calls attention to the fact that "Ochisi (Otcī´si) is a name applied to the Muskogee by Hitchiti-speaking peoples." [It is more likely that Elvas's Achese are the Hitchiti-speaking Uchise of later Spanish documents rather than the Muskogee-speaking Coweta that John R. Swanton favored.—JH]

107. *Ocute.* Called Ocuti by Fernández de Biedma (Bourne, II, 11). See Swanton, Bull. No. 73, pp. 174–175, who conjectures that the Ocute Indians were identical with the Hitchiti and that this town was the Aeykite of the French census of 1760 and

the Hitch-e-tee of a map of 1818. [In a 1717 census of native settlements just outside of St. Augustine, which contained post–Yamasee War immigrants from Georgia and South Carolina, a chief of Ocute was identified as speaking Yamasee, in circumstances that suggest that Yamasee and Hitchiti were the same language (see John H. Hann, "St. Augustine's Fallout from the Yamasee War," *Florida Historical Quarterly* 68 [1989]: 188–89). Other evidence suggests that Guale also was identical with or very similar to Yamasee and Hitchiti. Diego Camuñas, a native whom Spaniards employed as an interpreter for Guale and Yamasee from the 1670s to the 1690s, was also used in the 1680s as an interpreter for Hitchiti-speaking inhabitants of Apalachicola on the Chattahoochee River. Also a Yamasee, working in Apalachicola as a spy for the Spaniards, mentioned that he was able to pass as a local when he dressed as a local and did so because his language was so similar to that of the locals at Apalachicola.—JH]

108. *Altamaca.* Altapaha in Fernández de Biedma (Bourne, II, 10) and Altamaha in Rangel (*ibid.*, p. 89). The great river mentioned in the text was probably the Altamaha or Oconee. This seems to have been the eastward flowing stream mentioned by Fernández de Biedma (p. 10). See also Swanton, Bull. No. 73, p. 95.

109. *Hens.* Turkeys. Called *guanaxas* by Rangel (Bourne, II, 86). The word "turkeys" is to be understood in all cases where the word "hens" appears in the translation.

110. *Tamemes.* According to Buckingham Smith (*Narratives of the Career of Hernando de Soto,* p. 222), this is a word derived from the Mexican Indians which was in current use among the Spaniards. It is from "tlamama" or "tlameme," signifying porter or carrier of loads on the back.

111. *Patofa.* Tatofa in Rangel (Bourne, II, 91), who gives the name to the chief of the village.

112. *Youth.* Called Perico by Rangel (Bourne, II, 91).

113. *Coça.* Coosa. See Priestley, *The Luna Papers* (DeLand, 1928) for the connection of the Luna y Arellano expedition of 1559–61 with this region. See also Daniel Marshall Andrews, *De Soto's Route from Cofitachequi, in Georgia, to Cosa, in Alabama* (reprint from *Amer. Anthropologist,* XIX, No. 1, 1917), pp. 65–67.

114. *Rivers.* Identified as the Great Ohoopee and Cannouchee rivers by Lewis (*Spanish Explorers,* p. 170, note).

115. *River.* Identified as the Ogeechee River by Lewis (*Spanish Explorers,* p. 170, note 2). See Rangel's account of these crossings (Bourne, II, 93). Some of the swine were lost here.

116. *Inland.* Rangel (Bourne, II, 96) gives the date as Friday, April 23. His details differ somewhat from the text. On that day, Gallegos went upstream to the northwest and Añasco downstream to the southeast. Next day, Lobillo was sent inland toward the north.

117. *Aymay.* Hymahi in Rangel (Bourne, II, 96). The word is possibly identical with Yamassee.

118. *Cutifachiqui.* Called Cofitachequi by Rangel (Bourne; II, 98) and Cofitachiqui by Fernández de Biedma (*ibid.*, p. 13). Swanton identifies it with Kasihta. For information relative to this place and conjecture regarding its location, see Swanton, Bull. No. 73, pp. 216–225; and Andrews, *ut supra,* p. 57, who locates it at Silver Bluff. Lewis (*Spanish Explorers,* p. 172, note) says the word is a proper Creek word and means Dog-wood Town. Swanton (p. 216) says that the word was formerly considered to be a Yuchi word, but its appearance is Muskhogean, and the leading Yuchi authority has been unable to find any Yuchi word resembling it. The latest information relative to Cufitachiqui comes from Miss Mary Ross, of Berkeley, California, who has given much study to this region.

In a note written especially for this volume, Miss Ross says: "It has been an error to have located Cufitachiqui on the Savannah River near Augusta. More misleading has been a confusion of the location of that place with the site of Atlanta. A recent study of the Soto, Pardo, and Woodward documents supplemented by a consultation of maps relative to the old southeast, and confirmed by field work in the district named has settled the question. The 'pearl kingdom' made famous by Soto's encounter with the gracious princess of that realm was in the valley of the Congaree-Broad in South Carolina. The dramatic meeting between the don and the Indian maid took place somewhere in the general vicinity of the present town of Columbia.

"In the colorful accounts of the resolute march of Soto's men through the Florida wilderness, the provincial name for the land of the cacica was given as Cofitachyque, Cofachiqui, and Cutifachiqui. In reports on subsequent expeditions, the region is known variously as Cafatachiqui, Cano or Canosi, Caphatachaques, Chufytachique, Chufytachyqj, Chufytachyque, Chufytuchyque, Cofaciqui, Cofetazque, Cofitachiqui, Cosatachiqui, Cotachico, Tachequiha, Tatikequia, and other such appellations.

"Populous and numerous, the Cufitachiqui villages became renowned for their affluence and industry. For a full century and more that province served as a granary and way-station for expeditions en route to the interior. And on more than one occasion both Spaniards at Santa Elena (Parris Island) and Englishmen at Charlestown sought provisions and protection from the chieftains there. In times of strife the stalwart tribesmen '1000 bowmen' strong were no mean support against trouble making Westoes from the Savannah valley or wild folk from mountain fastnesses.

"Soto was the first European to covet the fruits of that Carolina land; but he was only the precursor of scores of other adventurous spirits seeking new fields to exploit. In the year 1566, Juan Pardo, intent on trans-continental trail blazing, passed through 'Canos or Cofetazque' in his effort to reach overland the distant mines of Zacatecas and San Martín. Copious streams, generous maize fields, rich vineyards, refreshing springs, and rumored mines of crystal, gold, and precious stones called forth the opinion from Pardo's men that therein was a 'land in which to plant a chief town.'

"Eight years later, Pedro Menéndez de Avilés subscribed to the same view when questioned about moving his estate to Pánuco, and he declared that he would keep his dwelling near the Atlantic seaboard. Should he change it would be to the fertile interior near 'Guatari Cano.' In fact, Menéndez planned to establish his Asturian colonists in the Carolina foothills beyond the reaches of the lowlands and marshes that so beset agricultural ambitions at Santa Elena.

"Virginians, too, soon after the days of John Smith, sought 'crystal hills' and pearl bearing streams toward the southwest. And a half century after Menéndez's day other Spanish officials renewed diplomatic relations with the Cufitachiqui leaders and entered into an alliance against the blue-eyed strangers rumored to be riding about the country and pushing in from the north and west.

"Time passed; but the importance of Cufitachiqui did not lessen. Sedentary and stable, the villages persisted and continued to attract other white men by their bounteous maize fields and lucrative trade in deerskin and furs. In 1670, Henry Woodward, surgeon and interpreter for the Charlestown or Cayagua outpost, visited the "Chufytachique" country and entered into a league of friendship. Woodward's enthusiasm exceeded that of his Spanish predecessors and fired the imagination of royal adventurers in England. Cufitachiqui, to the worthy doctor, 'would be a second Paradize' if cultivated. Its broad acres and tall warriors, 'biger and ruder' than the coastal Indians, were vital to Charlestown; while its 'red mould' hills gave promise of hidden treasure beneath outcroppings of 'black and white Marble.' Here were enviable prospects. Both Locke and Ashley were impressed, and step by step the white man pushed in and occupied the west.

"The memory of Soto's camp has lived on. But Cufitachiqui, like the other Indian realms that gave Carolina such a rich historical inheritance has disappeared. Only the red mould hills, pleasant valleys, copious streams, and strange outcroppings of 'anvil rocks,' or rich deposits of splendid blue granite, remain today to tell the tale of that wondrous past."—Mary Ross.

119. *Sister.* Fernández de Biedma (Bourne, II, 13) says that the cacica sent her niece to welcome Soto to her country. She presented him a necklace of five or six strings of pearls. One-half the town was turned over to the Spaniards, but after three or four days, the cacica suddenly went off into the woods.

120. *Hens.* See *ante,* note 109.

121. *Arrobas.* The arroba is a measure of capacity of approximately four gallons; or of weight, of approximately twenty-five pounds. Fernández de Biedma (Bourne, II, 14) says that after the cacica had gone away (see *ante,* note 119), Soto, failing to find her, ordered the graves to be opened. Rangel (Bourne, II, 100) notes that he and Soto together opened the temple where "they found some bodies . . . fastened on a barbacoa. The breasts, belly, necks and arms and legs full of pearls"—in all about two hundred pounds.

122. *Ayllón.* Lucas Vázquez de Ayllón, of a noble family of Toledo, and a man of considerable learning, went to Isla Española (Hispaniola) with Nicolas Ovando, where he amassed considerable wealth. He filled several important posts in the island, finally becoming a member of the audiencia. In 1520, when about to go to

Spain, he was appointed commander of the forces sent to Mexico at the same time that Diego Velázquez sent thither Pánfilo de Narváez in his memorable effort to wrest the command from Cortés. Favoring the latter, he soon returned to Española, as he found it impossible to reconcile the two elements. The same year, 1520, he outfitted an expedition for the purpose of coasting northward along the Atlantic, with Francisco Gordillo as captain and Alonso Fernández Sotil as pilot. His two ships fell in with Pedro de Quexos who had gone on a slave hunting expedition, and the three vessels, joining forces, landed on the mainland, and disregarding Ayllón's orders seized many Indians. Possession of the new coast was taken on June 30, 1521. On their return to Española, the Indians were set free. Ayllón himself, who had not gone personally on the expedition, went to Spain in order to obtain royal concession to explore and settle the new lands. He was granted license to explore the mainland between 35° and 37° by a royal cedula of June 12, 1523 (see *Col. de Doc. inéd. . . . Amer.*, XIV, 503–515), being awarded the usual privileges in such cases. In 1525, he sent Pedro de Quexos on an exploring expedition along the mainland, who explored the coast for a distance of 250 leagues. In July, 1526, Ayllón himself sailed from Española with a company of five hundred people and eighty-nine horses and made a settlement at San Miguel de Gualdape, in about latitude 33°. The colony, however, did not prosper, disease broke out, the Indians were hostile, and, finally, the leader died. It was one of the exploring parties sent out from the expedition which left the articles found by Soto's men. See Fernández de Biedma's mention of this expedition in Bourne, II, 14; Lowery, *Spanish Settlements, 1531–1561,* pp. 157–159; Bolton, *Span. Borderlands* (New Haven, 1921), pp. 12–19; and J. A. Robertson, *List of Documents* (Washington, 1910). Fernández de Biedma (Bourne, II, 14) says that the Spaniards found in the temple at Cufitachiqui "two wood axes of Castilian make, a rosary of jet beads, and some false pearls, which were taken from this country to traffic with the Indians." Rangel (*ibid.*, p. 100) says they found many glass beads and rosaries with their crosses as well as Biscayan axes of iron. See also Swanton, Bull. No. 73, pp. 32–34.

123. *Tierra Firme.* Havana later became the center at which the treasure and trading ships and fleets gathered for the return to Spain; and it was also the port whence the various vessels went to their respective ports in the Indies. For the early trade, see Clarence H. Haring, *Trade and Navigation between Spain and the Indies* (Cambridge, 1918); and Gervasio de Artiñano y de Galdácano, *Historia del Comercio con las Indias durante el Dominio de los Austrias* (Barcelona, 1917). Santa Marta was the second city to be erected in the new world (July 28, 1525).

124. *May 3.* Rangel (Bourne, II, 102) says that the expedition left Cufitachiqui on Wednesday, May 13; but as Bourne points out (p. 102, note 5) May 13 of that year fell on Thursday, and the date should be Thursday, May 13, or Wednesday, May 12.

125. *Chalaque.* Rangel (Bourne, II, 102) says they reached Chalaque in two days. The name appears in Garcilaso de la Vega's narrative both as Chalaque and Chalaques. As Charles C. Royce asserts ("The Cherokee Nation of Indians," in *Fifth*

Annual Report of the Bureau of Ethnology, Washington, 1887, p. 135), the word is apparently the same as "Cherokee." Royce also mentions (pp. 135–136) that the Dutch cartographer, Cornely Wytfliet lays down a site named Chalaqua on his map "Florida et Apalache" (Atlas, 1597) a short distance east of the Savannah River and immediately south of the Appalachian Mountains. In his "Carte de Mexique et de la Floride" (1703), Delisle locates Chalaque at about 33° north latitude. See also the Delisle map of 1718 reproduced in this volume [in Robertson, and herein].

126. *Hens.* See *ante,* note 109.

127. *Xualla.* Xuala in Fernández de Biedma (Bourne, II, 15) and Rangel (*ibid.*, p. 103); and Chouala in Garcilaso de la Vega. The word resembles the modern Cherokee word "Qualla." Rangel locates it on a plain between two rivers. It was in the territory of the Cherokees and has been variously located in northern Georgia and in North Carolina. James Mooney locates it in western North Carolina near the head of Broad River. Cyrus Thomas and others locate it in the Nacoochee Valley in Habersham County (see Lowery, *Spanish Settlements,* p. 230, note 3). Lewis (*Spanish Explorers,* p. 176, note 2) locates it above the junction of the Tuckaseegee and Oconna-Luftee rivers in Swain County, North Carolina. Wytfliet in his map (see *ante,* note 125) locates it to the west of and near the headwaters of the Secco or Savannah River.

128. *Country.* These distances appear to be greatly exaggerated. The Spanish league was somewhat less than three English miles.

129. *Guaxule.* Guasule in Fernández de Biedma (Bourne, II, 15) and Guasili in Rangel (*ibid.*, p. 106). The latter (p. 104) says: "Tuesday, May 25, they left Xuala, and on that day went over a very high range, and at nightfall they encamped at a little mountain." Royce (*Fifth Annual Report of the Bureau of Ethnology,* p. 135) says of the Indians of this region: "Assuming that these people, whose territory De Soto thus traversed, were the ancestors of the modern Cherokees, it is the first mention made of them by European discoverers and more than a century anterior to the period when they first became known to the pioneers of permanent European occupation and settlement." Lowery (*Spanish Settlements,* p. 230) gives the route after leaving Xualla as lying across the Blue Ridge and so down the upper courses of the French Broad to Guaxule, an Indian town which he locates in White County, Georgia. French (*Hist. Col. of Louisiana,* II, 101) and Belknap (*American Biography,* Boston, 1794, I, 189) place the crossing at or about north lat. 35° (see Lowery, p. 230, note 4).

130. *Petaca.* Described in Rangel's narrative (Bourne, II, 104) as "baskets covered with leather and likewise ready to be so covered with their lids, for carrying clothes or whatever they want to." This was probably an interpolation by Oviedo. The "petaca" was probably much like the "tampipi" used in the Philippine Islands.

131. *Cutifachiqui.* Rangel (Bourne, II, 105–6) says that the cacica escaped on May 26 after they had waded through a river and that on the same day and thereabout several desertions occurred. He says: "And that day there remained behind, it was

supposed intentionally, Mendoça de Montanjes and Alaminos of Cuba. And since Alonso Romo kept that day the rearguard and left them, the Governor made him return for them, and they waited for them one day. When they arrived, the Governor wished to hang them. In that region of Xalaque was left a comrade whose name was Rodriguez, a native of Peñafiel; and also an Indian slave boy from Cuba, who knew Spanish, and belonged to a gentleman named Villegas; and there was left a slave belonging to Don Carlos, a Berber, well versed in Spanish; and also Gomez, a Negro belonging to Vasco Gonçalez who spoke good Spanish. That Rodriguez was the first, and the rest deserted further on from Xalaque." This occurred, of course, before reaching Guaxule.

132. *Chiaha.* Chiha in Fernández de Biedma (Bourne, II, 15) and in Rangel (*ibid.*, p. 107); and Ychiaha in Garcilaso. A great deal of confusion seems to exist with regard to the location of this place. Swanton (Bull. No. 73, pp. 167–72) thinks there were at least three sites so named. Two of them are mentioned in the Soto narratives—one being that which had some relation to the settlement of Cufitachiqui and was known also as Lameco or Solameco (perhaps the Jalameco or Talimeco of Rangel—see Bourne, II, 98, 101—and the Talomico of Garcilaso, fol. 169). Of this name, Swanton says (p. 168), "I venture the suggestion that all these names are intended for the same word, Talimico or Talimiko, which again was probably from Creek Talwa immiko, 'town its chief' *wa* being uniformly dropped in composition." The "Chiaha" of the immediate text is that which lay down the river from Guaxule. Of it Garcilaso says (*La Florida del Inca,* fols. 181–182) that after a four days' stay in Guaxule where he informed himself of the country round about, Soto "went in a march of six days (at the rate of five leagues per day) to another village and province called Ychiaha, whose lord had the same name. The route taken on this march of six days was that following the water of the many creeks which flowed by Guaxule, all of which uniting within a short time made a large river, so that at Ychiaha (which was located thirty leagues from Gualuxe [*sic*]) it was larger than the Guadalquivir at Seville.

"This town of Ychiaha was located at the point of a large island more than five leagues wide which was formed by the river." For conjectures regarding the location of the town, see Lowery, *Spanish Settlements,* p. 231, note 2. Belknap (*American Biographies,* p. 192) thinks it was located on a branch of the Mobile River. Lewis (*Spanish Explorers,* p. 178, note 2) conjectures that Chiaha was located on the island at the junction of the Little Tennessee and Tennessee rivers, in Loudon County, Tennessee—that is, it is the hill village noted by Swanton.

133. *Canasagua.* Canasoga in Rangel (Bourne, II, 106). Lowery (*Spanish Settlements,* p. 231) calls it a frontier town of the Cherokees.

134. *July 5.* Hakluyt (p. 59) corrects this date silently to June 5, the date given by Rangel (Bourne, II, 107), which is the right date (see Bourne, I, 73, note 4).

135. *Them.* See *ante,* note 132.

136. *Quiet.* Hakluyt says (p. 60) "the weather was very hot."

137. *Slaves.* Of the stay in Chiaha, Rangel says (Bourne, II, 108): "The Indians spent fifteen days with the Christians in peace, and they played with them, and likewise among themselves. They swam with the Christians and helped them in every way. They ran away afterwards on Saturday, the 19th of the month, for something that the Governor asked of them; and, in short, it was because he asked for women. The next day in the morning the Governor sent to call the chief and he came immediately; and the next day the Governor took him off with him to make his people come back, and the result was they came back. In the land of this Chiaha was where the Spaniards first found fenced villages. Chiaha gave them five hundred carriers, and they consented to leave off collars and chains."

138. *Town.* See *ante,* note 137.

139. *Acoste.* Costehe in Fernández de Biedma (Bourne, II, 15), Coste in Rangel (*ibid.,* p. 109), and Acoste in Garcilaso (*La Florida del Inca,* fols. 184–185). Swanton (Bull. No. 73, p. 201) identifies the Indians of this region with the Koasati, who were closely related to the Alabama.

140. *Chisca.* Identified by Swanton (Bull. No. 73, pp. 288, 289) as a name for the Yuchi Indians (see also pp. 119, 120, 189, 202, 292–293). Swanton locates the province of Chisca "in the rough country in the eastern part of the present state of Tennessee."

141. *Chiaha.* Rangel (Bourne, II, 108) says the expedition left Chiaha on Monday, June 28, and after passing through five or six villages spent the night in a pine grove near a village.

142. *Come.* This incident as described by Rangel (Bourne, II, 109–110) is in fair accord with our text.

143. *Kid.* Evidently a buffalo robe.

144. *July 9.* On Friday, according to Rangel (Bourne, II, 111).

145. *Road.* Rangel (Bourne, II, 111) discloses the reason for the peaceful reception by the cacique of Tali, namely, that Soto had frustrated his attempt to send away the women and children, and the clothing. For the Tali Indians, see Swanton, Bull. No. 73, pp. 211–212.

146. *July 16.* Hakluyt (p. 55) says July 26; and the English translation (1686) of the French edition of 1685, the 15th. The town Coça (Coosa) has usually been located in what is now Talladega County, Alabama (see Bourne, II, 112, note 12, and Lowery, *Spanish Settlements,* p. 232, and note 3). Lewis (*Spanish Explorers,* p. 183, note) says, however, that this village may not have been in the same location as that of later times. The Luna expedition also reached this region about twenty years after Soto (see Priestley, *The Luna Papers,* index; also "Invasion of De Soto in Alabama" in De Bow's *Review of the Southern and Western States,* July, 1850). For the Indians called Coosa, see Swanton, Bull. No. 73, pp. 215, 241, 255. They have generally been considered a genuine Moskogee people. On the way to Coça, Rangel says (p. 111) they slept at a town called Tasqui, which Swanton (Bull. No. 73, p. 208) conjectures may have been occupied by the Tuskegee Indians. [Today the Little Egypt site in

northwestern Georgia is identified as the principal town of the Coosa chiefdom (see David J. Hally, Marvin T. Smith, and James B. Langford, Jr., "The Archaeological Reality of De Soto's Coosa" in Thomas, ed., *Columbian Consequences,* vol. 2, p. 122).—JH]

147. *Seeds.* Fernández de Biedma (Bourne, II, 16) calls Coça "one of the finest countries we discovered in Florida." Rangel (*ibid.*, p. 112) says: "There were in Coça many plums like the early ones of Seville, very good; both they and the trees were like those of Spain. There were also some wild apples like those called canavales in Extremadura, small in size."

148. *Carrying.* Fernández de Biedma (Bourne, II, 16) simply says: "The next morning we saw all the inhabitants, and having detained the cacique, that he might give us persons to carry our loads, we tarried some days until we could get them." Rangel (*ibid.*, pp. 112–113) corroborates the statements of the text, though very briefly.

149. *Tascaluca.* Taszaluza in Fernández de Biedma (Bourne, II, 16) and Tascaluça in Rangel (*ibid.*, p. 115). It is laid down on the 1718 map of Delisle. The name was applied both to the cacique and the region.

150. *Tallimuchase.* Talimachusy in Rangel (Bourne, II, 113). The name means New Town (Swanton, Bull. No. 73, p. 247). Rangel (Bourne, II, 113) says that a Levantine named Feryada deserted at this place.

151. *Ytaua.* Itaba in Rangel (Bourne, II, 113). The same author says that some women were bought at that place in exchange for mirrors and knives. Lowery, *Spanish Settlements,* appendix H, p. 452, suggests (following Mooney) that this region is identical with Yta or Etiwaw.

152. *Ullibahali.* Ulibahali in Rangel (Bourne, II, 113), and Olibahali in Dávila Padilla (*Historia de la Fundacion y Discurso de la Provincia de Santiago de Mexico, de la Orden de Predicadores,* Madrid, 1596, lib. I, Cap. LXII, pp. 245–246). Swanton (Bull. No. 73, pp. 192, 254) says it was a true Muskogee town and identifies it with Liwahali or Holiwahali, "a name which signifies 'to share out or divide war' (*holi,* war, *awahali,* to divide out)." See also Priestley, *The Luna Papers,* I, 225, where Fray Domingo de la Anunciación and others, writing to Luna y Arellano, at Coosa, August 1, 1560, says the town of Ulibaali, "the town mentioned so often by Soto's followers" was probably only five or six leagues away.

153. *Place.* Rangel (Bourne, II, 113–114) says there was a doubt as to whether Manzano had deserted or whether he lost his way. A Negro named Johan Biscayan, belonging to Rodriguez Lobillo, and who spoke Spanish, also deserted at this place. This Negro and one of the Spanish deserters lived for eleven or twelve years among the Indians, as was learned by one of the religious attached to the Luna y Arellano expedition (see Lowery, *Spanish Settlements,* p. 365, who cites Dávila Padilla).

154. *Toasi.* Tuasi in Rangel (Bourne, II, 114); identified as Tawasa by Swanton (Bull. No. 73, p. 137). Rangel notes that thirty-two Indian women were given to Soto at this place.

155. *Tallise.* Italisi in Fernández de Biedma (Bourne, II, 16) and Talisi in Rangel (*ibid.*, p. 115). A Creek town identified as Talsi (Tulsa) by Swanton (Bull. No. 73, p. 151).

156. *Indians.* Fernández de Biedma (Bourne, II, 16) says that the cacique made Soto a present of twenty-six or twenty-seven women at Talisi. See Rangel (*ibid.*, pp. 117–119), for an interpolated homily by Oviedo on the greed and lust of Soto's men.

157. *Casiste.* Also Casiste in Rangel (Bourne, II, 116). Identified by Swanton (Bull. No. 73, pp. 131, 218, 221) as a Lower Creek town inhabited by Kasihta Indians. Rangel says they reached this place on Tuesday, October 5.

158. *Time.* Rangel (Bourne, II, 116) says that after leaving Casiste they came to the towns of Caxa, Humati, and Uxapita. Caxa was the first town belonging to the district of Tastaluça (see Swanton, Bull. No. 73, p. 155).

159. *Built.* Both Fernández de Biedma (Bourne, II, 16) and Rangel (*ibid.*, pp. 120–121) mention the commanding presence of the cacique of Tascaluça. Lewis (*Spanish Explorers*, p. 186, note 2) says this is a correct Creek word meaning Black Warrior. Rangel calls the village where the cacique was found "Athahachi." The district is laid down by Delisle in his map of 1718. [Despite the quotation here, the term Tascaluça is not Creek but Western Muskogean (Choctaw/Chickasaw). The meaning Black Warrior is correct.—VJK]

160. *Motive.* This passage is translated by Hakluyt (p. 71) as follows: "How much the greater the will is, so much more giueth it name to the workes and the workes giue testumonie of the truth. Now touching my will, by it you shall know, how certain & manifest it is, and how pure inclination I haue to serue you." B. Smith translates as follows: "The greater the will the more estimable the deed; and acts are the living witness of truth. You shall learn how strong and positive is my will, and how disinterested my inclination to serve you."

161. *Piache.* Rangel (Bourne, II, 122) says Soto reached Piachi [*sic*] on Wednesday, and describes this town as a "village high above the gorge of a mountain stream." It was located near Mobile Bay (see Swanton, Bull. No. 73, p. 146). Lewis (*Spanish Explorers*, p. 188, note 1) thinks that Piache may have been located on the north side of the Black Warrior River. It was learned in this town (Rangel, p. 123) that a Spaniard and a Negro from the Narváez expedition had been killed.

162. *South.* See *ante*, note 128.

163. *Mavilla.* For various conjectures as to the location of Mavilla (Mauilla—a name surviving in the present "Mobile"), see Lowery, *Spanish Settlements*, pp. 233–234, and note 4, and Lewis, *Spanish Explorers*, p. 189, note 1. For the Indians of this district, see Swanton, Bull. No. 73, pp. 150–160. See also Peter J. Hamilton, *Colonial Mobile* (Boston, 1910), pp. 22–25, and *Mobile of the Five Flags* (Mobile, 1913), pp. 26–27.

164. *October.* Rangel (Bourne, II, 123) agrees with the text as to this date. The former adds that it was St. Luke's day.

165. *Foot.* Rangel (Bourne, II, 123) says that Soto was accompanied by only forty horse.

166. *Eighteen.* B. Smith, doubtless in a moment of distraction, translates (*Narratives*, p. 89): "of the Christians there were killed there two hundred."

167. *Together.* See Fernández de Biedma's description of the fight (Bourne, II, 18–21); and that by Rangel (*ibid.*, pp. 123–128). The first says twenty Spaniards were slain and the second, twenty-two.

168. *November 18.* Rangel (Bourne, II, 128) says Sunday, November 14, which is the correct date.

169. *Cabusto.* Rangel (Bourne, II, 128–129) says they reached a village called Talicpacana on Thursday, November 28 (correct date, November 18), which was the Taliepataua of the text. To reach Cabusto (Zabusta in Rangel), the Spaniards, according to the latter, crossed a river at a village called Moçulixa. Lewis (*Spanish Explorers*, p. 194, note 2) conjectures that Cabusto was located above the Sipsey River and west of the Tombigbee, and Moçulixa was located below the Sipsey and east of the Tombigbee.

170. *Chicaça.* Chicaza in Fernández de Biedma (Bourne, II, 22). The name is applied to a province, village, and river. Lowery (*Spanish Settlements*, pp. 235–236), following Gatschet, Irving, Shea, and Pickett, locates this region as lying "about the headwaters of the Yazoo and Mobile Rivers in what is now the State of Mississippi." Lewis (*Spanish Explorers*, p. 195, note 2) locates the town "about one mile northwest of the present Redland, in Pontotoc County, Mississippi." It was in the territory of the Chickasaws.

171. *Saquechuma.* Sacchuma in Rangel (Bourne, II, 132), who applies the name to the local chief of this district. Lewis (*Spanish Explorers*, p. 196, note) locates the province of Saquechuma on the lower Tallahatchie River and says that the town burned by the Indians was probably located in the present Tallahatchie County.

172. *Fuentes.* Of these four men, Reynoso (Reinoso) and Ribera (Pedro de Rybera) seem to have returned from Florida (see B. Smith, *Narratives of the Career*, pp. 297, 298). Francisco Osorio was a kinsman of Antonio Osorio, son of the Marqués de Astorga (so in Solar and Rújula, p. 327, instead of the brother, as given in our text [herein, vol. 1]). Reynoso is perhaps the Francisco de Reinoso noted by Solar and Rújula, p. 327, who was the son of Gonzalo or Gregorio de Reinoso and Isabel de Escobar, of Boadilla. The Fuentes of the text may have been Fernand Sanchez de la Fuente, the son of Garcia Gonzalez de la Vera and Juana Martin, inhabitants of Valencia de la Torre (Solar and Rújula, p. 313).

173. *Man.* Hakluyt (p. 84) mistranslates this passage, saying "was held for a tall man."

174. *Her.* Francisca Hinestrosa, the only Spanish woman in the expedition. Her husband, Luis de Inostrosa (Ynistrosa), son of Juan Fernández de Inostrosa and Guiomar de Torres, of Seville, returned from Florida (see Solar and Rújula, p. 318, and B. Smith, *Narr.*, p. 292).

175. *Jerkins.* See Fernández de Biedma's account of the disaster, in Bourne II, 22–23, and Rangel's, in *ibid.*, pp. 132–134.

176. *Field.* Called Chicacilla, which Lewis (*Spanish Explorers*, p. 199, note) conjectures was located about three and one-half miles north of Chicaça.

177. *1541.* Wednesday. Rangel (Bourne, II, 135), says the Indians attacked on Tuesday, March 15, in the morning watch, which is the correct date.

178. *April 25.* Rangel (Bourne, II, 136) says Tuesday, April 26—the correct date.

179. *Alimamu.* Alibamo in Fernández de Biedma (Bourne, II, 24) and Limamu in Rangel (*ibid.*, p. 136). The Indians of this region were the Alabama or Alibamo, an Upper Creek tribe (see Swanton, Bull. No. 73, pp. 191–201).

180. *Waiting.* Lewis (*Spanish Explorers,* p. 200, note) says the fort and ford were on the Tallahatchie River, somewhere near New Albany, in the present Union County, Mississippi.

181. *Quizquiz.* Hakluyt's translation (p. 89) is at fault here. Quizquiz is called Quizqui by Rangel (Bourne, II, 137). See Swanton, Bull. No. 73, p. 293.

182. *River.* This was the Mississippi, which is called Espiritu Santo by Fernández de Biedma (Bourne, II, 25).

183. *Flaunting.* Hakluyt (p. 169) says "shielding themselves"; and B. Smith (*Narratives*, p. 104), "covering themselves."

184. *Hereafter.* Lewis (*Spanish Explorers,* p. 204, note) places the crossing of the Mississippi either at the present Council Bend or Walnut Bend, in Tunica County, Mississippi, below Memphis. Bourne (II, 138, note 3) places it below Memphis and above the mouth of the Arkansas. See also Lowery, *Spanish Settlements,* p. 237, and note 2. The attempt to locate the point of the crossing has been the subject of considerable debate. See special bulletin, No. 1, of the Mississippi Historical Society, edited by Dunbar Rowland, namely, *A Symposium on the Place of Discovery of the Mississippi River by Hernando de Soto* (Jackson, Mississippi, 1927). Those who participated in the symposium were Theodore H. Lewis, J. P. Young, Charles A. Barton, and Dunbar Rowland. See T. H. Lewis, "Route of De Soto's Expedition from Taliepacana to Huhasene," pp. 19–20 of *A Symposium* (also in *Pubs. of the Mississippi Historical Society,* VI, 456–457).

185. *Casqui.* Icasqui in Fernández de Biedma (Bourne, II, 26); both Quarqui and Carqui in Rangel (*ibid.*, p. 138); and Casquin in Garcilaso de la Vega (fol. 231); Swanton (Bull. No. 73, pp. 213–214) connects the name with the Indians variously called Kaskinampo, Caskinampo, Kaskinoba, Caskemampo, Cakinonpa, Kakinonba, Karkinonpols, Kasquinanipo, and says that the name was also applied to the Tennessee River. See also Lewis, "Route of De Soto's Expedition," in *Pubs. of the Mississippi Historical Society,* VI, 457.

186. *Crossed.* Lewis (*Spanish Explorers,* p. 206, note) identifies the small river as Fifteen-Mile Bayou, and the locality as probably near the southeast corner of St. Francis County, Arkansas.

187. *Acorns.* Probably pecans.

188. *Gray.* Identified by B. Smith (*Narratives,* p. 223) as *Diospyros Virginiana* and *Diospyros Texana.* [The Portuguese that Robertson rendered as "gray" is *pardo.* Although *pardo* can mean "dark gray," it is used more commonly for "brown," the color of a mulatto, which is another of the meanings of *pardo.*—JH]

189. *Town.* Lewis (*Spanish Explorers,* p. 206, note) conjectures that this town was located near the mouth of the present Tyronza River. Of the town and the stay of the Spaniards there, Rangel says (Bourne, II, 138–139): "It was Saturday when we entered his village, and it had very good cabins, and, in the principal one, over the door, were many heads of very fierce bulls, just as in Spain noblemen who are sportsmen mount the heads of wild boars or bears."

190. *Suffered.* Of the cross, Rangel (Bourne, II, 139) says: "There the Christians planted the cross on a mound, and they received and adored it with much devotion, and the blind and lame came to seek to be healed."

191. *Flowing.* Lewis (*Spanish Explorers,* p. 208, note) identifies this as the present Tyronza River.

192. *Them.* The plight of the men is well described in an interpolation made by Oviedo in Rangel's narrative (Bourne, II, 130–131), as follows: "And that you may know, reader, what sort of a life these Spaniards led, Rodrigo Ranjel, an eye-witness, says that among many other great hardships that men endured in this undertaking he saw a knight named Don Antonio Osorio, brother of the Lord Marquis of Astorga, wearing a short garment of the blankets of that country, torn on the sides, his flesh showing, no hat, bare-headed, bare-footed, without hose or shoes, a buckler on his back, a sword without a shield, amidst heavy frosts and cold. And the stuff of which he was made and his illustrious lineage made him endure his toil without laments such as many others made, for there was no one who could help him, although he was the man he was, and had in Spain two thousand ducats of income through the Church. And the day that this gentleman saw him he did not believe that he had eaten a mouthful, and he had to dig for it with his nails to get something to eat.

"I could hardly help laughing when I heard that this knight had left the Church and the income above mentioned to go in search of such a life as this, at the sound of the words of De Soto."

193. *Cowhide.* Buffalo hide.

194. *June 19.* Rangel (Bourne, II, 139) gives the date of the arrival at Pacaha as Wednesday, June 29; but our text is here correct. Lewis (*Spanish Explorers,* p. 209, note) gives the probable location of Pacaha as in the vicinity of the present Osceola, Mississippi County, Arkansas, but not any farther toward the north (see also Lewis, "Route of De Soto's Expedition," p. 457).

195. *Above.* Inquiry as to the identity of the several kinds of fish mentioned in the text brought the following information from Dr. Lewis Radcliffe, acting commissioner of the Bureau of Fisheries at Washington: "The *bagre* no doubt refers to a species of catfish. Judging by the large size of the fish and its large head, as described,

it was most likely the mud catfish, *Leptops olivaris.* However, there is also a possibility that the author had in mind the blue catfish *Ictalurus furcatus.* Indeed, both species might have been seen in the vicinity, since both are of a large size and quite common in the rivers draining into the Gulf of Mexico. The word *barbo* is used in Spanish and French for several species of freshwater fish. The British name for those species is 'barbel.' The species to which these names are applied are wide-spread throughout Europe, including Portugal. Judging from the distribution of the species and the similarity of the names in England, France, and Spain, it seems quite likely that the name *barbo* is also applied in Portugal to the same fishes. None of the species of the barbels occur in American waters, but our species of suckers resembles in general appearance the European barbels, and to a lesser extent the same may be said in regard to our buffalofishes. There are several species of suckers and buffalofishes in American waters; but from the author's statement it is impossible to assert which one of these he had in mind. In a list of the common names of fishes in Portuguese, the name *choupa* is applied to *Sargus rondeletti* and *besugo* to *Pagellus acarne.* Neither of these species, both of which are spiny-rayed fishes, occurs in the waters of the United States. The Portuguese *choupa* is shaped something like our bream and the *besugo* resembles our black bass. Since the author evidently described only the larger fishes, two possibilities suggest themselves: he had in mind either the black bass (and in some of them, especially in large specimens, the body is fairly deep) or the fresh-water drum. Since he states that it was the 'most relished,' he probably had in mind the large-mouth black bass, *Micropterus salmoides.* The *pexe palla* was undoubtedly the spoonbill, *Polyodon spathula.* The description of the snout combined with the lack of scales, as stated by the author, applies to no other American species, and it fairly characterizes the spoonbill. [The official common name of the fish here called "spoonbill" is the paddlefish—VJK] The name *savel* (plural *saves*) is applied to two species of European shad, *Alosa alosa* and *Alosa finta.* A species of shad, *Alosa alabama,* occurs in the gulf drainage, although it is now quite rare. The author may have seen this or one of two other fishes, namely, the gizzard shad, *Dorosoma cepedianum,* and the menhaden, *Brevoortia patronus.* These two latter species resemble the shad in appearance, although they usually do not grow over a foot in length. There are several other clupeoid fishes in the waters of Florida, which have some resemblance to the shad, although they are of small size. It is impossible to identify the *pexe pereo* with any exactness. The names *peixe prego* and *peixe porco* are applied to species of sharks in Portugal. Judging from the author's comparison of the fish to a hog, a fish having a deep body is suggested. The following three species, which are found in these waters, are quite common and have rather deep bodies, namely, the fresh-water drum or gaspergou, *Aplodinotus gruniens,* the black drum, *Pogonias chromis,* and the jew-fish, *Promicrops itaiara.* The first named is a strictly fresh-water fish. The black drum is typically a salt-water fish, but is also common in brackish water; while the third is a salt-water species."

See also B. Smith, *Narratives,* pp. 223–226. It should be noted that the words "era de tamanho de Picoes," which have been translated "were as long as a pike" refer to "pike" the weapon and not "pike" the fish.

196. *Find.* See the accounts of these two chiefs in Fernández de Biedma (Bourne, II, 26–29) and Rangel (*ibid.,* pp. 136–146).

197. *Caluça.* Caluç in Fernández de Biedma (Bourne, II, 30). Swanton (Bull. No. 73, p. 214) says of this district: "This would seem to be the Choctaw or Chickasaw Oka lusa, 'black water,' from which we may possibly infer the Muskhogean connection of Casquin, but, on the other hand, the name may have been obtained from interpreters secured east of the Mississippi, and may be nothing more than a translation of the original into Chickasaw." The word apparently has no connection with the Calusa Indians of the Florida peninsula. Lewis (*Spanish Explorers,* p. 212, note) tentatively locates the province of Caluça in the northeastern part of the present state of Mississippi, extending from Baldwyn, Prentiss County, to the Tennessee River in Tishomingo County.

For the route of the expedition west of the Mississippi, see Theodore H. Lewis, "Route of De Soto's Expedition from Taliepacana to Huhasene," in *Pubs. of the Mississippi Historical Society,* VI (Oxford, Mississippi, 1902), pp. 449–467.

198. *Plums.* Probably persimmons.

199. *Cattle.* The bison.

200. *Quiguate.* Rangel (Bourne, II, 146) says that Quiguate was the largest village the Spaniards had seen in that region (in which he agrees with our text) and that it was located on the Casqui River.

201. *Mochila.* Rangel (Bourne, II, 144) says that Casqui gave one of his daughters to Soto and that Pacaha gave him one of his own wives, besides a sister and another Indian woman of rank. Oviedo (Bourne, II, 145) moralizes as follows: "But I could wish that along with the excellencies of the cross and of the faith that this Governor explained to these chiefs, he had told them he was married, and that the Christians ought not to have more than one wife, or to have intercourse with another, or to commit adultery; that he had not taken the daughter whom Casqui gave him, nor the wife and sister and the other woman of rank whom Pacaha gave him; and that they had not got the idea that the Christians, like the Indians, could have as many wives and concubines as they desired, and like the Indians, live as adulterers."

202. *Aquiguate.* See *ante,* note 200. Lewis (*Spanish Explorers,* p. 214, note 1) locates this town on the west side of the St. Francis River, in what is now the northern part of Lee County, or in the southern part of St. Francis County, Arkansas.

203. *Swamp.* Lewis (*Spanish Explorers,* p. 214, note 2) conjectures that this may have been Lake Mitchigamia of the French maps, which ceased to exist after the New Madrid earthquake. This lake is shown on the great Delisle map of 1718 on which the route of Soto is marked. The cartographer shows the route to have passed near a vague location which he calls Lac de Mitchigamia.

204. *Coligoa.* Coligua in Fernández de Biedma (Bourne, II, 31) and Rangel (*ibid.*, p. 146).

205. *Marshes.* "Lakes" in B. Smith's translation (p. 121) and in Hakluyt (p. 107).

206. *Leagues.* Hakluyt (p. 107) says "one hundred leagues."

207. *Streamlets.* Fernández de Biedma (Bourne, II, 31) says that on the way to Coligoa, they went at "night to the swamps, where we drank from the hand and found abundance of fish." Rangel says (*ibid.*, p. 146) the Spaniards left Quiguate on Friday, August 26, reaching their destination at the village of Coligoa on the following Thursday, September 1, journeying on the way from swamp to swamp to the number of four swamps. In these swamps or pools they found "no end of fish, because all that country is flooded by the great river when it overflows its banks." Lewis, *Spanish Explorers* (p. 215, note 1), conjectures that the four swamps of Rangel were the L'Anguille River, Big Creek, Bayou de Vue, and Cache River.

208. *Town.* Rangel (Bourne, II, 146–47) says that they came twice to the river of Coligoa before they reached the town itself; and he adds: "They found it populated, and from it they took much people and clothes, and a vast amount of provisions and much salt. It was a pretty village, between some ridges along the gorge of a great river. And from there, at midday, they went to kill some cows, of which there are many wild ones." Lewis (*Spanish Explorers*, p. 216, note 1) says the town lay in the valley of the Little Red River, and that before reaching it the Spaniards crossed the White River below the mouth of Little Red River, in what is now Woodruff County, Arkansas.

209. *Palisema.* According to Rangel (Bourne, II, 147), the Spaniards left Coligoa on Tuesday, September 6, and after recrossing the river and some mountains, reached a town called Calpista on Wednesday, "where there was an excellent salt spring which distilled very good salt in deposits." This spring, says Lewis (*Spanish Explorers*, p. 216, note 2), was located on the bank of Little Red River, in what is now Cleburne County. Palisema is called Palisma by Rangel (*ibid.*, p. 147), who says it was reached on Thursday (September 8).

210. *Tatalicoya.* Called Tutilcoya by Rangel (Bourne, II, 147), who says that on Saturday, September 10, the expedition encamped beside some water. On Sunday, they reached a town called Quixila, "where they rested over Sunday." They reached Tutilcoya on Tuesday. Fernández de Biedma (Bourne, II, 32) says they went under direction of their guides to some scattered settlements called Tatil Coya, where they found a river of considerable size which emptied into the Mississippi.

211. *Cayas.* Fernández de Biedma (Bourne, II, 32) says they went upstream to a great province called Cayas. This was evidently a district of scattered settlements, as noted in our text. There seems to have been some confusion in Rangel's account (see Bourne, II, 147) with regard to this district, which that author calls Cayase. Rangel says "they were never able to see that place or discover it; and subsequently they were told that they had left it near the river." Lewis (*Spanish Explorers*, p. 217, note

2) says that Cayas was located in what is now the northern part of Arkansas and Oklahoma. He connects the word with the appellation "Kansas" (see "Route of De Soto's Expedition" in *Pubs. of the Miss. Hist. Soc.*, VI, 458, note 20).

212. *Tanico.* Rangel (Bourne, II, 147) says that on Thursday, after having passed the night near a swamp, the Spaniards went to the district and town of Tanico, which was confused with Cayas by some. Tanico, according to Lewis (*Spanish Explorers*, p. 217, note 3) was on the east side of the Grand or Neosho River. It was probably a part of the district of Cayas.

213. *Pot.* Rangel (Bourne, II, 148): "One ought not to omit and leave in forgetfulness that in Cayase our Spaniards gathered baskets of dry sand from the river and strained water through it, and there came out a brine, and they boiled it down, and let it harden, and in that way made excellent salt, very white and of good flavour."

214. *Wounded.* Rangel (Bourne, II, 148) says the expedition left Tanico on Wednesday, October 5, reaching the town of Tula on Friday, October 7. On Saturday, the fight with the Indians occurred, during which one Hernandarias de Saavedra, grandson of the marshall of Seville, was wounded. Fernández de Biedma (*ibid.*, pp. 32–33) says that in going to Tula, they "passed over some rough hills." He says that the Indians wounded some seven or eight men and nine or ten horses; while the Spaniards killed some thirty or forty of the Indians. His account is quite similar to that of our text.

215. *Sheep.* These cattle were the American bison.

216. *Ridges.* Lewis (*Spanish Explorers*, p. 221, note) identifies these ridges as the Boston Mountains.

217. *Quipana.* Fernández de Biedma (Bourne, II, 34) says that after leaving Quipana the route lay eastward across the mountains and down to the plains. This town is called Guipana by Rangel (*ibid.*, p. 149). Lewis, "Route of De Soto's Exped.," p. 459, note 23, connects this word with "Pani" or "Pawnee." The province of Guahate mentioned below has not been identified.

218. *Catamaya.* Quitamaya in Rangel (Bourne, II, 149), which was reached on Monday, October 31.

219. *Autiamque.* Viranque in Fernández de Biedma (Bourne, II, 34) and Utiangue in Rangel (*ibid.*, p. 149). Rangel says that on Tuesday, November 1, they passed through a small village and reached Utiangue on Wednesday, November 2. The narrative by Rangel ends at this point. Lewis (*Spanish Explorers*, p. 222, note 2) locates Autiamque within thirty miles of Fort Smith, on the south bank of the Arkansas River.

220. *Safety.* Hakluyt (p. 115) translates this passage as follows: "They tooke some Indians which were gathering together the stuff which their wives had hidden."

221. *Autiamque.* The words "of Autiamque" were omitted by B. Smith.

222. *Tietiquaquo.* Lewis (*Spanish Explorers*, p. 223, note) says this town was located in the province of Chaguate (see *post*, note 250).

223. *Ortiz.* The death of Juan Ortiz is merely noted without comment by Fernández de Biedma (Bourne, II, 34).

224. *Ayays.* Lewis (*Spanish Explorers,* p. 225, note 1) points out that this province must not be confused with that of Aays, which was located south of Red River in Texas. Fernández de Biedma (Bourne, II, 34) says that after leaving Autiamque (Viranque), the Spaniards followed the course of the river to a province called Anicoyanque, which probably corresponds to the Nilco or Anilco of our text.

225. *River.* Lewis (*Spanish Explorers,* p. 225, note 2) says that the place where they crossed the river lay north of the present Pine Bluff, and was probably in the present Jefferson County.

226. *Swamps.* Hakluyt says the region had many lakes.

227. *Tutelpinco.* Located by Lewis (*Spanish Explorers,* p. 225, note 3) on Big Bayou Meto, in the present Jefferson County.

228. *Bastian.* Francis Sebastian in Hakluyt (p. 119). The name Francisco Sebastian occurs in the list given by Solar and Rújula, p. 309. He was the son of Alonso Sebastian and Juana Macias, both of the town of Villanueva de Barcarrota. The town of Tianto mentioned below has not been identified.

229. *Swamp.* Translated "lake" by Hakluyt (p. 120) and by B. Smith (*Narratives,* p. 136).

230. *Nilco.* Lewis (*Spanish Explorers,* p. 226, note) locates Nilco a few miles southeast of the present Arkansas Post, on the Arkansas River, in Desha County. There is a large mound there. See *ante,* note 224.

231. *Margaridetas.* Translated "margaritas" in Hakluyt (p. 120). Literally a small pearl; perhaps here a small trade bead made from shell.

232. *Swamp.* "Lake" in Hakluyt (p. 121) and in B. Smith (*Narr. of the Career,* p. 137).

233. *Guachoya.* See *post,* note 235.

234. *Quigaltam.* See *post,* note 298.

235. *Guachoya.* Guachoya is located by Lewis (*Spanish Explorers,* p. 227, note 1) in the neighborhood of the present Arkansas City, on the Mississippi River, in Desha County, and perhaps at or near the large mound north of that city. This place is called "Guachoyanque" by Fernández de Biedma (Bourne, II, 34–35), who says the town was "good, well and strongly fenced."

236. *April 17.* If the date of November 1 of the preceding year fell on Tuesday, as given by Rangel (see *ante,* note 219) is correct, then April 17 fell on Monday.

237. *Ri.* The Tamaliseu was probably the Arkansas; the Tapatu, the Mississippi; the Mico, perhaps the Coosa; and the Ri (evidently for Rio), the stream near where the expedition first entered Florida. There seems to be some confusion about this passage in B. Smith's translation.

238. *Were.* Hakluyt (p. 124) adds "every day," but these words are not in the original.

239. *Backward.* B. Smith (*Narr. of the Career,* p. 141) wrongly makes the reply of the chief a direct discourse; it is only a reported speech.

240. *Brazas.* The braza is a measure about equivalent to the fathom.

241. *Die.* Hakluyt (p. 127) translates this passage as follows: "These mens sinnes by Gods permission lighted on their own heads: who, because they would seeme valiant, became cruel; showing themselves extreme cowards in the sight of all men, when as most neede of Valour was required, and afterward they came to a shameful death."

242. *Alvarado.* See *ante,* note 10.

243. *Fitting.* Fernández de Biedma's only comment on the death of Soto is the dry remark (Bourne, II, 35): "The governor, at seeing himself surrounded, and nothing coming about according to his expectation, sickened and died. He left us recommending Luis de Moscoso to be our Governor." Cf. with this and the text, the touching remarks of Antonio Pigafetta after Ferdinand Magellan's death, in James A. Robertson, *Magellan's Voyage around the World by Antonio Pigafetta* (Cleveland, 1906), I, 177–179.

244. *River.* Garcilaso de la Vega (*La Florida del Inca,* fol. 272) says: Soto was buried in the river by Juan de Añasco, Juan de Guzmán, Arias Tinoco, Alonso Romo de Cardenosa, and Diego Arias. They were assisted by a Basque sailor and engineer, named Joannes de Abbadia. The corpse was buried with all secrecy (the men making signs as if they were going fishing) in the middle of the river in water having a depth of nineteen brazas and a width of a quarter of a league.

245. *Hogs.* This refers to Soto's property at the place of his death. See Soto's will (which was made in Cuba on May 13, 1539, shortly before the departure for Florida) in Solar and Rújula, pp. 207–221 (reproduced from the original manuscript in AI, 50-2-55/10, Papeles de Justicia, numero 750, pieza 1ª., fols. 42–51); and a translation into English made from the original manuscript, in B. Smith, *Narr. of the Career,* pp. 273–280. See also Solar and Rújula, pp. 223–273 (original in AI, 502-55/10, *op. cit.,* fols. 306–333), for the list of possessions left by Soto in Spain and the prices they fetched at auction. Garcilaso de la Vega (*op. cit.,* fol. 271) says that Soto had spent over 100,000 ducats on his expedition.

246. *Obtained.* Garcilaso de la Vega (*op. cit.,* fol. 270) notes that Moscoso had been deprived of the post of maestre de campo after the disaster at Chicaça.

247. *Leagues.* Hakluyt (p. 133) says wrongly "four hundred leagues."

248. *June 5.* Monday apparently fell on June 5.

249. *Catalte.* This region has not been identified, but it lay west of Guachoya. It is called "Catayet" on the map (see p. 418 [of Robertson—Ed.]).

250. *Chaguete.* Called Chavite (meaning "salt"—see Lewis, "Route of De Soto's Exped.," p. 461) by Fernández de Biedma (Bourne, II, 35–36), who says that they traveled for seventeen days from Guachoyante (Guachoya) to Chavite. Lewis (*Spanish Explorers,* p. 236, note) conjectures that this district may have been located on the

present Saline River in Saline County. The same author notes that the expedition turned south-southeast at this point. Fernández de Biedma says they turned "southwest-and-by-south."

251. *Reward.* B. Smith (*Narratives,* p. 152) omits everything in this discourse after this point.

252. *Lake.* Probably more of a marsh than a lake.

253. *Guzmán.* Apparently this was Francisco de Guzmán, son of Benito Rodriguez and Francisca Hernández, inhabitants of Seville. See Solar and Rújula, *op. cit.*, p. 289.

254. *July 4.* Fernández de Biedma (Bourne, II, 36) says it took the men three days to reach Aguacay, and that it lay due west from Chaguete. The same author adds: "After leaving this place, the Indians told us we should see no more settlements unless we went down in a southwest-and-by-south direction, where we should find large towns and food; that in the course we asked about, there were some large sandy wastes, without any people or subsistence whatsoever." July 4 fell on Tuesday.

255. *There.* Lewis (*Spanish Explorers,* p. 238, note 2) locates this place a short distance from the present town of Arkadelphia on the west bank of the Ouachita River.

256. *July 20.* July 20 fell on Thursday.

257. *Naguatex.* Hakluyt (pp. 136–137) says, "They pitched their Campe at noone betweene *Amaye* and *Naguatex* along the corner of a grove of very faire trees." Lewis (*Spanish Explorers,* p. 239, note) conjectures that this was on Prairie de Roane near the present town of Hope.

258. *Were.* Hakluyt (p. 137) says wrongly "and what order they kept."

259. *River.* Identified by Lewis (*Spanish Explorers,* p. 210, note) as the present Little River in Hampstead County.

260. *River.* Identified by Lewis (*Spanish Explorers,* p. 241, note) as the present Red River.

261. *People.* Lewis (*Spanish Explorers,* p. 242, note) identifies this ford as the present White Oak Shoals in Arkansas, three miles east of the Texas-Arkansas boundary.

262. *Six.* B. Smith (*Narratives,* p. 159) says wrongly "five."

263. [The Portuguese that Robertson translated as "miserable" is *proue*, which presumably was a misspelling of *pobre.*—JH] *Nisohone.* "Nisione" in Fernández de Biedma (Bourne, II, 36).

264. *Lacane.* Probably the "Came" of Fernández de Biedma (Bourne, II, 36).

265. *Nondacao.* Fernández de Biedma (Bourne, II, 36) uses the same form. This author says that the cacique of Nondacao furnished them a guide who purposely tried to lead them over rough country and off the road. The guide confessed that he did not know where he was guiding the Spaniards, but that he had been ordered to lead them into a region where they would die of hunger.

266. *Soacatino.* Fernández de Biedma (Bourne, II, 36) says: "We were obliged to

go where the Indian directed us, and went to a Province called Nisione, and to another called Nondacao, and another Came; and at each remove we went through lands that became more sterile and afforded less subsistence. We continually asked for a province which they told us was larger, called Xuacatino."

267. *Aays.* Properly Ayays. Fernández de Biedma (Bourne, II, 36–37) says: "We took another guide, who led us to a Province called Hais, where, in seasons, some cattle are wont to herd; and as the Indians saw us entering their country, they began to cry out: 'Kill the cows—they are coming'; when they sallied and shot their arrows at us, doing us some injury." Lewis (*Spanish Explorers,* p. 243, note) conjectures that this district is south of the present Gainesville, Texas, and that the town adjoined the "Lower Cross Timbers," on the prairie.

268. *Fight.* See preceding note.

269. *Nondacao.* Here, as elsewhere, the chief and his town are called by the same name. Hakluyt (p. 142) says "in Nondacao." It appears as "nõdacan" on the map (p. 418 [of Robertson—Ed.]).

270. *Christians.* Perhaps an echo of the Coronado expedition.

271. *Soacatino.* See *ante,* note 266. Fernández de Biedma (Bourne, II, 37) describes this district (which he also calls "Xacatin") as lying amid close forests and having little food. Lewis (*Spanish Explorers,* p. 244, note 1) conjectures that this region was located in the present "Upper Cross Timbers." It appears on the map (p. 418 [of Robertson—Ed.]) as Cehocatin.

272. *Southward.* Fernández de Biedma (Bourne, II, 37) says: "Hence the Indians guided us eastward to other small towns, poorly off for food, having said that they would take us where there were other Christians like us, which afterwards proved false." After this, he says they turned south and "travelled about six days in a direction south and southwest, when we stopped."

273. *Guasco.* Identified by Lewis (*Spanish Explorers,* p. 244, note 2) as Waco, Texas. If one gives the "w" sound to the Spanish "Gu," which is so often heard, and drops the "s" of "Guasco," the name "Waco" results. Lewis conjectures that this town was evidently located on the Brazos River, near old Fort Belknap.

274. *Naçacahoz.* This and the town of Naquiscoça mentioned above are conjectured by Lewis (*Spanish Explorers,* p. 144, note 3) to lie in the Brazos valley, southeast of Guasco.

275. *Naçacahoz.* Lewis (*Spanish Explorers,* p. 245, note 1) conjectures that this was the Double Mountain fork of the Brazos; and adds that the crossing was probably made at the south angle of the river, in the northwestern part of the present Fisher County.

276. *Daycao.* Lewis (*Spanish Explorers,* p. 245, note 2) conjectures that the "unpeopled region" or "wilderness," as it is translated by B. Smith, was a forest. He points out that the continuous forest from old Fort Belknap to the eastern slope of the "Staked Plains" was the only one through which the men could have gone for ten days to the westward.

277. *Alqueire.* A dry or solid measure of 138 deciliters. The liquid alqueire is equivalent to 84 deciliters.

278. *Arabs.* The word "Alarve" (Arab) has the derived meaning of "boor" or "glutton."

279. *Come.* Of the determination to return to the Mississippi River, Fernández de Biedma (Bourne, II, 38) says: "Reflecting that we had lost our interpreter, that we found nothing to eat, that the maize we brought upon our backs was failing, and it seemed impossible that so many people should be able to cross a country so poor, we determined to return to the town where the Governor Soto died, as it appeared to us there was convenience for building vessels with which we might leave the country."

280. *Montemor.* Estremóz is a town of Alemtejo, Portugal, twenty-three miles northeast of Evora. It is famous for its earthenware jugs and has a large trade in wool, and has many marble quarries rivaling those of Italy. Montemor is perhaps the Montemor Novo in Alemtejo, twenty-two miles north-northwest of Evora. See Lemos, *Encyclopedia Portugueza ilustrada.*

281. *Christian.* See *ante*, p. 237, and note 253.

282. *Aays.* See *ante*, note 267.

283. *Chilano.* This town has not been identified.

284. *There.* Probably ropes were made of this fiber.

285. *Aminoya.* Lewis (*Spanish Explorers*, p. 249, note 1) locates Aminoya above the mouth of the Arkansas River in the present Desha County. Hakluyt, in translating, uniformly uses the form "Minoya."

286. *Lethargy.* Perhaps malaria or dysentery.

287. *Sotis.* Hakluyt (p. 150) translates this passage "by their surname called Sotis."

288. *Fanegas.* The fanega is a dry measure of quantity equivalent to four alqueires (see *ante*, note 277), used for measuring grains and seeds. [*Fanegas* is often used as a measure of weight rather than volume, its weight is equivalent to 100 kilos. The *fanga*, the term for four alqueires of grain, was 1.57 bushels in Portugal and 4.12 bushels in Brazil.—JH]

289. *Daffodils. Abrotea*, literally "daffodil." Both Hakluyt (p. 151) and B. Smith (*Narratives*, p. 169) translate "hemp," which is more expressive.

290. *Tagoanate.* See *post*, note 293.

291. *Water.* Hakluyt (p. 151) translates this passage "because their places of refuge are in the water"; and B. Smith (*Narratives*, p. 170), "as their places of concealment were by the water's edge." The primary meaning of *colheita* is "harvest" or "fruits." It seems here to refer directly to the harvests which had perhaps been placed in *barbacoas* on islets. [There is no question but that *colheita* refers to harvest. The allusion to the "harvests" being "on the water" is probably simply a reference to the planted fields of as yet unharvested maize being close to the river in the floodplain, which most southeastern natives used for their agriculture.—JH]

292. *Them.* Hakluyt (p. 152) translates "for to goe to take them, they were neuer able." [The Portuguese that Robertson translated as "for there would have been no

remedy except to go to take them" is *porque pa lhas yr tomar nam auia remedeo.* From what precedes and follows this clause, the meaning of the Portuguese seems to be, "for there was no way for us to go to take them," which is close to the rendition that Hakluyt gave to this phrase. In the sentence that follows this passage, Elvas states that as soon as winter set in they were unable to move out with the horses needed for launching an attack to take the blankets.—JH]

293. *Taguanate.* Lewis (*Spanish Explorers,* p. 253, note) says this province lay on the White River, and that the town so named was probably located in the southern part of the present Monroe County in Arkansas, possibly at Indian Bay.

294. *Brigantines.* Fernández de Biedma (Bourne, II, 38) says: "We returned by the same road we had taken, until we came to the town; but we did not discover so good outfits as we had thought to find. There were no provisions in the town, the Indians having taken them away, so we had to seek another town, where we might pass the winter and build the vessels. I thank God that we found two towns very much to our purpose, standing upon the Rio Grande, and which were fenced around, having also a large quantity of maize. Here we stopped, and with great labour built seven brigantines, which were finished at about the end of six months. We threw them into the water, and it was a mystery that, calked as they were with the bark of mulberry trees, and without any pitch, we should find them stanch and very safe."

295. *Canoes.* Fernández de Biedma (Bourne, II, 38–39) intimates that the canoes with the horses were taken along in case a large town were found on the seacoast where the expedition might be supported, while two of the brigantines were sent to New Spain "with a message to provide us with vessels in which we could get away from the country."

296. *Twenty-two.* Fernández de Biedma (Bourne, II, 39) says twenty-six horses were taken.

297. *Right.* Lewis (*Spanish Explorers,* p. 255, note 1) says this arm of the river was a channel by which the Bayou Macon is connected with the Mississippi and that it is located in the northern part of the present Chicot County, Arkansas.

298. *Quigualtam.* Also spelt Quigaltam (see *ante,* note 234); "Quigualtanqui" in Garcilaso de la Vega, fol. 192. It lay on the opposite side of the Mississippi from Guachoya.

299. *Bluff.* Lewis (*Spanish Explorers,* p. 255, note) conjectures that this bluff was the present Vicksburg Bluffs.

300. *Twenty-five.* Hakluyt (p. 159) says wrongly "fifteen."

301. *Determine.* Fernández de Biedma (Bourne, II, 39) says of the assaults by the Indians: "The second day, descending the stream, there came out against us forty or fifty very large and swift canoes, in some of which were as many as eighty warriors, who assailed us with their arrows, following and shooting at us. Some who were in the vessels thought it trifling not to attack them; so, taking four or five of the small canoes we brought along, they went after them. The Indians, seeing this, surrounded them, so that they could not get away, and upset the canoes, whereby twelve very

worthy men were drowned, beyond the reach of our succor, because of the great power of the stream, and the oars in the vessel being few."

302. *Rest.* Hakluyt (p. 161) says "lingered behind."

303. *Sea.* Hakluyt (p. 162) says "until they came to the sea."

304. *Seventeen.* Fernández de Biedma (Bourne, II, 39) says they reached the sea in nineteen days. He says (p. 39–40) that encouraged by their first success, the Indians kept up their attacks "doing us much damage and wounding many people; for, as they found we had no arms that could reach them from a distance, not an arquebuse nor a crossbow having remained, but only some swords and targets [shields—Ed.], they lost their fears, and would draw very nigh to let drive at us with their arrows."

305. *So.* Lewis (*Spanish Explorers,* p. 259, note) points out that Garcilaso de la Vega increases this distance to 750 leagues, but that the real distance was about 720 miles.

306. *Sea.* Fernández de Biedma (Bourne, II, 40) says, "We came out by the mouth of the river, and entering into a very large bay made by it, which was so extensive that we passed along it three days and three nights, with fair weather, in all the time not seeing land, so that it appeared to us that we were at sea, although we found the water still so fresh that it could well be drunk like that of the river."

307. *Las Palmas.* Later called the Santander River and the River Soto la Marina, its present name. It enters the gulf 110 miles above Tampico. A large bar is formed at the mouth from the silt carried down by the current.

308. *Them.* This sentence is omitted by Hakluyt (p. 165).

309. *Sea.* Lewis (*Spanish Explorers,* p. 261, note) says that "at that time the Atchafalaya probably formed the lower course of Red River, the latter not having cut through to the Mississippi, and it was its current that they encountered."

310. *Keys.* Hakluyt (p. 166) mistranslates "creeks."

311. *Key. Ibid.* (p. 167).

312. *Fortune.* Hakluyt (p. 168) says "while they were in this tempest."

313. *Copee.* Cope, in Spanish. A name applied to various species of the genus *Clusia.* Two species, especially are known in Hispanic America, namely, *Clusia Rosea* or Cope grande; and *Clusia minor* or Cope chico. They are both found in Venezuela where they are called "cupay." Both kinds are used for their resinous qualities and are used, among other ways, in the calking of water craft. The text may refer, however, to some bituminous substance. This name apparently appears on the map [in Robertson] (p. 418).

314. *Islet.* Fernández de Biedma (Bourne, II, 40) says they went westward to some small islets.

315. *Better. Cf.* the procession made by the survivors of Magellan's ship, the *Victoria,* after landing in Spain in Robertson, *Magellan's Journey around the World by Antonio Pigafetta,* II, 189.

316. *Palmas.* See *ante,* note 307.

317. *Panico.* The River of Pánuco. This river, about 400 miles long, rises in the Valley of Mexico and enters the Gulf of Mexico six miles below the city of Tampico, now the great oil port of Mexico. The drainage of the Valley of Mexico, a stupendous accomplishment, takes place through a canal and tunnel emptying into one of the branches of the Pánuco River. This stream, notwithstanding the formidable bar at its mouth, is navigable for deep draft vessels to Tampico and to vessels of light draft to the city of Pánuco.

318. *Panico.* The town of Pánuco. This town was founded in 1520 at the orders of Cortés by Gonzalo de Sandoval, who called it San Sebastián del Puerto. Its Aztec name "Pánuco" means "place settled by persons who came by sea." It is located on the Pánuco River, about eighty miles from the Gulf of Mexico by water, but only about forty by land. Pánuco was the capital city of a former administrational unit of New Spain, also called Pánuco, which was bounded on the north by the Nuevo Reino de León and part of the audiencia of Guadalajara, on the east by the gulf, on the south by the provinces of Tlaxcala and Mexico, and on the west by the Reino de Michoacán. During the eighteenth century, it formed part of Nuevo Santander. In that century it had about 500 families and near the close of the nineteenth, about 9,000 inhabitants. The district was first visited by men of the expeditions of Garay. See Antonio de Alcedo, *Diccionario Geográfico Histórico de las Indias Occidentales* (Madrid, 1788), IV, 55; and Espasa, *Enciclopedia universal,* XLI, 900.

319. *Mendoza.* Antonio de Mendoza, the first viceroy of New Spain, was born in 1490, in the fortress of Alcala la Real along the Granada border. His father, Iñigo López de Mendoza, second conde de Tendilla, was captain general of the forces that were investing Granada. The family is said to trace back to the celebrated Spanish hero, the Cid, and thence to some of the best Roman and Gothic families. He was appointed viceroy of New Spain in April, 1535, and reached Mexico in October of the same year. In 1547, he was transferred to the viceroyalty of Peru, with his seat at Lima. He died in that city on June 21, 1552, and was buried beside Francisco Pizzaro, the great conqueror of Peru. In an age of narrow bigotry, he was characterized by an unusual breadth of mind (for that period), and was above all an excellent organizer and administrator. See Arthur S. Aiton, *Antonio de Mendoza* (Durham, 1927); and Ciriaco Pérez Bustamante, *Don Antonio de Mèndoza* (Santiago, 1928).

320. [Robertson's expression "they had ported there three hundred men" seems awkward. "Three hundred men had arrived in port there" would be better.—JH]

Men. Hakluyt (p. 173) says "three hundred and eleven men," thus giving the correct number as noted above. See also B. Smith (*Narratives,* pp. 292–299), "A Memoir of the names of persons who came from Florida, who they are, and of what countries natives." This shows a list of slightly over two hundred names. In the same volume, Smith publishes also two documents relative to the followers of Soto, as follows: 1. Letter to the king from the viceroy of New Spain, with testimony in behalf of Garcia Osorio, soliciting the royal favor, 1560, pp. 299–300. 2. Memorial of Alonso Vazquez to the king of Spain, petitioning for certain privileges, and permission to reside in Florida, together with the testimony of persons as to his services in the army of Hernando de Soto, during the invasion of that province, pp. 301–312.

321. *Mestitam Mexico.* Mestitam is undoubtedly a corruption of the word "Tenochtitlan," the Aztec name for the City of Mexico. The form of "Mestitan" occurs in Genaro Garcia's edition of Bernal Diaz del Castillo, *Conquista de la Nueva Espana* (Mexico, 1904), I, 460 and II, 362. There are many corrupted forms of the name. For the history of pre-Spanish and early Spanish Mexico, see Prescott, *Conquest of Mexico,* Charles Cullen's translation into English of Francisco Saverio Clavigero, *Historia Antigua de Mexico,* editions of which were issued in London, 1787, Richmond, 1806, and Philadelphia, 1817.

322. *Vera Cruz.* Hakluyt (p. 174) says "and other 60 from Panuco to the Port of Vera Cruz," omitting the three words "and from Mexico." The city of Vera Cruz, the chief seaport of Mexico, is located on the southwest shore of the Gulf of Mexico, one hundred and ninety miles from Mexico. Being on low, sandy, and marshy ground, it was a menace to health until recently, but is now sanitary and a modern city. Many of its buildings and its wall are of coral rock. It has a population of over 50,000; and is chiefly a commercial city, although it has some manufacturing industries. It was first visited by Europeans by Juan de Grijalva and next by Cortés (April 21, 1519), who landed at the point called by the natives Chalchiuhuecan on April 22. Because this was Good Friday and because of the wealth of the district, Cortés named it "La Villa Rica de la Vera Cruz." It was the point of departure for the conquest of Mexico. In modern times it has also been a place of entry for hostile troops on more than one occasion.

323. *East.* Hakluyt (p. 174) says "Panuco to the North."

324. *Food.* "Inda q̃ onestamente tiueram de comer." Translated by B. Smith (*Narratives,* p. 198): "particularly in respect of everything to eat."

325. *Tapile.* The proper form of the word is "topil" or "topile." It has the meaning of the Spanish word "alguazil," meaning "constable." It was early taken over into Spanish use. Ricardo del Castillo, *Los llamados Mexicanismos de la Academia Española* (Mexico, 1917), says (pp. 162–163) that the word is seldom used now in any state of Mexico. Eufemio Mendoza, *Apuntes para un Catálogo Razonado de las Palabras Mexicanas* (Mexico, 1872), p. 51, says it is used now only in a burlesque style. The word occurs in most of the Aztec dictionaries; e.g., Rémi Siméon, *Dictionnaire de langue Nahuatl ou Mexique* (Paris, 1885), p. 651.

326. *Meadows.* Hakluyt (p. 177) says: "it hath thinne woods, and very goodly meadows upon the Riuers."

327. *Swamps.* Translated "lakes" by B. Smith (*Narratives,* p. 201).

328. *Northeast.* Hakluyt (p. 178) says wrongly "northwest."

329. *Daycao.* See *ante,* pp. 252–253, and note 276.

330. *Others.* Hakluyt (p. 178) says "from those that grow more eastward."

331. *Acorns.* Pecans. See *ante,* note 187.

332. *Ligoacam.* William B. Rye, in his edition of Hakluyt's translation of the *Relaçam: The Discovery and Conquest of Terra Florida* (London, 1851), conjectures that this may refer to the *Lignum Guaiacum* (see p. 169, note 1). From the description of the fruit, it is probable that this was the alligator pear or avocado (Spanish, "aguacate").

333. *Walnuts.* See *ante,* note 198.

334. *Black birds.* Rye (*ut supra,* p. 169, note 5) conjectures that this black bird may be the winter cow-bird, *Molothrus pecoris.*

335. *Coast.* Not necessarily true, but it happens that the Calusa Indians who dwelt about the southern part of the Florida Peninsula and among the keys were the fiercest Indians of that region. See Hodge, *Handbook of the American Indian* (Washington, 1907); and Samuel Cole Williams (ed.), *Adair's History of the American Indians* (Johnson City, Tenn., 1930).

336. *Infante.* A reference undoubtedly to Enrique (1512–1580), son of King Manoel, the Fortunate, a cardinal and archbishop of Braga, Lisbon, and Evora, and inquisitor general. He was proclaimed king of Portugal in 1578; in 1580 Portugal passed to Spain after the defeat of Don Antonio, the pretender, and did not regain its independence until 1640.

Relation of the Island of Florida

by
Luys Hernández de Biedma

Newly Translated and Edited by
John E. Worth
With Footnotes by
John E. Worth
and
Charles Hudson

Introduction
Biedma's Account of the Expedition

by John E. Worth

Luys Hernández de Biedma accompanied the De Soto expedition as factor of the Crown, and while his role in the expedition appears to have been small, as judged by all of the documents, his brief relation is the only complete account for which the original document survives. It is located in the General Archive of the Indies in Seville, in Patronato 19, Ramo 3. The account comprises twenty pages written in an even hand and is personally signed by Biedma. While this manuscript was penned only a short time after the expedition, from Biedma's testimony before the Consejo de Indias in 1544, its contents were not published until the mid-nineteenth century. The first and only complete English translation from the original Spanish was published in 1866 by Buckingham Smith[1] and has been reprinted several times by various editors.

The following translation was drawn from microfilm of the original manuscript (at the P. K. Yonge Library of Florida History, University of Florida, Gainesville) and a nearly flawless printed transcription, both of which have been checked by this author during an examination of the original in Seville. Throughout, the goal has been to present as closely as possible in English the account as Biedma related it in Spanish. The following translation is therefore largely literal, with only occasional and minor restructuring of the original syntax in order to render specific passages into English more effectively. It is important to note that the original manuscript possesses no punctuation and no paragraphs, and thus these have been created based on grammatical structure and content. All names are preserved precisely as originally written. Interpolations by this editor are set off by brackets, and selected original Spanish terms are bracketed following their translation where they first appear in the relation. Where appropriate, certain common

[1]Buckingham Smith, *Narratives of the Career of Hernando de Soto in the Conquest of Florida* (New York: Bradford Club Series, No. 5, 1866).

Spanish terms remain untranslated. Footnotes have been added to provide additional information where precise meaning seems important or where meaning is ambiguous, and to provide supplementary commentary and information.

Relation of the Island of Florida . . . 1539[2]

by Luys Hernández de Biedma

We arrived at the port of Baya Honda and disembarked six hundred and twenty men and two hundred and twenty-three horses. As soon as we disembarked, we found out from some Indians that were captured that there was a Christian there in the land who was one of those who had gone with Pánfilo de Narváez, and we went in search of him; a *cacique* who was about eight leagues from the port had him. We came upon him on the road; he was already coming toward us, for when the cacique found out that we had disembarked there, he asked the Christian if he wished to come where we were. He told him yes, and [the cacique] sent nine Indians with him. He was naked like them, with a bow and some arrows in his hand, his body decorated like an Indian. As the Christians came upon them, they thought that they were Indians who came to spy on them; they went toward them, and they fled to a small forest [*montecillo*] that was nearby. The horses reached them, and they gave a lance-blow to an Indian and easily might have killed the Christian, because he knew little of our language, since he had forgotten it. He remembered how to call to Our Lady, and by this he was recognized to be a Christian.

We brought him with much joy to where the Governor was. He had been among those Indians for twelve years, and he also knew their language; he had been speaking it for so long that he was among us more than four days before he could join one word with another, since upon saying one word in Spanish, he would say another four or five in the language of the Indians, until finally he was again able to speak our language well. He knew little of the land and had neither seen nor heard of things only twenty leagues away. He told us upon seeing us that there was not a bit of gold in the land.

---

[2] The date here is a later filing note and refers to the beginning date of the events recounted in the relation. The exterior page of Biedma's relation includes the following brief descriptions: "Relation of the outcome of the armada which Captain Soto led" and "Relation of the outcome of the journey of Captain Soto, and of the quality of the land through which he walked."

All of us who had disembarked departed from the port of Baya Honda in order to penetrate the interior, except twenty-six on horseback and sixty foot soldiers that remained to guard the port until the Governor responded or sent for them. We went west[3] and then turned northwest. We had news of a cacique that the Indians told us everyone paid tribute to; he was named Hurripacuxi, and he was up to twenty leagues from the coast. We went from here, crossing some swamps [*ciénagas*] and rivers [*ríos*], another fifteen or twenty leagues from there to a town [*pueblo*] that the Indians made out to us to be very large, so much so that they told us that its people, shouting, made flying birds fall. We arrived at this town, which was called Etocale. It was a small town; we found some corn and beans and little dogs to eat, which was no small relief for the people, who were dying of hunger.

We stayed here seven or eight days, during which some excursions were made to capture some Indians who might guide us to the province of Apalache, which was widely known in all the land. They captured three or four Indians, but the one who knew the most did not know two leagues farther on from that town. We left from here traveling ever toward New Spain [Mexico], at a distance of ten or twelve leagues from the coast. We passed some towns in the five or six days that we traveled, until we arrived at a fair-sized village [*poblazón razonable*] called Aguacalecuen. We found all the Indians gone, having fled for the woods; here we halted another six or seven days in order to look for some Indians who might guide us. Going to look for some Indians, ten or twelve women were captured, among whom, they told us, one was a daughter of the cacique; for this reason the cacique came to us in peace and said that he would give us interpreters and guides for farther on, but he never gave them to us. We had to take him with us, and at the end of six or seven days that we traveled, about three hundred and fifty Indians came forth to attack us with bows and arrows, intending to take the cacique away from us. We killed some of them and apprehended all the rest. Among them there were some Indians who knew of the interior, and there they told us many great lies.

We crossed another river, which was in a province called Veachile, and we found some towns on the other bank, all abandoned, although we did not fail to find in them what we had need of, which was some food. We departed

[3]Biedma indicated direction using the terms *via* and *vuelta* interchangeably to signify way, or perhaps direction, in phrases such as *la via del Poniente,* or "the way of the west." This first reference to direction seems to be incorrect (since they landed on the west coast), although Biedma's directions elsewhere seem quite accurate.

from here for another town, which is called Aguile. This [town] borders on [*confina con*] that province of Apalache; a river divides the one province from the other. On this river we made a bridge of many pines tied to one another, and we crossed with great danger, because on the other side there were Indians who defended the crossing against us. When the Indians saw that we had crossed the river, they went away to the nearest town, which is called Yvitachuco, and waited there until we arrived in view of the town. Upon seeing us appear, they set fire to all the town and fled.

In this province of Apalache there are many towns, and it is a land of plentiful food; they call all this other land that we traveled through the province of Yustaga. We went to another town which is called Yniahyco, and here it seemed to us that it was time to find out about those who remained at the port, and that they should know about us, because we intended to plunge so far into the interior that we might not be able to have more news of them. We had already walked one hundred and ten leagues from where we left them up to there, and the Governor sent them a message to come where we were.

Here we went to look for the sea, which was about nine leagues from this town, and we found on the shore the place where Pánfilo de Narváez[4] made the boats, because we found the site of the forge and many bones of the horses, and the Indians told us through the interpreter how the other Christians had made those boats there. Juan de Añasco made certain signs in some trees that were on the shore of the sea, because the Governor ordered him to call the people who had remained at the port, and to send them by land the way we had come, and to come back by sea in two brigantines and a small vessel [*batel*] that was there, and to bring them to that province of Apalache; meanwhile we remained waiting there.

Juan de Añasco sent the people by land, and he came back by sea as the Governor commanded him, where he endured much hardship and danger, because he did not find that coast; he did not find a trace of what he had seen by land before he went there by sea, because the inlets [*ancones*] were shallow, and at high tide they had water but at low tide they were dry. We made a *piragua*[5] that each day went out two leagues into the sea to see if the brigantines were coming, in order to show them where they were to stop. Thanks to God they came to them by sea and the other people by land.

The brigantines having come, the Governor commanded that they go

[4]The Narváez expedition skirted the Gulf Coast in 1528.

[5]A *piragua* was a larger vessel than a canoe, but similarly long and narrow.

west, to see if they could find some port that might be near there, in order to know the coast, if they [the army] should find something in the interior. Francisco Maldonado, a nobleman from Salamanca, went in the brigantines, cruising the coast and entering all the coves [*caletas*] and inlets and rivers that he saw, until he arrived at a river where he found a good entrance, and a good port and a town of Indians on the seacoast. Some came to barter with him, and he captured one of those Indians and came back for where we were.

He spent two months on this journey, yet to all of us it became a thousand years through detaining us there so long, since we had news of the interior. When Maldonado came, the Governor told him that since we were going in search of the land that Indian told us was on another sea, he should return in those brigantines to the island of Cuba, where Doña Isabel de Bobadilla, the wife of the Governor, was, and that if within six months he had no news of us, he should come back in those brigantines and cruise the coast as far as the river of Espiritu Santo [the Mississippi], because we would have to return there.

The brigantines went to Cuba, and we headed north, in order to see what the Indians told us. We traveled five days through an uninhabited region [*despoblado*] until we arrived at a large and very swift [*muy corriente*] river. We could not make a bridge because of the strength with which it flowed, but we made a piragua in which we crossed. On the other bank we found a province, which is called Acapachiqui, very abundant in food of that which the Indians ate. We saw some towns of the province, and others we could not see because it was a land of very great swamps. Here we found a difference in the houses of the Indians; we found them as caves below the ground,[6] while up to there they were covered with palms and straw.

We went onward and came upon[7] two other rivers. We had to make bridges of tied pines on them, as we were accustomed to make them. We arrived at another province, which is called Otoa. We found a fair-sized town, larger than any we had found up to there. From there we went to other towns of another province, which was about two days from there,

---

[6] *Como cuevas debajo de tierra.* This probably refers to semi-subterranean structures with depressed floors, a type of architecture that archaeologists recognize to have been common in some regions at this time. Elvas also notes a difference in architecture but places it at Toa to the immediate north.

[7] The original manuscript has a word crossed out in front of *topamos,* or "we came upon." It appears to be *pasamo,* suggesting the first intention was to write *pasamos,* or "we crossed," which was corrected.

where we captured some people unawares, who had not heard about us. They agreed to come to serve us in peace so that we would return the people that we had taken from them. The Governor returned them, and the only ones they did not take from him were some interpreter guides for farther on. We spent five or six days in passing through this province, which is called Chisi, where we were well served by the Indians, from the little that they had.

From here we traveled another three days without seeing a village, until we came to another province, which is called Altapaha. Here we found a river that did not flow to the south like the others that we had crossed. It flowed east, to the sea, where the *licenciado* [lawyer] Lucas de Ayllón had come;[8] because of this we gave much more credit to what the Indian told us and believed all the lies that he had told us to be true. This province was well populated with Indians, and they all served us. The Governor questioned them about that province that we were searching for, which was called Cofitachique, and they told us that it was not possible to go there; there was neither a road nor anything to eat on the road, and we would all die of hunger.

We went onward to other caciques, who were named Ocute and Cofaqui, and they gave us some of the foods they had and told us that if we wished to go to make war on the lady of Cofitachique, they would give us all that we might want for the journey. They told us that there was no road by which to go, since they had no dealings with one another because they were at war; sometimes when they came to make war on one another, they passed through hidden and secret places where they would not be detected, and they spent twenty or twenty-two days on the road and ate only herbs and some toasted corn that they brought.

Having seen our determination, they gave us eight hundred Indians to carry our food and clothes, and other Indians to guide us; they headed straight to the east and traveled for three days. The Indian who had deceived us told us that in three days he would get us there. At the end of the three days we were already beginning to see the lie of the Indian. The Governor did not stop following the road that he had started on because of that, and he commanded that all should save as much food as they could, because he suspected what afterward happened, that we would be in great hardship and necessity. We traveled through this uninhabited region thirteen days, and at the end of them we arrived at some cabins [*cabañas*]. The Indians had al-

[8]Ayllón established a short-lived colony on the Atlantic Coast in 1526.

ready lost their bearings, and they did not know where to go or what road to give us.

The Governor went out to look for it and returned despairing of being able to find it; he made the people return about half a league from there to a large river, and there he began to give a pound of pork to each Christian as rations from some pigs that we were taking with us, and we ate it boiled in water without salt or anything else. And from here the Governor sent people in two directions to look for a road; one he sent upriver, north and northeast, and the other he sent downriver, south and southeast, and he gave to each one a limit of ten days to go and come back, to see if they found some road or saw a trace of a town.

He who went south and southeast came back in four days with news that he had come upon a little village [*poblezuelo pequeño*] with some food, and he brought from it three or four Indians who spoke with that Indian who deceived us, and they also understood the interpreter. This was no little thing for us because of the great necessity for interpreters that there is in the land. And he again affirmed the lies that he had told us, and we believed him through seeing the interpreter speak with those Indians. We all then departed to go to that little village and await there those who had gone in other directions to look for a road, and we were here four or five days, until all the people gathered. We found about fifty fanegas[9] of corn and some flour of toasted corn, and many mulberry trees loaded with mulberries, and some other small fruit.

We departed from here for the town of Cofitachique, which was two days' journey from this little village. It was on the bank of a river that we believe was the river of Santa Elena, where the licenciado Ayllón was. Having arrived at this river, the lady of the town sent us a niece of hers, and some Indians brought her on a litter with much prestige. And she sent a message to us that she was delighted that we had come to her land, and that she would give us whatever she could and had, and she sent a string of pearls of five or six strands to the Governor. She gave us canoes in which we crossed that river and divided with us half of the town. She was with us three or four days and then went away to the woods.

The Governor sent people to look for her, and when she could not be found, he opened a temple[10] that was there, where the important people of

[9]A *fanega* of corn equals approximately 100 pounds, making Biedma's amount roughly 5,000 pounds.

[10]*Mezquita*, probably referring to a temple or other public structure.

that land were buried, and we gathered from there a quantity of pearls; there must have been up to six and a half or seven arrobas[11] of them, although they were not good because they were damaged through being below the ground and placed amidst the adipose tissue of the Indians. Here we found buried two Castilian axes for cutting wood, and a rosary of beads of jet and some *margaritas* of the kind that they carry from here [Spain] to barter with the Indians.[12] All this we believed they had obtained from barter with those who went with the licenciado Ayllón.

According to the information that we had from the Indians, the sea was up to thirty leagues from there. We found out that the people that went with Ayllón scarcely went inland at all but rather stayed always on the seacoast, until Ayllón became sick and died. Afterward the people killed one another, each one intent on taking command, and many others [died] of hunger; one who had found himself there[13] told us that of six hundred men that Ayllón had settled in that land, not more than fifty-seven had escaped, largely because of losing a large ship loaded with provisions.

We were in the town of this lady for about ten or eleven days, and then it was advisable for us to leave from there in search of land where there was food, because here there was none, except a very limited amount for the Indians to eat, and we, with the horses and the people, used it up very quickly. We turned again north and traveled eight days through land poor and lacking in food until we arrived at a land that they call Xuala, and here we found little population, because of the land being rugged, but still we found some Indian houses. In these mountains we found the source of the great river by which we left,[14] and we believed it to be the river of Espiritu Santo. We went onward to a town that is called Guasuli, where they gave us a quantity of dogs and some corn, of which they had little.

From here we traveled four days and arrived at a town that is called

[11]One *arroba* equals approximately 25 pounds, placing the estimated weight of the pearls roughly between 160 and 175 pounds.

[12]Beads of jet, commonly used for rosaries, have not been recognized archaeologically prior to the mid-seventeenth century. The *margaritas* noted in the text were common trade beads but have not been positively identified. For further information, see Kathleen Deagan, *Artifacts of the Spanish Colonies of Florida and the Caribbean, 1500–1800* (Washington, D.C.: Smithsonian Institution Press, 1987).

[13]This individual might have been a survivor of the 1526 Ayllón colony who was also a member of the De Soto expedition.

[14]The members of the expedition believed that these were the headwaters of the Mississippi River, through which they would ultimately depart from Florida.

Chyha, which is very abundant in food. It is situated on an island in this river of Espiritu Santo, which from its source makes very large [islands]. In this province we began to find the towns palisaded [*cercados*], and here the Indians extract a great quantity of oil from nuts. We stayed here twenty-six or twenty-seven days, in order to give some relief to the horses, because they were very fatigued from little to eat and much labor. We departed from here, along the bank of the river, and arrived at another province that is called Costehe, where the towns are likewise on islands in the river.

From here we went to the province of Coça, which is one of the best lands that we came upon in Florida. Its cacique came forth to receive us on a litter with great festivity and many people, because he has many subject towns. The next day in the morning all the Indians fled. We captured the cacique, so that he would give us Indians to carry our burdens, but he detained us several days before he gave them to us. We found in this province plums like those from here in Castille, and a great quantity of wild vines, on which there were very good grapes. We departed from here toward the west and southwest, and went through towns of this cacique for five or six days, until we arrived at another province that is called Italisi. We found the people gone and went to look for them. Some Indians came to us, whom the Governor sent to call the cacique; he came to us and brought us as present twenty-six or twenty-seven women and hides of deer and whatever they had.

From here we headed south, drawing near the coast of New Spain, and we passed several towns until we arrived at another province that was called Tascaluza, of which the cacique was an Indian so large that, to the opinion of all, he was a giant. He awaited us in peace in his town. We made much festivity for him when we arrived and jousted and had many horse races, although he appeared to think little of all this. Afterward we asked him to give us Indians to carry the burdens, and he responded that he was not accustomed to serving anyone, rather that all served him before. The Governor commanded that he not be allowed to go to his house, but rather that he should be detained there; as a result he felt that he was detained among us, and because of this he committed the ruin that afterward he inflicted on us.

Because he said that he could not give us anything there, that we should go to another town of his, which was called Mavila, and that there he would give us what we requested of him, we headed for there, arriving at a large river [*río caudal*], which we believe is the river that flows into the bay of Chuse. Here we had news of how the boats of Narváez had arrived in need of water, and that here among these Indians remained a Christian who was called Don Teodoro, and a black man with him. They showed us a dagger[15] that the Christian had. We were here two days making rafts to cross this river, during which the Indians killed a Christian who was one of the Governor's guard. In a fit of anger, he [the Governor] treated the cacique badly and told him that he was going to burn him unless he gave him the Indians that had killed the Christian. He said that in his town of Mavila he would give them to us.

This cacique was an Indian who brought along many other Indians who served him, and he always walked with a very large fly-flap [*moscador*] made of feathers, which an Indian carried behind him in order to block the sun. We arrived at Mavila one day at nine in the morning. It was a small and very strongly palisaded town and was situated on a plain. There were some Indian houses on the outside of the palisade, but we found that the Indians had demolished all of them to the ground in order to have the field more clear. Some important Indians came forth to us upon seeing us and asked the Governor, through the interpreter, whether he wished to spend the night there on that plain or if he wished to enter within the town and said that in the afternoon they would give us the Indians for the burdens. It seemed to the Governor that it was better to enter in the town with them, and he commanded us all to enter in there, and so we did it.

Having entered within, we were walking with the Indians, chatting, as if we had them in peace, because only three hundred or four hundred appeared there, but there were a good five thousand Indians in the town, hidden in the houses. We did not see them, nor did the Indians appear. As they made festivity for us, they began to do their dances and songs. In order to dissemble, they had fifteen or twenty women dance in front of us. After they had danced a little while, the cacique arose and entered one of those houses. The Governor sent a message for him to come outside, and he said that he did not wish to. The Captain of the Governor's guard entered to bring him out, and he saw so many people within, and so ready for war, that he thought it a good idea to go out and leave him, and he said to the Governor that those houses were full of Indians, all with bows and arrows, ready to do some treachery.

The Governor called to another Indian who was passing by there, who likewise refused to come. A nobleman who found himself alongside him seized him by the arm in order to bring him, and then he [the Indian] gave a

[15] *Puñal,* or a poniard.

Spanish Swordsman, Arquebusier, and Pikeman about 1540. Fighting against soldiers equipped in this manner was demoralizing for native peoples who, however, showed great courage and ingenuity when facing them. The pikeman wears quilted cotton armor, which was much lighter than chain mail or plate armor and yet was effective protection from native archery. (Courtesy of Osprey Publishing, London)

pull that set himself free. Then he [the nobleman] put hand to his sword and gave him a slash that cut off an arm. Upon wounding this Indian, all began to shoot arrows at us, some from within the houses, through many loopholes that they had made, and others from outside. As we were so unprepared because we thought that we had met them in peace, we suffered so much damage that we were forced to leave, fleeing from the town, and all that the Indians brought us in our loads remained within, as they had unloaded it there. When the Indians saw us outside, they closed the gates of the town and began to beat their drums and to raise banners with a great yell, and to open our trunks and bundles and display from the top of the wall all that we had brought, since they had it in their possession.

As soon as we left the town, we mounted our horses and encircled the entire town, so that the Indians might not get away from us on any side, and the Governor decided that sixty or eighty of us should dismount, those of us who were best armed, and that we should form ourselves in four squads and assault the town on four sides, and that the first to enter should set fire to the houses, so that they might not do us more damage from within, and that we should give the horses to other soldiers who were not armed, so that if some Indians should come forth from the town in order to flee, they might overtake them. We entered within the town and set fire, where a quantity of Indians were burned, and all our supplies were burned, so that not one thing remained.

We fought that day until it was night, without one Indian surrendering to us, rather they fought like fierce lions. Of those who came out, we killed them all, some with the fire, others with the swords, others with the lances. Later, near nightfall, only three Indians remained, and they took those twenty women that they had brought to dance and placed them in front of themselves. The women crossed their hands, making signs to the Christians that they should take them. The Christians came to take them, and they turned aside, and the three Indians who were behind them shot arrows at the Christians. We killed two of the Indians, and one who remained alone, in order not to surrender to us, climbed a tree that was in the wall itself, and removed the cord from the bow and attached it to his neck and to a branch of the tree and hanged himself.

This day the Indians killed more than twenty of our men, and two hundred and fifty of us escaped with wounds, for we had seven hundred and sixty arrow wounds. We treated ourselves that night with the adipose tissue of the dead Indians themselves, since we had no other medicine, because all had burned that day. We stayed here treating ourselves twenty-seven or twenty-eight days, and thank God we all healed. We took the women and divided them among the most seriously wounded, in order that they might serve them.

We heard through news from the Indians that we were up to forty leagues from the sea. Many wished that the Governor would go to the sea, because they [the Indians] gave us news of the brigantines, but he did not dare, for the month of November was already half over and it was very cold, and he felt it advisable to look for a land where he might find provisions in order to be able to winter. In this [land] there were none, because it was a land of little food. We turned again north and walked ten or twelve days' journey, with great hardship from cold and from waters that we crossed on foot, until we arrived at a province, well-provisioned [*gruesa*][16] and with plenty of food, where we could halt while the fury of the winter passed, because more snows fell there than in Castille.

Having arrived at this province of Chicaça, the Indian warriors came forth to defend a crossing of a river that we had to cross, and they detained us there three days. In the end we crossed in a piragua that we made, and all the Indians fled to the woods. After seven or eight days, messengers from the cacique came to the Governor, saying that he and all his people wanted to come to serve us. The Governor received him well and sent a message for him to come in any case, and that he would give them many of the things he had brought. The cacique came and brought many Indians, who carried him on their shoulders. He brought us some little dogs and hides of deer. The cacique remained with us, and the other Indians went away again. Each day Indians went and came and brought many rabbits and whatever they could have in the land, and also at night some Indians were captured, who, under the pretense of being at peace, came to see the manner in which we slept and how we guarded ourselves.

Unaware of the treachery that they had intended, we told the cacique that we wished to depart the next day in order to continue our journey. He went away, and that night he came upon us, and as they already knew where we had placed our sentries, more than three hundred Indians entered in the town without the sentries detecting them, two by two and four by four, with some little jars [*ollillas*] in which they brought fire, in order not to be noticed or seen. At the time that the other Indians were arriving, the sentries detected the throng of people, and they sounded the call to arms; already these

[16]The term *gruesa* more precisely connotes corpulent, or stout, which seems to refer to the abundance of food and supplies.

others had set fire to one [house] in the town. They did us very great damage and killed that night fifty-seven horses and more than three hundred hogs and thirteen or fourteen men, and it was a great mystery of God why, without our resisting them or doing a thing, the Indians turned to flee and left us, because if they had pursued us, not a man of all of us would have escaped.

We then moved from there to a cabin, which was about one league from there. We found out that the Indians had decided to return that night upon us, except that thanks to God it rained a little, so that because of the water they abandoned their plan. We were so poorly supplied that although we still had some horses, we had neither saddle, nor lance, nor shield, because all had burned. Here we hurried to make shields and lances and saddles, as best we could and knew how. After five days the Indians, their squadrons formed with much order, turned again upon us and came to strike on three sides. As we were now more watchful, we detected them and came forth to them and routed them and did them some damage, so that thanks to God they did not return any more. We were here about two months, making what we had need of in the way of saddles and lances and shields, and then we departed toward the northwest for another province that is called Alibamo.

Here something happened to us that they say has never happened in the Indies, which was that in the middle of the road where we were to pass, without having food to defend nor women to guard there, but rather only to prove themselves against us, they made a very strong barricade[17] of poles in the middle of the road, and about three hundred Indians placed themselves there, with determination to die before they relinquished it. As they saw us appear, some Indians came forth from the barricade to shoot arrows at us and threaten us that no man would remain alive. From this we considered that barricade differently, and with the people that defended it, we believed they had some food there or something that they were guarding, of which we had much need, because we were expecting to cross an uninhabited region of twelve days' duration, in all of which there was not one thing to eat, except what we carried there. About forty of us dismounted and placed ourselves on two sides, so that at the sound of a trumpet we would charge the barricade all at once. We did it thus and entered, although we suffered some damage, for they killed seven or eight men and wounded twenty-five or twenty-six of us. We captured some Indians and others we killed, and we

[17]The term *albarrado* may refer to an earthen wall or trench, implying more than a simple wall of timber.

found out from them that they had done that only with the intent of proving themselves against us, and for no other purpose.

We looked for food there, although with difficulty, in order to enter into our uninhabited region. We walked through it for twelve days with great labor, because of the wounded and sick that we were carrying. We arrived one day at midday at a town that is called Quizquiz, so unexpectedly that they had no news of us. The Indian men were gone to do their labors at their cornfields. We captured more than three hundred women who were in the town and the pittance of hides and blankets that they had in their houses. Here we found the first little walnuts of the land,[18] which are much better than those from here in Spain. This town was near the river of Espiritu Santo. They told us that this and other towns there pay tribute to a lord of Pacaha, who was well known in all the land.

When they found out that we had taken those women, they came to us in peace and asked the Governor to give them back. The Governor did so and asked them to give us some canoes in order to cross that large river, and they said that they would give them to us, but they never did it. Rather, they gathered together in order to make war on us and came within view of the town where we were, but in the end they did not dare to assault us and turned back. We left that town and went to make camp on the bank of the river in order to organize how to cross it. We saw that on the other side was a great number of people ready to defend the crossing against us, and they had many canoes. We decided to make four large piraguas, so that each one of them would be able to carry sixty or seventy men and five or six horses.

It took us twenty-seven or twenty-eight days to make these piraguas. During this time the Indians each day at the hour of three in the afternoon placed themselves in two hundred and fifty canoes that they had there, very large and well shielded [*muy empavesadas*], and drew near the other shore where we were with a great yell. They shot all the arrows that they could and returned to the other bank. When they saw that we already had our boats ready to cross, they all fled and left the crossing undefended. In good order, we crossed the river, which was almost a league wide and nineteen or twenty *brazas*[19] deep. On the other bank we found some good towns. We went up the river, because in order to go to that province of Pacaha we had to turn upriver.

---

[18]Probably pecans.

[19]One *braza* (an armspan) equals approximately 5.5 feet, making Biedma's depth estimate roughly 104 to 110 feet.

Before we got to it, we arrived at another province of another lord, who was named Ycasqui, with whom he [Pacaha] was always at war. This cacique came forth in peace, telling us that he had been hearing of us for a long time, and that he knew that we were men from heaven and that their arrows could not do us harm, and that therefore they wanted no war with us, but rather wanted to serve us. The Governor received them very well and refused to let any soldiers enter in his town, so that they might not do it any damage, and we made camp on a plain in view of the town of the cacique. We were there two days.

The day that we arrived, the cacique spoke with the Governor, telling him that he knew that he was a man from heaven, and since he had to continue onward, he should leave a sign indicating whom he could ask for help for his wars, and whom his people could ask for water for their fields, because they were in great need of it, since their children were dying of hunger. The Governor commanded that they should make a cross of two very tall pines, and he told him that he should return the next day, that he would give him the sign of heaven that he asked him for, and that he should believe that he would lack nothing if he had true faith in it. The next day the cacique returned to us, saying many things because we delayed so much in giving him the sign that he had asked for, since he was so willing to serve us and follow us, and he made there such a great lament because they did not give it so quickly that he made us all weep from seeing the devotion and insistence with which he requested it. The Governor commanded that he and all his Indians should return in the afternoon and told him that we would go to his town and bring him the sign that he had requested.

He came in the afternoon with all his people. We went in procession up to the town, and they came after us. Having arrived at the town, we found that the caciques there were accustomed to have, next to the houses where they live, some very high mounds [*cerros*], made by hand, and that others have their houses on the mounds themselves. On the summit of that mound we drove in the cross, and we all went with much devotion, kneeling to kiss the foot of the cross. The Indians did as they saw us do, neither more nor less. They brought a great quantity of canes [*cañizos*] and made a wall around it. We returned to our camp that night.

The next day in the morning we traveled toward Pacaha, which was upriver. We walked two days, and then we saw the town on a plain, well palisaded and with a moat of water around it, dug by hand. We drew as near to the town as we could. When we were near, we halted, because we dared not enter in it, and walking around on one side and another, we saw that on one side many people were fleeing. Then we assailed the town and entered without any defense. Very few people were taken, because all had already fled. They were unable to keep the pittance that they had in a safe place, and all of it remained in the town. While we were halted in view of the town, because we dared not enter, we saw coming at our back a large squadron of Indians. We thought that it was people who were coming to the aid of the town, and we went toward them and found that it was the cacique we had left behind, where we had placed the cross. They were coming after us to aid us if we should need it.

We led him to the town, and he began to give so many thanks to the Governor for the cross that he had left him, saying that it had rained a great deal in his land the day before, and that all his people were so content that they did not wish to leave us but rather to go away with us. The Governor placed him in the town and gave him all that we found in it, which is much wealth for them, including some beads that there are of snail shells from the sea[20] and some small hides of cats and buckskin, and some corn that there was in the town, with which he sent him away happy to his land.

We were in this town twenty-seven or twenty-eight days to see if we could have a road north in order to traverse to the South Sea [the Pacific Ocean]. From here some excursions were made to capture Indians who might inform us. One expedition in particular was made to the northwest, because they told us that there were large villages through which we could go. But we traveled eight days through an uninhabited land of very great swampy lakes, where we did not even find trees, but rather some great plains, where was grass so tall and so strong that even with the horses we could not force our way through it. At the end of this time, we arrived at some Indian settlements [*ranchos*] that were covered with sewn reeds [*enea cosida*]. When they wish to carry them away, they roll up the reeds of the covering and an Indian man carries it, and the woman carries the framework of poles over which it is placed, and it is set up and taken down so easily that even if they moved every hour they could carry their houses with them.

We found out from these Indians that there were some little settlements [*ranchuelos*] of that sort across the land, and all they did was set up their house where there were many deer, or on a swamp where there were many fish, and when they had frightened away the game and could not catch fish

---

[20]*Caracoles de la mar.* The term *caracol marino* denotes the periwinkle shell, suggesting that these beads were made from periwinkles. Such beads are relatively common in the archaeological record.

as easily as at first, they moved from there with their houses and all that and went away to another place where they could find fresh game. This province was called Caluçi; they were people that paid little attention to sowing, because they maintained themselves on this fish and meat.

We returned to this town of Pacaha, where the Governor remained, and we found that the cacique had now come in peace. He was there in the town with him, and at this time the other cacique came from back where we had placed the cross. It was something to see, seeing both the caciques together, who were enemies. The Governor commanded each one of them to sit at his side. It was a marvelous thing what each one went through to win the right hand from the other.

Having seen that there was no road to traverse to the other sea, we turned south and returned with the cacique to where we had placed the cross, and from there we headed southwest to another province which is called Quiguate. This was the largest town that we found in Florida; it was on a branch of the great river. Here we tarried eight or nine days to look for interpreters and guides, still with the intention, if we were able, to traverse to the other sea, because the Indians told us that eleven days from there was a province where they killed some cows,[21] and that from there we would learn of interpreters in order to cross to the other sea.

We departed with these guides for that province, which is called Coligua, without any road, but rather they led us each night straight to some swamps of water from which we might drink, where we found a quantity of fish. We traveled over much flat land and other land of rugged mountains, and we struck pointblank at the town of Coligua, as if they led us by royal road, seeing that in all their life no man had passed through there. We found much food in this land and a great quantity of tanned cow tails and others for tanning. We inquired about a road in the direction we were heading and whether there was any village in that district, far or near. They were never able to tell us anything except that if we wished to travel where there might be a village, we had to turn west-southwest.

We turned again to where the Indians guided us, and we went to some scattered villages that were called Tatilcoya. Here we found a large river, and afterward we saw that it flowed into the great river [the Mississippi]. We had information that on this river upstream was a great province called Cayas. We went to it and found that it was all scattered population, though heavy, and several excursions were made. The land is very rugged with mountains.

[21]Refers to the bison.

An excursion was made in which the cacique and many people were apprehended. When we asked for news of the land, they told us that if we went upriver, we would come upon a well-provisioned province that was called Tula. The governor wished to go see if it was a place where the people could winter, and he went with twenty on horseback. He left all the rest in this province of Cayas.

Before arriving at the province of Tula, we crossed some rugged mountains and arrived at the town without their having heard anything of us. We began to apprehend some Indians, and they began to call to arms and make war on us. They wounded that day nine or ten horses and seven or eight Spaniards, and such was their ferocity that they joined together, eight by eight and ten by ten, and came at us like wounded dogs. We killed about thirty or forty Indians. It seemed to the Governor that it was not good to halt there that night, because he led very few people, and he returned by the road on which we had come to a clearing in a lowland that the river made,[22] having crossed a bad pass of the mountain range because there was fear that the Indians might take us at that pass.

The next day he arrived where his people were, and there were none of those Indians we had brought, nor did he find in that province Indians who could understand the interpreter. He commanded that all should prepare to travel to that province [of Tula]. We then went there. The day after we arrived, three very large squadrons of Indians came upon us at dawn, on three sides. We came forth to them and routed them and did them some damage, as a result of which they attacked us no more.

After two or three days, they sent the messengers as if in peace. Although we did not understand one thing for lack of the interpreter, through signs we told them that they should bring us interpreters for those [Indians] behind us, and they brought us five or six Indians who understood the interpreters that we brought. They asked us what people we were and what we were looking for. We asked them about some large provinces where there would be much food, because already the cold of the winter was greatly menacing us. They told us that the way that we were going, they knew of not one large village. They pointed out to us that if we wanted to turn east and southeast or northwest that we would find large villages.

Having seen that we did not have any other choice, we turned again southeast and went to a province called Quipana, which is at the foot of some very rugged mountains, and here we went east and traversed these

[22] *Un raso de una vega quel rio hacia,* probably referring to the floodplain.

mountains and descended to some plains, where we found a village suited for our purpose, because there was a town nearby that had much food, and it was on a large river that ended at the great river by which we left. This province was called Viranque.

Here we spent the winter. There were such great snows and cold weather that we thought we were dead men. In this town died the Christian who had been one of Narváez's men, whom we had found in the land and taken along as interpreter. We left from here at the beginning of March, since it appeared to us that the fury of the cold weather had abated, and we traveled downstream along that river, where we found other well-populated provinces with a quantity of supplies, until we arrived at a province that seemed to us to be one of the best that we had come upon in all the land, which is called Anicoyanque. Here another cacique, who was named Guachoyanque, came to us in peace. He has his village on the large river and wages much war with this other [province] where we were. The Governor departed then for this other town of Guachoyanque and took the cacique with him. It was a good town, well palisaded and strong. It had little food, because the Indians had hidden it all.

Here the Governor was already determined, if he were to find the sea, to make brigantines in order to send word to Cuba that we were alive, so that they might provide us with some horses and the things that we had need of. He sent the captain south to see if he could discover some road to go to look for the sea, because from the account of the Indians nothing could be found out about what there might be, and he returned saying that he did not find a road nor a way to cross the large swamps along the great river. The Governor, from seeing himself cut off and seeing that not one thing could be done according to his purpose, was afflicted with sickness and died.

The Governor dead, he left Luis de Moscoso appointed as Governor. We decided that since we could not find a road to the sea, we should head west, and that it could be that we might be able to get out by land to Mexico, if we did not find anything else in the land or any place to halt. We walked seventeen days' journey until we arrived at a province of Chavete, where the Indians made much salt; we did not find out anything about the west. From here we went to another province that is called Aguacay. We spent another three days' journey getting there, still going straight west. From here the Indians told us that we could not find more villages, but rather that we should descend southwest and south, because there we would find villages and food, and that going the way that we asked about there were some great stretches of sand [*arenales grandes*], and neither villages nor any food.

We had to return where the Indians guided us, and we went to a province that is called Nisione, and another that is called Nandacao, and another that is called Lacame, and across land more and more sterile and with less food. We went along asking about a province that they told us was large, which was called Xuacatino. This cacique of Nondacao gave us an Indian to guide us, with the intent of placing us where we could never get out, and so he guided us across rugged land and off road, until finally he told us that he no longer knew where he was leading us, and that his lord had commanded him to lead us where we would die of hunger.

We took another guide who led us to a province that is called Hais, where cows are in the habit of gathering at times, and as the Indians saw us enter through their land, they began to cry out that they should kill the cows that were coming;[23] they came forth to shoot arrows at us and did us some damage. We departed from here and arrived at the province of Xacatin, which was among some dense forests and lacked food. From here the Indians guided us east to other towns, which were small and had little food, saying that they were leading us to where there were other Christians like us. It seemed afterward to be a lie and that they could not have news of any others but us; since we had made so many turns,[24] in some of these they must have heard of our passing.

We turned south again, with purpose of living or dying or traversing to New Spain, and we walked about six days' journey south and southwest. There we halted and sent ten men on swift horses to travel eight or nine days, or as many as they were able, to see if they could find some town in order to replenish the corn so we could continue on our way, and they traveled as far as they could and came upon some poor people who did not have houses, but rather some miserable little settlements where they situated themselves, and they neither sowed nor gathered anything but rather maintained themselves only on fish and meat.

They brought three or four of these Indians. We found no one who could understand the interpreter. Having seen that we had lost the interpreter and that we found nothing to eat, that we were now lacking the corn that we had carried on our backs, and that it was [impossible[25]] for so many people to traverse so miserable a land, we decided to return to the town where Gover-

[23]Probably the Spaniards' horses.

[24]Here the term *vueltas* seems best translated as "turns," although it may also connote ways or even directions (as it is used in the rest of the relation), referring to multiple legs of the journey.

[25]While the text states *posible,* the context indicates this to be an error.

nor Soto had died, because there it seemed to us that it was possible to fashion vessels to leave the land. We returned along that same road that we had followed until we arrived at the town where the Governor had died.

Having arrived here, we did not find as good provisions as we thought, because we did not find food in the town, since the Indians had hidden it. We had to look for another town in order to be able to winter and fashion the ships. Thank God we discovered two towns much to our purpose that were on the great river and had a great quantity of corn and were palisaded, and there we halted and built our ships with much labor. We made seven brigantines and spent six months in finishing them. We cast off the brigantines in the river, and it was a thing of mystery that even though they were caulked only with the bark of those mulberry trees and without any pitch, we found them watertight and very good. We towed some canoes downriver with us in which we carried twenty-six horses, so that if at the seacoast we should find some village that could sustain us with food, from there we would send a pair of brigantines to give a message to the Viceroy of New Spain, so that he might provide us ships in which we could leave the land.

The second day that we were going downriver, there came forth to us about forty or fifty very large and swift canoes of Indians, among which there was a canoe that carried eighty Indian warriors, and they began to shoot arrows at us and pursue us, shooting more arrows at us. It seemed to some of those in our ships that it was cowardly not to attack them, and they took four or five small canoes of those that we were towing and went toward the canoes of the Indians, who, as soon as they saw them, encircled them as best they could and would not let them leave from among them. They upset the canoes in the water, and thus they killed this day twelve very honorable men, because we could not aid them, since the current of the river was so great and we had few oars in our ships. With this victory, the Indians came following us downriver, until we arrived at the sea, which took nineteen days' journey. They did us much damage and wounded many people, because since they saw that we did not have arms with which to do them damage from a distance, for we no longer had either arquebus or crossbow but only some swords and shields, they now had lost their fear and drew very near to shoot arrows at us.[26]

---

[26]The final section of Biedma's relation is written in a different hand than the bulk of the manuscript, and using different ink than both the text and the signature immediately below, suggesting that this final section was written by a different scribe (and may have been added after the signature, which is overlapped by this final section). It is possible that Biedma origi-

We came forth to the sea through the mouth of the river and went across a bay that the river makes, so large that we navigated three days and three nights with reasonable weather, and in all that time we did not see land. It seemed to us that we were far out at sea, and at the end of these three days and three nights we gathered water as fresh as from the river, which was good to drink. We saw some little islets toward the southwest side, and we went to them, and from there we went along the coast, gathering shellfish and looking for things to eat, until we entered the river of Panuco, where we were very well received by the Christians.

LUYS HERNÁNDEZ
DE BIEDMA[27]

---

nally intended to terminate the relation here, for he mentioned their departure from the river into the sea in the previous sentence.

[27]Following Biedma's relation is an appended four-page document entitled "Memorial of the persons who came from Florida, which persons they are, and from where they are natives." This list of 221 survivors of the De Soto expedition seems to be in a different hand and appears on distinctive paper that has been folded in a manner different from the Biedma relation, suggesting that it was added separately to Biedma's text. The list is presented and examined by Ignacio Avellaneda, *Los sobrevivientes de la Florida: The Survivors of the De Soto Expedition* (Gainesville: University of Florida, P. K. Yonge Library of Florida History, 1990).

Account of the Northern Conquest and Discovery of Hernando de Soto[1]

by

Rodrigo Rangel

(drawn from *Historia general y natural de las Indias*
by
Gonzalo Fernández de Oviedo y Valdés)

Newly Translated and Edited by
John E. Worth
With Footnotes by
John E. Worth
and *Charles Hudson*

[1]There is no separate title provided by Oviedo for the Rangel account, and thus this title was constructed from passages in chapter 26 of Oviedo's work (see chapter 6).

Introduction
Rangel's Account of the Expedition

by John E. Worth

Rodrigo Rangel,[2] a native of Almendralejo, accompanied the De Soto expedition as the private secretary of Hernando de Soto. The account of this expedition attributed to him is included in the massive work *Historia general y natural de las Indias* by Gonzalo Fernández de Oviedo y Valdés. As related below in chapter 6 of the account, Rangel gave a relation before the Audiencia Real in Santo Domingo soon after the expedition and was subsequently commanded to give a complete account of the De Soto expedition to Oviedo as the official royal historian of the Indies. The bulk of the Rangel account evidently derives from a detailed diary that he kept during the expedition, although some material appears to have been obtained by Oviedo through interviews with Rangel.

It is important to recognize that the text that follows is a product of Oviedo's hand, although it apparently follows the diary of Rangel closely. Certain passages were undoubtedly added by Oviedo, who often inserted personal commentary into the text of Rangel's account. These asides are easily extracted by the reader from Rangel's material.

The Rangel account is generally considered to be the most accurate of the four major extant accounts of the De Soto expedition. Notwithstanding this fact, the first and only published English translation of Rangel's complete text (first published in Spanish in its entirety in 1851[3]) was by Edward G. Bourne in 1904.[4]

The following translation is drawn from chapters 21 through 28 of Book XVII of Oviedo's *Historia general y natural de las Indias.* While minor

---

[2]While this name is spelled Rangel in the list of survivors of the De Soto expedition appended to the Biedma account, the printed version of Oviedo's text is spelled Ranjel, and this spelling is often found in the literature on the De Soto expedition.

[3]Gonzalo Fernández de Oviedo y Valdés, *Historia general y natural de las Indias* (Madrid: Imprenta de la Real Academia de la Historia, 1851).

[4]Edward Gaylord Bourne, *Narratives of the Career of Hernando de Soto,* 2 vols. (New York: A. S. Barnes & Co., 1904).

restructuring of the original syntax was necessary at times, the present translation is largely literal, following Oviedo's paragraph and sentence structure as closely as possible. All Indian names are preserved as originally printed in the Oviedo text, but the spelling of Spanish names and terms has been modernized. Where appropriate, certain Spanish terms remain untranslated. Interpolations by this editor are set off by brackets, and selected original Spanish terms are bracketed following their translation where they first appear in the account. Footnotes have been added to provide additional information where precise meaning seems important or where meaning is ambiguous, and to provide supplementary commentary and information.

ONE

HOW FERNANDO DE SOTO WENT TO GOVERN THE ISLAND OF CUBA OR FERNANDINA AS CAPTAIN GENERAL OF THEIR MAJESTIES, AND WITH TITLE OF *ADELANTADO* OF FLORIDA.

The Emperor our lord made as his Governor and Captain General of the island and province of Florida and its annexes on the mainland, to the northern part that the adelantado Juan Ponce de León[5] had discovered, Hernando de Soto, who was one of the soldiers of the Governor Pedrarias de Avila, and of whom, in the affairs of the mainland, mention is often made, because he was one of the earliest persons in those places, and in the end he found himself in the imprisonment of Atabaliba [Atahualpa], where he was one of those who gained a large part of those spoils.[6] And he put so great a portion of them in Spain, that it was rumored that he was seen with more than one hundred thousand pesos of gold in Castille, where for his services and merits he was very well treated by the Emperor our lord, and he made him a knight of the military Order of the apostle St. James and gave him other favors and made him his Governor and Captain General as stated. And being there in Castille, he married one of the daughters of Governor Pedrarias Dávila, whose name was Doña Isabel de Bobadilla, like her mother, a woman of great essence and goodness, and of very noble judgment and character, and with her he went to the island of Fernandina [Cuba], where he arrived in the month of [June[7]] of the year of fifteen thirty-nine. And after he had visited the island and its towns and provided what was suitable to the good state and sustenance of the land, he gave order to arm and cross to the mainland for the conquest, settlement, and pacification of those provinces that were entrusted to him by His Majesty; this history[8] will relate in the following chapters the things that occurred in this enterprise.

---

[5]Ponce de León explored the Florida coastline in 1513.

[6]Hernando de Soto served in Central and South America between 1513 and 1535.

[7]The month is missing from the text, but other sources indicate that the date was June 7, 1539 [1538].

[8]Referring to Oviedo's *Historia general y natural de las Indias,* of which these chapters are only a part.

TWO

THE DEPARTURE OF THE GOVERNOR HERNANDO DE SOTO FROM THE ISLAND OF CUBA, ALIAS FERNANDINA, FOR THE NORTHERN LAND OF THE MAINLAND, AND OF THE ARMADA AND PEOPLE THAT HE CARRIED FOR HIS DISCOVERY, AND OF THE HARDSHIP THAT THEY HAD IN DISEMBARKING, AND THE NUMBER OF HORSES AND OTHER THINGS HE CARRIED, AND HOW HE RECOVERED A CHRISTIAN, CALLED JUAN ORTIZ, WHO WAS LOST AND WALKED NUDE LIKE THE INDIANS.

Sunday, the eighteenth of May of fifteen thirty-nine, Governor Hernando de Soto left from the town[9] of Havana with a noble armada of nine ships, five with topsails, and two caravels and two brigantines. And on the twenty-fifth of the same month, which was the day of Whitsuntide,[10] land was sighted on the northern coast of the province of Florida,[11] and the armada dropped anchor two leagues from land, in four brazas[12] of depth or less. And the Governor boarded a brigantine in order to come see the land, and with him a gentleman called Juan de Añasco, and the principal pilot of the armada, called Alonso Martín, in order to reconnoiter what land that was, because they were doubtful of the port and which part they were in.[13] And not recognizing it, seeing that night was approaching, they wished to return to the ships, but the weather did not permit them, for it was contrary: so

[9]The term *villa* is used for Havana, in contrast to *pueblo,* which is typically used to describe larger Indian settlements in Florida.

[10]*Pascua del Espiritu Sancto.* The port at which the expedition landed would be named after the day when they sighted it.

[11]This passage refers to the northerly location of the coast of Florida with respect to the point of departure in Cuba.

[12]One *braza* equals roughly 5.5 feet, making the depth under 22 feet.

[13]This port had already been reconnoitered by Juan de Añasco.

they anchored near land and came ashore, and they found traces of many Indians and a hut like the large ones that have been seen in the Indies,[14] and other small ones. It was said later that it was the town [*pueblo*] of Oçita.

The Governor and those who were with him were in no little danger, because they were few and without weapons, and no less was the anxiety of those who remained on the ships to see their Captain General in such a state, because they could neither aid nor help him if he needed it. In short, to personally take so much care was carelessness and too much diligence or lack of prudence on the part of the Governor, because those things are the responsibility of other persons and not the person who has to govern and rule the army, and it would have been enough to command a subordinate Captain to go on that reconnaissance and to provide for the security of the pilot who had to reconnoiter that coast. And the ships there were in great danger, and all the armada, in which there were five hundred seventy men not counting the sailors, and with these, there were a good seven hundred men.

The next day, Monday, in the morning, the brigantine was well leeward of the ships and working to reach them but unable to. Baltasar de Gallegos seeing this, he shouted loudly to the *Capitana*[15] so that the Lieutenant General, who was a nobleman called Vasco Porcallo, would take proper precautions; but as they did not hear him, in order to aid the Governor, he commanded a large caravel, in which this gentleman came as Captain, to weigh anchor, and to go toward where the brigantine appeared. And although the Governor regretted that, it was well done, inasmuch as it was in his service and in order to aid his person. In the end, it arrived where the brigantine was, and the Governor was very pleased. By this time the port was already reconnoitered, and the other brigantine placed at the canal as signal for the ships, and the brigantine of the Governor went to the front and placed the caravel itself in the canal of the port. And he commanded that it should take a position at one side of the canal and the brigantine at the other, so that the ships might pass through the middle; [the ships], which were about four or five leagues from there, now began to set sail; and it was necessary that the Governor should go to show them the way, because the main pilot was in his brigantine, and because there were many shallows through there. Even with all of that, two ships struck [bottom], but as the bottom was sand, they did

[14]*Un buhio de los grandes que en Indias se ha visto.* This was probably a large public structure, or council house. Another similar structure was noted by Rangel in the town of Uriutina (see his chapter 4).

[15]Standard designation for the ship in an armada that carried the general.

not receive damage. This day the Governor and Juan de Añasco, who went as accountant of Their Majesties, had hard words, which the Governor concealed and endured.

The ships entered in the port with the sounder in hand, and although sometimes they struck [bottom], as it was silt,[16] they passed onward. In all this, they were detained five days without disembarking, but some people went ashore and brought water and grass for the horses. In the end, the shallows did not permit the loaded ships to arrive at where the town was, and they anchored four leagues back. Friday, which they reckoned to be the thirtieth of May, they began to unload the horses on land. The land where they disembarked is due north of the island of [Dry] Tortuga, which is in the mouth of the Bahama channel; and the cacique and lord of that land was named Oçita, and it is ten leagues to the west of the bay of Juan Ponce.[17]

As soon as some horses went on land, General Vasco Porcallo de Figueroa and Juan de Añasco and Francisco Osorio went riding to see something of the land, and they found ten Indians with bows and arrows, who also came, as warriors, to reconnoiter these Christian guests and learn what people they were; and they wounded two horses, and the Spaniards killed two of those Indians, and the rest fled.

Two hundred and forty-three horses went in that armada, and of those, nineteen or twenty died on the sea, and all the rest came ashore; and having disembarked, the General and several foot soldiers went with the brigantines to see the town, and a gentleman, called Gómez Arias, returned in one and gave good news of the land and said also that the [native] people were hidden.

On Sunday the first of June of the aforesaid year of fifteen thirty-nine, the day of the Trinity, this army traveled inland toward the town, carrying as guides four Indians that Juan de Añasco had taken when he went to discover the port; and they lost their bearings somewhat, either because they did not understand the Christians or because they did not speak the truth, for which reason the Governor took the lead with some on horseback; and as they did not have experience in the land, they tired the horses after deer and with the waters and swamps [*ciénagas*] that they crossed, and with the twelve leagues that they traveled before they arrived opposite the town. The inlet [*ancón*] of the port was between them [and the town], so that they were unable to go

---

[16]The text reads *lama*, which indicates that the bottom was covered with a fine-grained silt, or muck, contrasting with the *arena*, or sand, described earlier.

[17]On the east coast of Florida.

around the inlet, and thus scattered in many places, they slept that night very fatigued and in no military order.

During all that week the ships arrived near the town, unloading them little by little with small boats [*bateles*], and thus they unloaded all the clothing and supplies that they carried. There were some roads, but no one knew or guessed which they should take in order to find natives of the land. The four Indians that they had did not understand them except very little and by signs, and it was difficult to guard them, as they did not have shackles. Tuesday, the third of June, the Governor took possession of the land in the name of Their Majesties with all the formalities that are required, and he sent one of the Indians to persuade and invite in peace the neighboring caciques; and the same night two of the three Indians that remained fled, and it was much good fortune all three did not escape, which gave the Christians much concern.

The next day, Wednesday, the Governor sent Captain Baltasar de Gallegos, with the Indian that remained, to look for some people or a town or house. At the time that the sun was setting, going off road, because the Indian who was the guide led them wandering and confused, thanks to God they saw from afar as many as twenty Indians painted red (which is a certain red ointment that the Indians put on when they go to war or wish to make a fine appearance), and they wore many plumes[18] and carried their bows and arrows. And as the Christians ran forth against them, the Indians, fleeing, plunged into a forest [*monte*], and one of them came forth to the road shouting and saying: "Sirs, for the love of God and of St. Mary do not kill me: I am Christian, like you, and I am a native of Seville, and my name is Juan Ortiz." The pleasure that the Christians felt was very great, in that God gave them an interpreter and guide at such a time, of which they had great necessity. Delighted with this pleasure, Baltasar de Gallegos and all the Indians that came with him returned that night, very late, to the camp, and the Spaniards of the army became very agitated, believing it was something else and taking up arms; but having recognized who it was, the joy that all had was great, because they estimated that by means of that interpreter they would perform their tasks better.

Without losing time, the following Saturday the Governor determined to go with that interpreter Juan Ortiz to the cacique who had held him, who was called Mocoço, in order to make peace and bring him to the friendship

[18]The term *penachos* may refer to panaches, or bunches of feathers serving as a crest, rather than isolated plumes.

of the Christians. He [Mocoço] waited in his town with his Indians and wives and children, lacking no one, and complained to the Governor about the caciques Orriygua, Neguarete, Çapaloey and Eçita, all four of whom are caciques on that coast, saying that they menaced him because he took our friendship and was willing to give that Christian interpreter to the Christians. Using the same interpreter, the Governor told him that he should not be afraid of those caciques or of others, because he would help him, and all the Christians and many more who would come soon would be his friends and would help him against his enemies.

This same day Captain Juan Ruiz Lobillo set out with as many as forty soldiers, on foot, for the interior, and he attacked some settlements [*ranchos*] though could not take but two Indian women; and in order to rescue them, nine Indians followed him for three leagues shooting arrows at him, and they killed one Christian and wounded three or four without his being able to do them damage, although he had arquebusiers and crossbowmen, because those Indians are so agile and such fine warriors that in any nation of the world they would be seen as men.

THREE

HOW WAR BEGAN TO KINDLE AND WAS CRUELLY FOUGHT, AND HOW THE LIEUTENANT GENERAL RETURNED TO THE ISLAND OF CUBA, AND HOW THE GOVERNOR DEPARTED FROM THAT PORT OF SPIRITU SANCTO FOR THE INTERIOR, AND OF WHAT HAPPENED TO HIM AND HIS PEOPLE UNTIL THE TENTH OF AUGUST OF THE SAME YEAR OF FIFTEEN THIRTY-NINE.

This Governor was very given to hunting and killing Indians, from the time that he served in the army of Governor Pedrarias Dávila in the provinces of Castilla del Oro and Nicaragua, and he also found himself in Peru and took part in the imprisonment of Atabaliba, where he became rich, and he was one of those who returned to Spain richer, because he carried and put in a safe place in Seville about one hundred thousand pesos of gold; and he decided to return to the Indies only to lose them along with his life, and to continue the bloody tactics of times past, which had been his practice in the aforementioned places. Therefore, continuing his conquest, he commanded that General Vasco Porcallo de Figueroa should go to Oçita, because it was said that there was a gathering of people there. And this Captain having gone there, he found the people gone, and he burned the town, and he set the dogs on [*aperrear*] an Indian he brought as guide. The reader must understand that to set the dogs on [an Indian] is to make the dogs eat them or kill them, tearing the Indian to pieces. The conquistadors in the Indies have always used greyhounds or fierce and valiant dogs in war; and this is why hunting Indians was mentioned above. Therefore, that guide was killed in that way, because he lied and guided poorly.

While Vasco Porcallo did what has been said, the Governor sent another Indian as messenger to the cacique Orriparacogi. [The messenger] did not return because an Indian woman told him that he should not, and for that she was thrown to the dogs.

Among the soldiers there were diverse opinions about whether it would be good to settle there or not, because the land seemed sterile, as in truth that coast is reputed to be. On account of this, the Governor decided to send Captain Baltasar de Gallegos to Orriparagi [Orriparacogi] with eighty on horseback and one hundred foot soldiers, and he departed on Friday the twentieth of June.

Likewise the Governor sent Juan de Añasco, in the small vessels from the ships, along the seacoast with a certain number of foot soldiers, to break up a meeting that the Indians were holding, or to go and see what kind of affair it was. He found them on an island, where he had a fray with them. He killed nine or ten Indians with the light artillery[19] that he had, and they shot arrows and wounded as many or more Christians. Because he could not make them leave the island, he sent for aid, and the messenger was a nobleman called Juan de Vega. He asked for people on horseback, in order to take the mainland where they had to retreat, because with the people that he had and any others who might go, he intended to fight with the Indians. The

[19]The phrase *versos de la artilleria* refers to a light piece of artillery (the *verso*), half the size and caliber of the *culebrina*, a long and narrow artillery piece. These weapons were probably hand cannons.

Governor sent Vasco Porcallo with forty on horseback and some foot soldiers; but when this aid arrived, the Indians had already gone; and the Spaniards, in order not to have gone in vain, scoured the land and captured some Indians, whom they brought to the camp. Vasco Porcallo having come from that excursion, he had some unpleasantness with the Governor (which is not mentioned in this relation). The historian could not get the one who informed him [Rangel] to finish the story, for various reasons. And it was seen as a good measure that Vasco Porcallo should return to Cuba to attend to the affairs of the government there and to provide to the Governor and his army, when necessary, with what they might have need of. Many regretted the departure of this nobleman, because he was a willing friend and he did much for them.

The Governor had commanded Baltasar de Gallegos, that even though he might not find good land, he should write good news, in order to inspire the people. And although it was not of his disposition to lie, because he was a man of truth, in order to carry out the command of his superior and, even more, not to dismay the people, he always wrote two letters of different tenors: one of truth and the other of lies; but those lies, stated with such cunning, and with equivocal words, could be understood one way and the other, because it was commanded. Concerning this he said that the letter of truth had more power to excuse him, than the false one malice to incriminate him. And thus the Governor did not reveal the truthful items, saying rather that these that he did not reveal were news of great secrets, which later on would demonstrate much utility for all; and he showed them the equivocal and false letters and gave them some statements as seemed [best].

And those letters, although they did not promise anything with certainty, gave hopes and indications that stirred their desires to go forward and leave such uncertainties behind; but as the sins of man are the reason that the lie sometimes finds favor and credit, all fell into conformity and unanimously asked for entrance into the interior, which was what the Governor was scheming. And those who had been ordered to remain there with Captain Calderón regretted this greatly. There were forty on horseback and sixty foot soldiers left to guard the town and supplies, the port, and the brigantines and small vessels that remained, because all the large ships had been dispatched to Havana.

Having this agreement willingly, the Governor departed from the town and port of Spiritu Sancto (called thus for the day that the Governor and his armada arrived there), and this departure was on a Tuesday, the fifteenth of July of the same year of fifteen thirty-nine. And that day they spent the night at the river [*río*] of Mocoço, bringing behind them many pigs that had been brought over in the armada for food in an emergency. And they made two bridges on which this army crossed the river. The next day they went to the lake [*laguna*] of the Rabbit, and that name was given to it because a rabbit which appeared in the camp frightened all the horses, and they broke loose, fleeing back more than a league, leaving not one behind, and all the Christians scattered in order to go after the horses, unarmed. If Indians had attacked them, although they [the Indians] might be few, the Spaniards would have got what they deserved, and in return for their lack of caution, a shameful end to the war was prepared for them. Their horses having been recovered, they went the next day to the lake of St. John, and the next day, under a very strong sun, they went to a savannah [*sabana*], where they arrived very fatigued. A steward of the Governor, who was named Prado, died of thirst,[20] and many of the foot soldiers were in much hardship, and others would have accompanied the steward, if those on horseback had not aided them. The next day they came to the savannah of Guaçoco, and the soldiers went into cornfields and brought green corn, with which they were very happy, because it was the first that they saw in that land. Early the next day they arrived at Luca, a pretty town, and there Baltasar de Gallegos came to meet the Governor.

The following Monday, the twenty-first of July, they joined with the people that Baltasar Gallegos had. The Governor sent a messenger to Urriparacoxi, and a reply did not come; and on Wednesday, the twenty-third of the aforementioned month, the Governor and his army departed, and he went to Viçela, and passed it to sleep farther on; and on Thursday they spent the night at another town that is called Tocaste, which is on a large lake. And this same day the Governor went out with some on horseback headed for Ocale, because they had told him great news of the riches that he thought he would find there. And as he saw that the roads were broad, he thought that his hands were already on the prey. He commanded one of his soldiers, named Rodrigo Rangel (because, in addition to being a good soldier and a good man, he had a good horse), to return to the main army for more people to come and accompany him; and that squire went, although not without misgivings about what could happen, since only ten on horseback remaining with the Governor seemed few to him, and he was sending that nobleman alone and across a land of enemies and bad crossings; but even though some might take after him, he would either die or pass by force and would not

[20]Probably a victim of heatstroke in the July heat of peninsular Florida.

return without a reply. Because he thought it cowardly to ask for company, he bowed his head and obeyed. But I do not praise such determination, since in truth, in necessary and manifest matters, permission is given so that with reason one may express one's opinions to the prince and suggest how he would be better served, and how his commands could be better carried out.

What happened to this equestrian messenger this day he refused to say, because whatever he said would be in his own interest; but it suffices to say that his intention as a valiant man was well tested, and he came upon many Indians who were following the trail of the Governor, but he continued onward. And having arrived at the main army, the maestre de campo[21] gave him fourteen on horseback, with which the number of horses that the Governor had was increased to twenty-six.

The next day, Friday, the army moved along the trail of the Governor, and on the road they found two on horseback that the Governor sent to the maestre de campo, who was a nobleman called Luis de Moscoso, to command that he should not move, and they went back to sleep where they had come from, because there was a surprise attack [*guazábara*] (which is the same as a skirmish) with the Indians, and they killed a horse of Don Carlos Enríquez, son-in-law of the Governor, married to his niece, a native of Jeres de Badajoz, and they wounded some Christians. And they suffered much from hunger, for they were eating the ears of corn with the cobs (or wood, which it nearly is) upon which the kernels grow.

The next day, Saturday, the Governor found the roads broader and the land better, and he sent another two on horseback for another thirty men, and he sent to say that the army should move following his trail. And the maestre de campo sent Nuño de Tovar with thirty on horseback, and he moved according to the command the Governor sent him. The Governor, with the twenty-six on horseback who went with him, arrived on the day of St. Anne at the river or swamp[22] of Cale, and it was of great current and broad, and they crossed it with great difficulty, and where there was no need of a bridge, they crossed with the water at their chests and at the chin, with their clothes and saddles on their heads, a distance of more than three cross-

---

[21]The *maestre de campo,* or field master, was in charge of the daily affairs of the army and ranked under the commander (in this case, Hernando de Soto). The rank roughly corresponds to the modern brigadier general. Luis de Moscoso would later fill the vacancy created by the death of De Soto (see chapter 9).

[22]The description *río o ciénaga,* which is used in reference to both Cale here and Ivitachuco in chapter 4, probably refers to the floodplain swamp associated with the main channel of these rivers.

bow shots.[23] The thirty on horseback that Nuño de Tovar led crossed the following Sunday, and the current carried off a horse and it drowned. And seeing this, the rest crossed with ropes, as those who crossed first with the Governor had done. These people and their Governor arrived at the first town of Ocale, which was called Uqueten, where they captured two Indians: and then he provided that some on horseback and the mules that they had carried from Cuba should go with corn to aid those who were coming behind, since there they had found abundance; and it did not arrive at a bad time, because they found them in that swamp eating herbs and their roots, some roasted and others stewed, without having salt and, what was worse, without knowing what they were. They were glad for the arrival of provisions, and the great hunger and necessity that they had gave them a refreshment and very acceptable flavor, and of such savor that it revived their diligence and brought forth strength from weakness, and the last of the rear guard arrived the following Tuesday where Governor Hernando de Soto was. But they [the Indians] had already wounded some soldiers who strayed and had killed a crossbowman who was named Mendoza. Having joined the army, they went to Ocale, a town in a good region of corn; and there, going to Acuera for supplies, the Indians, on two occasions, killed three soldiers of the guard of the Governor and wounded others and killed a horse, and all that was due to poor order, since those Indians, although they are archers and have very strong bows and are very skillful and accurate marksmen, their arrows do not have poison [*hierba*] nor do they know what it is.

[23]The extreme range of a crossbow was perhaps 380 yards, making the distance of water crossed on foot over 1,000 yards.

FOUR

HOW GOVERNOR HERNANDO DE SOTO, PROCEEDING IN HIS CONQUEST, WENT ONWARD, AND HOW THE INDIANS WISHED TO KILL OR CAPTURE HIM THROUGH DECEIT, IN ORDER TO LIBERATE A CACIQUE HE HAD WITH HIM, AND HOW A CACIQUE GAVE A BLOW TO THE GOVERNOR WHICH BATHED HIS TEETH IN BLOOD. AND OTHER MATTERS SUITABLE TO THE DISCOURSE OF THE HISTORY ARE TREATED.

On the eleventh of August of the same year, the Governor departed from Ocale with fifty on horseback and one hundred foot soldiers in search of Apalache, because it was rumored that it had many people, and Luis de Moscoso remained behind with the rest of the army to see what happened farther on; and that day they went to sleep at Itaraholata, a good town with plenty of corn. There an Indian attacked Captain Maldonado and badly wounded his horse and would have pulled the lance from his hands if the Governor had not arrived by chance of fortune, although Maldonado was a good nobleman and one of the most valiant of that army; but the Indians of that land are very bellicose and indomitable and strong people.

The next day they went to Potano, and the next day, Wednesday, they arrived at Utinamocharra, and from there they went to the town of Mala-Paz, which name was given it because Juan de Añasco, having captured on the road thirty persons of that cacique, he [the cacique] sent the message that he wished peace, so that they might give them back to him, and he sent in his stead a vassal to negotiate with him. He [Añasco] believed that it was the cacique himself and gave his people to him. Following this, this Indian fleeing from the Christians the next day, a noble greyhound from Ireland plunged after him into the multitude of Indians that were on a densely wooded hill [*arcabuco*]. It rushed to the clamor and entered among all the Indians; and although it passed by many, not one did it seize but the one who had fled, who was among the multitude, and it held him by the fleshy part of the arm in such a manner that the Indian was thrown down and apprehended.

The next day the Christians arrived at a pretty town, where they found much food and many very delicious small chestnuts piled up. These are native chestnuts; but the trees which bear them are no taller than two palms of earth, and thus they grow in burrs covered with bristles.[24] There are other chestnuts in the land, which the Spaniards saw and ate, which are the same as those from Spain, and they grow on chestnut trees just as large and mighty, and with the same leaf and bristles or burrs, just as plump and of very good flavor.

This army went from there to a river that they call [the river] of the Discords, and he who gave this relation wished not to mention the reason, because he is an honest man, not disposed to relate the guilts or frailties of his friends. That day they made a bridge of pines, since there were many there, and the next day, Sunday, they crossed that river with as much or more hardship than the one at Ocale. The following day, Monday, they arrived at Aguacaleyquen, and Rodrigo Rangel and Villalobos, two gentlemen, equestrians but gentlemen (I say equestrians because in this army they were men on horseback), captured in a cornfield an Indian man and woman, and she showed them where the corn was concealed, and the Indian man led Captain Baltasar de Gallegos to where he captured seventeen persons, and among them an Indian woman, daughter of the cacique, for it seemed reasonable that this would make her father come in peace; but he wished to liberate her without that, and his deceptions and tricks were no less than those of these conquistadors. On the twenty-second of August a great multitude of Indians appeared, and the Governor, seeing that the land already showed itself to be more populated and better supplied, sent eight on horseback with all dispatch to call the maestre de campo, Luis de Moscoso, in order that with all the army [at Ocale] he should come to join with him; and the maestre de campo had no small diligence in carrying out that command, and on the fourth of September he arrived where the Governor was, and all were delighted to meet together; because as they had imprisoned the cacique, it was feared that the Indians would ally themselves: and it was not a bad thought, judging by what appeared later.

On the ninth of September they all departed together from Aguacaleyquen, taking with them the cacique and his daughter and a principal Indian, who was named Guatutima, as guide, because he said that he knew much of

[24]Probably referring to the chinquapin.

what was farther on and gave very great news about it. And they made a bridge of pines in order to cross the river of Aguacaleyquen, and they spent the night at a small town. The next day, Friday, they went to Uriutina, a town of pleasant view and with much food, and in it there was a very large hut, in the middle of which there was a large courtyard.[25] There was now good population through there. After they left from Aguacaleyquen, messengers from Uçachile, a great cacique, went and came, playing on a flute for ceremony. And on Friday, the twelfth of September, these Christians arrived at a town that they called [the town] of Many Waters, because it rained so much that they could not leave from there on Saturday or on Sunday. They left the following Monday, the fifteenth of that month, and found a very bad swamp and all the road very difficult, and they spent the night at Napituca, which was a very pleasant town, well situated and with much food. There the Indians made use of all their deceits and crafts to recover their cacique of Aguacaleyquen, and in the end the matter came to where the Governor saw himself in great danger; but their deceits and tricks were understood, and he did them a greater one, in this way.

Seven caciques from those districts, with their people, joined together and sent a message to the Governor saying that they were subjects of Uçachile, and that by his commission and their will, they wished to be friends of the Christians and to help them against Apalache, a strong province, an enemy of Uçachile and of them, and that to this end they had come, induced and requested by Aguacaleyquen (who is the cacique that the Christians held imprisoned), and that they were afraid to enter in the camp and be detained: therefore, the Governor should bring Aguacaleyquen with him and come forth to them to speak in a large savannah that there was there, to converse about this business. Their entreaties were understood and their message was accepted, and the Governor came forth to speak to them; but he commanded the Christians to arm and mount, and that at the signal of a trumpet they should attack the Indians. [The Governor] came forth to the savannah with only those of his guard and a chair to sit upon, and the cacique of Aguacaleyquen with him. Scarcely had the Governor seated himself, and the conversa-

---

[25]This description of a *gran patio* in the middle of a *gran buhio* seems to refer to an open court within a large aboriginal structure and mirrors various descriptions of aboriginal council houses, with a large open space in the center of the roof. For further information, see Gary N. Shapiro and John H. Hann, "The Documentary Image of the Council Houses of Spanish Florida Tested by Excavations at the Mission of San Luis de Talimali," in *Columbian Consequences: Archaeological and Historical Perspectives on the Spanish Borderlands East,* ed. D. H. Thomas, 511–26 (Washington, D.C.: Smithsonian Institution Press, 1990).

tion was beginning, when he saw himself immediately surrounded with Indians with their bows and arrows, and from many directions came innumerable others, in such a manner that the danger that the Governor was in was manifest. And before the trumpet could sound, the maestre de campo, Luis de Moscoso, struck his legs to his horse saying: "Come on, men, Santiago,[26] Santiago, and at them." And thus, all of a sudden, the people on horseback went lancing many Indians, and the stratagem only gained them the upper hand, allowing our men to strike first; notwithstanding, they [the Indians] defended themselves and fought like men of great spirit, and they killed the horse of the Governor and killed another belonging to a gentleman, called Sagredo, and wounded others. And after the fight lasted a good period of time, the Indians fled and took shelter in two lakes; and the Spaniards encircled one, and the other they could not, and they surrounded the first one, keeping vigil all night and until the morning when they [the Indians] surrendered, and they brought out from there as prisoners three hundred Indians and five or six caciques among them.

Uriutina in the end remained alone. He did not wish to leave until some Indians from Uçachile swam in for him, and they brought him out, and upon leaving, he asked for a messenger for his land, and [the messenger] having been brought, he spoke to him thus: "Look, go to my [people] and tell them that for me they should have no concern: that I have done, as a valiant man and lord, what there was to do and struggled and fought like a man until they left me alone; and if I withdrew to this lake, it was not to flee death or not to die as befits me, but rather in order to inspire those who were within and urge them not to give up: and after they gave themselves up, I never surrendered until these Indians from Uçachile, who are of our nation, begged me, saying that this was advisable to all. Therefore, what I charge and pray to them is that neither out of respect for me nor for another should they deal with these Christians, who are devils and who are more than a match for them, and that they should believe for certain that if I have to die, it will be as a valiant man." All of which was then referred and declared to the Governor by Juan Ortiz, the interpreter, who is that Christian whom the history has related they found in the land, by chance of fortune.

The Indians who were captured in the manner already stated were taken to be put in a hut, their hands tied behind. The Governor walked among them in order to meet the caciques, encouraging them in order to bring them to peace and concord, and having them untied so that they might be better

[26]The call to Santiago, or St. James, was a familiar battle cry of the reconquest in Spain.

treated than the other common Indians. One of those caciques, as soon as they untied him, the Governor being next to him, raised his arm and gave the Governor such a great blow that it bathed his teeth in blood and made him spit out much of it, for which they tied him and the other [caciques] each to poles and they were riddled with arrows. Other Indians did many other deeds, the full account of which could not be written, according to what he who found himself present told the historian; for which reason the Governor, seeing that with so few Indians and without weapons the Christians were so afflicted, and he no less so, spoke thus: "Oh help me God, and if only those lords of the Council were here so that they might see how His Majesty is served in these parts!" But it is because they know it, says the chronicler, that they have commanded the tyrannies and cruelties to cease, and to have better order in the pacification of the Indies, so that God, Our Lord, and the Imperial Majesty are better served, and the consciences of the conquistadors are at peace, and the natives of the land are not maltreated.

Tuesday, the twenty-third of September, the Governor and his army left from Napituca and arrived at the river of the Deer. This name was given to it because the Indian messengers from Uçachile brought there certain deer, since there are many and good ones in that land. And in order to cross this river they made a bridge of three large pines in length and four in breadth (these pines are perfect and like the very large ones from Spain), and when all the army had finished crossing the river, which was on the twenty-fifth of that month, they passed through two small towns the same day and one very large one that is called Apalu, and they arrived to spend the night at Uçachile. But in all these towns they found the people gone, and some captains went out to pillage [*ranchear*][27] and captured many people.

They departed from Uçachile the following Monday, the twenty-ninth of the month, and having crossed a large forest, they spent the night in a pine forest [*pinar*]. A lad, called Cadena, turned back without permission for a sword, and the Governor wished to have him hung for both offenses, but through the entreaties of good persons, he escaped [this punishment]. The next day, Tuesday, the thirtieth of the month of September, they arrived at Agile, a subject of Apalache, and they captured some women; and they are such that one Indian woman took a *bachiller*[28] named Herrera, who was alone with her and behind his other companions, and she seized him by the

[27] The term *ranchear* was a euphemism for pillaging, derived from the practice of quartering soldiers as an excuse to loot.

[28] Recipient of an academic degree.

genitals and held him very fatigued and submissive, and perhaps if other Christians had not passed and aided him, the Indian woman would have killed him. It was not that he wished to have intercourse with her as a lustful man, but rather that she wished to liberate herself and flee. Wednesday, the first of October, Governor Hernando de Soto left from Agile with his people and arrived at the river or swamp of Ivitachuco, and they made a bridge; and in a canebrake[29] on the other side was an ambush of Indians, and they shot three Christians with arrows; and they finished crossing that swamp the following Friday at midday, and there a horse drowned. And they went to sleep at Ivitachuco and found the town burning, for the Indians had set fire to it. Sunday, the fifth of October, they went to Calahuchi, and they took two Indian men and an Indian woman and jerked venison in great quantity, and there the guide who led them fled.

The next day they went forward carrying as guide an old Indian who got them lost, and an Indian woman led them to Iviahica, and they found all the people gone, and the next day two Captains left from there and found all the people gone. Juan de Añasco had left from this town, and eight leagues from it, he found the port where Pánfilo de Narváez[30] had embarked in the boats that he made. This he recognized by the skulls of the horses and site of the forge and cribs and mortars that they had made in order to grind the corn, and by crosses fashioned on the trees. And they wintered there and were there until the fourth of March of the year of fifteen forty, in which time came to pass many notable things with the Indians, who are most valiant men, and by what will now be told, the discerning reader will be able to surmise their great spirit and boldness. [For instance,] two Indians came forth against eight men on horseback; and they set fire to the town twice, and with ambushes they killed many Christians at other times, and although the Spaniards pursued them and burned them, never did they wish to come in peace. If they cut off the hands and noses of some Indians, they did not show more feeling than if each one of them was a Mucio Scévola, the Roman. Not one of them denied being from Apalache for fear of death. And upon taking one, when they asked him where he was from, he responded with pride: "Where am I from? . . . I am an Indian of Apalache," like one who gave to understand that he took offense from whoever might think that he was of another people but Apalache.

The Governor decided to go farther into the interior, because an Indian

[29] *Un carrizal,* referring to land covered in reed grass.

[30] Narváez skirted the Gulf Coast in 1528.

boy gave great news of what there was in the interior; and he sent Juan de Añasco with thirty on horseback for Captain Calderón and the people who had remained in the port, and they burned the supplies that they left behind and the town, and Captain Calderón came by land with all the people, and Juan de Añasco came by the sea, with the brigantines and small vessels, up to the port of Apalache. Saturday, the nineteenth of November, Juan de Añasco arrived at the port, and then Maldonado was dispatched in the brigantines along the coast to find a port to the west [*Hueste-Occidente*].

And at this time Captain Calderón arrived with all the people, minus two men and seven horses that the Indians killed on the road. Maldonado discovered a very good port and brought an Indian from a province that is next to that coast, which is called Achuse, and he brought a good blanket of sables (although they had already seen others in Apalache, but not like this).

Captain Maldonado was dispatched for Havana, and he left from Apalache on the twenty-sixth of February of fifteen forty, with an order and command from the Governor that he should return to the port that he had discovered, and to that coast where the Governor planned to come.

The province of Apalache is very fertile and very abundant in supplies, with much corn and beans [*fésoles*] and squash [*calabazas*], and diverse fruits, and many deer and many varieties of birds, and near the sea there are many and good fish, and it is a pleasant land although there are swamps; but they are firm because they are over sand.

FIVE

HOW GOVERNOR HERNANDO DE SOTO AND HIS PEOPLE DEPARTED FROM IVIAHICA IN SEARCH OF CAPACHEQUI, AND HOW THE GUIDE THEY HAD, WHEN HE DID NOT KNOW MORE OF WHAT THERE WAS FARTHER ON, MADE HIMSELF OUT TO BE POSSESSED; AND DIVERSE AND VERY NOTABLE THINGS ARE TREATED.

The departure from Iviahica, in search of Capachequi, began Wednesday, the third day of March of fifteen forty, and the Governor with his army spent the night at the river of Guacuca; and having departed from there, they went to the river of Capachequi, at which they arrived early the following Friday, and they made a canoe or piragua[31] in order to cross it; and the river was so broad that Cristobal Mosquera, who was the best thrower, tried but did not manage to throw a stone across it. And they took the chains in which they brought the Indians, strongly joined with some S hooks of iron, and having made one chain from all, they attached one end of the chain from one bank and the other one from the other, in order to cross the piragua, and the current was such that it broke the chain two times; and seeing this, they attached many ropes and from these made two, and they attached one to the stern and the other to the prow, and pulling from one side and from the other, the people and the clothing crossed. In order to get the horses across, they made long ropes and attached them to the neck; and although the current pushed them down, pulling the ropes drew them out, but with difficulty, and some half drowned. And on Wednesday, the ninth of March, all the army finished crossing the river of Capachequi, and they left to sleep in a pine forest. And the next day, Thursday, they arrived at the first town of Capachequi, which was well supplied, but among densely wooded hills or land very closed in with groves of trees [*arboledas*], and thus they passed on to sleep at another town farther on. And they came upon a bad swamp, next to the town, with a strong current, and before arriving at [the swamp], they crossed a very large stretch of water that came to the cinches and saddle pads of the horses, in such a manner that all the army was not able to finish crossing that day on account of the bad crossing. There one hundred[32] soldiers with swords and shields strayed away, and an equal number of Indians wounded one of them in the head and killed him, and they would have killed all of them if they had not been aided.

On the sixteenth of March they left from Capachequi and spent the night at White Spring. This is a very beautiful spring [*fuente*], with a great abundance [*gran golpe*] of good water, and it has fish. And the following day they spent the night at the river of Toa, where they made two bridges, and the horse of Lorenzo Suárez, son of Vasco Porcallo, drowned. And the following Sunday, the twenty-first of the month, they arrived at the crossing of the river of Toa, and two times they made a bridge of pines, and the great current broke them, and they made another bridge of timbers crossed in a cer-

[31] A *piragua* was a long and narrow vessel (larger than a canoe) typically made from a single piece of wood, although the gunwales were often made of planks or canes.

[32] This number [*cient*] seems much too large and may be a mistranscription of five [*cinco*], fitting more closely with the Elvas account.

tain way, which a gentleman, called Nuño de Tovar, described, at which all laughed, but it was true what he said; and having made [the bridge] in that way, they crossed very well. And on Monday all the army finished crossing, and they spent the night in a pine forest, although they were separated and in bad order. And early on Tuesday they arrived at Toa, a large town, and the Governor wished to go farther, but they did not let him.

Wednesday, the twenty-fourth of the month, the Governor left from there at midnight, secretly, with up to forty noblemen and gentlemen on horseback, and those whom for diverse reasons he had not wished to put under another Captain. And they traveled all that day until the night, when they found a bad and deep crossing of water, and although it was at night, they crossed it, and they walked that day twelve leagues; and the next day, which was Maundy Thursday, in the morning, they arrived at the province [*población*] of Chisi and crossed a branch of a large river, very broad, some of it on foot, and even a good part of it swimming, and they attacked a town that was on an island in this river, where they captured some people and found food. And because the place was dangerous, before canoes came they went back the same way they had entered, but first they had for lunch some hens of the land, which are called guanajas [turkeys], and loins of venison that they found roasted on a *barbacoa,* which is like on a grill.[33] And although it was Maundy Thursday, there was not one so Christian that he had scruples about eating the meat. And the boy Perico that they had brought from Apalache as guide led them there.

And they passed on to other towns, and at a bad crossing of a swamp, some horses drowned, because they were put in to swim with the saddles, while their owners crossed over on a beam which traversed the current of the water. And crossing thus one Benito Fernández, a Portuguese, fell from the beam and drowned. This day they arrived at a town where principal Indians came as messengers from Ichisi, and one of them asked the Governor and said three words, one after the other, in this manner: "Who are you? What do you want? Where are you going?" And they brought presents of hides, blankets of the land, which were the first gifts as a signal of peace; all of which was on Maundy Thursday and on the Day of the Incarnation. To the questions of the Indian, the Governor responded that he was a Captain of

[33]The term *barbacoa* refers to a framework of sticks that was used to cook meat, although other raised frameworks, such as a bench or corncrib, were often described using the same word. This term, which originated among the Arawak Indians of the Caribbean, survives today in the word *barbecue*.

the great King of Spain; that in his name he came to give them to understand the sacred faith of Christ, and that they should know him and be saved, and give obedience to the apostolic church of Rome and to the Supreme Pontiff and Vicar of God who resides there, and that in the temporal world they should recognize as king and lord the Emperor, king of Castile, our Lord, as his vassals, and that they would treat them all well, and with peace and justice, like his other Christian vassals.

On Monday, the twenty-ninth of March, they left from there for Ichisi, and it rained so much, and a small river swelled in such a manner, that if they had not made much haste to cross, all of the army would have been endangered. This day Indian men and women came forth to receive them. The women came clothed in white, and they made a fine appearance, and they gave to the Christians tortillas of corn and some bundles of spring onions exactly like those of Castile, as fat as the tip of the thumb and more. And that was a food which helped them much from then on; and they ate them with tortillas, roasted and stewed and raw, and it was a great aid to them because they are very good. The white clothing in which those Indian women came clothed are some blankets of both coarse and fine linen. They make the thread of them from the bark of the mulberry trees; not from the outside but rather from the middle; and they know how to process and spin and prepare it so well and weave it, that they make very pretty blankets. And they put one on from the waist down, and another tied by one side and the top placed upon the shoulders, like those Bohemians or Egyptians who are in the habit of sometimes wandering through Spain. The thread is such that he who found himself there certified to me that he saw the women spin it from that bark of mulberry trees and make it as good as the most precious thread from Portugal that the women in Spain procure in order to sew, and some more thin and even, and stronger. The mulberry trees are exactly like those of Spain, and as large and larger; but the leaf is softer and better for silk, and the mulberries better for eating and even larger than those from Spain, and the Spaniards also made good use of them many times, in order to sustain themselves. They arrived that day at a town of a cacique subject to Ichisi, a pretty town and with plenty of food, and he [the cacique] gave them willingly of what he had, and they rested there on Tuesday, and then on Wednesday, the last day of March, the Governor and his army departed, and they arrived at the Great River,[34] where they had many canoes in which they

[34]This is the only river that was denoted by the capitalized *Río Grande* in Oviedo's printed text, although the river beyond Quizqui (the Mississippi) was later termed *el río grande.*

crossed very well and arrived at the town of the lord, who was one-eyed, and he gave them very good food and fifteen Indians to carry the burdens. And as he was the first who came in peace, they did not wish to be tiresome. They were there Thursday, the first of April, and they placed a cross on the mound [*cerro*] of the town and informed them through the interpreter of the sanctity of the cross, and they received it and appeared to adore it with much devotion.

Friday, the second day of the month of April, this army departed from there and slept in the open, and the next day they arrived at a good river and found deserted huts, and messengers arrived from Altamaha and led them to a town where they found an abundance of food, and a messenger from Altamaha came with a present, and the following day they brought many canoes and the army crossed very well. And from there the Governor sent a message summoning the cacique Çamumo, and they said that he ate and slept and walked continually armed, that he never took off the weapons, because he was on the frontier [*frontera*] of another cacique called Cofitachequi, his enemy, and that he would not come without weapons, and the Governor replied and said that he should come as he might wish. And he came and the Governor gave him a large feather colored with silver, and the cacique took it very happily and said to the Governor: "You are from heaven, and this your feather that you give me, I can eat with it; I will go forth to war with it; I will sleep with my wife with it." And the Governor said to him that yes, all this he could do. This Çamumo and those others were subjects of a great cacique who is called Ocute. And this one with the feather asked the Governor to whom he had to give the tribute in the future, if he should give it to the Governor or to Ocute. And the Governor suspected that this question might have been asked with cunning, and he responded that he held Ocute as a brother, that he should give Ocute his tribute until the Governor should command something else.

From there he sent messengers to summon Ocute, and he came there, and the Governor gave him a hat of yellow satin, and a shirt, and a feather, and he placed a cross there in Altamaha, and it was well received.

The next day, Thursday, the eighth of April, the Governor departed from there with his army, and he took Ocute with him, and they went to sleep at some huts, and on Friday they arrived at the town of Ocute. And the Governor got angry with him, and he [Ocute] trembled with fear; and after that a great number of Indians came with supplies, and they gave the Christians as many Indian burden bearers as they wished, and a cross was placed, and they appeared to receive it with much devotion and adored it on their knees, as they saw the Christians do.

Monday, the twelfth of April, they departed from Ocute and arrived at Cofaqui, and principal Indians came with gifts. This cacique Cofaqui was an old man, full-bearded, and a nephew of his governed for him. The cacique Tatofa and another principal Indian came there, and they gave their presents and food, and all the *tamemes* that they had need of (in that language tameme means Indian burden bearer). On Thursday, the fifteenth of that month, Perico, the Indian boy who had been their guide since Apalache, began to lose his bearings, because now he did not know any more of the land, and he made himself out to be possessed, and he knew how to do it so well that the Christians thought that it was the truth; and a missionary that they had with them, named fray Juan el Evangelico, said it was so. But in fact, they had to take guides, which Tatofa gave them, in order to go to Cofitachequi across an uninhabited region [*despoblado*] of nine or ten days' journey.

Many times I am amazed by the gambling spirit, or tenacity or pertinacity, or perhaps I should say constancy, because it gives a better impression of the way these deceived conquistadors went on from one difficulty to another, and from another to yet a worse one, and from one danger to others and others, here losing a comrade and there three and over there more, and going from bad to worse, without learning their lesson. Oh marvelous God, what blindness and rapture under such an uncertain greed and such vain preaching as that which Hernando de Soto was able to tell those deluded soldiers that he led to a land where he had never been and had never set foot on it, and where three other Governors, more expert than he, had been lost, which were Juan Ponce, Garay,[35] and Pánfilo de Narváez, any one of whom had more experience than he in matters of the Indies, and they were persons of more credit than he in that; because he knew nothing either of the islands or the land of the North, knowing only the method of government of Pedrarias, in Castilla del Oro and Nicaragua, and of Peru, which was another manner of dealing with the Indians; and he thought that [experience] from there sufficed to know how to govern here on the coast of the North, and he deluded himself, as this history will relate.

Let us return to the history and route of this Captain or Governor. I knew well and spoke and communicated with him and the three mentioned

[35]Francisco de Garay made two unsuccessful expeditions from Jamaica to Florida in 1518 and 1519 and later became the Governor of Panuco in Mexico.

above, and the licenciado Ayllón,[36] who was also lost in that land of the North. Friday, the sixteenth of the month, this Governor and his people spent the night at a creek [*arroyo*] on the way to Cofitachequi, and the next day they crossed an extremely large river, divided in two branches, broader than a long shot of an arquebus,[37] and it had many bad fords of many flat stones [*lajas*], and it came up to the stirrups, and in places up to the saddle pads. The current was very strong, and there was not a man on horseback who dared to take a foot soldier on the rear. The foot soldiers passed across farther upstream on the river, through more deep [water], in this manner. They made a string of thirty or forty men tied one with another, and thus they crossed, the ones holding themselves to the others; and although some were in much danger, thanks to God not one drowned, because they aided them with the horses, and gave them the butt of their lance or the tail of their horse, and thus all came forth and slept in a forest.

This day they lost many pigs of those that they had brought tame from Cuba, which the current carried off. The next day, Sunday, they went to another forest or grove [*boscaje*] to rest; and the next day, Monday, they traveled without a road and crossed another very large river, and on Tuesday they spent the night alongside a stream, and on Wednesday they arrived at another extremely large river, and difficult to cross, which was divided in two branches, with bad entrances and worse exits. And now the Christians carried nothing to eat, and with great labour they crossed this river, and arrived at some settlements of fishermen or hunters, and the Indians that they brought lost their bearings, since neither they nor the Spaniards knew the road nor what way they should take, and among them there were diverse opinions. Some said that they should turn back; others said that they should go in another direction or by another way; and the Governor proposed, as he had always done, that it was better to go forward, without his or their knowing in what they guessed correctly or in what they erred. And being perplexed in this labyrinth, on Friday, the twenty-third of April, the Governor sent men to look for roads or towns in this manner: Baltasar de Gallegos went upriver to the northwest, and Juan de Añasco went downriver[38] to the southeast, each with ten on horseback and rations for ten days. And that day other Captains came from exploring, and they had not found anything. And

[36]Ayllón's ill-fated colony on the Atlantic Coast dated to 1526.

[37]An arquebus was a heavy matchlock gun.

[38]The text actually reads *el río arriba,* or upriver, but since this direction is opposite that of Gallegos, and since rivers on the southeastern Atlantic slope tend to flow northwest to southeast, Añasco is assumed to have gone downstream.

on Saturday the Governor sent Juan Ruiz Lobillo to the north with four on horseback, with rations for ten days; and he commanded that they kill the large sows that they had in the army, and they gave as rations one pound of meat to each man, and with it, the herbs and amaranths [*bledos*] that they looked for, and thus they supplied the best that they could in their need, not without great conflict and hardship, and the horses without any food, and they and their owners dying of hunger, without a road, with continual rain, the rivers continually swelling and narrowing the land, and without hope of towns or knowledge of where they had to go to look, calling and asking God for mercy.

And Our Lord remedied them in this manner: on Sunday, the twenty-fifth of April, Juan de Añasco came with news that he had found a town and food. They were very happy, and he brought an interpreter and guide, and thus the rations of the meat ceased, and each one fed himself as he was able, with unknown herbs and amaranths, so that the meat might remain for future use. And the Governor determined to depart then, and having written some letters and placed them in some gourds [*calabazos*], they buried them in a hidden place, and on a large tree left some letters that said where the Spaniards would find them. And thus they departed with Juan de Añasco on a Monday, the twenty-sixth of April. This day the Governor arrived with some on horseback (although few) at the town that is called Himahi, and the army remained two leagues back, the horses being tired. He found in this town a barbacoa of corn and more than two and a half *cahices*[39] of prepared *pinol*, which is toasted corn. And the next day the army arrived, and they gave out rations of corn and pinol; and there were infinite mulberries, because there were many mulberry trees and they were in season: this was a great help. And also they found in the savannahs some *morotes* like those that grow in Italy on some plants and next to the ground, which are like delicious and very fragrant strawberries, and even in Galicia there are many of these. In the kingdom of Naples they call this fruit *fraoles,* and it is a delicate and exquisite thing, and they esteem it. And apart from this, they found there by the fields infinite roses, and native ones like those of Spain; and although not of so many petals through being wild, they are not of less fragrance, but rather more delicate and mellow. This town they named [the town] of Succor.

The next day Captain Alonso Romo, who had also gone to explore, ar-

---

[39]One *cahiz* is equal to twelve *fanegas* (100 pounds of corn), making Rangel's amount approximately 3,000 pounds of corn.

rived and brought four or five Indians, and not one would make known the town of their lord nor disclose its location, although they burned one of them alive in front of the others, and all suffered that martyrdom, in order not to disclose it. The next day, Wednesday, Baltasar de Gallegos arrived with an Indian woman and news of a settlement [*poblado*]. The next day following, Lobillo came with news of roads, and he left behind two lost companions, and the Governor reprimanded him severely, and without letting him rest or eat, he made him return to look for them under penalty of his life if he should not bring them. And that was a better command, and better done and thought out than burning alive one of those Indians Alonso Romo brought, for not wanting to disclose his lord, because to such as he the Romans placed a memorial statue in the Forum, and to Christians such cruelty is permitted against no one, especially against an Indian who wished to die through being loyal to his fatherland and his lord; but later on all was repaid.

SIX

HOW GOVERNOR HERNANDO DE SOTO WENT TO THE TOWN OF JALAMECO, AND HOW THE *CACICA,* THE RULER OF THAT LAND, ENTERTAINED THEM AND PLACED ON HIS NECK A STRING OF PEARLS THAT SHE WORE ON HER NECK, AND HOW THEY FOUND MANY OTHERS, AND THROUGH THE FAULT OF THE GOVERNOR HE DID NOT FIND ALL THAT HE WISHED, AND OF THE TREES THAT THEY FOUND LIKE THOSE OF SPAIN, AND OTHERS OF THAT LAND OF COFITACHEQUI; AND HOW THEY WENT ONWARD AND HOW A CHRISTIAN CALLED RODRÍGUEZ AND A BLACK MAN AND OTHER SLAVES REMAINED IN THESE JOURNEYS, AND HOW THEY ARRIVED AT CHIHÁ, WHERE THEY FOUND PALISADED TOWNS AND CARRIED FROM THERE FIVE HUNDRED SLAVES,[40] AND HOW FARTHER ON THEY FOUND PEARLS IN RIVERS OF FRESH WATER, AND MANY OTHER PARTICULARS SUITABLE TO THE DISCOURSE OF THESE HISTORIES.

Let the reader not marvel how this historian proceeds so precisely through the journeys and rivers and crossings that this adelantado and Governor Hernando de Soto and his army experienced in those northern provinces and places; it is because among those gentlemen who found themselves in all that, there was one, called Rodrigo Rangel, of whom mention has been made and in future will be made, who served in that army, who, wanting to understand what he saw and how his life passed, like a wise man, wrote at

[40]The previous six lines were omitted by the editor of Oviedo and by Bourne for the sake of brevity.

the end of the day's journey, after his labours, all that which happened to them, and also for his recreation; and also because each Christian ought to do it in order to know how to confess and bring his sins to memory, in particular those who go to war; and also because those who have labored and passed through such excessive hardships, enjoy afterward, as eyewitnesses, communicating and sharing it with their friends, and in order to explain their own role, as they should. And so this Rodrigo Rangel came, after all those things already described and those that follow had happened, to this city of Sancto Domingo of the island Española and gave a relation of all these things in this Audiencia Real to the very reverend señor licenciado Alonso López de Cerrato, who presides in it,[41] and he commanded and charged that he should tell in writing and give an account of all to me, so that, as chronicler for Their Majesties of these histories of the Indies, this northern conquest and discovery might be compiled and made known, placed among their number, since so many novelties and unusual subjects come together for the delight of the prudent reader, and as a warning for many who in these Indies come to lose [their lives] following after a Governor who dispenses thus others' lives, as is apparent through these my studies and writings.

Let us come back to the events and the continuation of what we have in hand and is treated here. Friday, the last day of April, the Governor took some on horseback, the most rested, and the Indian woman Baltasar de Gallegos brought as guide and went toward Cofitachequi and spent the night hard by a large and deep river, and he sent Juan de Añasco with some on horseback to try to have some interpreters and canoes ready in order to cross the river, and he [Añasco] got some. The next day the Governor arrived at the crossing in front of the town, and principal Indians came with gifts, and the cacica, ruler of that land, came, whom the principal [Indians] brought with much prestige on a litter covered in white (with thin linen) and on their shoulders, and they crossed in the canoes, and she spoke to the Governor with much grace and self-assurance. She was young and of fine appearance, and she removed a string of pearls that she wore about the neck and put it on the Governor's neck, in order to ingratiate herself and win his good will. And all the army crossed in canoes, and they gave many presents of very well tanned hides and blankets, all very good, and a large amount of jerked venison and dry wafers, and much and very good salt. All the Indians walked covered down to the feet with very excellent hides, very well tanned,

[41]The reference to Cerrato was transcribed by the editor, J. Amador de los Rios, and did not appear in Oviedo's final manuscript.

and blankets of the land, and blankets of sable, and blankets of mountain lions,[42] which smelled; the people are very clean and very polite and naturally well developed. Monday, on the third of May, all the rest of the army arrived, and all could not cross until the next day, Tuesday, and not without cost and loss of seven horses, which drowned. These were among the most fat and strong, which fought against the current, but the thin ones, which let themselves go with the current, crossed better.

On the seventh of May, Friday, Baltasar de Gallegos went with most of the people of the army to Ilapi to eat seven barbacoas of corn that they said were there, which were a deposit of the cacica.[43] This same day the Governor and Rodrigo Rangel entered in the temple or oratory[44] of these idolatrous people, and having unwrapped some interments, they found some bodies of men tied on a barbacoa, the breasts and openings and necks and arms and legs covered in pearls; and as they were bringing them out, Rangel saw a thing like a green and very good emerald, and he showed it to the Governor, and he was very delighted. And he commanded that he should look out of the wall and call Juan de Añasco, accountant of Their Majesties, and Rangel told him: "My Lord, do not call anyone: it could be that there might be some precious stone or jewel here." And the Governor replied, somewhat angrily, and said: "Even if there were, do we have to steal it?" Juan de Añasco having come, they took out that emerald and it was made of glass,[45] and after that one, more and more beads of glass and rosaries with their crosses. They also found Biscayan axes of iron, by which they recognized that they were in the district or land where the licenciado Lucas Vázquez de Ayllón was lost. They brought out from there eight or nine *arrobas*[46] of pearls; and as the cacica saw that the Christians made much of them,

---

[42]The term *gatos de clavo,* or mountain cats, probably refers to the cougar (*Felis concolor*).

[43]This passage refers to the practice of storing surplus corn under the control of the chief, forming a basis for chiefly authority in a redistributive system.

[44]*La mezquita u oratorio,* probably referring to a charnel house or public structure such as a temple.

[45]Inexpensive glass beads were standard items of trade with Indians, and translucent green wire-wound seed beads are recognized by archaeologists to be markers for the early sixteenth century (see Kathleen Deagan, *Artifacts of the Spanish Colonies of Florida and the Caribbean, 1500–1800* [Washington, D.C.: Smithsonian Institution Press, 1987], and also Marvin T. Smith, "Chronology from Glass Beads: The Spanish Period in the Southeast, ca. A.D. 1513–1670," in *Proceedings of the 1982 Glass Trade Bead Conference,* ed. C. Hayes, 147–58 [Rochester: Rochester Museum and Science Center Research Records 16, 1983]).

[46]One *arroba* equals approximately 25 pounds, making Rangel's amount between 200 and 225 pounds of pearls.

she said: "Do you think this is a lot? . . . Go to Talimeco, my town, and you will find so many that you will be unable to carry them on your horses." The governor said: "Leave them here, and to whom God gives them by good fortune, may St. Peter bless them," and so they remained. It was believed that he intended to take that [place] for himself, because without doubt it is the best that they saw and the land of better disposition, although neither many people nor much corn appeared, nor did they tarry to look for them there.

Some things were made there as in Spain, which must have been taught by the Indians who went away to the licenciado Lucas Vázquez de Ayllón, because they made breeches and buskins,[47] and black gaiters [*antiparras*] with laces of white hide, and with fringes or edging of colored hide, as if they had been made in Spain. In the temple or oratory of Talimeco, there were breastplates, as well as corselets and helmets, made from raw and hairless hides of cows, and from the same [hides] very good shields. This Talimeco was a town of great importance, with its very authoritative oratory on a high mound; the caney or house of the cacique very large and very tall and broad, all covered, high and low, with very excellent and beautiful mats, and placed with such fine skill, that it appeared that all the mats were only one mat. Only rarely was there a hut which might not be covered with matting. This town has very good savannahs and a fine river, and forests of walnuts and oak, pines, evergreen oaks and groves of sweetgum, and many cedars. In this river it was said that Alaminos, a native of Cuba (although Spanish), had found a bit of gold; and such a rumor became public in the army among the Spaniards, and for this it was believed that this is a land of gold, and that good mines would be found there.

Wednesday, the thirteenth of May, the Governor left from Cofitachequi, and in two days he arrived at the province [*población*] of Chalaque; but he could not find the town of the lord, nor was there an Indian who would disclose it. And they slept in a pine forest, where many Indian men and women began to come in peace with presents and gifts, and they were there on Whitsuntide. And from there the Governor wrote to Baltasar de Gallegos by some Indians, [sending them] to the barbacoas that they had gone to in order to eat the corn, as was stated above, that they should follow the Governor. And on Monday, the seventeenth of that month, they departed from there and spent the night in a forest; and on Tuesday they went to Guaquili, and the Indians came forth in peace and gave them corn, although little, and

[47] *Borcequies,* a laced half-boot.

many hens roasted on barbacoa, and a few little dogs, which are good food. These are little dogs that do not bark, and they rear them in the houses in order to eat them. They also gave them tamemes, which are Indians who carry burdens. And on the following Wednesday they went to a canebrake, and on Thursday to a small savannah where a horse died; and some foot soldiers of Baltasar de Gallegos arrived, making known to the Governor that he was approaching.

The next day, Friday, they went to Xuala, which is a town on a plain [*llano*] between some rivers; its cacique was so well provisioned, that he gave to the Christians however much they asked for: tamemes, corn, little dogs, *petacas*, and however much he had. Petacas are baskets covered with leather (and also yet to be covered), with their lids, for carrying clothes and whatever they might wish. And on Saturday Baltasar de Gallegos arrived there with many sick and lame, and they needed them healthy, particularly since they now had the mountains [*sierras*] before them. In that Xuala it seemed to them that there was better disposition to look for gold mines than in all that they had passed through and seen in that northern part.

Tuesday, on the twenty-fifth of May, they left from Xuala and crossed that day a very high mountain range [*sierra*], and they spent the night in a small forest,[48] and the next day, Wednesday, in a savannah where they endured great cold, although it was already the twenty-sixth of May; and there they crossed, in water up to their shins, the river by which they afterward left in the brigantines that they made. When that river comes forth to the sea, the navigation chart states and indicates that it is the river of Spiritu Sancto; which, according to the charts of the cosmographer Alonso de Chaves, enters in a great bay, and the mouth of this river, in the salt water, is at thirty-one degrees on this side of the equator.

Returning to the history, from there where it is stated that they crossed the river in water up to their shins, the cacica of Cofitachequi, whom they took with them in payment of the good treatment that they had received from her, turned back, and that day Mendoza de Montanjes and Alaminos de Cuba stayed behind (it was said that it was done with deception); and because that day Alonso Romo led the rear guard and left them, the Governor made him return for them, and they awaited them one day; and when they arrived, the Governor wanted to hang them. In that [province] of Xalaque a comrade deserted who was named Rodríguez, a native of Peñafiel, and also a shrewd young Indian slave from Cuba, who belonged to a gentleman

---

[48] *Montecillo* may also denote a small hill, or hillock.

called Villegas, and a very shrewd slave of Don Carlos, a native of Barbary, and Gómez, a very shrewd black man of Vasco González; Rodríguez was the first, and those others farther on from Xalaque.

The next day they spent the night in an oak grove [*robredal*], and the following day, alongside a large creek, which they crossed many times; and the next day messengers came in peace, and they arrived early at Guasili, and they gave them many tamemes, many little dogs, and corn; and because this was a good resting place, the soldiers afterward called it, while throwing the dice, the House of Guasili, or a good encounter. Monday, which was the last day of May, the Governor left from Guasili and went with his army to an oak grove alongside a river, and the next day they passed through Canasoga and spent the night in the open. And on Wednesday they spent the night alongside a swamp, and this day they ate a very great number of mulberries. The next day, Thursday, they went alongside a large creek next to the river that they had crossed in the savannah (where the cacica went away), and now it was large. The next day, Friday, they went to a pine forest and a creek, where Indians from Chiaha came in peace and brought corn. And the next day, Saturday, in the morning, the Spaniards crossed the very broad river, across a branch of it, and entered in Chiaha, which is on an island of the same river.

Saturday, the fifth of June, was the day that they entered in Chiaha; and since from Xuala all their travel had been through a mountain range and the horses were tired and thin, and the Christians likewise fatigued, it was advisable to halt and rest there; and they gave them an abundance of good corn, of which there is much, and they gave them many *mazamorras*,[49] and considerable oil of walnuts and acorns, which they know how to extract very well, and it is very good and helped them very much for their sustenance, although some are wont to say that the oil of walnuts causes some flatulence; notwithstanding it is very delicious. The Indians were with the Christians fifteen days in peace; they played with them, and also among themselves; they swam in the company of the Christians, and in all they served them very well. They went away afterward one Saturday, the nineteenth of the month, because of a certain thing which the Governor asked them for; and in short, it was that he asked them for women. The next day in the morning, the Governor sent for the cacique, and he came then, and the next day the Governor carried him with him [as a hostage] to make the people return, and

[49]The term *mazamorras* refers to a porridge made with corn meal and sweetened with sugar or honey. This dish was probably similar to *sofkee*, a staple food for Creek Indians.

indeed they came. In the land of this Chiaha was where these Spaniards first found the towns palisaded [*cercados*]. Chiaha gave them five hundred tamemes, and they consented to leave off collars and chains.

On Monday, the twenty-eighth of June, the Governor and his people left from Chiaha, and they passed through five or six towns, and they went to sleep at a pine forest, in front of a town; but they had much hardship there in crossing a river that flowed very strongly, and they made a bridge or support of horses so that the foot soldiers might not be endangered, in the manner that will now be related. And it was thus: they put the horses in the river in single file, tail with head, and they held them still as much as they were able, and upon each one his master, and they received the impact of the current, and below them, where the water made no impact, the foot soldiers crossed, holding on to the tail, stirrup, cuirass, and mane of one after another; and in this manner all the army crossed well.

The next day, Tuesday, they passed through a town, and there they took corn and went onward to sleep in the open. The following Wednesday they crossed a river, and then a town and the river another time, and they spent the night in the open. And on Thursday the cacique of Coste came forth to receive them in peace, and he led the Christians to sleep in a town of his. He got angry because some soldiers looted, or more accurately, sacked some barbacoas against his will. And thus, the next day, Thursday, going toward his principal town of Coste, he slipped away and evaded the Spaniards and called his people to arms. On Friday, the second day of the month of July, the adelantado Governor arrived at Coste, which is a town on an island of the river, which there flows great and strong and is difficult to enter: and the Christians crossed the first branch without danger to any one of the soldiers (which was no small good fortune); and the Governor entered in the town carelessly and unarmed with a few unarmed men, and when the soldiers did as was their custom and began to climb on the barbacoas, in the instant that they began to do that, the Indians began to beat them and take their bows and arrows and come forth to the plaza. The Governor commanded that all should suffer it and be tolerant, because of the evident danger in which they were, and that no one should put hand to his weapons; and he began to quarrel with the soldiers, and in order to dissimulate, he also thrashed some of them, and he flattered the cacique and told him that he did not wish that the Christians should anger them, and that he wished to leave to take lodging at the savannah of the island. And the cacique and his [people] went with him, and as they had withdrawn from the town, in the clear, he gave the command to lay hands on the cacique and ten or twelve principals, and they put them in chains with their collars, and he threatened them and said that he would burn all of them, because they had laid hands on the Christians. From there at Coste, the Governor sent two soldiers north to see the province of Chisca, which was rumored to have great wealth, and they brought good news. There in Coste was found, in the trunk of a tree, honey from bees, as good as, or even better than can be had in Spain. In that river they found, in some clams that they gathered from it to eat, some pearls, and they were the first that those Christians saw from fresh water, although there are [pearls] in many parts of that land. Friday, the ninth of July, the adelantado and his army left Coste, and they crossed the other branch of the river and spent the night on its banks, and Tali was on the other side; and since the river flows together in one large channel, they could not cross it, and the Indians, believing that they had crossed, sent canoes, and in them their wives and children and clothes, on this side, well away from the Christians; but they [the Indians] were all taken suddenly, and as they went along with the current the Governor made them all turn back, which was the reason why the cacique came in peace, and he helped them cross to the other side in his canoes and gave to the Christians what they had need of. And thus he did in his land, through which they passed afterward; and they were there on Saturday, and they gave them tamemes, and they departed on Sunday and slept in the open.

On Monday they crossed a river, and slept in the open. On Tuesday they crossed another river, and on Wednesday another large river, and they slept in Tasqui. All these past days since they departed from alongside Tali, the cacique of Tali made [the Indians] bring out, from their towns along the road, corn and mazamorras and cooked beans, and everything he could. On Thursday they went to another small town and passed other towns, and on Friday the Governor entered in Coça. This is a great cacique with much land, and one of the best and most abundant [provinces] that they found in Florida; and the cacique came forth to receive the Governor on a litter, covered with white blankets of the land. Sixty or seventy of his principal Indians carried the litter on their shoulders, and none was an Indian of the plebeians or commoners, and those that carried him took turns from time to time, with great ceremony in their manner. In Coça there were many plums like the early ones of Seville, very good, and they and their trees like those of Spain. Also there were some small sour apples, like those that they call *canavales* in Extremadura. They were there in Coça some days, during which the Indians hid, and left the cacique in the power of the Christians along with some principal Indians; and they [the Spaniards] went to round them up and took many, whom they imprisoned in collars of iron and in chains: and in truth, as eyewitnesses testified, it was a thing of much pity to see it; but God forgets no evil thing done nor does it remain without punishment, as this history will relate.

On Friday, the twentieth of August, the Governor and his people left Coça, and there remained behind a Christian who was named Feryada, a Levantine; and they spent that night beyond Talimuchusi. And the next day, in a heavy rain, they spent the night at Itaba, a large town alongside a good river, and there they bartered for some Indian women, whom they gave them in exchange for mirrors and knives. Monday, the thirtieth of August, the Governor left from Itaba with his army and spent the night in an oak grove, and the following day they went to Ulibahali, a very good town, next to a large river. And many Indians of evil intent were waiting, intending to take the cacique of Coça away from the Christians, because they were subjects of his; and so that the land would not rise in revolt or deny them supplies, they took him with them, and they entered in the town very much on guard. The cacique of Coça commanded the Indians to lay down their weapons; and so they did, and they gave them tamemes and twenty Indian women, and they went in peace, although a gentleman from Salamanca, called Manzano, remained there, and it was not known if it was from his own will or from losing his bearings, going alone to pillage, inasmuch as he went on foot. He was unhappy, and he had requested other soldiers to remain with him, before they missed him. This was not known for certain, but it was said in the army after he was missing. Also a very shrewd black man, who was called Joan Vizcaíno, deserted Captain Juan Ruiz Lobillo there.

The day that they left from this town, they ate many grapes, as good as those grown from vines in Spain. In Coça and farther back they had eaten very good ones, but these from Ulibahali were the best. From this town of Ulibahali the Spaniards and their Governor left one Thursday, the second of September, and they spent the night in a pretty town hard by the river; and the next day, Friday, they came to Piachi, which is alongside a river, and there they awaited Lobillo for one day, who, without permission, had gone to look for his black man, and on coming back the Governor reprimanded him severely. On Sunday they left there and spent the night in the open, and the next day, Monday, they went to Tuasi, where they gave them tamemes and thirty-two Indian women. On Monday, the thirteenth of September, the Governor left from there, and they spent the night in the open, and on Tuesday they made another day's journey and halted likewise in the open, and on Wednesday they went to an old town that had double walls [*cercas*]

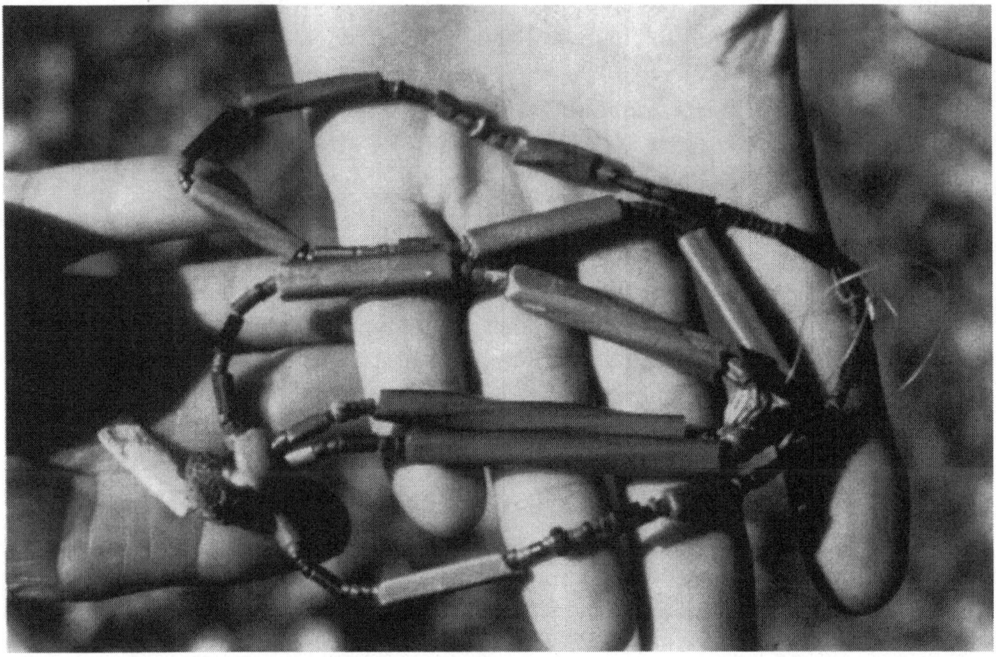

Spanish Glass Trade Beads. The Spanish conquistadors were well aware that Native American peoples generally placed a high value on gifts such as colored glass beads. Stores of cheap trade goods manufactured in Europe were routinely taken on expeditions to give away as presents, hoping to win the favor of local chiefs. The long tubular beads of blue glass shown here are of a type called Nueva Cadiz by archaeologists, who have found them at several sites in the region passed through by De Soto. Because this type of bead was no longer manufactured after about 1570, it is believed that some of the archaeological finds may mark the passage of De Soto's army nearby. (Courtesy of the University of Alabama Museum of Natural History)

A "Clarksdale" Bell. Small spherical bells made of sheet brass were used by Spanish explorers as gifts to native chiefs during the sixteenth century. This specimen was excavated from a Native American village site in the southeastern United States. Archaeologists have given this distinctive type of bell the name "Clarksdale," after a site near Clarksdale, Mississippi. Such finds may be used as evidence in the search for the route of De Soto's army. (Courtesy of the University of Alabama Museum of Natural History)

and good towers. And those ramparts [*muros*] are built in this manner: they sink many thick poles, tall and straight, next to one another; they weave them with some long sticks, and daub them within and without, and they make their loopholes at intervals, and they make their towers and turrets [*cubos*] spread out along the curtain and parts of the rampart as suits them; and at a distance, they appear to be one very excellent wall [*muralla*], and such walls are very strong.

The next day, Thursday, they spent the night in a new town next to the river, where the Spaniards rested that day. And the next day, Saturday, they went to Talisi, and they found the cacique and people gone. This town is large and fertile with much corn, and next to a large river. A messenger came there from Tascaluça, a powerful lord and very feared in that land, and then came a son of his, and the Governor commanded the Spaniards to mount, and that those on horseback should gallop, and sound the trumpets (more to impose fear, than to make ceremony with such a reception). Upon the return of those Indians, the adelantado sent with them two Christians instructed to observe and spy, in order that they might take counsel and be prepared.

On the twenty-fifth of September the cacique of Talisi came and gave what they asked him for, such as tamemes, women, and supplies, and there they freed the cacique of Coça, so that he might return to his land; and he was very angry and tearful because the Governor refused to give up a sister of his that they took, and because they had brought him so far from his land.

Tuesday, the fifth of October, they left from Talisi and spent the night at Casiste, which is a pretty town alongside the river. And the next day, Wednesday, they went to Caxa,[50] a wretched town on the bank of the river and at the boundary [*raya*] between Talisi and Tascaluça. And the next day, Thursday, they spent the night alongside the river, and a town that is called Humati was on the other side of the water. And the next day, Friday, they went to another new town [*población*], which is called Uxapita; and the next day, Saturday, they established their camp one league before arriving at the town of Tascaluça, in the open, and from there the Governor sent a messenger, and he came with the reply that he would be welcome whenever he wished to come.

The historian asked a well-informed gentleman who found himself present with this Governor and who went with him all through that northern land, why, in each place that this Governor and his army arrived, they asked

[50]While the printed text reads *la Caxa,* the article *la* is unique here before the name of this town and may have originally been a part of a longer Indian name *Lacaxa.*

for those tamemes or burden-bearing Indians, and why they took so many women, and these not old nor the most ugly; and after giving them what they had, why they detained the caciques and principal Indians, and why, where they went, they never halted or settled anywhere; saying that was neither to populate nor to conquer, but rather to disturb and devastate the land and take away the liberty of all the natives, and not to convert or make one Indian a Christian or a friend. He responded and said: that they took those burden-bearing Indians or tamemes in order to have more slaves and servants, and to carry their supplies, and whatever they stole or what they gave them; and that some died and others fled or weakened, and thus they had need to renew and take more; and that they wanted the women also in order to make use of them and for their lewdness and lust, and that they baptized them more for their carnal intercourse than to instruct them in the faith; and that if they detained the caciques and principal Indians, this was advisable so that the others, their subjects, would be quiet and not obstruct their thefts and prevent what they might wish to do in their land. As to where they were going, neither the Governor nor they knew, except that his intent was to find some land so rich that it might sate his greed, and to find out about the great secrets that the Governor said that he had heard about those places, according to many reports that had been given to him. And that as regards disturbing the land and not settling it, nothing else could be done until they came upon a site that would satisfy them. Oh, lost people; oh, diabolical greed; oh, bad conscience; oh, unfortunate soldiers; how you did not understand in how much danger you walked, and how wasted your lives and without tranquility your souls! Why did you not remember that truth that the glorious St. Augustine, deploring of the present misery of this life, says: "This life is a life of misery, decrepit and uncertain, a toilsome and unclean life, a life, my Lord, of evils, queen of the proud, filled with miseries and with dread; this is not life, nor can it be called that, but rather death, since in a moment it is finished by various mutations and diverse kinds of death"? Listen well, Catholic reader, and do not lament any less the conquered Indians than their Christian conquerors, or killers of themselves and of those others, and attend to the incidents of this ill-governed Governor, instructed in the school of Pedrarias de Avila, in the dissipation and devastation of the Indians of Castilla de Oro, graduate in the killing of the natives of Nicaragua and canonized in Peru, according to the Order of the Pizarros. And freed from all those hellish passages, and having gone to Spain loaded with gold, neither as a bachelor nor a married man could he rest, nor did he know how to, without returning to the Indies to spill human blood, not content with that already spilled, and to depart this life in the manner that farther on will be related; and giving cause for so many sinners, deceived by his vain words, to be lost with him. See how much more he wanted than what that queen or cacica of Cofitachequi, lady of Talimeco, offered him, where she told him that in that place of hers he would find so many pearls that all the horses of his army would not be able to carry them; and receiving him with such humanity, see how he treated her. Let us go on, and do not forget this truth that you have read, how in proof of how many pearls she offered him, this Governor and his people now carried eight or nine arrobas of pearls, and you will see what enjoyment they got of them in what follows.

SEVEN

IN WHICH IS RELATED WHAT HAPPENED TO THE ADELANTADO HERNANDO DE SOTO WITH THE CACIQUE OF TASCALUÇA, NAMED ACTAHACHI, WHO WAS SO TALL A MAN THAT HE SEEMED A GIANT; AND OF THE SURPRISE ATTACKS AND HARSH BATTLES AND ASSAULT THAT THEY GAVE TO THE CHRISTIANS IN THE TOWN CALLED MABILA AND FARTHER ON IN CHICAÇA. AND OTHER EVENTS SUITABLE AND NOTABLE FOR THE HISTORY ARE RELATED IN THIS CHAPTER.

On Sunday, the tenth of October, the Governor entered in the town of Tascaluça, which was called Athahachi, a new town; and the cacique was on a balcony that was made on a mound to one side of the plaza, about his head a certain headdress like an *almaizar*,[51] worn like a Moor, which gave him an appearance of authority, and a *pelote* or blanket of feathers down to his feet, very authoritative, seated upon some high cushions, and many principals of

[51] A type of turban.

his Indians with him. He was of as tall a stature as that Antonico of the guard of the Emperor our lord, and of very good proportions, a very well built and noble man; he had a young son as tall as he, but he was more slender. Always in front of this cacique was a very graceful Indian on foot, with a sunshade, on a pole, which was like a round and very large fly-flap, with a white cross similar to that which the knights of the Order of St. John of Rhodes wear, in the middle of a black field. And although the Governor entered in the plaza and dismounted and went up to him, he did not rise but rather was quiet and composed, as if he were a king, and with much gravity. The Governor sat with him a bit, and after a little while he rose and said that they should go to eat and took him with him, and Indians came to dance; and they danced very well in the way of the peasants of Spain, in such a manner that it was a pleasure to see.

At night he wished to go, but the adelantado told him that he had to sleep there; and he understood it and showed that he scoffed at such a decision, being lord, to give him so suddenly a restraint or impediment to his liberty; and concealing his intentions in the matter, he then dispatched his principal Indians, each one by himself, and he slept there to his sorrow. The next day the Governor asked for tamemes and one hundred Indian women, and the cacique gave them four hundred tamemes and said that he would give them the rest of the tamemes and the women in Mabila, the province of a principal vassal of his, and the Governor was content that the rest of that his unjust demand would be satisfied in Mabila. And he commanded that he be given a horse and some buskins and a cloak of scarlet cloth to keep him content. But as the cacique had already given him four hundred tamemes, or more accurately slaves, and was to give him one hundred women in Mabila, and those which they most desired, see what contentment could be given him by those buskins and mantle and the chance to ride on horseback, since he thought that he was riding on a tiger or on a ferocious lion, because horses were held in great dread among those people.

Finally, Tuesday, the twelfth of October, they left from that town of Atahachi, taking the cacique, as has been said, and with him many principals and always the Indian with the sunshade in front of his lord, and another with a cushion; and that day they spent the night in the open. And the next day, Wednesday, they arrived at Piachi, which is a high town, upon the bluff of a rocky river,[52] and its cacique was malicious, and he took a posi-

[52] *Un pueblo alto, sobre un barranco de un rio, enriscado.* The term *enriscado,* or craggy, may refer more to the bluff than to the river itself.

tion to resist the crossing; but in fact they crossed the river with difficulty, and two Christians were killed, and the principals who accompanied the cacique went away.[53] In that town Piachi it was found out that they had killed Don Teodoro, and a black man, who came forth from the boats of Pánfilo de Narváez.

On Saturday, the sixteenth of October, they departed from there and went to a forest, where one of the two Christians that the Governor had sent to Mabila came; and he said that there was a great gathering of armed people in Mabila. The next day they went to a palisaded town, and messengers from Mabila came who brought to the cacique much chestnut bread, for there are many and good chestnuts in his land. On Monday, the eighteenth of October, the day of St. Luke, the Governor arrived at Mabila, having passed that day through some towns. But these towns detained the soldiers, pillaging and scattering themselves, for the land seemed populous; thus only forty on horseback arrived in advance guard with the Governor, and since they were a little detained, in order for the Governor not to show weakness, he entered in the town with the cacique, and all entered with him. The Indians then did an *areito*, which is their kind of ball with dancing and singing.

While watching this, some soldiers saw them placing bundles of bows and arrows secretively in some palm leaves, and other Christians saw that the huts were filled high and low with concealed people. The Governor was warned, and he placed his helmet on his head and commanded that all should mount their horses and warn all the soldiers who had arrived; and scarcely had they left, when the Indians took command of the gates of the wall of the town. And Luis de Moscoso and Baltasar de Gallegos and Espíndola, Captain of the guard, and seven or eight soldiers remained with the Governor. And the cacique plunged into a hut and refused to come out from it; and then they began to shoot arrows at the Governor. Baltasar de Gallegos entered for the cacique, and he not wanting to leave, he [Gallegos] cut off the arm of a principal Indian with a slash. Luis de Moscoso, awaiting him at the door in order not to leave him alone, was fighting like a knight, and he did everything possible, until he could suffer no more, and said: "Señor Baltasar de Gallegos, come forth, or I will have to leave you, for I cannot wait for you any longer."

During this time Solís, a resident of Triana of Seville, and Rodrigo

[53]Bourne translated that these Indians were slain, but in actuality the text suggests that they escaped the Spaniards or may have been sent ahead by the cacique to warn the town of Mabila, as suggested by the Elvas account.

Rangel, had mounted. They were the first, and for his sins Solís was then shot down dead. Rodrigo Rangel arrived near the gate of the town[54] at the time that the Governor and two soldiers of his guard with him were leaving, and about him [the Governor] were more than seventy Indians, who halted out of fear of the horse of Rodrigo Rangel, and he [the Governor] wishing him to give it to him, a black man arrived with his own [horse]; and he commanded Rodrigo Rangel to aid the Captain of the guard who remained behind, who came out very fatigued, and with him a soldier of the guard, and he on horseback faced his enemies until he got out of danger. And Rodrigo Rangel returned to the Governor, and he drew out more than twenty arrows that he carried hanging from his armor, which was a quilted tunic of thick cotton; and he commanded Rangel to guard [the body of] Solís until he could bring him out from among their enemies, so that they might not carry him within, and so that the Governor might go to collect the soldiers. There was so much virtue and shame this day in all those who found themselves in this first attack and the beginning of this bad day. They fought admirably, and each Christian did his duty as a most valiant soldier. Luis de Moscoso and Baltasar de Gallegos left with the remaining soldiers through another gate.

In effect, the Indians ended up with the town and all the property of the Christians and with the horses that they left tied within, which they then killed. The Governor gathered all the forty on horseback who were there, and they arrived at a large plaza in front of the principal gate of Mabila, and there the Indians came forth, without daring to venture far from the palisade; and in order to draw them out, they pretended that those on horseback were fleeing at a gallop, withdrawing far from the ramparts, and the Indians, believing it, ventured from the town and from the palisade in their pursuit, desirous of employing their arrows, and when it was time, those on horseback turned around on their enemies, and before they could take shelter, they lanced many. Don Carlos wished to go with his horse up to the gate, and they gave his horse an arrow wound in the breast, and not being able to turn [his horse], he dismounted to draw out the arrow, and another came which struck him in the neck, above his shoulder, from which, asking for confession, he fell dead. The Indians did not dare to venture again from the palisade. Then, the adelantado encircled them on many sides until all the army arrived, and they entered it through three sides setting fire, first cut-

[54]This is the only Indian town in Florida that is denoted by the term *villa,* which was used earlier for Havana.

ting through the palisade with axes; and the fire traveled so that the nine arrobas of pearls that they brought were burned, and all the clothes and ornaments and chalices and moulds for wafers, and the wine for saying mass, and they were left like Arabs, empty-handed and with great hardship.

The Christian women, who were slaves of the Governor, had remained in a hut, and some pages, a friar, a cleric, and a cook and some soldiers; they defended themselves very well from the Indians, who could not enter until the Christians arrived with the fire and brought them out. And all the Spaniards fought like men of great spirit, and twenty-two of them died, and they wounded another one hundred and forty-eight with six hundred and eighty-eight arrow wounds, and they killed seven horses and wounded twenty-nine others. The women and even boys of four years struggled against the Christians, and many Indians hanged themselves in order not to fall into their hands, and others plunged into the fire willingly. See what spirit those tamemes had. There were many great arrow shots sent with such fine will and force, that the lance of a gentleman, named Nuño de Tovar, which was of two pieces of ash and very good, was pierced by an arrow through the middle from side to side, like a drill, without splintering anything, and the arrow made a cross on the lance.

Don Carlos died this day, and also Francisco de Soto, nephew of the Governor, and Juan de Gamez de Jaen, and Men Rodríguez, a good Portuguese gentleman, and Espinosa, a good gentleman, and another called Velez, and one Blasco de Barcarrota and other very honored soldiers; and the wounded were most of the people of worth and of honor. They killed three thousand Indians, in addition to which there were many others wounded, which they found afterward dead in the huts and by the roads. Nothing was ever learned of the cacique [Tascaluça], either dead or alive; the son was found lanced.

The battle having taken place in the manner stated above, they rested there until Sunday, the fourteenth of November, treating the wounded and the horses, and they burned a great part of the land. From the time that this Governor and his armies entered in the land of Florida up to the time that they left from there, all the dead were one hundred and two Christians, and not all, to my way of thinking, in true penitence.

On Sunday, the fourteenth of November of the aforesaid year, the Governor left Mabila, and the following Wednesday he arrived at a very good river, and on Thursday, the twenty-eighth,[55] they went across bad crossings and

[55]Should read November 18.

A Spanish Man-at-Arms. This type of armor was widely used by infantry during the sixteenth century. A victorious soldier was not above taking the armor of a defeated enemy if he thought it superior to his own. The illustrated helmet is probably of Italian manufacture. (From Albert F. Calvert, Spanish Arms and Armour, *London: John Lane, 1907)*

swamps and found a town with corn, which was called Talicpacana. The Christians had discovered on the other side of the river a town that seemed good to them from a distance, and well situated, and on Sunday, the twenty-first of November, Vasco González found a town, a half-league from this one, which is called Moçulixa, from which they had transferred all the corn to the other side of the river, and they had it in heaps, covered with mats, and the Indians were on the other side of the water, making threats. A piragua was made, which was finished on the twenty-ninth of the month, and they made a large cart to carry it up to Moçulixa, and having launched it in the water, sixty soldiers entered in it. The Indians shot innumerable darts, or more accurately arrows; but as this great canoe landed, they fled and did not wound but three or four Christians. They took the land easily and found plenty of corn.

The next day, Wednesday, all the army went to a town that is called Zabusta, and there they crossed the river in the piragua and with some canoes that they took there; and they went to take lodging in another town on the other end, because upriver they found another good town and took its lord, who was named Apafalaya, and brought him as guide and interpreter, and that bank was called the river of Apafalaya. From this river and province [*población*] the Governor and his people left in search of Chicaça on Thursday, the ninth of December, and they arrived the following Tuesday at the river of Chicaça, having passed many bad crossings and swamps and rivers and cold weather.

And so that you know, reader, what life those Spaniards led, Rodrigo Rangel, as an eyewitness, says that among many other needs of men that were experienced in this enterprise, he saw a nobleman named Don Antonio Osorio, brother of the Lord Marquis of Astorga, with a doublet of blankets of that land, torn on the sides, his flesh exposed, without a hat, bare-headed, bare-footed, without hose or shoes, a shield at his back, a sword without a scabbard, the snows and cold very great; and being such a man, and of such illustrious lineage, made him suffer his hardship and not lament, like many others, since there was no one who might aid him, being who he was, and having had in Spain two thousand ducats of income through the Church; and the day that this gentleman saw him thus, he believed that he had not eaten a mouthful and had to look for his supper with his fingernails. I could not help laughing when I heard him say that nobleman had left the Church and the aforementioned income in order to go to look for this life at the sound of the words of De Soto. Because I knew Soto very well, and although he was a man of worth, I did not hold that he would be able with such sweet talk or cunning to delude such persons. What did such a man wish, from an unfamiliar and unknown land? Nor did the Captain who led him know more of it than that Juan Ponce de León and the licenciado Lucas Vázquez de Ayllón and Pánfilo de Narváez and others more skillful than Hernando de Soto had been lost in it. And those who follow such guides, go from some necessity, since they find places where they could settle or rest, and little by little penetrate and understand and find out all about the land. But let us go on; small is the hardship of this nobleman compared to those who die, if they do not win salvation.

They found that the river of Chicaça was flowing out of its bed, and the Indians on the other side were up in arms, with many white banners. Orders were given to make a piragua, and the Governor sent Baltasar de Gallegos with thirty swimmers on horseback to go to look upriver for a place where they could cross and attack suddenly upon the Indians; but he was detected, and so they [the Indians] abandoned the crossing, and they crossed very well in the piragua on Thursday, the sixteenth of the month. And the Governor advanced with some on horseback, and they arrived very late at night at the town of the lord, and all the people were gone. The next day Baltasar de Gallegos arrived with the thirty who went with him. They were there in Chicaça that Christmas, and it snowed with as much wind as if they were in Burgos, and with as much or more cold.

Monday, the third of January of fifteen forty-one, the cacique of Chicaça came in peace and gave guides and interpreters to the Christians in order to go to Caluça, which had much renown among the Indians. Caluça is a province of more than ninety towns (not subject to anyone) of ferocious people, very bellicose and very feared, and the land is prosperous in those parts. In Chicaça the Governor commanded that half of the people of his army should go to make war on Sacchuma, and on their return the cacique Miculasa made peace, and messengers came from Talapatica.

And in the course of this war the time to travel arrived, and they asked the cacique for tamemes; and the Indians created such an uproar among themselves, that the Christians understood it, and the agreement was made that they would give them over on the fourth of March when they were to depart, and that day they would come with them. The previous evening, the Governor mounted his horse and found the Indians engaged in evil intrigue, and he recognized the treacherous intention that they had and returned to the camp and said publicly, "This night is a night of Indians; I will sleep armed and my horse saddled." And all said that they would do the same; and he called to the maestre de campo, who was Luis de Moscoso, and told him that he should take extra precautions with the sentinels that night, since it was the last. The Governor, upon leaving his soldiers, with whom he had made those arrangements, lay down undressed in his bed, and neither his horse nor any other was saddled, and all in the camp lay down to sleep without care and unarmed. The maestre de campo placed for the morning watch three on horseback, the worst of the worst, and on the worst horses in the whole army. And on the aforementioned day, the fourth of March, when the Indians had promised to give the tamemes, at break of day, fulfilling their word, they entered through the camp in many squadrons, beating drums as if it were in Italy, and setting fire to the camp, burning it and taking fifty-nine horses, among which, three of them they shot through both shoulders with their arrows. And the Christians behaved like careless people on this occasion, and few weapons, coats of mail, lances, and saddles survived the fire, and all the horses were driven away, fleeing from the fire and the clamor. Only the adelantado was able to mount, and he failed to cinch his horse, nor did he buckle his coat of armor, and Tapia de Valladolid along with him. The first Indian that he overtook, when he gave him a lance-blow, he [De Soto] fell upon him saddle and all. And if the Indians had known how to pursue their victory, this would have been the last day in the lives of all the Christians of that army and would have put an end to the demand for the tamemes.

Next the Spaniards passed to a savannah one league from that town in which they were, and they had huts and supplies, and they established camp on a slope [*ladera*] and hill [*cerro*] and made haste to set up the forge, and they made a bellows from hides of bears; and they tempered their weapons and made new saddle frames and provided themselves with lances, since there were very good ash trees there; and within eight days they had it all repaired.

They killed and burned alive up to twelve Christians in the aforementioned Chicaça. On Tuesday, the fifteenth of March, during the morning watch, the Indians attacked the Christians, determined to finish them, and they struck them on three sides; and as necessity had made them diligent, they were on guard and on watch. They fought with them valiantly and put the Indians to flight, and thanks to God the Christians did not suffer much damage, although a few Indians died. Some Spaniards showed themselves very valiant this day, and not one failed to do his duty, for a bad fate would have awaited anyone who in such a time did not defend his life well and who failed to show to his enemies the virtue and weapons of the Christians.

EIGHT

IN WHICH THE HISTORY RELATES ANOTHER ENCOUNTER WITH A BARRICADE, IN WHICH THE ADELANTADO FOUGHT WITH THE INDIANS, AND HOW HE ARRIVED AT A VERY LARGE RIVER, WHICH THE CHRISTIANS CROSSED, AND OF AN ORATION AND SPEECH WHICH THE CACIQUE OF CASQUI MADE IN FRONT OF THE ADELANTADO AND THE CHRISTIANS IN FAVOR OF THE CROSS AND THE FAITH, AND OF AN ARGUMENT BETWEEN THIS CACIQUE AND HIS ENEMY, NAMED PACAHA, OVER WHICH ONE OUGHT TO PRECEDE THE OTHER. THEY DEPARTED FROM UTIANGUE, AND MANY NOTABLE PARTICULARS ARE TOLD.

On Tuesday, the twenty-sixth of April of the year already stated of fifteen forty-one, Governor Hernando de Soto departed from the savannah of Chicaça and spent the night at Limamu, and they were there looking for corn, because the Indians had concealed it, and they had to cross an uninhabited region.

And on Thursday they went to another savannah, where the Indians had made a very strong barricade, and within it many Indian warriors all smeared and painted with colors that appeared very fine (and yet were bad, or at least they were harmful to the Christians); and they entered the barricade by force, with some casualties of dead and wounded on the side of the adelantado and his army, and many more, without comparison, on the side of the vanquished, and there would have been more, if the Indians had not fled. On Saturday, the last day of April, the army departed from the site of the barricade, and traveled nine days through an uninhabited region and a bad road through forests and swamps, until Sunday the eighth of May, when they arrived at the first town of Quizqui; and they took them unexpectedly and captured many people and clothes; but the Governor then set them free and made restitution to them all, for fear of war, although this did not suffice to make friends of those Indians. One league from this town was found another with much corn, and then, after another league, another, likewise with much corn. There they saw the great river.[56] On Saturday, the twenty-first of May, the army moved on to a savannah between the river and a small town, and they made camp, and began to make four piraguas in order to cross to the other side. Many of those conquistadors said that this river was a larger river than the Danube. On the other bank of the river, up to seven thousand Indians gathered to defend the crossing, and with up to two hundred canoes, all with shields [*escudos*], which were made of canes joined together, so strong and so tightly sewn that a crossbow would scarcely pierce them. Arrows came raining and the air was filled with them, and with such a yell, so that it seemed a matter of great dread; but when they saw that the work on the piraguas did not let up for them, they said that Pacaha, whose men they were, commanded them to remove themselves from there, and thus they left the crossing undefended. And on Saturday, the eighth of June,[57] all the army crossed that great river[58] in the four piraguas, and they gave many thanks to God, because in their opinion, nothing so difficult could ever be offered them again.

On Sunday, they went to a town of Aquijo; on Tuesday, the twenty-first of June, they left from there and passed through the province [*población*] of Aquijo, which is very beautiful and nicely situated. The next day, Wednesday, they passed through the worst road of swamps and water that they had seen in all Florida, and in this day's journey the people suffered much hardship.

The next day following, Thursday, they entered in the land of Quarqui and passed through many towns, and the next day, Friday, the day of St. John, they went to the town of the lord of Casqui, and he gave food and clothes to this army, and on Saturday they entered in his town; and he had very good huts, and in the principal [hut], over the door, were many heads of very fierce bulls, as in Spain they put heads of wild boars [*puercos javalíes*] or bears at the doors of the houses of the hunters. There the Christians placed the cross on a mound. They received it and adored it with much devotion, and I say with much devotion, because the blind and lame Indians

[56]*El río grande,* or the Mississippi.

[57]The date should be June 18.

[58]*Aquella gran ribera.* The term *ribera* refers to the bank or shore, but in this context river seems more appropriate.

came to ask for healing. The faith of these, said Rodrigo Rangel, would have been greater than that of the conquistadores, if they had been instructed, and in them more fruit would have been produced than what those Christians produced.

On Sunday, the twenty-sixth of June, they left from there for Pacaha, enemy of Casqui, and they spent the night at one town and passed others. And the following day they crossed a swamp, in which the Indians had a well-made bridge, broad and of ingenious construction; and on Wednesday they arrived at the town of Pacaha, a town and lord of great renown and very esteemed in those parts. That town [*población*] was very good and very well palisaded, with towers on the walls, and with a ditch [*cava*] roundabout, and most of it filled with water, which enters through an irrigation ditch [*aceiguia*] that flows from the river. That pond [*estaño*] had many very good fish of different kinds. The cacique of Casqui caught up with the Christians at the time that they entered the town, and they looted it ferociously. In Aquijo and Casqui and this Pacaha they saw the best towns that they had seen up to then, and better palisaded and fortified, and the people of more beauty, except for those of Cofitachequi.

The adelantado and his people being some days in Pacaha, they made some excursions into the interior, and the cacique of Casqui stole away one day when he saw the opportunity for it, without asking for permission, for which the Governor tried to make peace with Pacaha, and he came in [peace] in order to retrieve a brother of his whom the Christians had captured at the time they entered the town. And he struck an agreement with Pacaha that they should go to make war on Casqui, which was very gratifying to Pacaha. But Casqui had warning of that intent, and he came with fifty of his Indians in very fine array; and he brought a jester in front of himself for grandeur, who, saying and doing witty things, gave occasion for much laughter to those who saw him. The Governor displayed anger and harshness in order to please Pacaha, and he sent to command that he should not enter in the town. Casqui sent as a reply, that even though they should cut off his head, he would not stop from coming. Pacaha asked the Governor for permission to give a slash on the face to Casqui with a knife that he had in his hand, which the Christians had given him, and the Governor said to Pacaha that he should not do such a thing nor do him injury, because he would get angry with him; and he commanded that Casqui should come inside to see what he wanted, and because he [the Governor] wanted to ask him why he had gone without his permission.

Casqui arrived and spoke to the Governor in this manner, as related by the interpreter Juan Ortiz and other Indian interpreters that the Governor and the Christians now had: "How, my lord, is it possible that having given me the promise of amity, without my having done you any damage or given any occasion, you wish to destroy me, your friend and brother? You gave me the cross to defend myself from my enemies, and with that same [cross] you wish to destroy me." (He said this because the Indians of Pacaha, his enemy, who were against him with the Christians, wore crosses high on their heads so that they might be recognized.) "My Lord," said Casqui, "now that God heard us, by means of the cross; that the women and boys and all those of my land knelt down to it to ask for rain from the God who you said suffered on it, and he heard us and gave it to us in great abundance and saved our cornfields and seed beds; now that we have more faith in it and in your friendship, you wish to destroy those children and women who love you and your God so much? Why do you wish to use such cruelty without our meriting it? Why do you wish to lose the faith and confidence that we had in you, why do you wish to offend your own God and us, when on his behalf, you assured us in his name and received us as friends and we gave you complete faith, and we confided in the same God and in his cross and we held it in our guard and protection, and in the reverence and esteem that is suitable? To what end, to what purpose were you moved to do or think a thing so wrongful against people without guilt and friends of the cross and of yours?" And having said this, he fell silent. The Governor, his eyes softened and not without giving sign of tears, considering the faith and words of that cacique, responded to him through the interpreters in front of many Christian soldiers, who, with attention and not without tears, overcome with charity and faith, had heard all this, and he spoke thus: "Look, Casqui: we do not come to destroy you, but rather to make you know and understand the cross and our God, as you say; and these favors that he has done you are a small thing in respect to many other great ones that he will do for you, if you love him and believe in him; and thus hold it for certain, and you will find it and see it better each day. But since you went away without my permission, I thought that you held little regard for the doctrine that we had given you; and for the contempt that you had for it, I wished to destroy you, believing that you went away in pride, because this is the thing that our God most abhors and for which he punishes us most. Now that you come humbly, you may be certain that I wish you more good than what you think; and if you have need of something from me, tell me and you will see it, because we do what our God commands us, which is not to lie; and thus believe that I tell you the truth, because a lie is a very great sin among us. And do not be grateful to me or to my men for this good will, because if you believe what you say, God Our Lord commands that we love you like a brother, and that we do things for you, because you and your people are our brothers, and thus our God tells us."

The Indians were as amazed at this as the Christians were at what Casqui had said. At that point it was time to eat, and the adelantado seated himself and commanded both caciques to sit, and between them there was great contention about which of them would seat himself at the right hand of the Governor. Pacaha told Casqui: "You know well that I am a greater lord than you and of more honored parents and grandparents, and that to me belongs a better place than to you." Casqui responded thus: "It is true that you are a greater lord than I, and your ancestors were greater than mine. And since this great lord who is here says that we must not lie, I will not deny the truth; notwithstanding, you know well that I am older and more than a match for you, and I confine you in your palisade whenever I want, and you have never seen my land." In effect, this remained to be decided by the Governor, and he commanded that Pacaha should seat himself at his right hand, because he was a greater lord and more ancient in Estate, and there were in him and in his people good customs and, in their own way, the manner of courtly people.

Casqui had brought a daughter, a pretty girl, to the Governor. Pacaha gave him a wife of his, fresh and very virginal, and he gave him a sister and another principal Indian woman. The Governor made them friends and made them embrace and commanded that they should deal from one land to the other with their commodities and business, and so they agreed to do it. And with this the Governor departed from there on the twenty-ninth of June.

But I wish that, together with the greatness of the cross and of the faith that this Governor told to those caciques, he had told them that he was married and that the Christians are not to have more than one wife or access to another, or to commit adultery, and that he had not taken the young daughter that Casqui gave him, or his own wife and sister and another principal [woman] Pacaha gave him, and that he had not left them with the idea that the Christians, like the Indians, could have as many wives and concubines as they wished; and as those adulterers live, so do they end up.

Let us pass on: in my opinion, in a cacique of so much discretion as Casqui, it would have seemed well to baptize him and make him and his people Christians; and it would have been better to stay there, than to go forward to what this history will relate. Nor do I praise them for having gone on beyond Cofitachequi, for the same reason and for what has been said of that land.

Therefore, this army and its Governor having left from Pacaha, they spent the night at a town of Casqui, and the next day at the principal town of the same lord of Casqui, through which they had already passed, and they left from there on Sunday, the last day of that month, and went to a town of that province. And on Monday, the first of August, they arrived at another town that is alongside the river of Casqui, which is a branch that comes forth from the great river of Pacaha, and this branch is as large as the Guadalquivir. There Casqui came and helped them cross the river by canoe on Tuesday the second of August. They spent the night on Wednesday at a burned town, and the following Thursday, at another town next to the river, where there were many squash and much corn and beans. And the next day, Friday, they went to Quiguate, which is the largest town they saw in that land, next to the river of Casqui; and they found out afterwards that river was well populated below (although they did not manage to find it out then), and for that reason they took the road from Coligua, passing through an uninhabited region.

On Friday, the twenty-sixth of August, they departed from Quiguate in search of Coligua, and they spent the night at a swamp; and from swamp to swamp they made their journey of four swamps and four days, in which swamps or ponds there were large numbers of fish, because the great river floods all that area when it overflows its banks. And on Tuesday they went to the river that they call [the river] of Coligua, and on Wednesday likewise along the same river, and the following Thursday, which was the first of September, to Coligua, and they found the town populated, and in it they took many people and clothes and a great deal of food and much salt. It is a pleasant town among some mountains, on a gorge of a large river, and from there they went at midday to kill cows [buffalo], since there are many wild ones.

On Tuesday, the sixth of September, they departed from Coligua and crossed the river another time, and on Wednesday they crossed some mountains and went to Calpista, in which there was a spring of water from which very good salt is made, cooking it until it cakes. On the following Thursday they went to Palisma, and on Saturday, the tenth of September, they came forth to sleep at a [body of] water, and on Sunday they arrived at Quixila and rested there on Monday, and they went on Tuesday to Tutilcoya, and on Wednesday to a town alongside a large river, and on Thursday they spent the night alongside a swamp. And the Governor went in advance with some on horseback, and he arrived at Tanico; and the next day they [the army] went to the same province [*población*] of Tanico, which was very scattered but very abundant in supplies. Some wanted to say that it was Cayase, a large and palisaded town that was widely known, but they never were able to see or discover it, and afterward they told them that they had left it behind at one side of the river. From there the Governor went with thirteen on horseback and fifty foot soldiers to see Tula, and he returned from there rapidly, and they killed one of his horses and wounded another four or five, and he determined to go there with the army.

It should not be passed over or forgotten that there in Cayase our Spaniards gathered baskets of dry sand from the river and strained water through it, and brine came forth, and they cooked it and it caked, and thus they made very excellent and very white salt, and of high quality and delicious.

On Wednesday, the fifth of October, they left from the site of Tanico or Cayase and arrived on Friday at Tula, and they found the people gone; but they found many supplies. And on Saturday in the morning the Indians came to give them a surprise attack or battle. They brought long poles like lances, the points fire-hardened, and these were the best warriors that the Christians came upon; and they fought like desperate men, with the greatest courage in the world, and that day they wounded Hernandarias, grandson of the marshal of Seville, and thanks to God that the Christians behaved so valiantly, so that they did not receive much damage, although the Indians came to pillage the camp.

On Wednesday, the nineteenth of October, this army and the Governor departed from Tula, and they spent the night at two huts, and the next day, Thursday, at another hut, and on Friday at another, in which Hernandarias de Saavedra, who had been wounded at Tula, had a convulsion and died; and he died like a Catholic nobleman, commending his soul to God. The next day, Saturday, they went to Guipana, which is among some mountains, next to a river, and from there they went as far as they could to sleep, and all that [land] is mountainous from Tula on. The next day they came out of the mountains and entered the plains, and on Monday, the last day of the month, they arrived at a town that is called Quitamaya, and on Tuesday, the first of November, they passed through a small village [*poblezuelo*], and on Wednesday, the second of November, they arrived at Utiangue, which is a very well populated savannah of attractive appearance.[59]

---

[59]Here ends Book XVII of Oviedo's *Historia general y natural de las Indias.* The present chapter (Oviedo's chapter 28) is incomplete, and the two final chapters are known only from Oviedo's summary of their contents.

NINE

OF THE DEATH OF GOVERNOR HERNANDO DE SOTO, AND HOW LUIS MOSCOSO WAS SWORN IN AND OBEYED IN HIS PLACE; AND THE HARDSHIPS OF THOSE CONQUISTADORS AND OTHER THINGS ARE RELATED.

—The challenge of the cacique Quigudta to the Christians.
—Springs of water, from which salt is made.
—Hot rivers and salt which is made from the sand.
—Rugged and bellicose people.
—How the Christians made seven brigantines in order to go away and leave the land, how they left it, and of the flood of a river which lasted forty-three days.

TEN, AND LAST

OF THE OUTCOME OF THE PEOPLE WHO REMAINED FROM GOVERNOR HERNANDO DE SOTO, AND OTHER PARTICULARS.

—Of the animals of that land, and of the marvelous animal, called the sawyer,[60] and of the fish, in particular one called pala.[61]
—Of the fruits of that land and trees of sweetgum and sables and many other particulars.

[60]*El aserrador,* probably the beaver.

[61]Probably the paddlefish. See Robertson, *ante,* p. 206.

The Cañete Fragment: Another Narrative of Hernando de Soto

by Eugene Lyon

On Tuesday, August 14, 1565, in San Juan, Puerto Rico, one Rodrigo Ramirez, notary public, copied the Royal contract of Pedro Menéndez de Avilés. Menéndez, just named adelantado of Florida and on his journey to its conquest, had come to San Juan on his voyage from Spain and had some need for another copy of his contract. The *legajo,* or document bundle, of Seville's Archive of the Indies in which this document appears, and the particular piece in which it is found, seems to have been a depository for miscellany about Pedro Menéndez and the Florida conquest, ranging in date from 1565 to 1580.

Ramirez wrote across the bottom of the last sheet of the contract copy the following words: "There is in most parts of Florida much worked copper as in thin sheets (*hoja de Milán*); there are in the inland mountains great veins of silver, of very rich metal. Those who entered from Mexico by Copala toward Florida discovered great things, and found a place of more than twenty thousand citizens, and strong and high houses of seven floors and very strong walls. They found dies where they worked silver and many jewels of it and of gold; they had notice of kings crowned with golden crowns, far inland. . . ."

He added that this information had been gathered for the Spaniards in Menéndez's entourage, but "without hope of it."[1] There then follows the one-page Cañete fragment of a larger narrative about the journeys of Hernando de Soto, and several pages about the discoveries of Miguel de Legazpi in the Philippines. It can only be assumed that Pedro Menéndez de Avilés and his followers sought, as they prepared for their landing in Florida, to utilize past knowledge of the continent; it can further be assumed that

[1]From Archivo General de Indias, Seville, Patronato Real 19, No. 1, No. 15.

Ramirez, or Menéndez, had access to the full Cañete narrative at the time when he was copying the materials at San Juan.

Relation of Fray Sebastián de Cañete

Some of the things contained in the relation that Fray Sebastián de Cañete and the Captain gave are of the things they saw in Florida, going with De Soto. In the province of Mocozo they found a Spaniard who was 14 years among [the] Indians, and he had forgotten his [own] language. He had gone in search of Narváez. The lord of the province of Tascaluco was as large as a Spaniard mounted on a horse. The Adelantado De Soto died in the River of the Holy Spirit in the province of Guachoya.

The clothing that the Indians ordinarily wear are blankets of mulberry roots and of marten, very fine, and this in most parts; and hides of bears, wolves, lions, tigers, and of cows [probably buffalo—E.L.] near the plains. In all parts they found an abundance of food of the land, [such] as corn, beans and squash—infinite fruits of the land of those of Spain: there were four kinds of nuts—hazelnuts and chestnuts; in all the land a great quantity of grapes, and in some parts muscatel grapes, as sweet and flavorful as those of Spain. There are many acorns, and of this they make butter, and of nuts. [There is a] great quantity of woods and greater of plums, very good, and from them they make loaves like quince-sweet [*carne de membrillo*], and in most parts of all Florida they found much gold, which the Indian men and women have, and they offered it to the Spaniards.

There are not a number of pearls, because [he found? word partly destroyed at page margin] in the house of an idol they called El Cu in Cofitachiqui, they found more than 12 horse-loads of pearls, and the caciques of that town who were embalmed in El Cu, they had great sacks of pearls at the necks. They found much worked copper like fine sheets [*hoja de millión* [*sic*] *hoja de Milán*]. The people are very bright and well featured and of acute judgment in the places that they are accustomed [word off page edge].

They not only gave what was necessary to wear and eat for the men but to the horses they gave feather blankets, and in the houses there is a variety, according to the regions; in some parts toward the mountains there are houses with stoves [*estufas;* sweat-houses?], and in other parts they are of flat roofs as in Andalusia. There are elevated [*alzados?* the word is on a page edge and partly torn] places, and very great, and in Tanlo rado [? partly torn] one hundred; [in?] the province of Coza they traveled along the banks of a river four leagues through populated areas. [The] arms they ordinarily carry are [bows and] arrows, wooden clubs [*macanas,* here spelled *machanas*], and they are so skilled and spirited that in a skirmish that De Soto had in Macula [Mabila], where they killed 25 soldiers of his, was an Indian who went looking for the most valiant and best-armed Spaniard in order to kill himself with him. In Chicaza they came by night upon the Spaniards and took from them whatever they had, with the pearls.

In Cofitachiqui and in other places there were raisins from grapes and mulberries, of which there is a great quantity in all Florida. There are some plains in a certain part that extend more than 300 leagues, all filled with small cows [*vacas pequeñas:* probably buffalo] of very good meat, and there is trade in the hides inland. In all parts there are many turkeys [*gallinas de papada:* literally chickens with dewlap], deer, hares, rabbits, an infinite number of partridge, turtledoves [passenger pigeons?], and many other kinds of very good birds. There are many squirrels, bears, lions, tigers [panther?]; in all the rivers many fish and shellfish, mainly flounder [catfish?]. There are wild olive trees with fruit, liquidambar trees, *chinilla* [china? a species of sarsaparilla]; sumac to tan the hides [*cortir* [*sic*] *curtir*], even though they do not tan the deer hides with it, of which there are a great number in all the land. They greatly abominate those who lie and steal and married women who are bad. When they marry, they go to the house of the maiden's parents—he who wishes to marry with her—and says that they shall gather together her relatives; that he wishes to talk to them. Being gathered together and the marriage being carried out, they all give her to him. If, afterward, she is an adulteress, they return her, the same relatives of the husband, and having gathered her relatives together, the husband says to them, "You gave me this woman as good, and she is bad, and all of you as well; therefore [word off page] beware, patience; you all have to pay," and beginning with the adulteress, they kill them all. There is in everything much justice and reason, as is in Spain. . . .

* * * * * *

Examination of the text of the Cañete fragment and comparison of its contents with the texts of the four major "De Soto narratives" (Hernando Luis de Biedma, Rodrigo Rangel, the "Gentleman of Elvas," and Garcilaso de la Vega, "The Inca") raises many points of interest. In general the other narratives subordinate description to the running tale of exploration, rapine, battle, and disaster. By contrast, the Cañete fragment, even though quite short, devotes much of its space to description of the land, fruits, fauna, and even the mores of its native peoples. The thirtieth chapter of the Rangel diary, not extant in the Oviedo y Valdés version, appears to have contained some of this type of material, but the Cañete fragment is rich in it. As examples, one may cite the deity El Cu of the temple at Cofitachiqui, and the description of marriage customs and the treatment of adultery in the Cañete relation.

The research question of most import here is: Can the full narrative of Sebastián de Cañete be found? Judging by the promise of the fragment, the search for it seems most worth doing.

April 2, 1982

Parallel Itinerary of the Expedition

Originally published as Appendix E in the
Final Report of The United States De Soto Expedition Commission
by John R. Swanton, Chairman
Washington, D.C., 1939*

(Material not in original is put in parentheses; proper names retain the peculiar forms used by each writer)

Ranjel	Elvas and Biedma	Garcilaso
	(from Elvas unless otherwise stated; B = Biedma)	
	1538	
	Jan. 15, 1538, the Portuguese leave Elvas Vespers of St. Sebastian (Jan. 20), they reach Seville (Jan. 26–Mar. 15, enrollments made) Sunday, Morning of St. Lazarus (St. Laserain, now April 18 but before change in the calendar evidently) April 7, fleet sails from San Lúcar	The fleet sets sail from San Lúcar, Spain, April 6, 1538, accompanied by the Mexican fleet

Ranjel	Elvas and Biedma	Garcilaso
	1538	
	Easter Sunday (April 21), they reach Gomera in the Canary Islands	They reach Gomera in the Canaries in 15 days, i.e. April 21
	Sunday, April 28, leave Gomera	They stay 3 days and leave April 24
June, 1538, De Soto arrives at Santiago, Cuba	On Pentecost (June 9), they reach Santiago, Cuba (1 letter confirms this date; 2 others say June 7)	Sight Cuba at end of May; Mexican fleet parts from them 12 days before they land
	Early in Oct. the fleet with Isabel de Bobadilla, De Soto's wife, reaches Havana; followed by De Soto in Oct. or Nov.	De Soto leaves Santiago for Havana toward the end of August
	1539	
	End of March, 1539, most of cavalry reach Havana	Last of cavalry reach Havana by the middle of April
	(May 13, De Soto draws up his will and renews his compact with Hernan Ponce de Leon)	
(Sunday), May 18, 1539, fleet sails from Havana	Sunday, May 18, fleet sails from Havana	May 12, 1539, the fleet sails for Florida
(May 19–24, at sea)		They are 19 days at sea

Whitsuntide, May 25, they sight land of Florida; De Soto goes in pinnace to reconnoiter	On Festival of Espiritu Santo, May 25, they see the land of Florida	May 31, they sight land
Monday, May 26, vessels begin to enter the harbor		
May 27–29, continue entering		June 1, they send men ashore to get grass for the horses
Friday, May 30, begin to land the horses	Friday, May 30, the army is landed; Porcallo leads scouting party; Porcallo goes in pinnaces to town	June 2, they land 300 infantry and the disembarkation of men and supplies continues on the next day; De Soto takes formal possession of the country.
	Saturday, May 31, army starts for Ucita	They rest 8–9 days and then march to the town of Hirrihigua
Trinity Sunday, June 1, army goes toward village and spends night on other side of roadstead	Trinity Sunday, June 1, they reach Ucita	
(June 2, at Ucita)	(Succeeding events until August described by Elvas but not dated)	
Tuesday, June 3, De Soto takes possession of the country for the Crown of Spain		
Wednesday (June 4), Gallegos is sent to get natives and finds Juan Ortiz		They are joined by Juan Ortiz
(June 5–6, at same town)		
Saturday (June 7), De Soto visits Mocoço; Lobillo captures two Indian women		
(Sunday, June 8?), Mocoço is brought back to the port by De Soto; on this date or soon after it Porcallo is sent to disperse a gathering of Indians at Oçita		Mucoço visits the camp, probably on June 8, and G says he remained there 13 days (2 + 3 + 8), till June 21(?) or perhaps it should be 8 days, especially since he says these events

Ranjel	Elvas and Biedma	Garcilaso
	1539	
(Between June 8 and June 19 an Indian is sent with message to Urriparacoxi)		occured before Gallegos left to visit Urribarracuxi which was June 20 and Gallegos found Mucoço in his own town when he passed through
Friday, June 20, Gallegos is sent to the province of Urriparacoxi with 80 horse and 100 foot; Añasco is sent to disperse Indians on an island (Tuesday) July 8, Porcallo gets back from an expedition to relieve Añasco (Letter of De Soto) (Wednesday) July 9, Porcallo leaves for Cuba (Letter of De Soto)		In a little more than three weeks after landing Gallegos leaves to visit Urribarracuxi, reaches the town of Mucoço that night, and the town of Urribarracuxi in 4 days more. If this is correct it would have fallen on June 24. Gallegos sends four horsemen back who reach the port in 2 days; if Garcilaso's later figures are correct, this would be July 9 (see De Soto's Letter), the day Porcallo sailed; the day after he sailed the four horsemen arrived (July 10); Silvestre is sent to Gallegos with cavalry and to inform him that De Soto would follow on the 4th day, i.e. July 14
Tuesday, July 15, army leaves port of Espiritu Santo and camps on banks of River of Mocoço that night		July 14, De Soto sets out with the army and sights Mucoço's town on the morning of the 3d day

(Wednesday, July 16), at the Lake of the Rabbit (Thursday, July 17), at St. John's Lake (Friday, July 18), comes to plain (Saturday, July 19), comes to plain of Guacoço		
(Sunday, July 20), comes to Luca, a little village, early Monday, July 21, joined by soldiers of Gallegos (Tuesday, July 22), at Luca		De Soto reaches the province of Urribarracuxi
Wednesday, July 23, they set out and come to Vicela and camp beyond Thursday (July 24), sleep at Tocaste by a large lake; De Soto goes on with advance force on trail toward Ocale; Ranjel sent back for more horsemen and they are sent forward Friday, (July 25), army starts along trail but is turned back by two horsemen sent by De Soto		Scouts are sent out to reconnoitre the Big Swamp and return in 8 days The army reaches and crosses the Big Swamp in 2 days, 1 day being spent in the crossing; the scouts report impassable swamps ahead, so De Soto recrosses and leads an advance party along the edge of the swamp for 3 days, finally finding a crossing
Saturday, St. Anne's Day, (July 26), De Soto finds trails broad and sends two horsemen back for 30 cavalry for himself, ordering entire camp to move on; Tobar comes with cavalry; De Soto reaches the river or swamp of Cale, and crosses to Uqueten		Before crossing the Big Swamp De Soto sends 2 horsemen back for reenforcements and orders the army to follow; he then goes on across to Acuera (Ocale)

Ranjel	Elvas and Biedma	Garcilaso
	1539	
Sunday (July 27), Nuño de Tobar gets across to De Soto with his 30 horse		Reenforcements under Tovar reach Acuera (Ocale) the day after De Soto arrives
(July 28, De Soto is at Cale, the rest of the army moving forward)		The army takes 3 days to come up with them
Tuesday (July 29), last of stragglers reaches De Soto's camp		
(Wednesday, July 30–Sunday, Aug. 10, all remain at Ocale)	B says they stayed 7–8 days in Cale	They remain 20 days in Acuera, during which time scouts are sent about
(Monday) Aug. 11, De Soto goes on with 50 horse and 100 foot, the rest remaining under Moscoso; De Soto camps at Itaraholata	Aug. 11, 1539, De Soto goes forward from Cale and sleeps at Ytara	The entire army moves on (he ignores the separation of the army here)
(Tuesday, Aug. 12), at Potano	(Aug. 12), at Potano	
Wednesday (Aug. 13), reaches Utinamocharra	(Aug. 13), at Utinama	
(Thursday, Aug. 14), goes to the village of Bad Peace	(Aug. 14), at a village called Malapaz (Bad Peace)	
(Friday, Aug. 15), reaches a fair sized village	(Aug. 15), goes to sleep at Cholupaha, from abundance of corn there called Villafarta (in Portuguese)	They reach Ocali (Cholupaha) and remain there 6 days before the chief of the town comes in
(Saturday, Aug. 16), reaches "River of Discords"	Cross a river "before it" (the above village)	

Sunday (Aug. 17), crosses this river		
Monday (Aug. 18), arrives at Aguacaleyquen (Tuesday, Aug. 19–Thursday, Aug. 21, at Aguacaleyquen)	(Aug. 18, erroneously given as 17), arrive at Caliquen; B says 4–5 days from Cale	They march for $2^1/_2$ days and until noon of the third day when De Soto goes ahead with a picked force, travels steadily all night and next morning they reach Ochile (Aguacaleyquen) but do not make a formal entrance until the next day
(Friday) Aug. 22, many Indians appear and De Soto sends 8 horsemen back for the rest of the army (Saturday, Aug. 23–Wednesday, Sept 3 at same town) (Thursday), Sept. 4, the army comes up		The time spent in Ochile is left uncertain but it was 3 days before the chief's brother arrives They spend 8 days traveling through the lands of the first two brothers
(Friday, Sept. 5–Monday, Sept. 8, at same town)	B says they stayed in that town 6–7 days	
(Tuesday), Sept. 9, set out, cross on a bridge they had made and reach a small village where they spend the night	Sept. 10, cross a river	
(Wednesday), Sept. 10 (erroneously given as Friday), at Uriutina (Thursday, Sept. 11, at same town) Friday, Sept. 12, the army comes to a village called Many Waters because it rained so hard Saturday and Sunday, Sept. 13–14, they are kept there by rain		

Ranjel	Elvas and Biedma	Garcilaso
	1539	
Monday, Sept. 15, come to a bad swamp, have a toilsome journey, and sleep at Napituca; fight about the lakes occurs	Sept. 15, arrive at Napetaca; fight about the lakes occurs	They enter Vitachuco's main town (Napituca) the 9th day of travel. The two brothers stay there 2 days and then go home on the 3d; for 4 days more Vitachuco dispenses hospitality; on the 5th day he tells the interpreters of his intention to destroy the Spaniards 2–3 days later; he heads an outbreak 7 days after his first defeat
(Tuesday, Sept. 16–Monday, Sept. 22, at same town)		De Soto remains 4 days more in Vitachuco
Tuesday, Sept. 23, go on to the River of the Deer	Sept. 23, pass on to a river where a deer was brought as a present	He leaves Vitachuco and camps on the bank of the River of Osachile (River of the Deer); the river is 4 leagues from Vitachuco's town
(Wednesday, Sept. 24), building a bridge		
(Thursday, Sept. 25), finish bridge, cross, and the same day they pass through two small villages and one large one called Apalu and come at night to Uçachile	"Sept. 24," pass through Hapaluya and sleep at Uzachil	They finish building a bridge in 1½ days and reach Osachile on the 2d afternoon
(Friday, Sept. 26–Sunday, Sept. 28, at Uçachile)		They remain 2 days at Osachile
Monday, Sept. 29, pass a big forest (translator has a "high mountain," mistranslating "monte") and come at night to to pine wood		They travel 3 days and at noon of the 4th come to the boundary swamp of Apalache

Tuesday, Sept. 30, come to Agile, "subject to Apalache"	Axille, two days travel from Uzachil	Next day they camp in the woods on the borders of the province of Apalache
Wednesday, Oct. 1, come to the river or swamp of Ivitachuco and begin building a bridge	Oct. 1, leave Axille and have a bridge built	
(Thursday, Oct. 2, engaged in completing bridge and probably they began crossing)		
Friday, (Oct. 3), finish crossing at noon and come to Ivitachuco at nightfall finding it in flames	On Wednesday, the Day of St. Francis (an evident error as it was Friday, Oct. 3, when they crossed and the Day of St. Francis was Saturday, Oct. 4), they cross the river and reach Uitachuco	Next day they camp in a clearing in the forest on the Apalache side of the swamp Next day they camp on the edge of the cultivated ground
(Saturday, Oct. 4, spent at Ivitachuco)		
Sunday, Oct. 5, come to Calahuchi	Sunday, Oct. 25 (an evident error for Oct. 5, the 25th was on Saturday), reach Uzela	Next day they cross a second stream with steep banks and camp 2 leagues short of the Apalache town
(Monday, Oct. 6), come to Iviahica	Monday (Oct. 6), come to Anhaica Apalache	Next day (the 5th) they reach the Apalache capital (11–12 leagues from the swamp)
(Tuesday, Oct. 7), two captains go on and find all the people gone (Wednesday, Oct. 8–Friday, Nov. 28, at same town)		Two captains, Tinoco and Lobillo, are sent on scouting trips toward the north, one returning in 8 days and the other in 9 Añasco travels south 2 days to Aute He is misled by a guide twice, once for 8 days and again for 5, returning each time to Aute

Ranjel	Elvas and Biedma	Garcilaso
	1539	
		After obtaining a new guide it takes only 1 day to reach the former point of embarkation of Narvaez from Aute
	Friday, Oct. 17 (original has Friday Nov. 17), Juan de Añasco sets out with 30 lancers for Port of Espiritu Santo	The 30 horsemen leave Apalache for the port Oct. 20, 1539, and come to the port in 11 days
		Mucoço visits the camp at Ucita for 4 days being given many articles abandoned, and the dismantling goes on some time longer
		Añasco leaves in the pinnaces 7 days after his arrival at the port; Arias leaves, apparently at the same time, for Cuba
		On his march north Calderon reaches Mucoço's town in 2 days; next day Mucoço goes with them to the borders of his territory
		Calderon starts after Añasco has left and makes each day's travel as long as possible
		After coming to the Apalache country 1 day is spent in reaching the camp in the woods on the Apalache side
		The second day takes them to the open plain
		The 3d day takes them to the Apalache town, at sunset

Saturday, Nov. 29 (the original has 19, an error for the 19th was Wednesday), Añasco arrives at the port of Apalache with the pinnaces; Maldonado is shortly sent along coast to west	Saturday, Nov. 29 (the original has Sunday, Dec. 28, but the two dates have been transposed), Añasco arrives at the port of Apalache	Añasco arrives with the pinnaces 6 days before Calderon comes in A few days after Calderon's return Maldonado is ordered to explore the coast to the west and he returns in 2 months
	B says Maldonado was gone 2 mos.	
(Sunday, Dec. 28)	Sunday, Dec. 28 (in the original this date and the above have been transposed), an Indian sets fire to the town	

Itinerary of the Army on the Way North through Florida

From the Port of Espiritu Santo (Ucita)

	Leagues	
To the town of Muçoço	8–9	25
To Urribarracuxi	16–17	
To the Big Swamp	14–15	20
To Acuera	5–6	
To the River of Ocali (River of Discords)		17–20
To Ochile (Aguacaleyquen)		16
To Vitachuco (Napituca)		15
To the River Osachile (River of the Deer)		4
To the Osachile town (Uçachile)		6
To the Apalachee Swamp (Agile River)		12–14
To Anhaica Apalache		11
		126–131

Ranjel	Elvas and Biedma	Garcilaso
	1539	*Itinerary of the Thirty Lancers on the Way South through Florida* (As corrected—see p. 151 [of the *Final Report*]) From Anhaica Apalache To 2 leagues east of Apalachee Swamp .... 13 To 1 league south of Osachile town .... 13 To 8 leagues south of Vitachucho town .... 17 To within 5 leagues of the River of Ocali .... 18 To the River of Ocali and across it .... 5 To a point in the province of Acuera (Ocale).......... 20 To the Big Swamp .... 5–6 Crossing the Big Swamp ... —

To a plain north of Urribarracuxi	13
To a point 3 leagues north of Mucoço	15
To the Port of Espiritu Santo	11
	130–131

1540

(Monday, Dec. 29, 1539–Tuesday, March 2, 1540, at same town) Wednesday, March 3, De Soto leaves Iviahica and reaches the River Guacuca that night		A few days after Maldonado's return he is ordered to go to Havana and he leaves at the end of February, his directions being to meet De Soto at the Bay of Achusi in October
(Thursday, March 4), they depart from the River Guacuca Friday, (March 5), they reach the River Capachequi early and make a barge or piragua in which to cross (Saturday, March 6–Tuesday, March 9, spent in working on the barge and in crossing) Wednesday, March 10 (original has March 9, an evident error), finish crossing and go to sleep in a pine wood	Wednesday, March 3, De Soto leaves for the interior The 4th day of their journey they arrive at a deep river; B says after a march of 5 days	The army leaves Apalache about the end of March and journeys north

Ranjel	Elvas and Biedma	Garcilaso
	1540	
Thursday, (March 11), come to 1st village of Capachequi, pass it and come by nightfall to another village near a bad passage of water and a swamp	Thursday, March 11 (the original has Friday, March 11), come to a town named Capachiqui after 1½ days journey	They go on for 3 days and come to a small town "made into a peninsula" (Capachequi), "a dependency of Apalache"
(Friday, March 12–Tuesday, Mar. 16, at last village)		
(Wednesday), March 17, leave Capachequi and come to White Spring		
(Thursday, March 18), reach the River Toa, make 2 bridges and two bridges are broken, Tobar suggests another type which holds; horse of Suarez drowned		
(Friday, March 19 and Saturday, March 20, work building bridges)		
Sunday, March 21, start to cross		
Monday, (March 22), all get over and come by night to a pine wood		
Tuesday, (March 23), early in morning arrive at Toa, a large village	Tuesday, March 23 (original has Wed., March 21), they come to Toalli	
Wednesday (March 24), at midnight of 23–24 De Soto goes off with 40 horse (and infantry), and they cross a bad passage after dark, making 12 leagues	(Wednesday), March 24, De Soto leaves Toalli	De Soto goes on ahead with 150 men to reconnoitre the frontiers of the province of Altapahã (Ichisi)

(Thursday, March 25), Holy Thursday and this year the Day of the Incarnation, they come to a settlement of Chisi, cross a branch of a broad river, wading and a good part swimming, and reach a village on an id., breakfast on turkeys, leave and go to other villages and a bad passage where Benito Fernandez is drowned. Come to a village where messengers appear from Ichisi (Friday, March 26–Sunday, March 28, at this village)	Thursday, (March 25), in the evening come to a little stream where Benito Fernandez is drowned; just beyond a town called Achese where men and women plunge into river to escape; one captured understands Perico; B says Chisi province about 2 days march from Otoa (Toa)	
Monday, March 29, they go from there to Ichisi, having trouble crossing a small stream which rises rapidly in the rains, but reach a small village of Ichisi Tuesday, (March 30), rest at this village Wednesday, March 31, move on, come to Great River and cross in native canoes to the village of the Ichisi chief	B says they were 5–6 days going through this province	De Soto enters this province after a 2 days' march, passes through its territory for 2 days and on the morning of the 3d enters the first town; he is guided to another town and the rest of the army comes up some days later
Thursday, April 1, they set up a cross on the mound of the village Friday, April 2, they leave and sleep in the open country	They set up a cross in the town of Achese chief which was by a great river April 1 (should be 2) they leave and go through the country of this chief up along a well populated river valley	The army lodges 3 days in the town of Altapaha Leaving Altapaha they march for 10 days up along a river toward the north
(Saturday, April 3), come to a considerable stream and Altamaha sends messengers who guide them to a village where is food		

Ranjel	Elvas and Biedma	Garcilaso
	1540	
(Sunday, April 4), canoes are sent which take them across, and the chief Çamumo, comes; Ocute chief, being summoned, comes also	April 4, De Soto goes through the town of Altamaca; B says it was 3 days from Chisi to Altapaha	They then enter Achalaque, a poor province (Altamaha), which is confounded with a province entered later
(Monday, April 5, and Tuesday, Apr. 6, in this town)		
(Wednesday, Apr. 7, a cross is set up as before)		
Thursday, (April 8?), go on with Ocute and spend the night in some cabins		They march through the province of Achalaque 5 long days' journey
Friday, (April 9), come to village of Ocute where a cross is set up, though perhaps on a later day	April 10 (probably a day in error), De Soto arrives at Ocute	The 4th day after leaving the province of Achalaque they reach the first town of the province of Cofa (Ocute)
(Saturday, Apr. 10, and Sunday, Apr. 11, at Ocute town)		They remain 5 days in Cofa
Monday, April 12, leave Ocute and come to Cofaqui; another chief named Tatofa (Patofa) comes there	Monday, Apr. 12, leave Ocute	They travel for 6 days through the province of Cofa, the first day in company with the chief, and come to Cofaqui
(Tuesday, Apr. 13, and Wednesday, Apr. 14, at Cofaqui (or Patofa)		They remain 4 days in Cofaqui while a native army of allies is gathered
Thursday, Apr. 15, Perico, the guide, losing his bearings, pretends madness and Tatofa gives other guides for Cofitachequi		

Friday, Apr. 16, they go on and spend the night by a small stream		At the end of 2 days more they reach the edge of the wilderness between this province and Cofachiqui
Saturday, Apr. 17, they cross a very large river and pass the night in a forest (monte) (Smith has "hill" erroneously)	This is one of the two first rivers mentioned by Elvas	They march 6 days through a wilderness crossing two wide swift rivers
Sunday, (April 18), they come to another forest (monte) or grove to camp		
Monday, (April 19), they march without any trail and cross another very large river	The second of two large rivers mentioned by Elvas	
Tuesday, (April 20), they pass the night side of a small stream		
Wednesday, (April 21), they reach a very large river, hard to cross, divided into two streams, hard to enter and worse to get out of; reach fishermen's huts on the other side; lose their way	They had traveled 9 days instead of the 4 the guide said it would take; B says it took 13 days	About noon of the 7th day the trail gives out and they march until sunset when they come to a large unfordable river
(Thursday, April 22, seemingly spent in this camp)		
Friday, April 23, De Soto sends out Gallegos and Añasco on scouting expeditions; others go out without result		Scouts are sent out but Añasco alone finds a village after traveling up stream for 3 days
Saturday, (April 24), Lobillo is also sent out, toward the north		
Sunday, (April 25), Añasco brings news of a village and provisions	Sunday, (April 25), Añasco brings news of a small town 11–12 leagues off; B says he came back in 4 days	Añasco sends 4 horsemen back who get to camp in 1 day, a distance of "more than 12 leagues"

Ranjel	Elvas and Biedma	Garcilaso
	1540	
Monday, April 26, army sets out and De Soto with some horse reaches a village called Hymahi; army stays 2 leagues behind; most of the horses are exhausted	Monday, April 26, they set out for Aymay; De Soto reaches the town with the best mounts; the others sleep 2–4 leagues off	De Soto and the army overtake him in 1½ days; 5 days after they leave the other captains return to De Soto's old camp
(Tuesday, April 27), Romo returns with 4 or 5 Indians		
Wednesday, (April 28), Gallegos comes with an Indian woman and news of a populated region	Wednesday, (April 28), the three captains come in	In 2 days more they reach his new camp De Soto remains there 7 days, dismissing Patofa at the end of 5 days along with the Indian auxiliaries and staying 2 days longer
(Thursday, April 29), Lobillo comes with news of trails; is sent back after abandoned companions		
Friday, April 30, guided by the Indian woman, De Soto goes with some cavalry and spends the night near a large, deep river; Añasco goes on and secures guides and canoes in which to cross the river		He marches up the river and encamps "in a beautiful spot" among mulberries Añasco goes forward very early in the morning and after traveling 2 leagues, at 2 A. M. comes opposite the town of Cofachiqui; he gets back to camp a little before dawn
(Saturday, May 1), De Soto comes to the crossing and the niece of the Chieftainess, the "Lady of Cofitachequi," comes across to meet him; all cross in canoes	B says this place was 2 days from Hymahi	De Soto crossed the river that day.

(Sunday, May 2), De Soto at town; the rest of the army on the way	It was 2 days journey to the sea; B says about 30 leagues	In the course of the next day the army crosses
Monday, May 3, the rest of the army comes up and begins to cross		
Tuesday, (May 4), the army finishes crossing; 7 horses drowned		
(Wednesday, May 5), at Cofitachequi		Añasco is sent down the river after the chieftainess, is gone 1½ days and returns at the end of the 3d
(Thursday, May 6), do.		He goes again 3 days later, this time by canoe, and returns in 6 days, again without success
Friday, May 7, Gallegos and most of the soldiers go to Ilapi for 7 cribs full of corn; De Soto and Ranjel enter temple this day or soon afterward and discover mementos of Ayllon		Next day they enter the temple of Cofachiqui Two days later they go to the temple of Talomeco
(Saturday, May 8–Wednesday, May 12, at the same town)		De Soto spends 10 days more collecting information regarding the country beyond Gallegos and part of the army go to a storehouse 12 leagues away for corn
Thursday, May 13 (the original has "Wednesday, May 13," but Elvas has "May 3" and, though this is also wrong, the mistake is more likely to have been 3 for 13 than 3 for 12), De Soto sets out with part of the army	May 3 (evidently 13), De Soto goes on	De Soto leaves Cofachiqui and comes to the province of Chalaque in 8 days

Ranjel	Elvas and Biedma	Garcilaso
	1540	
Friday, May 14 (see above), they reach territory of Chalaque (or Xalaque) and sleep in a pine wood	In 7 days De Soto reaches the territory of Chelaque	
(Saturday, May 15), they remain at the same place		
Whitsuntide, (May 16), De Soto sends a message to Gallegos to follow with the rest of the army		Gallegos gets back to the highway in 5 days and continues on along it at the rate of 5–6 leagues per day though stopped 1½ days by a hail-storm
Monday, May 17, they leave and spend the night in a forest (monte)		Three days later he reaches the towns of Chalaque
Tuesday, (May 18), they come to Guaquili where they are given as food "dogs that do not bark"		
Wednesday, (May 19), they come to a region full of reeds		
Thursday, (May 20), they come to a small plain where some of the foot soldiers overtake them from Gallegos reporting that he would arrive soon		
Friday, (May 21), they reach Xuala	It took them 5 days to reach Xualla from Chelaque; B says it was 8 days from Cofitachique	Three days later Gallegos overtakes De Soto in Xuala; De Soto had arrived 2 days before

Saturday, (May 22), Gallegos comes up and there are many sick and lame		
(Sunday, May 23, and Monday, May 24 they remain at Xuala)	They stayed in Xualla 2 days	They remain in Xuala 15 days
Tuesday, May 25, they leave Xuala, cross a high ridge and camp at a little forest (monte-cillo)		On leaving they march 1 day through cultivated fields and 5 more over uninhabited mountains, the province of Xuala being 50 leagues across, and 20 leagues of mountains from Xuala to Guaxule
Wednesday, (May 26), they camp in a plain where they suffer cold and cross the river by which they afterwards left the country; woman chief of Cofitachequi escapes		
(Thursday, May 27), De Soto waits for Romo to bring up deserters		
(Friday, May 28), they pass the night in an oak wood		
(Saturday, May 29), they pass the night by a large stream which they had crossed often		
(Sunday, May 30), they reach Guasili early	Arrive at Guaxule at end of 5 days	The army is at Guaxule 4 days; chief's house on a mound
Monday, May 31, they leave and encamp in an oak wood by a river		
Tuesday, June 1, they camp in the open country beyond Canasoga	Canasagua reached 2 days from Guaxule	
Wednesday, (June 2), they sleep near a swamp; have many mulberries		
Thursday, (June 3), go along by a stream near the river (now very large) at which the woman chief went off		

Ranjel	Elvas and Biedma	Garcilaso
	1540	
Friday, (June 4), come to a pine wood on the stream and Chiaha Indians bring corn		
Saturday, June 5, in the morning they cross one arm of the river, which was very broad, and enter Chiaha, on an island; horses and men both worn out	March 5 days through unpopulated country and on 5th day of July (it should be June) enter Chiaha; B says it was 4 days from Guasuli	Traveling 6 days of 5 leagues each they reach the capital of the province of Ychiaha
(Sunday, June 6–Friday, June 18 at Chiaha)	During this time De Soto sends 2 men to Chisca;	Two men are sent north to Chisca, 30 leagues off, and return in 10 days
Saturday, June 19, Indians run off to avoid conscription		
(Sunday, June 20), De Soto compels the chief to bring his people back		
(Monday, June 21–Sunday, June 27, at Chiaha)	B says they were in Chiaha altogether 26–27 days	
Monday, June 28, leave Chiaha, pass through 5 or 6 villages and sleep in a pine grove, having much trouble in crossing a rapid stream		
Tuesday, (June 29), pass through a village and sleep in the open country beyond		
Wednesday, (June 30), pass over a river, through a village, over the river again and sleep in open country		

Thursday, (July 1), chief of Coste comes to meet them and takes them to one of his villages; same day (or next morning) the chief escapes to his village		
Friday, July 2, De Soto reaches Coste, on an island in the river, crosses first arm and enters with some hazard; trouble over corn-cribs; two men sent to view Chisca	July 2 enter Coste; sick brought down from Chiaha in canoes; men sent to Chisca return in 3 days	The day after their return the army marches 5 leagues along the island of Ychiaha to the capital of Acoste at the other end
(Saturday, July 3–Thursday, July 8, at Coste)		
Friday, July 9, leave Coste, cross other branch of the river and pass the night on its banks; on the other side was Tali	July 9, leave Coste and sleep at Tali	
Saturday, (July 10), at Tali; it was perhaps on that day that they drove back canoes trying to escape and enter town		
Sunday, (July 11), spend night in the open country		
Monday, (July 12), cross a river and sleep in the open		Next day they cross the river and enter the province of Coça
Tuesday, (July 13), cross another river		
Wednesday, (July 14), cross another large river and sleep at Tasqui, the chief of Tali provisioning them all the way		
Thursday, (July 15), pass another small village and then other villages		

Ranjel	Elvas and Biedma	Garcilaso
	1540	
Friday, (July 16), enter Coça	Traveling 6 days, they enter Coça Friday, July 16	They pass through the province of Coça, 100 leagues across, at the rate of 4–5 leagues a day, reaching Coça in 23–24 days
(Saturday, July 17–Thursday, Aug. 19, at Coça)	At Coça 25 days	They remain in Coça 11 or 12 days; later he says 10–12 days
Friday, Aug. 20, leave Coça and sleep beyond Talimachusy	Friday, Aug. 20, leave Coça and stop for night on a river bank, half a league beyond an uninhabited town called Tallimuchase.	
Saturday, (Aug. 21), go to Itaba in a heavy rain	(Saturday, Aug. 21), come to Ytaua, and are detained 6 days by a swollen river	
(Sunday, Aug. 22–Sunday, Aug. 29, at Itaba)		
Monday, Aug. 30, leave and come by night to an oak wood	Come to Ullibahali, a stockaded town	
(Tuesday, Aug. 31), at Ulibahali, a fine town by a large river		
(Wednesday, Sept. 1, at Ulibahali)		
Thursday, Sept. 2, camp at a small village near the river	Camp at a town subject to the lord of Ullibahali	
Friday, (Sept. 3), at Piachi near a river		

(Saturday, Sept. 4), wait a day at Piachi for Lobillo who went back for an escaped negro slave		
Sunday, (Sept. 5), go on and spend night in the open country		
Monday, (Sept. 6), come to Tuasi	Said to be 2 days from Ullibahali	
(Tuesday, Sept. 7–Sunday, Sept. 12, at Tuasi)		
Monday, Sept. 13, leave and sleep in the open		
Tuesday, (Sept. 14), again sleep in the open		
Wednesday, (Sept. 15), come to an old stockaded village		
Thursday, (Sept. 16), sleep at a new village close to a river		
(Friday, Sept. 17), remain at same village		
Saturday, Sept. 18, at Talisi, a big village; messengers come from Tascaluça including his son; two Spaniards sent back with him	Sept. 18, they reach Tallise	In 5 days they reach Talise
(Sunday, Sept. 19–Friday, Sept. 24, at Talisi)		They remain 10 days at Talise; Tascaluça's town was said to be 12–13 leagues away and approachable by two routes
(Saturday, Sept. 25), chief of Talisi comes and gives carriers and women		
(Sunday, Sept. 26–Monday, Oct. 4, at Talisi)	Said to have stayed there 20 days in all	
Tuesday, Oct. 5, leave and spend night at Casiste, a small village by the river	Sleep the first night at Casiste	

Ranjel	Elvas and Biedma	Garcilaso
	1540	
Wednesday, (Oct. 6), they come to Caxa, a poor village by the river bank and on a direct line from Talisi to the town of Tascaluça	Pass through another village next day and come to one in the province of Tastaluca	
Thursday, (Oct. 7), camp by the river opposite Humati		
Friday, (Oct. 8), come to a new village named Uxapita		
Saturday, (Oct. 9), sleep in the open 1 league short of Tascaluça's town	They rest in a wood 2 leagues from the chief's town	
Sunday, Oct. 10, enter Athahachi, "a recent village"		They cross the River of Talise and early on the 3d day come to Tascaluça's village
(Monday, Oct. 11), at Athahachi		
Tuesday, Oct. 12, leave with the chief and sleep in the open		
Wednesday, (Oct. 13), reach Piachi above the gorge of a mountain stream where Narvaez's men were killed	The second day from Tastaluca's town reach Piache near a great river	They march 3 days, making 4 leagues per day, and reach the chief's capital town on a peninsula in the river which passes by Talise
(Thursday, Oct. 14 and Friday, Oct. 15, at Piachi)		They spend all of the next day crossing
Saturday, Oct. 16, they leave and go into a forest (monte) where they meet one Spaniard of 2 sent from Piachi		

(Sunday, Oct. 17), come to a fenced village and messengers from Mabila reach them with bread of chestnuts		
Monday, Oct. 18 (St. Luke's Day), De Soto comes to Mabila, having passed through several villages, a populous region. Battle of Mabila.	Oct. 18 they reach Mauilla after a 3 days' march, the last continuously through an inhabited region. Battle of Mauilla	Early next day two scouts are sent to Mavila; De Soto follows and reaches the town by 8 A. M., Oct. 18, 1540, and the battle of Mavila follows; the sea coast said to be a little more than 30 leagues off
(Tuesday, Oct. 19–Saturday, Nov. 13, at Mabila).	They remain 28 days after the battle	They remain 23–24 days about Mavila, 8 days in rude huts and 15 days longer in abandoned Indian lodges
Sunday, Nov. 14, they leave Mabila.	Sunday, Nov. 18 (erroneous; it was the 14th), they leave Mauilla	
(Monday, Nov. 15), marching north through uninhabited country. (Tuesday, Nov. 16), the same. Wednesday, (Nov. 17), reach "a fine river".		
Thursday, (Nov. 18) the original has 28 by mistake), pass over bad places and swamps and reach Talicpacana; a village in sight on other side of river. (Friday, Nov. 19, at Talicpacana) (Saturday, Nov. 20, do.) Sunday, Nov. 21, Gonçalez finds a village named Moçulixa half a league distant from which the Indians had moved the corn to the other side of the river	Travel 5 days through a wilderness and come to Taliepataua in the province of Pafallaya	In 3 days they come to the province of Chicaça (meaning Pafallaya)

Ranjel	Elvas and Biedma	Garcilaso
	1540	
(Monday, Nov. 22–Sunday, Nov. 28, at Talicpacana at work on barge	A piragua is made in 4 days	
(Monday), Nov. 29, the barge is finished and carried on a truck to Moçulixa		
(Tuesday, Nov. 30), apparently on this day part cross and capture the corn, and cavalry secure the crossing above		
Wednesday, (Dec. 1), the army comes to a village called Zabusta where they cross, spend a night in a village on the other side; above was a fine village named Apafalaya like its chief	Town called Cabusto said to have been reached right after Taliepataua	Apparently it took them 5 or 6 days or more to cross the river (Pafallaya)
(Thursday, Dec. 2–Wednesday, Dec. 8, at Apafalaya)		
Thursday, (Dec. 9), set out for Chicaça		
(Friday, Dec. 10–Monday, Dec. 13, on the way to Chicaça), going through bad passages and swamps	March 5 days toward Chicaça	
Tuesday, (Dec. 14), reach the R. of Chicaça which was overflowing its bed	They come to a river; B says it was 10–12 days from Mauila	
(Wednesday, Dec. 15), make a barge and	They make a piragua in 2 days	

Gallegos leaves with cavalry and drives Indians from crossing		
Thursday, Dec. 16, they cross the river; De Soto going ahead with cavalry arrives late at night at a deserted village	Dec. 17, they cross the river and reach a small town the same day	After 4 more days travel they come to the province of Chicaça proper and enter the capital town at the beginning of December, 1540
(Friday, Dec. 17), Gallegos comes in, apparently the rest of the army also		
(Saturday, Dec. 18–Friday, Dec. 24, at Chicaça)		
(Saturday), Dec. 25, a heavy fall of snow as if it had been in Burgos, and the cold as bad or worse		
(Sunday, Dec. 26–Sunday, Jan. 2, 1541, at Chicaça)		They remain there almost 2 months
	1541	
Monday, Jan. 3, the Chicaça chief comes and offers guides and interpreters to take them to Caluça, a province of "more than ninety villages"		
Tuesday, Jan. 4–Wednesday, Mar. 2, at Chicaça, but an expedition is undertaken to Sacchuma and on their return its chief, Miculasa, makes peace, and messengers come from Talapatica		
(Thursday, March 3), De Soto asks the Chicaça chief for carriers	"Tuesday, March 8" (it should be Thursday, March 3), De Soto asks for carriers	
(Friday), March 4, at dawn the Indians fall upon the town and burn it, kill 50–60 horses	"Next morning" the Indians attack them	Toward the end of January, 1541, the Indians fall upon them

Ranjel	Elvas and Biedma	Garcilaso
	1541	
and destroy most of the equipment; the Spaniards move to a plain by a sloping hillside 1 league from the village and there refit		
(Saturday, March 5–Monday, March 14), engaged in refitting		Three days later they move 1 league off and establish themselves in a small town called Chicacilla
Tuesday, March 15, the Indians attack again during the morning watch	"Wednesday, March 15" (it should be Tuesday, Mar. 15), the Indians attack again: B says 5 days after first attack	Three days after their flight the Indians attack again
(Wednesday, March 16–Monday, April 25), at the same place	B says they remained about 2 mos.	They remain until the end of March (he says 4 months but this may mean "in all")
Tuesday, April 26, they leave and reach Limamu	April 25, they leave and sleep at a small town called Alimamu	At the beginning of April they leave Chicacilla
(Wednesday, April 27), send out scouting parties		
Thursday, (April 28), they discover and capture a strong barricade	(April 26), three scouting parties sent out; Añasco discovers the Alibamo barricade; it is taken the same day	They make 4 leagues the first day through level country and pass a quarter of a league beyond the inhabited region, though they seem to have encamped in a field; the Alibamo fort is attacked

Friday, (April 29), they remain near the barricade to recuperate		They remain there 4 days unable to march
Saturday, April 30, leave barricade	Start for Quizquis 3 days after they set out to hunt for corn	
(Sunday, May 1–Saturday, May 7, march through a deserted country and by a rough way, forested and swampy; 9 days in all	March 7 days through wilderness; B says it was a deserted country of 12 days across (error in Bourne's translation)	They march north 3 days
(Sunday), May 8, they reach the 1st village of Quizqui and capture it; 1 league beyond was another village and 1 league beyond that a third, and there they saw the Rio Grande		At the end of the 3 days they see the capital of the province of Chisca near the Chucagua (Mississippi River)
(Monday, May 9–Friday, May 20, they remain in that village)		They remain on the banks of the river for 20 days
Saturday, May 21, they move to a plain between the river and a small village and begin making barges		They march up the river slowly for 4 days making 12 leagues in all to a place where they can come down to the river
(Sunday, May 22–Friday, June 17), they work on the barges	They build 4 piraguas in 30 days; B says they took 27 or 28 days	They remain here 20 days or more making 4 barges (2 boats are finished in 15 days, and all 4 in 20) capable of holding 150 infantry and 30 cavalry
Saturday, June 18 (the original has June 8, an evident error), all cross		
Sunday, June 19, they come "soon" to a village of Aquixo	They reach a village a league and half from the point where they crossed	
(Monday, June 20), they remain at that village		
Tuesday, June 21, they pass by the main settlement of Aquixo, "beautifully situated"		

Ranjel	Elvas and Biedma	Garcilaso
	1541	
Wednesday, (June 22), they go through the worst tract of swamp and water they had seen in all Florida		After crossing they march for 4 days and on the 5th see "from some high hills" a town on the banks of a river, namely Casquin
Thursday, (June 23), they enter the land of Casqui (given in text as "Quarqui") and pass through small villages		They remain 6 days in the first town of Casquin
Friday, (June 24), St. John's Day, they come to the village of the lord of Casqui	They march 2 days through the province of Casqui before entering the chief's town	They march 2 days to the capital town 7 leagues up the river and on the same side
Saturday, (June 25), they enter his village and set up a cross on the village mound		On the 4th day the chief comes to ask them to make it rain
		In 2 days a wooden cross is finished and it is set up the next day
		That night rain falls and continues 2 days longer
Sunday, June 26, they leave for Pacaha, pass several villages and spend the night in one	They sleep in a town of Casqui; B says they camped 2 days in this town	After remaining 9 or 10 days they start on again on the day following
(Monday, June 27), they cross a swamp over which the Indians had built a bridge	They pass 2 other towns and come to a lake or swamp	They march for 3 days accompanied by a body of Indians until they reach a swamp
(Tuesday, June 28), they either stay in camp or move slowly forward		It takes 1 day to cross the swamp and they camp 1½ leagues beyond

Wednesday, (June 29), they come to Pacaha, a stockaded town by the Rio Grande	Wednesday, June 29 (the original has June 19, an evident error), they enter Pacaha; B says 2 days from Casqui	They travel on for 2 days and early on the 3d day come in sight of Capaha, seeing it from some high hills; it was a frontier and defence against Casquin; the Rio Grande (Mississippi) flowed 3 leagues above The Capaha Indians having fled to an island in the river, they wait 3–4 days for canoes; driven back by Indians but peace is made
(Thursday, June 30–Thursday, July 28), at Pacaha	They remained there 40 days; B says they remained 27–28 days; time occupied in making incursions inland, including one to the N. W. of 7 days (Elvas) or 8 days (Biedma)	Two Spaniards go to mountains 40 leagues from Capaha for salt and copper and return at the end of 11 days
(Friday), July 29, they leave and come at night to a village of Casqui		
(Saturday, July 30), they get back to the main village of Casqui	They lodge for one night near the chief's house	The army returns to Casquin and remains there 5 days
Sunday, (July 31), they leave and come to a village of Casqui	They pass the night in one of his towns	
Monday, Aug. 1, they come to another village of Casqui on the River of Casqui, a branch of the great River of Pacaha, and as large as the Guadalquivir	Next day they come to another town near a river	
(Tuesday), Aug. 2, the Casqui chief has them put across the River of Casqui in his canoes	Casqui sends canoes and they are carried over	

Ranjel	Elvas and Biedma	Garcilaso
	1541	
Wednesday, (Aug. 3), they sleep in a burned village		
Thursday, (Aug. 4), they sleep in another village, near the river		
Friday, (Aug. 5), they come to Quiguate, the largest village seen in that country; it was on the River of Casqui	Aug. 4, they come to Aquiguate, the largest town they saw in Florida; B says the same thing	They march down along the river for 4 days to the border of the province of Quiguate, and in 5 days more reach the capital town The Indians abandon the town 2 days later and return to it in 2 more
(Saturday, Aug. 6–Thursday, Aug. 25), at Quiguate	B says they remained 8 or 9 days	They remain in Quiguate 6 days and leave on the 7th
Friday, Aug. 26, they leave Quiguate for Coligua and spend the night by a swamp		
(Saturday, Aug. 27), they camp by another swamp		
(Sunday, Aug. 28), they camp near another swamp		
(Monday, Aug. 29), they spend the night near a fourth swamp		
Tuesday, (Aug. 30), they come to the River of Coligua		
Wednesday, (Aug. 31), they come to the same river again		
Thursday, Sept. 1, they come to the town	B implies it was 11 days from Quiguate	They march down along the Rio de

of Coligua, a populous place along the gorge of a river; at midday (probably of the same day) they go to kill some cows (bison)		Casquin for 5 days and arrive at the capital of Colima
(Friday, Sept. 2–Monday, Sept. 5), at Coligua		Within 2 days the Colima Indians revolt and flee
Tuesday, Sept 6, they leave Coligua and recross the river going S. W.		The Spaniards remain 1 day longer and then leave
Wednesday, (Sept. 7), they pass sierras and come to Calpista where was an excellent salt spring		
Thursday, (Sept. 8), they come to Palisema	It was 5 days from Coligoa	
(Friday, Sept. 9), they seem to have stayed at Palisema		
Saturday, Sept. 10, they go on to encamp by "a water"		
Sunday, (Sept. 11), they come to Quixila		
Monday, (Sept. 12), spend at Quixila		
Tuesday, (Sept. 13), they go on to Tutilcoya		
Wednesday, (Sept. 14), they go to a village along a large river		
Thursday, (Sept. 15), they camp near a swamp; De Soto goes on with some horsemen to Tanico the same day		At the end of 4 days they come to a river with salty sand along the shores
(Friday, Sept. 16), all go on to Tanico where were many scattered houses and by some it was thought to be Cayase	Reach a province called Cayas 4 days journey from Tatalicoya; the town was called Tanico; they remain there a month	They remain 8 days in this Province of Salt boiling down salt
(Saturday, Sept. 17–Friday, Sept. 30), at Tanico		

Ranjel	Elvas and Biedma	Garcilaso
	1541	
(Saturday, Oct. 1), De Soto goes on to Tula with 13 horse and 50 foot.	(Saturday, Oct. 1), De Soto goes to Tula with horse and foot	
(Sunday, Oct. 2), De Soto returns from Tula	B says it took 2 days to go to Tula and return	
(Monday, Oct. 3 and Tuesday, Oct. 4), at Tanico		
Wednesday, Oct. 5, the army leaves Tanico for Tula	(Wednesday, Oct. 5), the army leaves Tanico for Tula	They march 4 days more and at noon on the last day come within half a league of the capital of Tula
(Thursday, Oct. 6), on the march		
Friday, (Oct. 7), they come to Tula and find the town abandoned	The army takes 3 days from Cayas to Tula	
Saturday, (Oct. 8), the Indians attack them		The Tula Indians fight them (on the same day?)
		They enter the capital the day after the battle
		On the 4th night just before dawn the Tula Indians attack once more
(Sunday, Oct. 9–Tuesday, Oct. 18), at Tula		They remain 20 days in Tula
Wednesday, Oct. 19, they leave Tula and spend the night at two cabins		
Thursday, (Oct. 20), at another cabin		
Friday, (Oct. 21), they camp at still another cabin		

(Saturday, Oct. 22), they come to Guipana, between sierras near a river and go beyond for the night to a place where they can cross; sierras all the way from Tula	Quipana was 5 days march from Tula over sharp mountains	
(Sunday, Oct. 23), they leave the sierras and come out on the plains		
(Monday, Oct. 24–Wednesday, Oct. 26 (or Thursday, Oct. 27)), on the march toward Utiangue		They go on and in 2 days come to the province of Utiangue, continuing through it 4 days more to the capital; this was in the middle of October, 1541
(Thursday, Oct. 27, or Friday, Oct. 28), come to Anoixi, not named by Ranjel	At the end of 3 days they come to a town called Anoixi	
(Sunday, Oct. 30, or Monday, Oct. 31), come close to Quitamaya	In 2 days more come to Catamaya	
Monday, Oct. 31, come to a village called Quitamaya	Next day they enter the above named town and find it abandoned	
Tuesday, Nov. 1, they pass through a small village		
Wednesday, Nov. 2, they reach Utiangue, on a plain and well peopled all about	The day after entering Catamaya they arrive at Autiamque where they remain 3 months, and are "a month in snow"	
(*End of Ranjel Narrative*)		
		De Soto leads 100 cavalry and 150 infantry 20 leagues to the confines of the province of Naguatex on a foray lasting 14 days
	(Thursday, Nov. 3–Sunday, March 5, 1542), at Autiamque	They remain more than 5 months in Utiangue

Ranjel	Elvas and Biedma	Garcilaso
	1542	
	Monday, March 6, they leave Autiamque for Anilco; B says they left in the beginning of March	They leave Utiangue in the beginning of April, 1542
	(Tuesday, March 7–Wednesday, March 15(?)), travel south along river	In 7 days they travel 22–23 leagues and come to Naguatex, a different town from that against which De Soto had made a foray though it was in the same province
	(Thursday, March 16 (Elvas says in 10 days)), they come to Ayays and cross the river in a piragua	There they remain 15 or 16 days
	(Friday, March 17–Monday, March 20), they remain at Ayays on account of the snow	After 6 days a messenger comes from the chief and next day he sends some of his prominent men
	(Tuesday, March 21–Thursday, March 23), they travel 3 days through a deserted, low region full of lakes and bad passages	After 2 leagues travel Diego de Guzman is missed They march 5 days to the province of Guancane
	(Friday, March 24), all one day trying to find a crossing over a lake; Indians show a passage near Tutelpinco	They cross the province of Guancane in 8 days
	(Saturday, March 25), probably spent in crossing	
	(Sunday, March 26–Monday, March 28), they march 3 days to Tianto in the territory of Nilco; come into neighborhood of Nilco; chief's house set on fire by natives	They traverse 7 other provinces, 3 well settled and 4 not, until they come to the borders of Anilco; the distance across these must have been at least 120 leagues
	Wednesday, March 29, they enter Nilco and make headquarters there	They pass through the province of Anilco 20 days to the capital
	(Thursday, March 30–April 15 or 17), at Nilco	They remain at Anilco 4 days

Elvas and Biedma	Garcilaso
1542	
Sunday, April 17 (it should be Sunday, April 15 or Tuesday, April 17), they enter Guachoya	They march to Guachoya, a journey of 4 days, through an uninhabited country densely forested
(April 16 or 18–Sunday, May 20), at Guachoya; expedition to Nilco	After 3 days the Guachoya chief sends a messenger to De Soto and after 4 more days comes himself
(Sunday), May 21, De Soto dies	June 20, 1542, De Soto is attacked by a fever, in 3 more days he appoints his successor and in 7 more dies, aged 42; his body is sunk in the Chucagua (Mississippi), enclosed in a hollowed oak; he was "an hidalgo through all four lines"
(Monday, May 22 and Tuesday, May 23), at Guachoya	
(Wednesday, May 24), body buried inside a gate of the town	
Shortly afterward the body was committed to the river during the night	
(Thursday, May 25–Sunday, June 4), at Guachoya	
Monday, June 5, Moscoso leaves Guachoya, passes through the province of Catalte, and then through unoccupied country for 6 days (it should perhaps be 16); B says they took 17 days in going from Guachoyanque to Chavite	July 4 or 5 Moscoso leaves Guachoya and marches more than 100 leagues through many provinces of which they did not inquire the names
(Tuesday), June 20, at Chaguate (or Chaguete)	
(Wednesday, June 21–Sunday, June 25) they seem to have occupied in visiting a small town and in making salt	
(Monday, June 26–Saturday, July 1), in Chaguate proper (6 days)	
(Sunday, July 2–Tuesday, July 4, or Monday, July 3–Wednesday, July 5 (Elvas errs in saying that they arrived "Wednesday, July 4"), on the road to Aguacay; B says it was 3 days from Chavite	
(Date not given), they leave Aguacay and go to sleep at a small town, camping near a salt lake	
Next day they camp in an open grove between two mountains	
Next day they reach a small town called Pato	

Elvas and Biedma	Garcilaso
1542	
On the 4th day from Aguacay they come to the first inhabited place of a province called Amaye	
Saturday, July 22 or Thursday, July 20 (the text says erroneously "Saturday, July 20"), they leave Amaye and camp in luxuriant woods at midday where they fight with the inhabitants	
Next day they camp near a town by a river; this town was called Naguatex	
On the tenth day two bodies of cavalry are sent to take the fords and observe the villages on the other side	
In two days the chief who had been sent for arrives	
At the end of four days Moscoso sets out but finds the river running full much to his surprise and returns to his camp	
At the end of 8 days, the river having fallen, the army sets out and lodges in the fields	
After laying waste the towns of Naguatex, they leave and at the end of 3 days reach a hamlet of the poor province of Nissohone	
After traveling 2 days more they find the guides are misleading them, they substitute a woman taken in Nissohone, and in 2 days more reach Lacane, a miserable country	
They reach Nondacao, but in what way is not clear	
They leave Nondacao for Soacatino and in 5 days reach Aays (Hais)	They enter the province of Auche more than 100 leagues away where they remain 2 days
They are led 2 days out of the way by a guide who is then cast to the dogs and another substituted; next day they come to Soacatino	After traveling 2 days more they reach uninhabited country and pass through that for 4 days
	They travel 6 days more without a road to guide them
	They are misled by their guide and wander 8 days (but perhaps this includes the last 6)

They march for 20 days through a thinly peopled region (though this 20 may include part of the preceding itinerary) They reach a province called Guasco, apparently at the end of the 20 days; B says they were guided toward the east They reach a settlement called Naquiscoça In 2 days more they reach another called Naçacahoz (at least that was the name of the chief)	Then they march straight west to inhabited country They march 3 (or 6) days to the province of Vaqueros Marching more than 30 leagues through this they see lofty mountain ranges and forests
A captain and 15 horse set out in search of other white men reported by a female guide, but she confesses to have fabricated the story of her encounter with them They return to Guasco	
They journey 10 days toward the west to a river called Daycao; horsemen are sent across the river and find a wretched Indian camp, bringing back 2 Indians whose language no one could understand; B says they went 6 days to the south and southwest; and the horsemen went for 8–9 days as far as they could before reaching the Indian camp	Three scouting parties go out more than 30 leagues into the country and return in 15 days
They determine to retrace their steps at the beginning of October They return the same way they came, 150 leagues to the Rio Grande	The Spaniards return to the Chucagua on a course south of their route out They finally leave the province of the Vaqueros on their return and pass 20 days by long stages through different provinces They recross their own out trail in the middle of September without recognizing it after having been three months going and coming from Guachoya
Leaving Chaguate they recross the Rio Nilco at Aays, and follow it down to Nilco, discovering a new town called Chilano on the way	They have good weather on the march until they reach the borders of Guachoya at the end of October 1542, when very severe weather sets in with rain, cold, and wind

Elvas and Biedma	Garcilaso
1542	
	Then they have difficulty in crossing rivers and it takes 5–8 days to cross some of them; much snow falls
	This lasts from September to the end of Nov. when they reach the Rio Grande, the entire distance going and coming and with detours 350 leagues
They go from Nilco to Aminoya in the beginning of December, 2 days' journey, where were 2 towns half a league apart, near the Rio Grande and above Guachoya; they spend the winter there and build boats in which to leave the country	Arrived at the Rio Grande they take possession of 2 villages near each other surrounded by a fosse, 16 leagues above Guachoya and called Aminoya They spend 20 days in fortifying one of them
1543	
They plunder a town called Taguanate or Tagoanate, 2 days up river from Aminoya (by an error "fallen river" gives the opposite idea)	Near the end of Jan., 1543, orders are issued to cut timber for boats and they work on them until April
In March the river overflows so much as to reach Nilco, 9 leagues off, although more than a month had passed since rain fell. The Indians said that it extended an equal distance on the opposite side; for 2 months they are surrounded by water and can go on horseback only where the land is highest; they usually use canoes	The flood in the Rio Grande begins March 10, on Mar. 18 (Palm Sunday) it pours through the gates and inundates more than 20 leagues on each side of the river, extending 5–6 leagues beyond Anilco; it lasts 40 days and diminishes by degrees near the end of April; reaches greatest height Apr. 20; May 20 they still had to walk about barefoot, but by end of May it had retired within its bed
	Envoys of the hostile Indian league arrested at the beginning of June
The vessels are completed in June; it was then a long time since rain had fallen	The day of St. John the Baptist (June 24) the boats are launched
The canoes are tied together in twos, and 22 horses the best left, are taken in them; B says 26 horses were taken	They spend 5 days loading them until the evening of the Festival of St. Peter and St. Paul (June 28)

(Monday), July 2, 1543, they leave Aminoya in 7 boats in which go 322 Spaniards and 100 Indian slaves	They embark on the Festival of St. Peter and St. Paul (June 29)
They pass Guachoya the day they leave; Quigualtam said to be near an arm of the river which made out to the right; they come to land in a clump of trees and at dark retire to the vessels	
(Tuesday, July 3), they come to a town said to belong to Huhasene, a subject of Quigualtam	
(Wednesday, July 4 or perhaps still on July 3), they obtain corn and wait over a day	
(Thursday, July 5, or perhaps still on July 3), they have a skirmish with the Indians and burn a town under a bluff; B says 40 or 50 large swift canoes came out against them on the 2d day	They are attacked by a great body of Indians in numerous canoes, but after 10 days of fighting the enemy withdraw, they reach a town where they get much corn and release the remaining horses which are killed
(Friday, July 6, or Wednesday, July 4), Juan de Guzman and 10 other Spaniards are drowned in trying to repel Indian assailants in canoes; the rest pursue all night but	Esteban Añez and some companions attack the Indians but their canoes are upset and most of the company are drowned
(Saturday, July 7, or Thursday, July 5), at noon they get into another province but are treated as before and have to fight all of one day and one night	
Although using oars day and night the boats in which were the horses delay them so much that they kill all but 4 or 5 and cure their flesh (the 4 or 5 were probably killed by the Indians)	
(Sunday, July 8), at 10 A. M. these Indians (in 50 canoes) leave them and pursuit is taken up by 7 canoes from a small town near the bank but the Indians soon give it up	At sunrise of the 17th day of their voyage the Indians abandon the chase, having followed them without remission for 400 leagues
(In 17 days they went down 250 leagues by the river, "a little more or less"; near the sea they find it divided into two arms, each a league and a half broad; B says it took 19 days to reach the sea)	After three days more (the 17th–19th of their navigation) they descry the sea on the morning of the 20th; the time taken to the sea is given as 19 days and an additional night; the estimates of distances covered for each day and night are 20–40 leagues or more, but they finally agree on 25 leagues; they regard the distance from the point of embarkation to the sea as a little less than 500 leagues though Juan Coles estimates 700

Elvas and Biedma	Garcilaso
1543	
They cast anchor half a league before coming to the Gulf and are attacked by men with spears and atlatls	They stop 3 days at the mouth of the river and are attacked on the afternoon of the 4th by Indians, one of whom had an atlatl
After remaining there 2 days they go to the mouth of that branch and find 40 fathoms of water	They leave about 3 P. M. on the day after the attack
(Wednesday), July 18, they get under way for Mexico	
They sail all that day and the following night and the next day until vespers in fresh water (July 18–19)	They go on the rest of that day and until nearly sunset of the second day in fresh water
They stand out to sea and 4 days later return within sight of the coast	
Next day, after taking on water, they set forward again	
In 2 days they enter a basin like a cove	
They remain there unable to leave till the 4th day when they are driven ashore by a storm	They go on 7 or 8 days more until a storm forces them into a cove
Next morning they come to a creek where 2 boats going in advance had already found shelter and they remain there 2 days	At the end of 15 days more they reach four or five small islands not far from the mainland
They run on for 2 days and enter an arm of the sea where they land and pitch their boats with a "scum" the sea cast up	They remain there 8 days calking their boats
They spend 2 days at this place	
In 2 days more they enter an arm of the sea behind an islet	They spend 12 or 13 days from time to time fishing
They remain there 14 days waiting for fair weather	"Fifty three days had passed since our Spaniards had left the Rio Grande and entered the sea. They spent 30 of them in navigation and 23 in repairing the boats and in resting while they fished"
They navigate for 6 days	
In one or two (?) days more they reach the River of Panuco, entering it (Monday), Sept. 10, 52 days after leaving the Rio Grande; those who returned numbered 311	Next day, after sailing 25 or 26 hours two of the pinnaces are run aground south of Panuco
	The next day they learn they are in Mexico
	Eight days after the "shipwreck" of the two pinnaces they meet in Panuco
	Twenty-five days after entering Panuco they set out in separate bands for Mexico City

Selected Items from Narratives of the Career of Hernando de Soto in the Conquest of Florida

Translated by
Buckingham Smith
for the Bradford Club
New York, 1866

CONVEYANCE OF DOWER BY THE WIDOW OF PEDRÁRIAS DÁVILA TO HERNANDO DE SOTO, IN CONSIDERATION OF THE ESPOUSAL OF HER DAUGHTER.

Be it known to all who shall see this writing, that I, Doña Ysabel de Bobadilla, wife that was of Pedrárias de Avila, deceased,—be he in glory—Governor that was of Tierra Firme, my lord and husband, declare, that inasmuch as, by the assistance of Our Lord and His Blessed Mother, espousals of marriage are concerted and contracted, by words of assent, between Doña Ysabel de Bobadilla, my legitimate daughter and of said Pedrárias, with you, Señor Captain Fernando de Soto, being at this Court of their Majesties, native and resident of the City of Badajóz, by these presents, henceforth I promise and obligate myself to give you, and do henceforth give in dower and marriage with the said Doña Ysabel de Bobadilla, my daughter, for her and for her goods of dower, that you may keep and marry her with the consent and in the peace of the Holy Mother Church of Rome, that is to say, all the cattle with their young which the said Governor, my lord and husband, established and left at Panamá, in Tierra Firme, with all the cottage, the slaves who tend the cattle, the stud of horses with them in the fields, and every thing else that to said round cottage and stock is in all or in any wise belonging, with the increase of slaves, and whatever else is thereto pertinent, which the said Pedrárias de Avila, by a clause made of his will between living, in pure and perfect gift irrevocable in favour of said Doña Ysabel de Bobadilla, my daughter, that she thereby might the better and more honorably marry, as more fully may be found in the clause referred to of said will, which I deem here inserted and incorporated with the same force and vigour it would have were it written out word for word; of the which I, for what therein belongs to me and appertains, or that can appertain, by reason of any right of dower, paraphernalia, and goods, acquired during the matrimony existing between me and the said Pedrárias Dávila, my lord and husband, as well in whatever other manner, I consent publicly, and approve consent to the aforementioned donative made by Pedro Arias, and do so by good, lasting, and genuine signature, for this and in all time of the world, for evermore . . . Done at Valladolid, the 14th day of November, of the year 1536.

One of the witnesses to this release was Juan de Añasco. The document exists in full in the *Archivo de Indias.*

LETTER OF HERNANDO DE SOTO RESPECTING CONCESSIONS HE DESIRES SHALL BE OBTAINED FOR HIM AT COURT.[1]

✠

VERY MAGNIFICENT SIR:

That which Your Worship is to favour me in is as follows:

Inasmuch as His Majesty has not ceded to Francisco Pizarro more than two hundred and seventy-five leagues by Royal grant, of the six hundred that the said Governor Pizarro holds from Santiago, whence begins his government, to the mines of Callao, which divide his territory from that of Don Diego de Almagro, as will appear by an agreement made between them, must be taken off from the beginning of his government to the town of San Miguel, an extent may be of one hundred leagues, which region, from said town of Panamá, supposing now His Majesty should be pleased to grant it to me in government, is the most sterile and unprofitable of that country, although I am of opinion that by way of Quito there is good opening into the interior, whereby to serve His Majesty in the Provinces through which I came.

Your Worship, not being able to get what I have set forth, will try then for the government of Guatemala, with permission to make discovery in the South Sea, and for the title of Adelantado, with concession from His Majesty of the tenth part of whatever I may at my own cost discover in the sea, and conquer, with patent, and to my successors.

What Your Worship will send to the Señor Comendador, to be negotiated with His Majesty, is as follows:

The mantle of Santiago for Fernan Ponçe de Leon, and also for me.

All the Indians of Apportionment which said Hernan Ponçe de Leon and I hold by schedule from His Majesty, with other property in lands and houses,[2] in fee simple, and if possible with a title.

Let the government that may be got for me be in perpetuity if possible, and if not, then for the longest term Your Worship may be enabled to secure: And when you shall have acted on these instructions, and discovered where is the best chance of success, you will let me know how I am to treat with

[1]The original of these instructions, only the signature to which is in the handwriting of Soto, exists in the *Biblioteca Nacional,* at Madrid. It was no doubt written while he was in Spain, in the year 1536 or 1537.

[2]The words *se an de dar,* to be given, are here driven through with a pen.

these Lords of the Council in the business, and what I am to write to the Señor Comendador, and when.

CONCESSION MADE BY THE KING OF SPAIN TO HERNANDO DE SOTO OF THE GOVERNMENT OF CUBA AND CONQUEST OF FLORIDA, WITH THE TITLE OF ADELANTADO.

[Translation made from a copy in the *Archivo de Indias* at Sevilla, rubricated by the Secretary Samano.]

THE KING.

Inasmuch as you, Captain Hernando de Soto, set forth that you have served us in the conquest, pacification, and settlement of the Provinces of Nicaragua and Perú, and of other parts of our Indias; and that now, to serve us further, and to continue to enlarge our patrimony and the royal crown, you desire to return to those our Indias, to conquer and settle the Province of Rio de las Palmas to Florida, the government whereof was bestowed on Pánfilo de Narvaez, and the Provinces of Tierra-Nueva, the discovery and government of which was conferred on Lucas Vazquez de Ayllón; and that for the purpose you will take from these, our kingdoms and our said Indias, five hundred men, with the necessary arms, horses, munitions, and military stores; and that you will go hence, from these our kingdoms, to make the said conquest and settlement within a year first following, to be reckoned from the day of the date of these articles of authorization; and that when you shall leave the Island of Cuba to go upon that enterprise, you will take the necessary subsistence for all that people during eighteen months—rather over than under that time—entirely at your cost and charges, without our being obliged, or the kings who shall come after us, to pay you, nor satisfy the expenses incurred therefor, other than such as you in these articles may be authorized to make; and you pray that I bestow on you the conquest of those lands and provinces, and with it the government of the said Island of Cuba, that you may from there the better control and provide all the principal and important material for the conquest and settlement, whereupon I have ordered to be made with you the terms and contract following:

First, I give you, the said Captain Hernando de Soto, power and authority, for us and in our name, and in that of the royal crown of Castilla, to conquer, pacify, and populate the lands that there are from the Province of the Rio de las Palmas to Florida, the government of which was bestowed on Pánfilo de Narvaez; and, further, the Provinces of the said Tierra-Nueva, the government whereof was in like manner conferred on the said Licentiate Ayllón.

Also, purposing to comply in this with the service of God our Lord, and to do you honour, we engage to confer on you the dignity of Governor and Captain-General of two hundred leagues of coast, such as you shall designate, of what you discover, so that within four years, to be reckoned from the time you arrive in any part of the lands and provinces before mentioned, you shall choose and declare whence you would have the two hundred leagues begin; that from where you designate they shall be measured along the coast, for all the days of your life, with the annual salary of fifteen hundred ducats, and five hundred ducats gratuity, in all two thousand, which you shall receive from the day you set sail in the Port of San Lúcar, to go upon your voyage, to be paid to you from the duties and profits to us appertaining in those said lands and provinces which you so offer to conquer and colonize; and in that time should there be neither duties nor profits, we shall not be obliged to order that you be paid any thing.

Also, we will confer on you the title of our Adelantado over the said two hundred leagues which you shall thus select and make known for your government in the said lands and provinces you so discover and colonize, and will likewise bestow on you the office of High-Constable (Alguazil mayor) over those territories in perpetuity.

Also, we give permission, the judgment of our officers of said province being in accord, that you build there as many as three stone fortresses in the harbours and places most proper for them, they appearing to you and to our said officers to be necessary for the protection and pacification of that country; and we confer on you the Lieutenancy of them, and on one heir for life, or successor whom you shall name, with the annual salary to each of the fortresses of one hundred thousand maravedis, which you shall enjoy from the time they be severally built and finished and enclosed, in the opinion of our said officers; to be done at your own cost, without our being obliged, or any of the kings who shall come after us, to pay you what you may expend on those fortresses.

Again, inasmuch as you have petitioned us to bestow on you some portion of the land and vassals in said province you would conquer and populate, considering what you have served us, and the expenditure you will meet from this time in making said conquest and pacification, we receive the petitions favourably: hence we promise to bestow on you, and by these presents we do, twelve leagues of land in square in the said two hundred leagues you shall designate to hold in government in the said territories and provinces before declared, which we command our officers of the said province to assign, after you shall have designated the said two hundred leagues, to include no sea-port, nor the principal town, and that with the jurisdiction and title we shall confer at the time we give you the deeds.

Again, as has been said, you have petitioned us, that for the better governing and providing of all the principal and important matters for the conquest and settlement of said territories and provinces, I should order that there be given to you with them the government of the said Island of Cuba, which, to that end, we deem well, and is our pleasure, for the time it shall be our will, that you hold the government of said island; and for thus much we will order to be given you our provision by which you will be obliged to have a Chief-Justice, who shall be a lawyer, to whom we shall require you to pay yearly on that Island the salary of two hundred *pesos* of gold; and we give to you five hundred ducats annual gratuity for the government of said Island, while you hold the same, to be paid from the duties and profits we may have from the province you have thus to conquer, pacify, and hold in government; and if there be none there, we shall not be obliged to pay you that, nor any other thing more than the two hundred *pesos* of the said Chief-Justice.

Also, we give you liberty and right that you from these our kingdoms and lordships, or from the Kingdom of Portugal, or Islands of Cabo Verde, or Guinea, do and may pass, or whosoever may exercise your power, to the said Island of Cuba fifty negro slaves, not less than one-third of them to be females, free of the import duties that of right may belong to us at said island, upon paying the license of two ducats on each to Diego de la Haya, which sum by our order he is charged to collect.

Again, also, we promise that upon your arrival in that country of your government, which you have thus to conquer and settle, we give liberty and right to whomsoever shall have your power, that you may take thither from these our said kingdoms, or from Portugal, or the Islands of Cabo Verde, other fifty negro slaves, the third part of them females, free from all duties.

Also, we concede to those who shall go to settle in that country within the six years first following, to be reckoned forward from the day of the date of these presents, that of the gold which may be taken from the mines shall be paid us the tenth, and the said six years being ended, shall pay us the ninth, and thus annually declining to the fifth part; but from the gold and other things that may be got by barter, or in spoil got by incursions, or in any other manner, shall be paid us thereupon one-fifth of all.

Also we give, free of import duty, to the inhabitants of that country for the said six years, and as much longer as shall be our will, all they may take for the furnishing and provision of their houses, the same not being to sell; and whatsoever they or any other, merchants or traffickers, sell, shall go free of duty for two years, and not longer.

Likewise, we promise that for the term of ten years, and until we command otherwise, we will not impose on the inhabitants of those countries any excise duty, or other tribute whatsoever.

Likewise, we grant that to said inhabitants may be given through you the lots and grounds proper to their conditions, as has been done, and is doing, in the Island of Española; and we also give you license, in our name, during the time of your government, that you take the bestowal of the Indians of that land, observing therein the instructions and provisions that will be given to you.

Again, we bestow on the hospital that may be built in that country, to assist the relief of the poor who may go thither, the charity of one hundred thousand maravedis from the fines imposed by the tribunal of that country.

Again, also, according to your petition and consent, and of the settlers of that country, we promise to give to its hospital, and by these presents we do give, the duties of *escobilla* and *relabes*, existing in the foundries that may there be made; and, as respects that, we will order our provision to be issued to you in form.

Also, likewise we will order, and by the present command and defend, that from these our kingdoms do not pass into said country, nor go, any one of the persons prohibited from going into those parts, under the penalties contained in the laws and ordinances of our letters, upon which subject this by us and by the Catholic Kings are given, nor any counsellors nor attorneys to exercise their callings.

The which, all that is said, and each thing and part thereof, we concede to you, conditioned that you, the said Don Hernando de Soto, be held and obliged to go from these our realms in person to make the conquest within one year next following, to be reckoned from the day of the date of this charter.

Again, on condition that when you go out of these our said kingdoms, and arrive in said country, you will carry and have with you the officers of our exchequer, who may by us be named; and likewise also the persons, religious and ecclesiastical, who shall be appointed by us for the instruction of the natives of that Province in our Holy Catholic Faith, to whom you are to give and pay the passage, stores, and the other necessary subsistence for them, according to their condition, all at your cost, receiving nothing from them during the said entire voyage; with which matter we gravely charge you, that you do and comply with, as a thing for the service of God and our own, and any thing otherwise we shall deem contrary to our service.

Again, whensoever, according to right and the laws of our kingdoms, the people and captains of our armaments take prisoner any prince or lord of the countries where, by our command, they make war, the ransom of such lord or cacique belongs to us, with all the other things movable found or belonging to him; but, considering the great toils and perils that our subjects undergo in the conquest of the Indias, as some recompense, and to favour them, we make known and command, that if in your said conquest and government any cacique or principal lord be captured or seized, all the treasures, gold, silver, stones, and pearls that may be got from him by way of redemption, or in any other manner whatsoever, we award you the seventh part thereof, and the remainder shall be divided among the conquerors, first taking out our fifth; and in case the said cacique or lord should be slain in battle, or afterward by course of justice, or in any other manner whatsoever, in such case, of the treasures and goods aforesaid obtained of him justly we have the half, which, before any thing else, our officers shall take, after having first reserved our fifth.

Again, since our said officers of said Province might have some doubt in making the collection of our duties, especially on gold and silver, stones and pearls, as well those that may be found in sepulchres, and other places where they may be hidden, as those got by ransom and incursion, or other way, our pleasure and will is, that, until some change, the following order be observed.

First, we order that of the gold and silver, stones and pearls that may be won in battle, or on entering towns, or by barter with the Indians, should and must be paid us one-fifth of all.

Likewise, that all the gold and silver, stones, pearls, and other things that may be found and taken, as well in the graves, sepulchres, *ocues*, or temples of the Indians, as in other places where they were accustomed to offer sacrifices to their idols, or in other concealed religious precincts, or buried in house, or patrimonial soil, or in the ground, or in some other public place, whether belonging to the community or an individual, be his state or dignity what it may, of the whole, and of all other, of the character that may be and is found, whether finding it by accident or discovering it by search, shall pay us the half, without diminution of any sort, the other half remaining to the person who has found or made the discovery; and should any person or persons have gold, silver, stones, or pearls, taken or found, as well in the said graves, sepulchres, *ocues*, or Indian temples, as in the other places where they were accustomed to offer sacrifices, or other concealed religious places, or interred as before said, and do not make it known, that they may receive, in conformity with this chapter, what may belong to them, they have forfeited all the gold and silver, stones and pearls, besides the half of their goods, to our tribunal and exchequer.

And we, having been informed of the evils and disorders which occur in making discoveries and new settlements, for the redress thereof, and that we may be enabled to give you license to make them, with the accord of the members of our Council and of our consultation, a general provision of chapters is ordained and dispatched, respecting what you will have to observe in the said settlement and conquest, and we command it here to be incorporated in tenor as follows:[1]—

* * * * * *

Hence, by these presents, you, the said Captain Hernando de Soto, doing as aforesaid at your cost, according to and in the manner before contained, observing and complying with the said provision here incorporated, and all the other instructions we shall henceforth command you to obey, and to give with regard to that country, and for the good treatment and conversion to our Holy Catholic Faith of the natives of it, we promise and declare that to you will be kept these terms, and whatever therein is contained, in and through all; and you doing otherwise, and not complying therewith, we shall not be obliged to keep with you and comply with the aforesaid, nor any matter of it; on the contrary, we will order that you be punished, and proceed against you as against one who keeps not nor complies with, but acts counter to, the commands of his natural king and lord. In confirmation whereof we order that the present be given, signed by my name, and witnessed by my undersigned Secretary. Done at the town Valladolid, the twentieth day of the month of April, of the year one thousand five hundred and thirty-seven.

I THE KING.

ROYAL CEDULA PERMITTING JUAN DE AÑASCO TO TRAFFIC WITH THE INDIANS OF FLORIDA, SO LONG AS THERE ARE NO DUTIES ON IMPORTS IN THAT PROVINCE.

THE KING.

Inasmuch as thou on thy part, Juan de Añasco, our Comptroller of the Province of Florida, the government whereof I have conferred on the Captain Hernando de Soto, hast petitioned me to command that thou be permitted to traffic with the Indians of the Province, notwithstanding thou be our

[1]This Ordinance, first placed in the charter granted to Francisco Montejo for the conquest of Yucatan, dated the seventh day of December, of the year 1526, signed by the King, his Secretary, Francisco de los Cobos, Mercurinus cancellorius, fr. G. Epus. Oxemes, Dotor Caravajal, Epus. Canariensis, el Dotor Beltram, fr. G. Epus. Civitatem, was afterwards inserted in all like concessions, and is deemed to follow here.

Comptroller there, or in such way allowed as might to us be deemed proper, we by this present do license and empower thee, so long as in that Province we shall not be paid the duties of almoxarifadgo, to bargain, contract, and traffic with the Indians thereof, alone or in company, as thou wilt, and shalt deem proper, as well in the things of these our kingdoms, as in those which in that country may be produced or may exist there; observing in respect thereof the ordinances that are or may be enacted by our Governor and officers of that Province, to the extent that neither thou nor the said company treat or contract with our exchequer, directly or indirectly, under penalty of forfeiture of our favour, and of your goods to the fiscal advantage of our Treasury. Dated at Valladolid, the fourth day of the month of May, of the year one thousand five hundred and thirty-seven.

I THE KING.

WILL OF HERNANDO DE SOTO

In Dei Nomine, Amen.

Know ye who shall see this testamentary letter, that I, the Adelantado, Don Hernando de Soto, being of sound body and free mind, such as my Redeemer Jesus Christ has been pleased to bestow on me, believing firmly in what believes and holds the Holy Mother Church, in the most Holy Trinity, Father, Son, and Holy Ghost, three persons and one only true God, promising as a faithful Christian to live and die in His Holy Catholic faith, mindful of the blood that Jesus Christ shed for me as the price of my redemption, and endeavouring to repay and satisfy so great benefit, knowing that death is a natural thing, and that the more I shall be prepared for it the better will He be pleased, I declare that I commend my soul to God, who created it of nothing, and redeemed it with His most holy passion, that He place it among the number of the elect in His glory, and I order the body to the earth, of which it was made.

First, I command, should God take me from this present life on the sea, that my corpse be so disposed of, that it may be taken to the land wheresoever our Lord shall be pleased it shall come to port, and should a church be there, or should one there be built, that it be deposited therein until such time as there are arrangements for taking it to Spain, to the city of Xeréz, near Badajóz, where it be consigned to the sepulchre where lies my mother, in the Church of San Miguel; and in that church I order that of my goods a site and place be brought where a chapel be built that shall have for its invocation Our Lady of the Conception, in which edifice and work I desire there be expended two thousand ducats, one thousand five hundred in the structures and enclosure, and the five hundred in an altar-piece, representing the same Invocation of Our Lady of the Conception; and I order that vestments be made, with a chasuble, two dalmatics, an antependium and a cope, with three albs, and a chalice with its cover, both of silver, and two other chasubles for daily use, for which I direct there be paid of my goods other three hundred ducats; and I order that the mentioned vestments be of silk, of the color which to the patron and my executors, and to those of the said chapel, shall appear well; and I order that of my goods be bought a perpetual rent of twelve thousand maravedis, in good possession, which shall be given to a chaplain who shall say five masses each week for my soul, the souls of my parents, and that of Doña Ysabel de Bobadilla, my wife, and he shall be appointed by the patron of the chapel, with the understanding that should there be a clergyman of my line, who desires to be chaplain, it be given to him in preference to any other, and that he be the nearest of kin, should there be two or more.

Also, I order that if the body of my father or of my mother be in Badajóz, or in any other part whatsoever, not in that chapel, they be taken out and brought thence, and be entombed there where my body shall be, or should be placed, which is in the midst of the chapel, in such manner that the foot of the sepulchre adjoin the foot-stone of the altar; and thereon I order to be placed a tomb covered over by a fine black broadcloth, in the middle of which be put a red cross of the Commandery of the Order of the Knights of Saint Jago, that shall be for use on week-days, and another pall of black velvet, with the same cross in the midst, with four escutcheons of brocade, bearing my arms; which escutcheons I wish and order to be likewise placed on the chapel, altar-piece, and railing, and vestments, in such manner as to the patron and executors shall appear most becoming.

Also, to the end that this chapel and chaplaincy be kept in repair and appointment, the chapel and the income alike, I order that Doña Ysabel de Bobadilla, my wife, be the patroness; and, after her, should God give me children, I desire the patron to be my eldest legitimate son, or my eldest legitimate daughter, should I have no male child, that they, or either of them, who shall be the patron, may buy the site for, and make the said chapel, and do all the foregoing appertaining to it, and buy the said twelve thousand maravedis, and appoint the chaplain. And should God not grant me legitimate sons or daughters, I order that after the lifetime of my wife, the patron be Juan Mendez de Soto, my brother, and after his life, his eldest son; and if he be without a male child, I order that the successor to that patronage be the eldest son of Catalina de Soto, my sister; and should she have no male child, let the successor thereto be the eldest son of Maria de Soto, my sister; and if it happen of the designated patrons there should be no issue male, I order the patronage to succeed to the next nearest of kin, being always male.

Also, in order that the chapel, and vestments, and rent for the chaplaincy, may always be available, and that in each year, on All Saints' Day, a mass be sung, and another on All Souls' Day, with its vigil, and offerings of bread and wine, there shall be a perpetual rent of five thousand maravedis, on good possessions, to be bought with my goods, and I order that they be used in no other way than for what is expressed.

Also, I order that on the day my body is interred, it be followed by the *curas* and clergy of the parishes, with their crosses, and by the orders there may be in the city aforesaid, and that there be paid them what is customary; and I require that each *cura,* with the clergy of their church, sing a mass on that day, and they be paid what is usual; and I order that on the same day thirty masses be said for me, and that there be paid therefor what is customary.

Also, I order that there be said twenty masses of *requiem* in the said chapel, for the soul of the Captain Compañon, and that what is usual be paid for them.

Also, that there be twenty masses of Our Lady of the Conception said in the chapel.

Also, I order that ten masses of the Holy Ghost be said in the chapel.

Also, I order that ten masses be said of All Saints in said chapel.

Also, I order that ten masses be said, five of them of the Passion, and five of the Wounds, in the aforesaid, my chapel.

Also, I order that sixty masses be said for souls in purgatory, in my said chapel; all which masses shall be said by whom my executors shall please.

Also, toward the completion of pious works, I order to each of them one real.

Also, I order for the redemption of captives, two reals.

Also, I order, that inasmuch as I gave Ysabel de Soto in espousal to Don Carlos Enriquez, and it was understood should be given with her in marriage and for dowry whatever I might think best, I order that of my goods there be given to him three thousand ducats, which are the dowry of marriage of the said Ysabel de Soto, my cousin [niece; See *ante*, p. 179].

I confess to have received in dowry with Doña Ysabel de Bobadilla, my legitimate wife, seven thousand castellanos, of which, at the time of making this my will, I have received two thousand castellanos, the same being within my control; in Spain are deposited other two thousand in the House of Contratacion, and the remaining three thousand are in the possession of the debtor to whom was sold certain cattle in which the dowry was assigned.

Also, I admit that at the time I married Ysabel de Bobadilla, I sent her in marriage pledge six thousand ducats, all which, the seven thousand castellanos of dowry, as well as the six thousand ducats of *arras*, I order that she have and inherit of my goods, as her sole undivided property, that should belong to her of my said estate.

Also, I command that of my goods be given to my nephew, Pedro de Soto, five hundred ducats.

Also, I order that to a boy, who they say is my son, called Andrés de Soto, be given four hundred ducats from my goods.

Also, I order that to a daughter I left in Nicaragua, called Doña Maria de Soto, married to Hernan Nieto, be given one thousand ducats from my goods.

Also, I order to be given to Alonso Ayala, my mayordomo, from my goods three hundred ducats.

Also, I order that to Rodrigo Rangel, my secretary, be given, for the good service he has rendered me, three hundred ducats of my goods; to Castro, my carver, I order fifty ducats from my goods.

Also, I order two thousand ducats for the marriage of the maids of Doña Ysabel, who are Maria Arias, and Catalina Ximenes, and Mexia, and Arellano, and Carreño, which will be divided among them by Doña Ysabel de Bobadilla, my wife, as shall appear well to her, and as they shall have served her.

Also, I order to Doña Leonor de Bobadilla, in marriage, one thousand ducats, for the service that she and Nuño de Tobár have rendered, of which I desire she have five hundred, and he five hundred, to avoid delicacy or doubts.

Also, I order to Leonor de Bolaños two hundred ducats for her services.

Also, I acknowledge and declare that I have made a writing of companionship with the Captain Hernan Ponçe de Leon, in which are contained many things, as will appear by it, which was executed before Domingo de la (*illegible*), public notary, resident in Lima, and of that city, in the Province of Peru, which was amended and reaffirmed, with some additions, by another writing, made and executed before Francisco Sepero, and Francisco de Alcocer, notaries of His Majesty, in the town of San Christóbal, of the Havana, in the Island of Fernandina, named Cuba, which I have present: whence I say and declare, that of all the goods that to me belong, or can be mine, of which I have no exact knowledge, I admit that of the whole, one-half I possess are his; and of all goods whatsoever that he possesses and has, the half are mine, by reason of the partnership and brotherhood that we have formed, as contained in those writings.

Also, I declare that, in the event my body cannot be had for taking to Spain, for sepulture, as is set forth, it be no impediment or hindrance to the founding of that chapel and the chaplaincy aforesaid; but that all be done as in this my will is expressed and declared.

Also, I order, that this my will being executed in the manner set forth, of the remainder of my goods be purchased one hundred and fifty thousand maravedis of perpetual rents, in good possessions, which shall be joined with the other one hundred and fifty thousand maravedis of income which I have belonging to me of my share in the royal revenues from silk, in the city of Grenada, which, taken together, amounts to three hundred thousand maravedis, of which I wish and order to be made two parts, one, being one hundred and fifty thousand maravedis, Doña Ysabel de Bobadilla, my wife, to have and enjoy all her lifetime, and the other one hundred and fifty thousand maravedis be employed yearly in marrying three orphan damsels, daughters of some that be of my line, and to the fifth degree, the poorest that can be found; the which shall be employed by Doña Ysabel de Bobadilla, my wife, in their marriage, on whom I confer all my power complete to that full object, and they whom she shall elect and name, shall be elected and named as though I myself had done so; and if it happen that damsels shall not be found of my lineage to the fifth degree, I wish and order that they be any other damsels, orphans, daughters of nobility, of the poorest there may be in the city of Xeréz, near Badajóz, who likewise are to be selected and named by Doña Ysabel de Bobadilla, my wife; and I order that after her days the said rent of one hundred and fifty thousand maravedis I leave to her during life be united to the other hundred and fifty thousand maravedis, being three hundred thousand maravedis of rent employed in the marriage of six damsels yearly, in the same manner as hereinbefore declared of the three, to each of whom shall be given fifty thousand maravedis for their dowry—the half in money, the half in apparel and furniture; and for the better execution hereof, I leave for patrons and administrators of the three hundred thousand maravedis' rent, the very reverend fathers, the prior, or president, of the Convent of Santo Domingo, of the city of Badajóz, and the minister of the Convent of the Santisima Trinidad, of that city, and the prior of Sto. Agustin, of that city, and the guardian of San Francisco, which is within that city, who now are, or shall be, to whom I give my complete power to that end, and I order that the persons whom they name and designate stand named and designated as if by me; and I entreat them as favour, and charge their consciences, that this be done with all diligence, for it is in the service of Our Lord, mindful of all the foregoing contained above, that they be all six damsels of nobility of my line, the nearest of kin, and to the fifth degree, and should there be no relatives of my line within this grade, I desire they be daughters of nobility, orphan damsels, the poorest there are in the city of Xeréz, of Badajóz. And should there be no orphans that are of the poorest, I give such patrons the full power I have and possess, and of right belonging to me, to receive the said three hundred thousand maravedis, and have an administrator, that they may be collected, to whom shall be paid such salary for his trouble as they shall deem just; and, that there may be memory of this, I desire that each of these reverend fathers have one thousand maravedis of alms, which, with what will have to be given the administrator, shall be taken from the said three hundred thousand maravedis.

And in order to make compliance with and protect this my will, and the bequests in it contained, I leave as my executors Doña Ysabel de Bobadilla, my wife, Captain Hernan Ponçe de Leon, Juan Mendez de Soto, my brother, and Gutierrez Garay de Cardeñosa, and, in default of him, his son Hernan Gutierrez Cardeñosa, to whom and to each I give *in solidum* all my complete power, with general administration, and all its incidences and dependences, accidences, annexes and connexes, so much, in such case as may be requisite, that without authority of judge or superior, but of their own inherent, they may enter upon those my said goods, and take of them all that may be necessary, and sell them at public outcry, or otherwise, at very low, or bad price, to comply with all the requirements of this my will, according as they are therein contained, discharging them conformably to law.

Made in the town of San Christóbal of the Havana, on the tenth day of the month of May, in the year of the birth of Our Redeemer Jesus Christ one thousand five hundred and thirty-nine.

EL ADELANTADO DON HERNANDO DE SOTO.

All in this will contained is correct, and was set forth in the presence of Señor Fray Juan de Gallegos, and Señor Fray Francisco de la Rocha.

FRAY JUAN DE GALLEGOS.

FRAY FRANCISCO DE LA ROCHA.

Besides this, and over what is set forth, I order that all the debts that it shall appear at any time I owe, by information or truth spoken, be paid from my goods; and inasmuch as I caused some soldiers to be quartered of my armament in the city of Santiago, and the other towns of this Island, the inhabitants of which gave them subsistence, if any thing because of this should be asked, let there be paid of my goods whatsoever shall appear I am indebted in this behalf.

Made on the said day of May, one thousand five hundred and thirty-nine years.

EL ADELANTADO DON HERNANDO DE SOTO.

Witnesses: FR. JUAN DE GALLEGOS.
FR. FRANCISCO DE ROCHA.

Translated from a copy in the Lonja, at Sevilla, among the papers existing in the action of Ysabel de Bobadilla, widow, against Hernan Ponçe de Leon.

The name Maria de Soto seems not to be well transcribed from the original instrument, since the mention of Doña Mencia, as the sister of Hernando, is observed to occur several times among the voluminous papers in the suit, which is in conformity with what Salazar y Castro writes in his history of the House of Silva, that Maria Enriquez de Vargas brought with her in marriage the entailed estate of Manchada, with other lands from her parents, Don Alonzo Enriquez, Prefect of Badajóz, and Doña Mencia de Soto, sister of the Adelantado of Florida.

LETTER TO THE KING OF SPAIN FROM OFFICERS AT HAVANA IN THE ARMY OF DE SOTO.

[Original in the General Archive of the Indies, Seville.]

On the envelope is written:—

✠

TO THE S. I. C. MAJESTY

OF THE EMPEROR AND KING OUR LORD.

H. I. C. My.

We gave relation to Your Majesty from Saint Jago de Cuba of the favourable beginning of our expedition, which, it appears, the Adelantado Don Hernando de Soto brought with his good fortune, wherewith to serve in the matter of which he comes in control. Suffice it to say, that he has thought best to look both into the state of the Island and the population, as Your Majesty is informed; but with great toil and cost to himself, as he wished to travel throughout, visiting the towns, which had much need of attention. As well has he been detained, at great expense with his soldiers, longer than he wished, while providing himself, without loss of time, in every particular useful for his conquest, managing aptly in all matters, and setting every thing in complete order.

We inform Your Majesty, that to-day, on the eve of departure, he has large vessels in port, two caravels and two brigantines, in all nine sail, having lost two since our arrival. He carries in them two hundred and thirty-seven horses, besides some of relief; three hundred and thirty foot, as well as those mounted; in all, five hundred and thirteen men, without the sailors. With these go more abundant subsistence than could have been gotten out of Spain for an armada. There are three thousand loads of caçabi, twenty-five hundred shoulders of bacon, and twenty-five hundred hanegas of maize: moreover, there are beasts on hoof for the settlement, and for the butcher, to be in readiness on the return of the vessels, through which we are to receive large supplies. With this object, the Adelantado has bought many grazing farms, at the cost of much money, to be employed solely in affording us sustenance.

In order that Your Majesty may entertain good hopes of that country of Florida, we report, that directly upon our arrival here, in order that Juan de Añasco might go with fifty men to look for some port on the coast, he was elected to be the royal Comptroller; and although he passed through many hardships, because of the winter, he found the most convenient place that could be desired very near, only some seventy-five or eighty leagues from this land, inhabited and very secure. He brought four of the Indians, as interpreters, who are so intelligent that they already understand us, after a manner, and give grand expectations of that country, so much so, that all depart joyfully and contented.

The bearer of this letter is the Captain Hernan Ponçe de Leon, companion of the Adelantado, who has been a witness to all this, and is a person of whom Your Majesty can be informed in whatsoever may most interest you.

We will say no more at present, save that on arriving in the land of Florida, we will, by Divine pleasure, take particular care to give a very long relation of all that shall hereafter occur.

Our Lord guard and increase the S. I. C. life of Your Majesty with augmentation of more and greater kingdoms and lordships, as the servants of Y. M. desire.

From the town of San X^{o}bal of the Havana, the eighteenth day of May, of the year 1539.

From Y. S. I. C. M$^{y's}$

Servants, who your Imperial feet kiss.

JUAN GAYTAN	JNO. DE AÑ ASCO	LUIS FERNANDEZ DE BIEDMA
Rubrica.	*Rubrica.*	*Rubrica.*

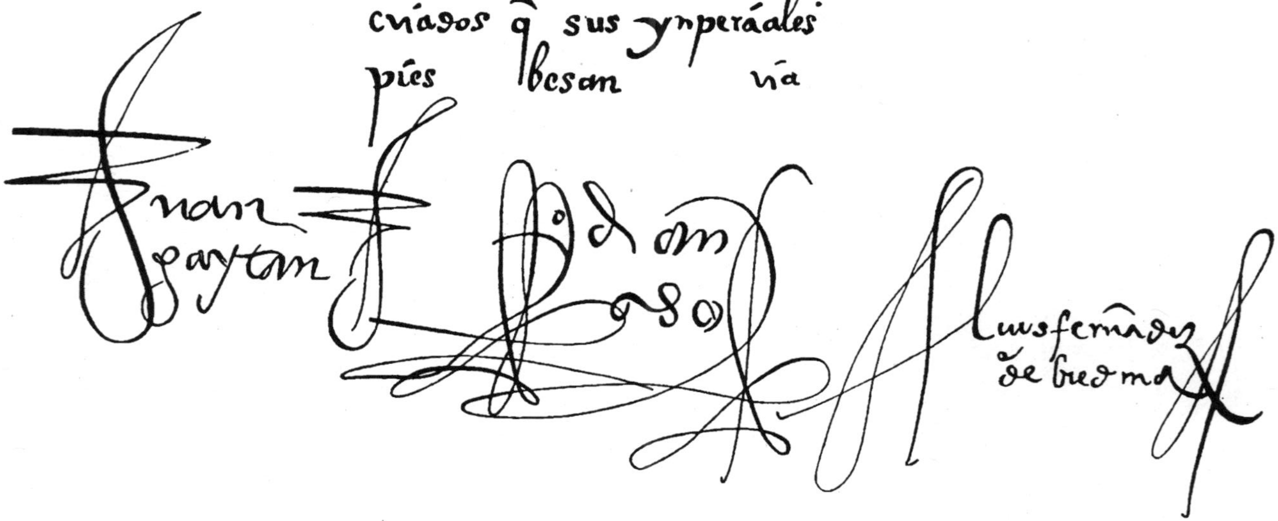

Facsimile of Signatures to Foregoing Document

LETTER OF HERNANDO DE SOTO AT TAMPA BAY TO THE JUSTICE AND BOARD OF MAGISTRATES IN SANTIAGO DE CUBA.

Very Noble Gentlemen:

The being in a new country, not very distant indeed from that where you are, still with some sea between, a thousand years appear to me to have gone by since any thing has been heard from you; and although I left some letters written at Havana, to go off in three ways, it is indeed long since I have received one. However, since opportunity offers by which I may send an account of what it is always my duty to give, I will relate what passes, and I believe will be welcome to persons I know favourably, and are earnest for my success.

I took my departure from Havana with all my armament on Sunday, the XVIIIth of May, although I wrote that I should leave on the XXVth of the month. I anticipated the day, not to lose a favourable wind, which changed, nevertheless, for calms, upon our getting into the Gulf; still these were not so continuous as to prevent our casting anchor on this coast, as we did at the end of eight days, which was on Sunday, the festival of Espiritu Santo.

Having fallen four or five leagues below the port, without any one of my pilots being able to tell where we were, it became necessary that I should go in the brigantines and look for it. In doing so, and in entering the mouth of the port, we were detained three days; and likewise because we had no knowledge of the passage—a bay that runs up a dozen leagues or more from the sea—we were so long delayed that I was obliged to send my Lieutenant-General, Vasco Porcallo de Figueroa, in the brigantines, to take possession of a town at the end of the bay. I ordered all the men and horses to be landed on a beach, whence, with great difficulty, we went on Trinity Sunday to join Vasco Porcallo. The Indians of the coast, because of some fears of us, have abandoned all the country, so that for thirty leagues not a man of them has halted.

At my arrival here I received news of there being a Christian in the possession of a Cacique, and I sent Baltazar de Gallegos, with XL. men of the horse, and as many of the foot, to endeavour to get him. He found the man a day's journey from this place, with eight or ten Indians, whom he brought into my power. We rejoiced no little over him, for he speaks the language; and although he had forgotten his own, it directly returned to him. His name is Juan Ortiz, an hidalgo, native of Sevilla.

In consequence of this occurrence, I went myself for the Cacique, and came back with him in peace. I then sent Baltazar de Gallegos, with eighty lancers, and a hundred foot-soldiers, to enter the country. He has found fields of maize, beans, and pumpkins, with other fruits, and provision in such quantity as would suffice to subsist a very large army without its knowing a want. Having been allowed, without interruption, to reach the town of a Cacique named Urripacoxit, master of the one we are in, also of many other towns, some Indians were sent to him to treat for peace. This, he writes, having been accomplished, the Cacique failed to keep certain promises, whereupon he seized about XVII. persons, among whom are some of the principal men; for in this way, it appears to him, he can best secure a performance. Among those he detains are some old men of authority, as great as can be among such people, who have information of the country farther on. They say that three days' journey from where they are, going by some towns and huts, all well inhabited, and having many maize-fields, is a large town called Acuera, where with much convenience we might winter; and that afterwards, farther on, at the distance of two days' journey, there is another town, called Ocale. It is so large, and they so extol it, that I dare not repeat all that is said. There is to be found in it a great plenty of all the things mentioned; and fowls, a multitude of turkeys, kept in pens, and herds of tame deer that are tended. What this means I do not understand, unless it be the cattle, of which we brought the knowledge with us. They say there are many trades among that people, and much intercourse, an abundance of gold and silver, and many pearls. May it please God that this may be so; for of what these Indians say I believe nothing but what I see, and must well see; although they know, and have it for a saying, that if they lie to me it will cost them their lives. This interpreter puts a new life into us, in affording the means of our understanding these people, for without him I know not what would become of us. Glory be to God, who by His goodness has directed all, so that it appears as if He had taken this enterprise in His especial keeping, that it may be for His service, as I have supplicated, and do dedicate it to Him.

I sent eighty soldiers by sea in boats, and my General by land with XL. horsemen, to fall upon a throng of some thousand Indians, or more, whom Juan de Añasco had discovered. The General got back last night, and states that they fled from him; and although he pursued them, they could not be overtaken, for the many obstructions in the way. On our coming together we will march to join Baltazar de Gallegos, that we may go thence to pass the winter at the Ocale, where, if what is said be true, we shall have nothing to desire. Heaven be pleased that something may come of this that shall be for the service of our Divine Master, and whereby I may be enabled to serve Your Worships, and each of you, as I desire, and is your due.

Notwithstanding my continual occupation here, I am not forgetful of the love I owe to objects at a distance; and since I may not be there in person, I believe that where you, Gentlemen, are, there is little in which my presence can be necessary. This duty weighs upon me more than every other, and for the attentions you will bestow, as befits your goodness, I shall be under great obligations. I enjoin it upon you, to make the utmost exertions to maintain the repose and well-being of the public, with the proper administration of justice, always reposing in the Licentiate, that every thing may be so done in accordance with law, that God and the King may be served, myself gratified, and every one be content and pleased with the performance of his trust, in such a manner as you, Gentlemen, have ever considered for my honour, not less than your own, although I still feel that I have the weight thereof, and bear the responsibility.

As respects the bastion which I left begun, if labouring on it have been neglected, or perhaps discontinued, with the idea that the fabric is not now needed, you, Gentlemen, will favour me by having it finished, since every day brings change; and although no occasion should arise for its employment, the erection is provident for the well-being and safety of the town: an act that will yield me increased satisfaction, through your very noble personages.

That our Lord may guard and increase your prosperity is my wish and your deserving.

In this town and Port of Espiritu Santo, in the Province of Florida, July the IX., in the year 1539.

The servant of you, Gentlemen.

EL ADELANTADO DON HERNANDO DE SOTO.

This document, which exists in copy only, written in a firm, clear hand, is to be found in the *Archivo de Indias,* and doubtless is that which accompanied the letter of the Licentiate Bartolomé Ortiz, dated at Santiago, the eighth day of November, 1539, addressed to the Emperor and Council of the Indias. In it he says:

"Directly as the Governor left here I fell sick in bed, and remained so three months, on which account I could not finish the bastion and bulwark he commenced. * * * It may be a month since the Governor of this Island wrote from the Port of Espiritu Santo to the Board of this City, stating his arrival in Florida, and its occurrences, a copy of which I send. He strongly urges the completion of the bastion at this port, but the magistrates oppose it; and, contrary to my commands, have ordered the assessment to cease, which is necessary for this purpose, and the following up of the wild Indians. * * *"

Notwithstanding the character in which the letter of the Adelantado is copied, the transcript seems to be faulty in omissions, and affords several evident mistakes of words.

LETTER TO CHARLES V FROM THE JUSTICE AND BOARD OF MAGISTRATES OF SANTIAGO DE CUBA, GIVING A STATEMENT OF OCCURRENCES ON THE ISLAND.

[Original in the General Archive of the Indies, Seville.]

On the envelope is written:—

TO THE SACRED IMPERIAL CATHOLIC MAJESTY,

THE EMPEROR KING OUR MASTER.

S. I. C. M.

On the seventh day of June, of the present year, the Adelantado Don Hernando de Soto arrived at this port with five ships, bringing six hundred men for the conquest of Florida. He laid before us a provision bestowing on him the government of this Island, which we receive as favour. Being mindful that he goes to serve Your Majesty in the settlement of that country, his people have been entertained among the inhabitants of the place in the best manner possible, and he now makes ready for his departure. May our Lord guide him thither, and give the success most for His service and that of Your Highness.

According to Your Majesty's command, he presented for his Chief Judge the Licentiate Bartolomé Ortiz, a civilian, long resident in these parts, of whom we hope that he will see the inhabitants receive good treatment, with considerations of justice and honour.

On the 5th of April just past, a French vessel, having seventy-eight men, entered this port, with the intention of robbing the city, at a time when it pleased God there should be found here a vessel belonging to Diego Perez, resident of Sevilla, which opposed her, the two with bombards fighting together a day and night, each killing three or four men for the other, the most of the townspeople in the mean while going to their farmhouses and bringing together their women and property, as in the city there was no military defence or support of any sort. With this resistance, that vessel went out and went off. Now we have news that she sailed to San X°val of the Havana, on this Island, burned all the town, the church inclusive, taking a certain amount in gold, the property of persons deceased, and another of the Crusade, with one hundred and fifty dollars, the proceeds of gate duties, belonging to Your Highness, besides doing other injuries to individuals. When she left this city, they said she would return; and as it may be that these or some other Frenchmen might dare as much, we resolve to make this known to Your Majesty, that the remedy may be applied in affording the protection of some artillery with which to make defence at the wharf, and give that security which a half dozen of large calibre and a dozen culverins we think sufficient to insure. These we beg that Your Highness will order to be sent to us, and the necessary ammunition from the House of Contratacion in Sevilla, with the haste possible; for if this town be burned or destroyed, the Island is ruined, and the injury is great. God will not permit that the Church and other stone edifices shall be consumed. They have cost much to erect, and could not be rebuilt in a long time.

We likewise make known to Your Majesty that, eight months since, twenty or thirty wild natives insurged, and have committed many atrocities, killing Christians, Spaniards, negroes, domestic Indians, and herds, and setting farms on fire. Although this Board has from the first sent a force against them, which killed many, they continue to do harm; and the Adelantado, having got this information, directly upon his arrival in this city sent out a troop of Spaniards, with negroes and tame Indians, at the cost of the assessment we have made here; and having also ordered out another party, from the town of San Salvador, the two are now in their pursuit. We hope these may be overtaken and chastised, that the evil may cease. Nothing has been heard as yet. Since there are no arms here nor on the Island, and standing in much need of some, it will be necessary that Your Highness require that from Sevilla there be provided for us as many as fifty thousand maravedis, the half for crossbows, shafts, strings, and appurtenances, the other half in lances and bucklers. We ask Your Majesty will order that the money be laid out in the Contratacion of Sevilla, and the arms sent to us in the first ship that comes to this city, when directly as they arrive we will pay the royal officers the amount thus spent.

Money has been requisite to make this war upon the Indians, who do so great mischief, and to protect us from the French vessels. The Board, being without any for the purposes, was obliged to raise as many as three hundred dollars gold by assessment of the community. We entreat that Your Majesty be pleased to deem the act properly done, the greater part being paid by the principal persons of the Island; and that, should one or two hundred more be found necessary, Your Highness will favour us by directing that we be authorized and empowered to raise the sum, which, beyond our great obligations, is a necessary measure for the welfare of the land.

From what has been already said, it may be seen how greatly this Island and people need that Your Majesty should order that they be favoured and assisted, lest every thing be lost, and they go away to Florida, Peru, and other parts to find support, which occasion, to many residents, appears to be at hand. Should Your Highness be pleased to permit that all the gold which is got by the Indians and negroes pay the tenth part during seven or eight years, the mines would be sought out and worked unattended by the frauds and deceptions practised at the time of melting the metal, many perjuring themselves in statements that it is got by the negroes, when it is procured by Indians. So small is the quantity obtained, because of the hindrance, that it does not annually amount to thirteen thousand dollars; and, making this concession, every one would strive to discover mines, and not cease to look after gold, as many have done, to engage in fields of other labour and pursuits, whence the income of Your Majesty is less, and the inhabitants continue very poor.

We entreat that it may serve Your Highness to command this favour: that a stone fortress be directed to be built in the Havana; and all the citizens of this place, with the residents, beseech that, in consideration of the want also here of one for defence, it serve you to direct that a fortress be built at this port, to be a permanency in the Island, so that, though many French vessels come, it may be able successfully to prevent their entrance here. This fabric would be the avoidance of many evils, put the inhabitants in heart to remain and settle here; or otherwise, Your Majesty may be assured that this city is in danger of being pillaged and burned, whenever it is the disposition of the French that it should.

The Bishop of the Island arrived here ten or twelve days after the Adelantado came; consequently we have rejoiced much, his presence giving us great consolation, and we trusting in God that it will be very profitable, both for the Island and its inhabitants. As he writes to Your Majesty, nothing remains to be said more than refer to what he states.

Sacred I. C. Majesty our Master. Be the Imperial person of Your Majesty preserved, and your dominion enlarged, as we your vassals desire.

From the City of Santiago, of the Island of Fernandina, the XXVI. day of July, of the year 1539.

From Y. S. I. C. Majesty's humble vassals, who kiss your royal feet and hands.

Juan de la Torre.
Ino. Armansa.
Lope Hurtado.
Andres Parada.
Thoribio de Castro.

By order of the Justice and Board of Magistrates:

X°val de Torres,
Notary Public, and of the Board.

El Adelantado Don Hernando de Soto

by Rocío Sánchez Rubio
Translated by Eduardo Kortright

Dra. Rocío Sánchez Rubio is a native of Badajoz. She is currently at the University of Extremadura. Her research interest is the emigration of Extremadurans to the New World in the sixteenth century. The following biographical sketch of De Soto was published in Spain in 1988 as Number 25 in the *Cuadernos Populares* series of the Junta de Extremadura.

This essay gives a good capsulized version of the life of Hernando de Soto and presents the Spanish point of view of the conquest. It is a point of view that allows for the expression of regional and national pride in the lives and accomplishments of the conquistadors. But it does not cover up the flaws of men such as De Soto, whose character encompassed as many notes of cruelty and caprice as of courage and nobility.

This essay should be read as a counterpoint to the immediately following biography of De Soto by Paul Hoffman, a senior American historian with much experience in the field. Yet the spirit and verve of Rocío Sánchez Rubio's article catches well the spirit and nature of the conquistador class, men, such as Hernando de Soto, who helped elevate Spain to a world-class power in the sixteenth century.

The finer points of modern archaeological debate—such as where exactly the De Soto *entrada* passed through the American Southeast and what was the effect of the Spanish expedition on Native American peoples—are addressed in this essay only in passing, if at all. However, for those wishing a general perspective on De Soto, his life and times, this is an informative place to begin.

The Conquistador

Like all human endeavors, the Spanish conquest of America was filled with "lights and shadows." Its principal figures have been caught between the Black Legend on the one hand and blind heroic adoration on the other, yet they deserve to be seen as they actually were: men of their times. Only in this way can a truly critical history of their accomplishments be written.

Despite the fact that the conquest was a collective event, individuals—the triumph of the hero—stand out from the rest. The common features that characterized these men allow us to talk of a "Generation of the Conquista." Born between 1474 and 1504, they left for America very young, issuing mostly from Andalusia, Castille, and Extremadura; second-born sons of the petty nobility, impoverished noblemen and commoners, their social and cultural origins were diverse.

Their heyday was between 1510 and 1545, coinciding with the reign of Emperor Charles V. Religious by conviction, their sword served not only the king, but also served God. They became divine instruments, waging a holy war that closely paralleled the one against the Turks during the same period.

They gained experience in the Antilles and became acclimated there before making the great leap to the mainland. The vast continents of the Americas were marked by diverse climates, topography, vegetation, and fauna, as well as sharp contrasts in the customs, attitudes, and rituals of their inhabitants. The constant challenges that the New World offered these conquistadors called for remarkable powers of adaptation. Through their efforts they learned to respect this new world they trod upon.

With few resources and lacking names or reputations, they left the Peninsula seeking honor, fame, and social and economic betterment in the New World. The great figures of the conquest were virtually unknown when they began their journeys to America. In their ambition and desire to stand out above others, they often refused to place themselves directly under the patronage of either the king's representatives or the leading captains. They did appeal to the monarch, but only to seek those offices and titles needed to undertake new adventures of conquest. Conflicts and lawsuits brought about by disputes over jurisdictional authority multiplied among the conquistadors, and these struggles for control of the subdued territories sometimes ended tragically.

Without financial support from the crown, they personally financed every new expedition. If too expensive for one, they often formed partnerships. In exchange, they shared overseeing and recruiting the members of the expedition, and the parties tacitly agreed to share the benefits obtained. Thus, the conquest was primarily the fruit of private enterprise.

In the following pages we will reconstruct the life of Hernando de Soto, a representative example of the Spanish conquistador. Many of the above-mentioned characteristics and circumstances can be applied to this Extremaduran. This is the story of a conquistador, a man whose life followed the knife edge between glory and failure; it was a life filled not only with wealth, triumph, and satisfaction, but also with toil, want, and suffering.

> The adelantado Hernando de Soto was . . . of more than medium build, of a very good appearance, looked well on foot and on horseback, he was of cheerful countenance, dark in color, skillful on both saddles, and more on the genet than the bridle. He was extremely patient in toil and in need, so much so that seeing the patience and suffering of their Captain General was his soldiers' greatest comfort in the midst of their own afflictions.
>
> He was fortunate in the individual journeys that he himself undertook, although not in the principal one, for life failed him at the greatest moment. . . . He was severe in punishing military misdemeanors; others he pardoned easily. He honored soldiers greatly, those who were virtuous and courageous. He was most courageous, so much that wherever he went he entered the fighting in pitched battle; he cleared the way with room enough for ten of his own to pass, and so they all admitted: that ten lances from all his army were not worth as much as his.
>
> This brave captain had in war a notable and most memorable trait, —in the sudden attacks that the enemy visited on his camp, by day he was always the first or second to go out in arms, and never third; and in those by night he never was the second, but always the first to appear having readied himself to go out [before retiring]. The alarm he always gave himself.
>
> —The Inca, Garcilaso de la Vega

Controversy over De Soto's Birth

Biographers are often frustrated by the lack of good documentation. Either the relevant documentation has not survived, or the existing sources contain contradictions, or both. The birth and childhood of people who later gained fame are often obscure. Such is the case with Hernando de Soto. Leonor Arias Tinoco, a native of Badajoz, gave birth to him some time between 1495 and 1500; the exact date is not known, since, in the Castille of the late fifteenth century, parish records were not regularly kept. These only became widespread after the Council of Trent in 1545.

Determining the place of De Soto's birth is even more problematic than fixing its date. As with many who figured prominently in the discovery and conquest of the New World—for example, another illustrious Extremaduran, Pedro de Valdivia, and even the great discoverer, Christopher Columbus—the uncertainty about De Soto's birthplace has given rise to polemics and disagreements. Three towns contend for the honor of being considered the birthplace of the Adelantado de la Florida: Jerez de los Caballeros, Barcarrota (formerly Villanueva de Barcarrota), and, to a lesser extent, Badajoz. We owe the confusion to three chroniclers who portray him as having been born in each of the above-mentioned places: Pedro Pizarro, the Fidalgo de Elvas, and the Inca, Garcilaso de la Vega. The first two were contemporaries of De Soto, and the third was not far removed from the events of his life.

Pedro Pizarro recorded the conquest of Peru, where Hernando de Soto played a significant role, and he identifies Badajoz as De Soto's birthplace. The Fidalgo de Elvas, who accompanied the *adelantado* in the expedition to Florida, declares De Soto a native of Jerez de los Caballeros, where his father, Francisco Méndez de Soto, was born. Finally, the Inca, Garcilaso, relates in his *Crónica sobre la conquista de la Florida:* "The adelantado Hernando de Soto . . . was a native of Villanueva de Barcarrota."

Over time, different authors have adopted the views of one or another of these three sixteenth-century chroniclers, so that each option gained a certain following. In the end, Garcilaso's view emerged as the most popular.

There are other important documents related to De Soto in the Archivo Histórico Nacional of Madrid and in the Archivo General de Indias of Seville. The first of these preserves the adelantado's papers of admission into the Order of Santiago. That honor was conferred upon De Soto by the king when the conquistador left for Florida, as a reward for the many services he had rendered. The heading of this document reads: "Santiago 1537. The adelantado Hernando de Soto, a native of *Xerez* . . . " [emphasis added]. The file includes the testimony of several persons who declared that they knew De Soto and his ancestors. While they mention his nobility and his more or less protracted stays in Badajoz, all of them confirm that Jerez was his birthplace. The Sevillan archives contain the last will and testament that Hernando signed on May 13, 1539, in San Cristóbal de la Habana, a few days before beginning the expedition to Florida. In it he made several bequests that were ultimately to be carried out in Jerez. Moreover, he stated his wish to be buried alongside his parents in the Church of San Miguel in Jerez. There can be no doubt that his ties to Jerez must have been important, whether he was born there or not.

But there are also arguments in favor of Barcarrota that lend credibility to that town's claims. De Soto's parents frequently traveled between Jerez and

Badajoz, spending the first years of their marriage in these two towns. However, it is difficult to believe that the bond between the conquistador and Barcarrota could have developed solely from such happenstance, especially when we consider the enthusiastic response among its inhabitants in enlisting for the expedition to Florida. And the honor and glory claimed by Barcarrota as the birthplace of Hernando de Soto is not lacking in concrete symbols; Barcarrotians still feel proud to preserve the house where their renowned son once "lived." The frequent contacts between this town and the "Society of Knights of Bradenton" in Florida, who annually travel from Florida to Barcarrota to commemorate De Soto, help to reinforce this belief. The meetings, colorful and picturesque, commemorate the expedition 450 years ago when the conquistador and a few hundred Spaniards landed on the coast of Florida to begin their memorable endeavor. These reunions also keep intact Barcarrota's claim to fame as the birthplace of the adelantado.

Whatever the place of his birth, De Soto was indisputably from Extremadura. Like him, many Extremadurans, some of them well known and written about (Pizarro, Cortés, Alvarado, Valdivia, Orellana, Balboa . . . and others, unfortunately anonymous), abandoned their homeland and undertook a great endeavor in search of the fame and fortune that were in such short supply in Extremadura, but so invitingly available to the bold and daring in the New World.

Encounter with the New World

If Hernando de Soto's birth is obscure, the first years of his life are impenetrable. The son of a noble family, though of modest means, his childhood was spent on horseback between Badajoz and Jerez de los Caballeros, accompanied by his three siblings: Catalina, María, and Juan Méndez de Soto. We do not know what sort of education he received; nevertheless, he must have been familiar with the "teachings" and rumors about America that circulated during his childhood and adolescence.

From the moment when Columbus first returned from the New World, a fascination with this exotic, unknown region spread through Castille. An expedition to the isthmus of Panama by another Extremaduran, Vasco Núñez de Balboa, opened the doors to the immense territory still to be discovered and to legends of wealthy kingdoms farther south. Balboa's expedition began in Nuestra Señora La Antigua, a town that Balboa himself founded on the coast of Darién (now Panama), and ended when he reached the South Seas—the name given to the Pacific Ocean. The Indians encountered during his trip across the isthmus all pointed Balboa to the existence of a great people to the south, possessing immense riches.

Pedrarias's Expedition

The reports brought back by the discoverer of the South Seas prompted King Ferdinand to organize a great expedition. His first measure was to name Pedro Arias de Avila governor and captain general of Castilla del Oro, the suggestive name given to this country, which captured the aura of wealth created by Balboa's reports. The offices granted to this native of Segovia, better known as Pedrarias Dávila, gave him the power to organize, subdue, and colonize the new territories. He was to settle in the Darién, in the aforementioned Nuestra Señora La Antigua.

Rumors of the wealth that could be obtained by participating in the expedition spread throughout Spain and proved very powerful in attracting volunteers. Besides the potential wealth offered by that part of the world, there were the many recompenses and benefices that the Catholic king would grant to anyone willing to embark in order to populate and colonize Castilla del Oro. The concessions of land, houses, and mansions, the right to participate in the apportionment of Indians, the exploitation of mines, the exemption from taxes and tariffs—these, among other privileges, facilitated the preparations. Hundreds of Castillians, blinded by the promises of wealth, rushed to enlist. Among those, still an adolescent, was Hernando de Soto. The resources deployed (twenty-five ships), the participating contingent (around two thousand people), and the direct involvement of the crown, which paid for and organized the preparations to the last detail, made this expedition unique in the history of America. This is even more striking if we consider that later enterprises involving discovery, conquest, or colonization were of a private nature; they were financed by the conquistadors themselves, the sovereign limiting himself to the legal recognition of the new possessions.

The expedition left San Lúcar de Barrameda on April 11, 1514; with De Soto traveled a group of individuals who, like him, gained renown in the conquest and exploration of the American continent: Bernal Díaz del Castillo (chronicler of the conquest of Peru), Diego de Almagro, Sebastián de Benalcázar, Hernando Luque, Gonzalo Fernández de Oviedo, and Pascual de Andagoya, to name but a few.

When the fleet arrived at La Antigua on June 29, Pedrarias Dávila took possession of the governorship of Castilla del Oro. Unfortunately, this site, which three months earlier had been idealized and had seemed a kind of paradise, turned out to be a veritable hell. The small colony was soon overwhelmed by this influx of adventurers from the Peninsula. Food soon became scarce, and the situation turned terribly critical. The words of Fernández de Oviedo, a direct witness of these events, are eloquent. He described the colony's experience and the prevailing atmosphere: "The men [were] starving in the streets. . . . Every day fifteen or twenty of them died . . . and in a short time more than five hundred men died. . . . Some returned to Spain and others moved to these our islands Española and Cuba and Jamaica and San Juan. . . . Those who died or departed were more numerous than those who were left in the land."

The Attainment of a Name

Hernando de Soto's early arrival in the New World allowed him to begin his brilliant military career by witnessing and participating in many different attempts at expansion into the lands of Central America.

In order to alleviate the difficult circumstances enveloping the small colony, Governor Pedrarias ordered incursions into the northern as well as the southern parts of the Darién. The expeditions to the south paved the way for the campaign that the Extremaduran (Trujillo) Francisco Pizarro launched years later to conquer the coveted Inca empire. De Soto must have figured in one of these expansionary incursions, especially given his ability as a rider, since the governor named him "Captain of the men on horseback." Other testimonies remain of his excellence in the saddle; the Inca Garcilaso de la Vega described him as "skillful on both saddles, and more on the genet than the bridle," later calling him "one of the best lances that have come to the New World, and few as good and none better, unless it were that of Gonzalo Pizarro." A famous episode occurred during the conquest of Peru when he used his skill as a rider to impress the Inca emperor, Atahualpa.

Bearing the title of captain, he must have been an eyewitness to the stormy relations between Pedrarias Dávila and Vasco Núñez de Balboa, as well as to the tragic end of their confrontations.

The quarrels between these men began with the arrival of the governor in La Antigua. They settled on a short truce in 1516 after the marriage by proxy of Balboa and María, Pedrarias's daughter. However, the truce was broken by Pedrarias, who accused Balboa of taking advantage of his title (as a reward for his services, the king had named Balboa adelantado of the South Seas and general of two provinces—he was still subject to the governor's authority, however), and that Balboa, furthermore, was infringing upon his jurisdiction by usurping the crown's land. Charged with treason and condemned to death, Vasco Núñez was executed in January of 1519.

After the death of Balboa, the center of operations was moved to Nuestra Señora de la Asunción de Panamá, a city founded by Pedrarias when he realized that movement to both the north and south would be more feasible from the Pacific Coast. Very soon this city, the first to be founded on the Pacific Ocean, replaced Nuestra Señora de La Antigua as the capital of Castilla del Oro. From here De Soto embarked on expeditions where—without yet playing a prominent role—he performed brilliant acts that increased his fame and merit in the eyes of the governor and his comrades. In the most significant episode, he personally rescued Master Espinosa, a lawyer, from the Indians during an expedition led by De Soto and Francisco Pizarro, which in 1520 attempted to expand the colony toward the territories of Costa Rica and Veragua.

Four years later Hernando was one of the captains under Francisco Hernández de Córdoba, whom Pedrarias had entrusted with the conquest of Nicaragua. De Soto again had the opportunity to demonstrate his personal loyalty to Pedrarias.

Hernández de Córdoba, after advancing without difficulty and having founded several towns and cities (León, Granada) in Nicaragua, tried to dissociate himself from the government of Castilla del Oro. He petitioned the king to make him the governor of Nicaragua; however, he found that the majority of his troops opposed him, including De Soto, who was imprisoned. He was freed by Captain Francisco Compañón, a lifelong friend of his. Together they returned to Panama and informed the governor of the chief expeditionary's behavior. Hernández de Córdoba was later executed in León, a city which he founded.

This display of absolute fidelity to Pedrarias increased De Soto's popularity to the point that the future adelantado of Florida began to become known outside the American territories. This, added to his participation in the expansion of Castilla del Oro throughout the Central American region, earned him prestige and respect in courtly circles. When he returned to Castille from Isla de La Española in 1526, Charles V could not find a better ambassador to send to Lisbon to rescue Gonzalo Gómez de Espinosa. This man, along with others, had accompanied Juan Sebastian Elcano in his voyage of circumnavigation, and they had been imprisoned by the Portuguese and lost their ship.

We do not know the outcome of his trip nor of his negotiations, nor do we know the date of his return to America. In 1529, De Soto was in Nicaragua again, where he lived as one of the richest and most influential inhabitants of León. This did not last long, however. Rarely were such men satisfied with the status gained at any given moment. They frequently exchanged the comfort and luxury that their previous expeditions had yielded for the privations, discomfort, and possible death that accompanied a new endeavor. Their desire for fame and greater riches drove them to invest their belongings in new expeditions. In 1531, Hernando de Soto participated in the final drive to conquer the Inca empire, an endeavor that up to that time had cost a great deal of effort.

The Conquest of Peru

The first years of Castilla del Oro were dominated by constant attempts to expand toward the south. In that direction lay the kingdom that, according to Panamanian Indians, possessed fabulous wealth. It was not until Asunción de Panamá was founded on the Pacific that access to Peru was made possible.

Following the failed expedition by Pascual de Andagoya in 1522, Francisco Pizarro, an Extremaduran (Trujillo) who had arrived in the Indies in 1502 and distinguished himself militarily under Pedrarias, began his incursions in 1524. He formed a partnership with Diego de Almagro, a native of La Mancha, and the Andalusian cleric Hernando Luque. After two unsuccessful attempts, the reticence and obstacles placed in Pizarro's path by Governor Pedrarias, by then an old man, became too much for him. He returned to Spain and received express authorization from the emperor: in 1530, by means of an agreement signed in Toledo, Pizarro was entrusted with the conquest of Peru and was named governor, captain general, and adelantado. Accompanied by his brothers and several contingents of Extremadurans, he returned to Panama to begin the preparations.

In order to launch an enterprise of that caliber, Pizarro had to seek people willing to participate in the expedition, and to risk their possessions and capital. Since Hernán Ponce de León was a member of the Pizarro group, it is only natural that his longtime friend, Hernando de Soto, was also included; the pair formed a partnership, agreeing to divide between them the profits obtained in battle. In this way, De Soto abandoned the privileges and comfort of León and was granted, through Ponce's exertions, the most important subordinate position in the army that embarked for Peru. In addition, he was promised that he would be made the lord of the first large town to be conquered.

Peru

All of the territory that lay to the south of Panama, beyond the Gulf of San Miguel, was known as Birú, Pirú, or Perú. The Tahuantinsuyu—a name used by the Incas to refer to their dominions—included today's Peru, Bolivia, Ecuador, and a part of northern Chile.

The Inca empire was forged from different tribes of the Quechua race and culture that originated in the Altiplano and Lake Titicaca. The Incas founded their capital in Cuzco, and from this city they expanded outward, subduing the length and breadth of Peru, Ecuador, and Bolivia. The expansion, which took place in less than two centuries, respected the traditions of each conquered tribe; however, the vastness of the territory and its topography were not propitious for political unity, and constant crises and conflicts drove the ruling caste to maintain an authoritarian and centralized regime.

Of the approximately eight million persons in Tahuantinsuyu, the inhabitants of the northern lands were the most troublesome. They were the last to be assimilated by the empire, and the political, economic, and social structures that the Incas tried to impose on them did not take root there.

At the time that the Spaniards began the conquest of Peru, the empire was experiencing its gravest crisis ever: the problem of dynastic succession. Upon the death of Huayna Capac, the last Great Inca, the unity of the empire was shattered by two of his children: Huáscar and Atahualpa. The first was the legitimate heir, since he was a *coya*'s son, that is, a queen's son. He controlled the greater part of the empire with the support of virtually the entire nobility of Cuzco. Atahualpa, the son of a *ñusta,* or royal maid, settled with his followers in Quito. Civil war was inevitable, and Atahualpa emerged victorious in the struggle when he took Huáscar prisoner. He proclaimed himself the only Inca and received the imperial *lauto*, a symbol of sovereignty.

Conditions That Favored the Conquest

The Spanish endeavors in the New World during the sixteenth century have been frequently characterized as heroic, and their principal figures have been elevated to the rank of demigods. Without belittling the daring and valor that they demonstrated, we have to admit that terms such as hero, feat, epic, geste, prowess, etc., so often used in relating the story of the conquest can be replaced in many instances by strategist, military expert, diplomacy, cleverness, and ability. These words give a more human dimension to the history of those events.

In the case of the conquest of Peru, it is unthinkable to suppose that a few hundred Spaniards could have single-handedly subdued a great and vast empire such as that of the Incas. The empire possessed an army of potentially thousands of male subjects, ready at any moment for the draft.

The conquistadors skillfully capitalized on the strife among the descendants of Huayna Capac. Pizarro, for example, gained the assistance of the defeated Huáscar's followers, who were the sworn enemies of Atahualpa. In a similar fashion, Pizarro won over different peoples under the control of the Incas who were discontented over the domination and demands by their Inca conquerors. In their view of things, the Spaniards were coming to liberate them from the yoke of the Incas. They expressed this belief at the mythological level as they identified the strangers with the "messengers of Viracocha," the emissaries of the god that created the world. Like that supreme being, the foreigners wore beards and had emerged from the waters (the ocean) where the god Viracocha had disappeared a long time before. Their reappearance could only mean one thing: the messengers would carry out the divine vengeance and would defeat the destroyers of the empire.

A similar situation arose during the conquest of Mexico. Hernán Cortés took advantage of the Indians' image of him as a demigod to establish his authority in the Aztec empire. In addition, he received help from the natives, who were tired of submission to the Aztecs, whom they viewed as their oppressors.

These circumstances, together with the weapons and horses they brought, gave the conquistadors the element of surprise that they needed to gain the fear and respect of the local people. However, as the Indians perceived that the newcomers suffered and died just like them and were therefore merely human, they gradually became less vulnerable to their initial beliefs. Yet, one must praise the Spaniards' effort and courage at times like these, alone in those unknown, inhospitable, and hostile places.

The Arrival of the Spaniards in Peru

On board three ships obtained for them by Hernán Ponce de León, the expedition led by Francisco Pizarro and Diego de Almagro embarked, heading south. It was January of 1531, and the group consisted of 180 soldiers, three friars, and thirty-seven horses.

Almost two years went by before Francisco Pizarro penetrated the land in Peru to which he had been named governor. The expedition, some of its members advancing by land and others by sea, reached Coyoacan. At this point it was determined that De Soto should return to Panama to recruit new contingents of troops. No problems were foreseen in the enlistment of men, given the riches that everyone expected to find. De Soto, having obtained some reinforcements, rejoined the ranks of the scouting expedition on the island of Puná, where the natives had killed some of the members of the expedition. According to the historian Diego de Trujillo, the first Spanish woman to tread on that soil was among the persons that arrived with Hernando de Soto; her name was Juana Hernández.

They all marched together until reaching Túmbez, the gateway to Peru, where they learned of the civil war then engulfing the empire. Advancing through the Tangarara Valley, the favorable terrain encouraged the Spaniards to found their first city, giving it the name San Miguel; it would later be moved to the Piura River valley, and would be known from then on as San Miguel de Piura. Other cities were established along their trajectory, always with a twofold purpose: to secure the colonization and, above all, to serve as bases or platforms from which new incursions could be launched.

Of the land conquered thus far, Hernando de Soto received the district and lordship of Túmbez. The promise made to him at the beginning of the expedition was thus fulfilled.

After five months in San Miguel, they left a detachment in that city as a base for their rear guard. They turned toward Cajamarca, near where the emperor Atahualpa was stationed with a large army. The Spanish troops numbered fewer than 180 men, and more than half did not have horses. Hernando de Soto, commanding forty soldiers, was sent on a reconnaissance mission into the mountains. De Soto and his scouts experienced *soroche,* the sickness of the high Andes caused by the altitude and the lack of oxygen. A number of De Soto's companions have left us a record of how, after crossing several localities, they came to a town called Caxas. Diego de Trujillo depicted their arrival and sojourn in this spot.

I went with him . . . and after twenty leagues we came upon a town called Caxas . . . and in it was one of Atabalipa's captains, with more than two thousand Indian warriors. And there were in that town three houses for secluded women who were called *mamaconas*. And since we entered and the women were taken out to the plaza, there were more than five hundred of them, and the captain gave many of them to the Spaniards, the captain of the Inca was greatly outraged and said: How dare you do this with Atabalipa staying twenty leagues from here?, because not one of you will remain alive. Then captain De Soto wrote to the governor about everything that was happening and about that Indian's arrogance. The governor responded that they should endure all his arrogance and we should lead him to believe that we were afraid of him. And so we brought him to Caruán, where everything about Atabalipa and his whereabouts became known.

Knowing where the Inca was stationed, Pizarro's armies continued their difficult march toward Cajamarca. "The going was so bad," wrote Hernando Pizarro, "that we would have made an easy match for them . . . , because even by making displays of ability we couldn't use the horses on the trail, and leaving the road rendered everyone, both on horseback and on foot, unstable and ineffective." The expedition halted for a few days in a town near Cajamarca. The chroniclers of the conquest of Peru give differing accounts of Atahualpa's reaction to the proximity of the Spaniards. According to some, the Inca was afraid, supposedly because it appeared that the prophecy of the arrival of the "children of the sun" was being fulfilled. In a more probable account, the emperor's attitude is portrayed as firm and menacing, since he was well aware of the small size of the foreign contingent advancing toward him. Even so, we may suppose that he felt some misgivings, although his position as emperor would not allow him to show them.

Encounter with Atahualpa and His Imprisonment

On November 15, 1532, the Cajamarca Valley lay at their feet. Far away, very near the baths at Konof, where hot springs still gush forth, they could see Atahualpa's encampment. The amazement and the impression that this sight caused was captured by Hernando Pizarro: "The Indians' camp looked like a very beautiful city. There were such a number of tents before our eyes that we all felt gripped by apprehension. We never would have imagined that the Indians could make a display of so much order, or possess such a number of tents and such magnificent ones. Until then nothing like it had been seen in the Indies, and despite the size of our Spanish army, the spectacle filled us with fear and confusion."

That same afternoon, once settled in Cajamarca, Pizarro sent Hernando de Soto as an ambassador; the Extremaduran thus became the first Castillian official to set eyes on Atahualpa. Francisco de Jerez, De Soto's companion, describes the meeting in his account of the conquest of Peru: "And the tyrant was at the door of his abode, sitting in a low seat and many Indians before him and women standing, almost surrounding him; and he had a woolen tassel that looked like silk . . . tied to his head with its cords . . . his eyes fixed on the ground without raising them to look anywhere."

Impatiently, the governor sent a second group, headed by his brother Hernando. The Inca's interview with the two Spanish captains has been described often enough, but the moment stands out when Atahualpa offered the governor's brother a cup of chicha: Hernando requested another for De Soto, stating that he was worthy of the same treatment. The emperor promised to approach Cajamarca the following day, and De Soto, before leaving, took part in a scene that impressed the Indian armies and Atahualpa himself: "A captain, Hernando de Soto, brought a small trained horse. . . . He exercised it about gracefully for a bit. The nag was spirited, foaming much at the mouth, at which, on seeing the rapidity with which it revolved, he (Atahualpa) marveled, although the people expressed more admiration among themselves. There was a great murmur, and a squadron of persons, seeing that the horse was coming towards them, drew back [the Indians had never seen a horse before]; which, those who did so paid for it that night with their lives because Atabalipa had them killed, because they had shown fear."

When the ambassadors returned, Pizarro and his men realized how untenable their situation was. They were eyewitnesses to the greatness, the resources, and the degree of organization of their enemies. It was then that Pizarro thought of capturing Atahualpa. He attempted to imitate Cortés, whose campaign in Mexico against the Aztecs had included the imprisonment of Moctezuma. Pizarro hoped that once he had been captured, the Inca's army would crumble and with it the empire.

The next day, in the midst of great pomp, Atahualpa headed for Cajamarca. The procession caused considerable admiration and made a great impression on the Spaniards. Father Valverde was chosen to read before the Inca a pronouncement whereby the Indians were required to accept the sovereignty of the Spanish monarchs and the true faith. Pizarro, like so many other expedition leaders of his generation, did not consider himself an intruder in Peru. Invoking the legitimacy of his titles, he was certain that those territories belonged to him, and that Atahualpa was obliged to obey his authority. As we can imagine, the emperor did not understand one word of the cleric's speech. He demanded that everything taken by the Spaniards since they entered his dominions be returned. Valverde offered him a Bible. Atahualpa, after turning its pages, threw it to the ground, extremely irritated, and the Spaniards then sprang their trap. They began to fire on Atahualpa's retinue while the cavalry charged into the plaza. Atahualpa's companions fled, unable to react from fear of the animals and of the noise and fire issuing from the weapons. The emperor was made a prisoner in a few moments.

During his captivity, Atahualpa maintained his status of emperor, still carrying out the functions of an absolute monarch. He was allowed to surround himself with the members of his court who had not been killed in the attack. The chroniclers, amazed by the ceremonies that accompanied all his acts, have left us a description of the rituals of his daily life.

Hernando de Soto and Hernando Pizarro became regular members of the Inca's coterie and held long conversations with him. Antonio de Herrera confirms this and describes the friendly and conciliatory climate that existed in the Spanish encampment: "Captain Hernando de Soto was one of those whom Atahualpa liked the most. Everyone tried to please him and found his conversation entertaining, because he had learned to play chess and throw dice and spoke admirably and asked witty and ingenious questions."

As the days of his captivity went by, Atahualpa observed the Spaniards' interest in precious metals. He offered, in exchange for his freedom, to fill the room where he was imprisoned with gold and silver in the space of forty days. Using safe conduct passes issued by the Inca, several of the Spanish captains crisscrossed Peru, gathering the precious metals. The ransom was never completely collected, since after some time Almagro proposed that they divide among themselves the riches obtained so far. Hernando de Soto was among those who benefited most from the division; his share amounted to about eighteen thousand gold pesos and eight hundred silver marks, an immense sum at that time.

Meanwhile, Atahualpa had his brother Huáscar killed, because he was afraid that Pizarro would enter into negotiations with him. The Spaniards used this act, together with false accusations of conspiracy, to condemn the emperor to death.

Death of Atahualpa and Entry into Cuzco

Once the ransom was divided, Hernando Pizarro was sent back to Spain. He was to report on the progress of the conquest and to deliver the king's fifth, for one-fifth of all the wealth obtained in the conquest belonged to the royal treasury and had to be deposited in the House of Trade of Seville as a mandatory tax. While the governor's brother returned to the Peninsula, Hernando de Soto was sent on a reconnaissance mission. The absence of both men, who were considered the Inca's best friends, has prompted certain authors to suggest that a premeditated plan existed to eliminate any possible defense for Atahualpa. Perhaps. In any case, the Spaniards charged the emperor with treason, believing that the army in Quito was preparing to attack them upon his command (these rumors later proved to have no basis in fact). The emperor was indicted and condemned to death, the sentence being carried out on July 26, 1533. Not all the Castillians were pleased by the execution; several of the chroniclers actually criticized it and questioned its legality. And even in Spain, in certain courtly circles, some regret became apparent over what was felt to have been an unwise decision.

With Atahualpa dead, anarchy spread. To prevent this, a new Inca had to be named, and the choice fell to Tupac Huallpa, another of Huayna Capac's sons.

The Spaniards had been in Cajamarca for eight months before the conquest of Peru began to roll again. With the aid of some of the Indians—mostly Quechua followers of the dead Huáscar—they began the march toward Cuzco, the capital of the empire. Advancing through Huamachuco, Andamarca, and Huaylá, they reached Jauja on October 11, where the newly elected Inca died. By then they were so close to Cuzco that De Soto was sent to reconnoiter the way, commanding a cavalry platoon. It was on this mission that he was violently attacked by the armies from Quito. Had it not been for Almagro's intervention, the attack could have cost him his life.

On November 14, 1533, the Spaniards and the Quechuas made their entrance into the capital. They were met with a display of gratitude from the inhabitants, who believed that the Castillians had come to avenge Huáscar and to restore the empire. It was here that Manco Inca Yupanqui, another of Huayna Capac's sons, was crowned emperor. Francisco Pizarro named Hernando de Soto lieutenant governor of the city of Cuzco as a reward for services rendered.

In this way the Spaniards took possession of the Inca empire. The sovereigns—Atahualpa and Huáscar—who had caused the civil war were dead; the armies from Quito were retreating; and the new sovereign, a survivor of the royal family, was agreeable to Spanish interests. The conquistadors spread through the territory, founding cities and completing the conquest.

Hernando de Soto's last action in Peru was to participate in the founding of Pizarro's new capital city of Lima in 1535. A year later he was on his way to Spain. We can be certain that he already had the adventure of Florida in mind.

Return to Spain

Hernando de Soto returned to Spain in 1536. He accomplished two things during his stay on the Peninsula: he married Isabel de Bobadilla, and he obtained the capitulación for the conquest of Florida.

The prestige and fortune he had obtained in the New World allowed him to make an alliance with one of the oldest Castillian families. De Soto married Isabel de Bobadilla, daughter of the renowned governor of Castilla del Oro, Pedro Arias de Avila, by then dead. The indenture for the dowry, preserved in the Archivo General de Indias, was granted in Valladolid on November 14, 1536; in it are enumerated all the possessions that Pedrarias's daughter brought to the union. The indenture, signed by her mother, by Isabel de Bobadilla, and by De Soto himself, reads as follows:

> . . . I give you and promise you as a dowry with said Ysabel de Bobadilla, my daughter . . . all the bovine cattle with their offspring that remained from said governor, my lord and husband in Panama, on the Mainland, with all his cattle and the slaves that tend it and the mares that accompany said cattle. . . .
>
> Likewise, I want him to have the totality of said cattle and herds that the convent and monastery of the devout house of Señor Santo Domingo, outside the city of Piedrahita, ceded in my favor, by reason of the habit and profession made and taken by fray Francisco de Bobadilla, my son, in said monastery. . . .
>
> . . . and I, said captain Hernando de Soto, who am present, concede and acknowledge by the present letter that I accept and receive this abovementioned contract and promise and obligate myself, said dowry having been given and delivered to me, to consider it . . . as the dowry of said doña Ysabel de Bobadilla, my spouse and wife. . . .

The belongings mentioned in the letter of dowry undoubtedly added to the great personal fortune that Hernando de Soto had already amassed in the conquest of Central America and Peru, allowing him to finance the expedition he was planning.

The Capitulación of la Florida

On April 20, 1537, in Valladolid, the king signed the agreement that granted Hernando de Soto the right to conquer and settle Florida. Years earlier, the same privileges had been given first to Pánfilo de Narváez, and after that to Lucas Vázquez de Ayllón.

The document, preserved in the Archivo General de Indias, stipulated the various conditions that were to be met for the proper completion of the expedition. The capitulación begins by expressing the esteem and trust that the monarch placed in De Soto, who by his earlier campaigns had amply demonstrated his ability to perform tasks of this nature: "Inasmuch as you, Captain Hernando de Soto, have served us in the conquest, pacification, and settlement of the provinces of Nicaragua and Peru and of other parts of our Indies, and now with the desire to serve us further and to continue and increase our patrimony and Royal Crown, wanted to return to the aforementioned Indies of ours to conquer and populate the province of Río de las Palmas up to Florida and the provinces and new lands. . . . "

Hernando de Soto was given a series of titles, ranks, and honors that endowed him with extraordinary powers concentrated in a single person. The same was done in every stage of the conquest of America. Thus, he was made governor and captain general of the territory that began at the coast and ended two hundred leagues inland; the delimitation of this area was left to him, and he was to fulfill the offices of Alguacil Mayor and Adelantado of the territory.

The title of adelantado carried with it multiple responsibilities. At the military level, as captain of the troops, he was in charge of defending the territory and maintaining peace and order. At the judicial level, he was empowered to represent the king himself. Besides these offices, he was granted the governorship of Cuba, "since from there you could govern better and provide everything that is essential and important for said conquest and settlement."

Five hundred men were to accompany De Soto, with arms, horses, munitions, and other things necessary for the expedition; the colonization would be carried out by giving the townspeople lands and lots, with the benefit of a tax exemption for the first ten years. They were still required, however, to pay the royal fifth of all the gold, silver, and other goods they found in those territories.

The dual purpose of the expedition (conquest and colonization) could be seen in the diverse makeup of the participants. Alongside experienced soldiers there traveled persons who had never left the Peninsula: there were representatives of the petty and medium nobilities and, most of all, laborers, "all of them young, for among them one could hardly be found who had gray hair, a thing very necessary for victory over the toils and difficulties that emerge in the new conquests," as Garcilaso wrote. With them came a small group of women who were to remain on the island of Cuba. Among these was Isabel de Bobadilla, the wife of the adelantado.

The makeup of the expedition matched, in general terms, the characteristics of any migratory movement: a marked predominance of male representatives—although in this case this was due to their mission of conquest—and a mass of young people, suited to the task at hand.

The capitulación also called for the presence of clergy, "for the instruction of the natives of that province in our holy catholic faith." We have already remarked that the sword of the conquistadors also served their religion. The adelantado would cover the cost of taking the clerics along, as well as pay for all the preparations and expenses of the expedition. The crown limited itself to granting the territories and titles, without ever risking money in the royal treasury. The document is clear in this respect: "all of it at your expense and mission, and neither we nor the monarchs that come after us shall be obliged to pay you or satisfy the expenses you may incur therein."

One must explain here that Hernando de Soto, along with so many other conquistadors, never expected to obtain financial aid from the king. All of them did, however, seek the legal recognition of their possessions and their heraldic confirmation:

> These titles and offices were published all over Spain, with much talk about the new enterprise that Hernando de Soto would undertake in going and subduing and winning great kingdoms and provinces for the Spanish crown; and since throughout it was said that the captain who would carry it out had been the conqueror of Peru, and that, not satisfied with the one hundred thousand ducats which he had brought over from there, he was spending them on this second conquest, all were amazed and considered it better and richer than the first: because of which from every part of Spain came many knights of very

illustrious lineage, many noblemen, many soldiers practiced in the military art, who in different parts of the world had served the Spanish crown, and many citizens and laborers; all of whom, with such good reports of the new conquest, and at the sight of so much silver and gold and precious gems that they saw being brought from the New World; leaving their land, parents, relatives, and friends, and selling their estates, they readied themselves and offered in person or by letter to go to this conquest, with the hope that was promised, that it was to be as rich or richer than the two previous ones of Mexico and Peru.

—The Inca, Garcilaso de la Vega

To ensure that the capitulación would be honored, the king sent officials from his treasury to accompany the expedition. They were in charge of collecting the king's fifth. The capitulación, like those granted to other conquistadors, contained extensive instructions in this respect. Juan Gaytán, Juan de Añasco, and Luis Fernández de Biedma were to travel with Hernando de Soto as accountants in the service of His Majesty.

Extremadurans Who Accompanied De Soto

The preparations began once the capitulación was confirmed. News of this new expedition spread throughout the Peninsula, and the response exceeded all expectations; it was not for nothing that De Soto had arrived from America a rich man, and with an aura of fame and prestige around him. His confidence in the successful completion of the endeavor encouraged hundreds of people, all wanting to change their luck and become rich, to enlist; a better advertisement than the expedition's organizer could not have been found.

The participation of the Extremadurans was enormous. Several factors contributed to the massive enrollment: news of the marvels that the New World offered; the fact that Hernando de Soto was from Extremadura; the tradition of the Extremadurans—many from Extremadura had accompanied Balboa, Cortés, Pizarro, and other captains, becoming rich in a short time. Those were the attractions of America. On the other hand, Extremadura's poverty relative to the other regions under the Castillian crown resulted in a constant emigration of its population during the sixteenth century toward the continent discovered by Columbus.

Of the approximately 600 persons who made up the expedition, more than half were natives or residents of Extremadura; specifically, there were 311 Extremadurans with De Soto, issuing from fifty-six towns. The passenger logs prepared by the House of Trade of Seville still preserve personal data for every one of them.

Regional differences can be observed in the enlistment figures, as the participation of the provinces, or even of certain sections, differed significantly. For example, the province now known as Badajoz contributed a greater contingent than that of Cáceres, and within the former, more departures were recorded from the southwestern section. Albuquerque and Barcarrota were, after Badajoz, the towns contributing the greatest number of persons. The ties between Badajoz and the conquistador have already been noted, so that its contribution is not unexpected. In addition, the fact that some of its citizens possessed the same last name as the adelantado is only natural; this coincidence could well imply that they were related in some way. By the same token, the meager participation by the inhabitants of Jerez de los Caballeros is surprising, given the many dealings that De Soto had with this town.

The Journey to Florida

Once the expedition assembled in Seville and the necessary permits were issued by the House of Trade, they traveled to San Lúcar de Barrameda. They embarked from this spot on April 6, 1538, a year after the capitulación was signed. The fleet under Hernando de Soto's command consisted of seven ships and three brigantines and was accompanied by twenty other ships that, after reaching Cuba, would head for their final destination, Vera Cruz. After stopping at La Gomera Island, the fleet arrived at Santiago de Cuba toward the end of May, and De Soto took over the governorship.

A year passed before the departure for the conquest of La Florida. Twice during this waiting period, De Soto sent Juan de Añasco, a seaman and cosmographer, in command of two brigantines to reconnoiter the ports and coves of Florida. This reconnaissance shows how De Soto's plan for the conquest was marked by exhaustive preparation, and how he attempted to leave nothing to chance or improvisation. In his exploration of the Florida coasts, Juan de Añasco captured four Indians who would later be used as guides and interpreters. The royal officers who accompanied the expedition reported this in a letter sent to the king, in which they inform him of the final preparations for the voyage: "He brought four as interpreters and they are so intelligent that we already understand each other somehow and they afford high hopes for that land, so much that everyone is very cheerful and happy to go."

While he waited in Cuba for the best time to set out for Florida, De Soto reaffirmed with Hernán Ponce de León the pact they had signed before the conquest of Peru, in which they swore to be brothers as well as partners. During this time, the adelantado also prepared his last will and testament. Signed in the city of La Habana only five days before the expedition departed, this document reveals interesting aspects of the Extremaduran's life. In it he mentioned his children, all of them illegitimate, since they were conceived before his marriage (Isabel de Bobadilla bore him no heirs). They were María de Soto, who lived in Nicaragua, Andrés de Soto, referred to by the adelantado as "a boy said to be my son," and Leonor de Soto, whose mother was Leonor, the daughter of the last Great Inca, Huayna Capac.

In other matters, the document records his wish to be buried in the Church of San Miguel de los Caballeros. In the event of his death during the attempt to conquer Florida, he requested that his body be brought to that church. He desired that a chapel be built in this same church, to be paid for out of his estate. The chapel was to be erected under the title of Nuestra Señora de la Concepción, who must have been the object of his devotion. He wished also to establish a chaplaincy, and he made several bequests intended for various relatives. In addition, his will contains a request in memory of his very close friend Francisco Compañón, who was dead by then.

Having completed all the details of the expedition, Hernando de Soto named his wife governor regent of Cuba during his absence. He left San Cristóbal de la Habana on May 18, 1539, bound for Florida, the land where, in the years before, hundreds of Spaniards had perished in the midst of the most dreadful misery.

Previous Attempts in Florida

Florida, the land called Bimini by the Indians, was the place where the Fountain of Eternal Youth was thought to be, one of so many myths born in the New World, such as those of the Country of the Amazons and of El Dorado. Before the sixteenth century, the geography of Florida had been unknown. It was discovered in 1512 by Juan Ponce de León, who named it La Florida, apparently because its fields were filled with flowers, and because he discovered it on an Easter Sunday (Domingo de Pascua Florida). La

Florida, to the Spanish, included all of the present-day Southeast of the United States. Ponce de León attempted to conquer it twice, in 1515 and 1521, but both occasions ended in failure.

A new attempt was made in 1526, led by Lucas Vázquez de Ayllón. Some time earlier, he had chartered three ships sent to enslave Indians to work in the mines of the Antilles. The success of that first slaving adventure encouraged him to ask the king for permission to proceed with the conquest. Unfortunately, his expedition never got very far inland, since Ayllón died on the coast. Hunger and struggles for power decimated his troops to the point that "out of six hundred men that Ayllón had brought into that land, no more than fifty-seven escaped."

In 1527, Pánfilo de Narváez left Spain with intentions of colonizing the coast of the Gulf of Mexico. After experiencing the devastating effects of a hurricane, he disembarked in Tampa Bay, in the same spot where De Soto would begin the conquest years later. The expedition of Narváez traveled through areas that De Soto would also explore later. Hunger, cold weather, and attacks by the Indians gradually destroyed them: only four survivors were left. After living with the Indians for several years, these men escaped and began a long journey, spanning the territory of what is now the United States from East to West. One of the survivors, Alvar Núñez Cabeza de Vaca, wrote in his work *Naufragios* about the suffering and tribulations they experienced in their walk across the continent.

These were the attempts to conquer Florida, considered one of the most inhospitable territories in the American continent. All of them had failed. Far from intimidating De Soto, however, they encouraged him to embark on an uncertain and dangerous adventure.

The Chroniclers of the Journey

The early stages of the conquest of America are well known to us, thanks to the many chronicles that survive today. In most cases, these testimonies were written by persons who participated directly in the events they related.

These soldier-chroniclers, in their desires to write memoirs of all that they witnessed, have left us valuable materials essential to our understanding of the different chapters of the Spanish conquest. They distinguished themselves by the quality of their works and by the attention to detail of their narratives. They not only preserved the most important events but also included geographic accounts of the areas they crossed and precise descriptions of their inhabitants. Likewise, there are reports written by the crown officials who accompanied each expedition; their chief function was to inform the king of the circumstances in which the conquest unfolded.

De Soto's expedition to Florida included several of these chroniclers. One of them was the Hidalgo de Elvas, an unknown writer who came originally from the city of Elvas in Portugal. Others accompanying De Soto were Alonso de Carmona, Juan de Coles (another Extremaduran), and Luis Fernández de Biedma, who was one of His Majesty's officials. The Hidalgo de Elvas published his chronicle in 1557, and it is the most complete of all those written about Florida. The works by Carmona and Coles, on the other hand, appear to be short narratives that survive only in quotations included in the account by Garcilaso de la Vega. They are, however, also of undeniable interest. Finally, the account prepared by Biedma is quite complete and detailed. The writing reflects its author's position, since he traveled with the expedition as a royal official whose account constituted a report to the king.

There is another important chronicle of Hernando de Soto's endeavor in Florida; its author, the Inca, Garcilaso de la Vega, did not participate personally in the expedition, but his sources are apparently the works by Carmona and Coles, as well as an anonymous author [presumed to be Captain Gonzalo Silvestre] who, like them, took part in the expedition. The Inca published his work in 1605, half a century after the events that he wrote about.

Writers with such varied backgrounds naturally interpreted the events in different ways, and this of course makes their chronicles differ in certain details. Some of these can be disregarded, but others are quite noticeable and significant. There is a veritable mêlée of dates and figures, and it is difficult to unscramble the discrepancies. Some of the chroniclers even omit events of unquestionable interest.

In light of this, whenever we are faced with contradictions of this nature, we follow here the account by the Hidalgo de Elvas. As we have already mentioned, it is the most exhaustive, and it was written by a direct witness. Quotations not otherwise attributed, come from Elvas.

The Many Faces of Florida

The chroniclers served as genuine ethnographers who described the land and its inhabitants, the customs, rituals, and prevailing ways of life.

The encounter with this inhospitable and alien land shocked the Spaniards, but their presence caused an even greater impact upon the indigenous population.

Charleton W. Tebeau estimates that at the beginning of the sixteenth century there were twenty-five thousand inhabitants in what later became Spanish Florida. This population was distributed throughout the territory as follows: around four thousand Calusa Indians (including such peoples as the Mayaimi, Ais, Jeaga, and Tequesta) occupied the southern part of the peninsula up to Tampa Bay; the Timucans, numbering slightly over fourteen thousand, lived scattered between Cape Canaveral, the Aucilla River to the west, and what is now Georgia to the north; finally, the Apalachees (together with their tributary peoples), estimated at sixty-eight hundred, settled between the Aucilla and the Ocklockonee rivers. These Indians had not yet discovered writing and were at a cultural level similar to that of the Neolithic. Aside from this, however, each group was quite different from the others: the Calusas, for example, isolated in the southern part of the peninsula, were not as advanced in relation to other cultures that settled more to the north.

The fertility of the soil was not uniform throughout the territory. The land toward the north, with its rich earth, was well suited for farming, whereas the southern terrain was poor, sterile, and marshy. Because of this, even though all these groups were hunters and gatherers, only the Timucans and the Apalachee practiced agriculture. They did this by burning the vegetation, opening clearings where they could plant beans, squash, and, above all, maize. The Hidalgo de Elvas describes the rooms where these products were stored: "They have barbacoas in which they keep their maize, which is a house built on high, on top of four sticks, made with boards like a loft and with reeds on the floor."

The tribes living near the coast included seafood in their diet to add variety to it. They deposited the shells, gathering them in heaps.

Florida's inhabitants lived in small settlements for long periods of time, and sometimes permanently. The dwellings were round in shape, and the materials used in their construction were diverse and showed how well they had adapted to the environment. Houses were built using wood, clay, palm leaves, weeds, and straw. Each town had a public house that served both as a meeting place and for holding ceremonies. The most characteristic structure that the Floridian Indians built was the mound, which was of two types: some mounds became the residence of the *cacique,* while others were set aside as burial places. The bodies of the dead were left there, open to the air, until only the bones remained, and these were later buried in cemeteries.

Besides the mounds, they also built sepulchral houses, called *mezquitas* by the Spaniards.

Their social system was based on the clan, a unit determined by blood ties. The tribe was composed of different clans and, headed by the cacique, constituted an independent sociopolitical unit, although there could be a higher entity that could unite several tribes under its authority. The office of cacique was hereditary and could be held by a woman. The cacique was entitled to collect taxes from the people; he presided over the meetings and decided the time for sowing, hunting, and gathering. Nevertheless, despite the many powers that fell to him, his authority was not absolute, and he had to seek the opinion of prominent members of the Indian community, who formed a kind of privileged caste within their society. The lowest layer of the social scale was formed by slaves captured in battles against other tribes, who were then employed in agricultural labor and similar tasks. Garcilaso, referring to these captives, remarks that "the nerves or tendons of their feet" were cut "to prevent their escape."

The Floridians worshiped the sun and the moon, and they venerated animals such as deer, serpents, and small reptiles or insects. They believed in a life after death, which they thought would be similar to the one they had led on earth. Occasionally they would offer human sacrifices to the sun. On these occasions, children and captives were the propitiatory victims for preventing calamities and obtaining divine favors.

Polygamy was permitted, although it was mainly practiced by caciques and the nobility. Adultery was severely condemned in women. Garcilaso tells us: "She was obligated to be most faithful to her husband, under penalty of the laws that they had established for the punishment of adultery, which in certain provinces ordained a cruel death and in others a very ignominious punishment."

This was, broadly speaking, the land that cost Hernando de Soto his life. His search for a new Incario was fruitless—the cultural development and degree of evolution of the Floridian Indians were centuries behind those of the Incas.

The Beginning of the Adventure

On May 30, 1539, the expedition disembarked at Tampa Bay, which they called Puerto del Espíritu Santo. De Soto, with his army of six hundred, took possession of the land in the name of Emperor Charles V, a formality that was repeated in every expedition made to the New World.

The first town they come upon was Ucita, where they found Juan de Ortiz, a Sevillan who had survived the expedition of Pánfilo de Narváez. Held by the Indians for twelve years, and undergoing enormous tribulations, he had managed to survive until the Spaniards freed him from his lengthy captivity. After the joy occasioned by this encounter, preparations began for the entry inland. De Soto sent the ships back to Cuba under orders to return with provisions at a later time. A group of men stayed behind on the coast, while the main body of the expedition penetrated inland, heading for the province of Paracoxis. De Soto had previously sent a group of men ahead of him to reconnoiter. These scouting missions were carried out throughout the campaign; their information was vital, since it prevented unpleasant surprises and saved them unnecessary marching. Similarly, the Indians who joined the expedition as guides and interpreters (*lenguas*) offered invaluable help, although their work was made difficult by the extent of the territory they covered, in addition to the fact that Florida had many faces to show them. As we have already mentioned, its tribes were very different from one another, each speaking a distinct dialect.

Advancing from Paracoxis, they reconnoitered new territory throughout the summer. They found, however, that the different settlements they crossed could barely support the Indians who lived in them, much less feed De Soto's troops. His men began to feel the ravages of hunger. The expedition was off to a difficult start, and far from improving, these conditions would only worsen during four interminable years, as the Hidalgo de Elvas relates: "[The troops] were badly beset by hunger and the bad terrain, as the land was very poor in maize, low and full of water, lakes, and thick bushes, and the provisions they had brought from the port had been exhausted."

The Portuguese chronicler attests to the difficulties of the journey: the dense vegetation and swamplands that composed the landscape made the progress of the troops slow and laborious, especially for the cavalry.

To the problems of topography were added the warlike nature of the tribes they encountered. De Soto's armies began to suffer casualties in skirmishes with the natives. The chroniclers have left us a long list of the Indian names of the towns and regions they crossed: Cale, Ytara, Cholupa, Napetaca. . . .

Hoping to find riches and precious metals there, the expedition headed north for the Apalachee region, where they found instead only the remains of the failed expedition of Pánfilo de Narváez. At this point, they had covered 110 leagues (some 450 km) since disembarking in Tampa Bay. The nearness of the sea and the good terrain prompted them to spend the winter in Apalachee: "There were great quantities of maize, squash and beans and dried plums of the earth, which are better than those of Spain and grow in the fields without anyone planting them . . . , the provision was collected which seemed that it would suffice to spend the winter."

During the stay in Apalachee, De Soto ordered the men who had stayed behind in the port of Espíritu Santo to come and join them; he also sent several brigantines to La Habana in order to inform the *gobernadora* of the progress of the conquest, and to bring back new supplies and provisions when they returned. We know, with the benefit of hindsight, that even though Francisco Maldonado, who was in charge of the voyage, returned several times, he could never contact De Soto or his expedition. At the end of March 1540, the adelantado broke winter camp at Apalachee and headed north toward Cofitachequi. It was there that they hoped to find the long-awaited riches, encouraged by statements made by the Indians. Again the going became difficult. They constantly encountered rivers that slowed their progress; in some cases it took them more than two days to ford them, and several Spaniards drowned during the crossings. Along the way, interpreters were not lacking to steer them incorrectly, and hunger and disease became chronic companions: "If a man fell sick there was nothing to help him get better and with a sickness that could have been easily remedied elsewhere he walked, spent, until he had not a well bone in him. And they died of sheer weakness, some of them saying: if I had a slice of meat or a few rocks of salt, I would not now be dying."

On the way to Cofitachequi they crossed a poor and unpopulated region. The scarcity of food was aggravated to the point that De Soto "began to distribute rations out of some swine we had brought," the Hidalgo de Elvas tells us. Each "Christian" received one pound of meat, which, "cooked in water with no salt," alleviated the emptiness of the Castillian stomachs for a while. It is strange to see how these men could want for food while marching beside an entire herd of swine that at one point contained hundreds of head. Nevertheless, these animals were not to serve as provisions for the troops, but rather as an important part of the colonization effort. Hernando de Soto's mission was not only to conquer, but also to populate the territories. Both phases of his mission were considered essential, and in the second—the colonization—the preservation of the swine played a significant role.

At this stage of the journey the number of members of the expedition had increased enormously with the addition of Indian guides, interpreters, and *tamemes* (those employed in carrying the cargo) from the villages they passed. The time came when there were more of these Indians than there were Spaniards. When the need for food became extreme, De Soto had to let many of them go, because "he did not have anything with which to feed them."

The Second Year in Florida

They arrived in April at Cofitachequi, where they found remains of the unsuccessful expedition led by Lucas de Ayllón. De Soto's army rested easily here. Located near a river, very close to the sea, its cacique was a woman, who received them with great splendor. The chroniclers agree in describing the good impression that these people made on them, both physically and culturally. The Spaniards admired the dresses, the cloaks made with colorful feathers, the good workmanship in leather and pearls that, even though they were perforated, could fetch a great price. Many of them, tired and disillusioned after wandering through wild and inhospitable territories without finding the promised wealth, began to view this land as appropriate for settlement. Their reasoning was solid: Cofitachequi was situated near the Atlantic Ocean, making it possible as a waypoint for ships traveling from New Spain, Peru, and the mainland on their way back to the Peninsula [Spain and Portugal]. Besides, the fertility of its fields ensured that everyone could be fed. Nevertheless, Hernando de Soto did not give up his determination to find a treasure like Atahualpa's, which had yielded such spectacular dividends. He was firm in his resolve, "and because he was a hard man and curt in his words, although he was glad to listen and to know everyone's opinion, after stating his own he did not want to be contradicted and he always did as he saw fit."

These were the first signs of division or disagreement among the Spaniards. The adelantado's authority and strict character drove them on in search of the long-awaited precious metals. They crossed the river where Cofitachequi was situated (which they called Espíritu Santo), heading northwest. In a few days the panorama again turned desolate. Along the way they found only scattered villages and impoverished lands, incapable of feeding the members of the expedition and their horses.

Advancing through rough terrain that obstructed their progress, they reached the river's source, arriving at Guaxule. This was as far north as they would ever go into what is now the United States. The three hundred dogs they were given there alleviated their near-continuous hunger. The enclosed towns and peaceful Indians of this region allowed them to regain their strength; "the horses arrived there so thin that in their weakness they could not carry their owners."

Throughout the entire journey, the adelantado constantly interrogated the natives about the existence of a land possessing great riches. The replies he received were always in the affirmative, and he was invariably shown in which direction to set out, somewhere far from the homes of those being interrogated. We may be certain that these answers concealed the desire of the Indians to be rid of him and his people; it is impossible to ignore the upheaval that this expedition caused in the settlements they crossed, or in the abuses they committed. De Soto's men were tired, hungry, and ever more discouraged. Food and women were requisitioned without any scruples.

The caciques were not always obliging when faced with the adelantado's demands, and this led to trouble. This happened in Tascaluça, for example. According to Fernández de Biedma, when the cacique, "an Indian so tall that everyone considered him a giant," was required to provide Indians for carrying the cargo, he answered "that he was not wont to serve anyone, rather, that everyone served him." In other places, De Soto had to resort to his diplomatic talents: in Acoste, he pretended to rebuke his own Spaniards for their vandalism in order to avoid being attacked by the Indians.

In the fall of 1540, while headed south toward the Bay of Mobile, they suffered the fiercest attack since their arrival in Florida at a town called Mauvilla: "The Indians fought with such energy that they returned many times to expel our men. The battle lasted so long that, tired and very thirsty, many of the Christians went to drink from a lake near the fence and returned to fight, and it was dyed with the blood of the dead."

The battle was tremendously bloody. On the Spanish side, according to Biedma, more than twenty men died and the wounded neared two hundred and fifty. A great number of horses were lost as well. Among the Indians the casualties must have been greater, given the superior weapons that De Soto's men carried. However, the figures quoted by the chroniclers are excessive and exaggerated; the twenty-five hundred enemy deaths they report surely betray their bias. The writers tried to emphasize the valor of the Castillian troops, although they also praised the daring of the Indians, who "fought like fierce lions."

In Mauvilla they stopped for a month so that the wounded could heal. There they heard that the sea was not far off, and entertained the hope that Maldonado had returned from Cuba and was waiting for them with provisions. In spite of this, Hernando de Soto decided to set out northward. The chroniclers disagree as to the reason for this decision. The king's official, Biedma, states that, as it was the month of November and the weather was quite cold, the governor thought it best to go and look for some new spot where they could find enough provisions to spend the winter. On the other hand, the Hidalgo de Elvas remarks that De Soto feared that news of his fruitless search, of not having yet found gold or silver, would reach Cuba. This news would give Florida a bad name, and no one would wish to go there; he therefore chose to continue searching before informing anyone of his situation.

This last version seems more probable if we consider the adelantado's resolve to succeed in his expedition at any cost. Besides, he knew his people's state of mind. He was aware that if they reached the coast, he risked a mass desertion.

The army crossed into present-day Mississippi and decided to spend their second winter at Chicaça, a small town of "no more than twenty houses." We can easily imagine the suffering of those undernourished, weakened men, tired by the constant marches, ravaged by the cold, and many of them wounded in the last encounter. The few buildings in the town were not enough to shelter all of them, and in spite of the fires they built, "they spent all night turning and tossing, without sleeping, because if they warmed themselves on one side, they froze on another."

The relations with the natives seemed to be peaceful. The Indians became so fond of pork meat "that each night the Indians came to some houses . . . where the pigs slept and they killed and took all the pigs they could."

Toward the end of the winter, however, the Spaniards were unexpectedly attacked by the Indians, who set fire to the already-battered winter quarters. Eleven Spaniards, fifty horses, and several hundred pigs perished during the fray. The material losses were irreparable, because "if by chance any of them had any clothing left from the war of Mauvilla, there they lost it in the fire." In addition to the wretched conditions they were already in, they were now faced with having to march half-naked. The Spaniards lost practically all of their supplies and most of their equipment in the fire resulting from the surprise attack on the town.

Elvas describes the battle in these words:

> The Indians came to the sleeping quarters, in four squadrons, each squadron separate from the rest. And when their presence was discovered they sounded a drum and attacked with great cries and with such speed that they arrived together with the night watch, who had been away from the camp. And

when they were found by those inside the town, half of their things were burning from the fire they set.

. . . And outside, behind the doors, they awaited the Christians, who left the houses with no time to arm themselves. And as they got up confused from their sleep, and the smoke and fire blinded them, they did not know where they were going, nor could they hit their target with the weapons, nor could they saddle their horses, nor could they see the Indians who threw them down. Many of the horses were burned in the stable, and those that could break their halters freed themselves.

The confusion and disorder were such that everyone fled wherever he could, without there being anyone to resist the Indians.

The Discovery of the Mississippi

In March of 1541, they continued their search for riches, having abandoned Chicaça. The attacks by the Indians came one after another, unceasingly, and only on a few occasions were they received peacefully by the natives. The chroniclers described the many bloody battles, which often followed the same pattern. The element of surprise and the lack of knowledge about their surroundings worked against the Spaniards, who continually suffered casualties. The Indians were a menacing sight in the eyes of the members of the expedition: their bodies, legs, and arms painted different colors, they were covered with tufts of feathers and wore horns on their heads; their faces were blackened and their eyes "bordered with red in order to look fiercer."

Weakened by the sheer number of trials, the morale of the Castillians gradually crumbled beyond repair. Their hopes of finding wealth disappeared, and in their place the shadow of death emerged. Yet even in spite of this, they remained faithful to the adelantado, who still clung firmly to his belief that he would find an Incario in Florida.

In June, the expedition arrived at the shores of the Mississippi, which they called the Río Grande because of its width and volume. De Soto and his men were the first Europeans to see it, and the surprise they felt was justified: "The river was around half a league wide, if a man stood motionless on the other side, one could not descry whether he be a man or something else. Its depth was great and its current very strong; the water was always muddy; in it many trees and pieces of wood floated down river, carried by the force of the waters and the current."

In time, the Indian name Meaot Massipi ("Father of the Waters") came to be used. It took the army a month to build canoes to cross the river.

Advancing westward through the swamps and lakes of the Mississippi basin, they reached the plains, where they marveled at the movable dwellings (*tipi*) used mostly by the Sioux and Comanches, who could quickly dismantle their semipermanent villages. They found empty settlements, abandoned by their inhabitants out of fear of the foreigners. In other places, however, the natives received them as demigods, convinced that they were the children of the sun. The cacique of Casqui, for example, asked De Soto to cure certain blind Indians and restore their eyesight, appealing to his divine powers. On occasion, De Soto described himself as a child of the sun. While this strategy was intended to intimidate the Indians, it did not always give the desired results. The cacique of Guayocha, a town on the shores of the Río Grande, put the adelantado's divinity to the test, by asking him to dry up the Mississippi. Only if he did this, he told De Soto mockingly, would he be convinced that he was indeed a child of the sun.

These two episodes show, once more, the Spaniards' precarious situation. They could not impose their authority effectively on the Indians. Biedma tells us,

> . . . We came to another province . . . called Ycasqui, this peaceful cacique came out to us, telling us that he had heard of us for a long time and that we were men from heaven, and that their arrows could not harm us and because of that they did not want to go to war against us, but to serve us. They were well received by the governor, and he did not want anyone to enter their town so that no harm would be done to it. . . . The cacique asked the governor . . . to leave them a sign to which he could come to ask for help in their wars and which his people could ask for water for their crops, which had great need of it, since their children were starving. The governor had a very tall cross made from two pine trees, and told him to come another day, and he would give him the sign from heaven, and he should believe that he would want for nothing if he placed a true hope in it. . . . We went in a procession to the town. . . . We erected that cross and we went with great devotion, going on our knees to kiss the cross in the town, the Indians did as they saw us do, no more and no less.

In their travels they came near Coligua, where they obtained salt from a lake filled with warm, briny water. This compound was vital for their survival, and they had not tasted it for several months. Coligua's inhabitants had not heard of the Spaniards, but when "they were in sight of the town . . . they fled." The Hidalgo de Elvas named this area Caya, since a river that ran through it reminded him of "the brook that runs through Extremadura." Here they were informed that to the west the inhabitants were few and widely scattered. On the other hand, to the southeast they would find large towns. De Soto decided to follow this route, intending at least to reach the sea and inform Cuba of the progress and whereabouts of the expedition. Although the governor was aware of their failure up to that point, he was not discouraged by it. In spite of the enormous effort they had invested, seemingly to no avail, he still hoped to rebuild his estate, to "turn and attack and discover, further ahead, toward the west." It was December 1542, and winter had overtaken them. They had lost half of their men, and more than a hundred and fifty horses. During their third winter in Florida, "it was so cold and there was so much snow," remarks Biedma, "that we thought we would die."

Death of the Adelantado Hernando de Soto

At the end of the third winter they advanced toward the southeast in search of the coast. Juan Ortiz—the man who had survived Narváez's expedition and had offered them invaluable services as an interpreter—died on the way. They again reached the Mississippi and stopped at Guayocha, the place where the cacique had tested De Soto. The governor sent out a party to look for the sea, and they returned, reporting enormous obstacles that had to be overcome: swamps, very dense vegetation, marshes, "which was received with great sorrow by the Governor when he saw the bad course of action he had for reaching the sea, and a worse one for surviving unaided on land, as his people and horses were diminishing, and with those thoughts he fell ill."

De Soto contracted what was probably typhoid fever, then called *tabardillo,* which killed him a few days later. He died filled "with sorrow for leaving them in such confusion, for that was what he was doing in leaving them in a land where they did not know where they were." It was June 25, 1542. Before his death, he made a new will, whose whereabouts is not known. He named his lieutenant—Luis de Moscoso, born in the town of Zafra—chief of the expedition. His death was deeply felt and greatly mourned by many, although, according to the Hidalgo, some were glad because with it came their liberation. Now they could return and leave behind the struggles, suffering, and poverty that had loomed over them ever since they set foot on that soil.

He was buried in secret, and his death was kept from the Indians. They noticed his absence and asked for him, and they were told "that he had gone to heaven, as he had often done in the past." However, they must not have been satisfied with this answer, because the Spaniards were still afraid that their captain's body would be desecrated. They disinterred it secretly and put it in the Mississippi, whose waters became a resting place for the intrepid Extremaduran.

The new captain, according to a custom of that time, sold the adelantado's belongings to his men: two male slaves, two female slaves, three horses, and 700 pigs. The buyers promised to pay whenever a distribution of riches were made. Obviously, Hernando de Soto's personal fortune was not limited to these possessions. Although in the journey to Florida he had invested an exorbitant amount of money, the failure of that enterprise would not have ruined him. Isabel de Bobadilla, having received news of her husband's death, made an inventory of the household goods, land, and livestock belonging to her husband. In a document dated December 6, 1543 in the city of San Cristóbal de la Habana, she listed all the possessions for which she had proof of ownership. She was aware that the inventory did not include property and goods that the adelantado had in the Kingdom of Castille and in other kingdoms of the crown. The lengthy enumeration includes a house and other outbuildings, land, slaves, livestock (horses, cows, pigs, sheep, and fowl), farming implements, furnishings, wardrobes, dresses and implements for household duties, gold and silver jewelry—in short, the inventory lets us glimpse the enormous fortune that Hernando de Soto's sword earned him in the different expeditions in which he participated.

> The death of the governor, Captain General Hernando de Soto, so worthy of lamentation, caused great sorrow and sadness among all his own. . . . Their sorrow and pain were doubled when they saw that they were forced to bury him in silence and in secret, which was not done in public so that the Indians would not know where it lay, because they feared they would do to his body certain ignominies and affronts they had done to other Spaniards. . . . Because of which they decided to bury him at night, with standing guards so that the Indians would not see or know where he was being left. . . . The next day, to hide the spot where the body lay and to conceal their sadness, they made it known to the Indians that the governor was in better health . . . , but as pleasure can only be badly feigned and grief cannot be hidden . . . , our men could not do so much that the Indians did not thus suspect the governor's death and the place where they had laid him. . . .
>
> As the Spaniards saw and noticed these signs . . . they thought it would be best to lay him to rest in the Río Grande. . . . They cut down a very thick

holm oak and at about half the height of a man they hollowed it out on one side where they could place the body, and the next night, with the greatest silence possible, they disintered him and placed him in the oak's trunk with boards nailed to embrace the body on the other side, and so he was left, as if in an ark, and with the many tears and sorrow of the priests and knights that were present in this second burial, they placed him in the middle of the river's current, committing his soul to God and they saw him then fall to the bottom.

—The Inca, Garcilaso de la Vega

The End of the Expedition

The main instigator and promoter of the expedition was dead. The number of soldiers had been reduced to less than half of the initial army, with virtually no horses remaining. Their hopes of finding the treasures and riches promised at the start of the journey had vanished. The majority of the Spaniards expressed their desire to renounce the conquest of Florida. Exhaustion and discouragement had reached their peak, and the death of the governor eliminated the last obstacle to the fulfillment of the thought in the minds and spirits of almost everyone: to return.

Two alternatives were considered. One was to go westward to New Spain [Mexico], attempting to repeat the journey that Núñez Cabeza de Vaca carried out years earlier; the other was to build ships and sail down the river to the sea. The better option seemed to be to set out across country for New Spain, since the descent of the Mississippi was risky—they had no one that could serve as mate or pilot, and they had no charts for navigation. Besides, on the journey by land it was still possible that they might find some treasure that could compensate for the sorrows they had encountered in that "accursed" place. So they started overland, but they again encountered the problems that had haunted them in their passage across most of Florida: difficult terrain, attacks by Indians, impoverished territories, hunger—all this, added to the fact that they did not know which route to follow or the true distance between them and New Spain, made them retrace their steps after having covered a good distance.

Back on the shores of the Mississippi, in Aminoya, they were forced to spend another winter. Building the seven brigantines that would carry them downriver took months. When this task was finished, they proceeded to kill the remaining horses (except for twenty-five of them) and the pigs that were left, since it was impossible to bring them aboard. For this same reason they

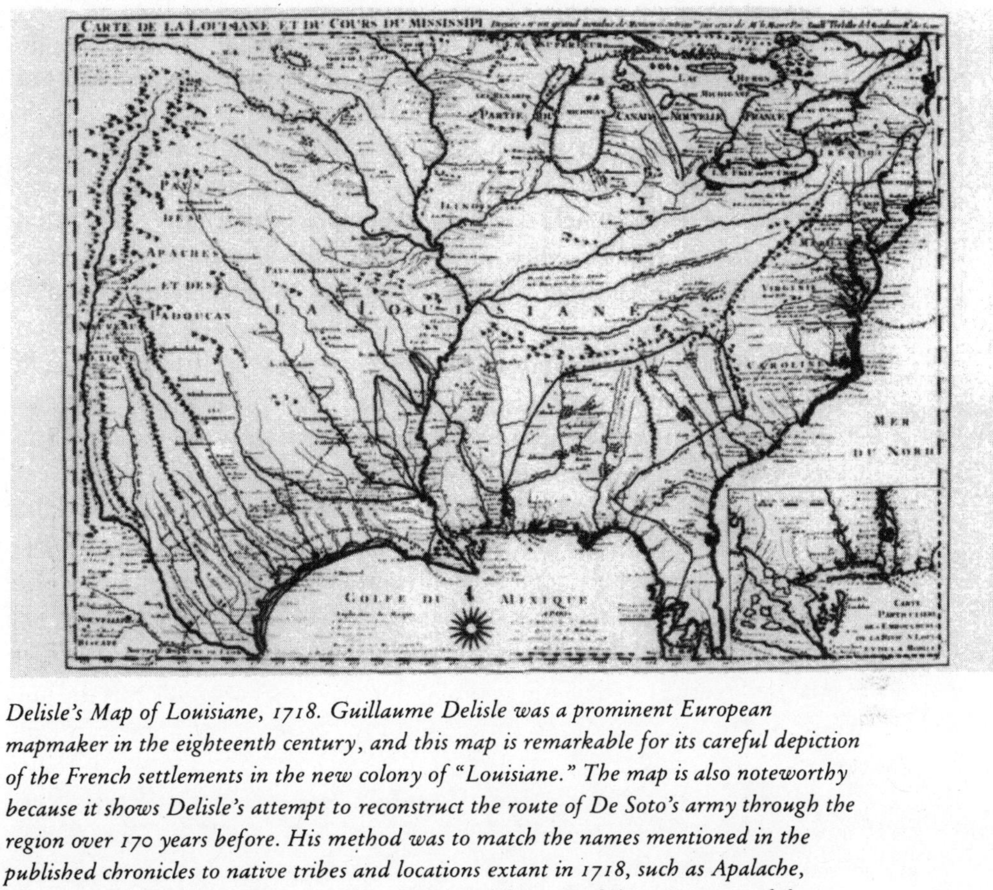

Delisle's Map of Louisiane, 1718. Guillaume Delisle was a prominent European mapmaker in the eighteenth century, and this map is remarkable for its careful depiction of the French settlements in the new colony of "Louisiane." The map is also noteworthy because it shows Delisle's attempt to reconstruct the route of De Soto's army through the region over 170 years before. His method was to match the names mentioned in the published chronicles to native tribes and locations extant in 1718, such as Apalache, Cheraqui (Chalaque), Conchaque (Coça) and Mobiliens (Mobila). (Courtesy of the Cornell University Library)

freed most of the Indians who had carried their cargo. This measure was inhumane in the opinion of the Hidalgo de Elvas, because many of these Indians were far from their own lands and were left at the mercy of other tribes. When they embarked, on July 2, 1543, the chronicler could not avoid describing the reaction of the unfortunate Indians who were not allowed on board the ships: "Most of them were left crying, which was very pitiful to behold, seeing that all those of good will had been Christians and would now be lost."

During their voyage downriver, they were continually attacked by the natives. They were unable to repel the attacks, since their firearms had been melted down and used in the construction of the ships.

After nineteen days, they reached the sea and decided to continue along the coast until they found New Spain. This was more feasible than crossing the gulf to reach Cuba, which would have been a risky adventure. Finally, on September 10, 1543, they sighted the mouth of the Pánuco River (in Tampico). Sailing into it, they noticed that there were Indians there, dressed in the manner of the Spaniards. The feelings of the members of the expedition on learning that these were indeed the shores of New Spain were captured by the masterly pen of the Hidalgo de Elvas: "The pleasure that everyone felt at this news cannot be entirely expressed, because it was as though at that moment they had been born."

The Spaniards, "dressed in deerskins that had been tanned and dyed black," had survived a hard journey "among infidels, without a single fortification where they could regain their strength, and without any other assistance." Hundreds of Castillians, including the man responsible for the enterprise, perished in the adventure they had begun four years earlier in Tampa Bay. Hernando de Soto died without realizing how wide was the gulf that separated the Peru of the Incas from the Florida he attempted to conquer.

So ended one of the most dramatic expeditions made by the Spaniards on American soil in the sixteenth century. Thousands of kilometers were explored in the southern part of the United States, covering the area now occupied by the states of Florida, Georgia, South Carolina, North Carolina, Tennessee, Alabama, Mississippi, Arkansas, Louisiana, and Texas. The expedition, although a failure from the standpoint of the conquest, brought about important geographic discoveries.

Hernando De Soto: A Brief Biography

by Paul E. Hoffman

Like many prominent persons of his time, Hernando de Soto's date of birth is unknown. Estimates range from 1496 to 1501.[1] But De Soto's own testimony in late October 1535 was that he was thirty-five, and thus born in 1500.[2] The idea that he was born in 1496 seems to have arisen from De Soto's testimony in 1536 that he was "about forty" and from an effort by later writers to make Lambert A. Wilmer's biographical "facts" fit with the date (1519) that De Soto was alleged to have gone to the Indies. Wilmer himself says that De Soto was born in 1500.[3] Until additional evidence turns up, a birth date of 1500 seems most likely.

The place of De Soto's birth remains controversial. Both Villanuevas in the immediate vicinity of Badajoz have claimed him on the basis of Garcilaso de la Vega's statement that De Soto was born in Villanueva de Barcarrota. Villanueva de la Serena is not mentioned in any account or document. Saying De Soto was born in Barcarrota seems to have been Garcilaso's droll way of resolving the rival claims of Jerez de los Caballeros and Badajoz. Barcarrota

[1]John R. Swanton, *Final Report of the United States De Soto Expedition Commission*, 1938, reprint with introduction by Jeffrey Brain (Washington, D.C.: Smithsonian Institution Press, 1985), 67; curiously, Swanton mentions that De Soto stated his age and place of birth in manuscript sources but fails to say what he said.

[2]Merits and Services interrogatory for Alonso Martín de San Benito, Lima, 26 October 1535, in José Toribio Medina, ed., *Descubrimiento del oceano Pacífico: Vasco Núñez de Balboa, Hernando de Magallanes y sus compañeros*, 3 vols. (Santiago, Chile: Imprenta Universitaria, 1913–20), 2:360.

[3]James Lockhart, *The Men of Cajamarca: A Social and Biographical Study of the First Conquerors of Peru* (Austin: University of Texas Press, 1972), 198; Wilmer claimed that De Soto came under Pedrarias's protection at age seventeen, spent six years at a university (Zaragoza), and then in 1519 [at the age of twenty-three] went to the Indies with his patron, who had returned to Spain in that year. Lambert A. Wilmer, *The Life, Travels and Adventures of Ferdinand de Soto, Discoverer of the Mississippi* (Philadelphia: J.T. Lloyd, 1858), 18–20.

is roughly halfway between them. Local lore to the contrary, there is no evidence De Soto was born or lived there.[4]

Solar and Rújula make a case for Jerez de los Caballeros on the basis of two documents. The first is De Soto's *expediente* for membership in the Order of Santiago. Among the testimony of nine witnesses is the explicit statement of Suero Vazquez de Moscoso that De Soto was born in Jerez and Alvaro Romo's less direct statement that De Soto's parents had lived in Jerez after their marriage and that he had seen Hernando in his parents' home there.[5] The second document is De Soto's will, in which he makes provision for the construction of a chapel in the church of San Miguel in Jerez de los Caballeros, in which he was to be buried and his parents reburied. His will does *not* say he was a native of that town.[6] To these Swanton added the statement of the Gentleman of Elvas that De Soto was born in Jerez de Badajoz.[7] Porrás Barrenechea notes that De Soto claimed to be a native (*natural*) of Jerez in testimony given at Seville in 1536, although in another place he said that he was a *vecino* of that town, which is not a claim of nativity.[8]

Finally, Badajoz was mentioned during his life as his birthplace. For example, the order for the investigation of his lineage preparatory to granting him membership in the Order of Santiago states that he was a native (*natural*) of Badajoz, and that is where the inquiry was conducted. Ordinarily, such inquiries were made in the person's hometown because that was where the most reliable witnesses as to his ancestry would be found. In a similar vein, his dowry agreement with Isabel de Bobadilla (November 14, 1536) states that he was a native (*natural*) and vecino (owner of a house) of Badajoz.[9]

The question of his birthplace thus resolves itself into the rival claims of

---

[4]Garcilaso de la Vega, *La Florida,* trans. Charmion Shelby, herein, vol. 2.

[5]Antonio del Solar y Taboada and José de Rújula y de Ochotorena, *El Adelantado Hernando de Soto: Breves noticias y nuevos documentos para su biografía* (Badajoz, Spain: Ediciones Arqueros, 1929), 133, 138.

[6]Ibid., 205–21, from a copy in Archivo General de Indias, Seville (AGI), Justicia 750; see also herein, vol. 2.

[7]"The Account by a Gentleman from Elvas," *True Relation of the Hardships Suffered by Governor Hernando de Soto & Certain Portuguese Gentlemen During the Discovery of the Province of Florida, Now newly set forth by a Gentleman of Elvas,* trans. and ed. James Alexander Robertson, herein, vol. 1. Cited hereafter as Elvas, *Relation.*

[8]Porrás Barrenechea, notes to the "Relación" of Diego de Trujillo, in *Biblioteca Peruana,* 1st Series 3 vols. (Lima: Editores Asociados, 1968), 2:64.

[9]Solar and Rújula, *El Adelantado Hernando de Soto,* 125 and 158, respectively; see also herein, vol. 2.

Jerez de los Caballeros and the city of Badajoz. De Soto's father was a native of the former, his mother a native of the latter.[10] His parents lived in both places during De Soto's infancy and boyhood, according to most witnesses in the Santiago expediente. De Soto's willingness to claim birth in both places means that no firm conclusion can be reached on the basis of his evidence. On a numerical count of the available sources, Jerez emerges as the "winner," but the official nature of the Santiago investigation lends weight to Badajoz (city). Perhaps the truth is that he was actually born in Badajoz, probably in his mother's family's house, but was almost immediately taken to and largely raised in his father's hometown of Jerez. We may agree with Lockhart that "all that we can assert categorically, given the usage of the times, is that De Soto felt himself to be from Jerez or its environs."[11]

There is little doubt that his parentage was noble, although much of the genealogy presented by authors such as Solar and Rújula must be viewed with great caution, coming as it does from eighteenth-century sources. The eighteenth century was a period when "historians" produced genealogies of some noble families that can be shown to be inaccurate at many points for which there is independent documentation.

De Soto is usually said to have been poor prior to going to the Indies. Heretofore, this claim was based on Oviedo's and Elvas's statements, repeated by Garcilaso, that De Soto went to the Indies with only a sword and buckler.[12] The veracity of this assertion is seemingly attested by Ruth Pike's note that De Soto (and his longtime partner, Hernán Ponce de León) borrowed money from a Genoese banker at Seville, probably so that he could equip himself and pay his fare in the Pedrárias fleet.[13] Obtaining such a loan suggests that De Soto may have been more short on cash than poor in the absolute terms that his biographers usually suggest. The point of Elvas's account, after all, is in its next sentence, which describes De Soto's return to Spain with a 180,000-*cruzado* fortune. De Soto, in short, was another "rags to riches" success story from the Indies.

De Soto went to Castilla del Oro with the expedition of Pedrárias (Pedro

[10]Solar and Rújula, *El Adelantado Hernando de Soto,* Expediente of Santiago, passim; all witnesses agree on this point.

[11]Lockhart, *Men of Cajamarca,* 199.

[12]Elvas, *Relation,* herein, vol. 1; Garcilaso de la Vega, *La Florida,* herein, vol. 2; Gonzalo Fernández de Oviedo, *Historia general de las Indias,* 1851, rpt., 5 vols. (Madrid: Biblioteca de Autores Españoles, 1959), does not comment on De Soto's economic status when he left Spain.

[13]Ruth Pike, *Enterprise and Adventure: The Genoese and the Opening of the New World* (Ithaca, N.Y.: Cornell University Press, 1966), 102, n. 1, and 194.

Arias de Avila) when it sailed on February 25, 1514. Swanton cites a witness in the Isabel de Bobadilla—Hernán Ponce lawsuit of 1539 to that effect.[14] Pike's discovery of the loans taken out in 1514 removes any remaining doubt.

By the date of De Soto's first known participation in an expedition, the worst of the "starving time" of the Pedrárias expedition was over, although hunger continued to plague the Spaniards for years afterward. Even though the Pedrárias expedition had been limited to twelve hundred persons, they were too many for the food resources of Darien and those they had brought. One estimate has it that by March 1515, when two caravels arrived from Spain with food, as many as seven hundred of the original twelve hundred had died or returned to the Antilles. Too, the Spaniards had fallen into a pattern of raids directed against the Indians in which finding food was almost as important as finding gold. Thus large numbers of men had been sent off with Luís Carrillo, Juan de Ayora (four hundred men), Pedrárias "El Mancebo," Francisco de Vallejo, Gaspar de Morales, and Balboa, to mention but the expeditions of 1514–15, evidently in the hope that they could live off the land for a time.[15] The subsequent history of the colony, to 1519, is a continuation of this pattern of "cabalgadas" in search of gold and food and slaves. All of these combined mixtures of negotiation (from a position of strength) and often a spectacular brutality.

De Soto's first known participation in a raid was with Vasco Núñez de Balboa's expedition of August 1515 into the Cueva Indian province of "Dabaiba," up the Rio Grande River in Panama.[16] Balboa took 190 men in a fleet of thirteen small boats. Expecting to find gold mines and a large native population, and hence food, the Spaniards were bitterly disappointed on

---

[14]Swanton, *Final Report,* 68.

[15]Pablo Alvarez Rubiano, *Pedrárias Dávila: Contribución al estudio de la figura del "Gran Justador," gobernador de Castilla del Oro y Nicaragua* (Madrid: Instituto Fernández de Oviedo, 1944), 209–10, 142–68. For gold presented for taxation, see Medina, ed., *Descubrimiento del oceano Pacífico,* 2:397–400, and, for slaves, 416.

[16]De Soto's testimony in Merits and Services interrogatory of Alonso Martín de San Benito, Lima, 26 October 1535, in Medina, ed., *Descubrimiento del oceano Pacífico,* 2:359–60; date from Alvarez Rubiano, *Pedrárias,* 171–73. If he had not already participated in Luís Carrillo's first expedition (end of 1514), or Pedrárias "El Mancebo"'s expedition (July–September 1514), this entrada would have been his introduction to dealing with Indians in frontier conditions. None of these three entradas was very profitable. Carrillo presented 1,155 p. 6 tomines, Pedrárias 535 p., and Balboa only 154 p. in gold objects of various finenesses for taxation. See Medina, ed., *Descubrimiento del oceano Pacífico,* 2:398, 400, 416 for treasury entries.

both counts. They returned to Santa Maria del Darien with only 150 *pesos de oro* and a few slaves.[17]

De Soto's next known participation in an expedition was in 1517. In September 1517, he was a member of Juan de Tavira's exploration of the Rio Grande. When Tavira drowned, the men elected Francisco Pizarro their captain. He got the survivors back to Darien. Shortly after returning from this disaster, De Soto apparently went to work with Balboa in his construction of boats at the Island of Pearls, an activity that may have kept him busy into 1518.[18]

Apparently by the time of the Tavira expedition, De Soto and Hernán Ponce, already a captain, had begun their company, which included Francisco Campañón. In June 1535, they said that it was then eighteen or nineteen years old, which puts its creation in 1516 or 1517.[19]

The basis for forming the company can be inferred from what little we know of these men at the time. In December 1515, Ponce left Acla as part of Licenciado Espinosa's 210-man expedition along the Pacific Coast to Natá and the province of chief "Paris" in search, among other things, of a treasure that Gonzalo de Badajoz was supposed to have buried in the land of Paris earlier in 1515. At one point in this expedition, noted as the most brutal toward the Indians up to that time, Ponce and Bartolome Hurtado and some men went off in canoes to islands off the coast. They returned with abundant loot and many Indian slaves.[20] Thus by the time Espinosa returned to Acla in April of 1516, Ponce was wealthy.[21] De Soto, on the other hand, probably still had relatively little wealth. He was young, was a foot soldier, and had participated in only one expedition (that we know about). Tavira's expedi-

---

[17]Ibid. Balboa to SM (Su Majestad; Your Majesty, the king), 16 October 1515, in Medina, ed., *Descubrimiento del oceano Pacífico,* 2:142–43.

[18]Alvarez Rubiano, *Pedrárias,* 191; Carl O. Sauer, *Early Spanish Main* (Berkeley, 1966), 259, 263; Testimony of De Soto, Lima, 26 October 1535, in Medina, ed., *Descubrimiento del oceano Pacífico,* 2:359–64, and 2:402, 411–12 for quinto entries.

[19]Swanton, *Final Report,* 68; see text of 1535 agreement in Solar and Rújula, *El Adelantado Hernando de Soto,* 80–82.

[20]Alvarez Rubiano, *Pedrárias,* 188; on p. 190 he confuses this side trip with another by other men during Espinosa's 1519 expedition. Cf., ibid., 276–78.

[21]Treasury records published by Medina, ed., in *Descubrimiento del oceano Pacífico* show that Espinosa's expedition turned in for taxation 725 p. of gold and paid 146 p. 5 t. 3 gr. (de oro) as the quinto on Indian slaves in April 1516; 55,298 p. 4 t. for taxation in March 1517; paid 1,724 p. 6 t. 11 gr. as the quinto on Indian slaves in June 1517; and turned in for taxation an undisclosed amount of pearls in this same period. Ibid., 2:400, 417, 401, 411.

tion of September 1517 promised him a golden return, but outfitting for it was probably up to each man. De Soto may have needed help, which Ponce might have supplied in return for an equal share of any booty. Later, Ponce may have funded De Soto's purchase of a horse, again in return for a share of any incomes De Soto gained from participation in raids or other sources. Such an arrangement with De Soto, and perhaps others, was not only standard business at that time, it may also have been attractive, because, according to Alvarez Rubiano, Ponce was posted at this time to the site of Panama city as Pedrárias's lieutenant, a position that probably kept him out of the field and so away from loot.[22] Ponce's title of captain, bestowed by Pedrárias, probably also dates from his success in 1515–16.[23]

De Soto and Ponce next appear in the account of Espinosa's expedition of July to October 1519, in which they both participated. This expedition of 115 men and thirty horsemen (De Soto among the latter) set out from Panama in search of gold and food. This is a commonly told incident in De Soto's biography because he is credited with leading a cavalry charge that saved Espinosa and a part of the force when they were in danger of being destroyed by the Indians of Utraboa (or Urraca). At the time, De Soto was part of the land party commanded by Francisco Pizarro. De Soto later served as a witness of the submission of cacique Paris (August 1) and of the truth of an account of the expedition (city of Panama, October 18).[24] Later in 1519, Espinosa included De Soto among the occupiers of the new town of Santiago, at Natá, the site of natural sources of salt. Francisco Campañón was given command of the new settlement. Santiago was about thirty leagues from Panama city. Herrera's account makes De Soto a hero for going for aid when Utraboa's (or Urraboa's) Indians attacked Santiago.[25]

---

[22]Alvarez Rubiano, *Pedrárias,* 189–90.

[23]Oviedo, *Historia general,* 3:207–8, stresses that only seven men had the title of captain when Pedrárias left Spain in 1514, but others, including Ponce and De Soto, were given the title afterward to honor an achievement or because "this name of captain was one of the principal sources of wealth or instrument for gaining [it]," that is, as a political favor.

[24]Swanton, *Final Report,* 69; account of the expedition in Medina, ed., *Descubrimiento del oceano Pacífico,* 2:272–317, with De Soto on pp. 292, 315–16, and *Colección de documentos inéditos, relativos al descubrimiento, conquista y organización, de las antiguas posesiones españolas de América y Oceanía, sacados de los archivos del reino, y muy especialmente del de Indias,* edited by Joaquín F. Pacheco, Francisco D. Cárdenas, and Luis Torres Mendoza, 42 vols. (Madrid, 1864–84) 20:56, 116 (cited hereafter as *DII*). Gold objects weighing 1,977 pesos were presented for taxation in November 1519. Medina, ed., *Descubrimiento del oceano Pacífico,* 2:404.

[25]Antonio de Herrera y Tordesillas, *Historia general de los hechos de los Castellanos en las*

As a resident of Santiago de Natá, De Soto disappears from available records for the next four years. The only hint of what he and his partners were doing are the entries in the treasury records showing Ponce submitting gold objects for founding and taxation.[26] Thus we do not know what role, if any, De Soto played in Lic. Juan Rodriguez de Alarconcillo's superficial *residencia* of Pedrárias (1520) nor in the two years of delays that Pedrárias imposed on Gil Gonzalez Dávila and Andrés Niño (January 1520 to January 1522) nor in their expedition to Nicaragua, January 1522 to June 1523.[27] We can be fairly certain, however, that De Soto heard of the ninety thousand pesos de oro that Gonzalez Dávila and Niño brought back, of how Gonzalez Dávila fled to Santo Domingo rather than surrender twenty percent of the haul to Pedrárias, and of the conviction of the men that Gonzalez Dávila had found a water route across Central America from the Gulf of Fonseca via the Nicaraguan lakes and the San Juan River to the Caribbean. Pedrárias likely had no difficulty recruiting De Soto for the old governor's own expedition to Nicaragua.

Once Gil Gonzalez Dávila was out of the way, Pedrárias lost no time in organizing his own expedition to grab the newly discovered riches and potential waterway in Nicaragua. Francisco Hernández de Córdoba, Governor Diego Velazquez's first explorer of Mexico, was given command, with De Soto, Campañón, and Gabriel de Rojas as captains. The expedition departed Panama at the end of 1523 and spent 1524 conquering western Nicaragua, founding the towns of Granada, León, and Segovia during the course of the year.

Nicaragua, even more than Castilla del Oro (the isthmus of Panama), made the fortunes of the partners in the Ponce–De Soto–Campañón company. De Soto's role, as it apparently had been on the isthmus, was making war and obtaining its spoils, while Ponce provided supplies and managed De Soto's wealth.[28]

In Nicaragua, De Soto continued to be a leading Indian fighter and seems to have emerged as a preferred leader of punitive expeditions. In addition, he occasionally led exploring parties. The chronicles are silent about these activities in the first three years of the conquest, aside from noting his involve-

---

islas y tierra firme del mar oceano, 1601, rpt., 17 vols. (Madrid: Imprenta Maestre, 1934–57), 5:355. See also Swanton, *Final Report*, 69.

[26]Mario Góngora, *Los grupos de conquistadores de tierra firme (1509–1530)* (Santiago de Chile: Universidad de Chile, 1962), 89.

[27]Alvarez Rubiano, *Pedrárias*, 270, 272–73, 319–27.

[28]Góngora, *Los grupos de conquistadores*, 48, 89.

ment in several expeditions associated with the struggle among the Spaniards for control of Nicaragua and Honduras; such expeditions inevitably involved subjugating and looting the Indians along the line of march.

The picture becomes clearer for the years 1527–30. In 1527, Diego López de Salcedo, who had seized the governorship of Nicaragua at a time when Pedrárias was undergoing his second residencia, used De Soto to suppress Indian rebellions.[29] Later that year, or early in 1528, De Soto was one of four captains sent to seek mines reported near Granada. They found good mines within fifteen leagues of the city. A second De Soto expedition later in 1528 had to return because of a shortage of food.[30] Finally, in 1530, Pedrárias sent De Soto and as many as a hundred men to suppress the Indian rebellion in the Islas de Petronilla up by the border with Guatemala. Apparently De Soto made two or three voyages for this purpose, each time returning with slaves. Juan Ruiz de Arce, one of the foot soldiers on at least one of these expeditions, was able to pay for his subsequent journey to Peru with his share of this (largely human) loot.[31]

De Soto's rewards for this leading role in the conquest of Nicaragua are, like his Indian fighting, poorly documented prior to 1527. The indirect evidence of his political position in these years (see below) suggests that he received one of the larger shares of the material and human loot. Some indication of what such a share might be is provided by a record of the agreement for the division of spoils from the first phase of the conquest. Dated at Hacoatega on May 1, 1524, this document called for the division of one hundred thousand pesos (weight?) of golden objects. De Soto was to receive one thousand pesos in fine gold for the services of his person, his horse, and a young black slave (*negrito*). Since it was recognized that the golden objects were of low karat, De Soto's share was to be much larger than the one percent suggested by the numbers. In the end, when reduced to sixteen-karat gold, this loot amounted to only 15,215 pesos. De Soto's share is not

[29]*Expediente*, Gov. López de Salcedo against Hernando de Saavedra and Capt. Diego de Albitez, Trujillo, 6 May 1528, in Andrés Vega Bolanes, ed., *Documentos para la historia de Nicaragua*, 17 vols. to 1957 (Madrid: Imprenta Juan Bravo, 1954–), 1:324, 344.

[30]Reply of Treasurer Rodrigo del Castillo to question 17 of Pedrárias's Interrogatory, León, 13 July 1528, *Documentos para la historia de Nicaragua*, 1:426; Pedrárias to SM, León, 15 January 1519, ibid., 456.

[31]Testimony in reply to question 81 of Lic. Francisco Castañeda's interrogatory from his residencia as alcalde mayor of Nicaragua, León, January 1536, *Documentos para la historia de Nicaragua*, 4:268, 330–31 (and other places), and Juan Ruiz de Arce, "Advertencias que hizo el fundador del vínculo y mayorazgo a los sucesores en el," in *Biblioteca Peruana*, 1st Series, 1:413.

known, but the ordinary soldiers got about twelve pesos de oro after the king's fifth, various fees, and the expenses of the outfitting of the ships had been deducted.[32] Clearly this division did not make his fortune. But later divisions, and *encomienda* grants, did. When he was captured by Gil Gonzalez Dávila in 1524, De Soto and his men had 130,000 pesos of low-grade gold objects with them, according to Herrera, although Oviedo does not mention a figure.[33] By 1525, he was wealthy enough, and important enough politically, to be named one of the two *alcaldes ordinarios* of León and, two years later, to be nominated as a perpetual *regidor* of that city's council.[34]

The first clear indication of De Soto's economic rise to prominence comes from the time of López de Salcedo. According to Gonzalo Fernández de Oviedo, who was in León at the time, López de Salcedo favored De Soto and Ponce with "very good caciques and Indians" so that they amassed great wealth. Apparently the governor's favor extended to regranting certain encomiendas held by other old settlers. One witness called in 1529 by Alcalde Mayor Francisco Castañeda said that De Soto had received the Indians of Hernán Gomez de Cortaya and that Ponce de León had been given ones belonging to Rodrigo Muriel. The alcalde mayor had restored the first to their former owner in the judgment of a lawsuit, and fear that he might do the same for Rodrigo Muriel caused the partners to reach an out-of-court settlement with him.[35] In addition, López de Salcedo allowed the shipment of Indian slaves from Nicaragua to Panama. Evidence from 1529 shows that the Ponce–De Soto partnership had an interest in the trade at that time (see below).[36] Certainly, De Soto's suppression of Indian rebellions in 1527 and 1530, noted above, would have provided captives to be sold.

In addition to their encomiendas, and interest in the trade in Indian slaves, the partners had interests in mines. Some years later, when Pedrárias was trying to justify not naming either De Soto or Ponce, by then very wealthy men and favored by Alcalde Mayor Castañeda, as regidores of

[32]Góngora, *Los grupos de conquistadores,* 48, 53, 89.

[33]Cited in Swanton, *Final Report,* 69–70; Oviedo, *Historia general,* 3:302.

[34]Replies to question 8, *Diligencias, re* election of Alcaldes for 1530, León, January 1530, in *Documentos para la historia de Nicaragua,* 2:500, 515, 545, 548; Instructions for Procuradores, León, 30 July 1527, ibid., 1:261.

[35]Oviedo, *Historia general,* 3:351; Información de parte de Castañeda, León, 17 September 1529, in *Documentos para la historia de Nicaragua,* 2:136. López de Salcedo helped himself as well as those he wanted to influence. Pedrárias charged that he took 9,000 Indians from others! Pedrárias to king, León, 15 January 1529, ibid., 1:451–52.

[36]Swanton, *Final Report,* 70, is certain of their participation in the slave trade.

León, he found witnesses to testify that when Ponce was alcalde ordinario in 1527 he spent most of the year at the mines of Gracias a Díos instead of attending to the duties of his office.[37] In 1528, Pedrárias sent De Soto and other captains to discover mines near Granada, apparently with some success. Ordinarily the discoverer of a mine, and his political superiors, enjoyed a share in it; that probably happened with any mines that De Soto discovered on this occasion.

Finally, by the spring of 1529, the Ponce–De Soto partnership had branched out into shipping. According to Licenciado Castañeda, at the end of March they had a ship, the *San Gerónimo,* ready for launching, a ship that was one of the largest yet built on the Pacific Coast. By that fall, he could charge that Pedrárias had taken control of the carpenters the partners had employed, in order to prevent them from building two or three more ships and engaging in exploration. Pedrárias, he claimed, wanted to monopolize the carrying trade from Panama to Nicaragua; in an earlier letter he listed the five ships (the *San Gerónimo* was not yet launched) engaged in that trade, only one of which belonged to Pedrárias.[38]

Aside from their offices in 1525 and 1527, De Soto's and Ponce's wealth is indicated by various levies that they, and other *encomenderos,* were required to pay in the years 1529–33. Thus in 1529, they were among six men each required to supply or support one soldier for a force being sent to "conquer" the mines of Gracias a Díos. Other encomenderos had to contribute only part of the support of a soldier. In 1532, De Soto and Ponce were among the nine men assessed fifty pesos de oro or more to pay for another force sent to guard the mines at Villa de Santa María de Buena Esperanza. The two most common assessments were thirty pesos (twenty-four instances) and twenty pesos (twenty-two instances).[39] Finally, in 1533, Ponce and De Soto together, in common with only two other encomenderos, were required to supply three Indians for training as Christians, who could in turn instruct their fellows. Fourteen other encomenderos had to supply two Indians each; the rest, only one each.[40] In sum, these levies indicated that Ponce and De Soto *each* had encomiendas that ranked them among the half-dozen richest men in León.

---

[37]*Diligencias,* León, January 1530, in *Documentos para la historia de Nicaragua,* 2:500, as question 10, with confirming testimony following.

[38]Castañeda to SM, 30 March, 5 October 1529, in ibid., 2:492; 2:209–10.

[39]Order of Pedrárias, León, 28 October 1529, in ibid., 2:225; Act of Cabildo, León, 8 January 1532, ibid., 3:258–69.

[40]Order of Lic. Castañeda, 28 September 1533, in ibid., 4:508.

The partners' wealth is also indicated by their house. It was located on León's principal street, next door to the cathedral. Too, in September 1529, they were the second owners in the town (Castañeda was the first) to rebuild with *tapieria* construction.[41]

De Soto's political role during his years in Nicaragua shows a man rapidly maturing from the position of a loyal subordinate to that of a man with political savy who established a degree of independence within the autocratic, not to say authoritarian, political system that Pedrárias maintained until his death in 1530. When Gil Gonzalez Dávila invaded Nicaragua from Honduras in 1524, Hernández de Córdoba sent Gabriel de Rojas and then De Soto to warn him off. Unlike Rojas, who avoided an armed confrontation with Gonzalez Dávila (because he said he lacked enough men), De Soto was drawn into the night battle of Toreba, where he and his men were captured by a trick and suffered a number of casualties.[42] Only Gonzalez Dávila's return to Honduras because of Cristobal de Olid's arrival there turned this defeat into a qualified victory. Nonetheless, De Soto received his reward: the position of alcalde ordinario in León. But he failed to exercise his office because, said his longtime friend Sebastian Benalcazar, De Soto knew that Hernández de Córdoba was affronted by his election.[43] Still the careful subordinate, De Soto avoided giving offense to the lieutenant governor.

A reason for Hernández de Córdoba's dislike for De Soto is suggested by De Soto's behavior later that year (1525), when Hernández de Córdoba decided to throw off Pedrárias's lordship over Nicaragua. De Soto, as alcalde, upheld Pedrárias's authority and was jailed. Campañón and nine other Pedrárias loyalists broke him out of jail and, after standing down Hernández de Córdoba and a small force that went in their pursuit, went overland to the Gulf of Fonseca, where they took a ship to Natá, from which they sent word to Pedrárias at Panama. De Soto and the others joined Pedrárias when he went to León early the next year and beheaded Hernández de Córdoba after the briefest of informal judicial proceedings.[44] Pedrárias then set about put-

---

[41]Ibid., 2:344, 137, respectively.

[42]Oviedo, *Historia general,* 3:302.

[43]*Diligencias,* León, January 1530, in *Documentos para la historia de Nicaragua,* 2:515, confirmed on 545, 548. Benalcazar did get him to walk about with the *vara* (the symbol of the office) for a few days at the very end of his year as alcalde, but apparently that was after Pedrárias had executed Hernández de Córdoba.

[44]Oviedo, *Historia general,* 3:169; documents in Medina, ed., *Descubrimiento del oceano Pacífico,* 1:225, 314, and 2:205, 357–360; Alvarez Rubiano, *Pedrárias,* 334; Swanton, *Final Report,* 70.

ting the province in order, according to his ideas, and asserting a claim to Honduras![45]

Pedrárias did not long enjoy his newly reestablished authority in Nicaragua. In August 1526, Pedro de los Ríos, his replacement as governor of Castilla del Oro, arrived on the isthmus. Pedrárias returned to Panama in January 1527, to begin his second residencia. He quickly persuaded Ríos that Nicaragua belonged to his (Ríos's) jurisdiction, even though Gil Gonzalez Dávila had been granted it as early as 1520 and again in 1524. But Gonzalez Dávila had died in 1526. Pedrárias's wife and other agents already had asked that Pedrárias be appointed governor of Nicaragua, but that grant had not been made. It is not clear whether officials at Panama knew that the Audiencia of Santo Domingo had appointed Diego López de Salcedo to go to Honduras and Nicaragua to resolve the multisided jurisdictional conflicts that had arisen in 1524 when Pedrárias, Hernán Cortés, Cristobal de Olid, and Gonzalez Dávila were contesting for control of the two provinces. In any case, getting Ríos to go to Nicaragua to claim it for Castilla del Oro not only got him out of Panama, giving Pedrárias a freer hand to attend to his affairs there, but also furthered Pedrárias's claims to the province.

The apparent ending of Pedrárias's rule in Castilla del Oro, and possibly Nicaragua, afforded De Soto and Ponce an important political opportunity that they seized, to their profit. Ríos arrived at León only a few days after López de Salcedo did, coming overland from Honduras. Both presented their titles and asserted a claim to govern Nicaragua. The *cabildo*, heavily stacked with Pedrárias's supporters (he had selected the regidores and the alcaldes ordinarios), decided that Ríos' title was limited to Castilla del Oro. López de Salcedo was installed as governor. Hernando de Soto was made the captain of his guard and proposed for the position of perpetual regidor. Hernán Ponce de León was already serving as alcalde ordinario. A redistribution of Indians was made, supposedly with the concurrence of the captains (De Soto and Ponce both held that rank) and principal persons. López de Salcedo and his new supporters, including De Soto and Ponce, were the chief beneficiaries.[46] De Soto and Ponce were beginning to assert a degree of political independence from their former commander, Pedrárias.

This situation did not last. On March 16, 1527, the queen signed orders making Pedrárias the governor of Nicaragua, permitting Pedrárias to remove his moveable property from Panama duty free, allowing him to leave an

[45]Oviedo, *Historia general,* 3:366–67.

[46]Ibid., 3:367.

agent to answer for him during his residencia, and allowing his servants and clients (*criados*) to freely immigrate to Nicaragua. In short, Pedrárias was allowed to move his operation to Nicaragua. López de Salcedo was instructed to concern himself solely with Honduras. At the same time, a new alcalde mayor, Francisco Castañeda, and a royal treasurer, Diego de la Tovilla, were named to provide checks on the old tyrant. In addition, Martín Enriquez, Martín de Medrano, and Diego de Madrigal were named permanent regidores of León, another way to restricting Pedrárias's power.[47]

The news of Pedrárias's appointment reached León late in 1527 or early in 1528. Martín de Estete, one of Pedrárias's faithful followers, organized others to prevent López de Salcedo from resisting Pedrárias's advent, as rumor and some of his actions seemed to suggest that he might. Still other men joined upon the rumor that López de Salcedo would flee to Honduras, defrauding his creditors in Nicaragua. De Soto joined this faction, whether initially or later in the conspiracy is not known. Such, comments Oviedo, was De Soto's payment for the good works that López de Salcedo had done for him.[48]

The crisis came to a head when Pedrárias landed on the Nicaraguan coast on March 24, 1528. López de Salcedo, after unsuccessfully trying to disperse the conspirators, fled to sanctuary in the cathedral, which is where Pedrárias found him upon entering León. López de Salcedo emerged from the church and publically acknowledged Pedrárias as the new governor. But he was not allowed to leave town. The cabildo and persons with claims against the former governor demanded that he post bonds to ensure them of payment in the settlement of lawsuits they were lodging. When he failed to do so, he was jailed, remaining in the fort until he agreed to pay certain claims. Pedrárias released him on January 8, 1529.[49]

Having changed loyalities at the right moment, De Soto continued to be an important member of León's society although he was likely less subservient to Pedrárias's will than formerly. Pedrárias's decision to send him to discover mines may have been an award, although the old man may also have hoped De Soto would place himself in a fatal position. But De Soto returned, apparently having found mines that added to his wealth.

De Soto soon confronted a more complex political situation, however.

---

[47]Alvarez Rubiano, *Pedrárias,* 353–55.

[48]Oviedo, *Historia general,* 3:351.

[49]Pedrárias to SM, León, 15 January 1519, in *Documentos para la historia de Nicaragua,* 1:448–51; Juan Perez de Tudela Bueso, "Vida y escritos de Gonzalo Fernández de Oviedo," in Oviedo, *Historia general,* 1:cviii.

The arrival of Lic. Castañeda, Treasurer Tobilla, and Veedor Alonso Perez de Valera later that spring challenged Pedrárias's exercise of authority. Tobilla seems to have accepted the old man's autocratic rule, but Castañeda and, even more, Perez de Valera challenged it. By mid-June (?) 1529, Perez de Valera had tried and failed to organize an opposition, even approaching De Soto. According to Ponce, De Soto had replied that "he would serve and support the lord governor as he had always done."[50] De Soto himself said during an investigation of this situation that he talked with Pedrárias often and intimately about persons and events, a comment suggesting that he continued in the man's good graces and thus in the role of loyal subordinate.[51]

On the other hand, De Soto and Ponce were careful to cultivate Lic. Castañeda, even though he found against De Soto in the Gomez de Cortaya lawsuit. In fact, De Soto praised the alcalde mayor for providing justice, where before Pedrárias had appointed judges with little learning or ability to decide suits.[52] De Soto and Ponce also befriended Francisco Hurtado, a royally appointed perpetual regidor. Hurtado became their informant about the business of the cabildo.[53]

De Soto and Ponce's increasingly independent (of Pedrárias) political position was further enhanced by Diego de Almagro's efforts during 1529 to recruit men and obtain new partners for his and Francisco Pizarro and Hernando de Luque's company for the exploration of Peru. Once a member, Pedrárias had been bought out after the first voyage had failed to provide much return. But after the second voyage turned up promising evidence of a complex, wealthy Indian society, the old man seems to have renewed his interest in the venture. When, therefore, Almagro sent Nicolás de Ribera and Bartolomé Ruiz to Nicaragua to solicit aid from Ponce, De Soto, and Pedrárias, the latter used his authority to try to either regain a share of the venture or again, as with Gil Gonzalez Dávila, to get the jump on a rival by organizing his own expedition before Pizarro and Almagro could get theirs going.

Ribera and Ruiz appeared in Nicaragua in June 1529, aboard a ship belonging to Almagro and Pizarro. After what may have been failed negotiations with Pedrárias, Ruiz began to openly recruit. Pedrárias issued orders

---

[50]Información, León, 17 September 1519, in *Documentos para la historia de Nicaragua,* 2:126.

[51]Ibid., 132.

[52]Ibid., 136.

[53]Ibid., 531.

that no person or ship could leave Nicaraguan waters without his permission and, in the case of ships, a register of all persons and cargo. With his ship anchored offshore, but using a bark from the Ponce–De Soto ship, now launched, Ruiz nightly ferried the daring from shore to ship. Eventually as many as 132 persons were aboard, with another 90 said to be waiting on shore.[54] Meanwhile, according to Alvarez Rubiano, Pedrárias tried to force Ponce and De Soto (and probably others) into a company that would sail to Peru, but these talks failed when Ponce and De Soto demanded command, probably for De Soto. Ruiz did, however, obtain Ponce's agreement to sail to Panama to await Pizarro's return and the negotiation of an agreement for the use of the *San Gerónimo.* With that acheived and as many Spaniards and Indian slaves as his ship could carry, Ruiz and his illegal passengers sailed for Panama. This development eventually provided a reason why the *San Gerónimo* should be sent to Panama.[55]

Scheming associated with Peru continued. Witnesses Pedrárias later called to support his refusal to select De Soto or Ponce or other persons that Castañeda supported for regidor and alcalde ordinario for 1530 testified that they had heard that Ponce, De Soto, and Castañeda had formed a company to build additional ships for the Peruvian venture. Ponce was said to have complained that summer that he could not make a living in Nicaragua, even though he held one of the better encomiendas. It was also alleged that De Soto's opposition to Pedrárias's plan to send Miguel Estete to "Morotega, Maslalata, and Cozcatan" was motivated by a desire to keep Spaniards in Nicaragua so that they could be recruited for a Peruvian venture under the Ponce–De Soto–Castañeda company. De Soto himself said that Estete was not fit to command and was being preferred only because he was a "criado" of Pedrárias and married to one of his female servants.[56] Estete eventually went anyway.

Since by this time Perez de Valera was no longer welcomed in León and wished to return to Spain, Ponce sought permission to take him to Panama in the *San Gerónimo.* Because there was no money to pay for her freighting, on August 19, permission was granted for the ship to carry Indian slaves to the Panama market. She was finally fully loaded by mid-October with 347

[54]Alvarez Rubiano, *Pedrárias,* 365–66; Inquiry, León, 3 July 1529, in *Documentos para la historia de Nicaragua,* 2:32, 37, 45–56.

[55]Swanton, *Final Report,* 71, follows Herrera in misdating these events to 1530.

[56]*Diligencias,* León, January 1530, in *Documentos para la historia de Nicaragua,* 2:507, 512–16, 532; De Soto's testimony, *Información,* León, 17 September 1529, ibid., 132–38.

slaves (some belonging to Ponce and De Soto) and fifteen *naborias,* besides her crew of nine, two of whom were black. Three Indian slaves also served with the crew. Apparently Ponce sailed with her.[57]

The final rounds in the drama of De Soto's political life in Nicaragua involved the selection of the alcaldes ordinarios of León for 1530 and his role as commander in the expeditions against the Petronilla islanders. The first, and perhaps the second, suggests some estrangement between Pedrárias and his former protégés. In brief, Castañeda proposed a number of candidates for alcalde ordinario and for regidor, but Pedrárias refused to appoint them, selecting instead men in whom he had confidence. Pedrárias justified this by long custom, from Castilla del Oro, and by having witnesses show that De Soto and Ponce, to discuss only the men of interest to us, had both failed to perform when they had been alcaldes on earlier occasions (1525(?) and 1527, respectively). The governor had his way.[58] Similarly, when he ordered De Soto to the Petronilla Islands, the captain obeyed. As has been noted, his purse was the better for it.

Probably by the time De Soto returned from the Petronilla campaign, Pedrárias was dead (March 6, 1530), a death that removed the last obligations that De Soto may have felt to the man he had served faithfully in Panama and whose patronage had sent him to Nicaragua and given him the opportunity to establish a more independent position, one from which he moved on to Peru.

Almagro's activities on behalf of the Pizarro–Almagro–Luque partnership came to a halt when Francisco Pizarro returned to Panama and told his associate that the Council of the Indies had insisted that only one man be in command of the projected conquest. Pedro Pizarro, not a wholly unbiased reporter, says that Almagro and Luque both withdrew from the company and began to claim as their own certain funds and supplies that had been accumulated against Francisco's return. Efforts by third parties to resolve the conflict got nowhere.

At that point, according to Pedro Pizarro, Ponce showed up with his ship (he erroneously says two ships) and a load of slaves. This was the *San Gerónimo,* whose preparations in the summer and fall of 1529 have been noted. Hernando Pizarro, acting for his brother, negotiated a contract for the use of the ship on terms very favorable to the Ponce–De Soto company. De Soto was to be made lieutenant governor of the chief Spanish town, and

---

[57]Ibid., 2:84–88, 264–77.

[58]*Diligencias,* León, January 1530, in ibid., 2:467–556.

Ponce would get a choice encomienda, in addition to the freight of the ship and any shares they earned from participation in the venture. This agreement, which made the trip to Peru possible without Almagro or Luque's participation, caused Almagro to back down and enter again into the old partnership, although with strained feelings and bad intentions, according to Pedro Pizarro.[59] In light of later events, it is difficult to see how the venture could have succeeded without Almagro's support from Panama during 1531 and 1532.

Preparations dragged on until the end of December 1530. The chroniclers who discuss the matter agree that many Spaniards did not want to go to Peru because they had heard reports of the hardships of the second voyage. Finally, either on December 27, 1530, or about January 1, 1531, the three ships, 180 men, and about thirty horses departed.[60] The *San Gerónimo* carried the five Pizarros, most of the foot soldiers, and as many of the horses as could be crammed aboard.[61]

For reasons that are unexplained except for Zarate's claim of adverse winds, the force was landed not on the Peruvian coast, but at San Mateo Bay in Ecuador, a good hundred leagues from the original goal, which seems to have been Tumbez.[62] The town of Coaque was captured, and perhaps three thousand pesos in loot, including several gold crowns, were sent back to Nicaragua and Panama to lure more men and capital into the venture. The *San Gerónimo* returned to Nicaragua at this time. Bartolomé Ruiz was her pilot.[63] In Nicaragua, Ponce already had two other ships, at least one named *La Concepción*, under construction.

The first relief to reach Pizarro came from Panama thanks to Almagro and Pedro Gregorio, a merchant. Probably in early November 1531, this ship brought a load of supplies, the royal treasury officials assigned to the expedition, about twenty men, and thirteen horses. Thus resupplied, the force marched south to Puerto Viejo, where, on November 15, they saw the two small ships that Sebastian de Benalcazar had used to reach the coast. He and

---

[59]Pedro Pizarro, *Relación*, in *Biblioteca Peruana*, 1st Series, 1:452, 454–55; see also Swanton, *Final Report*, 71, for Hernando Pizarro's own recollection of this contract.

[60]Lockhart, *Men of Cajamarca*, 6–7, n. 7.

[61]Zarate, "Historia del descubrimiento y conquista del Peru," *Biblioteca Peruana*, 1st series, 2:145.

[62]Ibid.

[63]Pedro Pizarro, *Relación*, in *Biblioteca Peruana*, 1st series, 1:456; Diego de Trujillo, "Relación," in ibid., 2:14; Ruiz and one of these crowns is mentioned in Lic. Castañeda's residencia in *Documentos para la historia de Nicaragua*, 4:56.

his force of thirty men and twelve horses had landed up the coast but soon joined Pizarro's army. That force, rapidly sickening, marched farther south, to Puna Island in the Gulf of Guayaquil. There on December 1, Hernando de Soto arrived with two ships, both called *La Concepción* according to the treasury records of the expedition. He had about a hundred men and twenty-five horses.[64]

Pedro Pizarro recorded that De Soto's arrival gave Francisco Pizarro and his men "great happiness and contentment," although the new arrivals felt quite differently, having left the "paradise" of Nicaragua to find themselves on an island with hostile Indians, little food, disease, and no gold or silver. De Soto, he says, refused to leave out of pride; his men were unable to leave.[65] Apparently the ships were sent north almost as soon as they had been unloaded. For his part, Francisco Pizarro may have regretted the bargain made at Panama. The Gregorio-Almagro and Benalcazar reinforcements showed that men, and horsemen, could be attracted to the venture. Ponce's price for the horses and men that De Soto had brought, in comparatively small numbers, may have begun to seem large.

Although preparations for a move to Tumbez began in February 1532, the army required months to make the journey and even more time before it was ready to enter the mountains to challenge the Inca empire. Finding Tumbez devastated, the Spaniards moved on, leaving Tumbez on May 16. They arrived in late July at Tangarara, the site of the first founding of the town of San Miguel (de Piura). There, on August 1, more supplies were received in the *Santa Catalina,* master Juan Pichón, and in the bark, *Santo Domingo,* master Juan de San Juan. Almagro seems to have been responsible for this aid, which made a venture inland thinkable. As a first step, the town of San Miguel was formally founded on October 4 with forty vecinos and about twenty other Spaniards as its residents. The old, infirm, and weak were left, although promised a share of any loot.[66]

Hernando de Soto's activities to this point are not recorded except for his service as judge at Tumbez when Francisco Pizarro wished to make a formal complaint against the treasury officials.[67] Far from being the sort of judicial authority that he had been unwilling to exercise in León in 1525, this judicial

[64]Lockhart, *Men of Cajamarca,* 7–9, and notes.

[65]Pedro Pizarro, *Relación,* in *Biblioteca Peruana,* 1st series, 1:459.

[66]Lockhart, *Men of Cajamarca,* 9.

[67]Testimony of Jeronimo de Aliaga, in *Pesquisa,* by Bishop Tomás de Verlanga, Lima, 20 August 1535, *DII,* 10:246.

role was the formal one of authorizing an inquiry before a notary. It required no exercise of judgment or impartiality.

As the army prepared to move inland, De Soto took up a role long congenial to his temperament, and which had earned him the respect of many men in Nicaragua: commanding forces sent to scout and combat Indians. Lockhart interprets the evidence to suggest that De Soto's dash and horsemanship and the personal loyality of most of the men who had come from Nicaragua under his command were winning him additional followers from among men raised in the western, Badajoz region of Extremadura, thereby creating a political threat to Francisco Pizarro's leadership, which was based on the allegiance of men from the Trujillo region of eastern Extremadura. To counter this development, "the Pizarros decided to give him his head, letting him ride out in command of the vanguard, where he might exceed his orders and plot mutinies, but was at least out of the way."[68] A few trusted loyalists were sent along to keep an eye on this restless subordinate.

Although Herrera credits him with an attack on the chiefs of Cango and Icotu, the first opportunity for De Soto to exercise his new role—which was also compatible with his position as Pizarro's putative lieutenant—was to scout Cajas, a town in the foothills about twenty leagues from San Miguel. His patrol found it devastated because it had supported Huascar in the war between him and Atahualpa. In addition to a small amount of gold seized as loot, De Soto allowed his men to indulge themselves with some of the five hundred women from the Holy Woman's building (the *acllas* and *mamaconas*), much to the anger of Atahualpa's envoy, who was in the town scouting the Spaniards when this outrage against Inca law and custom took place.[69]

During the march into the mountains and to Cajamarca, De Soto seems to have stayed with the main body of the army. But once at Cajamarca, Pizarro sent De Soto with fifteen horsemen and an interpreter to invite Atahualpa to visit him. At one point in the interview, De Soto is credited with charging his horse right up to Atahualpa's throne, then causing the beast to rear on its hind legs, froth from its flanks (or mouth) falling on the emperor. Another version has the animal's breath stirring the imperial fringe

[68]Lockhart, *Men of Cajamarca*, 84.

[69]Swanton, *Final Report*, 72, on the basis of Herrera, *Historia general*, dec. 4:178 and 5:7; question 8, Merits and Services interrogatory of Fernando Beltrán, Seville, 18 October 1536, in *Documentos para la historia de Nicaragua*, 3:466–87; see also John Hemming, *The Conquest of the Incas* (New York: Harcourt Brace, 1970), 30, 32.

(the sign of his office) on the man's forehead. At once an act of spontaneous intimidation, bravado, and foolish, infantile showmanship, the act fits well with De Soto's character as seen by many of his contemporaries and should be interpreted as a sign of one aspect of his personality.[70] Hernando Pizarro was right to worry about De Soto and to obtain permission to take twenty more horsemen to the Inca's camp.[71]

Following Atahualpa's capture and while his ransom was being gathered, De Soto seems to have accompanied Hernando Pizarro on the march to and from Pachacamac. The story that he was one of two Spaniards to go to Cuzco to collect part of the ransom is false, a case of later writers transferring an unusual deed to a man whose reputation fitted with such a deed.[72] The march to Pachacamac and back took from February to early April 1533. Among the trophies was Chalcuchima, one of Atahualpa's generals, who had agreed to accompany Hernando Pizarro from Jauja to Cajamarca.

Not long after Hernando Pizarro and his men returned to Cajamarca, Almagro appeared with some two hundred new men. Lockhart suggests that these men provided the Pizarros with enough loyal troops so that they could more effectively elbow aside potential rivals such as Benalcazar and De Soto. Thus in the division of the ransom during late July—the new men were excluded—Benalcazar and a number of lesser leaders received only modestly larger sums than the private soldiers. De Soto received 4 shares of the 217 distributed, while Francisco Pizarro claimed 13 and Hernando Pizarro, his actual second in command, took 7. The other Pizarro brothers, who had not exercised any leadership roles, received 2.5 shares each. But unlike Benalcazar, who took the hint and shortly left central Peru as the escort for the king's twenty percent of the ransom, De Soto stayed on. He still had the contractual promise of a lieutenancy in the best city the Spaniards might found.[73]

De Soto's general attitude toward Indians and his barely disguised efforts to gather a loyal following probably account for his next action: the burning

[70]I thus disagree somewhat with Swanton's assessment that "De Soto was still young and this looks very much like an outburst of boyish 'showing off.'" *Final Report,* 72.

[71]Hemming, *Conquest of the Incas,* 34. Atahualpa's willingness to talk with Hernando Pizarro, but his silence in response to De Soto's earlier speech, may well have galled the (slightly) older man. Hernando was about thirty, De Soto about thirty-two. Lockhart, *Men of Cajamarca,* 157, 190.

[72]Porrás Barrenechea, "Notes" on Pedro Pizarro, *Relación,* in *Biblioteca Peruana,* 1st series, 2:64; Swanton, *Final Report,* 72, repeats the traditional, false story.

[73]Lockhart, *Men of Cajamarca,* 80–81, 84.

of Chalcuchima. The Spaniards were convinced that he knew where a quantity of gold was hidden. When he denied any knowledge of it, De Soto took him aside and threatened to burn him if he did not tell where the gold was. When he again claimed ignorance of the matter, he was tied to a stake and a fire was begun that burned his arms and legs before he was removed, still denying he knew where any gold was to be found. On a previous occasion, in Castilla del Oro, De Soto was also said to have used fire to try to torture information out of an Indian leader. Some of his later actions in La Florida fit into this pattern of deliberate, even sadistic violence.[74]

Not long after this, in July, De Soto, Rodigro Orgoñez, Pedro Ortiz, Miguel Estete, and Lope Velez volunteered to scout for the Inca army under Ruminavi, which was reported to be marching toward Cajamarca with the intention of freeing Atahualpa. They found no evidence of the army at the place it was said to be.

While De Soto and his companions were gone, the 153 men who remained at Cajamarca and who were already planning to march on Cuzco, allowed fear to decide Atahualpa's fate. On the night of July 26, the Inca was garroted. De Soto, supposed by many writers of a romantic bent to have been opposed to the execution, seems to have commented only that it would have been better if he could have been shipped to Spain. He did not question that Atahualpa could not be left, alive, in Peru much longer. As Hemming has argued, the Inca had served his purpose and would have been a liability on the march to Cuzco. Hemming's careful review of how the various generations of sixteenth-century chroniclers treated this event suggests that De Soto's alleged position on this matter as well as Almagro's and the new arrivals' lack of sympathy for the man (and role in urging his execution) need to be dealt with cautiously. Panic at the realization of where they were and how few they were seems to explain why the Spaniards decided to kill Atahualpa.[75]

With Atahualpa dead and his ransom divided, the army left Cajamarca for Cuzco on August 11, 1533. On October 12, they reached Jauja. On the 24th, De Soto and a small force were dispatched to march ahead of the main body of the army, in the hope that he could seize and hold various bridges before the Inca army could destroy them. Thus given his head, De Soto bulled ahead, fighting the Inca at Vilcas, October 29, and at Vilcaconga on

---

[74]Hemming, *Conquest of the Incas,* 69–70; Porrás Barrenechea, "Notes," to Pedro Pizarro, *Relación,* in *Biblioteca Peruana,* 1st series, 2:97–98.

[75]Hemming, *Conquest of the Incas,* 76–85.

November 8 and 9. In the latter battle, unlike the first, his rash charges nearly cost him his men, the precious horses (who were worth more in battle than foot soldiers), and his life. Only the timely arrival of Almagro and forty horsemen saved him. He had disobeyed orders to wait for the body of the Spanish army at Vilcashuaman, apparently because he and his men wanted to be the first to get to Cuzco and its remaining loot (it had already been stripped to make up Atahualpa's ransom). For the rest of the march to Cuzco, De Soto kept company with the army. After another battle on the approach to Cuzco's valley, the army arrived at that city on November 15. Chalcuchima, saved in April from a fiery death and carried with the army as a hostage to ensure that his troops did not attack, was executed by burning on November 13, because Francisco Pizarro and De Soto were convinced (on purely circumstantial evidence) that he had been behind the attacks at Vilcas and Vilcaconga and the approaches to Cuzco.[76]

From Cuzco, where Manco Inca had been installed as puppet ruler, De Soto was sent on two expeditions to seek out Quisquis and his army of Ecuadorian Indians. This army had conquered Cuzco for Atahualpa during the civil war. Manco Inca was one of Huascar's relatives, now continuing the civil war with the help of his new friends. The first of these expeditions, in December 1533, involved fifty Spanish horsemen and five thousand Inca soldiers from Cuzco on a ten-day march to the southwest that failed to take them into contact with Quisquis. The second, from the end of January to early March 1534, involved Almagro, fifty Spaniards, Manco Inca (for part of the journey) and some twenty thousand native troops. The line of march was toward Jauja, but the army arrived three weeks after the Spaniards there (led by the royal treasurer Riquelme) had defeated units of Quisquis's army, with help from the local Indians and Quisquis's own blundering tactics. An attempt to dislodge Quisquis from a pass that he had fortified failed. De Soto and Almagro retired to Jauja to await Francisco Pizarro and Manco Inca.

Pizarro and Manco Inca reached Jauja in mid-April 1534. A subsequent attempt by Gonzalo Pizarro, De Soto, Manco Inca, eighty Spaniards and four thousand Inca warriors (mid-May to early June) to catch Quisquis, resulted in some fighting but not the engagement of the main body of his army, which was retreating toward Ecuador.[77]

Having conquered Huascar's empire and found an apparently compliant

[76]Ibid., 107–09.

[77]Ibid., 126–41, passim.

puppet ruler, Pizarro set about consolidating his power. To that end, on July 27, 1534, he issued instructions to Hernando de Soto for his position as lieutenant governor at Cuzco, the rich city promised to him in the negotiations at Panama in 1530.

Pizarro's instructions to De Soto indicate that his authority was to be quite limited. De Soto was to have no authority in legal cases, although he was to secretly inquire about any gold or silver that the eighty Spanish residents might have found and was to see to the enforcement of Pizarro's decrees concerning the good treatment of the Indians and their instruction in the Catholic religion. Too, he was to guard the city against Indian attacks or disorder.[78] Whether Pizarro really expected De Soto to meekly accept these limitations cannot be known.

Pizarro also turned his attention to the question of who would control Ecuador. As early as October 24, 1533, Sebastian Benalcazar, then at San Miguel preparing to sail for Panama and Spain, had learned that Alvarado was on his way from Guatemala to challenge Pizarro's conquest, on the claim that he was operating south of the area of his (Pizarro's) grant, in an area that Alvarado had been given by the king. This attempted claim jumping had been revealed by events in Nicaragua on the night of July 22. Alvarado had entered the Port of Posession and seized two large ships, Ponce–De Soto's *La Concepción* (returned from her trip with De Soto in 1531), and Pedro Bravo and Cristobal de Burgos's *La Vitoria,* along with the ship tackle and anchors for three smaller ships that were being careened. All five were being prepared to carry Captain Gabriel de Rojas and 180 or so men (with a hundred horses) to Peru on behalf of Lic. Castañeda, now Governor of Nicaragua after Pedrárias's death, and other, unnamed parties. Ponce and Bravo's efforts to get their ships back had failed, as had Luís de Moscoso's efforts on behalf of his cousin Alvarado to buy horses from Castañeda or, apparently, to bribe him to prevent Rojas from sailing for Peru until after Alvarado had gotten on his own way there. Rojas had left Nicaragua on September 16, sailing directly to San Miguel, although with only a few men.[79] Benalcazar sent him to tell Pizarro. Rojas arrived at Jauja just before Quisquis attacked in mid-February 1534. He conveyed his news upon Pizarro's arrival there in mid-April.

Acting on Rojas's information, Benalcazar set out for Ecuador about mid-

---

[78]*DII*, 42:132–34.

[79]*Información*, San Miguel, 24 October 1533, in *Documentos para la historia de Nicaragua*, 3:283–304; date from ibid., 4:459.

February 1534. He had two hundred men and sixty-two horses. Not long after, Almagro, informed of Alvarado's advance by Rojas, set off for the coast, where he learned in early April of Benalcazar's unauthorized departure from San Miguel. This news was in turn reported back to Pizarro. By late May 1534, Pizarro himself was laying plans to take the Spaniards not needed at Cuzco, Jauja, and San Miguel and march to Quito.[80] He soon abandoned these plans, preferring to let Almagro follow Benalcazar while he went to the coast to select a site for the "city of kings," which became Lima.

Alvarado's invasion of Ecuador went badly and was conducted with tactics learned in Central America, including the use of neck chains to keep Indian porters from running away. By the time he reached the highlands, Benalcazar had occupied Quito (June 22) and Almagro had joined him (July?). After a tense confrontation that almost produced a war, the rival camps agreed that Almagro, acting on behalf of the Pizarro-Almagro-Luque partnership, would buy out Alvarado's investment in ships and equipment for one hundred thousand pesos in gold. Alvarado's men, most of whom had probably paid their own ways, as was the custom then, were allowed to stay and join Pizarro's forces, but Alvarado had to return to Guatemala. Not long after signing this agreement on August 26, 1534, Almagro and Alvarado set out for Jauja to collect the money. Benalcazar, still loyal to Pizarro, was left to govern Quito.[81]

Almagro's bargain with Alvarado affected De Soto's rule at Cuzco in two ways. First, in following Pizarro's instructions, he had persuaded the residents to surrender enough gold and silver to make up the gift to Charles V that the cabildo had agreed to on August 4, 1534 (at Pizarro's request). Apparently the bargain he struck with the Spanish residents, at a meeting held in their church, was that he would not enforce Pizarro's orders against trade with and extortion from the various Indian groups if they would pay their shares. Once paid up, the thirty-four thousand marks of silver and twenty-six to twenty-seven thousand pesos de oro of the gift were sent to Jauja. But this fortune was diverted to buy out Alvarado.[82] De Soto's prestige among the Spaniards at Cuzco probably did not suffer for all of this because he was

[80]Hemming, *Conquest of the Incas,* 153; Pizarro and royal officals to cabildo of Panama, Jauja, 25 May 1534, in Raúl Porrás Barrenechea, ed., *Cartas del Peru (1524–1543)* (Lima: Sociedad de Bibliófilos, 1959), 114; this document is also found in *DII,* 10:134–43.

[81]Hemming, *Conquest of the Incas,* 159–64.

[82]*Pesquisa,* by Bishop Verlanga, Lima, 20 August 1535, *DII,* 10:246–72, especially 247–49, 256–57, 264, 272.

with them in continuing to loot, extort, and otherwise get all the gold and silver he could from the local population.[83]

The second effect of the Almagro-Alvarado bargain was Pizarro's decision of late 1534 to reward Almagro with the lieutenancy of Cuzco. De Soto had shown himself disobedient and had not taken kindly to the arrival of Juan and Gonzalo Pizarro, sent to maintain the Pizarro interest in Cuzco.

Almagro was on his way to Cuzco when word was received in early 1535 that his petition for a section of South America south of Pizarro's 270 leagues had been approved.[84] Almagro immediately concluded that Cuzco fell within his area and moved to occupy it (March 1535). De Soto's initial position was to resist this claim, but he apparently was persuaded of its justice (or at least his interest in supporting Almagro) and came to be viewed by Juan Pizarro as pro-Almagro.[85] Francisco Pizarro, who believed that Cuzco was in his grant, sent Melchor Verdugo to Cuzco with a formal revocation of his company agreement with Almagro and a new appointment of De Soto as his lieutenant, with Juan Pizarro as captain of the Spanish militia. Almagro ignored this, forcing Francisco Pizarro to go to Cuzco himself. Throughout these events, De Soto seems to have done nothing to cause the Almagro and Pizarro factions to disarm themselves. Civil strife was averted, but probably not because he exercised the authority of his office to try to prevent it. Rather, what little evidence there is suggests that De Soto was deeply involved in the partisanship of the time, doing nothing to cool passions.

Once in Cuzco in late May, Pizarro got Almagro to agree to occupy Chile under terms of an agreement they signed on June 12. Pizarro pledged to put up one hundred thousand pesos for the venture.[86] Chile was clearly outside of the limits of Pizarro's grant, whose exact boundary was to be determined by the bishop of Panama, Tomás de Verlanga, as the actual royal orders made clear when they arrived.[87]

---

[83]Swanton, *Final Report,* 73, notes that De Soto presided at the meeting of the Cuzco cabildo on 25 October 1534, during which the allotment of town lots was begun.

[84]Text, dated 21 May 1534 (*sic*), is in *Colección de documentos inéditos para la historia de Chile,* 4:224–39.

[85]Hemming, *Conquest of the Incas,* 174–76; queen to Francisco Pizarro, Madrid, 17 December 1535, in *Colección de documentos inéditos para la historia de Chile desde el viaje de Magallanes hasta la batalla del Maipo, 1518–1818,* 30 vols. (Santiago: Imprenta Ercilla, 1888–1902), 4:328.

[86]Text in ibid., 4:319–22.

[87]For some of the documents in this ongoing dispute, see ibid., 4:224–39, 318–19, 385–98, 407–18, and 5:279–80.

Pizarro also ordered the smelting of all precious metals, so that the royal fifth could be deducted. Hernán Ponce, now at Cuzco and acting for De Soto, presented some 18,500 pesos of gold of various finenesses on May 20. When smelted, they yielded gold worth 5,456,800 *maravedis,* from which the king got 1,080,448.[88] The Pizarros presented even larger amounts for smelting and taxation.

With Almagro agreed to go to Chile,[89] a move also supported by Manco Inca for his own reasons, the question arose as to whether Almagro would appoint an agent to conquer the coast from the Straits of Magellan northward. De Soto volunteered himself and two hundred thousand ducats. He and Ponce had just renewed their partnership (June 27).[90] Almagro got Rodrigo Orgoñez, by now a faithful follower, to propose to undertake this task, with one hundred thousand pesos de oro supplied by Almagro.

De Soto's motivation is not hard to discover. He was clearly out of the picture so far as a continued role at Cuzco. Moreover, the lack of Indian fighting since July 1534 had probably caused him to become restless. His ambition did the rest. Orgoñez wrote to a cousin that he and De Soto nearly came to blows, so intense were their desires to have a leading role in the new conquest. De Soto claimed Almagro had made certain, undisclosed promises to him, which he demanded be honored. But Almagro, probably with some pressure from Pizarro, refused. Instead, he openly preferred Orgoñez.[91] Orgoñez immediately wrote to his relatives in Spain to get them to press for a grant of five hundred leagues of coast, various offices for himself (patterned on Pizarro's grant), a habit of the Order of Santiago, confirmation of his encomienda at Pachacama, and the legitimization of his birth, to note but the more important items.[92]

Almagro's support of Orgoñez over De Soto was probably the bitterest humiliation De Soto had had to suffer. Although not all of the details may have been known, the fact of Orgoñez's illegitimacy and his shady, if profitable, career in the Italian wars was probably well enough known, along with

---

[88]*DII,* 10:504–5.

[89]Really western Bolivia and the mountains and coastal zone of modern Chile rather than the central valley of that nation.

[90]Date from the reaffirmation of the agreement, Havana, 13 May 1539, as published in Solar and Rújula, *El Adelantado Hernando de Soto,* 79–89.

[91]Rodrigo Orgoñez to Antonio de Vergara, Cuzco, 1 July 1535, in Porrás Barrenechea, ed., *Cartas del Peru, 1524–43,* 165.

[92]Orgoñez to Vergara, 1 July 1535; Orgoñez to his father, Cuzco, 2 July 1535, both in ibid., 165, 167, respectively.

his lack of distinction in the conquest of Central America. The insult to De Soto was apparent. Whether the shadow of Almagro's mother's *converso* origins, and arrest by the Inquisition for witchcraft, was also known is less certain, but if it was rumored, the insult would have been all the greater.[93] De Soto was noble, legitimate, and of old Christian stock and had a more distinguished record in the conquests of the Americas. And unlike Orgoñez, who had little money of his own, De Soto was rich and backed by Ponce's and the partnership's assets in Nicaragua. But Almagro preferred to support a man without De Soto's ability to become independent. On that, he and Pizarro were probably agreed, because both had seen De Soto's behavior in Peru.

De Soto remained in Cuzco until early July 1535. He thus saw Almagro's army depart on July 3, to be followed by Francisco Pizarro not many days later. In fact, De Soto probably traveled with Pizarro to Lima. In late August he was a witness in Bishop Verlanga's inquiry into how the royal revenues had been handled until that date. He reaffirmed that testimony on October 15 and was still in Lima on October 26, when he appeared in support of Alonso Martín de San Benito.[94]

In December 1535, De Soto sailed to Panama in his and Ponce's *San Gerónimo*. In March, he, many of his Peruvian followers, and a part of his fortune departed from Nombre de Díos in Damian de Soria's *Santi Spiritus*.[95] Another ship in the group carried more of his fortune under the watchful eye of Luís de Moscoso, later De Soto's successor in the La Florida venture. This ship was wrecked in the Jardines de la Reina, off southern Cuba, according to one report, or at the "point of Bime" in the Bahama Channel, according to another.[96] Even with some losses in that wreck, De Soto arrived at Seville with a large fortune, said to be between 100,000 and 180,000 pesos. He also carried letters recommending him as a man that the government could question to learn the facts of events in Peru.[97]

---

[93]Porrás Barrenechea, "Notes," to Pedro Pizarro, *Relación*, in *Biblioteca Peruana*, 1st series, 2:91–95.

[94]*Pesquisa*, *DII*, 10:269–72, 288; "Información de parte de Alonso Martín de San Benito," Lima, 26 October 1535, in Medina, ed., *Descubrimiento del oceano Pacífico*, 2:359–64.

[95]Listed as a 1535 return (1535 R # 44) in Huguette and Pierre Chaunu, *Seville et l'Atlantique (1504–1650)*, 8 vols. in 10 (Paris: SEVPN, 1955), 2:262. The unreliable nature of the records that the Chaunus used accounts for this dating discrepancy.

[96]Casa de Contratación to SM, Seville, 26 April 1536, in Porrás Barrenechea, ed., *Cartas del Peru, 1524–43*, 188–89; Swanton, *Final Report*, 73.

[97]Francisco Barrionuevo to Council of Indies, Nombre de Díos, 30 January 1536, ibid.; Bishop Verlanga to SM, Panama, 3 February 1536, in *Colección de documentos inéditos para la historia de Chile*, 4:330.

De Soto's first order of business upon reaching Seville was to outfit himself and his servants, and probably a number of his followers from Peru, with clothing signifying his wealth and pretensions to status. Elvas recalled that "he employed servants, including a major domo, grand master of ceremonies, pages, equerry, chamberlain, footmen, and all the other servants requisite for an establishment of a gentleman."[98]

Next, De Soto had to negotiate with the House of Trade concerning the "loan" that Charles V was demanding from all who returned with loot from the empire. In undertaking the Tunis campaign, Charles needed all the money he could find and so ordered seizures of remissions from Peru.[99] Juan Ruiz de Arce recalled that sixty of the men from Peru lent the crown some eight hundred thousand ducats, in return for which Charles assigned various revenues to them.[100] This is the origin of the three hundred thousand maravedis in "rents" on the Granada silk monopoly that De Soto acquired at about this time.[101]

With those matters settled, De Soto and others went to court, where they spent lavishly and petitioned for various benefits. De Soto's interest was in acquiring a province to govern and the right to carry out additional discoveries. While in Seville, he had entered his request for a grant south of Pedro de Mendoza's two hundred leagues; that is, for the area granted to Simón de Alcazaba in the summer of 1534. Alcazaba had died trying to reach it. This was the same area that Rodrigo Orgoñez was also soliciting.[102] It embraced the southern portion of Chile and the mouth of the Straits of Magellan.

Whether because he learned that the Bishop of Plasencia, Juan Rodriguez

---

[98]Elvas, *Relation,* herein, vol. 1; Swanton, *Final Report,* 75.

[99]Ramón Carande, *Carlos V y sus banqueros,* 3 vols. (Madrid: Sociedad de Estudios y Publicaciones, 1949–67), 3:170–79.

[100]Juan Ruiz de Arce, "Advertencias," in *Biblioteca Peruana,* 1st series, 1:435.

[101]Agreement of Ponce and De Soto, Havana, 13 May 1539, AGI, Justicia 750, printed in Solar and Rújula, *El Adelantado Hernando de Soto,* 79–89. Elvas says that Charles paid him 600,000 reales and interest from the silk monopoly and other monies from the House of Trade. Elvas, *Relation,* herein, vol 1. If the income were at the 3% rate normal on *juros* of the time, the principal sum was 10,000,000 maravedis or about 22,222 pesos de oro, about 20% of the fortune De Soto was said to have carried to Seville. Hernández Díaz, *Expedición de Hernando de Soto,* 32, documents of 4 December 1537 and 4 January 1538 grant Isabel de Bobadilla, the mother, power to collect 620,000 maravedis (1,377 p. 6 t. 3 gr. de oro @450 maravedis) that Charles V agreed to pay De Soto from the revenues of the treasury of Grand Canary Island.

[102]Casa to SM, n.d. [summer of 1536?], in Porrás Barrenechea, ed., *Cartas del Peru, 1524–43,* 185–86. Alcazaba's story is briefly noted in John H. Parry, *The Discovery of South America* (New York: Taplinger, 1979), 216.

de Fonseca, was interested in this area for his brother or some other captain he wished to patronize, or because he thought he saw a better opportunity, De Soto soon changed his petition to the 100 leagues north of San Miguel de Piura, the supposed beginning of Pizarro's 270 leagues. This was, he wrote an agent, "the most sterile and unprofitable [part] of that land," although he noted that "by way of Quito" it offered a good opening to the interior. If that were not available, he wanted Guatemala and the right to explore in the Pacific with the title of adelantado and ten percent of all goods discovered. He also wanted habits of the Order of Santiago for himself and Hernán Ponce de León and royal confirmation of their encomiendas, houses, and lands.[103] Evidently he was worried that Pizarro might deprive him of his Peruvian holdings.

While awaiting the decision of the Council of the Indies on his petition, De Soto entered into marriage with Isabel de Bobadilla, daughter of his old lord, Pedrárias, and of a woman of the same name. Much romantic nonsense has been written about De Soto and his new bride. Wilmer (1858) seems to be the origin of much of it in English, but as recently as 1986 Miguel Albornoz incorporated their supposed love story into his work on De Soto. According to these stories, the young people had become interested in each other during the years 1514–19 when mother and daughter (then a toddler) had been in Castilla del Oro. Their love had been temporarily frustrated by Pedrárias, who is alleged to have disapproved of De Soto and to have sent his daughter back to Spain to separate them.

In fact, De Soto's marriage to Isabel de Bobadilla was probably, like most such alliances, a calculated affair on both sides with the long-term preservation of property at issue. The dowry agreement was signed at Valladolid on November 14, 1536, at a time when De Soto's petition for a governorship in Ecuador or Guatemala was still pending (apparently). The possibility of a Guatemalan governorship would seem to be the point of the agreement. Isabel's sister María Arias de Peñalosa had married Rodrigo de Contreras y de la Hoz, governor of Nicaragua (1535–41). An alliance with a prospective governor of Guatemala would further solifidy the Pedrárias-Bobadilla interests in Central America. Isabel's relatively modest dowry of a Panamian ranch with a herd of cattle and horses worth seven thousand pesos de oro was only part of what she brought to the marriage. Through her De Soto gained access to the Bobadilla clan, still powerful in Segovia and the royal

---

[103]Ibid.; De Soto to "Magnifico Señor," n.d., n.p., in ibid., 273; translated in Swanton, *Final Report*, 75–76.

court, thanks to their services to Isabel the Catholic. De Soto offered not only the prospect of another Central American connection, but also six thousand ducats as a groom's portion (Isabel's if he died before her) and properties in Nicaragua and Peru that might pass to an heir.[104]

When the government finally acted, it offered De Soto not a governorship in one of the established colonies but the opportunity to conquer La Florida, roughly the southeastern quarter of what is now the United States.[105] Coupled with this was the position of governor of Cuba, which would serve as a supply base. Apparently Guatemala was denied to him because Bartolomé de las Casas, who held a low opinion of all Indian fighters and De Soto in particular, was trying to show that peaceful preaching would convert the Indians, even in the infamous "land of war" that had resisted the usual martial form of subjugation.[106] Too, Pedro de Alvarado was already governor of Guatemala. Ecuador and any part of South America were also denied to De Soto because other men were favored by court interests and, probably, because he was known to have bad relationships with Pizarro and Almagro. North America, on the other hand, was not claimed by anyone and the unpromising reputation of its coasts probably seemed analogous to the northern coast of Peru, which De Soto had said he wanted.[107]

After negotiations not recorded in surviving documents, the government issued his contract with a date of April 20, 1537. It is notable for being long on economic privileges and short, compared to Lucas Vázquez de Ayllón's, for example, on any emphasis on the Dominican theory of a peaceful approach to the native polities that might be found in La Florida. The contract did contain a copy of Charles V's decree of November 17, 1526, enjoining pacific treatment of the Indians, reading of the Requirement of 1514 to them

---

[104]Dowry agreement, Valladolid, 14 November 1536, in Solar and Rújula, *El Adelantado*, 157–214; Emilio Roig de Leuchsenring, *Hernando de Soto: Cuba y la conquista de la Florida* (Havana: Sociedad Colombista Panamerican, 1939), 13–14.

[105]The contract gave De Soto the areas formerly granted to Narváez and Ayllón. Narváez in turn had obtained Ponce de León's grant and Garay's Amichel, that is peninsular Florida and the northern coast of the Gulf of Mexico. The exact western boundary was defined by a royal decree of 30 December 1538 that set Río de las Palmas (the modern Soto La Marina) as the western border and Newfoundland as the northern border. Empress to viceroy of Mexico and others, 30 December 1538, AGI, CT 3309, Book for Florida, fols. 131v—132v.

[106]Lewis Hanke, *The Spanish Struggle for Justice* (Boston: Little Brown, 1949), 77–81.

[107]For the development of this reputation, see Paul E. Hoffman, *A New Andalucia and a Way to the Orient: The American Southeast in the Sixteenth Century* (Baton Rouge: Louisiana State University Press, 1990), 1–102.

until they understood it,[108] peaceful and honest trade, no forced labor or enslaving of Indians, and no recruitment of Spaniards from the Antilles for the expeditionary force. On the other hand, the contract permitted the establishment of encomiendas, the very device that had produced all the abuses that the decree wished to avoid! To help guarantee that Indian rights were respected, at least two friars were to go on every expedition. These religious commisars were to be consulted about all matters relating to the Indians.[109]

To sweeten the agreement, the crown ordered an investigation to determine whether De Soto qualified for the Order of Santiago. That inquiry, conducted at Badajoz in 1537, is an important source for his background and place of birth.

By early August 1537, De Soto was in Seville, beginning to purchase ships and to make other preparations for the journey.[110] He fixed rendevous for his expedition as Seville and January 1538. He then settled into the business of raising men, aided by the arrival of Alvar Núñez Cabeza de Vaca, one of three men to survive from Pánfilo de Narváez's ill-starred expedition of 1528 to Amichel. Asked to join the De Soto expedition, he eventually declined, but he did tell relatives that they might be well advised to join the venture. In other contexts he spoke of things that were only for Charles V's ear, which his hearers took to mean that he knew of great riches.[111] Men began to gather money to pay for their outfitting and journey. Some, like Garcia Osorio, sold real estate to support themselves and their relatives (a brother in this case), horses, foot soldiers, and servants.[112]

The Elvas narrative provides a graphic description of the gathering of the army (herein, vol. 1). The list of men and when they enrolled has been published, although it is not certain that all went on the expedition. Three or

[108]See Hanke, *Spanish Struggle for Justice,* 31–33, for the content of this document.

[109]Text in Solar and Rújula, *El Adelantado Hernando de Soto,* 91–117. The cedula is on pp. 103–16.

[110]José Hernández Díaz, *Expedición del Adelantado Hernando de Soto a la Florida: Notas y documentos relativos a su organización* (Sevilla: Instituto Hispano-Cubano de Historia de America, 1938), 13. See his pp. 13–31 for other contracts, especially with seamen for the ships. Hernández Díaz's documents came from only Oficio X, one of twenty-four notarial offices. Many more documents connected with this outfitting await discovery.

[111]Elvas, *Relation,* herein, vol. 1.

[112]Inquiry for Garcia Osorio, Mexico, 5 December 1560, AGI, Patronato 63 (photocopy in J. B. Stetson, Jr., Collection, P. K. Yonge Library, University of Florida).

TABLE 1. PROVINCES OF ORIGIN OF PARTICIPANTS IN CONQUESTS

PROVINCE	BOYD #	PERCENT	PERU #	PERCENT	DE SOTO #	PERCENT
Andalucia	6,419	34.2	34	20.2	92	13.2
Extremadura	2,973	15.9	36	21.4	341	48.9
New Castile	2,070	11.0	15	8.9	41	5.9
Old Castile	3,324	17.7	17	10.1	88	12.6
León	1,410	7.5	15	8.9	64	9.6
Basque	857	4.6	—	—	8	1.1
Galicia	309	1.6	—	—	12	1.7
K. of Aragon	304	1.6	2	1.2	3	0.4
Murcia	151	0.8	—	—	3	0.4
Navarra	81	0.4	2	1.2	—	—
Asturias	113	0.6	8	4.8	1	0.1
Canarias	39	0.2	—	—	—	—
Foreigners	698	3.7	2	1.2	8	1.1
Unknown	—	—	37	22.0	45	6.4
	18,743		168		698	

Sources:

Boyd: Peter Boyd Bowman, "Patterns of Spanish Emigration to the Indies until 1600," *Hispanic American Historical Review* 41 (1976): 585, table 1; columns 1 and 2 summed.

Peru: James Lockhart, *The Men of Cajamarca* (Austin, 1972), 28, table 3.

De Soto: John R. Swanton, *Final Report of the United States De Soto Expedition Commission* (rpt., Washington, D.C., 1985), 82.

four women also joined the expedition over and above Isabel de Bobadilla, De Soto's wife, and her ladies. Four men of possible Moorish origins have been noted. In all, about seven hundred persons sailed with the expedition, of whom eighteen had known civilian occupations (the majority tailors) and four were clergy.[113] Swanton has published a list and prepared a numerical analysis of some 698 names. Table 1 provides comparative information with all immigrants of 1493–1539, according to Boyd Bowman's compilation, and with the men of Cajamarca, as Lockhart has tabulated them. It is clear that, except for the very large percentage of Extremeños in the De Soto force

[113]Ignacio Avellaneda, *Los sobrevivientes de la Florida: The Survivors of the De Soto Expedition* (Gainesville: University of Florida, P. K. Yonge Library of Florida History, 1990), 7, which also contains prosopographical analyses of the 257 survivors.

(48.9 percent compared to 15.9 percent overall and 21.4 percent of the men at Cajamarca) and a correspondingly small number of Andalucians, De Soto's force had a composition not unlike that of Pizarro's at Cajamarca, while both differed by having fewer New Castilians and more Old Castilian and Leónese than the general pattern of immigration in that period.

Although most of the men provided their own weapons and supplies and probably contributed to their transportation costs, De Soto still had large expenses. At present little is known of them[114] aside from the fact that he pawned (or sold) the royal grant of income from the Granada silk monopoly in order to raise money. The purchasers may have been Genoese. One of their own, Cristobal Spinola, sold his goods and joined De Soto. Too, Elvas says that when he left Spain, De Soto was in debt, having arrived with a fortune![115]

As the fleet made up, it was assigned the task of accompanying a group of merchantmen. Spain was still at war with France, although her diplomats were close to arranging the Truce of Nice (July 14–16, 1538). Lacking the means to provide an escort as far as the Canary Islands, the crown took advantage of De Soto's force. Swanton has provided a table listing the ships, approximate size, and commanders in the De Soto fleet. This is reproduced here as table 2.

De Soto sailed from San Lucár de Barrameda on April 7, 1538. The trip was uneventful. Gomera, in the Canary Islands, was reached on Easter Sunday, April 21. After a week there gathering water and supplies, the convoy was off again, keeping company until well into the Caribbean, when the Mexican ships went their separate way, leaving De Soto's fleet to work its way to Santiago de Cuba. They arrived there on June 9.[116]

After a round of welcoming ceremonies, De Soto made provision for additional fortifications at Santiago, which had been raided some months before his coming, and attended to other governmental matters. That done, he divided his expedition, sending his family and the foot soldiers by ship to Havana while he took the horsemen, divided into several squadrons, overland to Havana. Although the men were supposed to pay for the provisions

[114]See Hernández Díaz, *Expedición del Adelantado Hernando de Soto,* 13–15, for expenses totaling 2,622 ducats for the purchase of two ships and of 653 ducats for the making of ship biscuit and for freight agreements whose value to De Soto is not indicated. These are but the tip of an iceberg of similar documents.

[115]Agreement, Havana, 13 May 1539, in Solar and Rújula, *El Adelantado Hernando de Soto,* 79–89; Ruth Pike, *Enterprise and Adventure,* 74–75; Elvas, *Relation,* herein, vol. 1.

[116]Swanton, *Final Report,* 100.

TABLE 2. SHIPS OF HERNANDO DE SOTO'S FLEET, SAN LUCAR, 1538

NAME	SIZE	COMMANDER
San Cristobal	800 *toneladas*	Hernando de Soto
La Magdalena	"no smaller"	Nuño de Tobar
La Concepción	> 500 toneladas	Luís de Moscoso
Buena Fortuna	"equally large"	Andre de Vasconcelos
San Juan	a "large ship"	Diego Garcia
Santa Barbara	a "large ship"	Arias Tinoco
San Antón	a "small galleon"	Alonso Romo de Cardeñosa
(not named)	caravel	Pedro Calderon
(not named)	two pinnaces	

Source: Swanton, *Final Report of the United States De Soto Expedition Commission*, 97.

they obtained, a trail of complaints followed them. De Soto, who went ahead, reached Havana about November 1. The rest of the cavalry did not arrive until March 1539, having spent the winter living off the land and its inhabitants.

Over that winter, De Soto sent Juan de Añasco to seek out a port on the west coast of Florida and attended to the fortification of Havana and other governmental chores. With Añasco's report and the cavalry at hand, De Soto pushed final preparations. By then he had acquired four agricultural properties that could supply maize, sweet potatoes, *cacabi* biscuit (a bread made from bitter manioc), beef, pork, mutton, turkeys, and chickens, in addition to any of those supplies that he bought from other Cuban producers. One of his properties, which also had fifty resident Indians held in encomienda, was used to raise horses as well as other livestock, maize, and manioc.[117] Almost on the eve of sailing, Hernán Ponce arrived aboard the *Santa Ana,* a ship in which he had bought a half-interest at Nombre de Díos. He was on his way back to Spain with the proceeds of De Soto's Cuzco properties (including slaves), sold to Almagro for four thousand pesos de oro, probably in early 1538 during Almagro's rebellion against Pizarro. Ponce had also given Almagro De Soto's encomienda at Cuzco because Almagro had purchased the

[117]Inventory and sale of goods, Havana, 6 December 1543, in Solar and Rújula, *El Adelantado Hernando de Soto,* 223–73; Irene A. Wright, *Historia documentada de San Cristobal de la Habana en el siglo XVI,* 2 vols. (Havana, 1927), 1:17.

other properties.[118] According to Elvas (repeated with elaboration in Garcilaso), Ponce had not intended to put in at Havana because he did not want to meet De Soto and only did so when adverse weather caused the ship's master to seek port.[119]

This story seems wrong on its face; ships from Tierra Firme almost never avoided a final food, water, and firewood stop at Havana, and a ship in as poor a condition as the *Santa Ana* supposedly was would surely have been brought to port before the long Atlantic crossing. On the other hand, Ponce might not have been particularly anxious to discuss their affairs with De Soto, because if he knew of the expedition he could have anticipated demands for money.

Whatever the truth of Ponce's motivations and feelings upon landing at Havana, he soon found cause for offense. On May 13, 1539, De Soto dictated his will. This made elaborate provision for charitable works and for De Soto's monument in the Church of San Miguel in Jerez de los Caballeros, but left nothing to Ponce. De Soto also induced Ponce to sign an agreement in which each accepted the other's actions in the nearly four years since they had renewed the company at Cuzco and waived all future claims for compensation under the partnership for any action taken to May 13, 1539. De Soto was particularly insistent that his expenses at court and in fitting the expedition be accepted and that he be released from any claim of extravagant spending. He did recognize that Ponce had a right to half of the income (150,000 maravedis) from the royal grant against the Granada silk monopoly, and a provision was made for Ponce to purchase for himself alone an equivalent income, using the partnerships' funds. This document so angered Ponce that he went to another notary and declared that he had signed it under duress and against his will and so would not be bound by it.[120] Subsequently confronted about this by Isabel de Bobadilla, Ponce renounced his renunciation, but then they became involved in a lawsuit about the company.[121]

Ponce's anger is understandable. Not only had De Soto squandered the

[118]Oviedo, *Historia general,* 5:196, noting that after Almagro's death in the battle of Las Salinas, 26 April 1538, Hernando Pizarro appointed Felipe Gutierrez as a regidor of Cuzco, assigning him the encomienda and giving these details of how Almagro had obtained it.

[119]Elvas, *Relation,* herein, vol. 1; Garcilaso, *La Florida,* herein, vol. 2.

[120]Letter of agreement, Havana, 13 May 1539, in Solar and Rújula, *El Adelantado Hernando de Soto,* 79–89.

[121]AGI, Justicia 750. This is the source for many of the documents found in volume 1 of this publication.

more than one hundred thousand pesos de oro he had taken to Spain, he had apparently run up large debts that the partnership—meaning Ponce—was obliged to pay. On top of that, De Soto was probably treating his former friend and one-time benefactor with a hauteur that had to have been offensive. And he was about to embark on a plunge into an area that had a reputation as a wasteland, one from which little profit might be expected.

De Soto sailed on May 18, to take advantage of favorable winds. The Florida coast was hailed on Sunday, May 25, the feast of the Holy Spirit. In due course the army was landed and began its great peregrination, as De Soto searched for mineral wealth or some other resource whose location would indicate which two hundred leagues of coast he should request from Charles V for the area of his government. His contract, it should be recalled, provided for exploration before he had to request a specific part of the continent for his territory.

Because this essay is a brief biography, the still controversial details of the landing point and the route will not be addressed. Suffice it to say that De Soto showed that he wanted to find minerals and would not settle for agricultural prospects (at Cofitachequi and Coosa), that he turned away from the coast rather than make contact with Maldonado and the supply ships he had at Achuse, and that he died west of the Mississippi River on May 21, 1542.

Led by Luís de Moscoso, De Soto's surviving soldiers, women, Indian slaves, horses, and pigs spent another sixteen months seeking riches, an overland route to New Spain, and building and sailing seven brigantines from Guachoya, on the Mississippi River, to the Rio Pánuco in New Spain. They reached that haven on September 10, 1543. Of approximately 600 Spaniards who landed in La Florida, only 311 survived to return to New Spain. Avellaneda's recent prosopographical study of the 257 survivors for whom some biographical data could be found reveals that they were what might be expected from what is known about those who embarked with De Soto in Spain. That is, the typical survivor was a male from Extremadura, about 24 years of age in 1539, able to sign his name, and a commoner who settled in New Spain or Peru after his adventure in Florida, and married.[122] Because there is no known list, we do not know the characteristics of the Indians who accompanied these Spaniards to New Spain. We do know that some of them later were sent to Guatemala whence they influenced Fray

[122]Avellaneda, *Los sobrevivientes de la Florida*, 67–74.

Luis Cancer's ill-conceived missionary voyage to Florida and the Luna expedition of 1559–62.[123]

The news of De Soto's death reached Havana on December 4, 1543, when the *Santiago,* master Ochoa Vizcayno, put in with a number of the surviving members of the expedition, including Rodrigo Rangel, and with letters from the viceroy of Mexico. Within two days, Isabel de Bobadilla had obtained not only depositions about that but also a court order for the inventory and sale of De Soto's and her property. The inventory was begun on December 6 and completed on December 12. Auction of the goods yielded 3,121 pesos de oro and 3 *tomines,* all of which Isabel claimed against the 7,000 pesos de oro value of her dowry. As many as eight of the purchasers, including Rangel, may have been survivors of the expedition.[124] The widow and her household left Havana the following spring.

What sort of person was Hernando de Soto? His contemporaries in Central America, Sebastian de Torres, Sebastian Benalcazar, and Gonzalo Fernández de Oviedo, offer a far from flattering picture, one that fits well with the more brutal aspects of his Florida venture and gives the lie to the romantic idealization of him as somehow different from other Spanish conquistadors. Torres and Benalcazar, both of whom had known him since 1514, testified in an admittedly partisan context in 1530 that De Soto would not make a good alcalde ordinario because "he is very excitable [*apasionado*] and thoughtless [*corto de razones*]" (Torres) and was an "excitable [*apasionado*], curt [*mal sufrido*] man" (Benalcazar).[125] That is, he was a man given to snap judgments, vehement support of persons and causes, and, likely, great anger and other emotions. In addition, he would not suffer gladly those he considered to be fools or bores. He was not, in short, the sort of thoughtful, objective, patient person who would make a good judge. Oviedo, who had seen him off and on since 1514, offered the opinion that he was "a good man in his person [that is, good looking] and very busy in this hunting [*monteria*] of Indians and he has sent many to hell. . . ."[126] The use of a term ordinarily denoting something akin to fox hunting, suggests Oviedo's assessment of De Soto's attitude toward his human prey.

These judgments are supported by a review of his biography. Incidents such as his rashness at the battle of Toreba (1524), before Atahualpa (1532)

[123]Paul Hoffman, *A New Andalucia and a Way to the Orient,* 100, 154.

[124]Solar and Rújula, *El Adelantado Hernando de Soto,* 223–73.

[125]*Diligencias,* León, January 1530, in *Documentos para la historia de Nicaragua,* 2:506, 515.

[126]Oviedo, *Historia general,* 3:351.

and at the Battle of Vilcaconga (1533), his near insubordination throughout the Peruvian campaigns and especially as lieutenant governor of Cuzco, his bidding war with Orgoñez over the right to invade southern Chile, and finally his almost reckless agreement to explore La Florida all indicate a man who did not think carefully about his options but plunged ahead. Such boldness, coupled with his skill as a horseman and fighter with the lance and sword, seems to have been admired by many of his followers because he (and they) seldom came to harm because of it. Probably vain, clearly ambitious, but handsome and apparently well spoken (on occasion), De Soto had most of the characteristics that might make a man charismatic, even a *caudillo* in the Hispanic world of his time. Such men draw some others to their orbits, while colliding with men of similar character or of superior social status.

That he was happy to engage in the "hunting of Indians" is well attested by events in Nicaragua, Peru, and La Florida and probably would be for Castilla del Oro if we knew more about his life there. Trained in Indian warfare in the schools of Balboa, Espinosa, and Pedrárias, he approached all Indians with the Central American tradition, which was one of brutal oppression directed against rulers, first of all.[127] On at least two occasions, he was party to, and probably led, the burning of Indians as a method of torture. He had no qualms about the Indian slave trade either in Central America, where slaves were branded on their foreheads, or in La Florida, although in the latter case he did not export any Native Americans because that would have required contacting his ships and thus admitting his failure in 1539–40 to find any minerals in the mountains, Ayllón's "Xapira."

This is not to suggest that he lacked social graces or that his personality did not change, even mellow a bit, with age. Clearly he was a man who knew how to act acceptably when the circumstances of the Spanish world required him to do so. As a youth and into his twenties, this meant being the loyal subordinate in Pedrárias's Castilla del Oro and Nicaragua, at least until about 1526 or 1527 when, legally of majority age (twenty-five was the age of majority), he began to be more independent. In Peru, where he was subject to the authority of a man of lower social origins than himself, he carried off his role of subordinate with great difficulty but just enough civility so that Pizarro did not have cause to take any action against him beyond sending trusted friends, even his own brothers, along with De Soto to keep him from striking out on his own. And once returned to Spain, where his role as a leading commander in Pizarro's forces was well advertised, he apparently

[127]Ibid., 2:165, says as much.

fitted into court life without difficulties, only to find that he was again treated like a subordinate when his petitions for a known, profitable governorship were denied. But he maintained his *amour propre* and his lavish household, putting a bold face on what must have been something of a disappointment. This behavior and his generally moderate conduct in La Florida toward the Indians (compared to his actions in Central America) suggest some moderation of his personality with age.

In sum, one has to agree with Raul Porrás Barrenechea that De Soto was "neither better nor worse than other conquistadores nor in any way a paradigm of goodness and gentleness."[128] Garcilaso and romantic writers who have followed his lead would have it otherwise, but a close reading of the available record shows us a man who delighted in his skill with a horse and lance when used against other human beings, was ambitious and greedy, and, in the view of contemporaries who knew him well, passionate and curt in his behavior toward others. Such a person would not be welcomed in the dens of many who, knowing only the romantic image, continue to idealize Hernando de Soto.

[128]Porrás Barrenechea, "Notes" to Pedro Pizarro, *Relación*, in *Biblioteca Peruana*, 1st series, 2:98.

Some New Translations of De Soto Documents from the General Archive of the Indies, Seville

Selected and Introduced by Rocío Sánchez Rubio
Translated by David Bost

Introduction

The documents presented here reflect several stages of Hernando de Soto's long American trajectory.* Appearing in chronological order as they were issued, the first of the collection relates his passage through Peru, where he had participated in the conquest under the command of Francisco Pizarro, also an Extremaduran. His active collaboration and leadership in some of the most important episodes of the Peruvian conquest, along with his proven loyalty, induced Pizarro to name him *Teniente de Gobernador* [lieutenant governor] of the city of Cuzco, the capital of the Incan empire. The post qualified him as supreme authority of the city surpassed only by Francisco Pizarro.

The naming [*nombramiento*] appears dated July 27, 1534, eight months after the Spaniards entered that city; it was issued in the nearby settlement of Jauja and signed by the governor. Instructions are included in the document for carrying out the post, specifying his obligations. As lieutenant governor of Cuzco, Hernando de Soto had the power to intervene in matters of jus-

*Included are: 1) a document naming De Soto as lieutenant governor of Cuzco [Archivo General de Indias, Seville (AGI). *Patronato.* Legajo 90-A]; 2) a Cédula Real from 1537 authorizing certain other ships bound for the Indies to accompany De Soto [AGI. *Indiferente General.* Legajo 1962, Folios 301 vto.–302]; 3) a Cédula Real from 1538 authorizing the same ships to leave by March 15 if De Soto was not ready (which he was not) [AGI. *Indiferente General.* Legajo 1962, Folio 331 vto.]; 4) authorization for Doña Isabel to bring three women slaves to Cuba in her personal service [AGI. *Indiferente General.* Legajo 1962, Folio 331]; 5) a lengthy interrogation for De Soto's admission to the Order of Santiago [Archivo Histórica Nacional. *Sección Ordenes Militares (Santiago).* Expediente No. 7855]; 6) a document in which De Soto granted wide authority to his wife to represent him in administering all his assets and properties [AGI. *Justicia.* Legajo 750 (A)]; and 7) an inventory of De Soto's assets drawn up by Isabel de Bobadilla after learning of her husband's death [AGI. *Justicia.* Legajo 750 (A)].

Spanish transcriptions of documents 5 and 6 have appeared before in Antonio del Solar y Taboada and José de Rújula y de Ochotorena, *El Adelantado Hernando de Soto* (Badajoz, Spain: Ediciones Arqueros, 1929).

tice, whether they be civil or criminal cases, and his authority extended to the Spanish population (residents or transients), as well as to the native population. Outside his jurisdiction were the defense of the city and conflicts brought about by indigenous uprisings. It is seen from this document that during this period Cuzco enjoyed ordinances that regulated municipal life not unlike those that also existed in Spain. In the instructions, for example, was the recommendation to Spaniards who had been awarded *repartimientos* and *encomiendas* of Indians not to commit abuses with their charges. This circumstance was entrusted to the care of De Soto, who was admonished to watch over the indigenous population and their treatment; he was also encouraged to begin the work of indoctrination and preaching of the Catholic faith among them.

For barely two years De Soto held the post of lieutenant governor. In 1536, he returned to Spain and obtained the royal authorization to begin preparations for the expedition to Florida. Related to these preparations are two royal *cédulas* issued in Valladolid on December 7, 1537, and February 25, 1538, respectively.

When the first of these cédulas was granted, all of the preparations had concluded for the expedition that De Soto would direct toward what is now the southeastern United States, the fleet and participants having joined together in San Lúcar de Barrameda. Through this document authorization was granted to the ships that were preparing to depart for the Indies in the company of the armada of the *adelantado*. With this concession the crown put into practice one of the means adopted in 1521 for the navigation of the Atlantic: the organization of convoys protected by warships to eliminate the dangers posed by pirates and corsairs and to safeguard the shipment of precious metals. Given the size of the armada that, under De Soto's command, was prepared to depart, and the material means within his reach, military protection was ensured.

The second of the cédulas issued from Valladolid is couched in terms similar to the first. Due to the delay of the expedition's departure, the crown again recommended that the ships preparing to depart for the Indies wait until March 15 so as to be able to travel under the guard of De Soto's armada, though it did grant the freedom to depart after that date even if De Soto's ships might not have left, which is essentially what happened. The expedition to La Florida would begin its navigation some days later on April 6.

In addition to the cédulas, we have included a document that is not directly related to Hernando de Soto but to his wife, Doña Isabel de Bobadilla, whom he married in 1536. It deals with a license that allowed her to bring along three women slaves for her personal service. The circumstance that these three slaves were white suggests with a high degree of probability that they were Moors. The reference in the document with respect to their having proved their Christian quality before their twelfth birthdays points equally in this direction.

Doña Isabel de Bobadilla, upon requesting a license for her slaves, was obeying the law of the time regarding the passage of slaves to the Indies. She was respecting the disposition that prohibited the passage of slaves without express consent of the king. Had she not done so, Doña Isabel would have incurred a penalty of one thousand pesos of gold, the fine levied against those who disobeyed.

Deposited in the Archivo Histórico Nacional of Madrid [National Historical Archives] is the proceeding leading to the concession to Hernando de Soto of the "*hábito e insignia*" [habit and insignia] of the Order of Santiago. In this proceeding are included the investigations that were brought about to prove that De Soto met the necessary requirements to make him worthy of such a distinction.

The basic requirement to accede to the habit and to be named *caballero* [knight] of the order consisted above all in demonstrating the quality of the individual, his condition of nobility [*hidalguía*] as well as that of his ancestors, and also his pure blood [*limpieza de sangre*]. The latter would be the central point around which revolved questions that the priest of Lobón—a village situated quite near the road between Mérida and Badajoz—asked various residents of the city, finally completing the charge with which the emperor had entrusted him. More than as king, the intervention of Charles V in this matter was motivated by his condition as "perpetual administrator" of the Order of Santiago.

The beginning of the proceeding had as a prelude—as the king indicated—the express petition of De Soto to enter the order as a caballero. De Soto's interest to rise to such a grade corresponds perfectly to the aspirations and wishes of that epoch to ascend the social ladder. The amount of money it would cost him should his request be found favorable mattered little to De Soto, in light of the distinction, prestige, and honorific relevance that he could obtain with this designation, given that there were many *hidalgos* in sixteenth-century Spain, while the number of people who could be presented as caballeros was somewhat lower. In any case, once such a distinction was obtained the aspirations of the Extremaduran would not end there. It is probable that De Soto envisioned the possibility of acceding to a domain [*señorío*] with a title—such as when Hernán Cortés was named Marqués del

Valle—if La Florida was revealed as a second Peru or Mexico and he managed to come out successful and triumphant.

Returning to the document, it contains the declarations that the cleric Juan Mexía took from nine people about a week after De Soto had set sail from San Lúcar de Barrameda. The witnesses are all mature, almost senile individuals: the youngest is more than forty years old, four are sexagenarians, and the oldest—Hernando Romo "el Viejo"—brings honor to his nickname and is said to be seventy years old. The profession and quality of the group are not explicit, but in accordance with the recommendation of the emperor to the priest, the latter was to search out testimony of people of "good fame and conscience." It only makes clear to us that one of them bragged about having the post of regidor and that another had obtained the degree of bachelor of law from the University of Salamanca. The fact that all, with one exception, signed the declaration with their own hands does not lead us anywhere, given that from such a circumstance it cannot be inferred with certainty who had control of the writing.

In spite of what might be supposed, in the testimonies contained in the interrogation little light is cast that might resolve the polemic surrounding De Soto's birthplace, even though he and his family, based on the declarations of the witnesses, are closely associated with Badajoz and Jerez; the third Extremaduran site in question is not mentioned at all—Villanueva de Barcarrota, the location indicated by Garcilaso de la Vega in his chronicle, *La Florida,* as the adelantado's birthplace.

In San Cristóbal de la Habana, moments before his departure for the Florida coast, Hernando de Soto endorsed a document granting wide authority to his wife Doña Isabel de Bobadilla. This document appears dated May 17, 1539, and through it Isabel was converted into the maximum representative of Hernando de Soto during his absence. The adelantado authorized his wife to administer all of his assets and properties in the kingdoms of Castille as well as on the island and Tierra Firme. Isabel de Bobadilla could henceforth collect and receive all money pertaining to the conquistador, rule and administer his Indians, carry out in his name contracts and companies, sell and pawn his assets, and represent him in civil and criminal cases. The adelantado also authorized his wife to send the support ships and necessary supplies to continue the conquest of La Florida.

This collection of documents closes with the inventory of assets drawn up by Isabel de Bobadilla after learning of her husband's death. Although the news had been sent through an official channel by means of a dispatch from the viceroy of New Spain, Isabel already knew of the details of the failed expedition and of the death of the adelantado from other people "who escaped and left La Florida."

The inventory, carried out on December 6, 1543, covers all of the assets—furniture, land, and livestock—that the couple possessed on the island to that moment, leaving aside the property in Castille and in other parts of the New World.

I

NAMING OF CAPTAIN HERNANDO DE SOTO AS LIEUTENANT GOVERNOR OF CUZCO, 1534.

What you, Captain Hernando de Soto, must do to fulfill the post of lieutenant governor of the city of Cuzco is as follows: Firstly, the things regarding the settlement of lawsuits, demands, denunciations, quarrels, and debates, and other civil and criminal matters that might occur among the Spanish, residents, and other persons in said city in all matters, as well as the matters that they as well as the natives under their control are subject to and other [matters] that require judgment, attention, and decrees through decisions. You will have your post without being involved in, nor being accustomed to, nor being aware of, anything involving the protection of said city, the pacification of the natives, or of war, should it occur, because I have provided for this, and I will provide the person who will be in charge of this as is contained in the instruction and provision that will be given.

ITEM: Because I left in place certain ordinances in said city of Cuzco and I am informed that some people have gone against them, you will secretly communicate which ones and who have broken them or have done anything other than what I left ordered, such as requesting and receiving gold, as well as other things, and how and in what way it is heard or done, you will send it to me so that I may see it and do what is right.

ITEM: If through such information you find that one or more have received gold or silver, you will determine and learn if it has been from their *caciques,* and if they have harassed them for it, and if they received it in the presence of a supervisor [*veedor*] and in the prescribed manner, and if they discovered it or brought it from another area. Having seen this, you will truthfully advise me, and above all you will send for and keep said gold and silver until you hear from me what will be well to do with it.

ITEM: Because Juan de Quincoçes has gone to said city on business related to the service of His Majesty, as you know and will see, you will give him all of the favors and help in such a way as to be carried out by my command, not impeding what has been said and stated above in this instruction.

ITEM: You will protect and carry out the ordinances that I left in place in said city, preventing anyone to take gold from his cacique or from anywhere else, or from harassing his Indians and caciques and from telling them to extract a lot of gold from the mines, or in asking or making them do more than what is necessary for their well being.

ITEM: You will have the responsibility and care to see that the Indians be well treated, not allowing that any harm or vexation be done to them by the Spaniards whose charge they may be in or by anyone else. You will especially see to it that they be indoctrinated and taught in the things of our Catholic faith, and you will let me know what might be needed to provide for their well being and for the maintenance and good governance of said city, taking special care with this matter.

It will be advisable to carry out all of the above and all related matters found in this instruction, and I trust that you will fulfill and resolve [such matters] with diligence and care as you see fit, deserving of service to His Majesty and the good governance of the republic of said city. Issued in the city of Jauja on the twenty-seventh day of the month of July, 1534. Francisco Pizarro. [AGI. *Patronato.* Legajo 90-A.]

2.

CÉDULA REAL PERMITTING THE SHIPS GOING TO THE INDIES TO GO IN THE COMPANY OF DE SOTO'S ARMADA, 1537.

Our officials, you who reside in the city of Seville in the Casa de Contratación of the Indies, on behalf of the adelantado Hernando de Soto, our governor and captain general of the province of Florida, it has come to my attention that he is ready to set sail on the January winds [*brisas de Henero*], because before now no ship has been able to enter the sea, and I have been requested to order that when he departs from the bar of San Lúcar all of the ships ready to go to our Indies go in his company, since traveling in the company of his armada they will go more safely protected from French corsairs, or as my wish might be. I took the above to be reasonable. Thus I command you to grant that said adelantado go as captain of the ships setting sail to continue their trip to our Indies at the time that he departs with his armada. Issued in Valladolid on the seventh day of the month of December, 1537. I the king. [AGI. *Indiferente General.* Legajo 1962, Folios 301 vto.–302.]

3.

CÉDULA REAL REQUIRING THE SHIPS GOING TOWARD THE INDIES TO DO SO IN THE COMPANY OF HERNANDO DE SOTO, 1538.

To those of their Majesties' Royal Council of the Indies, we order on behalf of the Crown that you, the officials who reside in the city of Seville in the Casa de Contratación of the Indies, that upon receiving this you notify the captains and masters and other seamen on that river [Guadalquivir?] or in the port of San Lúcar or in Cádiz that they wait until the fifteenth day of March of the present year and not leave without De Soto's armada. If Don Hernando has not set sail by the stipulated date, they may go whenever they wish, because this is suitable to His Majesty's service and the well being of his subjects. Issued in Valladolid on the twenty-fifth of February, 1538. Signed by the count and Beltrán Carvajal and Bernal Gutierre Velázquez. [AGI. *Indiferente General.* Legajo 1962, Folio 331 vto.]

4.

AUTHORIZATION FOR DOÑA ISABEL DE BOBADILLA TO BRING THREE SLAVE WOMEN TO THE ISLAND OF CUBA FOR HER SERVICE, 1538.

Our officials, you who reside in the city of Seville in the Casa de Contratación of the Indies, Doña Isabel de Bovadilla, wife of the adelantado Don

Hernando de Soto, our governor and captain general of the province of Florida, it has been communicated to me that she has three white slaves who are good Christians and women of good life and reputation whom she would like to bring with her to the island of Cuba to serve her and her household, and she has asked that I give her permission for this. Therefore, I order you to find out who these slaves are and to verify that they were Christians before they had turned twelve years old and that they are servants of said Doña Isabel. And allow them to travel with her to the island of Cuba without imposing upon her any impediment, having first paid Diego de la Haya, *cambio* [broker, purser, accountant] of our court, two ducats for the license of each one, inasmuch as it is his duty to collect this amount. Issued in the town of Valladolid on the sixteenth day of the month of February, 1538. I the Queen. [AGI. *Indiferente General.* Legajo 1962, Folio 331.]

5.

INTERROGATION FOR THE CONCESSION OF THE HABIT OF SANTIAGO TO HERNANDO DE SOTO, 1538

(transcription of Antonio del Solar and José de Rújula).

Don Charles, by divine clemency Emperor *sempers augusto,* king of Germany, Castille, León, Aragón, of the two Sicilies, of Jerusalem, Navarre, Granada, Toledo, Valencia, Galicia, Mallorca, Seville, Cerdeña, Córdoba, Córcega, Murcia, Jaén, of los Algarves, Algezira, Gibraltar, the Canary Islands, the Indies, islands and Terra Firme of the ocean, Count of Barcelona, Lord of Vizcaya and Molina, Duke of Athens and Neopatria, Count of Flanders and Tyrol, etc., perpetual administrator of the order and knighthood of Santiago by apostolic authority, to you Juan Mexía, priest of Lobón, friar of said order, health and grace. May you know that on behalf of the adelantado Don Hernando de Soto it was communicated to me that his purpose and will is to be in said order and to live in observance and under the rule and discipline of it, out of devotion that he has for the daring apostle Santiago, beseeching me to order that he be given the habit and insignia of said order, or as my wish might be. And because the person who is to be received into said order and be given its habit and insignia must be a noble [*hijodalgo*], according to traditional Spanish law and custom, and provided that he possess the qualities that the statutes of said order require, it was resolved in my council that I should send you this letter concerning said information, and I, trusting that you are an individual who will work to my benefit and who will faithfully and efficiently carry out what I have ordered and entrusted unto you, I considered it to be good. And through this letter I entrust unto you and order as is required [in the letter] you to go to the city of Badajoz, where it is said that the aforementioned adelantado Don Hernando de Soto was born, and that you receive through your office [*oficio*] any witnesses that you deem to be necessary, that they be people of good reputation and conscience, that they know the adelantado and his lineage, and that you ask him the questions contained in the interrogatory that you will be given with this letter, signed by Francisco Guerrero, secretary of my Council. And to the witness who answers the question, ask him how he knows, and if he believes it, how and why he believes it. And if they saw or heard tell something, let them say from whom and how, and how long ago, in such a way as to give a certain explanation to their statements and depositions. And send to my Council what these witnesses say and attest to, signed with your name, closed and sealed, so that I may see it and decide what has to be decided concerning it. I give you power to carry this out with its incidences and dependences, appurtenances and rights, and it must be carried out in the prescribed manner, subject to my grace, for twenty ducats of gold for pious works. Issued in the town of Valladolid, the twenty-eighth of March, 1538.

Count Don Garía Manrique, Licentiate Luxán, Licentiate Sarmiento, Doctor Anaya. I, Francisco Guerrero, chamber scribe of his imperial and Catholic Highness, had this written by his command in accord with those of his Council of the Orders.

The questions that are to be asked the witnesses who are to be received through the office regarding the habit of Santiago requested by Don Hernando de Soto are those herein contained. Above all, these witnesses must be assured that what they attest to will be known only to the gentlemen of the Council and no one else, that there will be no record of their statements, that it will not be brought before a scribe in the place where they live, that it will be brought only to the Council, and that it will not be made known outside the proceedings, as it is told. Having thus assured the said witnesses and first receiving from them a legal oath, ask them the following questions:

Firstly, if they know the aforementioned Don Hernando de Soto, where he was born, and whose son he is. And if they know his father and mother, and what their names are. And where they live, and if they know or knew De Soto's grandparents on both his mother's and father's side. And what their names were, where they lived and were born, and if the witnesses are related to any of them.

ITEM: If they know, believe, saw, or heard tell that the father of the adelantado Don Hernando de Soto and the father and mother of said father, naming each and every one of them, have been and are currently and generally reputed to be people of nobility [*hijosdalgo*], according to traditional Spanish law and custom, and that they have not been touched by the race of Jews, converts, Moors, or peasants.

ITEM: If they know, etc., that the mother of the adelantado Don Hernando de Soto and the father and mother of said mother, naming each and every one of them, have been and are currently reputed to be old Christians [*cristianos biejos*], without being touched by the race of Jews, converts, or Moors, as it is said.

ITEM: If they know, etc., that adelantado Don Hernando de Soto has a horse.

ITEM: If they know, etc., if adelantado Don Hernando de Soto has been challenged, and if the witnesses say that he has been challenged, may they declare how he overcame the challenge.

Francisco Guerrero.

In the town of Lobón, which is in the jurisdiction of the lord Santiago, on April 12 in the year of our Savior Jesus Christ, 1538, I, Juan Mexía, priest of the aforementioned town of Lobón, received a closed and sealed package of papers that Francisco Guerrero, secretary of the Council of the Orders, sent me through the mail, in which came a provision from the Emperor and King, our Lord, perpetual administrator of the order of Santiago, issued in the aforementioned Council and countersigned by the said secretary and sealed with His Majesty's seal, by means of which I am ordered to receive through my office the witnesses I determine to be necessary in order to know if the adelantado Don Hernando de Soto has the qualities that he should have for him to be given the habit of said order as is contained in said provision. And in this package came an interrogatory signed by the aforementioned Francisco Guerrero, with which I have to question and examine the witnesses; the provision and interrogatory are attached herein. And thus having received the aforementioned package with the said dispatch and with a letter that the secretary wrote to me on behalf of the gentlemen of the Council, so that through my office I secretly obtained this information from people of good reputation and conscience, that I not go before any scribe, that there be no record of any of it, that I get a clerk with no suspicion to do it, and that I send it closed and sealed to the Council signed by me and by those witnesses who can sign. And thus I, Juan Mexía, priest, with all humility and reverence, obeyed and accepted this provision and commission of His Majesty in fulfillment of what is contained within. I went to the city of Badajoz, and as discreetly and secretly as I could, I searched out and found people from whom the truth could be known, who were not indebted or unreliable regarding the information, which through my office I secretly did in the following way:

In the city of Badajoz, on the thirteenth day of April of the present year, I, Juan Mexía, priest, took and received legal oath from Hernando de León, resident of Badajoz; I read the provision and interrogatory to him, I attested to him what the opening part [of the interrogatory] contains, and I charged him under the obligation of his oath that he tell and clarify the truth about what he knew and about what he may be asked by me regarding the interrogatory. The oath executed, what he said and attested to is the following:

Being asked the first question, he said that he was more or less sixty years old, that he is not indebted to or related to anyone referred to in the first question. He said that he knows the adelantado Don Hernando de Soto, and that he knew the adelantado's father and mother, whose names were Francisco Méndez, his father, and Leonor Arias, his mother. He knew them to live in this city of Badajoz and in the city of Jerez. He also knew the adelantado to be in these cities in his parents' house. This witness did not know the father and mother of the adelantado's father, but he heard them say that they were natives of Jerez, but he did not know their names, and this is what he knows of this question.

This witness said that he knew the father and mother of the adelantado Don Hernando de Soto's mother, and their name was Hernando Gutiérrez and Cardeñosa. He knew them to be residents of this city of Badajoz for a long time, because they were neighbors of this witness and he had dealings and conversed with them every day.

To the second [question], this witness said that he knew the father of the adelantado who was named Francisco Méndez to live in this city of Badajoz and in the city of Jerez, and that he was regarded in these two cities as hidalgo and hijodalgo and was generally regarded as such until he died. And this witness knows that he was untouched by the race of Jews, Moors, or peasants, but rather having been regarded as hijodalgo, and as such was regarded, as has been said. And as for his parents, as already stated, he did not know them, except to hear that they were hidalgos.

To the third [question], this witness said that he knew adelantado Don Hernando de Soto's mother, and the father and mother of his mother, as has been stated, that his mother's name was Leonor Arias Cardeñosa, and the father and mother of the adelantado's mother were named Hernán Gutiérrez, and the mother and grandmother of the adelantado were named Cardeñosa. And this witness knows that they are old Christians and hidalgos and were regarded as such for as long as they lived in this city of Badajoz, and thus they are taken to be hijosdalgos, and that they are untouched by the race of Jews, Moors, or peasants. They were generally regarded as such in this city because they were neighbors of this witness.

To the fourth [question], this witness said that he knows that the adelantado Don Hernando de Soto has a horse because he has seen it, and his father and grandfather had one, and therefore it is the truth.

To the fifth [question], this witness said that he does not know anything, nor does he know anymore about this case, to which he swore an oath.

Hernando de León was sworn by me, Juan Mexía, priest, to secrecy, that he not ever say or reveal anything to anyone, under penalty of perjury, to which he promised and signed his name. Hernando de León.

In this city of Badajoz on the aforementioned day, month, and year, I, Juan Mexía, priest, received through my office the oath of Suero Vázquez de Moscoso, resident and regidor of the city of Badajoz. I read to him the provision and interrogatory, I attested to him what the opening part [of the interrogatory] contains, and I charged him that under said oath he tell and declare the truth about what he knew and about what he may be asked by me regarding the interrogatory. The oath executed, he said and attested to the following:

Being asked about the tenor of the first question from the interrogatory, he said that he knows the adelantado Don Hernando de Soto, and knows that he is a native of the city of Jerez, and knows that he is the son of Francisco Méndez and Leonor Arias Tinoca, and knows that said Francisco Méndez was a resident of the city of Jerez, and that said Leonor Arias was a native of this city of Badajoz. He did not know the father and mother of the adelantado Don Hernando de Soto's father but had heard of them. He knew

Hernán Gutiérrez and Juana González, father and mother of the adelantado's mother, and that they were residents of this city of Badajoz, whom he knew by sight, by dealings, and by conversation. And this witness is not a relative of any of them and is more or less fifty-three years old.

To the second, this witness said that he knew, as is already stated, the adelantado Don Hernando de Soto's parents. They were named, as is stated, Francisco Méndez and Leonor Arias Tinoca, and he knew them to be hijosdalgo, as the question declares, and were generally regarded as such in this city of Badajoz. And this witness knows that they were untouched by the race of the Jews, converts, Moors, or peasants, but rather they and their descendants were regarded as hijosdalgo.

To the third, this witness said that he knew the father and mother of the adelantado Don Hernando de Soto's mother. The father was named Hernán Gutiérrez Cardeñosa and the other, Juana González Tinoca, grandparents of the adelantado Don Hernando de Soto. He knew them to be hijosdalgo and were generally regarded as such in this city of Badajoz and throughout this land. They were untouched by the race of Jews, converts, Moors, and peasants, but rather were regarded as hijosdalgo and as old Christians and are thus regarded, and this is the truth because this witness knows it.

To the fourth, this witness said that he knows that Don Hernando de Soto has a horse and horses, because this witness has seen them.

To the fifth, he said that he knows no more of this case, to which he swore an oath. He was charged with secrecy, as with the first witness, and he signed his name here. Suero Vázquez de Moscoso.

In said city of Badajoz, the fourteenth day of April, 1538, I, Juan Mexía, priest, received through my office the oath of Hernando Morales, resident of the city of Badajoz, to whom I read the aforementioned provision and interrogatory, and I attested to him what the opening part [of the interrogatory] contains, and I charged him that under said oath he tell and clarify the truth about what he knew and about what he may be asked by me regarding the interrogatory. The oath executed, he said and attested to the following:

Being asked about the tenor of the first question, he said he knows the adelantado Don Hernando de Soto, that he knew his father, who was named Francisco Méndez, he knew the adelantado's mother who is named Leonor Arias Tinoca, that he knew them in the city of Jerez and in this city of Badajoz, and he also knew the adelantado in his parents' house. And this witness did not know the father and mother of the adelantado's father but had heard of them. He knew the father and mother of the adelantado's mother, who were named Hernán Gutiérrez Cardeñosa and she was Tinoca, not remembering her other name. He knew them to be residents of this city of Badajoz because he had dealings and conversation with them. He is probably forty-five years old and is not indebted to or related to anyone in the above question.

To the second, this witness said that he knew Francisco Méndez, father of the adelantado Don Hernando de Soto, in this city of Badajoz and in the city of Jerez. He knew him as an hijodalgo and had been regarded as such in these cities. And his descendants are regarded as hijosdalgo. And this witness knows that he is untouched by the race of Jews, converts, Moors, or peasants, but rather considered to be a very good hidalgo and hijodalgo. He did not know his parents, but this witness heard from his own parents and many other older men that they were very noble hidalgos and were regarded as such in this land, and this he knows.

To the third, this witness said that he knew, as has been stated, Leonor Arias, mother of the adelantado Don Hernando de Soto, and Hernán Gutiérrez and Fulana [so-and-so] Tinoca, his grandparents, father and mother of the adelantado's mother. And he knew them in this city of Badajoz to be hijosdalgo, and they were commonly reputed to be such hijosdalgo in this city of Badajoz and throughout this region, and regarded as old Christians. And they were untouched by the race of Jews, converts, Moors, or peasants and were untouched by any of the flaws referred to in the question, but rather were regarded, as has been said, as hijosdalgo and old Christians, and this is the truth.

To the fourth, this witness said that the adelantado Don Hernando de Soto has a horse and horses, because this witness has seen them.

To the fifth, he said that he does not know the content of the question, nor anything about it. He was charged with secrecy, as with the first witness, who promised it under the charge of said oath, and he signed it with his name. Hernando Morales.

In the city of Badajoz, on the fourteenth day of the current month and year, I, Juan Mexía, priest, through my office received in legal manner the oath of Alvaro Romo, resident of the city of Badajoz, to whom I read the provision and interrogatory, and I attested to him what the opening part [of the interrogatory] contains, and I charged him that under said oath he tell and clarify the truth about what he knew and about what he may be asked by me regarding the interrogatory. The oath executed, he said and attested to the following:

Being asked the first question, he said that he knows the adelantado Don Hernando de Soto and knew Francisco Méndez, his father, who was a native of the city of Jerez, and he also knew the adelantado's mother, who was named Leonor Arias, who was a native of this city of Badajoz. He knew them to live in Jerez after they got married, and there he knew the adelantado in the house of his parents. He did not know the adelantado's grandparents on his father's side but had heard tell of them. He knew Hernán Gutiérrez Cardeñosa and Hernán Gutiérrez's wife, the father and mother of the mother of the adelantado, his grandparents. And he knew them to live in this city of Badajoz until they died here. This witness is approximately fifty-five years old, more or less, and is neither indebted to nor relative of anyone referred to in this question.

To the second, this witness said that he knew, as has been said, Francisco Méndez, father of the adelantado Don Hernando de Soto, in the city of Jerez and in this city of Badajoz. He knew him as hijodalgo according to traditional Spanish law, and this witness regarded him as such for as long as he lived. He did not know his parents, as has been stated, other than to hear tell that they were hijosdalgo, and he heard this publicly in these two cities. And this witness knows that he was untouched by the race of Jews, converts, Moors, or peasants, having been regarded as stated, as hijodalgo, and this is the truth.

To the third, this witness said that he knew Leonor Arias, the adelantado's mother, and that he knew Hernán Gutiérrez Cardeñosa and his wife, whose name he does not remember, who are the parents of the adelantado's mother, his grandparents. He knew that they lived in this city of Badajoz, and that they and their descendants were generally regarded as hijosdalgo, because this witness has seen a judgment of nobility [*sentencia de hidalguía*] that other children and grandchildren of Hernán Gutiérrez have. They are regarded as hijosdalgo in said city. They are untouched by the race of the Jews, converts, Moors, or peasants, rather regarded as hijosdalgo and old Christians, and as such this witness has regarded them. Thus it is the truth to which he swore an oath.

To the fourth, he said that Don Hernando de Soto has a horse and horses, and this witness knows because he has seen them, and thus it is true.

To the fifth, this witness said that he does not know, nor does he know any more about this case. To the oath that he made, he was sworn to secrecy, as with the first witness, and he promised it under the charge of said oath. And he signed it with his name. Alvaro Romo.

In the city of Badajoz, on this day of the current month and year, the fourteenth of April, I, Juan Mexía, priest, through my office received in a legal manner the oath of Hernando Romo, the elder, resident of the city of Badajoz, to whom I read the provision and interrogatory, and I attested to him what the opening part [of the interrogatory] contains, and I charged him that under said oath he tell and clarify the truth about what he knew and what may be asked by me regarding the interrogatory. The oath executed, he said and attested to the following:

Being asked about the tenor of the first question, he said that he knows the adelantado Don Hernando de Soto from sight, from dealings, and from conversation. He knew Francisco Méndez, the adelantado's father, and knew Leonor Arias Tinoca, mother of the adelantado. And that Francisco Méndez was a native of Jerez de Badajoz, and that his wife, mother of the adelantado, was a native of this city of Badajoz. He did not know the father and mother of the father of the adelantado, the adelantado's grandparents, other than to hear tell of them. He knew Hernán Gutiérrez Cardeñosa, and the wife of said Cardeñosa, whose name he does not remember, but dealt and conversed with them because they were neighbors of this witness. They were the father and mother of Leonor Arias, mother of the adelantado, and grandparents of the adelantado, and were regarded as such in this city of Badajoz where they lived. He is seventy years old, more or less, and he is neither indebted to nor related to anyone referred to in said question.

To the second, this witness said that he knew, as has been stated, Francisco Méndez, the father of adelantado Don Hernando de Soto, and he saw him marry in this city of Badajoz Leonor Arias, his wife. And he was generally regarded as hijodalgo in this city and throughout this land, and as hidalgo and hijodalgo he was generally regarded. He heard publicly stated in this city that Francisco Mendez's parents were very good hidalgos. This witness knows that he had no trace of the race of Jews, converts, Moors, or peasants, but rather was hidalgo, as has been stated, because this witness dealt with and conversed with him many times and many days, because he was his neighbor, and this is the truth.

To the third, this witness said that he knew, as has been stated, Leonor Arias, mother of the adelantado Don Hernando de Soto, and he knew Hernán Gutiérrez Cardeñosa, and said Cardeñosa's wife, whose name he does not remember, who are the parents of Leonor Arias, and grandparents of the adelantado. They lived in this city of Badajoz until they departed from this life. This witness knows that they were hidalgos and hijosdalgo according to traditional Spanish law, and they were generally regarded as hijosdalgo in this city of Badajoz and in this land, and this witness regarded them accordingly. And he knows that their descendants are considered to be hijosdalgo, untouched by the race of Jews, converts, Moors, or peasants, but rather hidalgos, old Christians, and very noble, and this is true.

To the fourth, this witness said that he knows that the adelantado Don Hernando de Soto has a horse and horses, and this witness knows this because he has seen them.

To the fifth, he said that he does not know the content of the question or anything else about this case to which he swore an oath. He was charged with secrecy as with the first witness, and he promised it under the charge of the oath that he made and signed it with his name. Hernando Romo.

In the city of Badajoz on this day of the aforementioned month and year, I, Juan Mexía, priest, took and received in a legal manner an oath from Alonso González, resident of the city of Badajoz. I read to him the said provision and testimony, and I attested to him what the opening part [of the interrogatory] contains, and I charged him under the obligation of his oath that he tell and clarify the truth about what he knew and about what he might be asked by me regarding the interrogatory. The oath executed, he said and attested to the following:

Being asked the first question, he said that he knows the adelantado Don Hernando de Soto from sight, from dealings, and from conversation, and he knew Francisco Méndez and Leonor Arias Tinoca, his wife, parents of the adelantado Don Hernando de Soto. And the father was a native of the city of Jerez, near Badajoz, and he knew them to live in both of these two cities, but he did not know the father and mother of Francisco Méndez, grandparents of the adelantado, but had heard tell of them. And this witness knew Hernán Gutiérrez Cardeñosa and his wife, whose name he does not remember, father and mother of Leonor Arias, mother of the adelantado and his grandparents. These were residents and natives of this city of Badajoz and were there until they died, and this is the truth, because he knew them and dealt and conversed with them.

He said that he is sixty years old, more or less, and that he is neither indebted to nor related to anyone referred to in this question.

To the second, this witness said that he knew, as has been stated, Francisco Méndez, father of the adelantado Don Hernando de Soto, to live in this city of Badajoz and in the city of Jerez, and this witness knew him, and he was generally regarded in these two cities as hijodalgo, according to traditional Spanish law and custom, and was regarded as such until he died. He did not know the father and mother of Francisco Méndez, as has been stated, other than to hear publicly stated in this city of Badajoz that they were very noble hidalgos. And this witness knows that he is untouched by the race of Jews, converts, Moors, or peasants, but rather regarded as a very good hidalgo and hijodalgo. And this is the truth to which he swore an oath.

To the third, this witness said that he knew, as has been stated, Leonor Arias Tinoca, mother of the adelantado Don Hernando de Soto, and he knew Hernán Gutiérrez Cardeñosa and his wife, whose name he does not remember, father and mother of Leonor Arias, grandparents of the adelantado, and that they lived in this city of Badajoz until they died. This witness considered them and their descendants as old Christians and as very noble hidalgos and hijosdalgo. They are and were regarded as hijosdalgo, and this witness knows that they were untouched by the race of Jews, Moors, converts, or peasants, but rather were regarded generally as hijosdalgo and old Christians, and this is the truth to which he swore an oath.

To the fourth, this witness said that the adelantado Don Hernando de Soto has very good horses, and he knows because this witness has seen them.

To the fifth, this witness said that he does not know, nor does he know any more about this case. To the oath that he made, he was sworn to secrecy, as with the first witness, and he promised it under the charge of said oath. And he signed it with his name. Alonso González.

In the city of Badajoz on this day of the aforementioned month and year, the fourteenth day of said month and year, I, Juan Mexía, priest, received through my office in a legal manner an oath from Ruy Sánchez de Arjola, resident of the city of Badajoz, to whom I read the provision and interrogatory. I attested to him what the opening part [of the interrogatory] contains, and I charged him under the obligation of his oath that he tell and clarify the truth about what he knew and about what he might be asked by me regarding the interrogatory. The oath executed, he said and attested to the following:

Being asked the first question, this witness said that he has known the adelantado Don Hernando de Soto since he was born, and he knew Francisco Méndez and his wife very well, the father and mother of the adelantado, but that he does not remember her name. And that Francisco Méndez was from the city of Jerez, and that he knew them and knows that they were where he has said because this witness is a native of Jerez and now lives in this city of Badajoz. But this witness did not know the father and mother of Francisco Méndez, grandparents of the adelantado, but had heard tell of them many times in the city of Jerez, nor did he know the father and mother of the adelantado's mother but had heard of them, and they were natives of this city of Badajoz. He is sixty years old and is not a relative of anyone referred to in the aforementioned question.

To the second, this witness said that he knew, as has been stated, Francisco Méndez, father of adelantado Don Hernando de Soto, and he was a native of the city of Jerez, and this witness knew him to be hijodalgo, and he was generally regarded as hijodalgo in the city of Jerez and in this city of Badajoz. And this witness knew many relatives of Francisco Méndez in the city of Jerez, and that they were and are generally regarded as noble hijosdalgo. And this witness heard many people in general in Badajoz and Jerez say that the father and mother of the father of the adelantado were very noble hijosdalgo, and he knows that neither he nor his lineage was touched by the race of Jews, converts, Moors, or peasants, and this is the truth.

To the third, this witness said that he knew Leonor Arias, mother of the adelantado Don Hernando de Soto, and he knew her very well. And he knows that she was from a line of very good hidalgos who are his relatives that he has in this city, and as such regarded by this witness, and he knows that they are old Christians, and as such regarded by this witness. And he heard publicly stated in this city of Badajoz that the grandparents of the adelantado, his mother's parents, were very noble hidalgos, and this is what he knows.

To the fourth, this witness said that he knows Don Hernando de Soto to have a horse, and he always saw that Francisco Méndez, his father, had one.

To the fifth, he said that he does not know other than what has been said, nor does he know any more about this case. He was charged with secrecy, as with the first witness, and he promised it. He did not sign because he said that he did know how to sign, and I signed it. Juan Mexía.

In the city of Badajoz, the fourteenth day of the aforementioned month and year, I, Juan Mexía, priest, through my office received an oath in a legal manner from the *Bachiller* Alonso Romo, Bachelor of Law, resident of the city of Badajoz, to whom I read the provision and interrogatory, and I attested to him what the opening part [of the interrogatory] contains, and I charged him that under the obligation of his oath he tell and clarify the truth of what he knew and what he might be asked by me regarding the interrogatory. The oath executed, he said and attested to the following:

Being asked the first question, he said that he knows the adelantado Don Hernando de Soto from sight and conversation, and that this witness did not have that much knowledge of his parents, because he was young and was absent from this city of Badajoz in the city of Salamanca, but he saw them and knew them by sight in this city of Badajoz. And he knows that the father of the adelantado was named Francisco Méndez de Soto, and the mother Leonor Arias Tinoca, and thus he heard them called and named. They were residents of the city of Jerez, near this city. And he heard tell that they were married in this city and that Francisco Méndez, father of adelantado Don Hernando de Soto, died in it. He did not know the father and mother of Francisco Méndez, father of the adelantado, because they were from the city of Jerez. And this witness knew Hernán Gutiérrez Cardeñosa and his wife Fulana [so-and-so] Tinoca, whose name he does not remember, the parents of Leonor Arias, grandparents of the adelantado. And he knew them to live in this city of Badajoz a long time, because this witness as a child grew up on the street where they lived, and they were neighbors. This is the truth, and he is more than forty years old, and he is not indebted to or related to anyone referred to in this question.

To the second, this witness said that he knew, as has been stated, Francisco Méndez, father of the adelantado, and that this witness regarded him as hijodalgo, and as such was regarded in this city and in the city of Jerez where he was a native, because thus it is publicly declared and known in these two cities, and thus he always heard it said and never heard anything to the contrary. And he is regarded as an old Christian, untouched by the race of Jews, converts, Moors, or peasants, because if he had any of this, this witness would know it and would have heard tell, as has been stated, and this is what he knows of this question.

To the third, this witness said that he knew, as has been stated, Leonor Arias, mother of the adelantado, and he knew as well Hernán Gutiérrez Cardeñosa and Fulana [so-and-so] Tinoca, his wife, parents of Leonor Arias and grandparents of the adelantado. And he knew them all, as has been stated, in this city, and he regarded them as old Christians and hijosdalgo and as such were generally regarded in this city, and as such their children and grandchildren who are living are also regarded. And they were untouched by the race of Jews, converts, Moors, or peasants, because if they had been touched by any of the above, this witness would have known and heard tell, as has been stated, and thus it is publicly known and common opinion in this city and where they are known, and he never heard anything to the contrary, and this is the truth.

To the fourth, this witness said that he knows that the adelantado Don Hernando de Soto has a horse because this witness has seen it and has seen him sometimes lend it.

To the fifth, this witness said that he does not know any more than what has been stated, by the oath that he swore, and he signed it with his name. He was charged with secrecy, as was the first witness, and thus promised it under the charge of said oath. The Bachiller Romo.

In the city of Badajoz, this aforementioned day, month and year, the fourteenth day of April of said year, I, the aforementioned Juan Mexía, priest, through my office took and received an oath from Alonso de Medina, resident of the city of Badajoz, to whom I read the provision and interrogatory, and I attested to him what the opening part [of the interrogatory] contains, and I charged him under the obligation of his oath that he tell and clarify the truth about what he might be asked by me regarding the interrogatory. The oath executed, what he said and attested to is the following:

Being asked the first question, he said that he knows the adelantado Don Hernando de Soto from sight, dealings, and conversation, and that he knew Francisco Méndez and Leonor Arias Tinoca, his wife, father and mother of the adelantado Don Hernando de Soto. And this witness knew them to be residents in this city of Badajoz and in the city of Jerez, because Francisco Méndez was from Jerez, and his wife was from this city. And there he knew Don Hernando de Soto in the house of the aforementioned through his son. He did not know the father and mother of the adelantado's father because they were from the city of Jerez, but he had heard tell of them. He knew Hernán Gutiérrez Cardeñosa and his wife, whose name he does not have news of at the present, the father and mother of Leonor Arias, the adelantado's mother, and his grandparents. And he knew them to be residents for a long time in this city of Badajoz until they died. He is sixty-five years old, more or less, and is not a relative of anyone referred to in this question.

To the second, this witness said that he knew, as has been said, Francisco Méndez, father of the adelantado Don Hernando de Soto, and he knew this witness and he regarded him and was generally regarded as hijodalgo and had such a reputation in this city and in the city of Jerez. And he heard publicly stated in this city that his parents in Jerez were very noble hidalgos and that he is untouched by the race of Jews, converts, Moors, or peasants, because if he had any of this, this witness would know about it through the dealings that he had with him, but rather was regarded as hijodalgo and old Christian, and this is the truth.

To the third, this witness knew, as has been stated, Leonor Arias, mother of the adelantado Don Hernando de Soto, and he knew Hernán Gutiérrez Cardeñosa and his wife, whose name he does not have news of, parents of Leonor Arias and grandparents of the adelantado. And he knows them to have been regarded, as has been said, as old Christians and as hijosdalgo, and were regarded as such in this city of Badajoz while they lived. And at the present their children, grandchildren, and descendants are without any contradictions, and as such were and are generally regarded. He knows that they are untouched by any of the flaws contained in the question, because they were old Christians and very noble hidalgos. And this is the truth to which he swore an oath.

To the fourth, he said that he knows that the adelantado Don Hernando de Soto has a horse and horses, because this witness has seen them and thus it is true.

To the fifth, this witness said that he does not know, nor does he know any more of this case, to which he swore an oath, and he signed it with his name. He was charged with secrecy as with the first witness, and thus promised it.

The above information was compiled by me, Juan Mexía, priest, in the city of Badajoz, as it is declared, and is written on eight sheets of paper of an entire sheet [*pliego entero*], which has my signature. Above there are some flourishes in pairs and down below another flourish from side to side and at the beginning are found the provision and interrogatory, and in witness whereof I signed it here with my name. Juan Mexía. [Archivo Histórico Nacional. *Sección Ordenes Militares (Santiago).* Expediente No. 7855.]

6.

POWER GRANTED BY THE ADELANTADO HERNANDO DE SOTO TO HIS WIFE, ISABEL DE BOBADILLA, 1539

(from the transcription of Antonio del Solar y Taboada and José de Rújula).

May all who see this letter know how I, Don Hernando de Soto, adelantado and captain general of the conquest and land of Florida and on behalf of Their Majesty governor on this island Fernandina, currently a resident in this town of San Cristóbal de la Havana, from this island grant and recognize that I give all of my free, full, complete, and sufficient power, according to what I have and to what it rightly should be worth, to Doña Isabel de Bobadilla, who is my present legitimate wife, so that generally notwithstanding the people who with my power or through my commands have or might have the duty to administer and manage all of my assets, chattel, real estate, and seigniories of Castille, as well as in all of these parts, the islands of the Indies, the islands and Tierra Firme of the ocean, the aforementioned Doña Isabel de Bobadilla may be able above all others to manage, order, govern, and administer all of our assets and properties, those that we currently have and might have from now on, as well as those that in any manner may pertain to us and that benefit me and my positions just as I am able to do, manage, administer, oversee, and command. And for this may she name whomever she wishes to carry it out. And furthermore, may she demand and collect, receive and collect, both with and without court judgments, from any and all people who legally owe me, from their assets the following: any and all *maravedís*, weights of gold, jewels, pieces of gold, silver, and other metals, any valuable clothing, cloth, and silk, and any other chattel, real estate, and livestock, as well as annual rents and any other type that are or might be owed to me and that pertain or may pertain to me and that I am to receive in any form, as well as public contracts, companies, sentences, and conveyances, and any other public or private writings as well as others, and in any manner or for whatever reason, whatever titles and rights they may be. And furthermore, may she manage and administer and command any and all of my Indians and *naburías* [Indians as domestic servants] that I have in these parts of the Indies, islands, and Tierra Firme of the ocean, as well as black and white slaves, and may she demand and collect them from any person in whose power they may be with the interests and value of them and penalties that they might have incurred, in accordance with the command of Their Majesty in such a case. And from all that in my name she may receive and collect, may she give and execute a letter or letters of payment or receipt and of final payments. Such letters may be carried out when necessary and will be of the same worth were I myself to give and grant them, I being present. And in anything and any case that may seem to her to be worthwhile, may she deal with, contract with, or have any contracts and companies of quality and substance with any person or persons in any type of farming and commerce that seems to her to be most useful and profitable. And may she form said contracts and companies that seem appropriate to her, including those that up until now I have formed with anyone, as well as those that I may form from now on or that Doña Isabel de Bobadilla may form in my name. And furthermore, may she make any pacts and agreements, arrangements and promises, freeing transactions, releases, pardons, and any other cases or things that may come up, and may she execute them in the presence of any scribe with whatever entailments, firmness, conditions, penalties, agreements, and obligations that are necessary for their validation, and in order for this to be carried out, my person and my assets may be pledged, that by her executing these things I execute them and promise to resolutely carry them out and to accept them according to what is contained in them. And furthermore, may she sell, exchange, and pawn any of my assets that seem to her should be sold, exchanged, traded, and pawned to anyone she wishes and for the amount and for other things that may seem appropriate to her. And may she collect maravedís, weights of gold, and other things so that she might sell, pawn, exchange, and trade them, and she may execute any strong and firm letters of sale, exchange, and pawn in the presence of any scribes who concur that I should pledge my person and assets and with the conditions, penalties, agreements, and disclaimers of law that may be rightfully required, and through this letter I grant and promise to carry out, pay, and look after all that may be contained [in such letters]. And furthermore, may she buy any caravels, ships, and brigantines, and supplies and provisions for them, and all manner of munitions, both for the purpose of the conquest of La Florida as well as for any other purposes that may be worthwhile and necessary, and I may be obligated regarding them for any sum of weights of gold and other things that I may owe, which might be paid to people who are entitled to them by the due date that is agreed upon. And, above all, may she execute any strong and firm letters of obligation before any scribe with whatever entailments, firmness, corroborations, penalties, agreements, obligations, and disclaimers of law that may be necessary, and by her executing them I henceforth execute them and obligate myself to pay what is contained in them, according to and in the manner that such a contract and obligation may require. And furthermore, may she charter any ship or caravel that may be necessary to go to Spain or any other place, for the amount of weights of gold and maravedís that seem appropriate to her, and may she obligate me through [this money] to the person or persons with whom she might contract, that I will pay them back without fail by the due date that is agreed upon according to the agreements and conditions that are in the contract and writing. And furthermore, may she take and receive any servants, majordomos, administrators, applicants, and others for common service of my household that may seem appropriate to her, paying wages in installments or in any other manner seen to benefit my property and businesses, and she may dismiss whomever she wishes at any time, settling their account with payments from what they may owe to her, and she may collect any balances that she may have made to them. And furthermore, may she revoke any and all power and powers, both general as well as special, that I, from times past until today's date, have given to any person or persons, both in Castille as well as these parts and islands of the Indies and Tierra Firme of the ocean, if it seems to her that said persons or any one of them is not using said powers with the solicitude and fidelity that they should, and may she rectify and revoke and newly grant any power or powers that I have given and granted and revoked, it seeming necessary to her that they make use of them, that by Doña Isabel's revoking and renewing them, I henceforth revoke, renew, and ratify them in the way that she might enact them as it may seem to her. And furthermore, for those persons whose powers may be revoked, may she be able to restore their honor and good reputation according to and how they had it before and at the time that said powers were given and granted to them, and through this letter I restore them and consider them restored. And furthermore, may she get from scribes any power, and from other parties and authorities in whose power they may be, any writings, titles of privilege, and other pertinent writings, and, if any of the writings might be worthy of being annulled, may she annul them, in order to win from His Majesty any favors, be it conquests, settlement of lands, or any other provisions, privileges, cédulas, and commands that suit me, in order to capitulate with His Majesty all of those favors, duties, and offices that he might wish to give me and concede to me, and in order to eradicate and restrain any favors that may be won or wished to be won against my person and state. And furthermore, wherefor in all of my current and future civil and criminal suits, both in demanding as well as in defending, that I currently have and hope to have, against any and all person or persons of any quality or condition, and that such persons may have or plan to have against me in any way or for any reason, and for all that has been said and for each item, may she appear before His Majesty the Emperor, King Don Charles, and the Queen, Doña Juana, his mother, our lords, and before the president and judges [*oidores*] of his very high council, mayors and judges of his house and court, and before the president and judges of his royal *Audiencias* and chanceries who reside in these parts, the islands of the Indies, Tierra Firme, New Spain, and other parts, and before any and all mayors, judges, and justices, both higher as well as lower, ecclesiastics and seculars from any *fuero* and jurisdiction. And in the presence of them and any one of them, may she demand, respond, defend, deny, recognize, confront, protest, require, denounce, contest, ask for, take, and attain or in my name put forth, tell, and allege any other good reason, exception, and defense, and may she ask for, demand, and swear on my soul, both an oath of *calumnia* as well as *decisorio* [two types of legal oaths used in testimonies], and any other type of oath that I rightly should swear to, on the persons and assets of said debtors, conveyances and excisions, the sale and auction of their seized assets, may she put forth pleas and testimonies, and ask the other party or parties that they testify, and may she respond to those [testimonies] that may be put to me, in order to give and to present witnesses and evidence, to accuse, contradict, impute, and condemn those [testimonies] that may be given and presented to me, and to ask for the publication of them, and tell and contradict each and every one of them, both in statements as well as in person. And may she determine, ask for, and hear sentences, both interlocutory as well as definitive, and may she consent that those offered by me and those against me be appealed and that the appeal be carried out there or where it legally should be. And in order to request and protest costs and damages, and to swear to them and from them receive taxation, above all may she convoke other proceedings and measures legally required that I myself would do and could do being present, even if such actions according to law require my presence and special power and more copious and sufficient command. And furthermore, for all of the above may she employ and replace a prosecutor, or two or more, both before the contested case or cases, as well as afterward, and may she withdraw them when she wishes. And returning to assuming this power in and of itself, and the complete and sufficient power that I have over all of the above and everything fully related to it, I grant it and give it to said Doña Isabel de Bodadilla and to the substitute or substitutes named by her, with all of the incidences and dependences, appurtenances and rights, and with everything joined to it and concerning it, and with free and general administration I release them from any burden of satisfaction and guaranty under the legal clause that in Latin is *judiciun sisti judicatun solvi*, with all of its customary clauses. And in order to fulfill and to firmly have all that may be issued, procured, and granted by me and in my name in virtue of this power and not to go against it, I obligate myself and all of my chattel and real estate that I currently have and will have. And through this letter I give license, authority, power, and faculty to said Doña Isabel de Bobadilla so that through it she may make and execute all of the contracts and writings, enact and execute the other proceedings, both with and without court judgments, both regarding me as well as her and her own things. The letter issued in said town of San Cristóbal de la

Havana, the seventeenth day of the month of May, the year of our Lord 1539. Witnesses who were present at the above, Don Carlos e Nuño de Tovar and Alonso Romo, residing in [Havana], and the said adelantado stipulated the above and signed it with his name. [AGI. *Justicia.* Legajo 750 (A).]

7.

INVENTORY OF THE ASSETS LEFT BY THE ADELANTADO HERNANDO DE SOTO FOLLOWING HIS DEATH, 1543.

In the town of San Cristóbal de la Havana, that is on the island of Fernandina of the Indies of the ocean, on the sixth day of the month of December, the year of the birth of our saviour Jesus Christ, 1543, in the presence of the very noble gentleman Francisco Cepero, magistrate [*alcalde ordinario*] in this town on behalf of His Majesty, and in the presence of Fernando Florencio, notary of His Majesty, and notary for the public and council of this town, appeared Doña Isabel de Bobadilla, wife of the adelantado Don Fernando de Soto, who is said to be dead, may he be in glory, and she presented a petition in writing on his behalf, the tenor of which is as follows:

Very noble gentleman Francisco Cepero, magistrate in this town of Havana, I, Doña Isabel de Bobadilla, who was wife of the adelantado Don Fernando de Soto, may he have glory, appear before your mercy, and in the best form and manner that befit my rights, I ask that [it is possible that part of this sentence has been omitted] inasmuch as it is evident, two days ago the ship named Santiago came into this port, piloted by the Biscayan master Ochoa and Mateo de Bides. In this ship they brought me certain dispatches from the Viceroy of New Spain through which it was communicated to me that my lord and husband, the adelantado, had died. I am also informed through testimony and writings of Baltasar Hernández, notary of His Majesty, and through information of other people who are here who escaped and left La Florida. And keeping with what by law I am obligated, it is necessary to make an inventory of all of the assets that the aforementioned adelantado, my lord and husband, and I have at the present time, and that have resulted from our marriage. I ask your mercy, as I have asked, to be present at the report and to authorize said inventory, putting on it your decree and authority in such a form and manner that befit my rights, without anything being diminished, and I ask for this through testimony.

And said writing being presented in the manner that is stated, the magistrate next said that he would have the inventory done of all of the assets that in her request Doña Isabel de Bobadilla asks for within the legal time limit, and he said that this being done, he is ready to put his authority and judicial decree on it. Witnesses Alonso de Ayala, majordomo of Doña Isabel, and Rodrigo Rangel, her secretary.

And next, on the aforementioned day of the same month and year, the inventory of the assets of the adelantado and of Doña Isabel de Bobadilla, his wife, was begun and completed in the presence of said magistrate and in the presence of me, the notary, in the following manner.

After the above, on the twelfth of December of the same year, in the presence of the magistrate and in my presence, the aforementioned notary, Doña Isabel de Bobadilla appeared and said that after the presentation of her request, an inventory was made of all of the assets, property, clothing, and other things that the adelantado Don Fernando de Soto, may he be in glory, and she had on this island and in their home, as will appear on this inventory. Having carefully read it, the aforementioned magistrate received a legal oath from Doña Isabel de Bobadilla and she swore to it. And under the weight of said oath she said that the assets, property, and things contained in the inventory are those that the adelantado and she have on this island and in their home, and that she does not know of any more, and if any more come to her memory she will declare it. Witnesses to this were Rodrigo Ranjel, Alonso de Ayala, and Joan de Rentería. The tenor of the inventory is as follows:

The assets, chattel, and livestock that Doña Isabel de Bobadilla declared that she has and possesses and had and possessed until learning of the adelantado's death, may he have glory, are the following:

—one house in this town in which she lives
—another small house that serves as a storehouse next to the other one; both are covered with thatch; they are bounded by mayor Francisco Cepero's house on one side, and by Juan Márques' house and public streets on the other.

Slaves

—Isabel, Moorish slave
—Joanillo and his wife, Francisca, with one daughter, Margarita
—another child, son of Joanillo and an Indian slave—Manuel

—Francisco, *loro* [generally, someone of African descent], son of Manuel and an Indian slave
—Domingo
—Hernando
—Jorge
—Julián

Slaves outside the island

—Alonso
—Perico
—María
—Catalina
—Inés
—[illegible]

The things that are in Matabano are the following:

—fifty-six female and two male turkeys, that are fifty-eight in all
—two hundred head of pigs, one hundred large ones in the corral and one hundred branded pigs from this litter
—one ass
—nine horses used for burden
—fifty *fanegas* of corn
—five hundred bushels [*monton,* a heap or pile] of yucca [cassava] from this year

The things that are in Mayabeque

—four hundred fifty head of pigs, two hundred older ones and two hundred fifty from this year's litter, all branded
—sixty birds, among which are sixteen capons
—three more hens with thirty chicks
—eight pickaxes
—one shepherd's knife
—two hundred bushels of sweet potatoes
—five hundred bushels of yucca from this year

What there is in Bayonoa

—seventeen breeding cows, and four young bulls, three or four years old
—thirteen head [of cattle], eight old ones and five calves

What there is in Cogimar

—one cabin with a new doorway
—one stable with one *barbacoa* [lattice frame used for preserving grain] for corn
—twenty fanegas of corn
—seven *almudes* of planted corn not yet ready to harvest
—ten thousand bushels of yucca from last year
—one thousand bushels of old yucca of two years past
—five thousand bushels of yucca from this year
—five thousand bushels of sweet potatoes
—three pickaxes
—one *romana* [steelyard]
—three axes
—another seven pickaxes
—another five new pickaxes
—two cauldrons and one old pan
—two geese
—four turkeys
—ten birds
—sixty head of sheep, two rams, and twenty lambs
—one horse in the stable

The things that Doña Isabel de Bobadilla declared that she has in her chamber and at home

—a gilded chest and in it the following:
  —a new fruit holder made of *cortado* [a type of cloth]
  —a new cortado towel
  —a new cortado gown
  —a new cortado towel, I mean to say a new embroidered towel
  —another new mesh towel

—a used mesh fruit cover
—some new mesh sleeves with gold and silver thread lined with colored taffeta
—a ruffled traveling hat with some gold thread
—thirty *varas* of black ribbon
—a white box and in it the following things:
—a panel of damask table linen
—eight and one-half pounds of thread
—some Latin prayers of Our Lady
—twenty-five hundred pins
—two small mirrors made of steel
—some fringe trimmings for an old scarlet tablecloth
—two pair of white gloves
—some paper and wrapped in it a quarter [of a vara] of white cloth, I mean to say of silver
—and one collar of gold and pearls that is from a gorget
—more paper with a gold and black gorget and two of mesh
—more paper with a gold gorget and a hairnet
—more paper with a gold hairnet
—a large panel of damask table linen
—another two pair of large damask table linens
—four shirts, two gold and two black
—thirteen varas of Dutch linen
—four scarlet pillows and two pin cushions
—four black pillows with their pin cushions
—one yellow bolster pillow with its pin cushions
—four old green pillows with their pin cushions
—one new scarlet towel
—another old scarlet and gold one
—another gold and green embroidered one
—another pink one
—another old white embroidered one
—another with some old dark threads
—a calico Portuguese smock
—two panels of worn-out tablecloths
—four pieces of calico six varas long
—one collar for a shirt and black leggings
—some old embroidered black sleeves
—some worn-out gold sleeves

—an old towel
—some paper wrapped around ruffles that probably are three hats
—two and one-half varas of fine napkins
—some paper with four hats and two gorgets
—some more paper with some gloves and an embroidered cloth and a gold handkerchief
—twenty varas of colored taffeta in pieces
—a gorget of black velvet with nine gold eyelets that weigh three pesos
—some paper with two pieces of cloth that probably are ten varas long
—four old Dutch sheets of two and one-half sets
—seven French sheets, four new and three old
—four rather worn-out fitted sheets
—two other worn-out French sheets
—eight sheets made of *angeo* [a type of fabric] that are used on women's beds
—four old mattresses
—eight panels of small tablecloths, four of one and one-half varas and four of two varas
—two dozen old napkins
—four pounds of linen
—one hundred cakes of soap
—one small mesh bed
—two small towels, one white and one scarlet
—twelve embroidered strips of cloth for four colored sheets
—some green velvet shoes for women
—another black collar for a shirt and leggings
—a small box which these things are in:
—an outfit for saying mass consisting of an orange damask chasuble, two albs, two amices, one mesh frontal lined in colored linen, one altar, and two pair of corporals
—a leather-covered box which the following things are in:
—a blue damask country bed, sleeves and canopy valances of scarlet velvet, a bedspread for the same, and a front part with trimming
—three worn pieces of scarlet velvet that is the border for a tablecloth
—two sets of the damask blue tablecloth
—three tapestry cushions
—one scarlet brocade *raso* [a type of cloth] dress with its lace sleeves and some distaffs of the same and their rolls of cloth

—another yellow brocade raso dress with its lace sleeves lined in crimson raso
—two new tawny velvet cushions
—two more worn velvet ones
—an old black taffeta dress

—a leather-covered box that has the following:
—a worn scarlet petticoat
—a purple velvet dress with its smock
—a black velvet dress with two pair of lace sleeves, some lined in crimson raso, the others in yellow raso
—a black velvet open overskirt
—a black velvet cloak lined in taffeta
—two pair of small raso sleeves, some black and the others brown
—some white raso cone-shaped small sleeves
—other black knitted small sleeves
—others of gold pink cloth
—some sleeves covered in crimson fur
—a black velvet jacket
—a crimson raso bodice
—a worn-out black velvet hat trimmed in gold

—a leather-covered box with the following things:
—a writing desk lined with tawny velvet
—a damask-white dress with its white velvet smock
—a dress of crimson raso without sleeves
—a pink raso smock
—a pink raso pinafore
—another pinafore of Peruvian feathers with gold embroidery
—a pink raso petticoat
—five brushes

—another leather-covered box with the following things:
—a frizzed silk cape lined in black velvet
—a white serge capitular cloak
—a box with two dozen silk and flannel habits
—some white velvet stockings
—five pair of velvet shoes
—some velvet slippers
—a black silk sword belt
—two velvet caps

—a worn black velvet jacket
—another jacket of brown velvet and raso
—some Castilian clothing of raso lined in taffeta
—a velvet sleeveless smock, open with raso strips with fringes
—two pair of ankle boots
—an old blue harness with a protective cover, breastband, whitened headgear, and tassels on straps; it has no more than one stirrup strap and spur
—a scarlet cap
—a scarlet bonnet
—another white box which the following things are in:
—a green velvet hoopskirt
—some silver *angarillas* [suspended baskets] that for the sake of not being squandered, so that they are not falsely judged, they are not weighed; it has all of its harness, silver covering, and it does not have panels, it has a velvet covering and panels covered with velvet, headgear, checkreins for a mule, they are decorated with some silver flowers, they lack two pieces of the breaststrap with its supporting brace, it has a black velvet cushion
—another mule harness made of black cloth
—a wooden country bed
—some old bedclothing from this bed from Perú
—four *colones* [possibly German-made bed linen (from Cologne)]
—a Dutch bedspread of buckram
—a white box of embossed leather
—it has nine embossments of diverse colors
—another embossed leather box that has six embossments
—two embossed leather cushions
—four old torn tapestry cloths with figures
—two old rugs, one large, the other small
—two old blue velvet cushions
—there were the following copper things:
—three copper pitchers
—two stills
—one copper bread oven
—one large copper pot for a ship
—one new copper pot
—one larger pan with its iron handle
—another copper pan for making wax

—two skillets
—a casserole dish with a new top
—two other pot tops
—a vat for cooking pitch
—two brass candlestick makers
—two old plain tables with their benches
—a part of a table in pieces with its bench
—two small tables with their benches
—a small table with inlay
—three old chairs with backs
—three old padded white boxes
—two old white boxes in the house
—three *versos* [light artillery] with their iron chambers
—two bronze versos, one with its loading apparatus [*servidor*] and the other is fired without it
—twelve iron versos without their loading apparatus
—twenty-four lances
—two shields

The things of gold and silver that Doña Isabel de Bobadilla declared that she has at home and in pawn are the following:

—Eleven gold bracelets, one gold and pearl necklace, a gold sash, a medallion, some small necklace beads, a rosary, two ends of a sash, some earrings, fifty pieces of hairnet with sixteen other pieces of *cruzadillas* [probably a decorative fastener for hairnets] for the same hairnet and thirty-nine pieces of neckguards; they weighed two hundred ninety-five and one-half pesos of gold.
—There are six dozen gold nails that are on top of one another that they have in glass; two were broken, one of the larger ones and one of the smaller ones; because of not being falsely judged they were not squandered. These two weighed one peso and one *tomín*, all of them weighing forty and one-half pesos.
—There is a perfume box with some little bars and a small gold chain that, because of not being squandered, was not weighed; it might have had eight or ten pesos of gold, more or less.
—Two buckles plus another piece of gold from a sword belt, and one ducat weighed twenty-two pesos.
—The worked silver weighed one hundred twenty-two *marcos;* this included a broken jar, a broken chalice, two cruets, and the stirrups given

by Fernán Ponce, and the rest is silver service and for baptismal fonts. All of this is in the power of Juan de Rojas, pawned for four hundred seventy pesos of gold that are owed to him that were given for ordinary household expenses; these four hundred seventy pesos should take away from the value of said silver.

—two silver sauce boats that were not weighed that are used at home as salt dispensers

—a cross with relics and a ring that all weigh three pesos of gold

—a wooden crucifix that cost two pesos

—two *celcericas* [?] and one silver thimble weighing two and one-half *adarmes*

—a little bit of pearl that might weigh two adarmes

—a rosary with thirty-two gold beads that are very small and that weigh two pesos

—a small chest with inlay and in it the following things:

—a perfume bottle with a little civet

—a small box with an adarme of musk

—two and one-half adarmes of perfume

—one-half vara of Dutch linen

—two and one-half ounces and one-quarter of yellow silk

—two ounces of scarlet silk

—one and one-half ounces of thin thread

—one and one-half ounces of blue silk

—six small tablets of perfume

—two adarmes of black silk

—two unraveled handkerchiefs

—coral trimming for a cart

[AGI. *Justicia.* Legajo 750 (A)]

Indian Proper Names in the Four Narratives

Originally published in the
*Final Report of The United States De Soto Expedition Commission**
by John R. Swanton

Ranjel	Elvas	Biedma	Garcilaso
Oçita (and Eçita?)	Ucita	....	Hirrihigua.
Mocoço	Mocoço..............	....	Mucoço.
Orriygua (chief and probably province).	....	....	(Hirrihigus.)
Naguarete (chief and probably province).	....	....	
Çapaloey (chief and probably province).	....	....	
Orriparacogi, Orriparagi, Urriparacoxi.	Paracoxi	Hurripacuxi (De Soto has Urripacoxit).	Urribarracuxi.
Guaçoco	....	....	
Luca	....	....	
Viçela	Acela	....	
Tocaste	Tocaste	....	
Ocale (province) Cale (river or swamp).	Cale................	Etocale	(Acuera.)
Uqueten (town of Ocale)	....	....	
Acuera	....	Acuera (De Soto)	Acuera (for Ocale).
Itaraholata	Ytara	....	
Potano	Potano..............	....	Ocali (name misplaced).
Utinamocharra	Utinama	....	
("Mala-Paz")	("Mala-Paz")	....	
....	Cholupaha (Villafarta in Portuguese).	....	
Aguacaleyquen	Caliquen	Aguacalecuen	Ochile (name misplaced).
Guatutima (an Indian)...	....	....	
Uriutina	....	....	
("Muchas-Aguas")	....	....	
Napituca	Napetuca (or Napetaca).	....	Vitachuco (name misplaced).
Apalu	Hapaluya	....	
Uçachile	Uzachil (or Uzachill) ..	Veachile	Osachile.
Agile	Axille	Aguile	Ochile (see above).
Apalache	Palache (or Apalache) ..	Apalache (& Apalachi).	Apalache.
Ivitachuco	Vitachuco	Ivitachuco	Vitachuco (name misplaced).

*Reprinted with permission of the Smithsonian Institution Press.

Ranjel	Elvas	Biedma	Garcilaso
Calahuchi	Uzela		
Iviahica	Anhaica Apalache	Iniahico	
	Ochete		Aute.
Achuse	Ochus		Achusi.
Guacuca (river)			
	Yupaha (distant province).		
Capachequi	Capachiqui	Acapachiqui	
("Fuente Blanca")			
Toa	Toalli	Otoa	
Chisi, Ichisi (province)	Achese	Chisi	Altapaha (name misplaced).
("Rio Grande")			
Altamaha	Altamaca	Altapaha	Achalaque name (misplaced).
Çamumo (chief)			
Ocute	Ocute	Ocuti	Cofa.
Cofaqui	Cofaqui (chief)	Cofaqui	Cofaqui.
Tatofa (chief)	Patofa		Patofa (officer).
Hymahi	Aymay		
Ilapi			
Cofitachequi	Cutifachiqui	Cofitachique (or Cofitachyque).	Cofachiqui.
Talimeco			Talomeco.
Chalaque (or Xalaque)	Chalaque		Chalaques.
Guaquili			
Xuala	Xualla, Xuala	Xuala	Xuala.
Guasili	Guaxule	Guasuli	Guaxule.
Canasoga	Canasagua		
Chiaha	Chiaha	Chiha	Ychiaha.
Coste	Acoste (or Coste)	Costehe	Acoste.
Tali	Tali		
Chisca	Chisca		Chisca (name misplaced)
Tasqui			
Coça	Coça	Coça (or Coca)	Coça.
Talimachusy	Tallimuchase		
Itaba	Ytaua		
Ulibahali	Ullibahali		
Piachi			
Tuasi	Toasi		
Talisi	Tallise (& Talisi)	Italisi	Talise.
Casiste	Casiste		
Caxa			
Humati			
Uxapita			

Ranjel	Elvas	Biedma	Garcilaso
caluça	Tascaluca, Tastaluca	Taszaluza	Tascaluça.
ıahachi (or Atahachi)			
chi	Piache		
bila	Mauilla	Mavila	Mauvila.
icpacana	Taliepataua		
ıçulixa			
ɔusta	Cabusto		
afalaya	Pafallaya		
icaça	Chicaça	Chicaza	Chicaça.
			Chicacilla.
luça			
chuma	Saquechuma		
:ulasa (chief)	Nicalasa (chief)		
ıpatica			
ıamu	Alimamu	Alibamo	Alibamo.
izqui	Quizquiz	Quizquiz	Chisca (name misplaced).
uixo	Aquixo		
ıqui (also "Quarqui")	Casqui	Icasqui	Casquin.
aha	Pacaha	Pacaha	Capaha.
	Macanoche (woman's name).		
	Mochila (woman's name).		
	Caluça (2d province)	Caluç	
iguate	Aquiguate (or Quiguate).	Quiquate	Quiguate.
ligua	Coligoa	Coligua	Colima.
pista			
isma	Palisema		
ixila			
ilcoya	Tatalicoya	Tatil Coya	
ıico	Tanico		
ɣase	Cayas	Cayas	
a	Tulla	Tula	Tula.
ipana	Quipana	Quipana	
	Anoixi		
itamaya	Catamaya		
angue	Autiamque (and Autianque).	Viranque	Utiangue.
	Ayays		
	Tietiquaquo		
	Tutelpinco		
	Tianto		
	Nilco (or Anilco)	Anicoyanque	Anilco.
	Guachoya	Guachoyanque	Guachoya.

RANJEL	ELVAS	BIEDMA	GARCILASO
Quigudta	Quigualtam (or Quigaltam)	. . . .	Quigualtanqui.
	Tamaliseu (river)	. . . .	
	Tapatu (river)	. . . .	
	Mico ("river" at Coça)	. . . .	
	Ri ("river" in Ucita lang.).	. . . .	
	Catalte	. . . .	
	Chaguete (or Chagguate).	Chavite	
	Aguacay	Aguacay	
	Pato	. . . .	
	Amaye (or Maye)	. . . .	
	Naguatex	. . . .	Naguatex.
	Hacanac	. . . .	
	Nissohone (or Nisohone).	Nisione	
	Lacane	Came	Guancane (?)
	Nondacao	Nondacao	
	Aays	Hais	Auche (?)
	Soacatino	Xuacatino (or Xacatin).	
	Guasco	. . . .	
	Naquiscoça	. . . .	
	Naçacahoz	. . . .	
	Daycao (river)	. . . .	
	Chilano	. . . .	
	Aminoya	. . . .	Aminoya.
	Tagoanate (or Taguanate).	. . . .	

Glossary

adarme: approximately 179 centigrams.

adelantado: authorized to settle a new territory. Literally, "one who pushes forward." A military concept carried over from the Middle Ages. Recruits his own army and bears all costs of the expedition. Distributes land to loyal followers. Reserves an hereditary holding for his own family. Full military and civil authority. Responsible for the internal and external peace of the territory. Represents the king in his own person.

AGI [Also AI]: Archivo General de Indias in Seville. The chief depository in Spain of materials about the Spanish experiences in the New World.

alcalde: mayor; head of a town council.

almirante: second in command of a fleet. Sailed in the ship designated as *almiranta*, which guarded the rear of a convoy.

almud: an ancient land and grain measure; 0.8 bushels

alquiere: a measure of volume. Either a dry measure of 138 deciliters, or a liquid measure of 84 deciliters.

apu: a term like *curaca*, borrowed by Garcilaso de la Vega from Inca usage in Peru. In the present context, the noble office of war chief, subject to a principal chief.

arquebus [also *harquebus*]: "The earliest and mechanically the crudest of the hand-held firearms. It was fired by touching a piece of lighted matchcord, like a slow-burning fuse, to the powder hole. . . . A ball or shot fired from a harquebus had much greater velocity than an arrow or a crossbow bolt, but it was slow to load, not very accurate, and problematic in rainy weather. Because the matchcord had to be kept alight when action might occur, great quantities of it were required" (Charles Hudson, in *The Juan Pardo Expeditions*, Washington, D.C., Smithsonian Institution Press, 1990; 147–48).

arroba: either a measure of capacity, about 4 gallons, or a weight of about 25 pounds.

audiencia: the highest regional appeals court; a hearing at such a court.

barbacoa: a raised framework for smoking meat or fish [source of the modern word *barbecue*]; also the name of a wooden framework used to store corn above ground.

beheaded: although the Indians at times did behead their enemies, in Garcilaso, at least, this seems to mean to be scalped; the Spaniards had never seen scalping and had no word for it.

braza: a unit of measure; approximately one fathom.

cacique: an hereditary lord of vassals. A native term in an Arawak language, borrowed by the Spaniards in the conquest of the Antilles and later applied by them elsewhere in the Americas to various chiefs.

corregidor: a magistrate.

cow: a buffalo. The Spaniards had never seen a buffalo and had no name for it.

crossbow: "Although the crossbow could fire a small missile at high velocity and could be aimed and fired by a person of little skill or strength, an experienced Indian archer could fire an arrow with comparable penetrating power (because of the heavier weight of the arrow), and he could fire several arrows in the time it took a crossbowman to load and fire a single bolt" (Charles Hudson, in *The Juan Pardo Expeditions,* 147).

cruzada: a gold coin minted during the reign of Ferdinand and Isabella, equivalent to seven pesetas.

curaca: a district or provincial chief. A native term borrowed from the Quechua language of Peru. It is used interchangeably with *cacique* by the Inca, Garcilaso de la Vega.

encomienda: a grant of Indian tributary labor.

estado: a unit of measure equal to about 5 to 6 feet.

factor: an agent of the king; usually an accountant; reports to the king on the results of the expedition.

fanega: a grain measure equal to about 1.6 bushels.

fanega de tierra: a land measure equal to about 1.6 acres.

geira: a unit of land, roughly equivalent to the English acre.

league: a unit of land or sea measure. At least two versions of the Spanish land league were in use during the sixteenth century; which one is meant in a given context is a matter of dispute. The *legua legal* was 5,000 *varas,* equivalent to 2.63 U.S. miles or 4.19 km. The *legua común,* or common league, known to have been used as an itinerary measure, was equivalent to 3.45 miles or 5.57 km.

maestro de campo [also *maese de campo*]: camp master; chief administrative officer of the expedition. A military rank corresponding to a present-day colonel.

New Spain: the name the Spanish gave to Mexico and its borderlands.

oidor: a judge.

peso: a Spanish coin of varying value made of gold or silver; often rated at an ounce of pure silver.

piragua: a small, shallow-draft boat, meant to be rowed.

reales [*real,* sing.]: the real was a silver coin, first minted in Castile. Its value has varied.

repartimiento: a share received from the division of the proceeds of an expedition.

rodeleros: soldiers armed with sword and shield, from *rodela,* a round shield or buckler.

tameme: a native burden bearer or porter. Borrowed by the Spaniards from a native Nahuatl term used in New Spain, thenceforth applied elsewhere in the New World.

tercio: a Spanish regiment of infantry; sometimes the commanding officer of one. Garcilaso de la Vega served as tercio in a ship under Don Augostin Mexias during the period of the Spanish Armada.

Tierra Firme: the mainland of South and Central America.

tomín: 1/3 adarme; approximately 596 milligrams.

vara: approximately 33 inches.

vecino: a free Spanish citizen of a municipality, most often with voice and vote in municipal affairs.

Yelves: the city of Elvas in Portugal.

Introduction to Bibliography of De Soto Studies

by Jeffrey P. Brain and Charles R. Ewen

The search for the route of Hernando de Soto through the southeastern United States has become a consuming pursuit for many cartographers, historians, and archaeologists. Since the pioneering efforts of Guillaume Delisle in 1718, researchers have chased a variety of alternative routes.

In 1939, when John Swanton put together the *Final Report of the United States De Soto Expedition Commission,* the archaeological evidence was sparse. Nearly fifty years later, Brain (1985, xlvi) summarized the progress that had been made on defining the expedition's route since the commission's report and wryly remarked "that we are far more uncertain about the exact itinerary than the Commission was."

Five years after Brain's summary, De Soto scholars are still no closer to agreement on the route and, in fact, may have become more divisive in its interpretation than ever. Swanton himself foresaw this almost forty years ago, saying, "Hernando de Soto, his expedition, and the places he visited will probably be matters of discussion for years and years" (Swanton 1952a, 311). "Discussion" could be termed a euphemism for the heated debate that the study of the expedition's route has inspired. Indeed, the debate has polarized into two opposing factions: those that choose to adhere primarily to refinements of the route proposed by Swanton and those that support the route as reinterpreted by Charles Hudson of the University of Georgia and his associates. We will not attempt a discussion of the disputed points here; rather the reader is referred to the original references presented in our bibliography.

The Purpose of the Bibliography

This bibliography is intended to aid the scholar pursuing research on topics related to Hernando de Soto's entrada in the southeastern United States. It is not intended as a general guide to the Early Contact Period in the New

World. It was difficult to set the parameters of the bibliography. Including every reference that might conceivably have some bearing on De Soto–related research would have been beyond the scope of this work and certainly beyond the endurance of the compilers. Some general references have been included because they seemed to us to be useful research tools. There may be some personal bias in their selection, as the preponderance of archaeological references betrays the archaeological backgrounds of the authors.

A special effort was made to include those sources not readily available to the casual researcher. This so-called grey literature consists mainly of unpublished manuscripts in possession of the compiler, letters to other scholars or institutions, and archaeological contract reports on file at various federal and state agencies. Several scholars, who are actively pursuing De Soto–related research, were contacted and asked to contribute their most obscure references. Their responses resulted in the compilation of some truly arcane literature.

Pains have also been taken to include all points of view expressed by the various De Soto scholars. Opinions range widely concerning where the expedition went, who they encountered, and what constitutes evidence for these conclusions. Attempts were made to be impartial in the selection process, and all references are presented in an equal fashion. Readers are invited to examine the opposing hypotheses on the various topics and draw their own conclusions.

This introductory essay discusses the De Soto literature in a topical manner. During the compilation of the references it became apparent that there were several major themes pervading the literature. They are: the route of the army, archaeological investigations, artifact studies, biographical studies, and De Soto in explicitly fictitious literature. Many of the works included in the bibliography fit into more than one category, while others were idiosyncratic and hard to fit into any general category. Not all categories that appear in the bibliography (e.g., general anthropological and historical studies) appear in this essay; however, the intent is to get the researcher off to a good start. The reader should also consult the extensive bibliography published in Swanton's *Final Report* (1939, 337–43).

The Route of the Army

The route of the De Soto entrada is one of the longest-lived and most hotly contested issues in the study of the protohistoric Southeast. The earliest route version in this bibliography is Delisle's (1718) *Carte de la Louisiane et cours du Mississipi,* which graphically depicts what he thought was the track of the expedition. Other early studies of the route include Andrews (1917) and Fordyce (1929), with Swanton's 1939 report concluding the early period of research.

Tracing the entire route of the De Soto entrada is a daunting prospect, and many researchers have chosen to focus on a portion of the route. Most of these studies focus on either the search for an important site or the route within a particular state. It is these segmental studies that have provided and will provide synthesizers with their basic data. There are several key points that form the framework upon which the route is strung, and which have sparked the most heated exchanges.

The state of Florida figures prominently in the De Soto debates. Beginning with the landing site, the controversy is primarily over whether the expedition landed at Tampa Bay (Milanich 1984, 1988, 1989a, 1989b; Mitchem 1986; Swanton 1934, 1939) or farther south at Charlotte Harbor (Schell 1966; Tesar 1989; L. Williams 1986, 1989; Wilkinson 1960). A recent article (Leverette and Lawson 1990), however, suggests that De Soto landed on the east coast of Florida. Unfortunately, all of these speculations rest solely on the interpretation of the documentary evidence, since archaeological investigations have failed to corroborate any of them. There is less debate concerning the location of the first winter encampment. This is one of the few locations on the route for which there is general agreement, or at least not vehement disagreement. Preliminary documentation concerning the archaeological investigations of this site is provided by Ewen (1988, 1989a, 1989b, 1990, 1991), Ewen and Jones (1988), B. C. Jones (1988), B. C. Jones and Mitchell (1988), and Tesar and Jones (1989). General characterizations of the route through Florida appear in Blake (1987b), K. Johnson (1987), Milanich (1984, 1988, 1989a, 1990), and Milanich and Mitchem (1986). In attempting to trace the route of the earlier explorer, Pánfilo de Narváez, Scott (1981) provides useful data for interpreting the route of De Soto in Florida.

When the army left Florida and crossed into Georgia, their trail did not become any easier to follow. Much of the research concerning this part of the trail has focused on the prehistoric province of Coosa (Blake 1991b; Boyd and Schroedl 1987; Hudson 1988a, 1990a; Little and Curren, n.d.) and whether the Peachtree site in North Carolina is on the route (Anderson 1990; Eubanks 1989, 1990c; Little 1990; Setzler and Jennings 1941). Other more general works concerning the route through Georgia, the Carolinas, and Tennessee include: Andrews (1917b); Goff (1953); Hudson, Smith, and

DePratter (1984a, 1987); Hudson, Worth, and DePratter (1990); Melvin (1978); and M. Smith (1976).

Alabama holds the distinction for most avidly pursuing the route of De Soto in recent years. The Working Paper Series published by the Alabama De Soto Commission is perhaps the most useful set of recent publications pertaining to the expedition and to efforts made to locate evidence of its passing throughout the Southeast. Alabama also holds the distinction of being one of the first states to attempt to mark the route (Holmes, et al. 1989; D. Jones 1988) and yet having the least agreement as to exactly where the explorer went. Of particular concern is the location of Mauvilla, which though actively sought (Blake 1988b; Brannon 1929; DePratter, Hudson, and Smith 1985; Little 1988c) has still not been satisfactorily located. The hypotheses on where the route travels through Alabama are deeply divided, as is evident from such titles as Curren's (1988a) *A Rebuttal of the 'Georgia Reconstruction' of the Soto Route through Alabama* and (1988b) *A Rebuttal of the Blake Model* and Hudson's (1989a) *Critique of Little and Curren's Reconstruction of De Soto's Route through Alabama.* The various reconstructions of this section of the route include: Curren (1987, 1988c); Curren, Little, and Lankford (1981b); Hudson (1989b); Lankford (1977); Lankford, Curren, and Little (1980); Little (1988b, 1988e).

The route through Mississippi is no less controversial (Atkinson 1987; Brain 1984; Brain, Toth, and Rodriguez-Buckingham 1974; Evans 1940; Hudson, Smith, and DePratter 1989; Lewis 1927; Love 1921; Ward 1986; Weinstein 1985). The route through Mississippi, however, is only the precursor to the big question that transcends state boundaries and takes on a national concern. Where did De Soto "discover" the Mississippi River? This question has been addressed early by Rowland (1927a, 1927b), among others, in a symposium concerning that question. Other suggestions are offered in the segmental studies mentioned above.

Wherever they crossed, the diminished army spent the remainder of their sojourn criss-crossing Arkansas and may have even ventured into Missouri (Burgess 1967/1968; Eubanks 1990b) and Louisiana. The debate has been less bitter west of the Mississippi, but a definitive route is still to be marked. Works on the Arkansas portion of the route include: Akridge (1986); Dickinson (1986); Hudson (1985); Hudson and Morse (n.d.); Mixon (1917); Morse and Morse (1990); Swanton (1952b). Schambach (1989) discusses the route from southwest Arkansas into Texas, while Bryan (1956), Strickland (1942), J. Williams (1942), Woldert (1942), and others still in press (Hudson;

Kenmotsu, Bruseth, and Corbin; Schambach) follow the trail of De Soto's successor, Luis Moscoso, in Texas.

Charles Hudson, in 1988, under contract to the National Park Service, synthesized the segments he and his colleagues had researched and offered an alternative to the Swanton route (1988b). This was later published with DePratter and Smith (1989) and released as a final report by the Park Service in 1990. It was not without its detractors, as is evidenced in Curren (1991a), Little (1988d), and Little and Curren (1990c). The controversy eventually became such that the National Park Service declined to recommend that Congress designate the trail as a National Historic Trail, citing difficulties in marking its route because of lack of agreement among the principal researchers.

Archaeological Investigations

One advantage that contemporary researchers have over the 1939 De Soto Expedition Commission is that a great deal of archaeological work pertinent to the De Soto expedition has been conducted in the last fifty years. Most of it has been merely suggestive, rather than definitive, yet it has contributed to a better understanding of the De Soto entrada and the indigenous societies they met. The archaeological literature is divided into regional syntheses and site-specific investigations. Only a few of these studies will be mentioned here, and the reader is urged to consult the bibliography itself for a more thorough coverage of the archaeological literature.

Regional accounts that deal with the expedition itself and the protohistoric peoples of the Southeast are available for most of the route. These include: Brain, Toth, and Rodriguez-Buckingham (1974), "Ethnohistoric Archaeology and the De Soto Entrada into the Lower Mississippi Valley"; Curren (1984), *The Protohistoric Period in Central Alabama;* DePratter (1983), "Late Prehistoric and Early Historic Chiefdoms in the Southeastern United States"; Dye (1989b), *Towns and Temples along the Mississippi;* Morse and Morse (1983), *Archaeology of the Central Mississippi Valley;* Bruce Smith (1986), "The Archaeology of the Southeastern United States: From Dalton to De Soto, 10,500–500 B.P."; Marvin Smith (1987), *Archaeology of Aboriginal Culture Change in the Interior Southeast: Depopulation during the Early Historic Period;* and Walthall (1980), *Prehistoric Indians of the Southeast: Archaeology of Alabama and the Middle South.* Again, these references are intended only as the starting place for any research in their respective areas.

There are many individual site reports that claim a connection with the De Soto entrada. Some, if not all, of these will require further research to satisfy the skeptical or even the credulous. Thus cautioned, the reader may wish to consult the following works: for Anhaica (Ewen 1989a, 1989b; B. C. Jones 1988); for Coosa (Boyd and Schroedl 1987; DeJarnette 1958; Hudson et al. 1985, 1987b); for Casqui (H. Davis 1966; Klinger 1977; P. Morse 1981); for Mauvilla (Little 1988c); and for Cofitechequi (DePratter 1989). Along the general route there is a host of protohistoric sites, which the army may have visited or influenced in some way. The bulk of the archaeological site reports listed in the bibliography fall into this category.

One of the major questions concerning the impact of the expedition is whether or not De Soto and his men were responsible for spreading epidemic diseases throughout the Southeast and decimating the native inhabitants. This issue is dealt with on a regional level by Blakely and Mathews (1990), Dobyns (1983), Milner (1980), Ramenofsky (1982, 1987, 1990), and M. Smith (1984a, 1987, 1989a). On the site level, the immediate effects of the De Soto entrada are examined at the King Site in a volume edited by Blakely (1988) and at the Tatham Mound by Hutchinson (1990) and Mitchem and Hutchinson (1986, 1987). Not everyone blames the protohistoric demographic shifts on De Soto, however; Burnett and Murray (1991) point to natural factors in northeast Arkansas that may have contributed to the depopulation of that area.

Artifact Studies

Artifact studies are an important part of the De Soto literature. Because they are readily identifiable and afford tangible evidence of the passing of the expedition, Spanish artifacts are hailed by archaeologists as solid evidence of De Soto contact. Whether the Spaniards were ever actually at the site where these artifacts were deposited is another issue entirely since all of these artifacts are highly portable. Nevertheless, they are useful diagnostic tools, and much effort has been expended in their study. These artifact studies usually fall into one of two categories: 1) general studies on the kinds of artifacts that have been found at De Soto–related sites; 2) specific studies concerning a specific type of artifact (e.g., beads) and its relevance to De Soto research.

General studies attempt to answer the question "What kind of artifacts have been found on De Soto sites?" or sometimes "What kind of artifacts are likely to be found on De Soto sites?" These questions are addressed for the route-wide studies by Brain (1975); Curren, Little, and Corey (1991); DePratter and Smith (1987); Eubanks (1991a); Milanich and Mitchem (1986); Mitchem (1989a); Polhemus and Smith (1980); and M. Smith (1976). On a more site-specific level, M. Smith examines the European materials recovered from the King Site (1975) and the Little Egypt Site (1979). General guides for sixteenth-century artifacts in the Southeast include: Deagan (1987) and South, Skowronek, and Johnson (1988).

Many of these artifact studies focus on a single class of artifact. Beads are often used as a temporally diagnostic index artifact. Studies of De Soto–era beads have been undertaken by Eubanks (1991d), Floyd (1990), Francis (1986, 1987), Harris (1982), Mitchem and Leader (1988), M. Smith (1982, 1983, 1989b), and M. Smith and Good (1982). Metal artifacts found on protohistoric sites are also often associated with the De Soto expedition. Specific artifacts such as weaponry (Dickinson 1987, Little 1985, D. Morse 1988), bells (Heath 1991, Mitchem and McEwan 1988), and coins (M. Smith 1984b) are subsumed under this category. Other miscellaneous artifact studies include a curious Catholic/Aztec artifact (Langford 1990) and a debate over a spatulate axe from Demopolis, Alabama (Little et al. 1989a, 1989b; M. Smith 1989e).

Biographical Studies

Virtually every United States history text mentions Hernando de Soto, if only for his "discovery" of the Mississippi River. The man himself, however, has received short shrift in the literature, when compared to other explorers, and is, indeed, considered to be one of the lesser conquistadors by the Spaniards. Many of the biographies of De Soto were written in the late nineteenth century (Abbott 1898, Chadwick 1891, Villanueva 1892, Wilmer 1858) or early twentieth century (Bayle 1930; Graham 1924; W. Malone 1914; Solar y Taboada 1929). Later biographical sketches tend to be part of larger studies, such as Lockart's (1972) *Men of Cajamarca,* which examined the Spaniards involved in the conquest of Peru. Curiously, even with the 450th anniversary of the entrada and the 500th anniversary of the Columbus voyage at hand, few recent biographies of De Soto have been published.

Some biographical works have a definite agenda, of which the reader should be aware. For example, two works that tend to perpetuate *la leyenda blanca* or glorify the Spaniards' role in the New World are: *Hernando de Soto: Knight of the Americas* (Albornoz 1986) and *Hernando de Soto: El Centauro de las Indias* (Blanco Castillo 1955). These are of interest in that their interpretation of De Soto's exploits in the New World tends to conflict with the politically correct thinking of today. Another interesting biographical work is Avellaneda's (1990) *Los Sobrevivientes de la Florida: The Survivors of the De Soto Expedition,* which includes information concerning personal histories of the Spaniards who survived the expedition.

De Soto in Fiction

Although some may argue that many of the above-mentioned works constitute works of fiction, unless the author thinks so we have not included them as such here. The explicit works of fiction involving the exploits of Hernando de Soto are surprisingly few given the epic nature of the real-life expedition. Most of the early publications (John Jennings 1958, Littleton 1928, Lytle 1941, Steele 1956) are fairly standard action/romances. Such volumes have been the subject of a symposium paper by Ruiz-Fournells (1991). Recent works have told the story of the De Soto expedition in verse (Holford 1984, Peter 1983) or from the native point of view as in Piers Anthony's *Tatham Mound* (1991).

Conclusion

This brief introductory chapter is only intended to outline the scope of the available research pertaining to the De Soto entrada in the southeastern United States. The references mentioned in this chapter are only a fraction of the total volume of the literature related to De Soto. Our bibliography contains nearly seven hundred entries, but it also is not exhaustive. Nevertheless, we hope it may serve as a useful entry point for those pursuing research on De Soto.

Bibliography of De Soto Studies

by Jeffrey P. Brain and Charles R. Ewen

Abbott, John Stephens Cabot. *Ferdinand de Soto.* New York: Dodd, Mead, 1898.

Akridge, Scott. "De Soto's Route in North Central Arkansas." *Arkansas Archeological Society Field Notes* 211 (1986): 3–7.

Albornoz, Miguel. *Hernando de Soto: Knight of the Americas.* New York: Franklin Watts, 1986.

Anderson, David G. "Reply to Eubanks." *The Florida Anthropologist* 43 (1990): 13–35.

Anderson, David G., David J. Hally, and James L. Rudolph. "The Mississippian Occupation of the Savannah River Valley." *Southeastern Archaeology* 5, no. 1 (1986): 32–51.

Andrews, Daniel Marshall. *De Soto's Route.* Lancaster, Penn.: New Era Printing, 1917a.

———. "De Soto's Route from Cofitachequi, in Georgia, to Cosa, in Alabama." *American Anthropologist* 19 (1917b): 55–67.

Anthony, Piers. *Tatham Mound.* New York: William Morrow, 1991.

Atkinson, James R. *Post-Woodland Period Archeological Phases in the Upper Tombigbee River Valley between Tibbee/Line Creeks and Tupelo, Mississippi.* Natchez Trace Parkway, 1986. Ms. on file.

———. "The De Soto Expedition through North Mississippi in 1540–1541." *Mississippi Archaeology* 22 (1987): 61–73.

Atkinson, James R., John C. Phillips, and Richard Walling. *The Kellogg Village Site Investigations, Clay County, Mississippi.* Starkville, Miss.: Department of Anthropology, Mississippi State University, 1980.

Avellaneda, Ignacio. *Los Sobrevivientes de la Florida: The Survivors of the De Soto Expedition.* Gainesville: University of Florida, P. K. Yonge Library of Florida History, 1990.

Baber, Adin. "Food Plants of the De Soto Expedition." *Tequesta* 1, no. 2 (1942): 34–40.

Badger, R. Reid, and Lawrence A. Clayton, eds. *Alabama and the Borderlands: From Prehistory to Statehood.* University: University of Alabama Press, 1985.

Baker, Steven G. "Cofitachique: Fair Province of Carolina." M.A. thesis, University of South Carolina, 1974.

———. "Cofitachique: Fair Province of Carolina: An EthnoArchaeological Perspective." Paper presented at the annual meeting of the Society for Historical Archaeology, Charleston, 1975.

Bancroft, George. *History of the United States.* Vol. 1 (Boston 1839), 42–60.

Bandelier, A. F., ed. *The Journey of Alvar Nuñez Cabeza de Vaca.* New York: Allerton, 1922.

Barton, Charles A. "Where Did De Soto Discover the Mississippi River?" In *A Symposium on the Place of Discovery of the Mississippi River by Hernando de Soto in Jackson,* edited by D. Rowland, 1927.

Bayle, Constantino. *Hernando de Soto.* Madrid: Editorial Razon y Fe, 1930.

Bell, J. B., Jr., and T. D. Foster. *The Hernando de Soto Narrative.* Hernando, Miss.: Committee to Honor de Soto, 1989.

Billings, John S. *Silver Bluff, De Soto and Galphin, a Narrative Compilation of Some Old Documents.* Redcliff Plantation, S.C., 1955. Ms. on file.

Blake, Alan. *A Proposed Route for the Hernando de Soto Expedition Based on Physiography and Geology. Part II: Apalachee to Chiaha.* Vol. 4. De Soto Working Paper, Tuscaloosa: Alabama De Soto Commission, University of Alabama, State Museum of Natural History, 1987a.

———. *A Proposed Route for the Hernando de Soto Expedition from Tampa Bay to Apalachee Based on Physiography and Geology.* Vol. 2. De Soto Working Paper, Tuscaloosa: Alabama De Soto Commission, University of Alabama, State Museum of Natural History, 1987b.

———. *Legua Legal or Legua Comun: A Discussion.* Vol. 5. De Soto Working Paper, Tuscaloosa: Alabama De Soto Commission, University of Alabama, State Museum of Natural History, 1988a.

———. *A Proposed Route for the Hernando de Soto Expedition Based on Physiography and Geology. Part III: Chiaha to Mabila. Part IV: Mabila to the Mississippi River.* Vol. 6. De Soto Working Paper, Tuscaloosa: Alabama De Soto Commission, University of Alabama, State Museum of Natural History, 1988b.

———. "The Juan Pardo Expeditions: Proposed Routes Based on Geology and Physiography." *The Soto States Anthropologist* 91 (1991a): 45–79.

———. "Why Coosa Is Not in Northwest Georgia." *The Soto States Anthropologist* 91 (1991b): 99–108.

Blakely, Robert L., ed. *The King Site: Continuity and Contact in Sixteenth-Century Georgia.* Athens: University of Georgia Press, 1988.

Blakely, Robert L., and Bettina Detweiler-Blakely. "The Impact of European Diseases in the Sixteenth-Century Southeast: A Case Study." *Midcontinental Journal of Archaeology* 14 (1989): 62–89.

Blakely, Robert L., and David S. Mathews. "Bioarcheological Evidence for a Spanish–Native American Conflict in the Sixteenth-Century Southeast." *American Antiquity* 55 (1990): 718–44.

Blanco Castillo, F. *Hernando de Soto: El Centauro de las Indias.* Madrid: Editorial Carrera del Castillo, 1955.

Boorstin, Daniel J. *The Discoverers.* New York: Random House, 1983.

Boston, Barbara. "The 'De Soto Map.'" *Mid-America* 23 (1941): 236–50.

Bourne, Edward G., ed. *Narratives of the Career of Hernando de Soto in the Conquest of Florida.* New York: A. S. Barnes, 1904.

Boyd, C. Clifford, and Gerald Schroedl. "In Search of Coosa." *American Antiquity* 52 (1987): 840–44.

Boyd, Mark F. "The Arrival of De Soto's Expedition in Florida." *The Florida Historical Quarterly* 16, no. 3 (1938): 188–220.

Brain, Jeffrey. "Artifacts of the Adelantado." *The Conference on Historic Site Archaeology Papers* 8 (1975): 129–38.

———. "The Archaeological Phase: Ethnographic Fact or Fancy?" In *Archaeological Essays in Honor of Irving B. Rouse,* ed. R. C. Dunnell and E. S. Hall. The Hague: Mouton Publishers, 1978a.

———. "Late Prehistoric Settlement Patterning in the Yazoo Basin and Natchez Bluffs Regions of the Lower Mississippi Valley." In *Mississippian Settlement Patterns,* ed. B. D. Smith. New York: Academic Press, 1978b.

———. "La Salle at the Natchez: An Archaeological and Historical Perspective." In *La Salle and His Legacy: Early French Exploration and Settlement in the Lower Mississippi Valley,* ed. P. Galloway. Jackson: University Press of Mississippi, 1982.

———. "The De Soto Entrada into the Lower Mississippi Valley: Update of the Route and its Consequences." *Mississippi Archaeology* 19 (1984): 48–58.

———. "The Archaeology of the De Soto Expedition." In *Alabama and the Borderlands: From Prehistory to Statehood,* ed. R. Badger and L. Clayton. University: University of Alabama Press, 1985a.

———. "Introduction: Update of De Soto Studies since the United States De Soto Expedition Commission Report." In *Final Report of the United States De Soto Expedition Commission,* ed. J. R. Swanton. Washington, D.C.: Smithsonian Institution Press, 1985b.

———. *Working Paper Prepared for De Soto Symposium Convened by the Honorable Bob Graham, Governor of Florida.* Florida State Museum, 1986. Ms. in possession of author.

———. "The Effects of the Hernando de Soto Expedition on Native Americans." Paper presented at Congreso Internacional Hernando de Soto y Su Tiempo, Cáceres, Spain, 1991.

Brain, Jeffrey P., Ian W. Brown, and Vincas P. Steponaitis. *Archaeology of the Natchez Bluffs.* Peabody Museum, Harvard University, n.d. Ms. on file.

Brain, Jeffrey P., Alan Toth, and Antonio Rodriguez-Buckingham. "Ethnohistoric Archaeology and the De Soto Entrada into the Lower Mississippi Valley." *The Conference on Historic Site Archaeology Papers* 7 (1974): 232–89.

Brame, J. Y. "De Soto in Alabama, 1540," (with map). Part I. *Arrow Points* 13, no. 3 (1928).

———. "De Soto in Alabama, 1540." Part II. *Arrow Points* 13, no. 4 (1928).

———. "De Soto in Alabama, 1540." Part III (Conclusion). *Arrow Points* 13, no. 4 (1929).

Brannon, Peter. "The Route of De Soto from Cosa to Mauvilla." *Arrow Points* 2, no. 1 (1929).

Brooks, H. K. *Geology of Cape Canaveral.* Tallahassee, Fla.: Southeastern Geological Society, 1972.

Brose, David. "Mississippian Period Cultures in Northwestern Florida." In *Perspectives on Gulf Coast Prehistory,* ed. Dave D. Davis, 165–97. Gainesville: University of Florida Press, 1984.

Brose, David S., Ned J. Jenkins, and Russell Weisman. *Cultural Resources Reconnaissance Study of the Black Warrior–Tombigbee System Corridor, Alabama.* Department of Geography and Geology, University of South Alabama, 1982. Contract Report.

Brose, David S., and George W. Percy. "Fort Walton Settlement Patterns." In *Mississippian Settlement Patterns,* ed. B. D. Smith. New York: Academic Press, 1978.

Brown, Calvin S. *Archeology of Mississippi.* University: Mississippi Geology Survey, 1926.

Brown, Ian W. "Bells." In *Tunica Treasure,* ed. Jeffrey Brain, 197–205. Papers of the Peabody Museum of Archaeology and Ethnology, no. 71. Cambridge, Mass.: Harvard University Press, 1979.

Bryan, Frank. "Early Texas Travelers." *Central Texas Archeologist* 7 (1956): 57–108.

Bullen, Ripley P. *The Terra Ceia Site, Manatee County, Florida.* Vol. 3. Florida Anthropological Society Publications. Gainesville: Florida Anthropological Society, 1951.

———. "De Soto's Ucita and the Terra Ceia Site." *The Florida Historical Quarterly* 30, no. 4 (1952): 317–23.

———. "Tocobaga Indians and the Safety Harbor Culture." In *Tacachale: Essays on the Indians of Florida and Southeastern Georgia during the Historic Period,* ed. J. T. Milanich and S. Proctor. Gainesville: The University Presses of Florida, 1978.

Burgess, Charles E. "The De Soto Myth in Missouri." *Missouri Historical Society Bulletin* 24 (1967/1968): 304–5.

Burnett, Barbara, and Katherine Murray. "Don't Blame De Soto." Paper presented at University of Arkansas Anthropology Department Colloquium, Fayetteville, Ark., 1991.

———. "Death, Drought and De Soto: The Bioarcheology of Depopulation." In *The Hernando de Soto Expedition in the West, 1541–1543,* ed. Gloria Young and Michael P. Hoffman. Fayetteville: University of Arkansas Press, in press.

Bushnell, David I. *Villages of the Algonquian, Siouan and Caddoan Tribes West of the Mississippi.* No. 77. Bureau of American Ethnology Bulletin. Washington, D.C.: Smithsonian Institution, 1922.

Byrd, Kathleen M. "Report from Louisiana." *Chainmail* 3 (1989): 14–16.

Cabaniss, Frances A., and Allen Cabaniss. "The Middle Ages and Mississippi: A Note." *Journal of Mississippi History* 13 (1951): 212–25.

Caldwell, Joseph R. "Cherokee Pottery from Northern Georgia." *American Antiquity* 20, no. 3 (1955): 271–80.

Calvert, Albert F. *Spanish Arms and Armour.* New York: J. Lane, 1907.

Castañeda, Paulino, Mariano Cuesta, and Pilar Hernández. *Transcripción, estudio y notas del "Espejo de Navegantes" de Alonso Chaves.* Madrid: Instituto de Historia y Cultura Naval, 1983.

Castro, Florencia Vicente. "Caracteres psicológicos del indio y personalidad de la Conquista en la época de Hernando de Soto." Paper presented at Congreso Internacional Hernando de Soto y Su Tiempo, Cáceres, Spain, 1991.

Chadwick, Mara Louise Pratt. *Columbus and De Soto.* Chicago: Educational Publishing Company, 1891.

Chafe, Wallace. "Caddo Names in the De Soto Documents." In *The Hernando de Soto Expedition in the West, 1541–1543,* ed. Gloria Young and Michael P. Hoffman. Fayetteville: University of Arkansas Press, in press.

Chamot, Eduardo Dargent. "Oro y plata en el Perú de la Conquista." Paper presented at Congreso Internacional Hernando de Soto y Su Tiempo, Cáceres, Spain, 1991.

Chapman, Carl H., and Leo O. Anderson. "The Campbell Site: A Late Mississippian Town Site and Cemetery in Southeast Missouri." *The Missouri Archaeologist* 17, no. 2–3 (1955).

Chardon, Roland. "The Elusive Spanish League: A Problem of Measurement in Sixteenth-Century New Spain." *The Hispanic American Historical Review* 60, no. 2 (1980a): 294–302.

———. "The Linear League in North America." *Annals of the Association of American Geographers* 70 (1980b): 129–53.

———. "A Quantitative Determination of a Second Linear League Used in New Spain." *Professional Geographer* 32 (1980c): 462–66.

Charlevoix, Pierre F. X. de. *Histoire de la Nouvelle France.* Tome III. Paris: Ganeau, 1744.

Chatelain, Verne E. *The Defenses of Spanish Florida: 1565 to 1763.* Vol. 511. Washington, D.C.: Carnegie Institution of Washington Publication, 1941.

Clayton, Lawrence A. "The Spanish Heritage of the Southeast." *Alabama Heritage* 4 (1987): 2–11.

Connor, J. T., ed. *The Whole and True Discovery of Terra Florida.* Gainesville: University of Florida Press, 1965.

Cottier, John W. *The Alabama River Phase: A Brief Description of a Late Phase in the Prehistory of South Central Alabama.* Department of Anthropology, University of Alabama, 1970. Ms. on file.

Covey, Cyclone, ed. *Cabeza de Vaca's Adventures in the Unknown Interior of America.* 1961. Rpt. Albuquerque: University of New Mexico Press, 1983.

Crosby, Alfred W. *The Columbian Exchange: Biological and Cultural Consequences of 1492.* Westport, Conn.: Greenwood, 1972.

Cumming, William P. *The Southeast in Early Maps.* Princeton, N.J.: Princeton University Press, 1958.

Cumming, William P., R. A. Skelton, and D. B. Quinn. *The Discovery of North America.* New York: American Heritage, 1972.

Curren, Caleb B. *The Protohistoric Period in Central Alabama.* Camden: Alabama-Tombigbee Regional Commission, 1984.

———. *In Search of De Soto's Trail.* Report 1. Alabama-Tombigbee Regional Commission, 1986.

———. *The Route of the Soto Army through Alabama.* Vol. 3. De Soto Working Paper. Tuscaloosa: Alabama De Soto Commission, University of Alabama, State Museum of Natural History, 1987.

———. *A Rebuttal of the 'Georgia Reconstruction' of the Soto Route through Alabama.* Alabama De Soto Commission, 1988a. Ms. on file.

———. *A Rebuttal of the Blake Model.* Alabama De Soto Commission, 1988b. Ms. on file.

———. "An Attempt to Legislate History: The De Soto Commission and the National Park Service in Action." *The Soto States Anthropologist* 91 (1991a): 126–48.

———. "Spades Are Trumps." *The Soto States Anthropologist* 91 (1991b): 39–44.

———. *A Sword, a Malady, and a Cure.* Alabama-Tombigbee Regional Commission, 1991c. Ms. in possession of author.

Curren, Caleb B., ed. *Archaeology in Southwestern Alabama: A Collection of Papers.* Camden: Alabama-Tombigbee Regional Commission, 1982.

Curren, Caleb, and Keith J. Little. *Archaeological Investigations (1933–1980) of the Protohistoric Period of Central Alabama.* Alabama Historical Commission, 1981. Ms. on file.

Curren, Caleb B., Keith J. Little, and Pamela Corey. "Sixteenth Century Spanish Artifacts Recovered from Archeological Sites in the Pensacola/Mobile Bay Region." Paper presented at the 13th Gulf Coast History and Humanities Conference: Discovery and Exploration on the Gulf Coast, 1991.

Curren, Caleb B., Keith J. Little, and Harry O. Holstein. "Aboriginal Societies Encountered by the Tristan de Luna Expedition." *The Florida Anthropologist* 42 (1989): 381–95.

Curren, Caleb B., Keith J. Little, and George E. Lankford III. "The Route of the Expedition of Hernando de Soto through Alabama." Paper presented at the Southeastern Archaeological Conference, Asheville, N.C., 1981.

———. *Archaeological Research Concerning 16th Century Spanish and Indians in Alabama.* Camden: Alabama-Tombigbee Regional Commission, 1982. Ms. on file.

Curren, Caleb B., and Janet Lloyd. *Archaeological Survey in Southwest Alabama: 1984–1987.* Technical Report. Camden: Alabama-Tombigbee Regional Commission, 1987.

Curren, Caleb, and Rhonda Majors. *An Archaeological Reconnaissance of Monroe and Clarke Counties in Southwest Alabama.* Alabama Historical Commission, 1984. Ms. on file.

Curren, Caleb, and Lee McKenzie. *Archaeological Investigations at Three Sites in the 'Mauvilla Province.'* Alabama De Soto Commission, 1988. Ms. on file.

Davilla Padilla, Augustin. "[Narrative, ca. 1560]." In *Early History of the Creek Indians and Their Neighbors,* ed. John R. Swanton, 231–39. Bureau of American Ethnology Bulletin 73. Washington, D.C.: Smithsonian Institution, 1922.

Davis, E. Mott. "Archaeological and Historical Assessment of the Red River Basin in Texas." In *Archeological and Historical Resources of the Red River Basin,* ed. Hester Davis, 1. Fayetteville: Arkansas Archeological Survey, 1970.

Davis, Hester A. "An Introduction to Parkin Prehistory." *The Arkansas Archeologist* 7, no. 2–3 (1966): 1–40.

———. "An Archeological Inventory of Pulaski and Saline Counties, Arkansas." *The Arkansas Archeologist* 19 (1978): 36–43.

Davis, T. Frederick. "Juan Ponce de Leon's Voyages to Florida." *The Florida Historical Quarterly* 14 (1935): 5–70.

de Baillou, Clemens. "A Test Excavation of the Hollywood Mound (9 Ri 1), Georgia." *Southern Indian Studies* 17 (1965): 3–11.

Deagan, Kathleen A. *Artifacts of the Spanish Colonies of Florida and the Caribbean, 1500–1800.* Vol. 1: *Ceramics, Glassware, and Beads.* Washington, D.C.: Smithsonian Institution, 1987.

DeJarnette, David L. "An Archaeological Study of a Site Suggested as the Location of the Upper Creek Indian Community of Coosa Visited by Hernando de Soto in 1540." M.A. thesis, University of Alabama, 1958.

DeJarnette, David L., and Asael T. Hansen. *The Archeology of the Childersburg Site, Alabama.* Vol. 6. Notes in Anthropology. Tallahassee: Department of Anthropology, Florida State University, 1960.

DeJarnette, David L., Edward B. Kurjack, and Bennie C. Keel. "Archaeological Investigations of the Weiss Reservoir of the Coosa River in Alabama." *Journal of Alabama Archaeology* 19, no. 1 (1973).

Delanglez, Jean. "El Rio del Espiritu Santo." *Mid-America* 25, no. 3–4 (1943): 189–219, 231–49.

———. "El Rio del Espiritu Santo." *Mid-America* 26, no. 1–2 (1944): 62–84, 138–64.

Delisle, Guillaume. *Carte de la Louisiane et cours du Mississipi.* Paris: Chez l'Auteur, 1718.

DePratter, Chester B. "Late Prehistoric and Early Historic Chiefdoms in the Southeastern United States." Ph.D. dissertation, University of Georgia, 1983.

———. "Cofitechequi: Ethnohistorical Sources and Current Archaeological Knowledge." Paper presented at the 44th Southeastern Archaeological Conference, Charleston, S.C., 1987.

———. "Cofitachequi: Ethnohistorical and Archaeological Evidence." In *Studies in South Carolina Archaeology: Essays in Honor of Robert L. Stephenson*, ed. A. C. Goodyear and G. T. Hanson. Columbia: South Carolina Institute of Archaeology and Anthropology, 1989.

DePratter, Chester B., ed. "Explorations in Interior South Carolina by Hernando de Soto (1540) and Juan Pardo (1566–1568)." *South Carolina Institute of Archaeology and Anthropology Notebook* 19 (1987).

DePratter, Chester B., Charles Hudson, and Marvin T. Smith. "The Route of Juan Pardo's Explorations in the Interior Southeast, 1566–1568." *The Florida Historical Quarterly* 62 (1983): 125–58.

———. "The Hernando de Soto Expedition: From Chiaha to Mabila." In *Alabama and the Borderlands: From Prehistory to Statehood*, ed. R. Badger and L. Clayton, 108–26. University: University of Alabama Press, 1985.

———. "The Route of Juan Pardo's Explorations in the Interior Southeast, 1566–1568." *South Carolina Institute of Archaeology and Anthropology Notebook* 19 (1987): 37–51.

———. "The Juan Pardo Expeditions: North from Santa Elena." *Southeastern Archaeology* 9 (1990): 140–46.

DePratter, Chester B., and Chris Judge. "A Provisional Late Prehistoric and Early Historic Ceramic Sequence for the Wateree River Valley, South Carolina." Paper presented at the LAMAR Conference, Macon, Ga., 1986.

DePratter, Chester B., and Marvin T. Smith. "Sixteenth Century European Trade in the Southeastern United States: Evidence from the Juan Pardo Expeditions (1566–1568)." In *Spanish Colonial Frontier Research*, ed. Henry F. Dobyns, 57–77. Albuquerque: Center for Anthropological Research, 1980.

———. "Sixteenth Century European Trade in the Southeastern United States: Evidence from the Juan Pardo Expeditions, 1566–1568." *South Carolina Institute of Archaeology and Anthropology Notebook* 19 (1987): 52–61.

Detweiler-Blakely, Bettina. "Stress and Battle Casualties." In *The King Site: Continuity and Contact in Sixteenth-Century Georgia*, ed. Robert L. Blakely, 87–98. Athens: University of Georgia Press, 1988.

DeVorsey, Louis. "Early Maps as a Source in the Reconstruction of Southern Indian Landscapes." In *Red, White, and Black: Symposium on Indians in the Old South*, ed. C. Hudson. Southern Anthropological Society Proceedings, no. 5. Athens: University of Georgia Press, 1971.

Dibble, Ernest F., and Earle W. Newton, eds. *Spain and Her Rivals on the Gulf Coast*. Pensacola, Fla.: Historic Pensacola Preservation Board, 1971.

Dickinson, Samuel D. "Historic Tribes of the Ouachita Drainage System in Arkansas." *The Arkansas Archeologist* 21 (1980): 1–11.

———. "The River of Cayas: The Ouachita or the Arkansas River?" *Arkansas Archeological Society Field Notes* 209 (1986): 5–11.

———. "Arkansas's Spanish Halberds." *The Arkansas Archeologist* 24/25 (1987): 53–62.

———. "John Rison Fordyce." *Pulaski County Historical Review* 38, no. 3 (1990): 42–50.

Dobyns, Henry F. *Their Number Become Thinned: Native American Population Dynamics in Eastern North America.* Knoxville: University of Tennessee Press, 1983.

Donkin, R. A. "The Peccary: With Observations on the Introduction of Pigs to the New World." *Transactions of the American Philosophical Society* 75, part 5 (1985).

Duke, John Thomas. "De Soto and His Chroniclers." In "The Ouachita Basin: An Early History." Ph.D. dissertation, Texas A&M University, 1980.

Duthurburu, José Antonio del Busto. "Protagonismo de Hernando de Soto en la conquista del Perú." Paper presented at the Congreso Internacional Hernando de Soto y Su Tiempo, Cáceres, Spain, 1991.

Dye, David H. "1987 Excavations at Belle Meade (3CT30)." *Arkansas Archeological Society Field Notes* 219 (1987): 11.

———. "Death March of Hernando de Soto." *Archaeology* 42, no. 3 (1989): 26–31.

———. "Warfare in the Sixteenth-Century Southeast: The De Soto Expedition in the Interior." In *Columbian Consequences,* ed. David H. Thomas. Vol. 2. Washington, D.C.: Smithsonian Institution, 1990.

———. "Native Chiefdoms of the Southeast at the Time of Contact." Paper presented at the Congreso Internacional Hernando de Soto y Su Tiempo, Cáceres, Spain, 1991.

———. "The Hernando de Soto Expedition in the Mississippi Alluvial Plain." In *The Hernando de Soto Expedition in the West, 1541–1543.* ed. Gloria Young and Michael P. Hoffman. Fayetteville: University of Arkansas Press, in press.

Dye, David H., ed. *Towns and Temples along the Mississippi.* Tuscaloosa: University of Alabama Press, 1989.

Dye, David H., and Ronald C. Brister, eds. *The Protohistoric Period in the Mid-South: 1570–1700.* Vol. 18. Jackson: Mississippi Department of Archives and History Archaeological Report. 1986.

Early, Ann M. "Caddoan Settlement Systems in the Ouachita River Basin." In *Arkansas Archeology in Review,* ed. N. L. Trubowitz and M. D. Jeter, 15. Fayetteville: Arkansas Archeological Survey, 1982.

———. "Finding the Middle Passage: The Spanish Journey from the Swamplands to Caddo Country." In *The Hernando de Soto Expedition in the West, 1541–1543.* ed. Gloria Young and Michael P. Hoffman. Fayetteville: University of Arkansas Press, in press.

Eubanks, W. Scott, Jr. "Studying De Soto's Route: A Georgian House of Cards." *The Florida Anthropologist* 42 (1989): 369–80.

———. "The Lattimore Urn." *The Soto States Anthropologist* 90 (1990a): 112–23.

———. "The Missouri Omission." *The Soto States Anthropologist* 90 (1990b): 71–73.

———. "Swanton: Four . . . Hudson: Zero, A Response to Hudson, Smith, Anderson, and Chardon." *The Soto States Anthropologist* 90 (1990c): 3–32.

———. "Artifacts and the Spanish Explorers." *The Soto States Anthropologist* 91 (1991a): 86–92.

———. "De Soto, Still Another Look." *The Soto States Anthropologist* 91 (1991b): 149–90.

———. "More than a Footnote, Is Cofatachequi Really Cofetazque?" *The Soto States Anthropologist* 91 (1991c): 110–25.

———. "Spherical Turquoise Blue Glass Beads: Sixteenth Century Spanish?" *The Soto States Anthropologist* 91 (1991d): 81–85.

Evans, W. A. "The Route of De Soto across Monroe County, December, 1540." *Journal of Mississippi History* 2 (1940): 71–78.

Ewen, Charles R. *The Discovery of De Soto's First Winter Encampment in Florida.* Vol. 7. De Soto Working Papers. Tuscaloosa: Alabama De Soto Commission, University of Alabama, State Museum of Natural History, 1988.

———. "Anhaica: Discovery of Hernando de Soto's 1539–1540 Winter Camp." In *First Encounters, Spanish Explorations in the Caribbean and the United States, 1492–1570*, ed. Jerald T. Milanich and Susan Milbrath. Gainesville: University of Florida Press, 1989a.

———. "Apalachee Winter." *Archaeology* 42, no. 3 (1989b): 37–39.

———. "The DeSoto Apalachee Project: The Martin Site and Beyond." *The Florida Anthropologist* 42 (1989c): 361–68.

———. "Soldier of Fortune: Hernando de Soto in the Territory of the Apalachee, 1539–1540." In *Columbian Consequences*, ed. David H. Thomas. Vol. 2. Washington, D.C.: Smithsonian Institution, 1990.

———. "Soldier of Misfortune: Hernando de Soto in the Territory of the Apalaches." Paper presented at the Congreso Internacional Hernando de Soto y Su Tiempo, Cáceres, Spain, 1991.

Ewen, Charles R., and B. Calvin Jones. "Hernando de Soto's First Winter Encampment: Discovery and First Season of Excavation." Paper presented at the 53rd annual meeting of the Society for American Archaeology, Phoenix, 1988.

Ewen, Charles R., Richard Vernon, and Charles B. Poe. *Managing the Archaeological Resources of Leon County.* Historic Tallahassee Preservation Board, 1988. Ms. on file.

Fairbanks, Charles H. "Creek and Pre-Creek." In *Archeology of the Eastern United States*, ed. J. B. Griffin. Chicago: University of Chicago Press, 1952.

———. "Early Spanish Colonial Beads." *Conference of Historic Sites Archaeology* 2 (1968a): 3–21.
———. "Florida Coin Beads." *The Florida Anthropologist* 21 (1968b): 102–5.
———. "From Exploration to Settlement: Spanish Strategies for Colonization." In *Alabama and Its Borderlands: From Prehistory to Statehood,* ed. Reid Badger and Lawrence A. Clayton, 128–39. University: University of Alabama Press, 1985.
Fernandez, José. *Elvas Used 2.6 Mile League in Cuba: Report of Tests by University of Central Florida, Orlando.* Tallahassee: De Soto Committee, Bureau of Archaeological Research, 1983. Ms. on file.
Ferguson, Leland, ed. "Archaeological Investigations at the Mulberry Site." *South Carolina Institute of Archaeology and Anthropology Notebook* 6 (1974): 57–122.
Fisk, Harold. *Geological Investigation of the Alluvial Valley of the Lower Mississippi River.* No. 52. Vicksburg: Mississippi River Commission Publication, 1944.
Floyd, Bobby. "Big Beads and Snake Gorgets." *The Soto States Anthropologist* 90 (1990): 145–48.
Folmsbee, Stanley J., and Madeline Kneberg Lewis, eds. "Journals of the Juan Pardo Expeditions, 1566–1567." *The East Tennessee Historical Society's Publications* 37 (1965): 106–21.
Ford, James A. *Menard Site: The Quapaw Village of Osotouy on the Arkansas River.* Vol. 48, pt. 2. Anthropological Papers. New York: American Museum of Natural History, 1961.
Fordyce, John R. "Trailing DeSoto." *Bulletin of the National Research Council* 74 (1929): 67–74.
Francis, Peter. "Beads and the Discovery of the New World." *Center for Bead Research Occasional Paper* 3 (1986).
———. "Chevrons and the Conquistadors." *The Margaretologist* 1 (1987): 6–7.
Franco, Salvador Garcia. *La Legua Nautica en la Edad Media.* Madrid: Instituto Historico de Marina, 1957.
French, B. F., trans. *Historical Collections of Louisiana and Florida.* Part VI. New York: J. Sabin and Sons, 1869.
Fuller, Richard S. "The Bear Point Phase of the Pensacola Variant: The Protohistoric Period in Southwest Alabama." *The Florida Anthropologist* 38 (1985): 1–2.
Fuller, Richard S., Diane E. Silvia, and N. R. Stowe. *The Forks Project: An Investigation of the Late Prehistoric–Early Historic Transition in the Alabama-Tombigbee Confluence Basin.* Alabama Historical Commission, 1984. Ms. on file.
Garrow, Patrick H. "The Mouse Creek 'Focus': A Reevaluation." *Southeastern Archaeological Conference Bulletin* 18 (1975): 76–85.
Gibson, Jon L. "Evaluation of the Geographical Potential of the Lower Ouachita River Valley with Regard to the De Soto–Moscoso Expedition." *Louisiana Studies* 7 (1968): 203–12.
———. *Archaeological Survey of Portions of Little River, Boeuf River, and Big*

Creek, East Central and Northeastern Louisiana. Lafayette: Center for Archaeological Studies, University of Southwestern Louisiana, 1977.

Goff, John H. "Some Major Indian Trading Paths across the Georgia Piedmont." *Georgia Mineral Newsletter* 6, no. 4 (1953): 122–31.

Goggin, John M. "Are There De Soto Relics in Florida?" *The Florida Historical Quarterly* 32 (1954): 151–62.

———. *The Spanish Olive Jar: An Introductory Study.* Vol. 62. Yale University Publications in Anthropology. New Haven, Conn.: Yale University Press, 1960.

———. *Indian and Spanish Selected Writings.* Coral Gables, Fla.: University of Miami Press, 1964.

———. *Spanish Majolica in the New World.* Vol. 72. Yale University Publications in Anthropology. New Haven, Conn.: Yale University Press, 1968.

———. *An Introduction to Spanish Trade Beads and Pendants, 16th and 17th Centuries.* Harvard University, Peabody Museum, n.d. Ms. on file.

Goggin, John M., and William C. Sturtevant. "The Calusa: A Stratified, Nonagricultural Society (with Notes on Sibling Marriage)." In *Explorations in Cultural Anthropology: Essays in Honor of George Peter Murdock,* ed. W. H. Goodenough. New York: McGraw-Hill, 1964.

Graham, R. B. Cunninghame. *Hernando de Soto.* New York: Dial Press, 1924.

Greengo, Robert E. *Issaquena: An Archaeological Phase in the Yazoo Basin of the Lower Mississippi Valley.* Vol. 18. Memoir. Salt Lake City: Society for American Archaeology, 1964.

Gregory, Hiram F. "Plaquemine Period Sites in the Catahoula Basin: A Cultural Microcosm in East Central Louisiana." *Louisiana Studies* 8, no. 2 (1969): 111–34.

Griffin, John W. "Test Excavations at the Lake Jackson Site." *American Antiquity* 16, no. 2 (1950): 99–112.

Hall, John C. "The Search for Hernando de Soto." *Alabama Heritage* 4 (1987): 12–27.

Hally, David J. *Archaeological Investigation of the Potts' Tract Site (9-Mu-103), Carters Dam, Murray County, Georgia.* Vol. 6. Laboratory of Archaeology Series. Athens: University of Georgia, 1970.

———. "The King Site and Its Investigation." *Southeastern Archaeological Conference Bulletin* 18 (1975): 48–54.

———. *Archaeological Investigation of the Little Egypt Site (9Mu102), Murray County, Georgia, 1969 Season.* Vol. 18. Laboratory of Archaeology Series. Athens: University of Georgia, 1979a.

———. *Archaeological Investigations of the Little Egypt Site (9Mu102), Murray County, Georgia, 1970–1972 Seasons.* National Park Service, 1979b. Ms. on file.

———. "Archaeology and Settlement Plan of the King Site." In *The King Site: Continuity and Contact in Sixteenth-Century Georgia,* ed. Robert L. Blakely, 3–16. Athens: University of Georgia Press, 1988.

Hally, David J., and James L. Rudolph. *Mississippi Period Archaeology of the Georgia Piedmont.* Vol. 24. Archaeological Research Design Papers. Athens: Laboratory of Archaeology, University of Georgia, 1986.

Hally, David J., Marvin T. Smith, and James B. Langford, Jr. "The Archaeological Reality of De Soto's Coosa." In *Columbian Consequences,* ed. David H. Thomas. Vol. 2. Washington, D.C.: Smithsonian Institution, 1990.

Hann, John H. *Apalachee: The Land Between the Rivers.* Gainesville: University Presses of Florida, 1988a.

———. "Florida's Terra Incognita: West Florida's Natives in the Sixteenth and Seventeenth Century." *The Florida Anthropologist* 41 (1988b): 61–107.

———. *Transcription and Translation of the Apalachee Section of the Fidalgo de Elvas' True Relation of the Labors that the Governor Don Fernando de Soto and Certain Portuguese Gentlemen Experienced in the Exploration of the Province of Florida. Now Newly Made by a Gentleman of Elvas.* Florida Bureau of Archaeological Research, 1988c. Ms. on file.

———. *Transcription and Translation of the Apalachee Section of Garcilaso de la Vega's Florida of the Inca.* Florida Bureau of Archaeological Research, 1988d. Ms. on file.

———. *Transcription and Translation of the Apalachee Section of Luys Hernández Biedma's Report of the Outcome of the Journey that Hernando de Soto Made and of the Characteristics of the Land through Which he Traveled.* Florida Bureau of Archaeological Research, 1988e. Ms. on file.

———. *Translation of the Apalachee Section of the Account Written By Alvar Nuñez Cabeza de Vaca about the Expedition Led By Pánfilo de Narváez and about His Own Experiences.* Florida Bureau of Archaeological Research, 1988f. Ms. on file.

———. *Translation of the Apalachee Section of the Narrative about the De Soto Expedition Written by Gonzalo Fernandez de Oviedo and Based on the Diary of Rodrigo Ranjel, De Soto's Private Secretary.* Florida Bureau of Archaeological Research, 1988g. Ms. on file.

———. *Translation of the Florida Section of the Alvar Nuñez Cabeza de Vaca Accounts of the 1528 Trek from South Florida to Apalachee Led by Pánfilo de Narváez.* Florida Bureau of Archaeological Research, 1988h. Ms. on file.

———. *Summary Guide to Spanish Florida Missions and Visitas with Churches in the Sixteenth and Seventeenth Centuries.* Florida Bureau of Archaeological Research, 1989. Ms. on file.

Haring, Clarence H. *The Spanish Empire in America.* 2nd ed. New York: Oxford University Press, 1963.

Harrington, M. R. "A Pot-Hunters' Paradise." *Indian Notes* 1, no. 2 (1924): 84–90.

Harris, Elizabeth. "Nueva Cadiz and Associated Beads: A New Look." *Archaeological Research Booklets* 17 (1982): 3–15.

Harrisse, Henry. *The Discovery of North America: A Critical, Documentary, and Historical Investigation.* Rpt., Amsterdam: N. Israel, 1961.

Haynes, H. "The Alabama Stone." *American Antiquarian Society* 5, no. 3 (1888): 487–91.

Hayward, Hampton Dart, Caleb Curren, Ned J. Jenkins, and Keith J. Little. *Archaeological Investigations in the Proposed Pafallaya Province.* Vol. 1. Pensacola Archeological Laboratory Research Series, 1991.

Heath, Robert M. "Replication Experiments for the Manufacture of Sixteenth-Century Spanish Bells." *Mississippi Archaeology* 26 (1991): 39–55.

Hemmings, E. Thomas. *Human Adaptation in the Grand Marais Lowland: Intensive Archeological Survey and Testing in the Felsenthal Navigation Pool, Ouachita and Saline Rivers, Southern Arkansas.* Arkansas Archeological Survey, 1981. Contract Report.

Henige, David. "The Context, Content, and Credibility of 'La Florida del Inca.'" *The Americas* 43 (1986/1987): 1–23.

———. "Proxy Data, Historical Method, and the De Soto Expedition." In *The Hernando de Soto Expedition in the West, 1541–1543,* ed. Gloria Young and Michael P. Hoffman. Fayetteville: University of Arkansas Press, in press.

Herrera, José Tamayo. "El Cuzco que vio Hernando de Soto." Paper presented at Congreso Internacional Hernando de Soto y Su Tiempo, Cáceres, Spain, 1991.

Heye, George G., F. W. Hodge, and George H. Pepper. "The Nacoochee Mound in Georgia." *Contributions from the Museum of the American Indian, Heye Foundation* 4, no. 3 (1918).

Hodge, Frederick, and Theodore Lewis, eds. *Spanish Explorers in the Southeastern United States, 1528–1543.* New York: Charles Scribner's Sons, 1907.

Hodges, T. L., and Mrs. T. L. Hodges. "The Watermelon Island Site in Arkansas." *Texas Archeological and Paleontological Society Bulletin* 15 (1943): 66–79.

———. "Suggestion for Identification of Certain Mid-Ouachita Pottery as Cahinnio Caddo." *Texas Archeological and Paleontological Society Bulletin* 16 (1945): 98–116.

Hoffman, Michael P. "The Kinkead-Mainard Site, 3Pu2: A Late Quapaw Phase Site Near Little Rock, Arkansas." *The Arkansas Archeologist* 16–18 (1977): 1–41.

———. "Historic Indians of Arkansas." *The Arkansas Naturalist* 2, no. 10 (1984); 1–14.

———. "Identification of Ethnic Groups Contacted by the De Soto Expedition in Arkansas." In *The Hernando de Soto Expedition in the West, 1541–1543.* ed. Gloria Young and Michael P. Hoffman. Fayetteville: University of Arkansas Press, in press.

Hoffman, Paul E. "The Chicora Legend and Franco-Spanish Rivalry." *The Florida Historical Quarterly* 62 (1984): 419–38.

———. "Hernando de Soto y la conquista y colonización Española de Norteamérica en el siglo XVI." Paper presented at Congreso Internacional Hernando de Soto y Su Tiempo, Cáceres, Spain, 1991a.

———. *A New Andalucia and a Way to the Orient: A History of the American*

Southeast during the Sixteenth Century. Baton Rouge: Louisiana State University Press, 1991b.

Holford, Castello N. *Cofachiqui and Other Poems.* Bloomington, Ill.: L. D. Holford, 1984.

Holmes, Nicholas H., et al. *A Minority Report on the Trail Marking Program of the Alabama De Soto Commission.* Mobile, Ala., 1989. Ms. in possession of author.

Holstein, Harry O., Curtis E. Hill, Keith Little, and Caleb Curren. *Ethnohistoric Archaeology and Hypothesis Testing: Archaeological Investigation of the Terrapin Creek Site.* Alabama De Soto Commission, 1990. Ms. on file.

Horgan, Paul. *Conquistadores in North American History.* New York: Farrar, Straus, 1963.

House, John H. "Kent Phase Investigations in Eastern Arkansas, 1978–1984." *Mississippi Archaeology* 22 (1987): 46–60.

Howry, Jeffrey C. *Cultural Resources Mitigation Program for the Flint River Pulp Plant.* Atlanta: Environmental Research and Technology, 1979.

Hudson, Charles. "De Soto in Arkansas: A Brief Synopsis." *Field Notes: Newsletter of the Arkansas Archeological Society* 205 (1985): 3–12.

———. "Juan Pardo's Excursion beyond Chiaha." *Tennessee Anthropologist* 12 (1987a): 74–87.

———. "An Unknown South: Spanish Explorers and Southeastern Chiefdoms." In *Visions and Revisions: Ethnohistoric Perspectives on Southern Cultures,* ed. George Sabo III and William Schneider, 6–24. Athens: University of Georgia Press, 1987b.

———. *The Uses of Evidence in Reconstructing the Route of the Hernando de Soto Expedition.* Vol. 1. De Soto Working Paper. Tuscaloosa: Alabama De Soto Commission, University of Alabama, State Museum of Natural History, 1987c.

———. "A Spanish-Coosa Alliance in Sixteenth-Century North Georgia." *The Georgia Historical Quarterly* 72 (1988a): 599–626.

———. *A Synopsis of the Hernando de Soto Expedition, 1539–1543.* National Park Service, Southeast Regional Office, 1988b. Ms. on file.

———. *Critique of Caleb Curren's De Soto Route.* Alabama De Soto Commission, 1988c. Ms. on file.

———. *Critique of Little and Curren's Reconstruction of De Soto's Route through Alabama.* Vol. 12. De Soto Working Paper. Tuscaloosa: Alabama De Soto Commission, University of Alabama, State Museum of Natural History, 1989a.

———. *De Soto in Alabama.* Vol. 10. De Soto Working Paper. Tuscaloosa: Alabama De Soto Commission, University of Alabama, State Museum of Natural History, 1989b.

———. "Conversations with the High Priest of Coosa." In *Lamar Archaeology: Mississippian Chiefdoms in the Deep South,* ed. M. Williams and G. Shapiro. Tuscaloosa: University of Alabama Press, 1990a.

———. "A Synopsis of the Hernando de Soto Expedition, 1539–1543." In *De Soto*

Trail: National Historic Trail Study Final Report, ed. Wink Hastings. Atlanta: National Park Service, Southeast Regional Office, 1990b.

———. "The Expedition of Hernando de Soto through the American Southeast." Paper presented at the Congreso Internacional Hernando de Soto y Su Tiempo, Cáceres, Spain, 1991a.

———. *The Juan Pardo Expeditions: Exploration of the Carolinas and Tennessee, 1566–1568.* Washington, D.C.: Smithsonian Institution, 1991b.

———. "Reconstructing the Route West of the Mississippi River." In *The Hernando de Soto Expedition in the West, 1541–1543*, ed. Gloria Young and Michael P. Hoffman. Fayetteville: University of Arkansas Press, in press.

Hudson, Charles, Chester DePratter, and Marvin T. Smith. "Hernando de Soto's Expedition through the Southern United States." In *First Encounters: Spanish Explorations in the Caribbean and the United States, 1492–1570*, ed. Jerald T. Milanich and Susan Milbrath, 77–98. Gainesville: University of Florida Press, 1989.

———. "Reply to Henige." In *The Hernando de Soto Expedition in the West, 1541–1543*, ed. Gloria Young and Michael P. Hoffman. Fayetteville: University of Arkansas Press, in press.

Hudson, Charles M., and Joyce Rockwood Hudson. "Tracking the Elusive De Soto." *Archaeology* 42, no. 3 (1989): 32–36.

Hudson, Charles M., and Jerald T. Milanich. *Hernando de Soto and the Native Peoples of Florida*. Florida Museum of Natural History, n.d. Ms. on file.

Hudson, Charles M., and Dan F. Morse. *The De Soto Route West of the Mississippi River.* University of Georgia, n.d. Ms. on file.

Hudson, Charles M., and Marvin T. Smith. "Reply to Eubanks." *The Florida Anthropologist* 43 (1990): 36–42.

Hudson, Charles M., Marvin T. Smith, and Chester DePratter. "The Hernando de Soto Expedition: From Apalachee to Chiaha." *Southeastern Archaeology* 3 (1984a): 64–77.

———. "The King Site Massacre: An Historical Detectives' Report." Paper presented at the annual meeting of the Southern Anthropological Society, Atlanta, 1984b.

———. "The Hernando de Soto Expedition: From Apalachee to Chiaha." *South Carolina Institute of Archaeology and Anthropology Notebook* 19 (1987):18–28.

———. "The King Site Massacre Victims: An Historical Detectives' Report." In *The King Site: Biocultural Adaptation in Sixteenth-Century Georgia*, ed. Robert Blakely. Athens: University of Georgia Press, 1988.

———. "The Hernando de Soto Expedition: From Mabila to the Mississippi River." In *Towns and Temples along the Mississippi*, ed. David H. Dye and Cheryl Anne Cox. Tuscaloosa: University of Alabama Press, 1990.

Hudson, Charles, Marvin T. Smith, Chester DePratter, and Emilia Kelley. "The

Tristan de Luna Expedition, 1559–1561." In *First Encounters: Spanish Explorations in the Caribbean and the United States, 1492–1570,* ed. Jerald T. Milanich and Susan Milbrath, 119–34. Gainesville: University of Florida Press, 1989.

Hudson, Charles, Marvin Smith, David Hally, Richard Polhemus, and Chester DePratter. "Coosa: A Chiefdom in the Sixteenth-Century Southeastern United States." *American Antiquity* 50 (1985): 723–37.

———. "The Hernando de Soto Expedition: From Apalachee to Chiaha." *South Carolina Institute of Archaeology and Anthropology Notebook* 19 (1987a): 18–28.

———. "Reply to Boyd and Schroedl." *American Antiquity* 52 (1987b): 845–56.

Hudson, Charles M., John E. Worth, and Chester B. DePratter. "Refinements in Hernando de Soto's Route through Georgia and South Carolina." In *Columbian Consequences,* ed. D. H. Thomas. Vol. 2. Washington, D.C.: Smithsonian Institution, 1990.

Humble, Sallie L. "The Ouachita Valley Expedition of De Soto." *The Louisiana Historical Quarterly* 25 (1942): 611–43.

Hunter, Donald G., Jr., and William S. Baker, Jr. "Excavations in the Atkins Midden at the Troyville Site, Catahoula Parish, Louisiana." *Louisiana Archeology* 4 (1979): 21–52.

Hutchinson, Dale L. "Postcontact Biocultural Change: Mortuary Site Evidence." In *Columbian Consequences,* ed. David H. Thomas. Vol. 2. Washington, D.C.: Smithsonian Institution, 1990.

Iglesias, José Luis Pereira. "La Coyuntura socioeconómica de Extremadura durante la época de la conquista de America." Paper presented at the Congreso Internacional Hernando de Soto y Su Tiempo, Cáceres, Spain, 1991.

Irving, Theodore. *The Conquest of Florida under Hernando de Soto.* Philadelphia: Carey, Lea, and Irving, 1835.

Jefferson, Thomas. *Documents Relating to the Purchase and Exploration of Louisiana.* Boston: Houghton, Mifflin, 1904.

Jenkins, Ned J., and Teresa Paglione. *The Archaeological Reconnaissance of the Lower Alabama River.* Alabama Historical Commission, 1980. Ms. on file.

Jennings, Jesse D. "Nutt's Trip to the Chickasaw Country." *Journal of Mississippi History* 9 (1947): 34–61.

Jennings, John. *The Golden Eagle.* New York: Dell Publishing, 1958.

Jeter, Marvin D. "Tunicans West of the Mississippi: A Summary of Early Historic and Archeological Evidence." Paper presented at 4th Mid-South Archeological Conference, Memphis, 1983.

Johnson, Jay K., and John T. Sparks. "Protohistoric Settlement Patterns in Northeastern Mississippi." In *The Protohistoric Period in the Mid-South: 1500–1700,* ed. D. H. Dye and R. C. Brister. Vol. 18. Jackson: Mississippi Department of Archives and History, 1986.

Johnson, Kenneth W. *The Search for Aguacaleyquen and Cali: Archaeological Survey of Portions of Alachua, Bradford, Citrus, Clay, Columbia, Marion, Sumter, and Union Counties, Florida.* Vol. 33. Miscellaneous Project Report Series. Gainesville: Florida State Museum, 1987.

Jones, B. Calvin. "Southern Cult Manifestations at the Lake Jackson Site, Leon County, Florida: Salvage Excavation of Mound 3." *Midcontinental Journal of Archaeology* 7, no. 1 (1982): 3–44.

———. "The Dreamer and the de Soto Site." *The Florida Anthropologist* 41, no. 3 (1988): 402–4.

Jones, B. Calvin, and Mary L. Mitchell. "Hernando de Soto en la Florida." *Revista de Arcueologia* 9 (1988): 36–51.

Jones, B. Calvin, and John T. Penman. "Winewood: An Inland Ft. Walton Site in Tallahassee, Florida." *Florida Department of State, Bureau of Historic Sites and Properties Bulletin* 3 (1973): 65–90.

Jones, Douglas E. "Summary of De Soto Trail Commission Meeting." *Chainmail* 1 (1987): 3–12.

———. *Some Letters Concerning the National Park Study for a De Soto Historic Trail.* Vol. 13. De Soto Working Paper. Tuscaloosa: Alabama De Soto Commission, University of Alabama, State Museum of Natural History, 1989.

Jones, Douglas E., ed. *The Highway Route of the De Soto Trail in Alabama.* Vol. 8. De Soto Working Paper. Tuscaloosa: Alabama De Soto Commission, University of Alabama, State Museum of Natural History, 1988.

Jones, William K. "Notes on the History and Material Culture of the Tonkawa Indians." In *Smithsonian Contributions to Anthropology,* 65–81. Vol. 2. Washington, D.C.: Smithsonian Institution, 1969.

Judge, Joseph. "Exploring Our Forgotten Century." *National Geographic* 173 (1988): 330–63.

Kelly, Arthur R., and Robert S. Neitzel. *The Chauga Site in Oconee County, South Carolina.* Athens: Laboratory of Archaeology, University of Georgia, 1961.

Kenmotsu, Adele, James E. Bruseth, and James E. Corbin. "Moscoso and the Route in Texas: A Reconstruction." In *The Hernando de Soto Expedition in the West, 1541–1543,* ed. Gloria Young and Michael P. Hoffman. Fayetteville: University of Arkansas Press, in press.

Kenny, Michael. *The Romance of the Floridas: The Finding and the Founding.* New York: Bruce Publishing, 1934.

Ketcham, Herbert E. "Three Sixteenth Century Spanish Chronicles Relating to Georgia." *Georgia Historical Quarterly* 38 (1954): 66–82.

———. "Three Sixteenth Century Spanish Chronicles." *South Carolina Institute of Archaeology and Anthropology Notebook* 19 (1987): 29–36.

Kirkpatrick, F. A. *Los conquistadores Españoles.* Mexico City: Colección "Austral," 1958.

Klinger, Timothy C. "Parkin Archeology: A Report on the 1966 Field School Test Excavations at the Parkin Site." *The Arkansas Archeologist* 16–18 (1977): 45–80.

Knight, Vernon J., Jr. *A Report of Alabama De Soto Commission/Alabama State Museum of Natural History Archaeological Test Excavations at the Site of Old Cahawba, Dallas County, Alabama.* Alabama De Soto Commission, 1987. Ms. on file.

———. "Minutes: Meeting of the De Soto Trail Commission and the National Park Service De Soto Trail Project Advisory Committee, Holiday Inn South, Tuscaloosa, Alabama, June 28–29." *Chainmail* 2 (1988a): 5–11.

———. *A Summary of Alabama's De Soto Mapping Project and Project Bibliography.* Vol. 9. De Soto Working Paper. Tuscaloosa: Alabama De Soto Commission, University of Alabama, State Museum of Natural History, 1988b.

———. "Minutes: Meeting of the De Soto Trail Commission, Marriott Hotel, New Orleans, Louisiana, October 19, 1988." *Chainmail* 3 (1989): 3–8.

Krieger, Alex D. *Culture Complexes and Chronology in Northern Texas, with Extension of Puebloan Datings to the Mississippi Valley.* Publication No. 4640, Austin: University of Texas, 1946.

Langford, James B., Jr. "The Coosawattee Plate: A Sixteenth-Century Catholic/Aztec Artifact from Northwest Georgia." In *Columbian Consequences,* ed. D. H. Thomas. Vol. 2. Washington, D.C.: Smithsonian Institution, 1990.

Langford, James B., Jr., and Marvin T. Smith. "Recent Investigations in the Core of the Coosa Province." Paper presented at the LAMAR Institute Conference of South Appalachian Mississippi, Macon, Ga., 1986.

———. "Recent Investigations in the Core of the Coosa Province." In *Lamar Archaeology: Mississippian Chiefdoms in the Deep South,* ed. M. Williams and G. Shapiro. Tuscaloosa: University of Alabama Press, 1990.

Lankford, George E., III. "A New Look at De Soto's Route through Alabama." *Journal of Alabama Archaeology* 23 (1977): 10–36.

———. "Legends of the Adelentado." In *The Hernando de Soto Expedition in the West, 1541–1543,* ed. Gloria Young and Michael P. Hoffman. Fayetteville: University of Arkansas Press, in press.

Lankford, George E., III., Cailup B. Curren, and Keith J. Little. "De Soto's Route through Alabama: An Update." Paper presented at the Southeastern Archaeological Conference, New Orleans, 1980.

Larson, Lewis H., Jr. "Archaeological Implications of Social Stratification at the Etowah Site, Georgia." In *Approaches to the Social Dimensions of Mortuary Practices,* ed. J. A. Brown. Memoir No. 25. Washington, D.C.: Society for American Archaeology, 1971.

———. *Aboriginal Subsistence Technology on the Southeastern Coastal Plain during the Late Prehistoric Period.* Gainesville: The University Presses of Florida, 1980.

———. "The Pardo Expedition: What Was the Direction at Departure?" *Southeastern Archaeology* 9 (1990): 124–39.

Laudonnière, René. *Three Voyages.* Trans. Charles E. Bennet. Gainesville: University of Florida Press, 1975.

Lawson, Samuel J., III. "La Tama de la Tierra Adentro." *Early Georgia* 15 (1987): 1–18.

Leverette, Robert M., and Sam Lawson. "De Soto's Espiritu Santo: A New Look." *The Soto States Anthropologist* 90 (1990): 90–111.

Levy, Janet E., J. Alan May, and David G. Moore. "From Ysa to Joara: Cultural Diversity in the Catawba Valley from the Fourteenth to the Sixteenth Century." In *Columbian Consequences,* ed. D. H. Thomas. Vol. 2. Washington, D.C.: Smithsonian Institution, 1990.

Lewis, Clifford M. "The Calusa." In *Tacachale: Essays on the Indians of Florida and Southeastern Georgia during the Historic Period,* ed. J. T. Milanich and S. Proctor. Gainesville: University Presses of Florida, 1978.

Lewis, Theodore H., ed. "The Narrative of the Expedition of Hernando de Soto by the Gentleman of Elvas." In *Spanish Explorers in the Southern United States, 1528–1543,* ed. F. W. Hodge and T. H. Lewis. New York: Charles Scribner's Sons, 1907.

Lewis, Theodore H. "The De Soto Expedition through Florida." *American Antiquarian* 22, no. 6 (1900): 351–57.

———. "The De Soto Expedition through Florida (continued)." *American Antiquarian* 23, no. 2 (1901a): 107–11.

———. "The De Soto Expedition through Florida (continued)." *American Antiquarian* 23, no. 4 (1901b): 242–47.

———. "The Chroniclers of De Soto's Expedition." *Publications of the Mississippi Historical Society* 7 (1903): 379–87.

———. "Route of De Soto's Expedition from Taliepacana to Huhasene." In *A Symposium on the Place of Discovery of the Mississippi River by Hernando de Soto,* ed. D. Rowland, 1. Jackson: Mississippi Historical Society, 1927.

Lewis, Thomas, and Madeline Kneberg. *Hiawassee Island: An Archaeological Account of Four Tennessee Indian Peoples.* Knoxville: University of Tennessee Press, 1946.

Little, Keith J. "A Sixteenth Century European Sword from a Protohistoric Aboriginal Site in Northwest Georgia." *Early Georgia* 13 (1985): 1–14.

———. *A Critical Evaluation of the Hudson and Associates Use of Distance Statistics.* Alabama De Soto Commission, 1988a.

———. *A Critical Evaluation of the Placement of Casiste in the Talladega Springs Area.* Alabama De Soto Commission, 1988b. Ms. on file.

———. *A Critical Evaluation of the Proposed Locality of Mauvila in the Selma, Alabama Vicinity.* Alabama De Soto Commission, 1988c. Ms. on file.

———. "The Question Remains: W. S. Eubanks' Arguement for Sixteenth Century Spanish Contact at the Peachtree Site near Murphy, N.C. has not been Refuted by Hudson and Smith." *The Florida Anthropologist* 43 (1990): 152.

———. *A Critical Evaluation of Some Speculations Published by Blakely and Mathews in American Antiquity.* Pensacola Museum Foundation, 1991. Ms. on file.

Little, Keith J., and Cailup B. Curren, Jr. "Site 1Ce308: A Protohistoric Site on the Upper Coosa River in Alabama." *Journal of Alabama Archaeology* 27 (1981): 117–40.

———. "The Alabama De Soto Commission Debates: A Reply to the Criticisms by Charles Hudson." *The Florida Anthropologist* 43 (1990a): 181–88.

———. "Conquest Archaeology of Alabama." In *Columbian Consequences*, ed. D. H. Thomas. Vol. 2. Washington, D.C.: Smithsonian Institution, 1990b.

———. "Contemporary Politics of Sixteenth-Century Spanish Explorations: An Essay." *The Soto States Anthropologist* 90 (1990c): 87–89.

———. *The Moundville IV Phase: Cultural Change in the Wake of the Soto Expedition through Alabama.* Pensacola: Pensacola Archeology Laboratory, 1991.

———. *Coosa Rebuttal.* Alabama-Tombigbee Regional Commission, n.d. Ms. on file.

Little, Keith J., Caleb Curren, Curtis E. Hill, and Harry O. Holstein. *A Spatulate Axe from the Demopolis, Alabama Area.* Alabama De Soto Commission, 1989a. Ms. on file.

———. *A Reply to Marvin T. Smith.* Alabama De Soto Commission, 1989b. Ms. on file.

Littleton, Mary Brabson. *By the King's Command: A Romance of Ferdinand de Soto.* New York: P. J. Kennedy & Sons, 1928.

Lockhart, James. *The Men of Cajamarca: A Social and Biographical Study of the First Conquerors of Peru.* Austin: University of Texas Press, 1972.

López-Spínola, Maria Lourdes Díaz-Trechuelo. "La figura de Hernando de Soto en la Florida del Inca Garcilaso." Paper presented at the Congreso Internacional Hernando de Soto y Su Tiempo, Guadalupe, Spain, 1991.

Lorant, Stefan. *The New World: The First Pictures of America.* New York: Duell, Sloan, & Pearce, 1946.

Lorrain, Dessamae. *Archeological Excavations in Northwestern Crockett County, Texas: 1966–1967.* Report No. 12. Archeological Program. Austin: State Building Commission, 1968.

Love, William A. "Route of De Soto's Expedition through Lowndes County, Mississippi." *Publications of the Mississippi Historical Society Centenary Series* 4 (1921): 268.

Lowery, Woodbury. *The Spanish Settlements within the Present Limits of the United States.* New York: G. P. Putnam's Sons, 1901.

Lummis, Carlos F. *Los Exploradores Españoles del siglo XVI.* Mexico City: Editorial Porría, S.A., 1981.

Lyon, Eugene. *The Enterprise of Florida, Pedro Menéndez de Avilés and the Spanish Conquest of 1565–1568.* Gainesville: University of Florida Press, 1976.

———. *The Cañete Fragment: Another Narrative of Hernando de Soto.* St. Augustine Foundation, 1982.

———. *Santa Elena: A Brief History of the Colony, 1566–1587.* Vol. 193. Research

Manuscript Series. Columbia: South Carolina Institute of Archaeology and Anthropology, 1984.

———. "Pedro Menéndez's Strategic Plan for the Florida Peninsula." *The Florida Historical Quarterly* 647 (1988): 1–14.

Lytle, Andrew. *At the Moon's Inn.* 1941. Rpt. Tuscaloosa: University of Alabama Press, 1990.

———. "Introduction." In *Narratives of De Soto in the Conquest of Florida,* trans. Buckingham Smith. Gainesville: Palmetto Books, 1963.

Majó Framis, R. *Vida de los navegantes y conquistadores Españoles del siglo XVI.* Madrid: M. Aguilar, 1945.

Malone, James H. *The Chickasaw Nation: A Short Sketch of a Noble People.* Louisville: John P. Morton, 1922.

Malone, Walter. *Hernando de Soto.* New York: G. P. Putnam's Sons, 1914.

Manucy, Albert. *Florida's Menendez: Captain General of the Ocean Sea.* St. Augustine: The St. Augustine Historical Society, 1965.

Marban, Jorge A. *La Florida: Cinco siglos de historia hispanica.* Miami: Ediciones Universal, 1979.

Margry, Pierre. *Mémoires et documents pour servir à l'histoire des origines français des pays d'outre-mer.* Tome I. Paris: Maisonnueve et cie, 1879.

Marquardt, William H. "The Calusa Social Formation in Protohistoric South Florida." In *Power Relations and State Formations,* ed. Thomas C. Patterson and Christine W. Gailey, 98–116. Washington, D.C.: Archaeology Section, American Anthropological Association, 1987.

Marrinan, Rochelle A., John F. Scarry, and Rhonda L. Majors. "Prelude to De Soto: The Expedition of Pánfilo de Narváez." In *Columbian Consequences,* ed. D. H. Thomas. Vol. 2. Washington, D.C.: Smithsonian Institution, 1990.

Marshall, Richard A. *Proto-Historic Sites in Oktibbeha County, Mississippi.* Cobb Institute of Archaeology, n.d. Ms. on file.

Mathews, David S. "De Soto's Battle of Mabila: The Ulibahali Casualties from the King Site." M.A. thesis, Georgia State University, 1984.

———. "The Massacre: The Discovery of De Soto in Georgia." In *The King Site: Continuity and Contact in Sixteenth-Century Georgia,* ed. Robert L. Blakely, 101–17. Athens: University of Georgia Press, 1988.

Maynard, Theodore. *De Soto and the Conquistadores.* New York: Longmans, Green, 1930.

McCollough, Major C. R. "Dating Results for Two Sixteenth-Century Spanish Contact Towns in Tennessee." *Southeastern Archaeological Conference Newsletter* 30 (1988): 19.

McGimsey, Charles R., III. *A Report on the Quapaw in Arkansas Immediately Prior to the Treaty of 1818.* Miami, Ok.: Quapaw Tribal Council, 1964. Ms. on file.

———. "The Dupree Site in Retrospect." *The Arkansas Archeologist* 6, no. 1 (1965): 3–8.

Melvin, Richard. "Some New Thoughts on the De Soto Expedition in Georgia." Paper presented at the Annual Meeting of the Society for the History of Discoveries, Gainesville, Fla., 1978.

Milanich, Jerald T. "The Western Timucua: Patterns of Acculturation and Change." In *Tacachale: Essays on the Indians of Florida and Southeastern Georgia during the Historic Period,* ed. J. T. Milanich and S. Proctor. Gainesville: University Presses of Florida, 1978.

———. *Notes on the De Soto Route from Landing to Apalachee.* Florida State Museum, Gainesville, 1984. Ms. on file.

———. *Hernando de Soto and the Expedition in Florida.* Vol. 32. Miscellaneous Project Report Series. Gainesville: Department of Anthropology, Florida Museum of Natural History, 1988.

———. "Hernando de Soto and the Expedition in Florida: An Overview." *The Florida Anthropologist* 42 (1989a): 303–16.

———. "Where Did DeSoto Land?: Identifying Bahia Honda." *The Florida Anthropologist* 42 (1989b): 295–302.

———. "The European Entrada into La Florida: An Overview." In *Columbian Consequences,* ed. D. H. Thomas. Vol. 2. Washington, D.C.: Smithsonian Institution, 1990.

———. "The Hernando de Soto Expedition and Spain's Effort to Colonize North America." In *The Hernando de Soto Expedition in the West, 1541–1543,* ed. Gloria Young and Michael P. Hoffman. Fayetteville: University of Arkansas Press, in press.

Milanich, Jerald T., and Charles H. Fairbanks. *Florida Archaeology.* New York: Academic Press, 1980.

Milanich, Jerald T., and Susan Milbrath, eds. *First Encounters: Spanish Explorations in the Caribbean and the United States, 1492–1570.* Gainesville: University of Florida Press, 1989.

Milanich, Jerald T., and Jeffrey M. Mitchem. "Uncovering De Soto's Route: Bones, Beads, and Armor Point the Way." *The Florida State Museum News* 15 (1986): 3–7.

Milanich, Jerald T., and Samuel Proctor. *Tacachale: Essays on the Indians of Florida and Southeastern Georgia during the Historic Period.* Gainesville: University Presses of Florida, 1978.

Milner, George R. "Epidemic Disease in the Postcontact Southeast: An Appraisal." *Midcontinental Journal of Anthropology* 5 (1980): 39–56.

Mirsky, Jeannette. *The Gentle Conquistadors.* England: Karze & Ward, 1972.

Mitchem, Jeffrey M. "Tracking De Soto's Expedition." *The Florida State Museum News* 15 (1986): 1–11.

———. "Some Alternative Interpretations of Safety Harbor Burial Mounds." *Florida Scientist* 51 (1988): 100–107.

———. "Artifacts of Exploration: Archaeological Evidence from Florida." In *First*

Encounters: Spanish Explorations in the Caribbean and the United States, 1492–1520, ed. Jerald T. Milanich and Susan Milbrath, 99–109. Gainesville: University of Florida Press, 1989a.

———. "Redefining Safety Harbor: Late Prehistoric/Protohistoric Archaeology in West Peninsular Florida." Ph.D. dissertation, University of Florida, 1989b.

———. "The Ruth Smith, Weeki Watchee, and Tatham Mounds: Archaeological Evidence of Early Spanish Contact." *The Florida Anthropologist* 42 (1989c): 317–39.

———. "Initial Spanish-Indian Contact in West Peninsular Florida: The Archaeological Evidence." In *Columbian Consequences,* ed. D. H. Thomas. Vol. 2. Washington, D.C.: Smithsonian Institution, 1990.

Mitchem, Jeffrey M., and Dale L. Hutchinson. "Interim Report on Excavations at the Tatham Mound, Citrus County, Florida: Season II." *Florida State Museum Miscellaneous Project Report* 28 (1986).

———. "Interim Report on Archaeological Research at the Tatham Mound, Citrus County, Florida: Season III." *Florida State Museum Miscellaneous Project Report* 30 (1987).

Mitchem, Jeffrey M., and Jonathan M. Leader. "Early Sixteenth Century Beads from Tatham Mound, Citrus County, Florida: Data and Interpretations." *The Florida Anthropologist* 41 (1988): 42–60.

Mitchem, Jeffrey M., and Bonnie G. McEwan. "New Data on Early Bells from Florida." *Southeastern Archaeology* 7 (1988): 39–48.

Mitchem, Jeffrey M., Marvin T. Smith, Albert C. Goodyear, and Robert Allen. "Early Spanish Contact on the Florida Gulf Coast: The Weeki Wachee and Ruth Smith Mounds." In *Indians, Colonists, and Slaves: Essays in Memory of Charles H. Fairbanks,* ed. Kenneth Johnson, Jonathan Leader, and Robert Wilson. Special Publication No. 4. Gainesville: Florida Journal of Anthropology, 1985.

Mitchem, Jeffrey M., and Brent R. Weisman. "Excavations at the Ruth Smith Mound (8Ci200)." *The Florida Anthropologist* 37 (1984): 100–112.

Mitchem, Jeffrey M., Brent R. Weisman, Donna L. Ruhl, Jeannette Savell, Laura Sellers, and Lisa Sharik. *Preliminary Report on Excavations at the Tatham Mound (8-Ci-203), Citrus County, Florida: Season I.* Vol. 23. Florida State Museum Miscellaneous Project Report. Gainesville: Florida State Museum, 1985.

Mixon, Ada. "What Was Hernando de Soto's Route through Arkansas?" *The Arkansas Historical Association* 4 (1917): 293–311.

Mooney, James. "The De Soto Expedition—1540." *Bureau of American Ethnology Annual Report* 19 (1900): 23–27, 191–201.

Moore, Clarence B. "Certain Aboriginal Remains of the Alabama River." *Journal of the Academy of Natural Sciences of Philadelphia* 11 (1899): 289–348. Rpt.

———. "Aboriginal Sites on Tennessee River." *Journal of the Academy of Natural Sciences of Philadelphia* 16 (1915): 170–428. Rpt.

Moore, David G. "Late Prehistoric and Protohistoric Aboriginal Settlements in the Upper Catawba Valley." Ph.D. dissertation, University of North Carolina, 1990.

Moorehead, Warren K. *Archaeology of the Arkansas River Valley.* New Haven: Yale University Press, 1931.

———. *Etowah Papers.* New Haven: Yale University Press, 1932.

Morison, Samuel Eliot. *The European Discovery of America: The Northern Voyages.* New York: Oxford University Press, 1971.

———. *The European Discovery of America: The Southern Voyages 1492–1616.* New York: Oxford University Press, 1974.

Morrell, L. Ross. "Two Historic Sites in the Coosa River." *The Florida Anthropologist* 17, no. 2 (1964): 75–76.

Morse, Dan F. "The Nodena Phase." In *Nodena: An Account of 75 Years of Archeological Investigation in Southeast Mississippi County, Arkansas,* ed. D. F. Morse. Vol. 4. Arkansas Archeological Survey Research Series. Fayetteville: Arkansas Archeological Survey, 1973.

———. "Prehistoric Hunting Sites in Northeastern Arkansas." In *The Protohistoric Period in the Mid-South: 1500–1700,* ed. D. H. Dye and R. C. Brister. Jackson: Mississippi Department of Archives and History, 1986.

———. "Comments on 'Arkansas's Spanish Halberds' by Sam Dickinson." *Arkansas Archeological Society Field Notes* 222 (1988): 7–10.

———. "Report from Arkansas." *Chainmail* 3 (1989): 16–17.

———. "The Population of Arkansas in 1541–1543." In *The Hernando de Soto Expedition in the West, 1541–1543,* ed. Gloria Young and Michael P. Hoffman. Fayetteville: University of Arkansas Press, in press.

Morse, Dan F., and Phyllis A. Morse. *Archaeology of the Central Mississippi Valley.* New York: Academic Press, 1983.

———. "The Spanish Exploration of Arkansas." In *Columbian Consequences,* ed. D. H. Thomas. Vol. 2. Washington, D.C.: Smithsonian Institution, 1990.

———. *Another Synthesis of the De Soto Route in Northeast Arkansas.* n.d. Ms. in possession of author.

Morse, Phyllis A. "The Parkin Site and Phase." Paper presented at 45th Annual Meeting of the Society for American Archeology, Philadelphia, 1980.

———. *Parkin: The 1978–1979 Archeological Investigations of a Cross County, Arkansas Site.* Vol. 13. Arkansas Archeological Survey Research Series. Fayetteville: Arkansas Archeological Survey, 1981.

———. "The Parkin Archeological Site and Its Role in Determining the Route of the Expedition." In *The Hernando de Soto Expedition in the West, 1541–1543,* ed. Gloria Young and Michael P. Hoffman. Fayetteville: University of Arkansas Press, in press.

Moscoso, Fernando Rosas. "Clima y expansión European en la América meridional en tiempos de Hernando de Soto." Paper presented at the Congreso Internacional Hernando de Soto y Su Tiempo, Cáceres, Spain, 1991.

Myer, William E. "Indian Trails of the Southeast." *Annual Report of the Bureau of American Ethnology* 42 (1928): 727–857.

Nance, C. Roger. *An Archaeological Sequence at Durant Bend, Dallas County, Alabama.* Vol. 2. Special Publication. Moundville: Alabama Archaeological Society, 1975.

Nash, Charles H. "The Human Continuum of Shelby County, Tennessee." *The West Tennessee Historical Society Papers* (1961): 5–31.

National Park Service. *De Soto Trail: National Historic Trail Study Draft Report.* Atlanta: National Park Service, Southeast Regional Office, 1989.

———. *De Soto Trail: National Historic Trail Final Report.* Atlanta: National Park Service, Southeast Regional Office, 1990.

Neill, Wilfred T. "The Galphin Trading Post Site at Silver Bluff, South Carolina." *The Florida Anthropologist* 21, no. 2–3 (1968): 42–54.

Nuttall, Thomas. *Journal of Travels into the Arkansas Territory during the Year 1819, with Occasional Observations on the Manners of the Aborigines.* Philadelphia: T. M. Palmer, 1821.

Orr, Kenneth G. "Survey of Caddoan Area Archeology." In *Archeology of Eastern United States,* ed. J. B. Griffin. Chicago: University of Chicago Press, 1952.

Paisley, Clifton. *The Red Hills of Florida, 1528–1865.* Tuscaloosa: University of Alabama Press, 1989.

Payne, Claudine. "A Preliminary Investigation of Fort Walton Settlement Patterns in the Tallahassee Red Hills." *Southeastern Archaeological Conference Bulletin* 24 (1981): 29–31.

Pearson, Charles. "Evidence of Early Spanish Contact on the Georgia Coast." *Historical Archaeology* 11 (1977): 74–83.

Peebles, Christopher S. "Moundville and Surrounding Sites: Some Structural Considerations of Mortuary Practices." In *Approaches to the Social Dimensions of Mortuary Practices,* ed. J. A. Brown. Vol. 25. Memoirs of the Society for American Archaeology. Washington, D.C.: Society for American Archaeology, 1971.

———. *Excavations at Moundville, 1905–1951.* Ann Arbor: University of Michigan, 1979.

Peebles, Christopher S., ed. *Excavation in the Lubbub Creek Archaeological Locality.* Mobile: U.S. Army Corps of Engineers, 1981. Contract report on file.

Penman, John T. *European Glass Trade Beads of the Spanish Mission Period, Florida.* Florida Bureau of Archaeological Research, 1972. Ms. on file.

Pereyra, Carlos. *Las Huellas de los conquistadores.* Madrid: M. Aguilar, 1929.

Perttula, Timothy K. "The Long-Term Effects of the Entrada on Aboriginal Caddoan Populations." In *The Hernando de Soto Expedition in the West, 1541–1543,* ed. Gloria Young and Michael P. Hoffman. Fayetteville: University of Arkansas Press, in press.

Peter, Lily. *The Great Riding: The Story of De Soto in America.* Fayetteville: University of Arkansas Press, 1983.

Phillips, Philip. *The Menard Site on the Lower Arkansas River.* Report submitted to National Park Service, Washington, D.C. Cambridge: Harvard University, Central Mississippi Valley Archeological Survey, 1941.

———. *Archaeological Survey in the Lower Yazoo Basin, Mississippi, 1945–1955.* Vol. 60. Papers of the Peabody Museum of Archaeology and Ethnology. Cambridge, Mass.: Peabody Museum, 1970.

Phillips, Philip, James A. Ford, and James B. Griffin. *Archaeological Survey in the Lower Mississippi Alluvial Valley, 1940–1947.* Vol. 25. Papers of the Peabody Museum of Archaeology and Ethnology, Cambridge, Mass.: Peabody Museum, 1951.

Pickett, Albert J. *History of Alabama, and Incidentally of Georgia and Mississippi, from the Earliest Period.* 1851. Rpt. Sheffield, Ala.: Robert C. Randolph, 1896.

Polhemus, Richard R. *The Early Historic Period in the East Tennessee Valley,* n.d. Ms. in possession of author.

Polhemus, Richard R., and Marvin T. Smith. "Early Trade Goods from the East Tennessee Valley." Paper presented at the Annual Meeting of the Southeastern Archaeological Conference, New Orleans, 1980.

Popple, Henry. *A Map of the British Empire in America with the French and Spanish Settlements Adjacent Thereto.* London: W. H. Toms, 1733.

Price, G. R. Dennis. *Appendix to Design Memorandum No. 58: Nine-Foot Navigation Channel, Jonesville and Columbia Pools.* Vicksburg: U.S. Army Corps of Engineers, 1980. Contract report on file.

Price, G. R., and Lorraine Heartfield. *Archeological Test Excavation of Site 16OU15 Located on the Monroe to Sandy Bayou Levee, Ouachita River Levees, Ouachita Parish, Louisiana.* Monroe: The Research Institute, College of Pure and Applied Sciences, Northeast Louisiana University, 1977.

Priestly, Herbert I. *The Luna Papers: Documents Relating to the Expedition of Don Tristán de Luna y Arellano for the Conquest of La Florida in 1559–1561.* DeLand: Florida State Historical Society, 1928.

———. *Tristán de Luna, Conquistador of the Old South: A Study of Spanish Imperial Strategy.* Glendale, Calif.: Arthur H. Clark Company, 1936.

Quattlebaum, Paul. *The Land Called Chicora: The Carolinas under Spanish Rule with French Intrusions, 1520–1670.* Gainesville: University of Florida Press, 1956.

Quinn, David B. *North American Discovery, ca. 1000–1612.* Columbia: University of South Carolina Press, 1971.

———. *North America from Earliest Discovery to First Settlements: The Norse Voyages to 1612.* New York: Harper & Row, 1977.

———. "The Expedition of Hernando de Soto and His Successor, Luis de Moscoso, 1539–1543." In *New American World,* ed. David B. Quinn. Vol. 2. New York: Arno Press, 1979.

———. "Colonies from the Beginning: Examples from North America." In *Essays on the History of North American Discovery and Exploration,* ed. Stanley H. Palmer and Dennis Reinhartz, 10–34. College Station: Texas A&M University Press, 1988.

Quinn, David B., ed. *New American World. A Documentary History of North America to 1612.* New York: Arno Press, 1979.

Ramenofsky, Ann F. "The Archaeology of Population Collapse: Native American Response to the Introduction of Infectious Disease." Ph.D. dissertation, University of Washington, 1982.

———. *Vectors of Death: The Archaeology of European Contact.* Albuquerque: University of New Mexico Press, 1987.

———. "Loss of Innocence: Explanations of Differential Persistence in the Sixteenth-Century Southeast." In *Columbian Consequences,* ed. D. H. Thomas. Vol. 2. Washington, D.C.: Smithsonian Institution, 1990.

Rankin, Robert L. "Language Affiliations of Some De Soto Place Names." In *The Hernando de Soto Expedition in the West, 1541–1543,* ed. Gloria Young and Michael P. Hoffman. Fayetteville: University of Arkansas Press, in press.

Rankin, Robert L., Charles Hudson, and Karen Booker. "Linguistic Affiliations of the Juan Pardo Expedition Place Names." Paper presented at the annual meeting of the American Anthropological Association, Denver, 1984.

Reid, Bill. "Comments on De Soto and Pardo." *The Soto States Anthropologist* 90 (1990): 74–82.

———. "The Pardo Stone: A Postscript." *The Soto States Anthropologist* 91 (1991): 6–9.

Rementería, Carlos Díaz. "Bases jurídicas de las capitulaciones de descubrimiento y conquista." Paper presented at the Congreso Internacional Hernando de Soto y Su Tiempo, Guadalupe, Spain, 1991.

Ribault, Jean. *The Whole & True Discouerye of Terra Florida. A Facsimile Reprint of the London Edition of 1563.* Gainesville: University of Florida Press, 1964.

Robertson, James Alexander. *True Relation of the Hardships Suffered by Governor Fernando de Soto.* Trans. by James Robertson. DeLand: Florida State Historical Society, 1932.

Rojas-Mix, Miguel. "Iconografía del Adelentado Hernando de Soto." Paper presented at the Congreso Internacional Hernando de Soto y Su Tiempo, Guadalupe, Spain, 1991.

Rolingson, Martha A., and Frank F. Schambach. *The Shallow Lake Site (3UN9/52) and Its Place in Regional Prehistory.* Research Series. Fayetteville: Arkansas Archeological Survey, 1981.

Romans, Bernard. *A Concise Natural History of East and West Florida.* 1775. Rpt. New Orleans: Pelican Publishing Company, 1961.

Roper, James E. "Hernando de Soto: Update." Reprint of a paper read before *The Egyptians,* Memphis, 1976.

Ross, Lieutenant. *Course of the River Mississippi from the Balise to Fort Chartres; taken on an Expedition to the Illinois, in the latter end of the year 1765*. London: Robert Sayer, 1775.

Ross, Mary. "With Pardo and Boyano on the Fringes of the Georgia Land." *Georgia Historical Quarterly* 14 (1930): 267–85.

Rowland, Dunbar. "Did De Soto Discover the Mississippi River in Tunica County, Mississippi?" In *A Symposium on the Place of Discovery of the Mississippi River by Hernando de Soto*, ed. D. Rowland. No. 1. Jackson: Mississippi Historical Society, 1927a.

———. "A Second Chapter Concerning the Discovery of the Mississippi River by De Soto in Tunica County, Mississippi." In *A Symposium on the Place of Discovery of the Mississippi River by Hernando de Soto*, ed. D. Rowland. No. 1. Jackson: Mississippi Historical Society, 1927b.

Rubio, Rocío Sánchez. "Extremeños con Hernando de Soto en la expedición a la Florida." Paper presented at the Congreso Internacional Hernando de Soto y Su Tiempo, Cáceres, Spain, 1991.

Ruidíaz y Caravia, Eugenio. *La Florida: Su Conquista y colonización por Pedro Menéndez de Avilés*. Vol. 2. Madrid: 1893.

Ruiz-Fornells, Enrique. "La Figura de Hernando de Soto en la literatura Norteamericana." Paper presented at the Congreso Internacional Hernando de Soto y Su Tiempo, Cáceres, Spain, 1991.

Rye, William B., ed. *The Discovery and Conquest of Terra Florida by Don Fernando De Soto*. New York: Burt Franklin, 1851.

Sabo, George, III. "Indians and Spaniards in Arkansas." In *The Hernando de Soto Expedition in the West, 1541–1543*, ed. Gloria Young and Michael P. Hoffman. Fayetteville: University of Arkansas Press, in press.

Salo, Lawrence V. *Archaeological Investigations in the Tellico Reservoir, Tennessee, 1967–1968: An Interim Report*. Knoxville: Department of Anthropology, University of Tennessee, 1969.

Sánchez, D. Angel Rodríguez. "La sociedad castellana en tiempos de Hernando de Soto." Paper presented at the Congreso Internacional Hernando de Soto y Su Tiempo, Barcarrota, Spain, 1991.

Sánchez, Joseph. "La cartografía de la Florida en el siglo XVI y la expedición de Hernando de Soto." Paper presented at the Congreso Internacional Hernando de Soto y Su Tiempo, Cáceres, Spain, 1991.

Sánchez-Barba, Mario Hernández. "Hernando de Soto en el pensamiento historiográfico." Paper presented at the Congreso Internacional Hernando de Soto y Su Tiempo, Guadalupe, Spain, 1991.

Sauer, Carl O. *The Early Spanish Main*. Berkeley: University of California Press, 1966.

———. *Sixteenth Century North America: The Land and the Peoples as Seen by Europeans*. Berkeley: University of California Press, 1971.

Scarry, John F. "Fort Walton Culture: A Redefinition." *Southeastern Archaeological Conference Bulletin* 24 (1981): 18–21.

———. "Beyond Apalachee Province: Assessing the Evidence for Early European-Indian Contact in Northwest Florida." In *Columbian Consequences,* ed. D. H. Thomas. Vol. 2. Washington, D.C.: Smithsonian Institution, 1990.

———. "Mississippian Emergence in the Fort Walton Area: The Evolution of Cayson and Lake Jackson Phases." In *Mississippian Emergence: The Evolution of Ranked Agricultural Societies in Eastern North America,* ed. B. D. Smith. Washington, D.C.: Smithsonian Institution, 1991.

Schambach, Frank F. "The End of the Trail: The Route of Hernando de Soto's Army through Southwest Arkansas and East Texas." *The Arkansas Archeologist* 27/28 (1989): 9–32.

———. "The End of the Trail: Reconstruction of the Route of Hernando de Soto's Army through Southwest Arkansas and East Texas." In *The Hernando de Soto Expedition in the West, 1541–1543,* ed. Gloria Young and Michael P. Hoffman. Fayetteville: University of Arkansas Press, in press.

Schell, Rolfe F. *De Soto Didn't Land at Tampa.* Ft. Myers Beach: Island Press, 1966.

Schnell, Frank T. "An Archaeological Survey of Lake Blackshear." *Southeastern Archaeological Conference Bulletin* 18 (1975): 117–22.

———. "Late Prehistoric Ceramic Chronologies in the Lower Chattahoochee Valley." *Southeastern Archaeological Conference Bulletin* 24 (1981): 21–23.

Scott, Elizabeth. "The Route of the Narváez Expedition through Florida." *Florida Journal of Anthropology* 6 (1981): 52–63.

Sears, Elsie, and William H. Sears. "Preliminary Report on Prehistoric Corn Pollen from Fort Center, Florida." *Southeastern Archaeological Conference Bulletin* 19 (1976): 53–56.

Sears, William H. "Food Production and Village Life in Prehistoric Southeastern United States." *Archaeology* 24, no. 4 (1971): 322–29.

———. *Fort Center: An Archaeological Site in the Lake Okeechobee Basin.* Gainesville: University Presses of Florida, 1982.

Serrano y Sanz, Manuel. *Documentos históricos de la Florida y la Louisiana: Siglos XVI al XVIII.* Madrid: Victoriano Suárez, 1912.

Setzler, Frank M., and Jesse D. Jennings. *Peachtree Mound and Village Site, Cherokee County, North Carolina.* Vol. 131. Bulletin. Washington, D.C.: Bureau of American Ethnology, 1941.

Shapiro, Gary. "Trailing the Apalachee." *Archaeology* 41, no. 2 (1988): 58–59.

Sheldon, Craig Turner, Jr. "The Mississippian-Historic Transition in Central Alabama." Ph.D. dissertation, University of Oregon, 1974.

Sheldon, Craig T., and Ned J. Jenkins. "Protohistoric Development of Central Alabama." In *The Protohistoric Period in the Mid-South: 1500–1700,* ed. D. H. Dye and R. C. Brister, 18. Jackson: Mississippi Department of Archives and History, 1986.

Shields, E. Thomson, Jr. "El Adelentado de la Florida, Hernando de Soto: The Literary Character." Paper presented at the Congreso Internacional Hernando de Soto y Su Tiempo, Guadalupe, Spain, 1991.

Shipp, Barnard. *The History of Hernando de Soto and Florida. Or, Record of Events of Fifty-six Years, from 1512 to 1568.* Philadelphia: Collins, 1881.

Shogren, Michael G. *A Limited Testing Program at Four Mound Sites in Greene County, Alabama.* Vol. 11. De Soto Working Paper. Tuscaloosa: Alabama De Soto Commission, University of Alabama, State Museum of Natural History, 1989.

Silva-Santisteban, Fernando. "El Mundo Andino y la presencia de Hernando de Soto." Paper presented at the Congreso Internacional Hernando de Soto y Su Tiempo, Cáceres, Spain, 1991.

Smith, Buckingham. *Memoir de do d' Escalante Fonteneda respecting Florida.* 1854. Rpt. Miami: University of Miami and the Historical Association of Southern Florida, 1944.

Smith, Buckingham, trans. *Colleción de varios documentos para la historia de la Florida y tierras adyacentes.* London: Truebner, 1857.

———, trans. *DeSoto's Conquest of Florida.* New York: Bradford Club, 1866.

Smith, Bruce D. "The Archaeology of the Southeastern United States: From Dalton to De Soto, 10,500–500 B.P." In *Advances in World Archeology,* ed. Fred Wendorf and Angela E. Close. Vol. 5. Orlando, Fla.: Academic Press, 1986.

Smith, Hale G. *The European and the Indian: European-Indian Contacts in Georgia and Florida.* Vol. 4. Gainesville: Florida Anthropological Society Publications, 1956.

———. *Documentation Concerning the First Christmas in the United States Presented to the U.S. Postal Service Commemorative Stamp Committee.* Tallahassee: Department of Anthropology, Florida State University, 1975.

Smith, Marvin T. "European Materials from the King Site." *Southeastern Archaeological Conference Bulletin* 18 (1975): 63–66.

———. "The Route of De Soto through Tennessee, Georgia, and Alabama: The Evidence from Material Culture." *Early Georgia* 4, no. 1–2 (1976): 27–48.

———. "The Chevron Trade Bead in North America." *The Bead Journal* 3, no. 2 (1977a): 15–17.

———. "The Early Historic Period (1540–1670) on the Upper Coosa River Drainage of Alabama and Georgia." *The Conference on Historic Site Archaeology Papers* 11 (1977b): 151–67.

———. "European Artifacts from the Little Egypt Site." In *Archaeological Investigations of the Little Egypt Site (9Mu102), Murray County, Georgia, 1970–1972 Seasons,* ed. D. J. Hally. Atlanta: National Park Service, 1979.

———. "'Eye' Beads in the Southeast." *The Conference on Historic Site Archaeology Papers 1979* 14 (1982): 116–27.

———. "Chronology of Glass Beads: The Spanish Period in the Southeast, ca. 1513–

1670." In *Proceedings of the Glass Trade Bead Conference,* ed. Charles F. Hayes III, 147–58, Rochester Museum Research Records, 1983.

———. "Depopulation and Culture Change in the Early Historic Period Interior Southeast." Ph.D. dissertation, University of Florida, 1984a.

———. "A Sixteenth Century Coin from Southeast Alabama." *Journal of Alabama Archaeology* 30 (1984b): 56–60.

———. *Archaeology of Aboriginal Culture Change in the Interior Southeast: Depopulation during the Early Historic Period.* Gainesville: University Presses of Florida, 1987.

———. "Aboriginal Population Movements in the Early Historic Period Interior Southeast." In *Powhatan's Mantle: Indians in the Colonial Southeast,* ed. P. H. Wood, G. Waselkov, and M. T. Hatley. Lincoln: University of Nebraska Press, 1989a.

———. *Glass Beads from the Governor Martin Site.* Florida Bureau of Archaeological Research, 1989b. Ms. on file.

———. *In the Wake of De Soto: Alabama's Seventeenth Century Indians on the Coosa River.* Alabama De Soto Commission, 1989c. Ms. on file.

———. "Indian Responses to European Contact: The Coosa Example." In *First Encounters: Spanish Explorations in the Caribbean and the United States, 1492–1570,* ed. Jerald T. Milanich and Susan Milbrath, 135–49. Gainesville: University of Florida Press, 1989d.

———. *Review of "A Spatulate Axe from the Demopolis, Alabama Area" by Keith Little, Caleb Curren, Curtis Hill, and Harry Holstein.* Alabama De Soto Commission, 1989e. Ms. on file.

———. *Material Remains of the De Soto Expedition.* n.d. Ms. in possession of author.

Smith, Marvin T., and Mary Elizabeth Good. *Early Sixteenth Century Glass Beads in the Spanish Colonial Trade.* Greenwood, Miss.: Cottonlandia Museum, 1982.

Smith, Marvin T., and Steve A. Kowalewski. "Tentative Identification of a Prehistoric 'Province' in Piedmont Georgia." *Early Georgia* 8 (1979): 1–13.

Smith, Marvin T., and Robert C. Wilson. "Possible Markers for Luna's Route in Alabama." *Lamar Briefs* 5 (1985): 4–6.

Solar y Taboada, Antonio del, and José de Rújula y de Ochotorena. *El Adelentado Hernando de Soto: Breves noticias y nuevos documentos para su biografia.* Badajoz, Spain: Ediciones Arqueros, 1929.

Sotelo, Jorge Ortiz. "El Perú Marítimo en Tiempos de Hernando de Soto." Paper presented at the Congreso Internacional Hernando de Soto y Su Tiempo, Cáceres, Spain, 1991.

South, Stanley, Russell K. Skowronek, and Richard E. Johnson. *Spanish Artifacts from Santa Elena.* Vol. 7. Anthropological Studies. Columbia: South Carolina Institute of Archaeology and Anthropology, 1988.

Squier, E. G., and E. H. Davis. *Ancient Monuments of the Mississippi Valley.* Vol. 1. Contributions to Knowledge. Washington, D.C.: Smithsonian Institution, 1848.

Stahl, Jeremy D. "An Ethnohistory of South Florida, 1500–1575." M.A. thesis, University of Florida, 1986.

Steele, William O. *De Soto: Child of the Sun.* New York: Aladdin Books, 1956.

Steponaitis, Vincas P. "Ceramics, Chronology, and Community Patterns at Moundville: A Late Prehistoric Site in Alabama." Ph.D. dissertation, University of Michigan, 1980.

———. "Chronology and Community Patterns at Moundville." *Southeastern Archaeological Conference Bulletin* 24 (1981): 99–104.

Stowe, Noel R. *The Bottle Creek Site (1BA2).* Mobile: Archaeological Research Laboratory, University of South Alabama, 1982. Ms. on file.

Stowe, Noel R., Richard Fuller, Amy Snow, and Jennie Trimble. *A Preliminary Report on the Pine Log Creek Site: 1Ba462.* Mobile: Archaeological Research Laboratory, University of South Alabama, 1982.

Strickland, Rex W. "Moscoso's Journey through Texas." *The Southwestern Historical Quarterly* 46 (1942): 109–37.

Stuart, George. "Some Archeological Sites in the Middle Wateree Valley, South Carolina." M.A. thesis, George Washington University, 1970.

Sturtevant, William C. "Spanish-Indian Relations in Southeastern North America." *Ethnohistory* 9 (1962): 41–94.

Swanton, John R. *Indian Tribes of the Lower Mississippi River Valley and Adjacent Coast of the Gulf of Mexico.* Vol. 43. Bulletin. Washington, D.C.: Bureau of American Ethnology, 1911.

———. "De Soto's Line of March from the Viewpoint of an Ethnologist." *Proceedings of the Mississippi Valley Historical Association* 5 (1912): 147–57.

———. *Early History of the Creek Indians and Their Neighbors.* Vol. 73. Bulletin. Washington, D.C.: Bureau of American Ethnology, 1922.

———. "Ethnological Value of the De Soto Narratives." *American Anthropologist* 34 (1932): 570–90.

———. "The Landing Place of De Soto." *Science* 80 (1934): 336–37.

———. "Tracing De Soto's Route." In *Explorations and Field-Work of the Smithsonian Institution in 1934,* 77–80. Washington, D.C.: Smithsonian Institution, 1935.

———. "The Landing Place of De Soto." *The Florida Historical Quarterly* 16, no. 3 (1938a): 149–73.

———. "Picking Up De Soto's Trail." In *Explorations and Field-Work of the Smithsonian Institution in 1938,* 111–14. Washington, D.C.: Smithsonian Institution, 1938b.

———. *Final Report of the United States De Soto Expedition Commission.* Vol. 71. 76th Congress, 1st Session, House Document. Washington, D.C.: Government Printing Office, 1939a.

———. *Final Report of the United States De Soto Expedition Commission.* 1939b. Rpt. Washington, D.C.: Smithsonian Institution, 1985.

———. *The Indians of the Southeastern United States.* Vol. 137. Bulletin. Washington, D.C.: Bureau of American Ethnology, 1946.

———. "De Soto's First Headquarters in Florida." *The Florida Historical Quarterly* 30, no. 4 (1952a): 311–16.

———. "Hernando de Soto's Route through Arkansas." *American Antiquity* 18 (1952b): 156–62.

———. "De Soto and Terra Ceia, Florida." *The Florida Historical Quarterly* 31 (1953): 196–207.

Syme, Ronald. *De Soto, Finder of the Mississippi.* New York: Morrow, 1957.

Tebeau, Charlton W. *A History of Florida.* Coral Gables, Fla.: University of Miami Press, 1980.

Tesar, Louis D. *The Humber-McWilliams Site, A Pre-Columbian Burial Ground, Coahoma County, Mississippi: Exploration and Analysis 1975–1976.* Marshall, Tex.: Port Caddo Press, 1976.

———. *Did De Soto Sleep Here: And If So, Where?* Bureau of Historic Sites and Properties, 1979. Ms. on file.

———. "Fort Walton and the De Soto Entrada: Culture Change in the Tallahassee Red Hills Area of Florida." Paper presented at the annual meeting of the Southeastern Archaeological Conference, New Orleans, 1980a.

———. *The Leon County Bicentennial Survey Report: An Archaeological Survey of Selected Portions of Leon County, Florida.* Miscellaneous Project Report Series 49. Florida Bureau of Historic Sites and Properties, 1980b.

———. "Fort Walton and Leon-Jefferson Cultural Development in the Tallahassee Red Hills Area of Florida: A Brief Summary." *Southeastern Archaeological Conference Bulletin* 24 (1981): 27–29.

———. "The Case for Concluding That De Soto Landed near Present-day Fort Myers, Florida: The Conclusions Presented by Warren H. Wilkinson Reviewed." *The Florida Anthropologist* 42 (1989): 276–79.

———. *The De Soto Expedition in Apalache: In Search of the 1539–40 Wintering Site.* n.d. Ms. in possession of author.

Tesar, Louis D., and Donna L. Fichtner. "A Preliminary Report on Archaeological Investigations Conducted at the Humber Site (22Co601) in Westcentral Coahoma County, Mississippi." *Cottonlandia Notes* 1, no. 1 (1974).

Tesar, Louis D., and B. Calvin Jones. "In Search of the 1539–40 De Soto Expedition Wintering Site in Apalache." *The Florida Anthropologist* 42 (1989): 340–60.

Thomas, Cyrus. *Report on the Mound Explorations of the Bureau of Ethnology.* Twelfth Annual Report of the Bureau of Ethnology, 1890–1891. Washington, D.C., 1894.

True, David O., ed. *Memoir of D. d'Escalante Fonteneda respecting Florida, Written in Spain, about the Year 1575.* Coral Gables, Fla.: Glade House, 1945.

Varner, John G., and Jeanette J. Varner, eds. *The Florida of the Inca.* Austin: University of Texas Press, 1951.

———. *Dogs of the Conquest.* Norman: University of Oklahoma Press, 1983.

Villanueva y Cañeda, Luis. *Hernando de Soto.* Badajoz, Spain: 1892.

Walker, Winslow M. *The Troyville Mounds, Catahoula Parish, Louisiana.* Vol. 113. Bulletin. Washington, D.C.: Bureau of American Ethnology, 1936.

Walthall, John A. *Prehistoric Indians of the Southeast: Archaeology of Alabama and the Middle South.* University: University of Alabama Press, 1980.

Ward, Rufus A. "The Tombigbee Crossing of the De Soto Expedition." *Mississippi Archaeology* 21 (1986): 62–68.

Waselkov, Gregory A. *Coosa River Valley Archaeology.* Vol. 2. Auburn University Archaeological Monographs. Auburn, Ala.: Auburn University, 1980.

Wauchope, Robert. *Archaeological Survey of Northern Georgia, with a Test of Some Cultural Hypotheses.* Vol. 21. Memoirs of the Society for American Archaeology. Salt Lake City: 1966.

Weddle, Robert S., ed. *Spanish Sea: The Gulf of Mexico in North American Discovery, 1500–1685.* College Station: Texas A&M University Press, 1985.

Weinstein, Richard A. "Some New Thoughts on the De Soto Expedition through Western Mississippi." *Mississippi Archaeology* 20 (1985): 2–24.

White, Nancy M. "The Curlee Site (8JA7) and Fort Walton Development in the Upper Apalachicola–Lower Chattahoochee Valley in Florida, Georgia, and Alabama." *Southeastern Archaeological Conference Bulletin* 24 (1981): 24–27.

Wilkinson, Warren H. "Opening the Case against the U.S. De Soto Commission's Report." *Papers of the Alliance for the Preservation of Florida Antiquities* 1, no. 1 (1960a).

Willey, Gordon R. *Archeology of the Florida Gulf Coast.* Vol. 113. Miscellaneous Collections. Washington, D.C.: Smithsonian Institution, 1949.

Williams, J. W. "Moscoso's Trail in Texas." *The Southwestern Historical Quarterly* 46 (1942): 138–57.

Williams, Lindsey. *Boldly Onward.* Charlotte Harbor, Fla.: Precision Publishing, 1986.

———. "A Charlotte Harbor Perspective on De Soto's Landing Site." *The Florida Anthropologist* 42 (1989): 280–94.

Williams, Mark. *Hernando de Soto in Northeast Georgia.* 1989. Ms. in possession of author.

Williams, Mark, and Gary Shapiro, eds. *Lamar Archaeology: Mississippian Chiefdoms in the Deep South.* Tuscaloosa: University of Alabama Press, 1990.

Williams, Stephen. "On the Location of the Historic Taensa Villages." *The Conference on Historic Site Archaeology Papers* 1 (1967): 2–13.

———. "Armorel: A Very Late Phase in the Lower Mississippi Valley." *Southeastern Archaeological Conference Bulletin* 22 (1980): 105–10.

Wilmer, Lambert A. *The Life, Travels and Adventures of Ferdinand De Soto, Discoverer of the Mississippi.* Philadelphia: J. T. Lloyd, 1858.

Wilson, E. H. "Burned Rock Mounds of Southwest Texas." *Bulletin of the Texas Archeological and Paleontological Society* 2 (1930): 59–63.

Wilson, Jack H. "A Study of Late Prehistoric, Protohistoric, and Historic Indians of the Carolina and Virginia Piedmont: Structure, Process, and Ecology." Ph.D. dissertation, University of North Carolina, 1983.

Wilson, Robert C. "The Hightower Village Site (1Ta150), Talladega Co., Alabama." *Lamar Briefs* 4 (1984): 5.

———. *Preliminary Report on the Archaeological Investigations at the Hightower Village Site (1-Ta-150), Talladega County, Alabama, 1984 and 1985 Field Seasons.* 1987. Ms. in possession of author.

Woldert, Albert. "The Expedition of Luis De Moscoso in Texas in 1542." *The Southwestern Historical Quarterly* 46 (1942): 158–66.

Wood, W. Raymond. *The Denham Mound: A Mid-Ouachita Focus Temple Mound in Hot Spring County, Arkansas.* Vol. 1. Anthropology Series. Fayetteville: University of Arkansas Museum, 1963a.

———. "The Speers Site, 3GA2." *The Arkansas Archeologist* 4, no. 2 (1963b): 12–13.

Worth, John E. "Mississippian Occupation on the Middle Flint River." M.A. thesis, University of Georgia, 1988.

———. "Mississippian Mound Centers along Chickasawhatchee Swamp." *Lamar Briefs* 13 (1989): 7–9.

Young, Gloria. "History of the Study and Reconstruction of the De Soto Expedition Route." In *The Hernando de Soto Expedition in the West, 1541–1543*, ed. Gloria Young and Michael P. Hoffman. Fayetteville: University of Arkansas Press, in press.

Young, Gloria, and Michael P. Hoffman, eds. *The Hernando de Soto Expedition in the West, 1541–1543*. Fayetteville: The University of Arkansas Press, in press.

Young, John P. *De Soto and Chickasaw Bluffs.* Memphis, Tenn.: Mississippi Historical Society, 1918.

———. "De Soto at Chickasaw Bluffs." In *A Symposium on the Place of Discovery of the Mississippi River by Hernando de Soto*, ed. D. Rowland. Jackson: Mississippi Historical Society, 1927.

Index

This index is divided into four sections: Biedma, Elvas, Rangel, and Supporting Materials. (Each narrative has its own index section, because the spellings of proper names have not been standardized across narratives.) The Supporting Materials section contains all the materials not found in Biedma, Elvas, or Rangel, including Cañete fragment entries, which are listed individually and collectively (under *Cañete fragment, items in*).

For each entry, alternate spellings are indicated by brackets—for example, **At[h]ahachi**—or parentheses—for example, **Atabaliba (Atahualpa)**. For a comparison of alternate spellings across narratives in both volumes, see "Indian Proper Names in the Four Narratives" beginning on page 499 of this volume.

BIEDMA

ELVAS

RANGEL

SUPPORTING MATERIALS

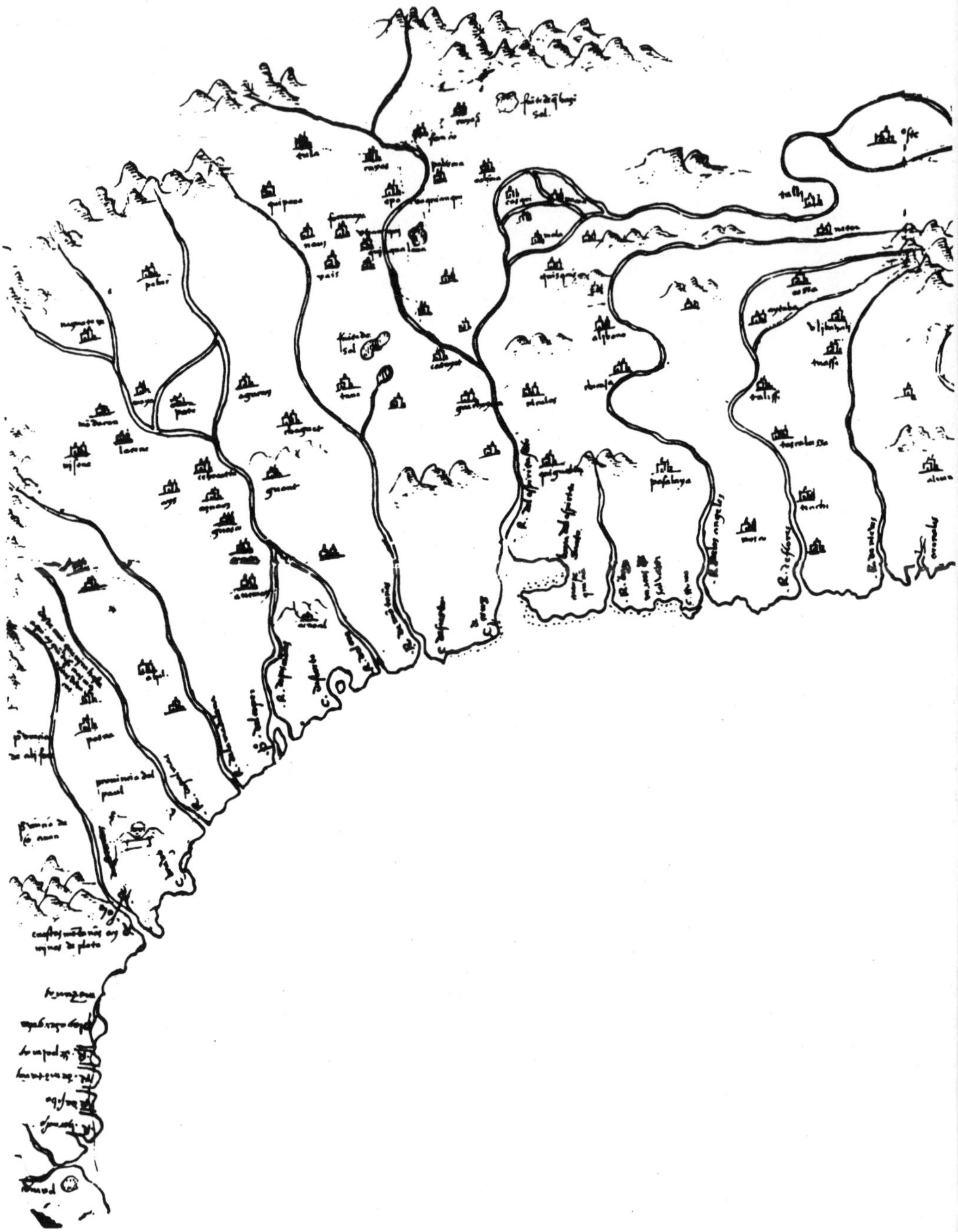

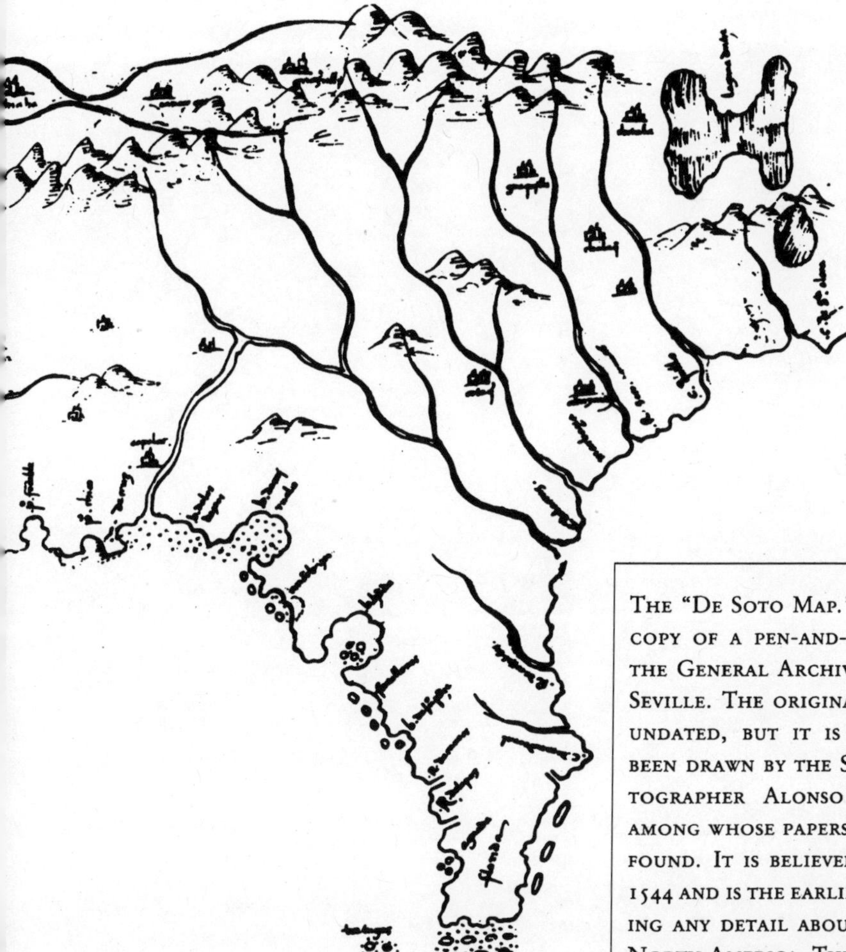

The "De Soto Map." This is a modern copy of a pen-and-ink-sketch map in the General Archive of the Indies in Seville. The original is unsigned and undated, but it is believed to have been drawn by the Spanish royal cartographer Alonso de Santa Cruz, among whose papers it was originally found. It is believed to date around 1544 and is the earliest known map giving any detail about the interior of North America. The source of the information was obviously one or more of the survivors of the De Soto expedition. The rendering of the coast comes from other contemporary sources, and the author has attempted, with limited success, to match the coastal river mouths and bays to the rivers crossed in the interior by De Soto's army. (Courtesy o the Smithsonian Institution)